In the Classroom

An Introduction to Education

Arthea J. S. Reed (at right in the photo), called "Charlie" by her friends and family, is a professor and chairperson of the Department of Education at the University of North Carolina at Asheville, where she has taught for thirteen years. She received her Ph.D. at Florida State University, her M.S. at Southern Connecticut State University, and her B.A. at Bethany College in West Virginia. She has taught in grades two through twelve in the public schools of Connecticut, Ohio, and West Virginia. She is the author of *Reaching Adolescents: The Young Adult Book and the School* (Holt, 1985) and *Comics to Classics: A Parent's Guide to Books for Teens and Preteens* (IRA, 1989), and numerous monographs and articles. For six years, she was the editor of *The ALAN Review,* a journal in the field of adolescent literature published by the National Council of Teachers of English. She was the codirector for eight years of the Mountain Area Writing Project, a site of the National Writing Project, and is currently chairperson of the National Council of Teachers of English, Promising Young Writers Program. She was named the Ruth and Leon Feldman Professor by her peers at UNCA for service to education in 1985 and was listed in Who's Who in American Education in 1989.

Verna E. Bergemann is professor emeritus and past-chairperson of the Department of Education at the University of North Carolina at Asheville, where she taught for twelve years. Prior to coming to UNCA, she was a professor of education at the State University of New York at Oswego for thirteen years. She earned her Ed.D. at the University of Maryland, her M.A. at the State University of New York at Buffalo, and her B.A. at the State University of New York at Brockport. She taught elementary school in Niagara Falls, New York, and Los Alamos, New Mexico. She has worked with beginning teachers as a helping teacher, as a cooperating teacher in a university laboratory school, and as a consultant with the North Carolina Department of Public Instruction. She has been a professor of education at three universities. In addition, she is the author of numerous articles and activity workbooks for teachers. For many years she has worked closely with volunteer organizations that attempt to improve adult literacy. In 1989, she was named Woman of Distinction and Woman of the Year by the city of Asheville for her outstanding contributions to literacy education.

In the Classroom

An Introduction to Education

Arthea J. S. Reed and Verna E. Bergemann

University of North Carolina, Asheville

DPG

The Dushkin Publishing Group, Inc.

To Our Teachers

Minnie Bergemann

Martha Staeger

Dora Wakeman

John Taylor

Printed in the United States of America

Library of Congress Catalog Card Number: 91-77534

International Standard Book Number (ISBN) 0-87967-931-X

First Printing

Credits appear on pages 601–603, which constitute a continuation of the
copyright page.

Preface

Like the Clerk in Chaucer's *Canterbury Tales*, we would gladly learn and gladly teach; in fact, we would encourage every student in the foundations course of education or in the introductory course to adopt this motto, too. In writing this book for those courses, we have included a number of features designed to be informative, to provide glimpses of life in the classroom, and to challenge students to analyze points of views that may be different from their own.

This book combines in one volume the features of both a foundations of education text and an introduction to teaching text. The following features of each chapter enhance this dual approach:

Chapter Outlines   Provide overviews for instructors and students of the material in each chapter.

Chapter Objectives   Allow students to understand what information is available in each chapter.

Opening Anecdotes   Introduce the content of the chapter in story format, an advanced organizer for the material to follow.

Boldfaced Vocabulary   Introduces students to essential concepts within the context of the chapter; also included in the end-of-book glossary.

Viewpoints   Range from poetry to excerpts of essays and articles; used to elaborate material in the text, illustrate another point of view, or enhance a concept.

Point-Counterpoint   Presents two sides of a controversial argument discussed within the chapter; encourages students to question the issues presented and to extend their learning beyond the text.

Cross-Cultural Perspectives   Broaden the student's perspective through information about education in such cultures as Canada, France, and Japan.

In the Classroom   Presents diary entries or stories of real teachers in actual classroom situations, intended to illustrate a specific idea in a chapter.

Points to Remember   Keyed to the chapter objectives; helps students review material during their reading.

For Thought/Discussion Questions following each chapter to help students reflect on the content of the chapter.

For Further Reading/Reference Annotated bibliography at the end of each chapter.

Because students today are expected to spend a fair amount of time observing in classrooms, each copy of our book is accompanied by *A Guide to Participation and Observation In the Classroom*. This guide is designed to help education students objectively observe teachers, students, and student/teacher interaction, using a variety of field-tested materials. In addition, tools to augment the beginning teacher's technique in tutoring and small group work are included.

We have also written an instructor's resource guide, *Teaching and Testing With In the Classroom*, to provide a variety of approaches for using the text, including a point-counterpoint approach, an "in the classroom" case-study approach, and a discussions/reflections approach. Course syllabi and teaching ideas and materials are provided for each of the three approaches. We also include summarizing questions for each chapter, classroom activities for small and large group discussion, and individual investigations for independent study. *Teaching and Testing With In the Classroom* contains a test bank of approximately 1,500 items, which are also available on disk as *EZ-TEST®* to *Accompany With In the Classroom*.

ACKNOWLEDGMENTS

Without the help and support of many individuals, a book like this could never be published. First and foremost, each of us thank the other for the contribution she has made. We began the project as friends and colleagues and completed it believing even more strongly in each other. Next, without Marcuss Oslander, the developmental editor of this text, the book would still be years away from publication. It is hard to explain in a few words all of the encouragement and help she provided us. We will always be grateful! In addition, we cannot help but mention all the terrific people at The Dushkin Publishing Group, Inc. Working with them is what most writers believe publishing a book should be. From our first trip to Connecticut, where we met with Rick Connelly, Irving Rockwood, John Holland, and Marcuss, to the final revisions, everyone has been involved in the project. We could not have asked for better support!

We also must thank the staff of UNCA's Ramsey Library. Mel Blowers generously gave us the freedom to use its space, personnel, and resources. Bill Buchanan and Anita White-Carter tirelessly found us books, addresses, phone numbers, government documents, legal case summaries, and more items than we can begin to mention. The rest of the staff cooperated in every way. We feel very privileged to work with such wonderful colleagues.

This book profited greatly from the astute and careful reviews given it by the following professionals in education. We are grateful for their help.

Barbara Arnstine	California State University-Sacramento
Timothy J. Bergen, Jr.	University of South Carolina
Lloyd L. Coppedge	Northeastern State University
Anthony A. DeFalco	Long Island University–C. W. Post Campus
J. Merrell Hansen	Brigham Young University
Joseph T. Kelly	University of Idaho
Max L. Ruhl	Northwest Missouri State University
David L. Rush	Eastern Kentucky University
Toni Ungaretti	Johns Hopkins University

Thanks to the UNCA teacher education students who helped field-test our many observation and participation tools. Special thanks to our colleagues at UNCA, Gene Arnold and Jim McGlinn, who used various drafts of the chapters in their introductory classes and provided us with helpful feedback.

Thanks to Judy Carver who tirelessly typed and retyped, copied, answered numerous telephone calls, and mostly kept the troops at bay while we were writing.

We could not have written this book without the numerous teachers, administrators, students, and parents, many of whom are mentioned in the text, who provided us with their special insights into teaching, schooling, and learning. We thank each of you. One person at the U.S. Office of Education deserves special mention. W. Vance Grant, statistician specialist, answered our numerous difficult questions and frequently provided us with statistical data long before its publication.

Thanks to the UNCA administrators, particularly Larry Wilson, who gave us the opportunity to complete this work, and to the graphics staff who provided us with many printed materials.

Finally, no author can complete a work of this magnitude without the loving support of friends and family. Particular thanks to Libby and Don who kept up our spirits and read the many drafts of our manuscript.

Arthea J. S. Reed
Verna E. Bergemann

Brief Table of Contents

Contents

3

BECOMING A TEACHER 56

4

THE TEACHING PROFESSION 86   86

II FOUNDATIONS 122

5

THE HISTORICAL FOUNDATIONS OF U.S. EDUCATION 124

6

TWENTIETH-CENTURY U.S. EDUCATION 156

7

THE PHILOSOPHICAL FOUNDATIONS OF EDUCATION 194

III   SCHOOLS AND CURRICULUM   232

8

EFFECTIVE SCHOOLS   234

9

THE CURRICULUM   266

IV STUDENTS AND LEARNING 304

10

THE STUDENTS 306

11

LEARNING   348

V   SOCIETY AND SCHOOLS   380

12

SOCIETY'S EFFECT ON THE SCHOOLS   382

13

SCHOOLS RESPOND TO SOCIAL CHANGE   426

VI SCHOOLS AND GOVERNANCE 468

14

THE POLITICAL INFLUENCES ON EDUCATION 470

15

FINANCIAL AND LEGAL ASPECTS OF EDUCATION 504

APPENDIXES

In the Classroom

An Introduction to Education

1 What Is Teaching?

This chapter will explore the process of teaching. We will ask the question: Is teaching an art or a science? We will also examine teaching from the perspective of a variety of teachers and look specifically at a week in the life of one teacher and a year in the life of another.

2 Who Can Teach?

Not everyone can teach; not everyone should teach. What is it that makes Mary MacCracken and Jaime Escalante effective teachers? Is it possible to learn how to be an effective teacher? This chapter attempts to answer these questions. As you read it, think about whether you possess the values and can learn the skills that will allow you to become an effective teacher.

3 Becoming a Teacher

This chapter will first examine how contemporary teachers are educated and the importance of fieldwork in the training of teachers. We will then look at alternatives to traditional teacher-training programs. Finally, we will investigate teacher education reform movements of the 1980s and 1990s.

4 Is Teaching the Profession for You?

Most teacher-training institutions claim to be educating students for a profession in teaching. At the same time, not everyone agrees that teaching is a profession because it lacks some qualities generally associated with a profession. In this chapter we will review some of these qualities and discuss some developing issues that are certain to have an effect on professionalizing teaching.

*If we accept the status quo and maintain a conservative view toward change, we will not progress. In fact, we'll probably regress. We have an **obligation**, as educators, to constantly seek better ways of **doing things**. If that means putting our heads on the chopping block, so be it. Either we stand for something or we stand for nothing. If we stand for something it should be so important that any sacrifice to preserve and further it is worthwhile. And, as educators, we are under a moral and ethical responsibility to stand for something.*

Very truly yours,
Jack Crowley

PART I

Teachers and Teaching

1

What Is Teaching?

Margery had taught college composition in a small Southern college for three years. Every semester the students read essays and used them as models for their own writing. And every semester Margery graded six compositions written by each student and saw little progress from one to the next. One hot summer she decided to find a remedy.

She reread and analyzed the papers of students from previous semesters, listing common errors and cataloging them into levels of difficulty. For example, she decided that it was easy for students to learn that each paragraph needs a topic sentence. However, it was difficult for them to understand that the topic sentence need not start the paragraph. She realized that the more difficult the writing skill, the more frequently it was incorrect in the student's first paper and also the same student's final paper.

Margery then determined which skills should be taught for the first, second, third, and each subsequent composition. She developed increasingly complex skill checklists which she gave to the students before they began writing each composition. This not only helped students focus on the skill, but she also used these checklists to grade the papers. If a student's composition contained an error related to a skill that had yet to be taught, the student's grade would not suffer. However, if the skill had been taught, and the error still appeared, the student's grade would reflect the error. Once a skill was taught, the student was expected to have mastered it in each subsequent composition.

She also decided to allow the students to work in pairs and evaluate rough drafts of their compositions using the checklists. In addition, she would meet with the students in conferences and allow them to identify potential errors against their checklists.

Margery's efforts paid off. The students' writing improved significantly from composition to composition. And when she compared the final compositions of students who had used the new method to final compositions from previous semesters, writing improvement was marked. This, in turn, resulted in an improvement of the students' attitudes. And their grades reflected this. Margery had never given so many "A's," and she felt good about giving them. The students had earned them.

Jack Snyder was a septuagenarian when he started teaching. He never had any children of his own and, as a free-lance writer, spent most of his time communicating with adults. Crusty, sarcastic, opinionated, he was *not* a "grandfatherly" type. In the city where he lived, the school system relied heavily on volunteers to share skills, hobbies, travel or work experiences, and other valuable enrichments not otherwise available or possible in the classroom.

Jack was taking a writing course at the university when the call went out for volunteers to come into the schools and work with classes in creative writing. Jack was asked, but dismissed the idea instantly. He had hardly talked to a child in sixty years!

Midwest winters are bleak, and retirement schedules leave a lot of time for leisure, so Jack finally decided to volunteer. He didn't sleep the night before his first class—a fourth grade in an inner-city school. He went through the nightmares and jitters that all beginning and many experienced teachers suffer "the night before." He awoke to a snowstorm that snarled traffic, paralyzed the city, and postponed his first class until the next day. Two straight days and nights with no rest; he could hardly eat; his head swam with fears and fantasies. He had no experience to draw from, no education courses, no guidebooks in his library to inspire him. Dread overcame anticipation. He finally . . . stood in front of the room with all those quizzical, "show me" children's eyes staring at him.

"To tell the truth, I'm scared," he admitted to the class. "I'm not used to talking to kids so it may take me a little while. Be patient with me, please."

Silence.

He picked up the chalk [and] . . . wrote across the top of the board:

RULES

The class moaned.
1. No loitering
2. No trespassing
3. No drinking
4. No smoking
5. No writing in Greek or Latin

By this time, the class was delighted. They relaxed and smiled at each other. . . .
6. No rules, except . . .

The class stiffened. What now?

Jack . . . erased the entire board except for Rule 6, to which he added: everyone must write.

And they did! Stories, poems, plays, books, comics, and songs flew from their pencils. They [wrote] assembly programs, television shows, and holiday plays. In one term he taught six classes in creative writing in various schools and was invited to many more. . . . Jack enriched the lives of the children he taught. When he was out sick for a week, he received many original poems, stories, pictures, and cards—an outpouring of the love and concern that the children felt for him.

From: M. B. Chenfeld. 1987, *Teaching Language Arts Creatively*, 2nd ed., 38–39. Used with permission.

CHAPTER OBJECTIVES

After studying this chapter, you should be able to:

- Describe teaching as an art.
- Describe teaching as a science.
- Explain why it is important to distinguish between the art and the science of teaching.
- Explain why teaching requires both art and science.
- Define effective teaching research.
- Define teaching.
- Explain why teaching today can create contradictory feelings and demand contradictory actions.
- Understand the daily activities of a typical teacher in today's schools.
- Understand the yearly successes and failures of a typical teacher.

Both Margery and Jack are very successful teachers. Each helps students become good writers. However, both approach their similar tasks in different ways. This chapter will explore the process of teaching. We will ask the question: Is teaching an art or a science? We will also examine teaching from the perspective of a variety of teachers and look specifically at a week in the life of one teacher and a year in the life of another.

TEACHING AS ART AND SCIENCE

For many years, educators have debated whether teaching is primarily an art or a science. As early as the latter part of the nineteenth century, psychologist William James clearly asserted that teaching is an art rather than a science.

> I say moreover that you make a great, a very great mistake, if you think that psychology, being the science of the mind's laws, is something from which you can deduce definite programmes and schemes and methods of instruction for immediate schoolroom use. Psychology is a science, and teaching is an art; and sciences never generate arts directly out of themselves. (W. James, in *Woodring*, Ed., 23–24)

Educational historian Ellwood P. Cubberly in *An Introduction to the Study of Education and Teaching* (1925) disagrees with James: "At its basis [the teaching process] is a science" (p. 230). According to Cubberly, the teaching process is based in the behavioral sciences. He says, "Teaching, at bottom, is the giving or withholding of stimuli, that certain desired responses in human beings may be produced." Although Cubberly asserts that the practice of teaching is an art, he, unlike James, believes that the art is generated from the science. "Science is a body of principles explaining the nature of some act; art is a body of percepts and skills enabling us to do some special work" (p. 231).

Today, educators still disagree about whether teaching is an art or a science. This argument is particularly important in discussions of how teachers are trained and evaluated. One side of the issue asserts, "Teaching is an art, and, therefore, it cannot be taught or evaluated." According to proponents of this point of view, teaching is intuitive; either an individual can do it well or cannot.

The other side of the issue contends that teaching is a science and, therefore, can be examined, taught, and evaluated. Proponents of this point of view believe researchers can determine teaching strategies that are successful, which can then be taught and their effectiveness evaluated. As Beverly C. Pestel in the *Journal of Chemical Education* says, "We have an obligation to our students . . . to know what the research [on teaching] says and then apply those principles to our teaching. Our teaching practices require the same attention to the current research as do our laboratory practices, for each is a science in its own right" (June 1990, 490).

How do teachers who call teaching an art describe it? Perhaps, a visit to the fourth-grade classroom of Jones Ledbetter will help you understand the art of teaching. Everyone agrees that Jones is a master teacher. He has been named teacher of the year. Parents lobby to have their children placed in his class. Carolyn Harris, his principal, appoints him to all the major school committees. However, she must also evaluate his teaching performance. Each time she does so she agonizes over how to describe what he does.

Teaching
as an Art

The Artist/Teacher Improvises

Jones seems to break all the traditional rules. He rarely opens his class with an objective or a review, which is required by the evaluation instrument used in his school district. In fact, Carolyn wonders if he ever opens his class at all. When she enters his classroom, all the children are busy. She frequently finds Jones sitting on the floor with four or five children reading an article from the day's newspaper. Sometimes he circulates around the room, stopping to kneel on the floor as he reads a child's classwork. At other times, he works with the children on art projects at the tables in the back of the room. When Carolyn enters, the children rarely notice her; Jones never does. They simply continue their work.

N. L. Gage, in a lecture given at Teachers College, Columbia University, states that artistry in teaching requires a departure from the rules.

> As a practical art, teaching must be recognized as a process that calls for intuition, creativity, improvisation, and expressiveness—a process that leaves room for departures from what is implied by rules, formulas, and algorithms. In teaching, by whatever method it proceeds—even in the fixed programs of computer-assisted instruction—there is need for artistry: in the choice and use of motivational devices, clarifying definitions and examples, pace, redundancy, and the like.
>
> When teaching goes on in face-to-face interaction with students, the opportunity for artistry expands enormously. No one can ever prescribe successfully all the twists and turns to be taken as the lecturer, the discussion leader, or the classroom teacher uses judgment, sudden insight, sensitivity, and agility to promote learning. (1978, 15)

The Artist/Teacher Focuses on Motivation and Pacing

The children seem happy and rarely misbehave. Jones keeps things continuously moving in the classroom. When a child is off task or appears to be disturbing another, Jones simply looks up at the child and either winks or smiles. Only once has Carolyn observed Jones leave one group of children to deal with a disruptive child, and that time he simply walked over and gently put his hand on the child's arm. He looked up at Jones, nodded, walked up to Jones's desk, wrote his name in the notebook there, and returned to his seat.

The Artist/Teacher Bases Activities on Student Behavior

According to Jones, what works one day may not work the next. He tells Carolyn, "I cannot determine the order of activities. On some days when the children are hyper, quiet time is the most appropriate way to begin the day, whereas on days when they seem down, a physical activity is more appropriate." If he hears an important news report in the morning, this may become the basis of his social studies lesson for the day. When Jones reads a new book to the students, it is frequently one suggested by a child. If the day is sunny and warm, Jones might suggest that it is a perfect day to begin a unit on plant life with a nature walk in the woods. Carolyn has to admit that what he does seems to be effective. Jones's students never visit the office with behavioral problems and attendance in his classroom is the best in the school.

The Artist/Teacher Is Intuitive and Difficult to Evaluate

What Jones does in his classroom may be difficult to measure. Jones's teaching cannot be evaluated using instruments that examine the content of a lesson. Nor can his teaching be evaluated according to the progress of his students. Jones's students score as well as other students on standardized tests but do not score significantly better.

The definition of teaching as art emphasizes the qualities of insight and intuition. These, however, are not the only qualities necessary to successful teaching.

Teaching as a Science

Proponents of the point of view that teaching is a science contend that most people can learn the skills of teaching, can implement them in the classroom, and can be evaluated based on how well they teach. For example, in the anecdotes at the beginning of the chapter, Margery might be called a practitioner who carefully analyzes what is to be taught and learned, whereas Jack might be considered an intuitive teacher who decides what is taught based on the circumstances of the day. Therefore, it could be said that Margery is a scientist/teacher and Jack is an artist/teacher.

A visit to another classroom in Carolyn Harris's school may help us better understand the scientist/teacher. Carolyn believes that Sarah Smather is an outstanding teacher. Sarah is like an expert engineer in her first-grade classroom.

The Scientist/Teacher Organizes Instruction

In Sarah's classroom it is easy to observe and understand what she is doing. She begins every lesson with a review of the previous lesson and a statement about what is to be learned.

Sarah's class is well organized and orderly. Each day begins the same way: She reads to the children, sometimes a short article from the newspaper, sometimes a poem or a children's book. Then the children take their workbooks from their desks and begin the assignments, which are carefully printed on the chalkboard in the color that represents their learning group.

The Scientist/Teacher Sets Acceptable Levels of Performance and Behavior

Sarah always begins by working with the red learning group in the small reading circle at the back of the room. She faces the class so that she can observe any rule infractions. Although there rarely are any, Sarah does not hesitate to call a child's name, saying, "Jennifer, you know that it is a rule not to bother another child while he is working. Go write your name on the board." Jennifer understands that if her name is called again, a check will be recorded after it,

The artistic teacher knows how to motivate students in both traditional and unusual ways. Through insight and intuition these teachers will determine what approach their students will best respond to in a particular situation and will be willing to implement it.

and she will miss fifteen minutes of recess. This is the **assertive discipline** plan used throughout the county (see chapter 13, pp. 426).

When Carolyn asks Sarah why she always begins the day working with the red learning group, Sarah explains that they are nonreaders and cannot follow the instructions on the board, and need her help and encouragement more than the other children. She works with this group for nearly half an hour before moving to the blue learning group, with whom she works for only fifteen minutes. They already know how to read and write.

The Scientist/Teacher Manages a Classroom

At the end of the reading period, Sarah and the children review the stories they have read that day, sometimes acting them out. Sarah thinks it is important for each of the small learning groups to talk about what they are learning, but not while they are working on their lessons. Sarah carefully organizes her lesson plans, knows exactly what the students are doing at all times, follows school rules, uses the discipline plan devised by the county, and carefully monitors and evaluates her students' progress. When Carolyn asks Sarah how she teaches, Sarah replies, "I use the six-point lesson plan. I think it makes sense. It's orderly and young children like routine. It also makes it easy to monitor the students' progress. I think of teaching as a science."

David Berliner agrees with Sarah that the science of teaching must take precedence over the art since the management of the contemporary classroom is such a difficult task.

> Classrooms are workplaces: complex and dynamic workplaces that require management by an executive of considerable talent. Teachers are not usually thought of as executives. But it's time they became universally recognized as such. . . . Management is "running the place." In the new style of corporate management, less emphasis is on raw materials and manufacturing and more on managing and using the resource of personnel in such a way [as] to create something of value that did not exist before. (Berliner 1989, 105, 106)

Teaching as an Art and a Science

Most contemporary educators agree with the authors of this text that teaching must be both artistic and scientific. Why? Look back at the anecdote at the start of the chapter. What Jack does in the classroom is wonderful, but not enough. Jack's students must learn that writing is not always fun; that frequently it is hard work to revise and rewrite. Indeed, they must learn the difference between something that is well written and something that is creative but lacks accuracy and clarity. If they do not, they will not know where to begin when told to revise. They will be frustrated when their work is not "right" the first time. They will never achieve excellence in their writing.

On the other hand, what Margery does is good, but not good enough. She is teaching, basically, a structured kind of writing, the five-paragraph theme. Unfortunately, five-paragraph themes have limited usefulness. The students in Margery's composition class may be paralyzed when asked to begin their writing with what is inside their heads and hearts. They will not know where to start. They may want to know: "How do I get an idea?" "How long does the paper have to be?" "Does it have to be typed?" "How many paragraphs should it have?" Like Jack's students, they are unlikely to achieve excellence in writing.

Both Margery and Jack are good teachers, but if they do not modify their approaches, neither will help their students become independent, successful writers. Jack must add some of the science of writing and teaching to his work. Margery must add some of the art of writing and teaching to her work. The master teacher must be a scientist of the art of teaching.

The best teachers have clear objectives but improvise tactics for reaching those objectives. They know when it is essential to deal directly with facts and when it is important to enrich lessons to stimulate interest. They design learning activities based on the needs, interests, and abilities of the students. They frequently modify approaches when students appear to be experiencing difficulty. They base the standards they set on the objectives to be reached, but they encourage all students to exceed these objectives. Although substitute teachers and evaluators can follow their lesson plans, when artist/scientist/teachers implement the plans the lessons are varied and subject to change.

The Artist/Scientist/Teacher

Landon McMillan is a teacher of ninth-grade social studies who combines the qualities of an artist and a scientist. The ninth-grade curriculum emphasizes U.S. government. Landon believes that the students must be involved in the democratic process if they are to understand how the government works. For the first two weeks of each school year, Landon and his students monitor the

(continued on page 12)

Point/Counterpoint

TEACHING AS AN ART

1. Improvises tactics for reaching objectives.
2. Digresses from topic to enrich lesson, stimulate interest.
3. Bases learning activities on student behavior.
4. Focuses on motivation and pacing.
5. Uses intuition and hunches to modify usual practices.
6. Sets high standards for self and students.
7. Lessons are varied, subject to change.

From: "Teaching as an Art" adapted from L. J. Rubin 1985

TEACHING AS A SCIENCE

1. Follows clearly stated behavioral objectives.
2. Deals directly and objectively with facts.
3. Bases learning activities on objectives, order, and relationships.
4. Focuses on willingness to accept facts, a search for order.
5. Uses objectivity to guard against wishful thinking.
6. Sets acceptable performance levels for students based on objectives.
7. Lessons can be replicated.

POSTSCRIPT

Educators who believe that teaching is primarily an art contend that it is intuitive and difficult to analyze and evaluate, whereas those who believe it is primarily a science contend that it is a series of skills that can be taught, and evaluated. This controversy is central both to the education of teachers and to on-the-job evaluation and promotion. Many educators argue that teachers should not be rewarded or promoted based on evaluations of their teaching, since teaching is an art and cannot be evaluated. Others argue that this is ridiculous, that teachers must be evaluated and rewarded for teaching excellence that can be analyzed, observed, and measured.

The authors of this book contend that teaching is both an art and a science. As such, some elements of teaching, the science, can be analyzed, taught and evaluated, whereas other aspects of teaching, the art, are intuitive and insightful. Therefore, teachers must be trained in the science of teaching, and must be encouraged to develop the science so fully that the art evolves from their fluidity.

The art of teaching may be intuitive; however, it will not develop fully until the teacher is so comfortable employing the skills of effective teaching that artistry emerges. Similarly, the artistry of teaching may be difficult to analyze without knowing the skills required in effective teaching. Think about observing teaching in terms of critiquing a painting or a piece of music. To the untrained eye and ear the work of some contemporary artists may look or sound like child's play. However, when you recognize the essential elements of the work, as does a trained observer, you will see the skill and artistry.

Miró, Joan. *Painting.* 1933. Oil on canvas, 68¹/₂″ × 6′ 5¹/₄″. Collection, The Museum of Modern Art, New York. Loula D. Lasker Bequest (by exchange).

We can best understand the process of effective teaching as both an artistic and scientific endeavor if we compare it to the process of understanding a painting. In order to appreciate and respond emotionally to this Miró painting, we must first recognize its concepts of color and design.

local newspapers for an issue of local interest. This fall the students select cutting down of trees for timber in a nearby national forest. For many years the lumber companies have selectively harvested trees and planted new ones to replace them. Recently, however, local environmentalists have expressed concern that the foresting of trees is removing the natural habitats of several endangered species. Landon and his students read as much as they can about this issue and decide to make it the focus of their year's study in government.

The Artist/Scientist/Teacher Focuses on Objectives But Improvises Tactics

Once the students have selected the topic, Landon gives them a list of objectives for the year that is based on the topic and the state's competency goals for ninth-grade social studies.

1. To understand how the federal government influences environmental issues.
2. To understand how the federal courts affect environmental issues.

3. To understand how the state government influences environmental issues.
4. To understand how the state and local courts affect environmental issues.
5. To understand how local governments influence environmental issues.
6. To understand how interest groups interact with government to affect environmental issues.
7. To understand the role of Joe and Joanne Citizen in environmental issues.
8. To understand the role of the media as the "watchdog" of government.
9. To involve ourselves in government as it relates to this environmental issue.

He tells the students they will learn about how a democratic government works by being actively involved in this social and political issue, but doesn't tell them exactly how to accomplish this goal. Instead, Landon begins the unit by having the students discover what they already know about the issue. Then they make a list of things they need to learn. Landon suggests that they continue reading newspapers and current news magazines. He tells them to search for additional sources as they read. He advises them to write to agencies or individuals mentioned in the articles for more information. He also suggests that they discuss the issue with their families. "Perhaps," Landon suggests to his students, "we can invite local adults who deal with this issue to class." He tells the students to begin to formulate their own opinions as they read. Later in the unit the students will debate the issue based on their opinions and the new knowledge they have gained. "Ultimately," he tells the students, "the goal of this class is to help you understand the democracy in which you live so that you can take your role as an active citizen of the United States."

The Artist/Scientist/Teacher Assists Students in Reaching Objectives

The students are next divided into groups, each with a different aspect of the topic to investigate. One group is to search recent news magazines for related articles from various regions of the country. Another is to develop an annotated bibliography of available resources. A third is to develop a historical timeline of the forestry industry in the United States. Another is to make a list of various business, political, and environmental groups interested in the issue and write to them for information.

The Artist/Scientist/Teacher Bases Standards on Objectives

The groups are given nine sheets of paper and told to head each with a different objective. The students will list appropriate information and bibliographic data under each objective. Landon knows that the students are expected to master library research skills in ninth-grade social studies; therefore he incorporates these skills into the unit.

After the students gather information, they post their lists and discuss them with the class. Landon and the students synthesize the information and develop a course outline and bibliography. Landon monitors the students' progress by observing them in the library and ensuring that each student is involved in the group process. As the year progresses he will use a variety of evaluation techniques including informal oral presentations, formal oral presentations, mock court hearings, debates, papers explicating a single point of view, papers explaining several points of view, production of newscasts, interviews with key people, tests, research papers, and a final project requiring each student to take an active role in the issue.

The Artist/Scientist/Teacher Encourages Students to Exceed Set Standards

Not only will Landon ensure that each of the objectives he and the students set together is met, but he will also ensure that the students know the terms, concepts, and skills required to do well on statewide tests. They will read and discuss appropriate chapters in the state-adopted textbook, and as they read the chapter on the presidency, for example, they will examine how the president affects environmental policy.

By the end of the year, Landon's students will know the content required in the ninth-grade social studies curriculum based on state competency objectives and those set by Landon and the students. In addition, they will have become participants in the democratic process.

Landon McMillan utilizes both his artistic and scientific qualities in teaching. He understands what Theodore R. Sizer says about the artist/scientist/teacher in *Horace's Compromise: The Dilemma of the American High School.*

Teaching is a complex craft, one class never being quite the same as another. Treating teaching as mere technology either reduces its goals to brute training of the children in rote skills or permits great inefficiency. Standardized high school teaching is wasteful. That students differ is inconvenient, but it is inescapable. Adapting to that diversity is the inevitable price of productivity, high standards, and fairness to students. . . . Like writing, teaching is science, art, and craft. There are certain rules and conventions, so many and of such complexity that their orchestration becomes less of science than of craft. Good teachers sense when progress is being made, not so much by objective tests, as by impression born of a wide variety of signals from the students. The intuitive, the serendipitous, the mysterious ordering of things that suddenly makes a learner say, I see! To the extent that others evoke them, these visions are evoked by artists, artist-teachers. (Sizer 1984, 191–192)

1.1 POINTS TO REMEMBER

- Artist/teachers are intuitive, improvise tactics, digress from topics, base learning on student behavior, focus on motivation and pacing, and set high standards for self and students.

- Scientist/teachers follow clearly stated objectives, deal directly with objectives and facts, seek order and relationships, guard against wishful thinking, and set expectations for performance based on objectives.

- Teaching as an art is intuitive; teaching as a science is based on developed skills. The training of teachers requires the development of skills; the evaluation of teachers requires the analysis of skills.

- The artist/scientist/teacher helps students understand what their best work can be and teaches them to achieve it by setting attainable goals.

DEFINING TEACHING

Throughout the 1980s, dozens of studies were done, interviewing and observing teachers, and previous studies were synthesized in an attempt to determine what differentiates effective or good teaching from ineffective or poor teaching and to delineate the characteristics of effective teachers. This body of research has come to be called *effective teaching research*. (The characteristics of effective teachers, as cited in this research, are discussed in chapter 2.) Although some educators contend that effective teaching studies are an attempt to make teaching more scientific, it is interesting to note that many of these studies conclude, as many teachers themselves believe, that much about teaching cannot be measured, that the science of teaching is not what makes the profession enjoyable. To give an idea of what teaching is like from teachers' perspectives, the authors of this text asked numerous practicing classroom teachers to write about what teaching means to them. Their definitions include self-examination, guidance, enablement, helping, sharing information, and drudgery and disappointment.

Teaching Is Self-examination

Scribner Jeliffe, a high school social studies teacher at a midwestern independent school with forty years of teaching experience, says that teachers help students examine themselves, and, therefore, much of what a teacher does cannot be seen or heard.

> At the core of teaching is the sense of bringing to the students what they need to know to advance their self-examination. We must explore the outer reaches of ourselves in order to understand what is within. To that end, a teacher brings written and visual materials together to provide both background content and a central problem for the students and a congregation of interested partners, the class. I have been impressed by how much teaching takes place when the teacher is silent. As a student recently put it, (I have learned that) "I am my own best teacher and my own best student."

Teaching Is Guiding

Alida Woods, a fifth-grade teacher with sixteen years' teaching experience, says that the teacher is a guide and a partner.

> Teaching is a high calling . . . in education, as the Latin indicates, we "lead out"—(*e ducare*)—and, in so doing, we guide, facilitate, hold, and light candles as we journey forth, *with* and beside our students.

Both Alida Woods and Scribner Jeliffe discuss aspects of teaching that cannot be measured easily. How can we measure the teaching that takes place when the teacher is silent? Will we recognize a teacher's leading out when we see it? If the leading out is successful, it is likely that neither the observer nor the student will know it is occurring. Instead, children will assume responsibility for themselves because of the guidance the teacher has given.

Teaching Is Enabling

Educator Ken Macrorie spent seven years seeking teachers whose students did "good works." Macrorie defined good works as "what learners write,

Alida Woods is a fifth-grade teacher with sixteen years teaching experience. She believes a teacher is a guide and a partner in the process of learning.

speak, or construct that counts for them, their fellow learners, their teachers and persons outside the classroom" (1984, xi). He wondered what it is about the interaction of these teachers with their students that brought out the students' best work. The twenty teachers, from elementary to college level, had many things in common. In particular, they each believed in "pretty much the same ideas and were using pretty much the same methods—although they were teaching, for example, woodworking to rich kids in Pennsylvania or history to poor kids in California, space engineering to university students in Michigan or mathematics to sixth graders in Massachusetts. They were not *teachers* in the usual sense—persons who pass on the accepted knowledge of the world and get it back from students on tests, but *enablers* who help others to do good works and extend their already considerable powers" (p. xi). According to Macrorie, enablers write and talk to students as equal human beings so that mutual trust and respect develops. They help their students produce "good works" rather than meet minimum competencies and do well on standardized tests. Another common element of teachers who help students do good works is the development of a classroom social life that is "intense and valuable" and is characterized by "intellectual rigor." According to Macrorie, the classrooms of enablers are exciting and enjoyable (pp. xii–xiii). Kathleen Hespelt, a fifth-grade teacher with twenty-five years of teaching experience, further explains enabling as "exposing students to enough knowledge about themselves and the world to allow them to want to learn more so life will be enjoyable and rewarding."

V I E W P O I N T S

Teaching

Terrific		Tough
Elating		Exhausting
Amusing		Arduous
Challenging		Complex
Happiness	and	Heartbreaking
Intriguing		Imprecise
Noble		Nerve-wracking
Glorious		Grueling

From: Kathleen Hespelt, Isaac Dickson Elementary School

Teaching Is Helping

Carol Meehan, a fourth-grade teacher with eighteen years' experience, says teaching involves "helping each child learn in developmentally appropriate ways. A teacher is a facilitator who challenges children to achieve their unique potential." Macrorie, Hespelt, and Meehan agree that the best teachers assist students in finding their own unique abilities and provide them with the resources to develop others.

Teaching Is Sharing Information

Mary Futrell, president of the National Education Association from 1979 to 1989 and herself a teacher, believes that the pleasure of sharing knowledge puts teachers in a position to receive the affection and respect of students; they become role models. "Having others follow in your example is a heady reward" (Futrell 1989, 26).

Rene Caputo, a first year elementary school teacher of Spanish, says:

Teaching is an exciting process of helping students discover new sounds with which they can communicate. It involves creating an environment in which students can safely suspend the absoluteness of their everyday realities to enter a world in which previously learned rules do not apply and everything has a new name.

My first year of teaching has been extremely exhausting: teaching between eleven and fourteen classes each day, carrying my materials from room to room, learning the layouts and organizational structures of three schools, and trying to memorize 650 new faces and their accompanying names. There were definite moments when I was ready to give up.

My students kept me coming back. I had never met so many loving, interesting, and inquisitive people before. It was an exhilarating experience to challenge each other in our exploration of another culture and language, to share videos, games and songs, to laugh as we acted out fairy tales together. I learned that a teacher needs to be prepared and flexible, and above all, care deeply about her students and her subject.

Teaching Is Part Trade, Part Professionalism

While some teachers feel very positive about what they do and offer inspiring comments about their profession, others feel that teaching has its

CROSS-CULTURAL PERSPECTIVE

What Is Teaching Like in Great Britain?

According to Michael Durham in a London *Sunday Times* article titled "Swapping Chalk for Cheese: Teachers Over the Wall" (June 4, 1989), many teachers are leaving the profession in Great Britain because it involves many duties other than teaching children.

After eleven years as head of physical education at Thomas Tallis comprehensive school in Southeast London, Chris Stanley, 33, decided he had had enough. He quit teaching and started a new career as a constable in the Metropolitan Police.

The workload and stress of teaching in a secondary school had begun to tell. "I loved the job and the classroom at first," said Stanley. "But as you progress in teaching you tend to move away from what you are good at. Then came new responsibilities like assessment, pupil profiling,

the GCSE [General Certificate of Secondary Education] and all the rest.

"A lot of these ideas are very good ones, but they were brought in against a background of staffing cuts. My department shrank from seven to four despite all the extra work.

"The day started at 7:30 in the morning with the paperwork and post. I rarely had a proper lunch break and I never got home until after six. On cricket evenings, it was much later. Sometimes I ran games on Saturdays too. I was tired out and I never had any time for my own kids."

. . . Life in the classroom has probably never been so unpopular. Most teachers trying to make it "over the wire" into other jobs blame their discontent on evermore arduous workload, such as the GCSE and national curriculum.

Their work has not been made any easier by gradually worsening school discipline, cuts in money and manpower, lack of support and low public esteem. And to cap it all, they complain of low pay.

From: Durham, London *Sunday Times* (June 4, 1989), F4.

negative side as well. Heavy workloads, a great deal of paperwork, and low pay have discouraged some who teach. A few of their comments follow.

Educational researcher John Goodlad says, "Teaching functions in a context where the [teacher's] beliefs/expectations are those of a profession but where the realities tend to constrain, likening actual practice more to a trade. . . . By its very nature a profession involves both considerable autonomy in decision making and knowledge and skills developed before entry and then honed in practice" (1984, 194). In Goodlad's three-year "Study of Schooling" in *A Place Called School: Prospects for the Future,* he interviewed 1,350 teachers and found that most went into teaching with professional values but "encountered in schools many realities not conducive to professional growth."

Stephanie Petrovich, a middle school social studies teacher, had similar experiences: "The teaching profession . . . stifles the creative energy of its teachers, often causing immense feelings of despair within the ranks. Teachers are not treated professionally, nor are they allowed to devote their time to the task of teaching. As a result of continued pressure by bureaucrats within the school system, school administrators, and the general public, as well as increasing work loads and low pay, teachers are embittered and apathetic toward their careers."

For many teachers such as Alida Woods and Carol Meehan, teaching is a rewarding, challenging, and noble profession, whereas for many teachers like

Stephanie Petrovich in the United States and Chris Stanley in Great Britain, teaching is not what they thought it would be. Educational policies, such as testing expectations, standardized curriculums, and unending paperwork, make the task of teaching less rewarding than they expected. Their delight in the work they do with children is diminished because of the policies that seem to get in the way of teaching and learning.

A WEEK IN THE LIFE OF A TEACHER

As the effective teaching research clearly shows, "teaching is a complex craft, one class never being quite the same as another" (Sizer 1984, 1919). And there is no doubt that David Berliner is correct when he says, "Classrooms are workplaces: complex and dynamic workplaces that require management by an executive of considerable talent" (1989, 105). Most teachers agree that, regardless of the rewards, teaching is a difficult task.

Teachers must bring to classrooms their knowledge of the subject matter, children, how to teach, how to manage and control, how to communicate, and how to motivate. They have accumulated lifetimes of experiences in which they have failed and succeeded. Every minute of every day, teachers synthesize knowledge and experience with their values and beliefs into what researchers call a teaching style.

What Does It Take to Be a Teacher?

Children gain an appreciation of the language and learn to enjoy reading simply by having stories read to them or performed. This storyteller has the rapt attention of most of his first-grade audience.

Students come into the classroom with varying amounts of knowledge, diverse skills and experiences, wide-ranging social, ethnic, and religious backgrounds, failures and successes, dreams and fears, values and beliefs, abilities and disabilities. Some children have been loved and nurtured; others have been abandoned, abused, and forced to sustain themselves. Some have been taught and have learned; some have been taught and not learned; some have learned without teaching; others have neither been taught nor learned. The teacher's task is to make learning possible for all students. Sharon Cascio, a third-grade teacher in Sebastian, Florida, writes in her diary after a particularly difficult day: "I *do* come back the next day as I have for sixteen years. I *do* care that they [the children] be all that they can be! I get upset when they don't (feel *I* have failed, not the students), and I rejoice when they do. I instruct, explain, guide, lead, praise, lecture, scold, comfort, listen, counsel and advise. I teach!"

What Are Some of the Joys and Frustrations of Teaching?

The authors of this text wanted you to be able to view a week in the life of a teacher from the perspective of that teacher, not from what research says teachers do. So we asked Sharon Cascio to keep a diary for us and for you, a diary of each day for a week where we see recorded the joys and frustrations of teaching. We hope you will be able to glean from it an understanding of the great skill and artistry needed to successfully negotiate a week as a teacher.

IN THE CLASSROOM

From the diary of Sharon Cascio, third-grade teacher, Sebastian, Florida, sixteen years' teaching experience.

January 23

8:00   Good morning to co-workers; small talk about our various weekend activities. . . . Conversations involving Super Bowl results and half-time show. . . .

8:40   Enter students. Good morning all around. Just like adult counterparts, their conversation includes Super Bowl discussion, the half-time show, their weekend activities and the movie *Brotherhood of the Rose* that followed the Super Bowl. I can't believe they were allowed to stay up that late and watch a violent film. Nothing should surprise me, but I still state my disbelief. . . .

9:15   Begin teaching three reading groups—reading groups go well: Group #1—introduction to new story (vocabulary and background). Then they go off to the four corners of the room to read it silently. All settle in favorite spots (under craft table, one in the closet, one always sits at my desk while her friend sits under my desk, several lying on the floor by my bookshelves and by my filing cabinet . . .).

10:30   Give individual help to two students who are still having trouble counting money. We work with Milton Bradley coin set and practice counting coins I place on the table.

10:55 PE with PE teacher while I have planning time; cranking out papers on Xerox machine; check spelling papers from morning seat work, and grade math make-up tests. . . .

1:50 Follow up Indian tribe activity. Filmstrip on Hopi and Apache tribes of Southwest shown and discussed. Loved the music and the Pueblos. Started project involving five tribes discussed to date. They will choose a tribe and make a shadow box or large mural depicting environment, food sources, shelter of their tribe. They can work independently or with a partner. Students busy deciding which tribe to do and if they want to go it alone or with a comrade. They will let me know their decisions tomorrow.

2:30 Story time, *Owl Moon*—they love the pictures. . . .

3:35 After getting work together for tomorrow, I leave with about one hour worth of work to do at home. . . .

Reflections:
Three students went home sick during the day. Flow of lessons stopped each time as I jotted down their assignments and got them ready to leave. . . .

January 24

8:15 To room—get report cards back with memo from principal, "Nice job! Good comments." Makes me feel like I got an "A.". . .

8:55 Correct last night's homework—100 percent brought in homework. Every team gets a point—even team four brought it in. . . .

10:30 Small group instruction on cause-effect skill. Try sequence approach, what happened 1st, 2nd. Much better. Record books read for January "Book It" program, so they can get new books this P.M. in library. Fourteen children meet minimum reading requirement (200 pages for pleasure) for this month and receive Pizza Hut coupons. *Amelia Bedelia* series, mysteries, and books on Indian tribes (carry over from social studies, "read more about it") popular this week.

11:00 English lesson—quick review of verbs (pronoun-verb agreement). "Killer bees" (2) interrupt lesson twice. Girls screaming, they get in their hair, in their eyes, etc. General chaos. Takes forever to shoo bees out the window, secure the fort, calm students. Never do get to my science lesson. Oh, well, adapt, regroup, adjust.

Reflections:
—Another student goes home sick—traveling virus. . . .

—Prior to bee chaos—was a slower pace in A.M., found myself rephrasing instructions and questions, had to allow for more response time than normal before they finally answered my questions. My expression "yoohoo you're in la la land" was used a few times in A.M.

—Didn't bring home paperwork. It's my birthday!

January 25

8:40 Enter students, their usual talkative selves. One student throws up immediately; galloping virus strikes again. Three Indian projects arrive already—complete and beautiful. I'm impressed; the class is impressed; the three are proud! The rest of the class vows to get theirs done. Student comes back from clinic—will go home. Now I have four absent for the day—work will be gathered and sent to siblings in other classes at end of the day. . . .

Reflections:
—One girl who signed on using another student's name was also eating candy in class on Tuesday and received name and check by name for not

following room rules on Monday. What's going on? Never any problem before; now 3 days in a row. Talk to fifth-grade teacher who has older sister—find out if sister is acting out too. I don't like my student's attitude: very moody, snapping at her friends, sharp tone to me Monday and Tuesday.
—Talked to another student who during course of day hit a child in face with pencil point and another child in back with chair legs. All accidents, but she has problems with invading other people's space—clumsy—she has got to be more alert, careful. She agreed; was sorry and will be more aware of people around her. Step back a little.

January 26

8:00   Spoke to fifth-grade teacher. The sibling in her class is exhibiting similar behavior. Feel there is a need for Crisis Intervention (counseling by school psychologist). Fifth-grade teacher will bring the child's name before Teacher Support Team (TST) which meets every Friday morning. . . .
8:20   Complete TST paperwork (scheduling, writing up a preliminary recommendation report, etc.); read memos. Put assignments on board.
8:40   Enter students, all excited. Twenty some, all talking at once, telling me why two of my boys are in the office—incident on playground—boy #1 hit boy #2 in eye. . . . A third boy comes up all upset because he traded another boy his game for three erasers. He now wants the game back and the boy won't fork over. Since the other boy goes to another school and the trade occurred at home, I state that I know he's upset but there is nothing I can do. I suggest he talk to his mom and ask her advice. Also talk about trading on impulse and how we often regret decisions. He says he'll never "do that again." Lesson learned the hard way. . . .
1:40   Back in room to work on Social Studies projects. Difficult time working together. *Very* noisy, lots of movement . . . , spilling of paints and water, lots of paper rolled into balls and discarded in trash can. After 30 minutes of nonproductive . . . behavior, I throw in the towel. I've had it for today. I order *clean up*. . . .
3:10   Last bus arrives. "What a day!" I'm exhausted—mentally drained. . . .

January 27

8:00   Prepare for TST meeting; get files from records room. Team meets with fifth-grade teacher. History of child abuse in family. HRS (Health and Rehabilitation Services) has been involved in the past. . . . Team recommends child receive Crisis Intervention counseling immediately. I fill out necessary forms; team signs names.
8:25   January birthday breakfast. . . . Enjoyed by all.
8:40   Children in room; more Indian projects come in; quickly glance at memos—will take care of them during planning period; one child says he's sick, feels very hot; off to clinic; announcements, attendance; Pledge, etc. Check homework; 100 percent bring it in again today. Three days of four everyone did it and brought it to school the next morning! . . .
11:00 Science lesson (finally get to it this week); follow up activity for unit on plants. Show two filmstrips, one on plants in different environments; we tie it into social studies and talk about which environment's plants different Indian tribes would have seen and used. . . .
3:15   All have left with "Have a good weekend; see you on Monday." I stay and straighten the room, check plan book for next week (could a substitute follow?). . . . I consult with teacher who will be going to the computer conference to choose which seminars we will attend. . . . I return to the room to grade the spelling test papers (14 A's). I put these A papers on the

"Good Job" bulletin board. I also put up a Black History Bulletin board that I have ready for February's Black History Month.

4:00   I leave. It wasn't exactly a good day today. Many sloppy, rushed and incorrect math papers and extremely poor paragraphs despite what I thought were "clear" directions. I really had to count to ten silently several times as I felt my blood pressure rising. I remind myself that they *did* do well on the spelling test, *Weekly Reader* story discussion and science discussion. It [positive-negative feeling] seems to balance out at the end of the day.

Sharon's week shows that all teachers must possess the skills of the scientist/teacher and the intuition and flexibility of the artist/teacher. Sharon carefully plans each day. However, she must be flexible enough to work with students who have difficulty counting money. She must deal with unexpected illness and unplanned-for interruptions. If we examine Sharon's diary, we can see a teacher who possesses the attributes of both the artist and the scientist.

A YEAR IN THE LIFE OF A TEACHER

The school year typically comes to an end in May or June, depending on the geographic location of the school. During the approximately 180 days of that school year, the teacher works hard to ensure that every child learns. This is not easy. At the end of some school years, the teacher looks back with pride at the accomplishments of the students, at his or her success as a teacher. But, at the end of other school years, the accomplishments are harder to see. Some years it seems that the harder the teacher works, the more distant the goals become.

Upon reflection, each school year is made up of good and bad days, small and large successes, and small and large failures. Some of the students achieve more than ever dreamed possible; others fail to reach their potential. Sometimes the rewards far outweigh the frustration; sometimes they don't. Sue Nix, a sixth-grade teacher, chronicles a school year in which she laughed and cried.

IN THE CLASSROOM

From the diary of Sue Nix, sixth-grade teacher, Oswego, New York, sixteen years' teaching experience.

November 1

9 A.M. - Kids are tired today. They are moving slower than usual. . . .

11 A.M. - Fun science today—but I guess I always feel that way. Demonstrating, using students, is a great motivation.

12 noon - Kids love to play with science equipment. I can use a few minutes here to get some board work ready for them. . . .

12:45 P.M. - Almost lunch time. Math was great! They are comprehending decimal *process* very well—but not the decimal place *values*. I still think it takes more maturity and expertise than they have at this age. . . .

3:00 P.M. - Afternoon went by quickly. One of the reading groups and I discussed science topics related to space and the environment. The subject of destruction of our ozone layer was of great interest to them. After much discussion, the kids were excited to try to do something about the problem. Problem solving is the main concept I emphasize in science. Right away they wanted to develop a plan *they* could control. Right away they brainstormed and categorized, made decisions involving value judgments and formed a feasible plan of action. It was one of those wonderful moments in teaching—rewarding and real. I'm glad I'm here.

November 2

2:30 P.M. - Stupid, stupid books! The skill is taught one way and tested in a completely different way. First in math where they don't follow their own rules and then in reading where "cause and effect" suddenly asks for "signal words," a term never mentioned or previously taught!

November 3

8:50 A.M. - Parent Conferences coming up next week. I always find them informative. They give good insight into children and why they are what they are. Report cards are due then too—and Book Wheel folders and science projects. Almost too much!

10:10 A.M. - What a complete hassle school can be at times! Here I am, all ready to do a great review activity and lesson for science before tomorrow's test, and, suddenly, the schedule is changed because an artist is visiting the fifth grade. . . .

2:45 P.M. - What do I do with Jake? He is perpetually late, running behind on everything he does. . . . It took him almost twenty minutes to get ready for orchestra and he was that late. . . .

December 10

10:15 A.M. - Office called to say that Jayne's mom won't come in for conferences at all. What is the matter with people? Don't they care at all? She has three children in this school and refuses to come in. Jayne is rapidly moving backward in math and reading. She writes me in her daily diary that everything is wrong in her life. She takes everything negatively. . . . The reading teacher and I both see this inward negative trend . . . and we planned to talk to her mom together. Now, no mom. . . . I hurt for some of these children.

January 30

9 A.M. - It is good to be back. After being out with Andrew sick and then the snow day and Friday's funeral, I feel so disorganized. I'll spend the morning getting back on track. Stephanie's late again! When she comes in she's so down, but won't talk to me. Mom's nasty note about my report card comment sure lets me know I'll get no help for Steph from her. . . .

10:45 A.M. - Being out last Friday morning, I did not get to review for the test with the science classes. As a sub, Sam seems to have handled it well. So far, tests look good. It was nice having him in for me. As a former student teacher of mine, he already knows the routines and expectations. . . .

11 A.M. - Projects are wonderful! Each student shows his/her own individual talent and personality, and out of four classes, everyone did one! . . .

12:15 P.M. - My math students suffer when I'm out. You really need to know them to get results and they forget so easily. How can I turn math into a fun project? Not possible, I guess. No matter how cutesy the approach or novel the lesson, it's everyday dull practice that keeps coming up.

February 3

9:30 A.M. - Science has to change today—no candles! Talked to Donna about contract negotiations. Why do the sides play power games with each other? We stress honesty and integrity with kids and yet, when it comes to solving adult differences, we turn to deceit. . . .

12:30 P.M. - Tough math today—test day! But the kids are doing quite well. I'm pleased.

1:15 P.M. - Talked to Darryl about Robbie. He's going to drive him home tonight and discuss what is happening and see if we can figure out "why." . . .

May 1

11:05 A.M. - Well, so far today I've had two meetings, a beautiful coffee hour, a visit to two Speedway race cars, and one science class. Normally, that would make for a great morning! But this group of kids is so difficult to be around. Just as you begin to enjoy someone or something, it's always interrupted by a demand for counter-attention in a negative sense. I love kids and I love being around them—but this year, those with "problems" are the rule, not the exception, and caring about them is draining. Couple that with the curriculum pushing being done by New York State and the limitations placed on a classroom teacher of schedules and adhering to someone else's rules, and I'm really frustrated. I can't seem to live up to my own standards. There's just too many things and people needing my attention. . . .

2 P.M. - Practicum girl comes tomorrow. She has a nice way about her. Tomorrow she will try a science lesson. It will be fun to watch. College students have been much better lately (last two years). They seem ready and eager to work hard, listen, and accept advice. That's nice to have back. For a while, it was like someone "owed" them success! Now they just ask to work. Parents as Reading Partners starts today. I'll read to those who don't go with younger kids. I still have two parents who have not come in or contacted me to get report cards! What makes anyone think they will enforce reading at home!

May 2

12 noon - Good science classes today. It's so strange. I do the same thing with all four groups—yet often one or two will remember something that others act like they never heard! . . . Terri, my practicum student from the college, really did a nice job. As with most college students, discipline will be her biggest problem. . . .

2 P.M. - I have a new student. He is from another District where I find out he was labeled emotionally handicapped with 20 percent of his time spent with a resource teacher. But, no one here seems interested in giving me support services to keep him mainstreamed. Frustrating! He does a nice job— sometimes, and other times—he's a master at playing games. But, I'm finding that he has a good sense of humor and, as long as he is dealt with in a fair way and the "why" he's wrong is explained, he seems fine. He has quite a bit of ability. I even find myself questioning his E.H. (Educable Hand-icapped) classification. Meeting on Friday will be interesting to get information.

May 4

9:20 A.M. - Meeting with Middle School principal about kids for next year! Best meeting we've ever had. We finally have some definite answers, so we can make better decisions about where these kids can go next year. Hurray!!

10 A.M. - Science experiment from Tuesday didn't work! Spent some time with college practicum student turning the "mistake" into a positive experience for kids. It's amazing how college students are all so afraid to make an error. They don't see what a good thing that can be.

11:30 A.M. - One more science class to go! Terri has done such a good job of accepting my suggestions and controlling the situation! I'd like her to come back as a student teacher. . . .

2 P.M. -I've so much to do. Already today I have had three meetings! I really am tired of so many directions to go in.

Sharon Cascio and Sue Nix both find that teaching can be rewarding as well as frustrating. As much as a teacher might try, she or he cannot have control over traveling viruses, killer bees, and parents who don't show up for conferences. Most teachers realize that enabling, guiding, and helping are ideals that can be reached only occasionally and usually for brief periods of time, but are willing, nevertheless, to work toward those goals. To give a child encouragement, to light a tiny flame of recognition, to shape, even minutely, the mentality of the future is worth all the time and effort it takes.

1.2 POINTS TO REMEMBER

- Effective teaching researchers observe and analyze what good teachers do to determine the skills common in most good teachers.

- Teaching is many things. First and foremost, it is interacting with students. It is guiding, enabling, and helping students achieve their best work. Much of what a teacher does cannot be seen, heard, or evaluated.

- Teachers frequently find themselves forced to limit their interaction with students, their reason for teaching, to deal with the bureaucratic tasks of the profession. Most find these actions contradictory and frustrating.

- The day-to-day activities of a teacher include all the skills of the scientist/teacher, including planning and management, and all the attributes of the artist/teacher, including intuition and flexibility.

- A year in the life of a teacher is a series of small victories and disappointments. Students do better than expected; others do not achieve as much as the teacher anticipates. Teachers frequently measure their own success based on the successes and failures of their students.

FOR THOUGHT/DISCUSSION

1. Discuss why there is a disagreement among educators about whether teaching is an art or a science.

2. Compare and contrast the characteristics of the artist/teacher and the scientist/teacher.

3. How do you feel about making mistakes? How will you react to your students when they make mistakes?

4. What is your personal memory of a good teacher?

5. Discuss the joys and frustrations of teaching as presented in the two diaries.

FOR FURTHER READING/REFERENCE

Bedwell, L. E., Hunt, G. H., Touzel, T. J., and Wiseman, D. G. 1984. *Effective teaching: Preparation and implementation.* Springfield, IL: Charles C. Thomas. A descriptive discussion of the science of teaching and the scientist/teacher.

Fenstermacker, G. D., and Soltis, J. F. 1986. *Approaches to teaching.* New York: Teachers College Press. An exploration of the art and science of teaching.

Freedman, S. G. 1990. *Small victories: The real world of a teacher, her students, and their high school.* New York: HarperCollins. A true story of a master artist/teacher depicting the joys and frustrations of teaching multicultural and socially deprived students in inner-city Manhattan.

Highet, G. 1950. *The art of teaching.* New York: Vintage. Examinations of teaching as an art and the artist/teacher.

Zahorik, J. A. 1987. Teaching rules, research, beauty, and creation. *Journal of Curriculum and Supervision, 2* (3), 274–284. An exploration of not only the art and science of teaching but also the product and process of the art and the science of teaching.

Art Bouthillier in *Phi Delta Kappan.*

"Lemme guess . . . first day at school with braces, right?"

2

Who Can Teach?

Mary MacCracken is a teacher of emotionally disturbed children. She is loving and warm, frequently hugging the children. She wants the children to learn to be independent. She knows they will never achieve great academic success, so she uses her time with them in the classroom to encourage them to be the best they can be. She chronicles one school year in her book Lovey: A Very Special Child. *The excerpt below tells about the start of the first day in school.*

Brian was the first to arrive. He came so quietly that if I hadn't been watching I wouldn't have known he was there. He came to the hall door and stood just outside it, his hands hidden in his pockets so I couldn't tell whether they were trembling or not. Each year I think I've outgrown the ridiculous soaring excitement I felt the first time I came to the school and saw the children. And then each year I find I'm wrong. The same spin-jolting, rocking delight hits me and spins me around, and I have to be careful not to somersault across the room when the children come.

"Hey, Brian, I'm glad to see you." I walked across the room toward him, waiting for his smile, thin and sweet, to come and warm his pinched little face.

But Brian didn't smile. He didn't even come into the room. "Why are we in here?" he asked. "This isn't our room. This isn't where we were last year."

It's so hard for our children to handle new situations. Their sense of self is so small, their beings so fragile, that if their outer surroundings change, they fear that they themselves will fall apart.

"Listen," I said. "This is the best room we've ever had. Don't spurn luxury. Look, we've got a whole coat closet, instead of just hooks."

Brian took a step or two into the room and peered at the coat closet. "I liked just the hooks," he said.

"And we've got blocks and trucks and a whole toy kitchen—a stove and a sink and tables—and now, look here, our own door. How about that? No more having to go through the office when we want to sneak out before lunch to ride our bikes."

Brian was all the way in the room now. "Do we still have the bikes?"

"Sure. We've even got a couple of new ones." They weren't really new, the church ladies and the Junior Leaguers had donated them, but they were new to us.

Within the next minute Rufus arrived. He looked tan and healthy and had obviously had a good summer.

"Hey, Mary," he announced, "maybe we're going to get a cat. I'm almost not 'lergic any more and my mom says as soon as I'm not 'lergic we can get one." He turned toward Brian. "And I'll bring it in here, Brian, so you can see it."

Rufus walked comfortably around the room, commenting on everything, and I could see Brian loosening up, his fears diminishing. The children did so much for each other without realizing it. Rufus's explorations freed Brian to begin his own, and soon both boys were settled on the floor taking out books and papers and small supplies that I'd put in their individual cubbies.

From: M. MacCracken, 1976, *Lovey, A Very Special Child*, 11–12.

Jaime Escalante teaches high school mathematics to Latino students in East Los Angeles. Many teachers assume these students cannot learn and, therefore, go easy on them. Escalante disagrees, and his results have been well-documented in the book Escalante *by Jay Mathews and the film* Stand and Deliver. *These excerpts from the book discuss some initial frustrations and later successes.*

For his first AP [Advanced Placement] class Escalante collected a few members of the previous year's mathematics analysis course and one or two students who claimed to have taken the prerequisite course at East Los Angeles College. He had fourteen enrolled in the first-period class by the fall of 1978, but many, including Escalante, felt like babes lost in the woods.

Heiland [a student] brought him a copy of an old calculus AP free-response test, the problems requiring written answers that make up the latter half of the three-hour examination. Escalante fingered the green paper gingerly. It had seven questions. He knew this group could not come close to answering any of them. He wondered how far he could take them in just eight months.

He assumed his sharpest look and addressed the class: "You're going to be able to do this class, but you need to brush up your Algebra 2, your math analysis, your trigonometry. You don't know anything in this class. . . .

"First period starts at eight o'clock. We open the doors here at seven. We start at seven-thirty. Then from eight to nine we have regular class. I'd like to change this textbook, but no way. I got to be honest, I don't understand myself this book. So we going to have to give you a lot of handouts and you have to take a lot of notes and keep a folder. Every morning we have a five-minute quiz. [Now several students began to exchange looks.] And a test on Friday."

He began the routine. To his surprise, in two weeks he was down to seven students.

. . . That day two more boys approached him defiantly. "We gonna drop, Mr. Escalante." They watched closely for his reaction.

"But you gotta *try*," he said.

"Nah," the taller boy said. "I don't want to come at seven o'clock. Why should I?"

. . . Only five students in Escalante's calculus class—three girls and two boys—lasted through the spring. It was a test not only of their patience but of the district's and the principal's.

CHAPTER OBJECTIVES

After studying this chapter, you should be able to:

- Identify the characteristics of an effective teacher.
- Discuss how the skills and values of an effective teacher can be developed.
- Explain how effective teaching research contributes to defining teaching skills.
- Define teaching style.
- Differentiate teaching style from teaching method and content.
- Identify the characteristics of instructor-centered, content-centered, student-centered, teacher-student-centered, and content-student-centered teaching styles.
- Analyze the potential benefits and dangers of effective teaching research.
- Identify different teachers' job expectations revealed by cultures-of-teaching research.
- Defend teacher diversity.
- Discuss why systematic classroom observation is important.
- Discuss the criteria of objective observation.

Administrators were not supposed to sanction such tiny classes.

Escalante still insisted the students see him before and after school, but he had to treat them more gently now. He assured them repeatedly they could handle AP questions. He gave them what sample questions he could find from past examinations.

. . . From the beginning Escalante knew he had to soften calculus's granite-hard image. His principal devices were humor, nonchalance, and an appeal to the team spirit. The class motto appeared in a huge poster on his wall: CALCULUS NEED NOT BE MADE EASY; IT IS EASY ALREADY.

In May 1979 all five Escalante students sat down in the English classroom just inside the main door of the school and took the AP calculus examination. One girl, Leticia Arambula, could barely speak. She was mortified. She had panicked and answered only a handful of multiple-choice questions. By the time she opened the free-response booklet, her mind had gone blank.

Escalante knew how quick East LA youths were to wallow in self-doubt. He comforted her. She had not been the best student and was slow in finding her answers to daily quiz questions. But she worked hard and did her homework.

The counseling office called him in July with the results. The Educational Testing Service scored the examination on a five-point scale. A 5 was best, a 1 was worst. A 3 or better meant a student could be said to have passed a college-level calculus course and would receive credit for one at most major universities. In Escalante's class, the grading report said, there were two 4s and two 2s. Leticia Arambula had received a 1.

Escalante resolved to do better. (1988, 100–110, 114–116)

From: J. Mathews, 1988, *Escalante: The Best Teacher in America*, 100–110, 114–116.

Escalante and his students did do better. In May 1980, all nine students who had enrolled in the class took the test in the spring. One student received a 4, five received 3s, and two received 2s. One, who took the calculus BC exam, reserved for those with more than a year of preparation, passed with a 3.

In May 1981, fifteen students took the test and the results were: One 5, four 4s, nine 3s, and one 2. By the fall of 1986, there were 151 calculus students in Escalante's school and at least 400 others in the developing process. Escalante, through his persistence and effective teaching, proved that the students of East Los Angeles could learn high level mathematics.

Perhaps you are familiar with the nineteenth-century British playwright and satirist George Bernard Shaw's comment about teachers, "He who can, does. He who cannot, teaches" (1903, 230). This remark makes the assumption that teachers cannot do what they teach. Also inherent in this assumption is

Jaime Escalante teaches Latino students high-level mathematics in East Los Angeles. His persistence and dedication have enabled him to communicate the subject matter to his students effectively and, more importantly, to instill in them a sense of self-confidence that has enabled them to succeed.

that anyone can teach. Shaw was wrong. Teachers like Mary MacCracken and Jaime Escalante prove he was wrong. Although they are entirely different in terms of how they teach, each possesses the attributes and skills of an effective teacher.

Not everyone can teach; not everyone should teach. What is it that makes Mary MacCracken and Jaime Escalante effective teachers? Is it possible to learn how to be an effective teacher? This chapter attempts to answer these questions. As you read it, think about whether you possess the values and can learn the skills that will allow you to become an effective teacher.

WHAT IS EFFECTIVE TEACHING?

As educational researchers Donald Kauchak and Paul Eggen point out, "Education has always been one of the most rewarding professions—but at the same time, it continues to be one of the most difficult in which to perform well. . . . An effective teacher combines the best of human relations, intuition, sound judgment, knowledge of subject matter, and knowledge of how people learn—

When teachers do not share an identity with their students, not only do they have to understand the culture and social environment of the children but they also must determine the most effective means of teaching them the material.

all in one simultaneous act" (1989, 3–4). Effective teachers make the very difficult task of teaching appear easy. They are able to teach all kinds of children so effectively that children, in fact, do learn. But although, in theory, effective teaching seems easy to define, its practical aspects are still being researched and analyzed.

Shared Identity   According to Philip Jackson in *The Practice of Teaching*, teaching may appear simple, except for what he calls "the assumption of shared identity." **Shared identity** means that "when teachers are working with students who are very much like themselves, there is relatively little to learn about teaching, at least insofar as technique is concerned, that is not supplied either by common sense or by knowledge of the material to be taught. When working with children like themselves, teachers can teach as they were taught, using techniques that worked for them. But when teacher and student are *not* alike in important ways—that is, when the presumption of shared identity is invalid . . . [t]he knowledge called for under those circumstances is genuine knowledge about teaching per se" (1986, 26).

We can see the lack of shared identity between students and teachers in the anecdotes above. Mary MacCracken's students are emotionally and mentally disabled. In order to work with them, she must understand their level of development and select an appropriate means for helping them grow beyond it.

Jaime Escalante's students are from the East Los Angeles Latino ghetto and, since most of their parents are Mexican immigrants who speak little

English, they are the children of two cultures. Escalante says that most of them give up easily in their new environment. However, as a physics teacher in a Catholic high school in Bolivia, he had seen that when students band together to strive for a common goal, they can succeed. Although Escalante's background is very different from his students, he has learned about their culture and developed ways to motivate them. Through his hard work, dedication, knowledge of and ability to communicate the subject to his students, he has convinced them that they too, can succeed.

In order for teachers to be effective with students who do not share their identity, it is important to determine the traits and skills of effective teachers.

Effective teaching research is a new field of study that developed in the early 1980s. Educational researchers are attempting to determine, through extensive observation and interviews of effective teachers and synthesis of research on teaching completed in the 1960s and 1970s, the common characteristics possessed by teachers who are judged to be effective.

Although the term *effective teaching* was coined by researchers in the 1980s, studying what makes teachers successful began in the 1960s. The earlier research focused on the process of teaching by examining a variety of teaching behaviors. For example, from 1959 until 1967, Ned Flanders and his associates focused their research on the effects of teacher indirectness (questioning, praising, and accepting rather than lecturing) on student success. In 1963, Donald Medley and Harold Mitzell's research led to the development of tools for systematically observing and measuring the attributes of teacher behaviors as they relate to changes in student achievement. By 1971, Barak Rosenshine was actively examining these attributes. This research and other similar studies provided the foundation for the effective teaching research of the 1980s and 1990s, which defined effective teaching as that which leads to student success, usually measured by nationally normed standardized tests. In addition, researchers use evaluation of teachers by administrators and trained teacher observers, teacher-created portfolios, and the opinions of teaching peers, among other means, to determine the common characteristics of successful teachers.

Effective Teaching Research

Educator Philip Jackson believes that many of the skills and traits identified by researchers in effective teachers can be directly examined, taught, and learned. Many of them relate to the study of pedagogy, the methods of teaching, and constitute the science and the art of the profession. Effective teaching research concentrates primarily on those teacher behaviors that positively influence student performance. Because not all studies agree on all the qualities of effective teachers, only those generally agreed upon will be discussed here.

Effective teachers are knowledgeable, have a strong general background, and understand the subject material at a high level. They understand how children and adolescents learn and they know how to encourage student learning. They have the ability to impart knowledge through appropriate instructional techniques and understand that different approaches are appropriate in different situations. They are flexible in making instructional decisions. They model what is to be learned, set appropriate goal levels for academic

Effective Teaching Research and Teaching

achievement, concentrate on a few dominant goals, have a clear instructional focus, offer an overview of each lesson, explain exactly what is expected of students, allow for practice, give feedback, and allow for review and closure. Effective teachers know how to question, motivate, enrich, and stimulate student learning. They use a limited amount of seat work, teach for mastery, have detailed lesson plans with a variety of activities, and revise and reteach based on student achievement.

Effective teachers have clear and consistent communication and management skills. They use classroom time effectively and efficiently either on instruction or on student task development. Effective teachers spend limited time in transitions. They are organized, set a brisk instructional pace, monitor student work and progress, are good managers, and help students cope with problems. They are in control of the students and the environment. They use praise more than criticism, are good decision makers, and select and direct activities rather than students.

Although most effective teaching research has emphasized measurable teacher behaviors that produce measurable student learning, much effective teaching research has also identified elements of a teaching personality that cannot be measured. For example, the research has revealed that effective teachers also have sound moral character, like children, want to teach, are sensitive, are tenacious, balance the needs of the individual with the needs of the class, are self-confident, are patient, are energetic, have empathy and warmth, are enthusiastic, set high goals for themselves and their students, improvise, are intuitive, are efficient, take pride in what they do, and devote as much time as possible to what they enjoy about teaching. The characteristics of the effective teacher are listed in table 2.1. If you do not already possess them, can you learn them or develop them? In the next section we will discuss how you learn and develop the qualities of effective teaching.

Learning to Be an Effective Teacher

Most characteristics of the effective teacher can be taught, learned, and evaluated. For example, there are many ways to ask questions. Far too many teachers simply ask and answer their own questions, or they pose questions that require only factual answers. Students learn little if all questions are answered by the teacher, or if they require only the mere recall of information. (Question: Who was the first president of the United States? Answer: George Washington.) This kind of direct questioning results in low-level cognitive learning. High-level questions, on the other hand, require students to apply their knowledge, analyze, synthesize, and evaluate, and result in higher order thinking skills. (Question: If Thomas Jefferson had been elected the first U.S. president, what differences might we find in our democracy? Answers: As with most high-level questions, there are many possible answers. One might revolve around Jefferson's economic policies, which differed from Washington's. Washington supported Alexander Hamilton's approach of expanding manufacturing in the Northeast, whereas Jefferson supported a westward expansion and an agrarian economy. Another answer might discuss Jefferson's egalitarian view of citizens. It is likely, for example, that Jefferson would have given more power to the states, particularly in education. He would have also encouraged better relations between the president and Congress and opposed a two-term presidency.)

TABLE 2-1

Effective Teaching Skills

Measurable

has knowledge of subject matter
Hall 1981; Sizer 1984; Bennett 1986

has strong general background/
understands subject at a high level
Manatt 1981; Rubin 1985; Bennett 1986; Futrell 1989

understands how child/adolescents learn
Hall 1981; Rubin 1985; Futrell 1989

has ability to impart instruction/
understands that different approaches are appropriate in different situations
Walberg et al. 1979; Rubin 1985; Kauchak and Eggen 1989

is flexible in instructional decisions
Flanders 1970; Walberg et al. 1979; Rubin 1985

models what is to be learned
Manatt 1981; Kauchak and Eggen 1989

sets appropriate goal levels of academic achievement
Brophy and Good 1986; Kauchak and Eggen 1989

concentrates on a few dominant goals
Rubin 1985

has clear instructional focus
Rubin 1985; Kauchak and Eggen 1989

provides overview of lesson
Stanford Studies, Gage et al. 1960–1982; Brophy and Evertson 1973; Brophy and Good 1986

explains exactly what is expected
Bennett 1987

provides for practice
Kauchak and Eggen 1989

gives feedback
Stanford Studies, Gage et al. 1960–1982; Good and Grouws 1975; Stallings 1977, 1978; Kauchak and Eggen 1989

provides for review and closure
Stanford Studies, Gage et al. 1960–1982; Canterbury Studies 1970; Brophy and Evertson 1973; Stallings 1978; Kauchak and Eggen, 1989

knows how to question
Soars and Soars 1968; Canterbury Studies, Wright and Nuthall 1970; Rosenshine and Furst 1971; Brophy and Evertson 1973; Stallings 1977; Manatt 1981; Kauchak and Eggen 1989

motivates students
Walberg et al. 1979; Rubin 1985

enriches and stimulates student learning
Rubin 1985

limits amount of seat work
Manatt 1981

teaches for mastery
Walberg et al. 1979; Manatt 1981

gives detailed lesson plans with a variety of activities
Manatt 1981

revises/reteaches instruction based on student achievement
Brophy and Evertson 1973; Good and Grouws 1975; Walberg et al. 1979

has clarity of communication
Stanford Studies, Gage et al. 1960–1982; Canterbury Studies, Wright and Nuthall 1970; Rosenshine and Furst 1971; Good and Grouws 1975; Walberg et al. 1979; Sizer 1984; Rubin 1985; Brophy and Good 1986; Futrell 1989; Kauchak and Eggen 1989

is consistent in communication
Kauchak and Eggen 1989

has governing powers
Hall 1981

uses time effectively and efficiently; most time spent on instruction and task
Soars and Soars 1968; Rosenshine and Furst 1971; Brophy and Evertson 1973, 1979; Beginning Teacher Evaluation Studies, Denham and Lieberman 1973–1977; Stallings 1974, 1977, 1978; Good and Grouws 1975; Walberg et al. 1979; Manatt 1981; Rubin 1985; Brophy and Good 1986; Bennett 1987; Kauchak and Eggen 1989

limits time in transitions
Brophy and Evertson 1973, 1979; Good and Grouws 1975

monitors student work and progress
Brophy and Evertson 1973; Beginning Teacher Evaluation Studies 1973–1977; Good and Grouws 1975; Brophy and Good 1986

is organized
Beginning Teacher Evaluation Studies 1973–1977; Kauchak and Eggen 1989

has brisk instructional pace
Good and Grouws 1975; Junior High Study 1980; Rubin 1985; Kauchak and Eggen 1989

provides good management
Good and Grouws 1975; Manatt 1981; Rubin 1985; Kauchak and Eggen 1989

(continued on p. 36)

helps students cope with problems
  Rubin 1985; Bennett 1987
is in control and bases control on
student behavior
  Flanders 1970; Rubin 1985; Brophy
  and Good 1986
uses praise more than criticism
  Stanford Studies, Gage et al.
  1960–1982; Rosenshine and Furst
  1971; Stallings 1978; Manatt 1981
is good decision maker
  Rubin 1985; Kauchak and Eggen
  1989
selects and directs activities, not
students
  Manatt 1981

Not Measurable

has sound moral character
  Hall 1981; Bennett 1986
likes children and wants to teach them
  Bennett 1986
is sensitive
  Futrell 1989
has tenacity
  Futrell 1989
balances the needs of the individual

with the needs of the class
  Futrell 1989
has self-confidence
  Sizer 1984; Rubin 1985
has patience
  Sizer 1984
has energy
  Sizer 1984
is empathic and warm
  Sizer 1984; Kauchak and Eggen
  1989
has enthusiasm
  Reinhartz and VanCleaf 1986;
  Kauchak and Eggen 1989
sets high goals for themselves and their
students
  Rubin 1985; Bennett 1987
has ability to improvise
  Rubin 1985; Reinhartz and VanCleaf
  1986
is intuitive
  Rubin 1985
is efficient
  Rubin 1985
takes pride in what he does
  Rubin 1985
devotes as much time as possible to
what she enjoys about teaching
  Rubin 1989

Research on effective teaching has discovered many skills that can be measured as well as numerous skills that can't effectively be measured but which, nevertheless, are observed in classrooms where students are learning the material. Both types of skills are listed here with their researchers.

There are some characteristics of effective teachers that are not easy to learn, but because many of them are values they can be developed. In *Taxonomy of Educational Objectives: Affective Domain*, educator David Krathwohl says we develop values by first becoming aware of them. For example, once we recognize that sensitivity toward others is an important characteristic of the effective teacher, we can nurture it.

According to Krathwohl, the next step is to respond to this sensitivity with careful observation and attempted imitation. How does the sensitive teacher respond when a child has difficulty understanding a problem? How does he or she talk to students or react to misbehavior? Once we have determined how the sensitive teacher responds to students, an attempt should be made to respond to students in a similar manner.

The third stage in developing a value, according to Krathwohl, is expressing the value both orally and in writing. Although we might not consider ourselves particularly sensitive to others, we certainly can recognize sensitivity in others. According to Krathwohl, we can develop our own sensitivity by talking and writing about those individuals who embody the value. For example, when keeping a log of classroom observations, write about the importance of sensitivity in teaching and how the teacher practices sensitivity. We can discuss sensitivity in teaching with our instructors and our peers, read

Sensitivity is one of the characteristics of the effective teacher that can be developed by observing how sensitive teachers behave in different situations in the classroom. Sensitivity is one way of reaching students who have a tendency to resist learning or who may be intimidated by the learning process, their peers, or their teachers.

about sensitive teachers, like Mary MacCracken, and plan how to develop sensitivity with our students.

The next stage in developing a value is its organization within what Krathwohl calls a values complex. In other words, how does one value fit into the hierarchy of values we have already established in our lives? For example, if sensitivity is an important teaching attribute, how is that achieved within a framework of maintaining classroom discipline? How can students be made aware of the inappropriateness of their behavior with sensitivity? Go back and observe in the classroom of a sensitive teacher. Are the students well-behaved? What does the teacher do to be a sensitive disciplinarian?

It is also helpful to read about teachers who must deal with potential conflicts between two values. Mary MacCracken's book *Lovey: A Very Special Child* provides a good example. Mary is warm, loving, and sensitive to the needs of her emotionally disturbed students, who come to trust her and rely on her. She enjoys and feels rewarded by their trust. However, she begins to understand that her students are very vulnerable. What happens to them when she is not there to tell them what to do or help them solve their problems? Although she wants them to come to her when they need her, she believes she must teach them independence. She decides to teach Brian, who will attend a new school the next year, to ride the bus by himself. The students do not want to learn to be independent, and their parents complain that Mary is not being sensitive to their fears. She must find a way of proving to the students that she is being sensitive to their needs at the same time that she is teaching them the importance of doing things on their own.

She does this by first taking all the children in her car to the school Brian will attend the next year. Later, she and the children take the bus to the school. She lets Brian pay for his own fare. The children are fearful; Brian doesn't want to give the bus driver the money; the bus driver criticizes Brian's lack of discipline, and Mary wonders if it is worth it. "It had taken the whole afternoon, that one miserable bus ride. In some ways it didn't really seem worth it" (1976, 184). But the children and Mary continue to ride the bus together for several weeks. Finally, she puts Brian on the bus alone while she follows in the car with the other children. He is afraid, but she continues to encourage him. For many days, they follow Brian on the bus to his new school. Soon Brian is making the trip with confidence, and the other children are begging to go with him. Mary has combined her sensitivity with her concern for doing what is best for the children even in the face of the children's and their parents' protests.

According to Krathwohl, the final stage in value development is "characterization by a value complex." This simply means that a value such as sensitivity becomes an integral part of the personality.

This is certainly true of Mary in the example above. Sensitivity is so much a part of Mary's personality that she is able to display it even when others tell her she is being insensitive. She may question whether her intuition is correct, but she continually assesses her actions and determines that what she is doing is important to her students. "At night, before I slept, [Brian's] pale, worried face peered at me from the window of the bus, and I'd think, I want him back, riding in the car with us, safe and happy. But the next day I'd drive him to the bus station and pick him up at the other end" (p. 186).

It is the rare individual who possesses all the attributes of the effective teacher listed in table 2.1, but many of them can be developed through teacher training programs, reflective reading, and careful observation.

2.1 POINTS TO REMEMBER

- Research shows that effective teachers have sound moral characters, like children, and want to teach them. They are sensitive, tenacious, self-confident, and patient. They possess energy, warmth, and enthusiasm. They set high goals for themselves and their students. They are intuitive, efficient, and take pride in what they do.

- Effective teaching values can be developed by recognizing them, responding to them orally and in writing, observing others who possess the values, and practicing by imitating those who possess them.

- Research identifies effective teachers as knowledgeable, with a strong general background. They are flexible, model what is to be learned, and set appropriate goals. Their lessons have a clear instructional focus. They know how to question and motivate students. They have good communication and management skills.

TEACHING STYLE

If we look back to the anecdotes at the beginning of the chapter, we see two effective teachers who approach teaching in very different ways. Both have a similar goal, which is to ensure that their students succeed at the highest possible level. However, each achieves this goal in unique ways based on his or her background, values, knowledge of subject matter and students, understanding of the environment in which he or she teaches, and ability to impart information. Each has developed a personal **teaching style**.

According to Louis Rubin, the author of *Artistry in Teaching*, every teacher has a special way of doing things, a manner or style that makes the teacher what he or she is.

> Style is a composite of the teacher's demeanor and conduct, apparent in the things teachers emphasize, in the procedures they use and in their reactions to opportunity, adversity, failure, success. It is reflected in both good teaching and bad, because each teacher-practitioner goes at his or her work differently. (p. 19)

Rubin further claims that every instructional goal can be accomplished in a variety of ways, depending on one's values, self-image, and conception of teaching role. The teacher's manner or style evolves over a period of time from experience and involves the individual's personality, talent, and ideology. This personal style nourishes the effective teacher. "Great teachers are inspired by the significance they attach to their work and by the pleasure they take in fostering intellectual growth" (p. 20).

Method

Diane Ravitch in *The Schools We Deserve* writes: "Teachers do things in the same way because they all came up through the years of the same type of schooling—they 'model' their own teachers. The pressure in schools is to stay in line with everybody else" (1985, 68–69). John Goodlad's extensive three-year study of 1,350 teachers in thirty-eight very different schools seems to confirm Ravitch's point. His study found that the methods used by all these teachers are more similar than they are different. However, Goodlad's study also concluded that "able teachers, under favorable circumstances, do make an important difference in students' learning, especially in those areas not likely to be attended to in the family" (1984, 167).

Barbara B. Fischer and Louis Fischer (1979) claim that one of the reasons educators, such as Ravitch, frequently make the assumption that all teachers are alike is that they tend to think in terms of teaching methods rather than teaching styles. Teaching methods include such techniques as lecturing, asking questions, grouping students, conducting discussions, assigning readings, and giving homework and tests. Most teachers use all these methods at one time or another. A teacher's style is not the specific methods employed but is, instead, the unique way in which the teacher organizes and uses these methods.

For example, two teachers may employ the teaching method of discussion. One teacher acts as the discussion leader, asking directive questions that lead to specific, planned answers. The other allows the students to direct the discussion. This teacher may begin the discussion with an open-ended question and only reenter it to suggest opposing views or alternative solutions or problems. The first teacher expects specific answers from the students; the second wants the students to come up with as many answers as possible. The unique ways in which the teachers employ the discussion technique is based on each teacher's individual teaching style.

Content   Teaching style, according to the Fischers, is a "pervasive quality in the behavior of the individual, a quality that persists though the content may change" (p. 245). In other words, two teachers may present the same material but in totally different ways. For example, one may teach the causes of the Civil War by using a simulation in which students play the roles of various social and political groups and attempt to determine the causes of the war based on their interactions. Another may have the students read from a variety of sources to determine the causes of the Civil War. The goals and the content are the same; however, each teacher achieves the goals in a unique way. Their uniqueness constitutes teaching style and is achieved primarily by how content is organized, emphasized, and delivered, based on the teacher's philosophy of learning and teaching.

CATEGORIZING TEACHING STYLE

In order to understand how individual teachers teach, many educational researchers have attempted to create broad categories under which to group various teaching styles. The five broad categories are instructor centered, content centered, student centered, teacher-student centered, and content-student centered. Within these broad categories, other researchers have described several specific teaching approaches that fall within the major style. See table 2.2 for a delineation of styles and researchers who studied them.

Instructor-Centered Teaching Styles   **Instructor-centered teaching** and learning implies that the teacher is the model of the way in which a learner should approach a particular field or subject. The teacher is viewed as an ego ideal and a socializing agent. He or she is sometimes dramatic in discussions and lectures with the focus on his or her interpretation of the material. Therefore, evaluation is more subjective, with both **cognitive** (development of concepts) and **affective** (development of values) orientations to the content and the presentation (Bergquist and Phillips, p. 18).

According to Fischer and Fischer, the **task-oriented** style assumes that "teachers prescribe the materials to be learned and demand specific performance [related to teacher-determined competencies] on the part of the students." Learning is frequently defined and charted on an individual basis. An explicit system of accounting keeps track of each student's progress (p. 250).

Teachers who exhibit the **emotionally exciting teaching style** or the **nonemotional teaching style** either show intense emotional involvement or no apparent emotional involvement in the presentation of subject matter. Emotionally exciting teachers conduct class in an active and intense manner. Their counterparts, on the other hand, conduct class in a subdued and unemotional tone, where rational processes predominate. Learning is dispassionate although just as significant as in the emotionally charged classroom.

Content-Centered Teaching Styles   According to Bergquist and Phillips, **content-centered teaching** and learning implies that the primary task of instruction is to cover the material of the course or subject in a coherent and systematic manner. The teacher is viewed as an

TABLE 2-2

Teaching Styles by Broad Categories

Instructor-Centered Style	Student-Centered Style

Instructor-Centered
    Bergquist and Phillips 1975
Task-Oriented
    Fischer and Fischer 1979
Emotionally Exciting or Nonemotional
    Fischer and Fischer 1979
	Student-Centered
	    Bergquist and Phillips 1975
	Inferential
	    Blue 1986
	Child-Centered
	    Fischer and Fischer 1979

Content-Centered Style	**Teacher-Student-Centered Style**

Content-Centered
    Bergquist and Phillips 1975
Expository
    Blue 1986
Subject-Centered
    Fischer and Fischer 1979
	Cooperative Planning
	    Fischer and Fischer 1979
	
	Content-Student-Centered Style
	
	Learning-Centered
	    Fischer and Fischer 1979

Many educational researchers, listed here, have organized teaching styles first into broad categories, then into various approaches within those categories. Not any one of the teaching styles has proven to be exclusively effective.

expert or a formal authority; the goals of the course are based on the demands of the material. The teacher's primary methods are lectures and formal discussions. The students are usually measured objectively against the material (p. 18).

The **expository style**, according to Blue, involves a variety of lecturing techniques, lecture-recitation being the most prominent. Directive questioning is an important aspect of the expository style as well as is a strong reliance on textbooks and structured assignments. Most of the talk in the classroom is teacher oriented. Teachers impart information, keeping sequence and content under their control. The sequence is determined by the text and subject matter. Teachers are openly didactic, appeal to the learners' rationality, and don't believe that learners can be left to their own devices. The major goal of expository style teaching is academic achievement related to content taught (pp. 55–56).

The **subject-centered** teacher focuses on the content nearly to the exclusion of the learner. The goal of this type of teaching style is to "cover the subject," even if the student does not learn (Fischer and Fischer, p. 251). This classification is very similar to Bergquist and Phillips's content-centered teaching style, but there the student's learning is central.

Student-centered teaching and learning, according to Bergquist and Phillips, implies that the teacher is a facilitator and has a person-to-person relationship with each student. This method places a heavy emphasis on learning contracts drawn up between student and teacher that define goals, resources, and means of evaluation. Instruction is tailored to the needs of the student. Student-run group discussions, role playing, simulations, fieldwork, and independent study

Student-Centered Teaching Styles

are key instructional methods. This style emphasizes student-to-student and student-to-teacher interaction. Student experience is an important component. Both cognitive and affective goals are emphasized.

The **inferential style**, according to Blue, is primarily student centered. The teacher employs inquiry, discovery, discussion, simulations, values clarification, brainstorming, and independent study. The classroom of the inferential-style teacher is characterized by communication in which the teacher (sender) attempts to see the students' (receivers') points of view. The teacher encourages self-directed activities, delegates control to students whenever and wherever possible, attempts to allow for the students' psychological needs, engages the learners' sympathy, resorts to heuristic methods (use of experiment and trial and error), and believes that learners, with guidance, can educate themselves. The goal of this type of instruction is learner independence.

The **child-centered teaching style**, in its purest form, according to the Fischers, requires the teacher to provide a structure within which children can pursue whatever interests them. The curriculum emerges from the children's interests. This classification is similar to Bergquist and Phillips's student-centered teaching style, but in that style the curriculum does not emerge from the children; it is planned by the teacher.

Teacher-Student-Centered Teaching Style

In the **teacher-student-centered teaching style** both the teacher and student share equally in the planning of instruction. In this **cooperative planning** teaching style, teachers plan "the means and ends of instruction with student cooperation" (Fischer and Fischer, p. 250). Teachers encourage and support student participation in the learning process, and in guiding students' learning listen to their needs with respect.

Content-Student-Centered Learning Style

Content-student-centered learning styles balance the objectives of the material to be learned with the needs of the students. The **learning-centered** teacher has equal concern for the students, the curricular objectives, and the material to be learned. These teachers reject the "overemphasis" of the child-centered and subject-centered styles. The goal is to assist students, whatever their abilities, to develop toward curricular goals and autonomy in learning (Fischer and Fischer, p. 251).

Knowing the broad categories of teaching styles allows us to understand how the various approaches facilitate learning. Yet, according to educator Donald C. Orlich, "If there is one truism in teaching, it is there is no *one way* to teach anything or anyone" (1985, 5). In fact, the research indicates that, while there are many characteristics common to effective teachers, there is not yet one definitive style that will work for all teachers, in all situations, all the time.

Student-Centered Teaching

Influence of Effective Teaching Research on Teaching Style

The studies of Ned Flanders (1970), Barak Rosenshine and Norma F. Furst (1971), Herbert J. Walberg, Diane Schiller, and Geneva Haertel (1979), and Kenneth Macrorie (1984) found that student-centered teaching styles had a positive impact on student attitudes and achievement. In other words, teachers who allowed students to work on their own and to discover what they were to learn on their own were more effective than teachers who directed student learning. Jere Brophy and Thomas Good (1986) examined and synthesized earlier important effective teaching research and reported that one important variable that contributed to student achievement was the involvement of students in organizing and planning their own instruction, an essential component of inferential and student-centered instruction.

Instructor-Centered Teaching

Studies conducted by Robert S. Soars and Ruth M. Soars (1978), Jane Stallings (1974, 1977, 1978), Carolyn Evertson et al. (Junior High Study, 1980), and C. Denham and A. Lieberman (1980), and the Beginning Teacher Evaluation Study conducted between 1973–1977, determined that more direct, instructor-centered teaching benefits student achievement. In fact, the Stalling's teaching of basic skills (reading) in the secondary school study (1978) found a negative correlation between student achievement and choice of activities, one of the most important elements of student-centered instruction. Why do studies on effective teaching disagree on which teaching styles are most likely to promote student achievement?

Conclusion: Individual Teaching Styles

These studies of effective teaching seem to prove that, although successful teachers may possess many similar traits and characteristics, they do not necessarily apply them in the same way all the time. In other words, different styles of teaching are appropriate in different settings with different students.

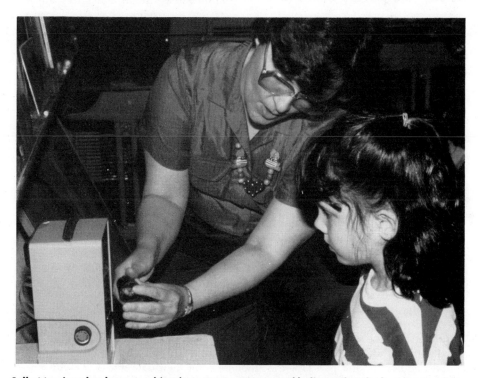

Sally Morrison has been teaching for seventeen years and believes that the best approach is not to utilize one particular teaching style but to be flexible and adapt various styles to the needs of a particular class or to a particular student in a class.

As Sally Morrison, a second-grade teacher with sixteen years teaching experience states,

> Meeting individual needs should be a full-time job. This includes being aware of individual needs, desires, and problems as well as talents. A teacher asks that the children do work to the best of their abilities, whatever the level, thus accomplishing their full potential. While letting the children be themselves, it is important to bring forth the "best self," bringing out and developing pride, responsibility, self-awareness and accomplishment. The teacher expects and gets each child's "best."
>
> It is important for goal setting to be a combined effort of student and teacher. Classes are provided with immediate goals and opportunities to put learning into practice. A teacher should have a sequential and thorough program to provide basic skills with numerous and varied activities which provide zest and flavor to the child's work. This way the child's work is not only *valid* but enjoyable. The teacher uses avenues of approach which appeal most to the child—love and affection, music and rhythm, color and motion, arts and crafts, puppetry, simple humor or whatever the individual best and most effectively responds to.

Morrison acknowledges that effective teachers adjust their teaching styles not only to different groups of students but to individual students within the group. In addition, she notes that there are some elements of instruction that are planned and implemented by the teacher (expository or instructor-centered instruction) and other elements that are jointly planned and implemented by child and teacher (inferential or student-centered instruction). Like all good teachers, Morrison can flexibly adjust pace, methodology, and interactive techniques depending on the needs of the individual child.

IN THE CLASSROOM

Gerry Young teaches middle school science in North Pole, Alaska. She claims to have begun teaching the way she was taught, moving lock-step through the textbook. Now however, she teaches science on a 25-acre natural lab that she has designed and developed.

Her lab began as a nature trail, with the help of a few small grants, several years ago. But, when she saw the benefit her students derived from their interaction with the environment, it became an outdoor classroom, in which the students observed, collected data, inferred, predicted, tested hypotheses, and applied their findings to their lives.

Today, it is not only a classroom, but an actual outdoor laboratory in which the students are keeping weekly records of local weather and snow depths for a Federal-State Cooperative Snow Survey. The Cooperative uses, according to Gerry, "core samples of the local snowpack to measure water density and accumulation. The information helps officials estimate how much groundwater will be available for agricultural needs" (p. 13).

Gerry's students are participating in the real world of science and understand the importance of, and take pride in, their accuracy. "Back in the classroom—which a colleague describes as part museum, part herbarium, part aquarium, and part lab—the students enter their data into a computerized data base" (*Learning*, Sept. 1989, p. 15).

Recently Gerry's students began testing the acid content in the snow. Unexpectedly, they found a low pH, indicating the possibility of future environmental damage because of slow acidifying precipitation. The students searched for pertinent variables. They hypothesized that local oil refineries could be affecting the acid content of the snow through their emission of sulfur dioxide. They also hypothesized that exhaust emissions or wood burning stoves could cause the increased acidity. They asked students at other Alaskan schools to test their hypotheses by measuring the acid content of snow near their schools. Over 70 schools participated in the first study of acid rain and snow in Alaska.

Gerry Young uses the teacher-student learning style very effectively. Her students not only learn about the environment but have the potential to make an impact on it.

BENEFITS OF EFFECTIVE TEACHING RESEARCH

Documenting the common, observable attributes of effective teaching is one step toward helping us better understand what it takes to be a good teacher. And for the first time, researchers are using the teacher as the basis for making this determination. In earlier decades, it was not unusual to measure successful teaching by studying what it takes to be successful in business, medicine, or law on the assumption that success in one field automatically extends to success in other fields. For example, in the early 1970s, thousands of educational administrators were trained by the American Management Association for the purpose of adapting the skills used in business management to education. These administrators then trained classroom teachers in the use of the management-by-objective concept in their instructional programs and in their classrooms (Chabator and Montgomery 1972).

According to Theodore Sizer, until the qualities that make a teacher good are accessible to everyone, teachers will not be empowered. In other words, teachers must understand from their successful peers what skills and traits are likely to make them successful, and they must be given the opportunity to develop them. Those who are judged to be effective must help other teachers develop essential teaching skills. Until this occurs, Sizer maintains, teaching will fail to be a profession.

Danger of Conformity in the Implementation of Effective Teaching Research

Some educators worry that documenting the qualities of effective teachers will lead to a situation where *all* teachers are required to fit into a particular mold. In addition, since most of the researchers select effective teachers based on the achievement of their students, usually measured by standardized tests, they worry that the unmeasurable qualities of teaching, its art, will be left out of the formula for developing effectiveness and rob teachers of their individual spontaneity. If this is the case, critics suggest, teachers will have less control and will be less happy in the profession. These critics are concerned that if effective teaching research is used to require teachers to become model effective teachers, the best and brightest teachers will leave the profession.

According to Louis Harris in the 1988 *Metropolitan Survey of the American Teacher*, "There has been a dramatic increase in the number of teachers with less than five years' experience who say they are likely to leave [the profession]. In 1987, 20 percent of those with less than five years of teaching experience said that they were likely to leave teaching, compared to 34 percent—more than one out of three—in 1988" (p. 13). As all the teachers quoted in chapter 1 indicate, what they find rewarding about teaching is using their own ingenuity, their own unique style, to help students learn. Critics of prescribed teaching content and methodology, including potential misuse of effective teaching research, suggest that this increase in those who want to leave teaching may be a result of less flexibility in making personal teaching decisions.

The danger in effective teaching research lies not in the research or in the information gained, but rather in how this research is used by educators. If we attempt to make all teachers clones of a model effective teacher, the danger will be realized. As Richard Turner says, "A widespread problem in school districts, in schools of education, and in educational research is the idea that there is a single best style of teaching and that teachers should be highly skilled in that style" (1979, 258).

On the other hand, if the research is considered useful by teachers and prospective teachers in developing their skills, it is likely they will become better at what they do. In fact, the development of one's skills will enhance one's personal teaching style. "Some teachers are superb lecturers, others are excellent discussion leaders, others are at their best in one-to-one tutorial sessions. Some teachers are witty, others impress us with their honesty, others with erudition. Some are firm. Others relaxed and informal. . . . Good teaching is not one way of acting but many ways" (Jackson 1986, 14).

Point/Counterpoint

CONTENT-CENTERED TEACHING

Marva Collins taught in two inner-city Chicago schools. She believed it was most important that impoverished black children learn how to read. She focused on the teaching of phonics. According to Collins, an experienced black teacher, children should be taught all the regular and irregular patterns of English and the phonetic rules and their exceptions before they learn a single word. She taught the skills of reading by focusing on content and paying attention to the individual needs of her students.

A child who doesn't know how to read can't do anything. But children do not learn to read by osmosis. It requires work—hard, boring work without any shortcuts. It is drill and more drill. Repetition and memorization. . . .

On the first day of school the children learned to read, write, and spell *Meet me*. On the second day I used the same method to introduce a new initial consonant, the letter *s*. The children pronounced the consonant and vowel sounds in *See me*, and then they went to the board and wrote the words as I dictated. Having learned the *ee* spelling for the vowel sound *e*, the class went on to learn that *ea* also says *e*. I wrote *e* on the board, putting a macron over the *e* and a slash through the silent letter, and the children read and wrote *See me eat*. (p. 93)

By November, I saw the daily regimen of phonics drills beginning to work. It was a tedious, repetitive method of teaching reading, tedious for me as well as for the children. But there was no substitute for its effectiveness. (p. 65)

Each child at the school got the work he or she needed. . . .

If a child was having difficulty with homonyms such as *to* and *too*, the appropriate worksheet would be on the desk the next morning. (p. 117)

From: Collins and Tamarkin, 1982

STUDENT-CENTERED TEACHING

Pat Conroy, a young white teacher who was educated in white schools and had no experience teaching black children, taught impoverished black youngsters on Yamacraw Island off the coast of South Carolina in the preintegration 1960s. He shared the teaching in the two-room elementary school with Mrs. Brown, a black teacher with many years' experience teaching black children who warned him about his students, "You've got to treat them stern." Conroy taught the older children in grades five through eight and found that the student-centered approach he believed to be successful with the children was often in conflict with Mrs. Brown's teacher-centered approach. Indeed, Conroy found his teaching style in conflict with the administration and the school board. He says of a speech he gave to the school board at the end of his first year on Yamacraw [fictional name for Daufuskie Island], "I then recited the litany of ignorance I found the first week. 'Six children who could not recite the alphabet. Eighteen children who did not know the President. Eighteen children who did not know what country they lived in. . . .' I slammed twenty-three of these strange facts down their throats, hoping they would gag and choke on the knowledge . . ." (p. 260). He blamed the school board and the administration for their lack of concern for these children, and the teaching style of Mrs. Brown for the students' lack of knowledge. His own style attempted to counter these problems.

I have read a number of books by teachers who had brilliant success by using certain methods. I would stumble upon an idea in the morning that seemed surpassingly clever and relevant, then find it foolish and absurd by the afternoon. Or what appeared ordained by the gods in autumn seemed commonplace and senseless by spring. What fired the imagination of my students one week bored and stultified them the next. So there was constant shifting in emphasis, approach, and material. The one great knave that I hunted was boredom, and if I caught him lurking anywhere in the room, in corners, by blackboards, behind the covers of books, or in glazed, anesthetized eyes, we went to something else quickly, shifted in midstream, danced, sang, fought, or milked rats. But always we spoke of the world beyond the river. The cities with their stables of cars, their flow of people, their massive stores, their baseball teams, and their hidden dangers. . . . Always we turned outward to where they would drift when they left Yamacraw, to the world of lights and easy people, to the dark cities that would devour their innocence and harden their dreams.
The one goal I developed the first week that never changed was to prepare the kids for the day when they would leave the island for the other side. (pp. 234-235)

Conroy attempted to do this by bringing visitors to his classroom. Guests who talked about their lives, read stories, taught the children Mozart, taught them to play soccer. And Conroy took the children on trips. At first they went across the river to celebrate Halloween in Conroy's hometown of Beaufort, South Carolina. Late in the year Conroy and the children visited Washington, D.C., despite the protestations of Mrs. Brown.

Mrs. Brown, whose primary job on the island seemed to be crapehanger, forbade all plans to leave the island for any reason. "Those children have had their fun. Now it's time to work. Fun time is over. They need drill in readin', writin', and 'rithmetic. They don't need no Washington, D.C. The state department says we gotta get through the books. You aren't even usin' the books, Mr. Conroy. Not even usin' the books." (pp. 236-237)

From: Conroy, 1972

POSTSCRIPT

The argument between Mrs. Brown and Pat Conroy relates to which teaching methods are most successful and what content must be taught. It is likely that Marva Collins and Pat Conroy would have a similar disagreement. However, they are arguing about more than methods and content; they are arguing about teaching style.

The teaching style of Marva Collins is based on her firm belief that in order to succeed all children must be taught how to read. And, indeed, she believes that all children *can* be taught to read. There is no doubt that she has successfully taught many who had been called hopeless by other teachers. In fact, as her coauthor, Civia Tamarkin, reports in the book's preface, "a segment of CBS *60 Minutes* had named her the miracle worker who had succeeded where other teachers had failed" (pp. 9-10).

Pat Conroy's teaching style is based on his belief that teaching methods such as those prescribed by elementary school textbooks and state departments of education have not worked; in fact, they have produced massive ignorance. He found that his fifth through eighth graders couldn't read in spite of having been force-fed phonics since first grade, and many couldn't even spell their names. Nor did they know any facts about the state or country in which they lived. His success is more difficult to measure than is Marva Collins's. Even he admits that students' progress in terms of language is limited. However, he contends that continued efforts such as his will make them more able to cope with life.

Who is correct? We'll leave that up to you to decide. However, we think you'll agree that both Marva Collins and Pat Conroy were effective teachers who based their individual teaching style on firmly held personal beliefs and values, a philosophy of teaching and learning.

Cultures-of-Teaching Research

Another recent trend in research on teaching may mitigate the potential cloning danger of implementing effective teacher research. Sharon Feiman-Nemser and Robert Floden, in reporting on what they call cultures of teaching, examine how teachers define their work situations.

These researchers are finding a great deal of variety in how teachers view their work—differences related to age, experience, social and cultural background, gender, marital status, subject matter, and wisdom and ability. However, they are also finding that the extrinsic and intrinsic rewards of teaching are not the same for all teachers.

Extrinsic Rewards

The extrinsic (external) rewards of teaching include relatively high salary, short working hours, elevated status, and significant power. According to cultures-of-teaching studies, "Teachers vary in the importance they attach to both extrinsic and intrinsic rewards. Even the supposedly objective benefits of money and status are not valued equally by all teachers" (Feiman-Nemser and Floden, p. 510). Frequently these differences stem from the teacher's economic and social status and gender.

The fact that most teachers are women has, according to these studies, negatively affected the status of teaching and the self-image of teachers. Women carry a "double burden in society" by combining career with home and family. "The study of teaching careers using male professionals and businessmen as templates has not done justice to teaching, an occupation dominated by women" (Feiman-Nemser and Floden, p. 523). Cultures-of-teaching studies have found that the extrinsic rewards that are crucial in some professions do not necessarily apply to all teachers, perhaps because 68 percent of teachers are women (83 percent of elementary teachers and 49 percent of secondary teachers).

Intrinsic Rewards

The cultures-of-teaching studies (Lortie 1975; Biklen 1983; Feiman-Nemser and Floden 1986) show that the intrinsic (internal) rewards of teaching include knowing that students are learning, having an emotional attachment to them, enjoying interaction with colleagues, deriving satisfaction in performing a valuable service, enjoying teaching activities themselves, and learning from teaching.

Many teachers find that the intrinsic rewards of the classroom outweigh extrinsic rewards. According to Feiman-Nemser and Floden, "The primary importance of career ambition may be appropriate for some occupations, but these characteristics need not be desirable in all teachers" (p. 523). Biklen found that women teachers frequently rejected promotions to administrative positions because they were highly committed to teaching and maintained that if they did move to administration, the quality of their work would suffer. "The point is to offer an array of rewards that will meet many teachers' needs" (Feiman-Nemser and Floden, p. 523).

Value of Diversity in Teaching

The cultures-of-teaching studies and concerns over the danger of implementing effective teaching research make the recommendations of Daniel Duke in *Teaching: The Imperiled Profession* (1984) very important if we are to maintain a diverse, talented teaching force. According to Duke, we must begin valuing diversity in teaching instead of acting as if there were one best kind of teacher—there is "no approach to teaching that has been shown to be uniformly effective for all ages of students or all subjects" (p. 138). We must begin thinking of teaching not only as a set of technical skills—such as problem solving, hypothesis testing, decision making, information processing, logical analysis, and resource allocation rather than as a way to impart subject matter—but we also must begin thinking of teachers as discipline-based scholars as well as instructor-teacher-historians, teacher-child development specialists. Duke suggests that not all teachers should be expected to teach the same students. "Perhaps teachers should be spending more time assessing their different strengths and matching them with the strengths of particular students" (p. 138). He suggests that teachers' schedules could be flexible enough for them to teach late afternoons and evenings. Adult students as well as younger students might be encouraged to attend school. Duke maintains that at least some teachers should act as coaches so as to learn effective motivating techniques. "Coaches do not rely much on asking questions, yet they often manage to elicit outstanding performances from their players" (p. 140). Duke further suggests that teachers may possess differing skills at age fifty-five than they had at age twenty-two. Therefore, he questions whether it might be possible to give different-age teachers different teaching responsibilities. Perhaps, more experienced teachers would assume new teaching roles such as supervisor or adjunct university professor. Duke concludes that his suggestions are only a few of the possible ways in which the teaching profession can begin to value the diversity of its teachers.

OBSERVING IN CLASSROOMS

One important technique for learning about effective teaching is to observe effective teachers at work in their classrooms. This is a skill, however, that needs to be developed in order to yield the best results. One needs to know what to look for, how to look for it, and how to be objective in one's analysis.

In the following excerpts, two different university students observe the same teacher in a second-grade classroom. Note how, in their analysis, they came to different conclusions.

CROSS-CULTURAL PERSPECTIVE

Japanese Teachers Do More Than Drill

Many Westerners believe that Japanese educational successes are due to an emphasis on rote learning and memorization, that the classroom is rigidly disciplined. This is far from reality. An American teacher walking into a fourth-grade science class in Japan would be horrified: children all talking at once, leaping and calling for the teacher's attention. The typical American wonders, "Who's in control?"

But if one understands the content of the lively chatter, it is clear that all the noise and movement is focused on the work itself—children are shouting out answers, suggesting other methods, exclaiming in excitement over results, and not gossiping, teasing, or planning games for recess. As long as it is the result of this engagement, the teacher is not concerned over the noise, which may measure a teacher's success. (It has been estimated that American teachers spend about 60 percent of class time on organizing, controlling, and disciplining the class, while Japanese teachers spend only 10 percent.)

A fifth-grade math class I observed reveals some elements of this pedagogy. The day I visited, the class was presented with a general statement about cubing. Before any concrete facts, formulae, or even drawings were displayed, the teacher asked the class to take out their math diaries and spend a few minutes writing down their feelings and anticipations over this new concept. It is hard for me to imagine an American math teacher beginning a lesson with an exhortation to examine one's emotional predispositions about cubing (but that may be only because my own math training was antediluvian).

After that, the teacher asked for conjectures from the children about the surface and volume of a cube and asked for some ideas about formulae for calculation. The teacher asked the class to cluster into its component *han* (working groups) of four or five children each, and gave out materials for measurement and construction. One group left the room with large pieces of cardboard, to construct a model of a cubic meter. The groups worked internally on solutions to problems set by the teacher and competed with each other to finish first. After a while, the cubic meter group returned, groaning under the bulk of its model, and everyone gasped over its size. (There were many comments and guesses as to how many children would fit inside.)

The teacher then set the whole class a very challenging problem, well over their heads, and

---

Sarah's Observation Log

As soon as the bell rang the children moved quietly to their seats. They seemed to know exactly what to do, exactly what was expected of them. They put their books in their desks and folded their hands on top of the desk as Mrs. Menotti instructed the two class monitors to collect the lunch money and the picture money. She reminded them to have each child check off his name on the list when his money was turned in. As the students did this Mrs. Menotti read the morning announcements. All the time she read she was monitoring the students collecting the money. There were no disruptions and the students seemed to collect the money in an orderly fashion. She did not call the roll, but I saw her put the attendance on the outside of the classroom door. Because the children have assigned seats, she can simply look to see who is not present. All of this was accomplished in less than ten minutes.

Mrs. Menotti told the children she would meet first with the red reading group in the reading circle. The other children would find their assignments on the board written in the color of their reading group. What a great idea! I'll have to remember this one. The children quietly took out their books and all but two began to work while Mrs. Menotti was telling the reading group what to do.

gave them the rest of the class time to work on it. The class ended without a solution, but the teacher made no particular effort to get or give an answer, although she exhorted them to be energetic. (It was several days before the class got the answer—but the excitement did not flag.)

Several characteristics of this class deserve highlighting. First, there was attention to feelings and predispositions, provision of facts, and opportunities for discovery. The teacher preferred to focus on process, engagement, commitment, and performance rather than on discipline (in our sense) and production.

Second, the *han:* assignments are made to groups, not to individuals (this is also true at the workplace) although individual progress and achievement are closely monitored. Children are supported, praised, and allowed to make mistakes through trial and error within the group. The group is also pitted against other groups, and the group's success is each person's triumph, and vice versa. Groups are made up by the teacher and are designed to include a mixture of skill levels—there is a *hancho* (leader) whose job it is to choreograph the group's work, to encourage the slower members, and to act as a reporter to the class at large.

The regular classroom is a place where the individual does not stick out, but where individual needs are met and goals are set. Children are not held back nor advanced by ability; the cohesion of the age group is said to be more important. Teachers focus on pulling up the slower learners, rather than tracking the class to suit different abilities.

So where is the competitive selection principle served? In the *juku. Juku* are tough competitive classes, often with up to 500 in one lecture hall. The most prestigious are themselves very selective and there are examinations (and preparation courses for these) to enter the *juku.* Some *juku* specialize in particular universities' entrance exams, and they will boast of their rate of admission into their universities. It is estimated that one-third of all primary school students and one-half of all secondary school students attend *juku.*

The "king of *juku,*" Furukawa Noboru, the creator of a vast chain of such classes, says that *juku* are necessary to bridge the gap of present realities in Japan. He says that public schools do not face the fact of competition, and that ignoring the reality does not help children. While there is considerable grumbling by parents, and while it is clear that the *juku* introduce an inegalitarian element into the process of schooling (since they do cost money), they do, by their separation from the regular school, permit the persistence of more traditional modes of learning, while allowing for a fast track in examinations.

From: White, 1987

When she looked up and saw one child not working and another talking to the child next to him, she went to the board and wrote their names on it. The children immediately got to work.

Though I couldn't really hear the reading group I could see the flip chart on which Mrs. Menotti had written letter combinations that would be used in the story. I could tell that each child was reading round robin fashion and that Mrs. Menotti interrupted only when the child needed help sounding out a word.

Since the rest of the class was working quietly in their workbooks, I took this time to look at the classroom. I was impressed with how neat and organized it was. All the desks were in neat rows. In the right front of the room is the reading circle. Mrs. Menotti sits so that she can see the children in the circle and the rest of the room. On the walls are colorful posters. The bookshelves are very carefully organized. On the bulletin board behind Mrs. Menotti's desk is a neat display of student work. All of the work on the board is very nicely done and displayed. There is an overhead projector in the front of the room. Also there are maps and a globe. There are lots of dictionaries and books in the book cabinets. There are no papers on the floor and the children keep their books in their desks. Mrs. Menotti keeps the shades drawn most of the way down so the children are not distracted.

Only once during the reading group did Mrs. Menotti have to stop to reprimand a student. It was one of the same students as earlier and she went to the board to put a check next to his name and reminded him that it was not art time and he shouldn't be drawing and should be working in his workbook. He put his drawing in his desk, but I noticed that he did not concentrate on his workbook, but doodled around the edge of the pages. At one point I noticed that he was doing his drawing inside his desk. Mrs. Menotti did not seem to notice, and I wondered if I should tell her.

After about twenty minutes the reading groups changed in an orderly fashion. The blue group went to the reading circle and the red group took out their books and began doing the assignments written in red on the board.

I was really impressed by the order and organization in this classroom. Almost all the students were quiet and actively involved in their work. Mrs. Menotti was able to work with the few students in the reading group. I hope I can have an orderly classroom like this one some day.

Steve's Observation Log

The same morning Steve observed in Mrs. Menotti's classroom. Here are some excerpts from his observation log:

I got to the classroom about ten minutes before the bell was to ring. I introduced myself to Mrs. Menotti. Though she seemed friendly and told me to make myself at home, I had the feeling that she was distracted and rather cool. The children were having a wonderful time talking and giggling in small groups. The boys in the group nearest me were talking about the soccer game. They were really excited that they had won. I already knew that I'd like these children. They were enthusiastic, bright-eyed and bushy-tailed.

When the bell rang, everything changed. The atmosphere became rigid. Mrs. Menotti stood in the front of the room staring at the class. She didn't say anything, but her message was clear, "It's time to get to work." The students stopped talking and moved to their desks which were in rigid rows. Mrs. Menotti never smiled or said "good morning"; she just told the two monitors to collect lunch and picture money as she read the announcements. I noticed that the students selected as monitors appeared to be upper class students in expensive looking clothes. While they were taking the money one of them seemed to be giving some of the less well-dressed children a hard time, but Mrs. Menotti did not seem to notice. Since the children's seats seemed to be assigned she took attendance without calling roll. Though the class is orderly, it seems as if the children might as well not be there. The only ones Mrs. Menotti has called by name are the monitors. I think my first impression was right; Mrs. Menotti is a very cold woman.

I couldn't help notice how cold the classroom is. The only work of the children that is displayed is behind Mrs. M's desk where the children can't go easily. It looks like perfect penmanship papers to me. The only other decoration in the room is mass-marketed posters that look like they've been here since Mrs. M started teaching twenty years ago. The shades are down and the only light in the room is artificial. I would hate to be a student here and my sense is the children don't much like it either. I've not seen one smile since the bell rang.

When it was time to go to reading group Mrs. Menotti called the red group to the circle. Is this class ability grouped? I think so. It looks like all the children in the red group wear designer clothes. The two monitors are in that group. When they get in the group Mrs. M notices two boys who have not yet started to work in their workbooks. It seems that one boy can't read the assignment on the board, and I can understand why. He's in the yellow group so the assignment is written in yellow and hard to see from where he sits. However, Mrs. M does not ask why he is talking, she just puts his name on the board. I notice a tear in his eye. I am beginning to dislike Mrs. Menotti. Another boy is fussing in his desk. He doesn't seem to be able to find his book, so his name goes on the board too.

I watch the reading group for about ten minutes and it looks deadly. Mrs. Menotti has letter combinations on the flip chart. As the children read in order she points to the letters and asks them to make the sound. It seems to me these children read very well and do not need this kind of instruction. Since I am bored I decide to walk around to see what kind of seat work the kids are doing. Each group seems to be working on a different page in the same workbook. I can tell who the "smart" kids are. They can tell, too. At one point, Mrs. Menotti stops the reading group to yell at the same boy who could not see the board earlier. He is still not doing his work. I noticed earlier that he was drawing and he's a really good artist. But, she does not acknowledge his ability, instead his name gets a check and she tells him he can come in after school to do his seat work. So much for the value of art in this classroom!

It's no wonder so many kids drop out of school before they graduate. Mrs. Menotti has already decided that Shane, the artist, will be one of them. What hope is there for Shane?

Conclusion

Both Sarah and Steve observed the same class during the same period of time; each saw a totally different Mrs. Menotti in a radically different situation. Sarah's Mrs. Menotti was well organized, and the classroom environment was conducive to work and study. Steve's Mrs. Menotti distanced herself from the students, and the environment was controlled and nonproductive. How could two students from the same university class see such different things in the identical classroom?

Defining Observation

Most simply, observation is the act or practice of paying attention to people, events, and/or environment. The difficulty with observation is simply that every individual brings to an event his or her psychological perception of it.

However, not all observation is subjective. It also can occur systematically and be conducted fairly objectively. The fact that Sarah and Steve were required to observe in Mrs. Menotti's classroom means that the observation was deliberate, and, therefore, more formalized than everyday observation. However, it was not systematic. **Systematic observation** is long-term observation involving visiting a classroom many times and observing many different situations. It is planned, objective, and is goal or question oriented. The observers identify beforehand what they are looking for and how they will carry it out. Sarah and Steve did neither. Thus, their observations may simply have reinforced their existing prejudices, thereby "arresting or distorting the growth from further experiences" (Evertson and Green, p. 95).

Objectivity in Observation

Because teachers and classrooms are so different, observation can be difficult. If the observer tries to do more than record exactly what he or she has seen, the conclusions will be filtered through his or her prejudices and biases.

The criteria for objective observation are *(1) observe an entire event or sequence, (2) set goals, limits, and guidelines prior to the observation, (3) record observations completely and carefully, and (4) record objectively without bias or prejudice.*

The goal of the systematic observer, then, is to gather as much data as possible over a period of several observations about the classroom, the students, the teacher, and the curriculum. The more data collected, the easier it will be to get a complete picture. The methods of obtaining as objective a point of view as possible involve anecdotal observation, structured observation, and interview. **Anecdotal observations** focus on the situation and specifically on who says or does what rather than on personalities or interpretations of events. **Structured observations** are informal and require that observers look for and record specified information that is called for on such things as checklists, sociograms, and profiles. The **interview** is a technique that seeks to find information through direct questioning. This method can be extremely valuable in understanding a procedure one has observed or the rationale behind it. The interview must be planned for and conducted as objectively as possible.

The specific tools and techniques you need to conduct these observations are available in the observation guide that accompanies this text.

Systematic observation of teachers, students, and classrooms gives preservice teachers the opportunity to learn from effective teachers at work. They can use in their own development what they have learned through their observations.

2.2 POINTS TO REMEMBER

- Teaching style is a composite of what the individual teacher believes about teaching and learning and how this philosophy is translated in the classroom.
- Teaching methods are techniques. Teachers can use similar methods and teach identical content even when they have very different teaching styles.
- Teaching styles can be categorized in numerous ways. The most common means is by determining whether the teacher, learner, or content is the central focus of the teaching.
- Some studies of effective teaching claim that teacher-centered teaching is more effective than student-centered teaching; others claim the reverse. This is probably because different styles of teaching are effective in different situations with different students.
- Effective teaching research can help teachers develop the traits and skills of effective teachers. On the other hand, if it is assumed that there is one type of effective teacher, the implementation of the research could limit the teacher's ability to develop a personal teaching style.
- Cultures-of-teaching research reveals that some teachers consider job advancement to be very important; others are more interested in intrinsic rewards such as interpersonal and professional relationships.
- Teachers develop their own personal teaching styles depending on their strengths and the needs of their students. Since students differ, it is important that there be significant diversity among teachers.
- Systematic observations help preservice teachers learn a great deal about teaching. They are planned, objective, and are goal and question oriented, helping students avoid biased judgments of the teaching they observe.
- Objective observation of teaching requires that students observe numerous lessons and record what they observe carefully, completely, and without bias; that they observe the entire event or sequence and set limits, goals, or guidelines for the observation.

FOR THOUGHT/DISCUSSION

1. How can teachers learn to understand their students if they have no shared identity?

2. Must all effective teachers have the same qualities? Why or why not?

3. How can research into teaching styles help teachers improve instruction?

4. How is it possible for observations of classroom situations to be understood in terms of one's own bias?

FOR FURTHER READING/REFERENCE

Carter, J. M. 1987. *Confessions of a space cadet: The transformation of a teacher.* Lanham, MD: Hamilton Press. A personal story about how a high school teacher became an effective professional.

Collins, M., and Tamarkin, C. 1982. *Marva Collins' way.* Los Angeles: J. P. Tarcher. A journalist relates the story of Marva Collins, an inner-city teacher who has successfully taught children and adults whom other educators and schools had given up on.

Conroy. P. 1972. *The water is wide.* Boston: Houghton Mifflin. A moving saga of Pat Conroy's year of teaching the children on isolated Yamacraw Island off the coast of South Carolina. This book was made into the popular motion picture *Conrack.*

Delbosco, J. S. 1986. *Effective teaching practices: An instructional handbook for teachers and supervisors.* Huntington, NY: Diamond Designs. A cookbook approach to developing a broad range of teaching skills and values.

Joyce, B., and Weil, M. 1986. *Models of teaching.* 3rd ed. Englewood Cliffs, NJ: Prentice-Hall. An interesting delineation with numerous examples of various models and styles of teaching. The book illustrates how many different approaches to teaching can be successful.

James Warren in *Phi Delta Kappan.*

"I expect you all to be independent, innovative, critical thinkers who will do exactly as I say."

3

Becoming a Teacher

Long before the effective teaching movement of the 1980s, John C. Crowley (1970) wrote this letter to his student teacher. In it Crowley summarizes what it takes to become an effective teacher.

Dear Bill:

Well, your baptism by fire is about over. You have passed through that vague state appropriately mislabelled as "Student Teacher." Soon you will return to the more familiar and secure world of the college campus.

I hope your teaching experience was of some value. Throughout the time we worked together I made repeated plans to sit down with you and have a long talk—a "tell it like it is" type session. Unfortunately, except for between-class chats and noontime gab sessions, our talks never did get down to the nitty-gritty. So, with due apologies for a letter instead of a talk, this will have to do.

If you leave here feeling to some degree satisfied and rewarded, accept these feelings. You have worked diligently and consistently. For your part you have a right to feel rewarded. Teaching offers many intangible bonuses; feeling satisfied when a class goes well is one of them. The day teaching no longer offers to you the feelings of satisfaction and reward is the day you should seriously consider another profession.

Mingled with these feelings is also one of discouragement. Accept this too. Accept it, learn to live with it, and be grateful for it. Of course certain classes flopped; some lesson plans were horror shows; and some kids never seemed to get involved or turned on. This is not a phenomenon experienced only by student teachers. We all encounter this. The good teacher profits from it—he investigates the reasons for failure and seeks to correct himself, his approach, or his students. And in so doing, the good teacher further improves and gets better.

Bad teachers develop mental calluses, blame it on the kids, and sweep the failures under the rug. Always be discouraged and unsatisfied; it's the trademark of a good, professional teacher.

I don't know if you plan to make teaching your career—perhaps, at this point, you don't know yourself—but if you do, I'm sure you will do well; you have the potential. In the event you do elect a teaching career, I would offer these suggestions:

1. Develop a philosophy for yourself and your job. Why do you teach? What do you expect of yourself and your students? Do not chisel this philosophy in stone. Etch it lightly in pencil on your mind, inspect it frequently. Do not be surprised that it changes—that can be a good sign. Be more concerned with the reasons for a change rather than the change itself. Unless you base your teaching on a foundation of goals and ideals, you are wasting time. . . .

2. Do not be just "a teacher," be a professional teacher. Teaching is the most rewarding, demanding, and important job in the world. We deal with the minds of men and the future of the world. It is not a task to be taken lightly. Demand professionalism of yourself and your associates. Do not shut

yourself up in a classroom, isolated from and ignorant of the real world. Be prepared to teach at any time, in any place, to anyone. Ferret out ignorance with the zeal of a crusader and the compassion of a saint. Teach as if the fate of mankind rested squarely upon your shoulders and you'll know, in part, what I mean.

3. Always be a learner. Never assume you know all the answers or enough material to teach your class. Read constantly. Do not become an encapsulated specialist. Vary the material. Talk to others. Most of all, learn to listen to your students . . . not to what they say but to what they mean.

A good teacher learns as much from his students as he teaches to them. Do not discourage dialogue. Do not be so dogmatic as to accept only your own views. Do not use the textbook as a mental crutch. . . .

4. Develop the feeling of empathy. Try to feel how the student feels. Do not lapse into the warm complacency of a seating chart, names without faces. Do not accept the cold facts of a rank book, marks without personality. . . .

[See] the boy in the back of the room. Bad teeth, poor complexion, shabby clothes. No known father, a promiscuous mother, and a cold-water flat in a bad part of town. Of course he acts up and appears rebellious; wouldn't you? How have we alleviated his problems by assigning detention time and writing a bad progress report? How does it feel to sit in class day after day hungry, ill, knowing that when the last bell rings it will be back to the sewer?

Is it any wonder that Jacksonian Democracy, the English morality plays, or Boyle's Law leaves these kids cold? But if they are to eventually move into society we must reach them, and the first step comes when we, as teachers, understand them. . . .

5. Finally, alluding to the misadventures of Don Quixote, I would counsel—"Do not be afraid of windmills!" As a conscientious, professional teacher you will find your path constantly bestraddled with windmills of one type or another.

These may come in the form of other teachers, guidance departments, administrators, department heads, school committees, parents, or heaven knows what. They will obstruct, criticize, belittle, and attack you for a variety of reasons and motives. If you think you are right, do not back down! Always be willing to go as far as necessary to defend your convictions and beliefs. Do not avoid experimentation for fear of mistakes or criticism!

If we accept the status quo and maintain a conservative view toward change, we will not progress. In fact, we'll probably regress. We have an obligation, as educators, to constantly seek better ways of doing things. If that means putting our heads on the chopping block, so be it. Either we stand for something or we stand for nothing. If we stand for something it should be so important that any sacrifice to preserve and further it is worthwhile. And, as educators, we are under a moral and ethical responsibility to stand for something.

After studying this chapter, you should be able to:

- Explain what coursework is included in most teacher education programs.
- Explain why fieldwork is important in the training of teachers.
- Examine some of the technology used in teacher training.
- Discuss why there is diversity in how teachers are educated and trained.
- Examine the differences among the teachers' college model, liberal arts model, and competency-based model to teacher training.
- Discuss the variety of five-year programs.
- Examine alternative approaches to teacher training.
- Identify reasons that alternative approaches are controversial.
- Compare and contrast the teacher education reforms suggested by reform commissions of the 1980s and 1990s.
- Discuss outcomes of the reform reports including changes in coursework required, national certification of teachers, and national accreditation of teacher education programs.

Well, I hope these words of advice have proved helpful. Repeating an earlier statement, you have great potential and I personally hope you put it to use as a teacher.

I know of no other job that compares with teaching. We need every promising candidate who comes along. It goes without saying of course that should you need a letter of recommendation I will be only too glad to supply it. Having participated in your student teaching experience I also feel morally obliged to assist you should you, at some future date, require and want assistance. It's there for the asking.

Very truly yours,
Jack Crowley

In Jack Crowley's letter to Bill the emphasis is on both the skills and attributes of the effective teacher. Crowley would no doubt agree with Robert N. Bush of Stanford University when he asserts, "I am inclined to doubt that genuine artistry in teaching can develop without a thorough underpinning of scholarly, scientific study and training in many of the specific aspects of teaching" (1967, 35). Crowley also tells Bill, "Unless you base your teaching on a foundation of goals and ideals, you are wasting time."

In spite of their institutions' commitment to help preservice teachers develop all the characteristics of effective teachers, many critics of teacher education believe that teachers are ill-prepared for the challenges of the contemporary classroom. These critics have suggested many reforms. According to researchers Kenneth R. Howey and Nancy L. Zimpher in *Profiles of Preservice Teacher Education* (1989), "critics of teacher education, always plentiful, now have the floor. 'Reform' proposals abound" (p. 1).

This chapter will first examine how contemporary teachers are educated and the importance of fieldwork in the training of teachers. We will then look at alternatives to traditional teacher-training programs. Finally, we will investigate teacher education reform movements of the 1980s and 1990s.

TEACHER EDUCATION PROGRAMS IN THE 1990S

Most contemporary teachers are educated in colleges and universities. Nearly 1,200, or 70 percent of all four-year colleges and universities in the United States, have state-approved teacher certification programs (NCES 1989b, 237). **Certification** is a procedure whereby the state evaluates and reviews a teacher candidate's credentials and provides him or her a license to teach. More than 60 percent of these institutions are private and grant bachelor's degrees only, and

38 percent are public (NCES 1989b, 237). Although private colleges represent the largest percentage of institutions training teachers, 78 percent of all bachelor-level teachers are trained in public institutions (p. 236).

Coursework

Teacher education programs generally have three components: general liberal arts, major and minor fields of specialization, and professional studies. In 1989 the Association of Colleges for Teacher Education reported that elementary teacher certification students took, on the average, 40 percent of their coursework in general liberal arts, 32 percent of their coursework in professional studies (methodology, foundations, fieldwork, and psychology), 9 percent in student teaching, and 15 percent in an academic concentration. Secondary teacher certification students took 40 percent of their coursework in general liberal arts, 39 percent in major and minor fields of specialization, and 21 percent in professional studies (AACTE 1989).

There is, however, significant diversity around the country in the number of hours required in academic and professional studies. For example, in 1988, California required 84 semester hours in general education for elementary certification, 12 in methodology, and an equal number in field experiences; while Mississippi had no specific coursework requirements. The highest number of semester hours in professional studies for elementary certification are required by Puerto Rico (90), Oregon (64), Missouri (60), and Utah (58). The highest number of semester hours in general education for elementary certification are required by Indiana (95–100), Iowa (95–100), North Dakota (91), Alabama (60–87), Maryland (80), and Colorado (75) (Council of Chief State School Officers 1988).

In a study of twenty-nine colleges and universities with teacher education programs in eight states, John Goodlad and his associates (1990) found that undergraduate programs leading to teacher certification were usually between 120 and 132 semester hours in length. Of the twenty-nine institutions, which ranged in size from 900 to 35,000 students, 24 had four-year undergraduate programs in education. Five required a fifth-year certificate. Most of these programs required two years of general studies, a concentration in an academic discipline for secondary certification students, and some academic coursework for elementary certification students. Goodlad found that the number of methods courses required of teacher certification students had decreased in recent years. His study concluded that fieldwork, however, was increasingly important in the teacher certification programs he reviewed.

Fieldwork

The dominant approach to teacher training today is based on **fieldwork**, the concept that effective teaching requires a combination of teaching skills, knowledge of subject matter, and appropriate personality traits and values.

A survey of former and current teachers, conducted by Louis Harris and Associates for the Metropolitan Life Insurance Company in 1985, found that 50 percent thought it was more important for preservice teachers to spend time on teaching skills than on subject matter; however, 50 percent thought the opposite. The dilemma of how to balance coursework and fieldwork has still not been solved, and the percentage of each varies throughout the country.

According to Louis J. Rubin, to become effective teachers, education students must have more direct exposure to public school classrooms, which can help develop their "capacities for innovation, spontaneity, perception, and intuition" (p. 165). Rubin contends that prospective teachers should observe how mentor teachers exhibit patience, adjust and readjust teaching demeanor to a student's actions, sense how to avoid problems, invent solutions, experiment with numerous instructional and evaluation strategies, and honor individuality (pp. 164–165).

Educational Research Supports the Importance of Fieldwork

Research supports the belief that classroom-based experiences are important in the training of teachers. A study of forty prestudent teachers found that their field experiences positively affected their interpersonal skills as they worked with students, other teachers, and administrators (Austin-Martin, Bull, and Molrine 1981). In another study, Dennis Sunal reported that elementary preservice teachers who participated in field experiences as well as methods studies were better able to model specific teacher roles than their peers who had not participated in the field experiences (1976). According to a research study conducted by Marvin Henry, Indiana State University students who participated in a program that required field experiences as teaching aide–observers (twenty–thirty hours), as observers of youth in their cultural setting (ten–twenty hours), as teaching assistants (ten hours minimum), and as reading tutors (ten hours minimum), were better prepared than their peers who had not participated in the field experience. They felt more confident about their ability to assist students with reading problems and perceived themselves as better prepared to teach students with disabilities. In addition, they experienced fewer problems during student teaching (1988).

Although most educators and administrators agree on the importance of classroom-based field experiences for preservice teachers, they frequently disagree on how much field experience is appropriate, when in the student's program it should occur, and what should be accomplished. As John Goodlad's study revealed, the trend in contemporary teacher education programs is toward increasing the number of hours spent in the schools, beginning field experience early in a student's program, and requiring a greater variety of experiences than in the past.

Technology in Teacher-Training Programs

According to Isabel Bruder (1989), although the use of technology in teacher-training programs is still in its infancy, an increasing number of teacher preparation institutions are experimenting with it. Most programs focus on how computer technology can be used to enhance classroom instruction. Gary Bitter (1989) contends that such topics as the microcomputer in education, computer-assisted instruction, and trends in teaching with computers should be taught to teacher education students.

According to Bruder, however, because of time and other constraints, most programs in teacher education are not training preservice teachers adequately in the use of the computer. In fact, much of this training does not occur until the graduate level or in inservice programs sponsored by schools and universities.

Despite concerns that not enough is being done, the use of technology in the training of teachers has grown significantly since the early 1980s. In a report of the Southern Regional Education Board, *Changing the Education of Teachers*, between 1981 and 1987 colleges and universities in fifteen southern states greatly increased the amount of training teachers received in the classroom use of computers (Hawley, Austin, and Goldman 1988).

In addition, technology is being used in a great many new ways to enhance teacher training and student learning. One example is Indiana University's Center for Excellence in Education, which is becoming a national demonstration center for the application of technology to education. For example, it uses videotapes of student teachers to assist them in improving their teaching and to introduce various teaching strategies in methods courses. Also, teleconferencing is allowing university and public school faculties to expand course offerings and consult each other about administrative and instructional issues.

At the University of North Carolina at Asheville students videotape lessons and later discuss them with peers and faculty advisers. In addition, a microcomputer network allows university students to communicate with students in elementary and middle schools. In one class, for example, university students are assigned the same novel as children in a middle school classroom. In another instance, a university student who is working with two middle school students in a predominantly black urban school has assigned a novel for them to read. Two other middle school youngsters in a predominantly white rural school have been assigned the same book. The children will correspond about the book via the computer network, and the university student will monitor their correspondence on a computer at the university, allowing all of them access to ideas and opinions not otherwise easily obtained.

Student teachers at Miami University in Oxford, Ohio, can access a computer network from their student-teaching site that allows them to find curricular information on courses they took in their freshman year. They also have access to videotapes of teachers dealing with classroom management problems that they can use in analyzing their own techniques.

3.1 POINTS TO REMEMBER

- Most teacher education programs require students to complete a series of courses in general liberal arts, a specialty area or major, coursework in education and psychology, and significant fieldwork.
- Classroom-based fieldwork helps preservice teachers develop their own effective teaching skills and personality traits by allowing them to work with and model mentor teachers.
- Technology in teacher training is used to reinforce fieldwork and to introduce teaching strategies via videotape. In addition, telecommunication networks are employed to allow university faculty, school-based personnel, and teacher education students to confer without leaving their own institutions.

APPROACHES TO THE TRAINING OF TEACHERS

Requirements for state **accreditation** of teacher education programs, a procedure whereby the state evaluates the curriculum and standards of an institution and provides it a professional license to grant degrees (discussed on page 81), have led to a general consistency in requirements for teacher certification. However, within each state there is a great deal of diversity in how these requirements are met by individual institutions. For example, a state may

One common aspect of most teacher-training programs is the opportunity for students to practice teaching under the tutelage of an experienced professional. It provides the student with not only a role model but also practical insights into the daily operations of a classroom. This student teacher is helping seventh graders with their science laboratory problems.

require that all teachers have competency in working with disabled youngsters. Institutions can determine how and when that competency will be met: in a specialized course, during fieldwork, in the education or psychology department, through independent research projects, or other alternative approaches.

Therefore, the goals of teacher-training programs may be similar; however, the approaches employed may be very different. The National Council for Accreditation of Teacher Education (NCATE), the national agency that evaluates and accredits teacher education institutions, calls these approaches the "knowledge bases for professional education" (NCATE 1990, 45). The concept of knowledge bases assumes that there are many ways to prepare teachers effectively. NCATE's requirement for accreditation is that each institution's "professional education programs are based on essential knowledge, established and current research findings, and sound professional practice" (p. 45). It is up to the institution to decide how to interpret these elements.

Howey and Zimpher (1989) examined a variety of models of teacher education. These are briefly described in the following section.

Teachers' College Model

The first of these is the *teachers' college model*, which emphasizes a core of professional courses. Contemporary teachers' colleges are usually separate schools or colleges within large universities. In many instances, they were historically the largest within the university because the universities themselves were originally normal schools, institutions dedicated to the training of teachers. Many institutions have designed model programs for teacher training. One such example is EXEL, Experimental Elementary Education at Ball State University in Muncie, Indiana. This is a cooperative program with the Muncie schools in which students complete a sequence of professional classroom experiences beginning as early as the freshman year. Early and frequent field experiences are required by most teachers' colleges.

Most students in teachers' colleges major in education, usually in an area of specialty: elementary education, foreign language education, or special education, for example. Frequently, secondary certification students take some or all of the same major courses as others in their discipline. However, most elementary certification students take courses specifically designed to be adapted to the methods employed in the elementary schools.

The **liberal arts model** features a core liberal arts curriculum in the belief that in order to succeed students must become "capable and cultured human beings" (J. S. Mill). Thus, a large number of courses taken by students in liberal arts programs are interdisciplinary, integrating various arts and sciences disciplines.

Liberal Arts Model

All Colorado College teacher education students, for example, major in a discipline within the arts and sciences. At Luther College elementary certification students complete twenty to twenty-four hours in an area of concentration from anthropology to philosophy. Further, the students' professional studies are heavily based in psychology and include coursework in curriculum, instructional strategies, and foundations of education.

Extensive fieldwork in addition to student teaching is required. At Washington University (St. Louis, Missouri) students are required to do fieldwork in specific courses such as mathematics or anthropology. "Experience in schools is used to illustrate both important ideas in liberal studies and basic educational

The liberal arts approach to teacher preparation emphasizes the process of inquiry and analysis. It is firmly grounded in subject matter disciplines and integrated with fieldwork. This teacher utilizes the seminar approach to engage his students fully in the process of thinking about and analyzing a topic.

issues" (Johnston and associates, p. 128). In Educational Psychology students observe classroom control for five hours as an example of creating a viable social system. In Sociology of Education, teaching decisions are examined in the context of the school as a political organization, subject to community mores. In this way, the subject matter, the focus of the liberal arts model, can be utilized in developing teaching methods.

According to Joseph S. Johnston, Jr., and his associates in a review of liberal arts teacher education programs for the Association of American Colleges, an integrated liberal arts program for arts and sciences majors who are prospective teachers can take many shapes. However, there are several broad characteristics that define the integrated liberal arts teacher education program.

> Each of its principal parts—general education, arts and science major, and professional education—is internally coherent. They also are carefully coordinated and, to an extent, merged with one another. The program emphasizes rigorous and sustained study in the arts and sciences. It also engages undergraduates with this subject matter in ways that specifically support their efforts to prepare themselves as teachers. Study in the liberal arts is improved for all students by a new attention to teaching and learning and to the processes—not merely the products—of disciplinary enquiry. (Johnston and associates 1989, 4)

Competency-Based Model

Competency-based models center on developing teaching behaviors that are specifically geared to motivate students to learn to the best of their abilities. The goals of the University of Toledo program, for example, were adapted from a statement of quality education from the Pennsylvania State Board of Education. The goals read as follows:

Each teacher should be prepared to help every child:

1. Acquire the greatest possible understanding of himself and an appreciation of his worthiness as a member of society.
2. Acquire understanding and appreciation of persons belonging to social, cultural, and ethnic groups different from his own.
3. Acquire to the fullest extent possible for him mastery of the basic skills in the use of words and numbers.
4. Acquire a positive attitude toward school and toward the learning process.
5. Acquire the habits and attitudes associated with responsible citizenship.
6. Acquire good health habits and an understanding of the conditions necessary for the maintenance of physical and emotional well-being.
7. Acquire opportunity and encouragement to be creative in one or more fields of endeavor.
8. Understand the opportunities open to him for preparing himself for a productive life and . . . take advantage of these opportunities.
9. Understand and appreciate as much as he can of human achievement in the natural sciences, the social sciences, the humanities, and the arts.
10. Prepare for a world of rapid change and unforeseeable demands in which continuing education throughout his adult life should be a normal expectation. (Howey and Zimpher 1989, 80–81)

These original goals were later organized into five contexts: organization, education technology, contemporary learning-teaching processes, societal factors, and research. In addition, more than two thousand behavioral objectives related to these broad contexts were generated by the faculty of the University of Toledo College of Education.

Competency-based teacher education programs, like the one at the University of Toledo, require cooperative relationships between the university and the public schools since a significant portion of the preservice teachers' time must be spent in public school classrooms. The overriding goal of such programs is to bring about educational change through improved teaching.

Each course in the competency-based education sequence must bring the preservice teacher closer to reaching the competencies. The University of Toledo accomplishes this by developing a set of educational modules, each designed to help the students reach the specified learning outcome or objective.

As in other education programs, students in competency-based programs are required to complete a definite sequence of general education or liberal studies courses that usually includes composition, the humanities, the natural sciences, the social sciences, and mathematics. Moreover, most students must also complete courses in their area of specialization, such as early childhood, language arts, mathematics, science, or social studies.

Also inherent in a competency-based program is the measurement of student success based on behavioral objectives. In the University of Toledo program, for example, students take written tests that are related to the behavioral objectives of each educational module within their education course sequence. The tests may be self-assessments or career explorations. They may also deal with coursework or be based on the student's observation in the schools.

Five-Year Degree Models

In recent years the concept of a **five-year degree** in education, frequently culminating in a master's degree, has gained popularity. However, in 1991 no states required a master's degree for *initial* certification, according to Elmer Knight, past president of the National Association of State Directors of Teacher Education. The following states were among those that required a master's degree after a period of time to continue teaching: Arizona, California, Connecticut, Massachusetts, New York, and Oregon.

The master's degree program at the University of New Hampshire provides an interesting model for an integrated undergraduate-graduate five-year program for elementary and secondary teachers. According to University of New Hampshire director of Teacher Education Michael D. Andrew (1990), this five-year, two-degree program begins with a teacher assistance experience during the freshman or sophomore year followed by a required course in the foundations of education. The program concludes with a year-long, twelve-credit teaching internship, at least six credits of electives in education, and a final project or thesis. The baccalaureate degree, with a major outside education, is completed in four years. With the exception of the initial teaching assistance experience, the foundations course, a course in human development, and a course titled "Alternative Perspectives on the Nature of Education" (a study of how children and adolescents learn), the rest of the program is completed at the master's level.

A more traditional model for fifth-year programs is the Master of Arts in Teaching (MAT). Students enter the MAT program after completing a bachelor's degree, with or without training in teaching. The basic idea of the Master of Arts in Teaching is that it is primarily a disciplined study of the arts and sciences; at the same time, the student applies this knowledge to theoretical and practical approaches to teaching. The emphasis is on practice teaching as a vehicle for developing methodology. The Association of Master of Arts in Teaching Programs has eight institutional members: Brown University in Rhode Island, the University of Chicago, Claremont Graduate School in California, Colgate University in New York, Duke University in North Carolina, North-western University in Illinois, Reed College in Oregon, and Vanderbilt University in Tennessee. Although there are other institutions that offer Masters of Arts in Teaching programs, these eight programs have in common the traditional liberal arts approach to the MAT, a firm commitment to academic excellence in a subject area first, and then its application to teaching/learning methods.

Alternative Approaches

Although the models discussed in the previous section are the most common, there are numerous other approaches to teacher education. Michigan State University, for example, has four alternative approaches to the standard teacher education program. They offer special attention to the challenges of fostering academic learning, teaching in heterogeneous (mixed group) classrooms, promoting personal and social responsibility, and professional decision making under conditions of multiple and competing demands and expectations. Each of these alternative paths to teacher training requires different coursework designed to lead students toward different teaching situations.

Many of the **alternative approaches** to teacher training have arisen because of shortages of teachers in certain disciplines, such as mathematics and science, and in certain geographic regions of the country. Frequently, these programs take advantage of revised state certification requirements for entering teaching. According to the report *Redesigning Teacher Education: Opening the Door for New Recruits to Science and Mathematics Teaching*, all these nontraditional programs "strive to reduce or overcome some of the potential barriers to entry into teaching" (Darling-Hammond, Hudson, and Kirby 1989, viii). Many of these programs focus on the retraining of professionals in other fields who wish to enter teaching.

The barriers that these programs attempt to help preservice teachers overcome include coursework in pedagogy, extensive field experiences prior to initial certification, and financial constraints of a career change. The requirements for these alternative routes to certification vary from state to state and program to program.

Teachers for Rural Alaska is one interesting alternative approach to teacher certification. It is a fifth-year program designed to train secondary teachers for small rural high schools with predominantly native populations. Students who enter the program already have bachelor's degrees in the arts and sciences.

It emphasizes reflective, inquiring thinking processes, including (1) identification of crucial problems and dilemmas in rural, cross-cultural teaching, (2) developing a wide repertoire of teaching methodologies, (3) using the research base to develop methodologies, (4) tailoring instruction to culturally different students, and (5) reflecting upon and learning from their own practices. Students work with master teachers, participate in reflective seminars linked to

Wendy Kopp, the founder of Teach for America, hopes to improve and expand her alternative teacher preparation program. Many who have participated feel that the program has accomplished its goal of reaching students in areas of the country that desperately need teachers.

an apprenticeship, take courses that focus on concrete teaching problems, use case studies to develop reflective inquiry skills, assess skills through videotaped teaching, and student teach in rural villages throughout Alaska (Kleinfeld and Noordhoff 1988).

Another alternative teacher-training program that has received a good bit of national publicity is the brainchild of recent Princeton University graduate Wendy Kopp. It is her contention that the best college and university graduates do not go into teaching and that many of these graduates are undecided as to a career. Therefore, with the support of various industries and private foundations, she founded Teach for America. The program is designed to train liberal arts graduates to teach in inner-city and rural public schools, where it is difficult to employ quality teachers. Students enrolled in this program possess baccalaureate degrees and take an eight-week intensive training course in Los Angeles. The training includes seminars with education specialists from universities and active public school teachers. Participants do fieldwork in California's year-round public schools. After completing the program, they are qualified to teach in the public schools of twenty states and receive the same salary as other starting teachers. In states in which they are not immediately qualified to teach, they may be required to complete additional coursework prior to teaching or during a probationary period in which they can teach but are not yet certified (Chira 1990).

V I E W P O I N T S

Alternative Teacher-Education Project Draws Mixed Reviews in First Year of Placing Recent College Graduates in Schools

Soon after Katherine K. Plunkett entered her classroom at Crestworth Elementary School here [Baton Rouge, LA] last fall, she knew she was in trouble. The 1987 graduate of Vassar College couldn't bring her kindergartners under control. Some of the 5-year-olds were running around, several were fighting, and another was climbing a bookshelf.

Ms. Plunkett came here as part of a new program called Teach for America, an alternative teacher-education plan that aims to recruit the brightest graduates from the nation's campuses and send them on two-year teaching stints to some of the nation's toughest schools.

The year was rougher than Ms. Plunkett expected, but it didn't dampen her desire to teach.

"I don't think just because I've had a bad year or a hard month, I'm going to give up," Ms. Plunkett says.

Across town, in an elementary school surrounded by barbed wire, however, Catherine M. Krahnke, a Teach for America recruit from Lehigh University, wants out.

Her year was soured by first graders she couldn't control, and by a few colleagues who resented that she hadn't spent years in college preparing to be a teacher. Teach for America recruits are primarily recent liberal-arts graduates who received just eight weeks of teacher training last summer.

"As hard as I expected it to be, I don't think I was prepared for what it was like," says Ms. Krahnke. One day this spring, she had to break up a fight between two students' mothers. One of the mothers had a gun.

Ms. Krahnke and Ms. Plunkett are among 15 recruits who were sent here last fall by Teach for America. About 500 recent graduates were placed in 25 inner-city and rural school districts throughout the nation that could not find enough certified teachers. The districts

accepted and paid the recruits as first-year teachers. In exchange for signing on with Teach for America for two years, the recruits may defer a portion of their student-loan repayments.

The organization says nearly 90 per cent of the new teachers survived their first year in Baton Rouge, New Orleans, Los Angeles, New York City, and several rural towns in North Carolina and Georgia. But the program's first year has drawn mixed reviews. Many of the recruits have been frustrated by their experiences, while others say the program has helped solidify their plans to make teaching a career.

Wendy Kopp, the founder and director of Teach for America, says she realized the first year would uncover lots of difficulties, and says she and her staff are working to improve the program.

"We have learned an incredible amount across the board," says Ms. Kopp. "We're fine-tuning every part of our operation."

Teach for America has drawn tremendous interest across the country, primarily because of its unusual beginnings. Ms. Kopp, a 1989 Princeton University graduate, first proposed the idea in her senior thesis. She was interested in coming up with an innovative way to create a new supply of quality teachers desperately needed by the nation's schools.

Much to the surprise of her professors, and of those who for years have been working to attract people to teaching, Ms. Kopp quickly put the plan into place. She raised more than $1 million by convincing the heads of some of America's largest companies that her idea would work. And she sparked the interest of hundreds more graduates than the program had room for.

Some teacher educators have criticized the plan, saying that underprepared teachers are not what the nation's schools need. They point to the frustrations of some of this year's recruits as evidence of the problems inherent in alternative teacher-education programs.

One of the biggest complaints of the new teachers is that they didn't receive adequate training or have enough time to prepare for their new jobs. Most of those sent here, for example, didn't arrive until a day or two before classes. Some didn't get here until the night before.

On her first day, Lori A. Donoho learned she was the only mathematics teacher at Northdale Magnet Academy. It is an alternative school for students who had trouble in regular classrooms because of learning disabilities or discipline problems. Her students ranged in age from 14 to 21, making Ms. Donoho, a 1990 graduate of Emory University, only two years older than her oldest students. Her challenge didn't end there.

Ms. Donoho was assigned to teach six periods a day, and in three of them she had to divide the class into two subjects. For example, in one period Ms. Donoho had to teach Algebra I to some students and consumer math to others. She ended up writing roughly nine lesson plans each day. She says she had planned and taught no more than 20 lessons in her student-teaching experience at the Teach for America training institute. . . .

Ms. Plunkett says she certainly wasn't ready for what she came up against in her poor school district here. Many of her students were covered with ringworm and lice bites from dirty living conditions. Ms. Plunkett found herself comforting a girl whose abusive mother had burnt her leg with an iron. And the young teacher was frustrated by a youngster who had spent two years in kindergarten but still couldn't write her name. . . .

Many of the new teachers say they also had problems getting guidance from their schools. Some of the districts—because of personnel constraints or budget cutbacks—were unable to follow through on agreements to pair an experienced teacher with each Teach for America recruit. Some recruits grabbed the teacher in the classroom next door

for help. But others found they weren't accepted when their colleagues learned how they had been trained.

Says John C. Darby, a 1990 graduate of Emory University who taught third grade at Buchanan Elementary School here: "I told people, and I felt like it put them off."

Most school officials acknowledge that they would prefer to have certified teachers in every classroom. But the reality is that they need teachers. Many school officials say that if Teach for America can get quality people into teaching, they will support the program.

Officials of the Inglewood Unified School District in California were excited when they first heard of Ms. Kopp's idea, and they signed up for 38 recruits last fall. They say Teach for America offers a new market of highly motivated people with diverse experiences who can bring fresh ideas to the classroom.

"It was a workable alternative when we couldn't find enough credentialed teachers," says Althea L. Jenkins, Inglewood's assistant superintendent for personnel services. "We were grateful to find some who wanted to give the profession a try."

Ms. Kopp says expertise will come to those of the recent graduates who stay with teaching. Like all beginning teachers, she says, Teach for America recruits must learn on the job.

"We don't know of a way in this country to prepare people to be expert teachers before they walk into a classroom or to be prepared for what they will see," says Ms. Kopp. "We really believe teachers are made through experience." Ms. Kopp believes some of the recruits will stay long enough to become excellent teachers. A Teach for America survey shows that 23 per cent of the new teachers who survived the first year plan to stay in teaching for at least five years beyond the initial two-year commitment they made to the program.

Teach for America officials say they have made some dramatic improvements as the program enters its second year.

The curriculum for this summer's training institute is being revised to create a better balance between theoretical concepts and classroom management. Experienced teachers from specific regions will travel to the institute to instruct the new recruits on their schools' problems.

Instead of spending all eight weeks at the institute, the recruits will attend a six-week training session in California and will then travel to their schools for a one-to-two-week induction period. Each region also will have a support director—an experienced teacher from the area who will actually observe the new teachers and offer pointers.

The institute projects that 650 to 700 new corps members will be selected from 3,100 applicants this summer. Schools in five new areas—the Rio Grande Valley; Houston; Miami; Oakland, Cal.; and towns in Arkansas—have signed up to accept recruits for the 1991–92 school year.

Teach for America officials say that even the recruits who choose to leave teaching after their two-year commitment can become advocates for education by telling others what they have seen on the front lines of American education.

Says Ms. Kopp: "They are going to take this experience with them and see the world through a whole new lens."

From: Nicklin, 1991

Controversy Surrounding Alternative Teacher-Training Programs

One major concern about alternative approaches to teacher training is that the limited pedagogical training of preservice teachers may become the norm, and thus, the skills of those entering the profession through college and university programs will be held in lower regard than the nonteaching skills possessed by teachers entering from other professions. The result of this could well be the devaluation of characteristics such as sensitivity and ability to teach for mastery and the loss of empowerment. In addition, many educators resent these programs because the assumption is that the skills learned in professional education programs are unimportant or that they can be learned in a few weeks (AACTE Policy Statement June 1989; Buechler March 1990).

The National Education Association (NEA), the largest professional organization of teachers, endorses what it calls a *"nontraditional route to teacher licensure* while reaffirming its position calling for a fully licensed and qualified teacher in every classroom." The NEA "recognizes that adults will change jobs several times in their lifetimes and that there will be mid-career individuals coming into teaching. . . . [However, NEA's] goal is to avoid substandard licensure programs that will put anyone short of a fully prepared professional at the head of every public-school classroom." To do this, NEA suggests that nontraditional programs be developed that "rigorously prepare an individual to obtain a standard, full teaching license" (NEA July 5, 1990).

The American Association of Colleges for Teacher Education maintains in a 1989 policy statement that alternative paths to licensure are possible through collaborative programs between collegiate teacher education institutions and the public schools without lowering standards or decreasing expectations and requirements. The organization cites such previous successes as Experienced

Teacher Fellowship Programs and Teacher Corps. In these programs, novice teachers worked with mentor teachers to develop the skills of teaching prior to taking on their own classes. According to AACTE, "these nontraditional programs provide professional training for prospective teachers, and have the same standards and experiences of competence as a traditional teacher education program. The fundamental differences between an alternative and traditional program are in the target audience, the training design, and the length of training, not in program content, rigor or expected outcomes" (June 1989, 2).

In a summary of *Redesigning Teacher Education: Opening the Door for New Recruits to Science and Mathematics Teaching* (Darling-Hammond, Hudson, and Kirby) Lynn Olson says,

> In general, the authors found, those programs that follow a more "traditional" approach were rated as most effective by program participants. Such programs provided substantial coursework before recruits enter the classroom and a gradual assumption of teaching duties under supervision of an experienced mentor.
>
> In contrast, alternative-certification programs that give minimal amounts of time to education coursework, and expect recruits to learn most of their skills on the job, received the lowest rating. (1989, 26)

In spite of these findings, alternative programs in teacher training are growing in number and popularity. In the article "The Other Certification: More Benefits than Risks?" Patricia Graham, a member of the development committee for the South Carolina Critical Needs Certification Program, concludes that the South Carolina alternative teacher-training program works because it is "supervised by the state Department of Education and directed from a college campus. College professors and public school faculty work to provide assistance and assessment to new teachers. Field coordinators visit the new teachers in their schools, observe and evaluate their lessons, meet with mentors and administrators, and serve as part of the support system" (1989, 78).

3.2 POINTS TO REMEMBER

- Requirements for certification of teachers are consistent within individual states. However, institutions are usually allowed to interpret state requirements to meet the needs of their students.
- The foundation of the teachers' college approach is methodology and fieldwork.
- The foundation of the liberal arts approach is the development of critical thinking skills through academic study.
- Competency-based approaches to teacher training contend that there is a series of skills that all successful teachers must be able to meet.
- Fifth-year programs are housed in colleges and universities; some are continuations of bachelor's programs; others are separate master's programs.
- Alternative teacher education programs are often developed to meet the need for more teachers than traditional programs can supply. Some are within colleges or universities, and students in these programs complete the same basic requirements as traditional students.
- Some educators worry that alternative paths to teacher education will diminish the professionalism of traditionally trained teachers.

REFORMS IN CONTEMPORARY TEACHER TRAINING

By most measures, American education is failing to educate its young people. Average SAT scores have fallen nearly one hundred points in the last thirty years, and the most recent tests of the National Assessment of Education Progress (NAEP) indicate that serious deficiencies exist in high school seniors' knowledge of English, mathematics, science, history, and geography. Among the many areas of reform suggested to improve American education is that of teacher training.

Despite the commitment of educators to study what it takes to be an effective teacher and to design teacher-training programs that develop a student's knowledge, attributes, and skills, cries for reform came from many educators, politicians, and business leaders during the 1980s and early 1990s. Each of the reports suggested goals of reform such as five-year teacher training programs; increased number of credits in liberal arts courses; majors or concentrations in arts and sciences disciplines; master's degrees for recertification, professional certification, or permanent certification; and increased length of school-based internships, but how best to train effective teachers remained elusive and much of the content of the reform was controversial. Some of these reports are discussed in the following section.

Holmes Group   *Tomorrow's Teachers*, the report of the Holmes Group, made up of fifty deans of colleges of education, one from each state, acknowledged that their suggestions had been made before. In fact, the name of the group honored Henry W. Holmes, dean of Harvard Graduate School, who had suggested many similar reforms in the 1920s. The members of the Holmes Group of 1986 did make many of the same recommendations as Holmes himself in the 1920s and other reform commission reports of the late 1950s and early 1960s. However, they expected different outcomes because the deans of some of the most influential research colleges and universities made up the group. These men and women could influence teacher education reform in their institutions, and, thereby, across the nation.

The Holmes Group identified the following goals for teacher education: to make the education of teachers intellectually more solid; to recognize differences in teachers' knowledge, skills, and commitment, in their education, certification, and work; to create standards of entry to the profession— examinations and educational requirements—that are professionally relevant and intellectually defensible; to connect our own institutions [universities] with the schools; and to make schools better places for teachers to work and to learn (1986, 4).

Responding to these goals, the Holmes Group proposed a three-tier system of teacher certification (see table 3.1 on pages 74–75). The first tier would include novice instructors who would have a five-year, nonrenewable teaching certificate and would have completed a minimum of a four-year degree in an arts and sciences discipline and several months of intensive pedagogical study (the four-year undergraduate education major would be eliminated). These entry requirements would be flexible to allow professionals from other fields to become teachers. During the first year of teaching, novice instructors would teach under the supervision of a fully certified professional.

Entry to the second tier (professional teacher) would require successful teaching for five years; satisfactory examination scores in general education, professional education, and the individual's arts and sciences discipline; and a master's degree in teaching that would include advanced coursework in the arts and sciences discipline, classroom teaching of children considered to be at-risk in the educational setting, and a full year of supervised teaching. Also, candidates for this level would demonstrate on-the-job performance and would prepare portfolios to document their successful teaching.

To reach the final tier, career professionals, teachers would be able to document extensive and outstanding experience as a professional teacher. Also, they would have completed further specialized study, usually a doctorate, in an arts and sciences discipline or another educational specialty such as supervision or administration. This level of professionalism would require completion of research, oral examinations, and portfolios of practical competence in teaching. Moreover, teachers at this level would use their expertise to improve the teaching of novice instructors at the entry level.

The Carnegie Forum on Education and the Economy Task Force on Teaching as a Profession

The Carnegie Forum on Education and the Economy Task Force on Teaching as a Profession was established in 1985 and consisted of fourteen members from business, education, and politics. Unlike the Holmes Group, only one member of the Carnegie task force represented higher education. In 1986 the task force issued its report, *A Nation Prepared: Teachers for the 21st Century*, which included the following suggested reforms:

1. "Create a National Board for Professional Teacher Standards, organized with a regional and state membership structure made up of a majority of members elected by Board-certified teachers, to establish high standards for what teachers need to know and be able to do, and to certify teachers who meet that standard." The Board would set standards for awarding teacher's certificates attesting to high levels of competence and advanced teacher's certificates for outstanding teaching competence and demonstrated leadership abilities. It would award national certification to teachers that initially would be voluntary.
2. "Restructure the teaching force, and introduce a new category of Lead Teachers with the proven ability to provide active leadership in the redesign of the schools and in helping their colleagues to uphold high standards of learning and teaching."
3. "Require a bachelors degree in the arts and sciences as a prerequisite for the professional study of teaching." States should abolish the undergraduate degree in education and develop Master in Teaching degrees, which should emphasize systematic study of teaching and include extensive school-based experiences.
4. "Develop a new professional curriculum in graduate schools of education leading to a Master in Teaching degree, based on systematic knowledge of teaching and including internships and residencies in the schools." (p. 55)

(continued on p. 75)

TABLE 3-1

Major Reports on Teacher Education: 1981–1986

The Need for Quality, 1981
Meeting the Need for Quality, 1983
Improving Teacher Education: An Agenda for Higher Education and the Schools, 1985

Southern Regional Education Board

- The four-year undergraduate program should continue as the typical entry into teaching. Requirements should be more rigorous and courses more meaningful.
- Beginning teacher programs which are joint efforts of higher education and the schools should continue.
- Evaluating the results of new models to prepare beginning teachers, including state programs for alternative certification of liberal arts graduates and selected fifth-year programs, should be encouraged.

Professional level	Educational requirements	Type of certification
Provisional Teacher	4-year teacher education or liberal arts degree	Provisional
Professional Teacher	Completion of beginning teacher program that includes on-the-job coaching and assessment	Renewable

A Call for Change in Teacher Education, 1985

National Commission for Excellence in Teacher Education
(Also known as the AACTE report)

Professional level	Educational requirements	Type of certification
Provisional Teacher	Degree level is left open; sufficient to integrate liberal studies, subject specialization, and professional studies	Provisional, non-renewable
Professional Teacher	Completion of one-year paid internship	Renewable tenured certification

Tomorrow's Teachers, 1986

Report of the Holmes Group

Professional level	Educational requirements	Type of certification
Instructor (Novice)	Bachelor's in arts and sciences plus several months of intensive pedagogical studies. The 4-year undergraduate education major and degree would be abolished; a new 5-year "master's in teaching" program would be created	5-year non-renewable certificate; would be supervised by professional teacher
Professional Teacher	Master's in teaching (including full year of supervised teaching)	Renewable tenured certificate
Career Professional	Doctorate in education plus extensive and outstanding experience as professional teacher	Renewable tenured certificate

A Nation Prepared, 1986

Carnegie Forum on Education and the Economy

Initially states would license entry-level teachers who hold bachelor's degrees in arts and sciences. A professional lead teacher would supervise beginning teachers. The 4-year undergraduate education major and degree would be abolished; a new 5-year "master's in teaching" program would be created.

A National Board for Professional Teaching Standards would be created to develop the standards (educational program standards, certification tests, performance assessment criteria, etc.) for teachers. Initially teachers would seek National Board Certification on a voluntary basis. The Forum's hope is that eventually such certification would become the norm.

The Board would issue two levels of certification beyond initial state licensure.

Professional level	Educational requirements	Type of assignments
Board Certified Teacher	Master's in teaching	Majority of teaching force (10-month contract)
Advanced Certificate	Additional advanced study to meet performance standards of the Board	Lead teachers (12-month contract) or Advanced Certificate holders (10-month contract)

From: Southern Regional Education Board, 1986. *Major Reports on Teacher Education: What Do They Mean for the States?* Atlanta, GA: author.

This table briefly summarizes the major reports calling for reform in education from 1981–1986. It is organized so that at each professional level, the educational requirements are listed as well as the type of certification obtained at that level.

National Commission for Excellence in Teacher Education

The 1985 report *A Call for Change in Teacher Education* differs from the other reform reports in that it was written by the professional organization of colleges of education, the Association of American Colleges of Teacher Education (AACTE). The seventeen members of the commission included college presidents, chancellors, deans, representatives from the professional organizations of teachers, state superintendents, a governor, legislators, and a representative from the National School Boards Association.

The report made recommendations related to five themes: supply and demand of teachers, programs for teacher education, accountability for teacher education, resources for teacher education, and conditions necessary to support the highest quality of teaching. Many of the report's recommendations related directly to the training of teachers:

1. "Each teacher education program should be an exacting, intellectually challenging integration of liberal studies, subject specialization from which school curricula are drawn, and content and skills of professional education." The report does not suggest the elimination of the four-year degree in education. Instead, it suggests that education students should have a liberal arts background "equivalent to that of the best-educated members of their community." The report falls short of suggesting the requirement of an undergraduate arts and science major. Instead, it focuses the content of the arts and sciences on practical considerations of teaching and unlike the previous reports discussed, suggests that teachers should gain practical teaching skills during the undergraduate program. (p. 14)
2. "Following their completion of a teacher education program and the awarding of a provisional certificate, new teachers should complete an induction period or internship of at least a year's duration for which compensation is provided." (p. 15)
3. The report suggests that with the help of state funding, colleges and universities should "consider major structural changes, not just course modification; and states should be willing to adjust existing regulations, with appropriate monitoring, to test the new models." (p. 16)

CROSS-CULTURAL PERSPECTIVE

France Makes Universities the Center of Its New Approach to Teacher Education

France has embarked on a new approach to teacher education, seeking to increase elementary-school teachers' knowledge of their subject matter while strengthening secondary-school teachers' instructional skills.

Officials also hope to bring as many as 250,000 more people into the teaching profession over the next 10 years to replace a big group of retirees and otherwise compensate for a growing shortage of faculty members.

At the core of the new approach is additional university preparation for all teachers. In a radical break with past practice, prospective teachers for both elementary and secondary schools will receive the same basic education in newly created University Institutes for Teaching Training. A nationwide system of *écoles normales* that has been used for the preparation of elementary-school teachers will be eliminated.

"We want all teachers to have a good university background and solid professional training," says Daniel Bancel, an adviser to Education Minister Lionel Jospin.

The changes, which are scheduled to be instituted throughout the country next year [1991], have already been introduced at the Universities of Grenoble, Lille, and Reims.

Bernard Vallet, an adviser to the Grenoble project, says the goal is "a common course of pedagogical study" for all schoolteachers. In the past, the *écoles normales* have concentrated on instructional technique, while universities—which have educated secondary-school teachers—have focused on subject-matter preparation, with little attention to technique.

The premise underlying university programs in the past has been that knowledge of a subject was essentially all that a high-school teacher needed. The students were expected to be capable of handling the work.

Elementary-school teachers, on the other hand, were believed to need a minimum of subject-matter preparation but a maximum of pedagogical skills, so they could maintain classroom discipline and keep pupils interested in their work.

The preparation of elementary-school teachers has included two years of university education, followed by two years of pedagogical training in an *école normale*. Those planning to become high-school teachers have been required to complete three years of university education, followed by an examination of their academic knowledge, an ad-

4. Unlike the Carnegie Commission Report, the AACTE report suggests that the states should continue to certify teachers and approve teacher education programs. However, it also contends that voluntary national accreditation of teacher education programs should be strengthened.

5. This report, unlike the others, suggests that funding for research and development in teacher education is essential and must be provided by federal and state governments.

Southern Regional Education Board

The Southern Regional Education Board (SREB) produced three major reform reports from 1981 through 1985. The board is made up of representatives from fourteen southeastern states. The three reports of the SREB, *The Need for Quality* (1981), *Meeting the Need for Quality* (1983), and *Higher Education and the Schools* (1985), suggested that:

1. Four-year, undergraduate programs be viewed only as entry to the teaching profession.

ditional year of university courses, and a year of theoretical and on-the-job training.

Under the new system, all students will need three years of university education to qualify for admission to the university institutes. There they will have a year of in-depth study in their chosen fields of specialization, along with some courses in the theory of teaching.

Next the students will take an examination tied to the level of education for which they are preparing. Those who pass will become "civil-service interns" and be required to sign a contract in which they promise to teach in a public school, probably for five years.

An additional year of university training, including student teaching, will follow, after which students must pass an aptitude test.

Courses for prospective elementary- and secondary-school teachers will differ, notes Mr. Vallet.

"The knowledge requirements for a kindergarten teacher are not the same as those for a teacher of high-school physics," he says.

The reforms have been well received by most teachers and university students, but some criticisms also have been expressed. Representatives of faculty unions are worried that too little money will be provided for the changes.

Guy Odent, general secretary of the National Union of Higher Education Teachers, wonders whether the universities have adequate facilities for the new institutes.

"Space is already a problem at most universities," he says.

The government does expect to make use of the *écoles normales*, but Mr. Odent notes that those schools are not on university campuses, and that sometimes they are not even in university cities.

In addition, some faculty unions question plans for the institutes to award degrees in education, rather than in the students' original fields.

The students "should have a degree that gives them more options—not just teaching," says Mr. Odent. "They should be able to continue their education and/or go into research if they want to."

Others, including the Education Ministry, disagree. Says Mr. Vallet: "We are here to train teachers, so it stands to reason the students should get a degree in education."

Student leaders, meanwhile, say they are concerned about what will happen to those who do not pass the examinations after their first year at the institutes.

"A total of 30,000 to 35,000 students will be admitted each year, but only 25,000 will be hired after the exam," says Olivier Rey, vice-president of the country's largest student organization, UNEF-ID.

Mr. Vallet concedes that a system should be devised to give university credit to students who fail the examination so they can continue their education and obtain master's degrees elsewhere.

From: Brett, 1990

2. Four-year, undergraduate programs be revised and higher standards be developed.
3. States, universities, and schools develop collaborative programs to support and monitor teachers in their first years of teaching.
4. Alternative certification programs for liberal arts graduates be developed especially where shortages in the supply of teachers occur.
5. Fifth-year teacher education programs be developed.
6. Establishment of two types of certification, provisional for teachers with three or fewer years of teaching and professional after the completion of a beginning teaching program and advanced coursework.

There is no doubt that the reform reports of the 1980s have influenced teacher training, as the Holmes Group had suggested they would. Few future teachers will have baccalaureate degrees in some form of education but instead will have degrees in arts and sciences disciplines and second majors or minors in

Results of the Reform Reports of the 1980s

Teacher-training programs in France are in the process of being revised so that all teachers will receive university training in a subject discipline as well as training in pedagogical techniques. This elementary school teacher in Paris received only two years of a university education, then studied teaching methods for two years at an *école normale*.

education. Some may not begin teaching until they have completed a fifth year of training or a master's degree. Entrance and exit requirements for teaching candidates will be more rigorous. Although professional coursework will decrease, most teacher education students will spend many hours in school field experiences. An increasing number will have paid or unpaid internships after completion of bachelor's degrees but prior to professional licensure. Teachers will be carefully evaluated not only in the college or university but in the public school classroom as well. Many will be trained through collaborative programs in the colleges and universities and public schools. These changes can be seen in the reform initiatives that occurred after the publication of the Holmes Group's report at some of the institutions whose deans had participated in the group's study and at some of the one hundred institutions that were added to the Holmes Group after the publication of the study (see table 3.2).

(continued on p. 80)

TABLE 3-2

Reform Intitiatives by Program Type in Holmes Groups Schools

	Connections to arts and sciences	Teacher and school collaborations	Professional development schools	Internships	Professional studies	New organizational partnerships
Four-year programs						
Arizona State University		•	•	•	•	•
Catholic University of America		•	•		•	
SUNY at Buffalo	•	•			•	•
Teachers College					•	
Tulane University	•	•				
University of California at Berkeley		•	•		•	
University of California at Davis		•			•	•
University of Houston		•	•		•	
University of Louisville		•	•			
University of Maine	•	•	•	•		
University of Massachusetts at Amherst		•	•	•	•	
University of Mississippi		•	•			
University of Missouri at Columbia	•					•
University of New Mexico		•		•		
University of North Dakota	•					
University of Vermont		•				
University of Wisconsin at Milwaukee		•	•		•	•
Virginia Tech		•				•
Post-baccalaureate programs						
Bank Street College	•				•	•
Kent State University		•	•	•		
University of Alaska		•			•	
University of Colorado at Boulder	•	•	•	•		•
University of Iowa	•	•				•
University of Kansas					•	
University of Minnesota					•	
University of Pennsylvania		•			•	
University of Washington		•	•			•
Five-year programs						
Louisiana State University	•	•	•			
Ohio State University		•	•	•	•	•
Oklahoma State University	•	•	•	•		

(continued on next page)

Five-year programs (continued)

	Connections to arts and sciences	Teacher and school collaborations	Professional development schools	Internships	Professional studies	New organizational partnerships
Rutgers University	•	•			•	
Texas A & M	•	•		•		
Trinity University	•	•	•		•	
University of Cincinnati	•	•	•	•	•	
University of Illinois at Chicago	•	•	•	•	•	
University of Illinois Urbana/Champaign	•	•	•		•	
University of Kansas	•	•		•	•	
University of Maryland		•			•	
University of Nebraska at Lincoln	•	•	•		•	•
University of Nevada at Reno	•	•		•		
University of New Hampshire	•	•		•	•	
University of Oklahoma	•	•	•	•		
University of Pittsburgh	•	•			•	
University of Rochester	•	•	•			•
University of Southern California		•	•	•	•	
University of Tennessee	•	•	•	•	•	
University of Utah	•	•		•	•	
University of Virginia	•			•	•	
University of Wisconsin at Madison		•			•	
University of Wyoming	•	•				
Virginia Commonwealth	•			•	•	

From: R. J. Yinger and M. S. Hendricks, "An Overview of Reform in Holmes Group Institutions," *Journal of Teacher Education* (March–April, 1990), 22.

The nature of major educational reforms in teacher training implemented by many institutions of higher learning are illustrated in this table by a representative group of those institutions that participated in the Holmes Group study. Organized first by the length of time students spend in the program, the table then shows which of these programs participate in the initiative. In almost every instance, the reform involves a collaboration between the teacher education institution and either the department of arts and sciences within the university, the public schools, or other teacher-training institutions.

A National Board of Professional Standards

Other changes in teacher education can be traced to these reform reports. A National Board of Professional Standards, suggested by the Carnegie Forum, was established in 1987. Although the board did not establish a national curriculum for teachers, it developed five core propositions of what teachers need to know and should be able to do. They include commitment to students and their learning, knowledge of subject and how to teach it, ability to manage and monitor student learning, ability to think systematically about the practice of teaching and to learn from experience, and membership in the learning community. To be board certified, teachers must possess at least a baccalaureate degree at an accredited institution and three or more years of successful teaching experience. The board is developing a variety of assessment techniques for determining the effectiveness of the classroom teacher. By 1993, the board plans to develop the standards for board certification of teachers. Certification of teachers by the National Board of Professional Standards remains voluntary; national certification does not replace state licensing.

Levels of Certification

Another change that can be directly linked to the teacher education reform reports is the creation of a variety of levels of certification, from initial or provisional certification to permanent or professional certification. Each of the reform reports suggested this type of distinction, linking teacher performance and increased responsibility to each subsequent certification level. Likewise, additional training or higher education is also linked to each higher level of certification. All the reports suggested that salary increments also be tied to this hierarchy of certification levels. According to Elmer Knight, past president of the National Association of State Directors of Teacher Education, by 1991 most states had adopted some type of tiered approach to levels of teacher certification (telephone conversation, February 20, 1991).

The Knowledge Base Debate

Although a move toward increased requirements in liberal arts courses for teacher education students and a decrease in professional coursework at the undergraduate level can be said to be a result of the reform reports, there is still a raging debate over what standards should be set and what coursework is appropriate for the preparation of teachers. No states have done away with four-year baccalaureate programs leading to teacher certification, nor have they required master's degrees for initial certification. However, the content of degree programs for teachers is definitely changing. The debate over what teachers should know and be able to do is a direct outcome of the reform reports, and it has led to a change in how teacher education programs are accredited.

Accreditation of Teacher Education

Because of the diversity of teacher preparation programs around the country, many teacher education reform reports of the 1980s suggested that training programs should be more consistent in their requirements for coursework and field experiences. To encourage consistency, a move toward national evaluation and accreditation of teacher education programs was suggested by many of these reports.

National Accreditation   The reform reports' call for more rigorous standards for all teachers has led to changes in the national accreditation of teacher education programs. The National Council for Accreditation of Teacher Education (NCATE), the major review board for college and university programs in teacher education, in the mid-1980s made its requirements for the accreditation of teacher education programs more rigorous.

NCATE requires that each institution receiving accreditation meet eighteen standards under five major headings. These include (1) knowledge bases for professional education (design, delivery, and content of the curriculum in

(continued on page 83)

Point/Counterpoint

TEACHER EDUCATION REFORM MUST FOCUS ON COURSE CONTENT AND METHODOLOGY

In this new pursuit of excellence, . . . Americans have not yet fully recognized two essential truths: first, that success depends on achieving far more demanding educational standards than we have ever attempted to reach before, and second, that the key to success lies in creating a professional equal to the task—a profession of well-educated teachers prepared to assume new powers and responsibilities to redesign the schools for the future. Without a profession possessed of high skills, capabilities, and aspirations, any reforms will be short lived. (1986, 2)

The fundamental requirements for proficient teaching are relatively clear: a broad grounding in the liberal arts and sciences; knowledge of the subjects to be taught, of the skills to be developed, and of the curricular arrangements and materials that organize and embody that content; knowledge of general and subject-specific methods for teaching and for evaluating student learning; knowledge of students and human development; skills in effectively teaching students from racially, ethnically, and socioeconomically diverse backgrounds; and the skills, capacities and dispositions to employ such knowledge wisely in the interests of students. (1989, 13)

From: Carnegie Forum on Education and the Economy 1986 and National Board for Professional Teaching Standards 1989.

TEACHER EDUCATION REFORM MUST FOCUS ON MORAL ISSUES

We are, I believe, very much in a cultural, political, and moral crisis and hence, ipso facto, in an educational crisis. Indeed, it is imperative that we confront the nature of this crisis or, more accurately, that we attend to how a number of critical, cultural, and educational issues and problems are perceived and interpreted. . . . The recent flurry of educational reports do not, for example, reflect or propose anything approaching a fundamental reconceptualization of the schooling process, much less anything in the way of a serious social/cultural critique. Instead they suggest rather minor reforms directed at amelioration rather than transformation. It is indeed ironic that these reports are highly critical of the intellectual excellence of schools and yet themselves offer relatively superficial responses to the roots of the problems they identify. (pp. 1, 5)

The educational crisis is rooted in the moral and spiritual crisis of the culture as reflected in the value confusions and contradictions. . . . Our culture's insistence on competition, individual success, and privatism is reflected in a school program, which puts cultural considerations of achievement, order, control, and hierarchy over educational values of free inquiry, the development of a critical and creative consciousness, and the struggle for meaning. (p. 93)

From: Purpel, 1989

POSTSCRIPT

Purpel argues that if we do not address what he calls the "value confusions and contradictions" of society, we may be forced "to confront the possibility of a new world or of no world" (p. 93). His argument focuses on the moral values of a society, whereas the various reports of most of the commissions focus on the intellectual content of most school programs and teaching methodology. The argument is an old one and is not easily resolved. It may be, however, that the answer is not as elusive as it appears. Moral values can be integrated into a curriculum by choice of materials and the direction of the teacher. Indeed, in many classrooms the focus is both intellectual and moral. But without specific standards for the implementation of this approach, it is not likely to occur on a regular basis around the country, assuming, of course, that someone can come to an agreement about which moral values are essential in a society.

general education, specialty studies, and professional studies); (2) relationship to the world of practice (field-based experiences, continuing contact with and evaluation of graduates, and cooperative relationships with the public schools); (3) students (rigorous admissions requirements, monitoring of progress, extensive advising services, and measurements of competence upon completion of the program); (4) faculty (appropriate qualifications including education and experience, a reasonable work load to allow for scholarship and service as well as teaching, a program of faculty development, and rigorous evaluation of faculty); (5) governance (support from all levels of the institution and congruence of its mission and that of the teacher education program) and resources (adequate resources and financial support) (*NCATE* 1990).

The goal of NCATE's standards for teacher education programs is to ensure that all programs meet specific national standards: "(1) to require a level of quality in professional education that fosters competent practice of graduates, and (2) to encourage institutions to meet rigorous academic standards of excellence in professional education." Accreditation by NCATE does not assume that all teacher education programs look alike. NCATE does not require a specific number of hours in liberal arts or in professional courses. Instead, it requires rigorous standards no matter the approach used to the training of teachers. Therefore, even in those institutions accredited by NCATE the debate over the composition of teacher education programs continues.

State Accreditation NCATE accreditation, like national certification of teachers, is voluntary, although an increasing number of states require it. On the other hand, state accreditation of teacher education programs is required although only two states have formal evaluation processes. Consequently, state

The requirements for teacher certification vary from state to state, but most include tests to assess basic knowledge and observation to assess professional skills. This student teacher is being observed by her mentor teacher.

education agencies have more control over the content and requirements of teacher education programs than national accreditation agencies. For example, within each state, there are certain requirements that must be met by all teacher-training institutions. In thirty-six states and the District of Columbia, assessments of teacher preparation of individual candidates are required prior to initial or provisional certification (National Center for Education Statistics 1989, 127–128). These assessments include tests of basic skills, professional skills, content knowledge, and/or in-class observation. As a result, institutions of teacher training must design their programs to prepare students to pass these state-mandated assessments. Therefore, consistency in teacher-training requirements can be seen within the institutions of most states, but not across the nation. (See appendix 2, p. 544, for a table listing state-by-state requirements for initial teacher certification and appendix 3, p. 548, for a table listing second-stage certification requirements.)

3.3 POINTS TO REMEMBER

- The reform reports of the 1980s suggested teacher education reforms that included increased academic training of teachers, five-year teacher education programs, additional fieldwork, and collaborative relationships for the training of teachers among schools, colleges, and universities.

- All the reform reports suggest more rigorous entrance and exit requirements for teacher education students. All suggest a tiered approach to the certification of teachers, with a mentoring program in the first years of teaching.

- The Holmes Group and the Carnegie Forum suggest requiring a five-year approach to certification and elimination of the education degree leading to certification.

- The Southern Regional Education Board and the National Commission for Excellence in Teacher Education contend that degrees in education can be maintained with more rigorous standards in all degrees.

- The reform reports have resulted in changes in how teachers are educated and certified. National certification of teachers is nearly a reality, and national standards for accreditation of teacher education programs are far more demanding than they were less than a decade ago. No states have adopted the five-year approach to initial teacher certification.

Art Bouthillier in *Phi Delta Kappan.*

"Think of this as a TV talk show. The band and the audience are off and you are my guests who'll answer my questions."

FOR THOUGHT/DISCUSSION

1. Which do you believe is more important in the development of teaching skills—fieldwork or coursework? Why?
2. If your teacher preparation program does not include training in computer-assisted instruction and other aspects of computer technology, do you feel it is necessary to acquire this knowledge on your own? Why or why not?
3. Do you believe that national standards for teacher preparation would stabilize and upgrade the profession or cause it to stagnate and become predictable? Explain your position.
4. Explain the basic concerns of traditionally prepared and certified teachers about alternative routes to certification.

FOR FURTHER READING/REFERENCE

Bloom, A. 1987. *The closing of the American mind.* New York: Simon and Schuster. A discussion of how universities have failed students by not acquainting them with the great traditions of philosophy and literature that can stimulate critical thinking and nurture self-knowledge.

Good, T. L. 1990. Building the knowledge base of teaching. In *What teachers need to know: The knowledge, skills and values essential to good teaching,* ed. D. Dill and Associates, 17–75. San Francisco: Jossey-Bass. A discussion of how motivation, organization, management, and effective communication are essential for building the knowledge base of teaching.

Goodlad, J. I. 1990. *Teachers for our nation's schools.* San Francisco: Jossey-Bass. A description of teacher education programs in twenty-nine colleges and universities from small, private liberal arts colleges to large research institutions.

Sikula, J. 1989. *Alternatives, yes. Lower standards, no!: Minimum standards for alternative teacher education programs.* Washington, DC: Association of Teacher Educators. A list of twenty-three recommendations for alternative teacher certification programs.

Sirotnik, K. A. 1990. Society, schooling, teaching, and preparing to teach. In *The moral dimensions of teaching,* ed. J. I. Goodlad, R. Soder, and K. A. Sirotnik, 296–326. San Francisco: Jossey-Bass. A discussion of the moral purposes of public schooling and their implications for teacher education.

Tom, A. R. 1987. *How should teachers be educated? An assessment of three reform reports.* Bloomington, IN: Phi Delta Kappan. Discussion of three teacher education reform reports: the Holmes Group, the Carnegie Forum, and the National Commission for Excellence in Education.

4

The Teaching Profession

This letter is in response to one written to Margaret T. Metzger by Clare Fox, Metzger's former student, who is interested in pursuing a career in teaching.

Dear Clare,

I look forward to teaching. By mid-August I start planning lessons and dreaming about classrooms. I also wonder whether I'll have the energy to start again with new classes. Yet after September gets underway, I wake up in the morning expecting to have fun at work. I know that teaching well is a worthwhile use of my life. I know that my work is significant.

I am almost 40 years old, and I'm happier in my job than anyone I know. That's saying a lot. My husband, who enjoys his work, has routine days when he comes home and says, "Nothing much happened today—just meetings." I never have routine days. When I am in the classroom, I usually am having a wonderful time.

I also hate this job. In March I want to quit because of the relentless dealing with 100 antsy adolescents day after day. I lose patience with adolescent issues: I think I'll screech if I have to listen to one more adolescent self-obsession. I'm physically exhausted every Friday. The filth in our school is an aesthetic insult. The unending petty politics drain me. Often I feel undermined on small issues by a school system that supports me well on academic freedom. . . .

A curious irony exists. I am never bored at work, yet my days are shockingly routine. I can tell you exactly what I have done every school day for the past 18 years at 10:15 in the morning (homeroom attendance), and I suspect I will do the same for the next 20 years. The structure of the school day has changed little since education moved out of the one-room schoolhouse. All teachers get tired of the monotonous routine of bookkeeping, make-up assignments, 22-minute lunches, and study-hall duties. I identify with J. Alfred Prufrock when he says, "I have measured out my life with coffee spoons." My own life has been measured out in student papers. At a conservative estimate, I've graded over 30,000—a mind-boggling statistic which makes me feel like a very dull person indeed.

The monotony of my schedule is mirrored in the monotony of my paycheck. No matter how well or poorly I teach, I will be paid the same amount. There is absolutely no monetary reward for good job performance, or any recognition of professional growth or acquired expertise. My pay depends on how long I've taught and my level of education. I work in a school district in which I cannot afford to live. I am alternatively sad and angry about my pay. To the outside world it seems that I am doing exactly the same job I did in 1966—same title, same working conditions, same pay scale (except that my buying power is 8 percent less than it was when I earned $5,400 on my first job). To most people, I am "just a teacher."

86

But this is the outside reality. The interior world of the teacher is quite different. Although you have to come to some terms with the outward flatness of the career, I want to assure you that teachers change and grow. So little research has been done on stage development of teachers that the literature recognizes only three categories—intern, novice, and veteran. This is laughably oversimplified. There is life after student teaching; there is growth after the first year. You will some day solve many of the problems that seem insurmountable during your exhilarating student teaching and your debilitating first year.

Sometimes I am aware of my growth as a teacher, and I realize that finally, after all these years, I am confident in the classroom. On the very, very best days, when classes sing, I am able to operate on many levels during a single class; I integrate logistics, pedagogy, curriculum, group dynamics, individual need, and my own philosophy. I feel generous and good-natured toward my students, and I am challenged by classroom issues. But on bad days, I feel like a total failure. Students attack my most vulnerable points. I feel overwhelmed by paperwork. I ache from exhaustion. I dream about going to Aruba, but I go to the next class. . . .

To me, teaching poses questions worthy of a lifetime of thought. I want to think about what the great writers are saying. I want to think about how people learn. I want to think about the values we are passing on to the next generation. Questions about teaching are like puzzles to me; I can spend hours theorizing and then use my classroom as a laboratory.

I am intellectually challenged by pedagogical problems. I have learned to follow the bizarre questions or "wrong answers." Some questions reveal chasms of ignorance. For example, "Where is Jesus' body?" or "Before movies were in color, wasn't the world dull just being in black and white?"

And then there are all the difficult, "normal" situations: students and parents who are "entitled," hostile, emotionally needy, or indifferent; students who live in chaotic homes, who are academically pressured, who have serious drug and alcohol problems. The list goes on and on. No school of education prepared me for the "Hill Street Blues" intensity and chaos of public schools. I received my combat training from other teachers, from myself and mostly from the students. You will too. . . .

Clare, when you consider a life's work, consider not just what you will take to the task, but what it will give you. Which job will give self-respect and challenge? Which job will give you a world of ideas? Which job will be intellectually challenging? Which job will enlarge you and give you life in abundance? Which job will teach you lessons of the heart?

With deep respect,

Margaret Metzger

From: M. T. Metzger and C. Fox, "Two Teachers of Letters" (1986), *Harvard Educational Review* 56 (4), 351–354.

CHAPTER OBJECTIVES

After studying this chapter, you should be able to:

- Describe the qualities of a profession.
- Define teacher autonomy.
- Explain what is meant by teacher empowerment.
- Explain why autonomy and empowerment are important.
- Discuss why collegial time is important to teachers.
- Define incentive pay.
- Discuss the importance of accountability to professionalism.
- Describe a merit pay system.
- Describe a career ladder or differentiated staffing program.
- Describe a master teacher program.
- Discuss the pros and cons of incentive pay programs.
- Discuss changes in teachers' salaries.
- Discuss trends in the demand for new teachers.
- Define some positive and negative aspects of a career in teaching.
- Examine the in-service expectations for teachers.
- Discuss ethnic diversity in the public schools.
- Examine advancement opportunities for teachers.
- Discuss the role of political and professional development organizations.
- Identify other careers within the teaching field.

Most teacher-training institutions claim to be educating students for a profession in teaching. At the same time, not everyone agrees that teaching is a profession because it lacks some qualities generally associated with a profession. In this chapter we will review some of these qualities and discuss some developing issues that are certain to have an effect on professionalizing teaching.

TEACHING: A PROFESSION

If teaching is a profession, it should possess the characteristics of a profession. Simply stated, this means that teaching must have the same basic characteristics as other professions such as accounting, medicine, and the law. Researchers have identified those characteristics as:

1. *a body of knowledge and the ability to apply that knowledge in the classroom*
   Ayers 1990; Feinberg 1990; Darling-Hammond 1988; Shanker 1987; Stinnett and Huggett 1963; Becker 1962; Bestor 1985
2. *autonomy to make decisions that affect life in the classroom and empowerment to make decisions that affect operation of the school*
   Carnegie Foundation 1990; Metropolitan Life Survey 1989; Maeroff 1988; Bennett 1986; Sizer 1984; Becker 1962
3. *a well-established set of collegial and peer relationships*
   Carnegie Foundation 1990; Sockett 1990; Maeroff 1988; Shanker 1987; Bennett 1986
4. *ability to communicate to the public his or her actions, practices, and judgments*
   Sockett 1990; Bennett 1986; Sizer 1984
5. *high standards, a code of ethics, and a character and personality that are admired and respected*
   Goodlad 1990; Sockett 1990; Shanker 1987; Stinnett and Huggett 1963; Becker 1962; Bestor 1955
6. *commitment to the welfare of students; caring and compassionate relationship with students*
   Ayers 1990; Darling-Hammond 1988; Stinnett and Huggett 1963
7. *commitment to a lifetime teaching career*
   Freidson 1986; Stinnett and Huggett 1963
8. *accountability for the quality of teaching and the progress of students*
   Sockett 1990; Gallup and Elam 1988
9. *membership in professional organizations*
   Stinnett and Huggett 1963; Becker 1962

As professionals, teachers need to possess numerous qualities. Among them are a set of high standards, a personality and character that are admired and respected, and the ability to impart knowledge to a group of diverse students. This junior high school English teacher seems to have many of these characteristics.

10. *opportunity to use his or her own discretion and freedom to teach without direct supervision*
    Sockett 1990; Shanker 1987; Bennett 1986

In addition, the field of education, in order to be considered a profession, needs to acquire the following characteristics:

11. *controlled recruitment into the field of teaching and extensive training*
    Feinberg 1990; Goodlad 1990; Freidson 1986; Stinnett and Huggett 1963; Becker 1962
12. *working conditions, salary, benefits, and comparable performance*
    Sockett 1990; American Federation of Teachers 1989; National Education Association 1989a; Carnegie Forum 1986; Goodlad 1984; Boocock 1980
13. *continuous retraining for intellectual growth and development*
    Stinnett and Huggett 1963
14. *objective evaluation and performance rewards*
    Brandt 1990; Southern Regional Education Board 1991; Chance 1986; Rosenholtz 1986; Wise et al. 1984

Perhaps the best way to look at teaching is as an emerging profession. Of the fourteen professional qualities listed above, nine have clearly been attained. However, five are still being developed. We will examine each of the qualities of the teaching profession that have not been met: autonomy, empowerment, collegial and peer relationships, evaluation and rewards, and accountability.

Teacher Autonomy   **Autonomy** assumes that teachers have the discretion to make decisions related to the life of the classroom. According to Gary Fenstermacher in *The Moral Dimensions of Teaching* (1990), a teacher must have the autonomy to formulate his or her own plans, act on these plans, assess them, and act again. A teacher who lacks autonomy may be told which books to use, which questions to ask, and which pages in the workbook students are expected to complete, and thus feel in less control than someone with autonomy.

According to Barry Bull in *The Moral Dimensions of Teaching*, teacher autonomy includes both freedom and responsibility: freedom to instruct the young when parents no longer have exclusive rights to do so and responsibility to develop those characteristics, abilities, and understandings expected by the "democratic polity." This responsibility, according to Bull, also requires resisting those policy directives that are not relevant to the purposes of public education. Bull further maintains that the responsibility to resist directives should be shared among the state, local school boards, the schools, and teachers. However, he contends that the centralized system of schooling mitigates against directives and regulations of the school board reaching teachers who are seldom aware of all the issues involved in the decisions. If teachers are to be autonomous in their classrooms, there must be decentralization of authority.

The more autonomy teachers have in making decisions important to their teaching, the more likely they are to have a positive image of their role. The more positive their image of themselves as teachers, the more satisfied and successful they are likely to be. According to David Goslin, teachers in smaller schools usually have a good deal of autonomy in the classroom; however, the larger the school, the less the teacher's autonomy (1965, 29). Sarane Boocock (1980) found that teachers' relatively low status in the school hierarchy (below principals, supervisors, and other administrators) gave them little control over their working conditions, even those in their own classrooms.

Elementary teachers in a 1986 poll conducted by *Instructor Magazine* suggested that autonomy, along with improved public understanding, respect, and professionalism, were the most important qualities needed in the teaching profession. Although elementary teachers found their jobs to be "deeply gratifying" and demanding, some days to the point of exhaustion, they were frustrated by their lack of involvement in decision making. Fewer than 30 percent of those surveyed said they made most of the major decisions about texts and supplementary materials. Only 24 percent said they were "meaningfully" involved in the subjects and grades they taught, and only 16 percent said they frequently received useful guidance from the principal on instructional matters (1986, 6).

Teacher Empowerment   Gene is a first-year teacher certification student at a large university. However, Gene is not a typical student. He is forty-three years old and has already had a successful career as a banker. On the first day of class, he sits down with Maryjane Montgomery, his adviser, to discuss his decision to make a career change. "Why have you decided to go into teaching?" Maryjane asks.

"I guess I always wanted to teach," replies Gene. "What I liked best about my job at the bank was training and supervising our new employees. A teacher

Teachers who directly participate in the development of school policy, curriculum, and textbook selection have autonomy, a quality necessary for a positive self-image and success in the classroom. These teachers are discussing curriculum at a department meeting.

has the power to make a real difference for people. I can't think of a more rewarding profession."

After Gene leaves Maryjane's office, she finds herself wondering if Gene is making the right decision. She respects Gene's decision but is fearful he might be disappointed in teaching. Will he find teaching as rewarding as he hopes? Will he have the "power," as he calls it, to make a real difference? She hopes so; she knows that Gene is the type of person who should be in the classroom.

Teacher empowerment is a relatively new phrase that frequently is used as a synonym for professionalism. It goes a step beyond autonomy. It assumes that teachers are decision makers and that they help make school policy decisions that will influence life in the classroom and the school, including student placement, student evaluation and grading, selection of texts and other materials, attendance procedures, subject matter to be taught, curriculum development, teaching methodology, in-service training, evaluation of peers, and selection of school-based administrators.

However, teachers report that they have a limited role in school decision making. For example, in the *Instructor Magazine* poll, 47 percent said they made none of the decisions regarding their own in-service training; 61 percent had no opportunity to observe their peers teach. Similar results were reported in a 1990 Carnegie Foundation poll of 21,698 public school teachers. Ninety percent of the teachers surveyed indicated that they had no say in issues like teacher evaluation or selection of new teachers and administrators. Just 20 percent felt they had any influence at all in tailoring school budgets (see table 4.1, overleaf).

A 1990 poll of 21,389 teachers from each of the fifty states and Washington, D.C., conducted by the Carnegie Foundation for the Advancement of Teaching

TABLE 4-1

Percent of Teachers Who Think They Have "a Great Deal" of Influence Over School Policy: 1987–1988

	Total teachers	Public	Private
Discipline policy	14.6	12.9	27.4
Content of inservice training	11.7	11.2	15.8
Policy on grouping students by ability	13.1	11.5	25.5
Curriculum	14.4	12.7	27.2

From: U.S. Department of Education, National Center for Education Statistics, School and Staffing Survey, 1987–88.

Empowerment, the ability of the teacher to make policy decisions regarding the curriculum, grouping of students, and discipline, is important in developing a professional attitude. Most teachers, however, don't feel they have any influence over these important decisions.

found "no significant growth in teacher participation [in school decision making], and in some cases . . . a slight decline" (p. 51). When polled, many teachers reported that they were "slightly" or "not at all" involved in setting student promotion and retention policies (71 percent); in setting budgets (8 percent); in the selection of new teachers (90 percent); in the evaluation of teacher performance (92 percent); and in selecting new administrators (93 percent).

Standardized Approaches Limit Teacher Empowerment

Teachers in the late 1980s and early 1990s voiced concern that standardized approaches to curriculum development, standardized testing of students, and standardized planning and evaluation of teaching, found in most states, limited teacher decision making, thus forcing them to comply with state and school mandates. According to a mail survey of teachers in all fifty states, teacher morale was low in spite of reforms such as incentive pay plans adopted by many of those states (Carnegie Foundation for the Advancement of Teaching 1988, 11). In fact, careful examination of the survey shows that teacher morale was lowest in states where reforms reflected a top-down administrative structure, which made teachers feel as if they lacked autonomy and had no control over decisions that affect their teaching and evaluation.

> The input of teachers must give shape to the forming of education; it cannot be left to others to make all the important decisions. Flesh and blood require more nurturing than do plastic and steel. Unless teachers are treated with humaneness and dignity, the education of children cannot fulfill its potential. In part, taking greater regard of teachers and what they have to say means enhancing their role. Knowledgeable teachers who act as professionals can improve the education of their students. This is the reason why teachers should be empowered. (Maeroff 1988, viii)

V I E W P O I N T S

Teacher Empowerment

Deborah Peterson began teaching fourteen years ago in Crowley, Louisiana, and returned home to Baton Rouge two years ago to take a job as a sixth-grade teacher at Capital Middle School.

Peterson and her colleagues are just beginning to experiment with some of the tenets of the school reform movement. She is also experimenting with different instructional strategies in order to engage the attention of every child. "I think we're realizing now that we are going to have to deal with things differently than in the past. At one time I was not receptive to the idea of having different things going on in a classroom. But we must compete against outside forces for a student's attention."

Let me tell you what a group of teachers is trying to do at Capital Middle School, and you tell me whether or not it's teacher empowerment.

Capital has a high percentage of at-risk students from low socioeconomic situations. The school's success indicators were the lowest of any school in Baton Rouge. When I got here a couple of years ago, morale was very low. A few of us realized that if we were going to do something to boost student morale, the teachers had to boost their own. We had to realize that we were in a position to change a school that everyone did nothing but complain about.

A few of the sixth-grade teachers began to talk about ways to stimulate improvement. At the same time the Southern Regional Council came along with grant money for middle schools with at-risk populations through a local agency called Volunteers in Public Schools (VIPS). We applied for a grant to build achievement, encourage good behavior, and raise academic standards.

While we would have made progress on our own, the grant money was catalytic. It gave us a sense that we could do much more for students than we could have done alone. It also meant that the community and the administration backed us up.

Teachers formed a volunteer steering committee dedicated to changing the school. Some, perhaps, signed up out of curiosity, but many were very determined that we could make a difference.

We tackled our problems one by one. For example, kids wouldn't come to class on time so we set up a "tardy room." The idea was this: If kids came to school late, they'd go directly to the tardy room. The teacher on duty would work with the kids in whatever way he or she chose to impress upon them that being on time was important. An important point: Each teacher gives up a prep period to monitor the room.

The tardy room works beautifully. We started out with twenty-five or thirty kids in the room every period. That number was cut at the end of the school year to 6. Sometimes this year there aren't any students in the room. We are proud of the success because this is something we made work.

Teacher empowerment is a pretty simple concept: It's active involvement of teachers in the school decision-making process and assuming responsibility for that involvement. We wanted to cut down on tardiness. We came up with an idea, and we implemented it.

To make change in a school, there has to be a team approach. You have to find people who are going to work with you. If you take an authoritative attitude, you're going to have the respect that authority commands. But to have authority you have to have credibility. And you have to know how to approach people. If you force your opinion, you're not going to have any success. But if you go into a situation with a genuineness of heart, people will be willing to work with you.

From: Peterson, 1990

Collegial and Peer Relationships

Arlene Plevin reports that teachers find collegial relationships important to their professional development, particularly at the beginning of each school year, when every member of the educational team essentially starts over again with new students with diverse personalities presenting exciting challenges. Having time to share ideas with colleagues can lead to the development of new, different, and exciting lessons and exercises.

Plevin (1988) reports that some schools and school districts are attempting to create more opportunities for collegial exchange. Traditional class scheduling and in-service days are being modified to meet this need. In some secondary schools, for example, all teachers in a single subject area have the same planning period so that they can meet together to share ideas and plan the curriculum.

Although it is clear that some schools are working toward developing increased time for collegiality, others are not. For example, the 1989 Metropolitan Life Survey showed that team teaching (two or more professionals teaching a single course together) has increased in 45 percent of the schools and decreased in 25 percent of the schools since 1985. Similarly, 39 percent of the teachers responding to the 1989 survey reported that structured collegial time in their schools had decreased since 1985, whereas 41 percent reported that it had increased.

Another means of providing teachers with more collegial time is planned observation of peers. Thirty-seven percent of those teachers responding to the 1989 Metropolitan Life Survey reported that their school was better in 1989 than in 1986 at having teachers observe one another and provide feedback. However, 33 percent of the teachers said that their school was worse than in 1986.

Incentive Pay

Incentive pay, or **performance-based**, programs are designed to give teachers increased compensation for success in teaching, for accepting additional responsibilities, and/or for obtaining additional educational degrees. These programs are an outgrowth of the reform reports of the 1980s that suggested that school improvement required better teaching and greater student achievement. Hence, incentive pay programs attempt to link rewards to performance.

In 1990, twenty-five states had increased funding for incentive pay programs that linked financial rewards for teachers and administrators to performance and increased work loads. Ten states had incentive programs that rewarded schools and their staffs for schoolwide innovation or improvement. In 1991, the Southern Regional Education Board reported that most incentive pay programs had focused on increased student achievement and reduced dropout rates.

According to a 1990 study by Richard Brandt, the plans have affected teaching in the following ways:

- *Teacher evaluation has changed. Because few systematic procedures existed, evaluation schemes were developed not only to help teachers, but to make decisions about performance. . . .*
- *There are very few instances where incentive pay has been primarily dependent on student achievement. . . .*
- *Principals are spending more time in the classroom dealing with instruction; some teachers are taking on new roles that expand their responsibility beyond*

their own classroom; and the teacher is no longer teaching behind the door because of expectations of monitoring [by the principal] in some programs.

- *Programs have caused more differentiation in pay among teachers in a district. . . .*
- *Teacher attitudes have often initially been negative, but attitudes have become more positive where programs are seen to have been well implemented.*
- *Teachers are most hostile to programs that are performance-based and highly selective. . . . (1990, 245–255)*

All incentive pay, or performance-based, compensation programs are designed to improve teaching by providing the best teachers with financial incentives.

Teacher Accountability

Teacher evaluation and assessment of student performance are frequently tied to systems of incentive pay. The assumption is that quality teaching leads to greater student achievement and should be rewarded.

Teacher accountability, then, means that teachers are responsible for the quality of their instruction and the progress of their students. Usually, teacher performance is measured through classroom-based observation and evaluation by administrators and trained teacher evaluators. Student progress is typically measured by performance on nationally normed standardized tests. In the 1990 Gallup poll of the Public's Attitude Toward the Public Schools, 70 percent of those surveyed favored requiring public schools in their communities to conform to national standards and goals. However, only 36 percent believed national standards and goals could be accomplished by the year 2000. Likewise, in a 1989 survey of two thousand teachers, conducted by the Metropolitan Life Insurance Company, 61 percent of the teachers surveyed indicated that they support teacher accountability for the academic success of students (Harris and Associates 1989, 75).

Despite the support of teacher accountability for student achievement, there is significant disagreement about whether it is possible to evaluate excellence in teaching and whether it is appropriate to assume that teaching excellence necessarily leads to student achievement. For example, assume that Jane and Robert teach second grade in the same elementary school. Jane teaches a class of students who tested above grade level in kindergarten and first grade. Robert's class tested below grade level. Evaluators believe that both are very good teachers. However, when the standardized tests are administered in the spring, Robert's students have fallen even further below grade level and Jane's students have risen further above. Hence, in their incentive pay system, Robert will receive an average salary increase and Jane will receive an above average increase. Is this fair? Robert contends it is not. He says that studies show that children who are below grade level continue to fall further and further behind no matter how good their instruction. He also maintains that his children do not test well because their backgrounds render the tests inappropriate. According to Robert, the children are unfamiliar with many of the words on the tests because the words are not used in their homes. In addition, Robert says that he has to work harder than Jane to be a successful teacher. He also contends that it is not fair to make him accountable when he cannot make decisions about the textbooks and the curriculum. He says that if he could teach these children as he would like to, he would throw away the basal readers, take them on weekly field trips, use written material related to those field trips, introduce them to all kinds of music and visual arts, and read to them at least an hour per day. "Only then," says Robert, "can I be accountable for the progress of the children."

Results of Incentive Pay Programs

Historically educators have complained that the only way to advance themselves professionally was to quit teaching and enter administration. One of the goals of incentive pay, or **performance-based**, compensation plans, therefore, is to give teachers increased professional opportunity without requiring them to leave the classroom. For example, in an incentive pay system a teacher's salary is based on seniority and also on educational advancement and teaching excellence. This gives teachers the opportunity to advance financially and in status among their peers without leaving the classroom. Furthermore, many incentive pay programs offer opportunities to pursue higher education. In some states, school districts provide training for teachers that can lead to merit increases or simply reimburse teachers for educational expenses. Three of the most common incentive pay programs are merit pay, career ladder, and master teacher programs.

Point/Counterpoint

EXTERNAL REWARDS TO IMPROVE TEACHING

The concept of return on investment is an ancient idea and practice. Only in teaching, as a form of public service, has it met with extreme resistance in modern times. Despite the persistent recommendations of national commissions in both education and business over the past twenty-five years, including the *Nation at Risk* report, schools have systematically resisted the effort to improve the quality of teaching through realistic incentive systems.

John Goodlad reports in *A Place Called School* (1984) that although only 2 to 4 percent of elementary and secondary teachers selected in his study chose teaching for economic reasons, 18 to 25 percent left teaching for economic reasons. Opportunities to remain in education and receive higher salaries, except in school administration, do not exist for the teacher.

Moreover, more women are choosing fields other than teaching because of their increased opportunities. And the profession has traditionally relied upon women to fill teaching positions.

In former years, the uniform salary schedule did reduce what were major inequities among teachers. One was the large discrepancy between the salaries of elementary and secondary school teachers. Another was salary discrimination based on sex. Training and years of experience became the new criteria for eliminating those inequities. Now, however, having nearly eliminated inequities through uniformity, the single-step salary schedule stands in the way of promotional excellence. . . .

A multiple-step salary schedule, on the other hand, adds criteria for promotion to another level of teaching excellence and adds criteria for maintaining proficiency at that level. . . .

The multiple-step salary schedule serves as both a guide and goal, urging good teachers to seek the next level of instruction and offering them examples of how to attain it. Those who have had to submit to collegial evaluation have clearly had to demonstrate performance. . . .

What is clear is that the single-step salary schedule, by itself, progresses in a linear fashion and acknowledges nothing except years of continuity in service. Variable pay scales, on the other hand, with both merit pay and differentiated pay levels for differing responsibilities, are the most important reform needed to promote and reward teaching excellence. . . .

Let's assume schools were able to identify outstanding examples of teaching. The logical next step would be proportionate rewards, including nonpay incentives. In the long run, of course, it is pay incentives that will likely maintain and increase precisely those teaching skills that the school wants promoted, and which will in turn increase student learning performance. (pp. 406–408)

From: Sharpes, 1987

INTRINSIC REWARDS TO IMPROVE TEACHING

Effective incentive systems should reflect the principles that intrinsic rewards are more powerful than extrinsic ones and that encouraging collegiality is preferable to rewarding individual teachers. . . .

Too many recent policies have tried to induce improved school performance by threatening teachers' job security or concentrating financial rewards on individual behavior. The result has been an unbalanced and often unreliable incentive system that frustrates and alienates as many teachers as it succeeds in rewarding. While some aspects of teaching can be improved by isolating individual teachers and encouraging them to concentrate their efforts on a small group of students, the most serious problems confronting today's schools call for coordinated work efforts by teachers who are able to work closely with trusted colleagues and who take pride and sense of personal identity from participating in the total school organization.

Incentives capable of improving accountability, encouraging professional development, strengthening recruitment and retention, and expanding teacher job definitions are readily available in most school settings. Too few managers have the capacity to nurture and support an effective incentive system, however. While monetary rewards may be important, they are viewed as the most important incentives for good teaching only by policymakers and school managers who do not understand the potency of intrinsic satisfactions for teachers and who constantly disrupt the development of needed collegial groups and strong organizational structures by rewarding teachers for self-centered and organizationally subversive actions. Good schools are the best incentives for good teachers. (pp. 74, 78)

From: Mitchell and Peters, 1988

POSTSCRIPT

Educators continue to argue about whether incentive pay programs are appropriate in education. On the one hand, they argue that without incentive pay programs teachers are and will continue to leave teaching for more lucrative professions. On the other, they worry that incentive pay programs will erode those aspects of teaching that make it intrinsically rewarding: collegiality and interpersonal relationships. Those who favor incentive pay, including merit pay and career ladders, contend that without extrinsic recognition for a job well done, the best teachers will become frustrated. Why work so hard to achieve success in teaching when the teacher down the hall who puts in half the number of hours makes the same salary and has the same benefits? Those opposed are concerned that attempting to reward teachers requires evaluating teachers. According to opponents, evaluation of teachers requires the quantification of teaching results, which cannot be easily quantified and counted. However, in spite of the arguments, it is clear that the number of incentive pay systems have increased. In the next several years, it will be interesting to observe whether they continue or whether they are discontinued, as were many of the merit pay systems of the past.

Merit Pay

One method of financially rewarding teachers for doing their job well is **merit pay**. They do not require a teacher to have increased responsibility or extra assignments. Generally, merit pay is not incorporated into the teacher's base salary but is awarded in the form of an annual bonus. In addition, merit pay programs do not attempt to develop a hierarchy of job classification but simply reward teachers for job-related achievement.

One of the greatest difficulties in a merit pay system has always been determining the best evaluation system to identify those who deserve a pay increase. Whether conducted by a supervisor, based on student achievement data, or determined by a teacher's portfolio, there is no system that is completely objective. Thus, complaints of favoritism may arise, or worse, moral and ethical complacency may develop in order to appease those in authority who may be scheduled to evaluate a teacher's performance. Furthermore, whatever collegiality exists in a particular school environment may be threatened by the necessity to compete with one's colleagues rather than cooperate with them.

Merit pay is not a new concept. In the early 1920s, 40–50 percent of school districts in the United States had merit pay plans. However, by the 1930s many of these plans had been replaced by more uniform pay scales. Complaints about merit pay systems included questions about the evaluator's judgment and differentials in the salaries of males and females. However, during the school reform movement of the 1950s, merit pay plans, based on teacher performance, were reintroduced. In 1968, 11 percent of all school districts had merit pay programs. By 1976, only 4 percent of all schools awarded merit pay. Today, although some merit pay programs exist, most incentive pay programs are not merit or bonus systems but instead base salary differences on measurements of performance, increased responsibilities, and higher levels of education or training.

Career Ladder

Much more elaborate than merit pay plans are **career ladder** plans that create a new structure for a teaching career, allowing teachers to pass through several stages, each with greater responsibilities and more pay. These plans are also called **differentiated staffing**. Promotion from one level to the next is based on an objective assessment of professional achievements. A hierarchy of job classifications and a differentiated salary schedule result.

For example, as a level-one classroom teacher, or intern, a teacher might be paid at a base of $24,000. Before advancing to level two, the professional level, the teacher would be expected to have successfully completed several years of teaching and to have been evaluated by other teachers and administrators based on a state- or district-designed evaluation instrument. Moreover, he or she would be required to obtain additional education to reach level two. This level also carries increased responsibility, such as curriculum development or teacher mentoring. The base for this level might be $27,000. At level three, the career professional level, the teacher might be required to assume responsibilities as a teacher evaluator or curriculum supervisor. In addition, she or he is likely to be required to obtain a master's degree and additional areas of certification. At this level, the base might be $32,000.

Career ladders are a relatively new concept. However, some states have had career ladder programs since the early 1980s. Tennessee's career ladder, instituted statewide in 1983, began as a merit pay program to attract the best candidates and to identify and keep superior teachers. By 1987, 39,000, or 84 percent, of Tennessee's teachers had a career ladder certificate, with 6,200 teachers at the top two levels. Although involvement in Tennessee's career ladder program is no longer mandated by law, the majority of tenured teachers participate and have received training in the evaluation system. Most teachers remain at the lowest level since promotion to the upper levels is done sparingly by outside evaluators. During 1988–1989, only one of five eligible teachers or administrators had achieved levels two or three, and salary supplements ranged from one thousand to seven thousand dollars for a twelve-month contract. Teachers at levels two and three had additional opportunities for summer employment. But today teachers at all levels have equal opportunities for summer employment, removing one of the incentives for achieving higher levels on the career ladder.

Master Teacher

Superior performance can be achieved through **master teacher** plans. Although such plans do not establish a graduated career structure, they give one group of teachers increased responsibility for which they are usually provided additional compensation. The programs are also called lead, mentor, or head teacher plans. In California, mentor teachers spend 40 percent of their time working with other teachers on curriculum and instruction and conducting workshops and peer evaluations. Other master teacher plans restructure the teaching pattern of the school. In these plans, the teaching staff might be divided into teams with one master, mentor, head, or lead teacher assuming a leadership function. In other plans, mentor teachers might assume responsibility for the guidance of neophyte teachers in the school. Although these plans are not usually associated with a differentiated staffing pattern, they do highlight differences in teacher performance, responsibility, and salary that run counter to the egalitarian manner in which schools have been traditionally organized.

Opposition to Incentive Pay

Although the majority of teachers support some type of teacher accountability for student achievement, a large percentage do not support the current incentive pay plans. In 1989, 48 percent of teachers surveyed by the Metropolitan Life Insurance Company believed that methods used to select teachers for merit pay tended to be unfair and nonobjective. This, however, was down from the 56 percent who found the methods unfair in 1986. Similarly in 1989, 60 percent of teachers surveyed believed that career ladder systems created "artificial and unfortunate distinctions among teachers." This was down from 72 percent in 1986. If so many teachers do not support performance-based compensation plans, can the programs be considered incentives toward improving teaching and keeping the best teachers in the classroom? On the other hand, as these plans are becoming more widely employed, are they more acceptable to the teachers who are participating in them? It will be some time before we know the answers to these questions and the level of success of performance-based compensation plans. Table 4.2, overleaf, shows the types of incentives favored by teachers.

Salaries

Teachers' salaries are increasing both in and out of incentive pay programs. But, are they keeping up with inflation and the salaries of other professionals?

A study of elementary economic principles reveals that an increased demand for teachers and a limited supply of teachers, such as we have in the 1990s, should lead to increased salaries. Historically, this has not been the case.

TABLE 4-2

**SASS (Schools and Staffing Survey) Data on Public School Teacher
Favorability Ratings of Pay Incentives**

Pay incentive program	Statistic[1]	Favorability rating			
		Strongly favor	Mildly favor	Mildly oppose	Strongly oppose
1. For Added Responsibilities	Percent	57.8%	28.7%	5.7%	6.9%
	Std Error	.33	.22	.14	.16
2. Teaching in Shortage Field	Percent	23.7%	28.6%	20.6%	27.0%
	Std Error	.20	.28	.25	.26
3. Teaching in High-Priority Location	Percent	40.5%	36.3%	12.3%	11.0%
	Std Error	.30	.29	.18	.19
4. Career Ladder Progress	Percent	39.1%	30.7%	12.2%	18.0%
	Std Error	.33	.27	.21	.24
5. Individual Merit Pay	Percent	27.0%	26.2%	16.5%	30.4%
	Std Error	.31	.29	.20	.28
6. Group Merit Bonus	Percent	33.5%	30.1%	14.7%	21.8%
	Std Error	.28	.29	.18	.24

[1]The unweighted sample sizes on which these data are based are about 40,000 teachers in the public sector and about 6,500 in the private sector. The statistics tabulated pertain to weighted estimates of over 2,200,000 public school teachers and close to 300,000 private school teachers in the United States.

From: E. Boe, "Teacher Incentive Research With SASS," paper presented at meeting of the American Education Research Association (April 1990).

Several programs for determining which teachers should receive pay in addition to their salary have been implemented through the years in various school systems around the country. None have been totally effective or totally acceptable. This table lists the major programs and, by showing the percentage of teachers who approve or disapprove of them, gives a favorability rating for each.

In the 1960s, when the demand for teachers exceeded the supply, teaching salaries remained low. Although teaching salaries have risen dramatically in the last several decades, they have not kept pace with those for other professions (see figure 4.1), nor have they kept pace with inflation (see figure 4.2, p. 102).

As early as the mid-1800s, educator and politician Horace Mann recognized the need for improved teacher salaries. Mann claimed that in the 1840s female teachers were paid less than many female laborers in factories. He recognized that the quality of teachers would not improve until salaries improved. Figure 4.1 (p. 101) indicates that the problem of relatively low salaries for teachers when compared to other professions still exists in the late twentieth century. If Mann was correct, incentive pay programs will do little to improve the quality of teaching unless overall teaching salaries increase.

FIGURE 4-1

Average Teacher Salary Grows at About the Same Rate as Other Professions in 1988

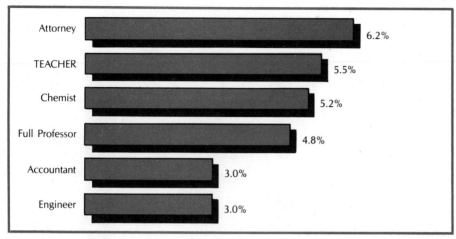

Average Teacher Salary in 1988 Falls Short of Earnings in Other Professions

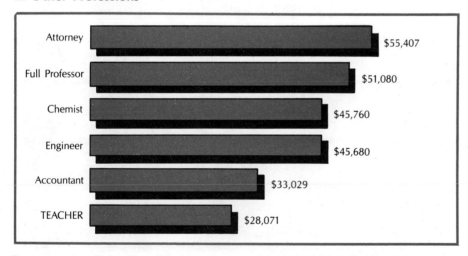

From: American Federation of Teachers, *Survey and Analysis of Salary Trends* (1989).

While it is encouraging that teachers' salaries have risen at about the same rate as other professions, they remain, for the most part, considerably below the salaries of other professions.

Again in the 1980s, as many times before, the call for increased teacher salaries was made by the commissions suggesting reforms in teaching and teacher training. According to a U.S. Department of Education report in 1987, "reports of teacher shortages in selected specialities and the possibility of a general teacher shortage in the future have increased the perceived importance of teacher salaries as an incentive in attracting and retaining capable teachers" (p. 50).

FIGURE 4-2

(A) Inflation Closes in on Teacher Salaries

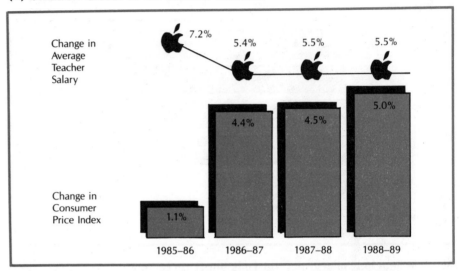

(B) Average Teacher Salary Barely Exceeds 1972 Levels
Average Teacher Salary in 1989 Dollars

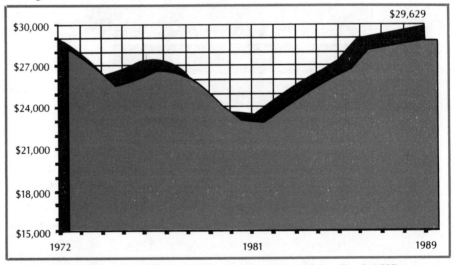

From: American Federation of Teachers, *Survey and Analysis of Salary Trends* (1989).

Teacher salaries have not kept pace with the cost of inflation as measured by the consumer price index, which shows the percentage of change in cost of goods and services over a given period of time (A). When adjusted for inflation, a teacher's salary in 1990–1991 increased only 27 percent from 1980–1981 (B).

In 1990–1991 the highest paid teachers in the United States lived in Alaska and earned an average of $43,406, while the lowest paid teachers lived in South Dakota and made $22,363. The average teaching salary in 1990–1991 was $32,880, up 87.3 percent since 1980–1981 when the average salary was $17,544. However, when adjusted for inflation, the increase over that period was only $7,054 or 27 percent, according to the American Federation of Teachers.

FIGURE 4-3

The Average Teacher Salary Compared to the Average Experience Level of Teachers

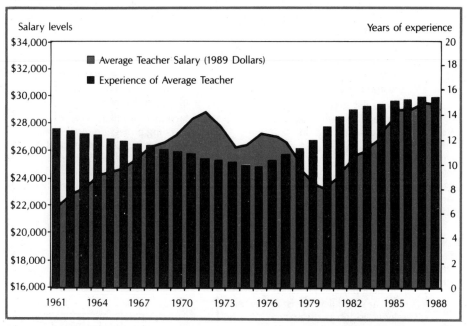

From: American Federation of Teachers, *Survey and Analysis of Salary Trends* (1989), p. 35.

In an effort to attract more people to the teaching profession, beginning teachers' salaries have had to keep pace with inflation. The salaries of experienced teachers have not kept pace, however, with the result that many of the best teachers are leaving the profession for higher-paying jobs.

Ironically, the inability of teaching salaries to keep ahead of inflation affected teachers with experience more than it did beginning teachers. In order to attract new teachers to the profession, entry salaries have been kept relatively high when compared to salaries of experienced teachers (see figure 4.3). John Goodlad called the low ratio of teaching salaries after ten years to beginning salaries the "flatness" of the profession. He warned that this trend would ensure that teaching remains a "marginal profession" because the best teachers would leave for better-paying jobs (1984).

In part, as a response to the concern for the flatness of teacher salaries, reform in how salaries are allocated was initiated in many states in the 1980s. This reform, allowing differentiation in pay for teachers based on performance and increased responsibilities, was highly touted by the Reagan and Bush administrations. Reagan's secretary of education, William Bennett, and most of the reform commissions of the 1980s contended that teachers should be paid based on quality of performance rather than seniority. It was hoped that performance-based compensation plans would keep the best teachers in teaching.

4.1 POINTS TO REMEMBER

- The qualities of a profession include a body of knowledge, controlled recruitment, freedom to use one's own discretion, autonomy from direct supervision, empowerment to make decisions, well-established collegial relations, ability to communicate with the public, high standards and a code of ethics, good working conditions and benefits, commitment to the welfare of students, commitment to a career, accountability for performance, continuous retraining, objective evaluation of performance, and membership in professional organizations.

- Teacher autonomy gives teachers the freedom to use their own discretion about decisions related to life in the classroom and to teach without direct supervision.

- Teacher empowerment is the freedom and responsibility for teachers to make decisions regarding the operation of the school that affect life in the classroom. These may include decisions about student placement, curriculum, hiring, promotion.

- Autonomy and empowerment are required in a profession in order to increase self-worth and ultimately to improve the process of education.

- Collegial time allows teachers to share ideas with other professionals and grow through the process.

- Incentive pay is awarded for excellent teaching performance, student achievement, and/or increased responsibilities.

- As professionals, teachers are accountable for their own success or failure, giving them the freedom to make their own decisions and the responsibility for accepting the consequences.

- A merit pay system awards teachers on a scheduled basis for excellence in job performance.

- A career ladder, or differentiated staffing, program moves teachers through various professional levels that are related to job performance, increased responsibilities, and additional education and results in increased salary.

- Master teacher plans, also called mentor teaching plans, require experienced teachers to work as mentor, lead, or head teachers.

- Incentive pay plans may make the teaching profession more competitive with other professions but have yet to develop an equitable and objective method of determining who should receive incentive pay.

- Teachers' salaries have been increasing but have not been keeping ahead of inflation. The gap between the salaries of teachers and other professionals is still wide.

TEACHING AS A CAREER

When we think in terms of a career, we think in terms of a life's work. According to Alan Eck of the U.S. Bureau of Labor Statistics, the average U.S. adult will change jobs five or six times during his or her working life (telephone conversation, February 22, 1991). However, it is generally true that the longer the length of training, the longer the individual will remain on the job. Since teaching requires at least four years of academic training and a baccalaureate degree, it is likely that many individuals will remain in classroom teaching or will seek other positions in education. In the 1988 Metropolitan Life Insurance survey of current teachers, 26 percent said they anticipated leaving the profession, but according to Vance Grant of the National Center for Education Statistics, only 4.1 percent of all teachers left teaching in 1987–1988 (telephone conversation, July 19, 1990). This, according to Alan Eck, is down from 4.65 percent in 1986–1987 (ibid.). In *The Metropolitan Life Survey of The American Teacher 1990*, Louis Harris found that most new teachers (90 percent of over one thousand teachers interviewed) view teaching as a long-term career choice, not merely a job (see figure 4.4).

FIGURE 4-4

Intention to Remain in Teaching

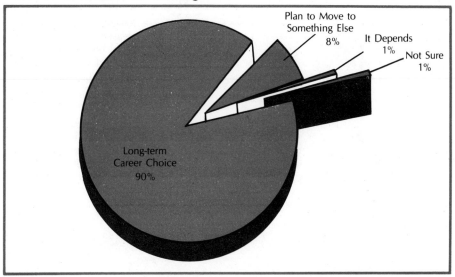

From: Metropolitan Life Insurance Company, *The Metropolitan Life Survey of the American Teacher 1990* (1990), p. 6.

Teachers, interviewed by Louis Harris and Associates, were asked: "At this time, do you view teaching as a long-term career, or something you expect to do for a few years and then move on to something else?" Their responses indicate that most teachers expect to remain in the profession for a long time.

In 1987 the public schools in the United States had more than 4 million employees, more than half of whom were classroom teachers (National Center for Education Statistics 1990b). The schools also employed nearly 199,000 administrators, nearly 129,000 administrative support personnel, over 194,000 school and library support staff, over 335,000 instructional aides, over 70,000 guidance counselors, nearly 48,000 librarians, and more than 1 million other support personnel. However, the proportion of teachers to the total public school staff had declined from 65 percent in 1959 to 52.8 percent in 1987. Of those teachers employed by the public schools in the mid-1980s, 85 percent were white; more than two-thirds were female. Many people believe that teacher's salaries remain lower than those of other professions simply because the majority of teachers are women. Many between the ages of thirty-six and forty-five had taught for ten to twenty years.   The relative maturity of the teaching force means that in the next two decades there will be critical shortages as teachers with twenty or more years of experience begin to retire.

According to the Carnegie Foundation for the Advancement of Teaching (1990), the oversupply of teachers experienced in the early 1970s reversed itself by 1982 and the demand will continue to increase relative to the supply throughout the 1990s (see figure 4.5, overleaf). By 1994, according to the U.S. Department of Education, the supply should peak with a need for 281,000 more teachers than there are graduates of teacher-training programs. By the mid-1990s a large portion of the teaching professionals of the 1980s will have retired; consequently, the demand for new teachers will continue to grow.

Who Are Today's Teachers?

FIGURE 4-5

Trends in Projected Demand for New Hiring of Teachers, by Level

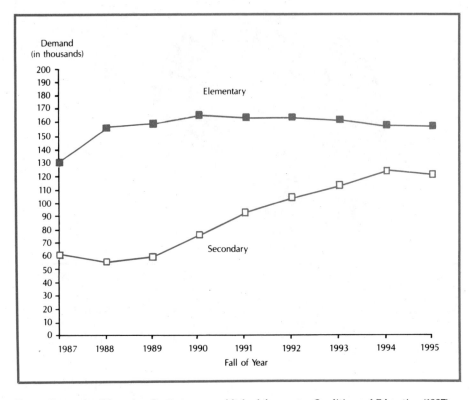

From: Center for Education Statistics, unpublished forecasts, *Conditions of Education* (1987).

The projected demand for new hiring of elementary school teachers increased in the late 1980s and is expected to decline in the first half of the 1990s, while the projected demand for new hiring of secondary school teachers is expected to increase in the first half of the 1990s.

Positive Aspects of a Teaching Career

Research has shown that there are many reasons that teachers who continue in teaching do so. Below we will examine some of those reasons and cite sources for seeking more information.

1. *Teaching fulfills a desire to work with young people and help them grow and develop.* (Metropolitan Life Insurance Company 1990; Plevin 1988; Ream 1977; Lortie 1975)
2. *The personal rewards involved in watching young people grow and develop are significant.* (Metropolitan Life Insurance Company 1990; Isaacs 1990)
3. *Personal relationships with young people are important.* (Metropolitan Life Insurance Company 1989)
4. *Teachers can continue to explore a subject area of interest or work with an age level of students with whom they are intrigued.* (Metropolitan Life Insurance Company 1989; Ream 1977)

(continued on p. 108)

CROSS-CULTURAL PERSPECTIVE

Sequoyah Writes

One day on a trip to the village, Sequoyah fell into conversation with some of his tribesmen.

The white man, he told them, had a method of putting thoughts on paper by a series of signs or marks.

He bent down and picked up a stone and began to scratch figures on it with his knife.

"I can teach the Cherokee to talk on paper like the white man," he said.

His clansmen laughed at him and told him he was crazy. But he said no more then. And on his way home he thought more and more about it.

Over the years he had observed that many things found out by man had become lost to his people because there was no way to preserve them.

Although ignorant of the writings and teachings of philosophers, he knew that what the white man wrote down on paper remained and was not forgotten.

Sequoyah thought if he could make things fast on paper it would be like catching a wild animal and taming it.

He was so intrigued by the thought that he determined to devote the rest of his life to solving the riddle of written speech.

The year was 1809 when he plunged into his long and lonely task. . . .

He sought at first to make a character for each word, but in a year he had thousands of characters which even he could not decipher. Finally, he began attempting to develop an alphabet based on syllables in the Cherokee language. . . .

One day on a public road he found a piece of newspaper, this Cherokee who was unable to read or speak one word of English. He found characters on it that gave him an idea.

He picked out the Roman letters. He adopted them in lieu of many of his own. He did this without knowing the English name or meaning of a single one of them. He added curls and dashes to them, turned them upside down, and drew them in his own fashion.

Thus he completed a Cherokee alphabet, or syllabary. It was a system in which characters

Despite great odds, Sequoyah continued working on the Cherokee alphabet so that he could teach other Native Americans how to read and write.

represented sounds out of which words could be compounded—a system in which single letters would stand for syllables.

A dozen years had gone into the work and now he was ready to make his invention known to his people.

The first scholar was his own daughter. In only a few days she was able to read and write Cherokee.

In 1821 he gave a public demonstration before a gathering of tribal heads. They accepted his miracle. And soon the entire Cherokee nation was reading and writing Cherokee. . . .

In 1824 the legislative Council of the Cherokee Nation voted a medal to be struck and presented to Sequoyah "as a token of respect and admiration for your ingenuity in the invention of the Cherokee alphabetical characters." . . .

When Sequoyah was 75 years old he set out on an expedition to Mexico in search of a "lost" tribe of Cherokee.

Alone, he fell sick with fever in 1842 and halted his ox cart near San Fernando in northern Mexico. There he died. He was buried near the Rio Grande. . . .

The language he taught his people to read and write is still spoken by the old ones here on the 65,000-acre Qualla Boundary, but there are only a few still around who can read and write Cherokee.

From: Parris, 1989

5. *Teaching is intellectually rewarding; lifelong learning goals are achieved.* (Plevin 1988; Harbaugh 1985)
6. *Success in working with young people enhances one's sense of dignity and esteem.* (Lortie 1975)
7. *Teaching allows one to use intuition and insight in diagnosing and helping to solve students' academic, social, and psychological problems.* (Ayers 1990; Bullough 1988; Plevin 1988)
8. *The school calendar allows teachers to pursue other interests and professional development.* (Ream 1977)
9. *Teaching allows for geographic flexibility.* (Harbaugh 1985)
10. *Teaching provides a fair to good salary and good fringe benefits.* (Carnegie Foundation 1990; Harbaugh 1985)
11. *Incentive pay increments based on performance can be rewarding.* (Brandt 1990; Carnegie Foundation 1990; Harbaugh 1985)

Frustrations of a Teaching Career

Although the majority of new teachers plan to stay in teaching for a career, a large percentage of these teachers will leave the profession. What causes them to leave? Researchers have found the following problems and concerns to be frustrating enough that teachers who had planned to remain in the classroom depart because of them.

1. *Some teachers believe that too many parents treat teachers as adversaries and are not involved in their children's education.* (Carnegie Foundation 1990; Metropolitan Life Insurance Company 1990; Harbaugh 1985)
2. *Some teachers feel unprepared to teach students from a variety of ethnic backgrounds.* (Metropolitan Life Insurance Company 1990; National Coalition of Advocates for Students 1988)
3. *Some teachers do not feel qualified to teach the students with disabilities who are mainstreamed into their classrooms.* (Harbaugh 1985)
4. *Many teachers believe that they do not have enough scheduled preparation time.* (Carnegie Foundation 1990; Metropolitan Life Insurance Company 1989)
5. *Some teachers believe their classes are too large.* (Carnegie Foundation 1990; Harbaugh 1985)
6. *Fiscal resources have declined, and many teachers spend their own money on supplies and other educational materials.* (Carnegie Foundation 1990; Metropolitan Life Insurance Company 1989)
7. *Support services such as counseling are not always available.* (Carnegie Foundation 1990; Metropolitan Life Insurance Company 1989)
8. *Many teachers believe they do not have autonomy in making decisions about the classroom.* (Bull 1990; Brandt 1990; Fenstermacker 1990)
9. *Some buildings and materials are outdated.* (Carnegie Foundation 1990; Goodlad 1984)
10. *Salaries are not comparable to those in other professions.* (Carnegie Foundation 1990; American Federation of Teachers 1989; Goodlad 1984)
11. *Some feel that incentive pay plans lack objective evaluation.* (Brandt 1990; Carnegie Foundation 1990; Bullough 1988; Darling-Hammond 1988; Chance 1986; Rosenholtz 1986)

IN THE CLASSROOM

The following excerpt recounts one incident in Christine Emmel's first year of teaching. Emmel, who had a traditional white, middle-class upbringing, taught five life-science classes to noncollege-bound students in an inner-city Los Angeles high school. She was emergency certified as part of the Los Angeles Unified School District's teacher intern program.

I prefer to regard myself as a "first-year veteran," having pulled through the horrendous initiation that Maywood [High School] had in store. Gang violence, vandalism, overwhelming rates of teen motherhood, phenomenal records of truancy, student fights, theft, and extreme student hostility in the classroom were just a few of the charms of this particular institution.

I knew I'd be O.K. . . . if I could just turn in my fifth period to the deck and get a new hand. Fifth period was to be my point of surrender—surrender to the frustration of feeling totally powerless over their behavior, surrender to my own feelings of self-doubt and inadequacy.

In the face of my problem with this class, I decided to try "relating" to the students humanistically; this was a suggestion gleaned from several more experienced teachers.

I told the students that I wanted to talk something over with them, meanwhile easing myself into what I hoped was a nonthreatening "I'm your friend" stance. I proceeded to explain, or rather purge, my feelings—how I felt as though they were pitted against me and resistant to what I was trying to teach them, how I felt "real bad" about it and wished we could have a friendlier and more enjoyable class. I finished by "relating" my need for their cooperation, since I wanted to help them, and couldn't under the current terms of our relationship.

What a feeling to finally speak the truth of my feelings—and to them! I looked into their faces, trying to gauge their reaction. Feeling so good about opening up myself, I could only hope for the best. Alas, as usual, reality corrected my forever idealistic expectations, in the form of [her student] Geri's comment: "Well, if you weren't such a bad teacher . . ." This cutting remark, in the face of my vulnerability, plus a few smirks and other unsympathetic comments, were enough to push me past my limit.

And so, I cried in front of fifth period—something I never dreamed I'd do and certainly one of my more horrible imaginings. I'd never let them know I could be pushed that far—and yet, here I was, uncontrollably watering the dirty tile floor! I quickly exited to the hallway, to attempt to regain some equanimity. I hoped no other teachers had decided to keep their doors open that day. After a few moments of agonized "I blew it" thoughts in the empty corridor, I stepped back into my room, heart pounding. In the first second of opening the door, I heard the sound of fake sobs from within. So much for the damned "humanistic" approach! Clearly, neither I nor my students were at a point where this tactic could succeed.

What I learned from this experience is still not altogether clear to me. Once again, however, I was permitted to see that school, just like life, goes on no matter what. I felt I had lost a battle that day and had admitted total defeat in an utterly humiliating way. But a new day of school and fifth period would dawn again . . . and it did. Nothing is irrevocable, and my striving for successful classroom management continued, even though I thought that one day was "The End."

Patricia Norton, a health teacher for more than 20 years and a mentor teacher, reacted this way:

First of all, I needed to calm down from the outrage I felt upon learning that Christine, with her background and total lack of experience, was sent to such a difficult situation in the first place! I know of no other business where the employers show such a lack of concern about a person's suitability to a particular job. I was beginning to think that the sink-or-swim attitude in education was phasing out with the advent of mentor programs, but I see, as in Christine's dilemma, that the mentality is still alive and well.

Certainly, in a situation like Christine's, a mentor teacher from that school—one who knows the students and the problems—should have spent time with her initially. It was terribly unfortunate that she came to the point of surrender and helplessness.

As to the advice by Christine's colleagues about solving the fifth-period problem by "showing her human side," I think that the interpretation of what that meant needed more defining. An approach that comes from weakness, as hers was interpreted by the students, never works. She needed to come from whatever strength she had left.

I admire Christine's tenacity to hang in there and learn that experience helps. It sounds as if she really has what it takes to be a teacher. (Shulman and Colbert 1988)

TRENDS IN TEACHING

Although the ideals of professionalism have yet to be fully implemented in the teaching field, several trends in the 1990s point to an awareness of difficulties and a concerted effort in most parts of the country to improve the conditions under which teachers work. As one indication, an NEA Blue Ribbon Task Force on Educational Excellence established by Mary Futrell, former NEA president, concluded that if teaching is going to be a full-fledged profession, a career in teaching will look like this by the year 2000: (1) teachers will demand more from students and place more responsibility on them; (2) a school's faculty will be deployed in ways that permit individual students to receive help in a timely fashion; (3) the number of students per teacher will be small enough to allow ample time to plan each child's programs; (4) teachers will no longer be isolated from one another; (5) teaching will be an attractive, lifelong profession, and teachers will be professionally compensated; (6) teachers will be encouraged to participate in the development of school policy and programs; (7) there will be no hierarchical staffing systems within the profession, only an exciting mix of equally important roles—such as curriculum development, helping new teachers . . . ; (8) decisions about instruction will be made at the school level, not by bureaucracies in school system central offices and state capitals; and (9) starting salaries will not be less than $24,000 (Futrell 1989, 5–6, 8, 10, 14–15, 25).

Mid-Career Teaching   An interesting trend in teaching is the "growing number of professionals . . . turning to teaching in mid-career, taking pay cuts in order to pursue their late-found vocation" (Tifft 1989). This trend can be attributed, in part, to increasing salaries and efforts by many states to speed up the certification process through the development of alternative programs, which frequently count professional experience or expertise toward obtaining teaching credentials. (See chapter 3, pages 70–71, for a discussion of the controversy surrounding alternative certification routes.)

Although professional rewards, such as salary and autonomy, are important to these career changers, it is clear from the salary cuts they take that these are not the crucial motives. Tom Carlyle, who quit a management job in publishing to teach high school math, says, "Getting these kids through high school is much more satisfying than working behind a desk" (Tifft 1989).

After initial certification, all fifty states and the District of Columbia require that teachers meet additional educational requirements at various stages in their teaching careers. In 1991, forty-five states had a second level of teacher certification (required in thirty-five of the forty-five). Requirements for this second level of certification varied among the states and included teaching experience, additional course work, state examinations, and success on assessments of performance. Eleven states required a master's degree for this second level of certification; three required a fifth year of study; others required from six to thirty semester units of credits. Also, in forty-three states a continuing education requirement had to be met after the second stage of certification. The most common requirement was six semester hours every five years or 120–150 hours of staff development every five years. In 1987, 46.3 percent of all teachers had a master's or specialist degree as compared to only 23.1 percent in 1961 (National Center for Education Statistics 1990, 76). The teaching profession has embraced Mortimer Adler's message in *The Paideia Proposal* (1982): "The teacher who has stopped learning is a deadening influence rather than a help to students being initiated into the ways of learning" (p. 59). In-service training programs are specifically designed to improve teaching and management skills. They may be conducted at the school site or in conjunction with a university and involve case studies, films of classroom teachers at work, and role-playing. Teachers analyze how to deal most effectively with the situations presented.

Staff Development

Today's school population is diverse, particularly in urban centers. In California, Texas, Florida, and New York nearly half of all schoolchildren are from minority groups (Hodgkinson 1989, 65). According to James Banks in a lecture at the University of North Carolina at Asheville, in 1990 students of color were the majority in twenty-five of the fifty largest public school systems in the United States. By the year 2020, students of color will constitute 46 percent of the nation's public school population (lecture, March 1, 1991).

In many schools it is not unusual to find several races and numerous religions represented and many students speaking English as their second language or not at all. In 1987–1988, 1,105,561 of the nation's total school population of 39,911,968 were enrolled in bilingual programs. In addition, 1,041,702 students were enrolled in English as a second language (ESL) programs (National Center for Education Statistics 1990).

In 1988–1989 in Miami, Florida, 166,761 students were registered in bilingual programs and 52,000 in special ethnic heritage programs (National School

Diverse School Population

Many American classrooms are becoming ethnically diverse. The teacher must be able to provide opportunities for these students to appreciate their own cultural heritage and at the same time to adjust to their adopted American culture.

Boards Association 1989, 24, 39). In Delray Beach, Florida, students speak as many as five different languages. The students are the children of migrant workers, illegal aliens, and newly arrived immigrants. In an ESOL (English for Speakers of Other Languages) classroom, the children in Pine Grove Elementary School are given the opportunity to learn English through a computer program called C.A.R.E. (Computer Assisted Reading in English).

Therefore, it is important that teachers, too, come from diverse backgrounds and cultures. Likewise, it is essential that today's teachers be knowledgeable about the cultures and backgrounds of the students they teach, and, in many parts of the country, that they be bilingual.

Advancement Opportunities

Sarah has been teaching for fifteen years. When she began her career she expected to stay in the classroom no more than five or ten years. But she soon discovered that she was an excellent teacher. After her third year of teaching she began a master's program at a local university. Even after earning her degree she continued to enroll in other educational programs. One summer she went on a tour of the Soviet Union; another summer she was a fellow in a writing project for teachers. All of this made staying in the classroom more and more attractive. And then, her state adopted an incentive pay plan. Within three years her salary jumped nearly 50 percent. During this time she evaluated new teachers as part of her school's mentor teacher program, supervised six preservice teachers from the university, served on the teaching evaluation committee, and worked on the development of a new integrated language arts curriculum. Sarah believes that she is making a real contribution to her profession. And now she has been asked to serve as a teacher evaluator for the

(continued on p. 114)

V I E W P O I N T S

Hidden Minorities

When I was in junior high school, I absolutely loved my history class and I idolized my teacher. That is, until one afternoon.

His lecture that day covered various groups of immigrants that came to America in the early 1900s. He told us that many Greeks arrived during those years. Since their families were so large, there wasn't much time for each individual. Therefore, according to my teacher, the children did not do well in school and many ended up on welfare. The cycle then repeated itself with their children.

As my teacher spoke, I grew numb. I, as well as my brothers and sisters, worked hard to earn As and Bs in all our classes. Our family was not on welfare, and my grandparents were among those Greek arrivals in the early 1900s.

I never did tell that teacher that I was Greek. I did think a little less of him, however, from that point. . . .

Recently, something happened in my own classroom that made me remember those past experiences. My seventh grade speech class was reading poetry aloud. One boy chose Shel Silverstein's *The Gypsies Are Coming*. As he began to read, many students started laughing and staring at Eric in the back of the room. I interrupted and asked for an explanation. After a moment of silence, one of them said, "Eric's a Gypsy" and volunteered negative information about Gypsies.

Eric and I had something in common: we were all members of hidden minorities. Most people are polite (or two-faced) enough to silence their remarks about a racial or ethnic group in the presence of members of that group. We usually know if there is a black person or an Oriental present. But there are many other groups that are not easy to identify. We cannot always tell by a person's name either. Many ethnic surnames were changed to give them a more "American" sound.

I decided to do something about the incident that had happened in my class. That evening I did some research at the library. The next day I gave each of my students an opportunity to talk about his or her heritage. I added my comments on each group and also revealed what I had learned about Gypsies. . . .

Chances are you have hidden minorities in your classroom, too. What can you do to keep these children from being hurt? First of all, let your students know that you expect respect for all ethnic groups. Don't tolerate any ethnic jokes.

Secondly, make stereotypes and prejudice common topics in your classroom. Discuss some common stereotypes. Talk about how ethnic prejudice has led to social injustice, slavery and war throughout history. Devote a bulletin board to a different ethnic group every few weeks. Highlight famous people from the group, facts about the country where the group originated, how they have been treated and special accomplishments.

Finally, schedule an ethnic pride day. Students can bring in flags, clothes, foods, etc., from the countries of their origins. Students who don't know their own ethnic background can choose any interesting group. Some activities may include breaking a piñata, eating Chinese egg rolls, learning to play a Korean game, listening to a student's grandmother speak about early German settlers in your town, and reading Irish folktales. It is amazing what you and your students can learn in one day!

As a teacher, you are in a position to do something about hidden minorities. By taking a little time in the classroom this year, you can help your students develop a lifelong appreciation of our country's rich ethnic heritage.

From: Nicholas, 1988

district's career ladder program. Although she believes that teaching will never be a profession until teachers are evaluated by teachers, she is in a quandary. She had decided not to complete the residency required for a Ph.D. in administration because she did not want to leave the classroom. This new evaluator position is full time, the pay is significantly more than for teaching, but it means leaving the classroom. Sarah must make a difficult decision, one facing many excellent teachers who are in a position to advance their careers but at the expense of what they do best—teach. Thus, while advancement opportunities are available to teachers in most systems, they must often give up classroom teaching.

PROFESSIONAL ORGANIZATIONS

Professional organizations for educators serve two purposes—political power and professional development. The National Education Association (NEA) and the American Federation of Teachers (AFT) are the political arms of the profession. Over 80 percent of all public school teachers belong to either the NEA or the AFT. These two organizations research issues related to education, take public stands on these issues, lobby for federal and state legislation, defend members in school-related legal cases, organize local chapters, and bargain with school boards for improved benefits for teachers.

Organizations primarily devoted to the professional development of teachers include the National Council of Teachers of English (NCTE), International Reading Association (IRA), National Science Teachers Association (NSTA), National Council of Teachers of Mathematics (NCTM), National Council for the Social Studies (NCSS), National Middle Schools Association (NMSA), Association of Childhood Education International (ACEI), and Association of Supervision and Curriculum Development (ASCD). They publish journals and books, fund research, conduct conferences and meetings, provide teachers with materials, sponsor special interest groups, give awards and scholarships, sponsor state or local chapters, suggest criteria for teacher certification, evaluate teacher certification programs, among other activities, with the goal of improving the profession. (See appendix 4, p. 551 for a list of professional organizations, addresses, and student membership information.)

Political Professional Organizations

The NEA and the AFT are the political watchdogs of the teaching profession. Both the NEA, established by Congress in 1906, and the AFT, organized in 1916 by the American Federation of Labor, have similar national education legislative agendas but significant differences in their membership and approaches (see table 4.3).

For example, in 1989 the NEA's legislative agenda included a commitment to excellence in education—with high standards for teaching and learning whereby the student becomes an active participant in achieving mastery of subjects sufficient for problem solving, decision making, and further educational growth; continued federal support for education; continued support of free public education; a national health care insurance plan to be supported and funded by the U.S. Congress; and establishment of study committees to monitor media activities and to promote positive educational programming. In addition, the NEA opposed federal and state-mandated parent choice plans in

(continued on p. 116)

TABLE 4-3

NEA and AFT: Similarities and Differences

Similarities	Differences
1. Promote professional excellence among educators and excellence in all aspects of education.	1. NEA opposes merit pay based on performance; AFT supports it if politics are left out and evaluations are fair.
2. Support national education goals.	2. AFT has relationship with AFL-CIO; NEA is an independent organization.
3. Work for increased salaries and increased fringe benefits for teachers.	3. AFT membership includes noneducational workers such as nurses, custodians, clerical staff, and social workers; NEA membership does not.
4. Work for increased state and federal financial support for public schools.	4. NEA has a national staff of 500; AFT's staff is 50.
5. Supports the concept of a licensed educator in every position.	5. NEA works closely with school administrators, including them in membership; AFT contends that affiliation with administrators interferes with collective bargaining.
6. Support the development of a diversity of programs: developmentally handicapped; special education; global and multicultural education; sex, drugs, and AIDS education; adult education; vocational and career education; fine arts; counseling; athletics and health; pre-Kindergarten education; before- and after-school programs.	6. AFT has a permanent national leadership (Albert Shanker has been president since 1973); NEA elects a president every two years, eligible for two additional terms.
7. Work toward teacher autonomy and empowerment in making decisions affecting classroom technique, class size, workloads, selection of instructional materials, and objective evaluation procedures.	7. AFT has larger membership in larger cities; NEA's membership is in smaller cities and suburban and rural areas.
8. Oppose legislation related to tuition tax credits to subsidize private schooling.	
9. Promote continued intellectual development of teachers through inservice and advanced degrees.	
10. Promote use of instructional materials and activities related to cultural diversity in classrooms.	
11. Use of collective bargaining rights, due process, and grievance procedures for teachers.	
12. Exercise of academic and professional freedom to explore and discuss divergent viewpoints.	
13. Support career ladder plans in principle (i.e., different levels of compensation for different responsibilities).	
14. Support elected officials that have strong education platforms.	
15. Publish monthly journals and express views in other professional literature.	

The National Education Association (NEA) and the American Federation of Teachers (AFT) are the two primary organizations that represent teachers in negotiations with the school board, conduct research on policy issues, and lobby the legislature for improved school policies. While they have more similarities than differences, the differences may be crucial to your selection of one or the other to represent you when you become a professional teacher.

which parents select schools for their children, **tuition tax credits** for parents of private school children, and **voucher plans** that would fund education by giving parents financial vouchers they could use at a school of their choice (see chapter 13, p. 441).

The 1990 legislative agenda of the AFT focused on some of the same issues. The members supported a renewal of the federal role in recruiting and retaining qualified teachers through scholarships, loans, sabbatical programs, and induction programs that allow new teachers to work with master teachers. The AFT supports the government and schools working together to keep "disappointed" teachers through salary increments, transferability of pensions, enrichment and renewal programs, and incentive programs for school innovation. The legislative agenda for 1990 also supported increased and improved multicultural and multilingual education, the phasing out of standardized tests as measurements of student progress and teacher accountability, and restructuring of schools through shared decision making.

In 1990, both the NEA and the AFT resolved to support the national education goals for the year 2000 adopted by President Bush and the fifty governors (see chapter 6, pp. 188–191). In 1991, the NEA began to identify programs throughout the nation that are working toward these goals: all students will start school ready to learn; 90 percent of high school students will graduate; student mastery of subject matter will improve dramatically; mathematics and science achievement will improve significantly; all adult citizens will be literate; and all schools will be disciplined and drug free.

Professional Development Organizations

There are numerous organizations devoted primarily to the professional development of educators. These organizations publish journals, monographs, and books and conduct conferences and workshops. Special interest groups within the organizations publish opinion statements. They suggest standards for certifying teachers and for reviewing the certification programs of colleges and universities through the National Council of Accreditation of Teacher Education review process. They also survey teachers to determine trends, publish directories of leaders in the profession, and distribute press releases related to educational issues. Membership in these organizations is voluntary.

Following are some examples of the work of these organizations.

- In 1989, the National Council of Teachers of Mathematics (NCTM) published *Curriculum and Evaluation Standards* to help mathematics teachers better understand when to use technology such as computers and calculators in teaching mathematics.
- In 1990, NCTM developed Standards for the Improvement of Mathematics Education by the year 2000. They were related to the national goals for education endorsed by President Bush and the fifty governors.
- In 1988, the National Middle Schools Association (NMSA) conducted a survey of the educational approaches, practices, and trends in the nation's middle schools and published a summary of their findings in *Education in the Middle Schools.*
- In 1990, the National Science Teachers Association (NSTA) worked jointly with the Association of Science Education and the NCTM to establish specific goals for classroom teachers for the improvement of both mathematics and science education by the year 2000.

- In 1990, the National Council of Teachers of English (NCTE) approved a policy advocating a class size of twenty and a daily work load of not more than eighty for English and language arts teachers. NCTE proposed legislation that required that school districts applying for categorical funds have a plan to reduce class size and teaching loads for English and language arts teachers.
- In 1990, the Association for Childhood Education International (ACEI) developed new initiatives to increase parental involvement in education. In particular, ACEI developed activities for collaboration with the Parent Teachers Association (PTA) in addressing problems related to parents and the education of young children.

TABLE 4-4

Alternative Careers in Education

Position	Job Description	Training
Childcare Specialist	Work with pre-K children in day care centers and pre-schools	Dependent on position and state requirements. In public schools, minimum of bachelor's degree.
Vocational Instructor	Work in high schools and community colleges and state and federal training programs to help students explore the world of work: distributive education, health occupations, technical occupations, automotive repair, computers, robotics, agriculture, etc.	Bachelor's or advanced degrees in specialization; work experience. If position is part-time, degree may not be required.
Computer Technologist	Work with students and teachers as specialists in computer education.	Bachelor's degree: work in computers, education, and psychology.
Adult Basic Education	Work with adults to meet requirements for high school diploma (GED) and English as a Second Language (ESL), sometimes called English for Speakers of Other Languages (ESOL).	Bachelor's degree from approved teacher training program.
Industry	Develop and run training programs for employees: academic, mental, physical, health, or leisure.	Bachelor's or advanced degrees.
Teacher of Special Children	Work with developmentally handicapped, physically, mentally, and emotionally handicapped children in small groups. Work with classroom teachers to plan programs for special children.	Bachelor's and master's degrees in specialty.
Bilingual and English as Second Language	Work with students who do not speak English or speak English as a second language.	Bachelor's degree with concentration in variety of languages.
Teaching Specialist	Teaching in the arts, foreign languages, reading, mathematics, and writing.	Bachelor's or master's degree in area of specialty.
Counselor	Work with faculty to identify student problems, help students make career decisions and give tests. Counsel students in academic and personal concerns.	Advanced degree in guidance/counseling; frequently teaching experience.

Educational Social Worker	Liaison between students, families, agencies, and schools to help solve problems and promote learning.	Bachelor's and master's degrees with specialty in sociology and education.
Psychometrist and School Psychologist	Administer individual and group tests, develop guidance programs, interpret test results to teachers and administrators, and work with teachers and referred students.	Advanced degree beyond master's in guidance/counseling and psychology.
Librarian and Media Specialist	Work in libraries and media centers with teachers and students in the use of books, videos, microfiche, movies, filmstrips, slides, computer, and the library.	Bachelor's degree in library or media education.
	Specialists organize and administer the library and media center.	Master's degree in library or media education and professional library experience.
School Health Services	Diagnostic work and health care for students: nurses, dental hygienists, speech and hearing specialists, audiologists, and athletic trainers. Also work in preventative health programs.	Bachelor's degree or master's degree in specialty.
Dietician	Plan for and provide nutritious meals for students.	Bachelor's degree with specialty in nutrition.
School Administrators	Principals have responsibility for daily operation of the school—its finances, discipline, curriculum, and transportation. District-wide administrators are specialists in charge of finance, curriculum, transportation, psychological services, special education, and personnel. Superintendent oversees all aspects of education in school district.	Advanced degree in administration and supervision; usually experience in teaching.
Supervisor	Work directly with teachers to improve teaching by helping, counseling, providing inservice workshops on curriculum development, and evaluating teaching.	Advanced degree in supervision; teaching experience.
Independent School Personnel	Work in independent/private schools in teaching, admissions, business management, or fundraising.	Bachelor's or master's degree in specialty
Coach (full- or part-time)	Work with athletic teams	Bachelor's degree
Dean	Counseling and discipline	Bachelor's or advanced degree
Physician	Health services	Medical degree
Attorney	Legal services	Law degree
Director of Student Activities	Extracurricular activities	Bachelor's degree

This table lists the numerous career opportunities available in education other than classroom teaching.

OTHER CAREERS IN EDUCATION

In addition to classroom teaching, there are numerous career opportunities in education. Table 4.4, beginning on page 117, indicates the type of position, a brief description of the job, and training requirements.

A career in teaching can be very rewarding. Although the salaries have not yet reached the level of other professions, they are increasing across the country and becoming competitive. It is a developing profession; therefore, those beginning a teaching career in the 1990s may have a voice in how the profession will develop as more and more schools and school districts empower teachers to make decisions that affect life in their classrooms. As you make the decision about whether teaching is the career for you, you will need to balance the positive aspects of a career in education against the frustrations you are likely to encounter.

If one is interested in working with young people, but doesn't necessarily want to teach, other careers in education are available. This vocational guidance counselor, for example, advises students on job opportunities, helps the student match his or her skills with available jobs, and helps with the application procedure.

4.2 POINTS TO REMEMBER

- The demand for new teachers is likely to exceed the supply throughout the 1990s.

- There are many positive attributes of a career in teaching. They include working with young people and watching them grow, exploration of a subject or working with an age group that intrigues the teacher, achieving lifelong learning goals, a sense of dignity and worth, a school calendar that allows pursuit of professional interests, geographic flexibility, a fair to good salary and good benefits, and the potential for incentive pay increments.

- A career in teaching also has some potential frustrations. They include parents who may treat teachers as adversaries, feeling unprepared to work with the multiculturalism of today's student population, lacking qualifications for working with disabled students, not enough time to prepare for teaching, classes that are too large, limited fiscal resources, lack of support services, lack of autonomy, outdated buildings and materials, salaries not comparable with other professions, and subjective evaluation of teaching.

- In-service educational expectations vary from state to state. However, all states require that teachers continue their education and training after they enter the profession.

- Today's classrooms are ethnically diverse. Twenty-five of the nation's fifty largest school districts have a majority of students of color. In some school districts, a majority of the schoolchildren do not speak English.

- Through incentive pay programs and differentiated staffing, teachers have the potential to advance in status while remaining in the classroom. Teachers can become mentor teachers, work on advanced degrees, and/or participate in school-based decision making.

- The American Federation of Teachers (AFT) and the National Education Association (NEA) are the largest professional organizations for teachers. They are the political watchdogs of the profession and help ensure teachers' rights.

- Professional organizations such as the National Council for the Social Studies and the National Middle School Association are organizations for those who teach specialized subjects, certain groups of students, and/or a range of grade levels. These organizations help teachers grow professionally through workshops, conferences, publications, and position statements. They also propose national and state legislation related to their particular educational concerns.

- There are numerous careers in education other than teaching. A bachelor's degree and limited experience are generally required for vocational teachers, some childcare specialists, and some computer technicians. An advanced degree is needed for such professionals as counselors and social workers. Administrators and some counselors require teaching experience as well as an advanced degree.

Reprinted with special permission of King Features Syndicate, Inc.

FOR THOUGHT/DISCUSSION

1. Do you believe that teacher accountability can be determined by measuring student achievement on a standardized test? Why or why not?

2. Which, if any, of the incentive pay programs contribute to the professionalization of teaching? How?

3. What are some of the trends in teaching that will contribute to its becoming a full-fledged profession?

4. When you become a teacher, will you belong to the NEA or the AFT? What reasons would you give for choosing one over the other?

FOR FURTHER READING/REFERENCE

Brandt, R. M. 1990. *Incentive pay and career ladders for today's teachers: A study of current programs and practices.* Albany: State University of New York. The author presents case studies that discuss implementation of incentive pay programs in various school districts where these programs have been in effect for five or more years.

Bullough, R. B., Jr. 1988. Evaluation and the beginning teacher: A case study. *Education and Society* 6 (1, 2), 71–78. A case study of how an enthusiastic beginning teacher was disillusioned by the evaluation of her work by her principal and her experienced peers.

Flinders, D. 1989. *Voices from the classroom: Education policy can inform policy.* Eugene, OR: ERIC Clearinghouse on Educational Management, University of Oregon. Flinders presents three case studies of high school teachers at work in their classrooms and argues that the realities of the classroom should be the basis of educational policies for the improvement of classroom teaching.

Kramer, R. 1988. *Maria Montessori: A biography.* New York: Addison-Wesley. A biography of a powerful professional teacher who worked toward reforms to improve the profession and who made significant contributions to teaching in the early decades of the twentieth century.

Maeroff, G. I. 1988. *The empowerment of teachers.* New York: Teachers College Press. The author describes the power of professionalism that teachers take into their classrooms and examines the role of teachers in the reform of the teaching profession.

5 The Historical Foundations of U.S. Education

The past is never totally past. It invariably informs the present. Thus whatever educational problems and issues exist in today's society can be said to be a product of both the recent and distant past. We study the history of education to learn from our past, to learn of our origins. This chapter discusses the historical roots of the American educational system.

6 Twentieth-Century U.S. Education

There are no easy solutions to the problems created by the growth of democracy and the concept of equal education for all. As society changes, the system of education must find ways of dealing with a complex and burgeoning student population. This chapter discusses the historical developments of education, and the proposals for reform that have been suggested in the twentieth century.

7 The Philosophical Foundations of Education

This chapter focuses on the philosophies that have informed educational thinking and that allows teachers to look forward to ways that thinking might be used to creatively restructure what goes on in the classroom and in schools. As Roland Barth says in a recent issue of *Phi Delta Kappan*, "Let go of the trapeze. Think otherwise. Become an independent variable. Lick the envelope. Bell the cat. Fly the cage. Leave your mark" (1991, p. 128).

Dear Molly,

Tomorrow the doors of the world begin to open to you. Your father and I have only one request as you begin your college years: Don't close the doors.

You will meet people who are very different from your family and friends. They will look different, have different values, express different ideas, talk differently. . . . Although we do not suggest that you embrace either the person or her ideas, we want you to listen and to think. What does she believe? Where does he come from? How has her life been different from yours? What does he know that you do not know? Listen and learn, Molly.

With love and respect,
Mom

PART II

Foundations

5

The Historical Foundations of U.S. Education

The following letter to Martha Jefferson was written by her father, Thomas Jefferson, in Annapolis, on November 28, 1783. In it, he admonishes his daughter to follow a daily plan of study conducted by tutors he provided. Although Jefferson proposed several plans for public education, they ironically did not include girls beyond three years in elementary school.

Dear Patsy,—After four days' journey, I arrived here without any accident, and in as good health as when I left Philadelphia. The conviction that you would be more improved in the situation I have placed you than if still with me, has solaced me on my parting with you, which my love for you has rendered a difficult thing. The acquirements which I hope you will make under the tutors I have provided for you will render you more worthy of my love; and if they cannot increase it, they will prevent its diminution. Consider the good lady who has taken you under her roof, who has undertaken to see that you perform all your exercises, and to admonish you in all those wanderings from what is right or what is clever, to which your inexperience would expose you: consider her, I say, as your mother, as the only person whom, since the loss with which Heaven has pleased to afflict you, you can now look up; and that her displeasure or disapprobation, on any occasion, will be an immense misfortune, which should you be so unhappy as to incur by any unguarded act, think no concession too much to regain her good-will. With respect to the distribution of your time, the following is what I should approve:

From 8 to 10, practice music.

From 10 to 1, dance one day and draw another.

From 1 to 2, draw on the day you dance, and write a letter next day.

From 3 to 4, read French.

From 4 to 5, exercise yourself in music.

From 5 till bed-time, read English, write, etc.

Communicate this plan to Mrs. Hopkinson, and if she approves of it, pursue it. As long as Mrs. Trist remains in Philadelphia, cultivate her affection. She has been a valuable friend to you, and her good sense and good heart make her valued by all who know her, and by nobody on earth more than me. I expect you will write me by every post. Inform me what books you read, what tunes you learn, and enclose me your best copy of every lesson in drawing. Write also one letter a week either to your Aunt Eppes, your Aunt Skipwith, your

Aunt Carr, or the little lady from whom I now enclose a letter, and always put the letter you so write under cover to me. Take care that you never spell a word wrong. Always before you write a word, consider how it is spelt, and, if you do not remember it, turn to a dictionary. It produces great praise to a lady to spell well. I have placed my happiness on seeing you good and accomplished; and no distress this world can now bring on me would equal that of your disappointing my hopes. If you love me, then strive to be good under every situation and to all living creatures, and to acquire those accomplishments which I have put in your power, and which will go far towards ensuring you the warmest love of your affectionate father.

P.S. Keep my letters and read them at times, that you may always have present in your mind those things which will endear you to me.

From: J. G. DeRoulhac Hamilton (Ed.), *The Best Letters of Thomas Jefferson* (1926).

Thomas Jefferson (1743–1826), member of the Virginia Legislature and the Continental Congress, governor of Virginia, secretary of state, vice-president, and president of the United States, believed that the purpose of education was to develop an informed citizenry. Only through education, he believed, would people have the understanding necessary to exercise the rights and responsibilities of a member of a democratic society.

CHAPTER OBJECTIVES

After studying this chapter, you should be able to:

- Discuss the importance of studying the history of education.
- Discuss the contributions of the early Greeks and Romans to the history of education.
- Understand how education developed in the medieval period and the Renaissance.
- Explain the influence of Rousseau, Pestalozzi, Herbart, and Froebel.
- Define the terms *popularization, multitudinousness,* and *politicization* as they relate to the history of U.S. education.
- Explain how interpretations of the history of education have changed.
- Explain how the colonial New England schools influenced the popularization of U.S. education.
- Determine how the schools of the Southern colonies influenced the politicization of U.S. education.
- Understand how the schools of the Middle Atlantic colonies developed the concept of multitudinousness.
- Explain the influence of Benjamin Franklin, Thomas Jefferson, and Noah Webster on U.S. education.
- Discuss the impact of Horace Mann and Henry Barnard on the development of U.S. public education.
- Discuss the impact of the common school movement on the popularization of U.S. education.
- Understand how schools in the North during the mid- to late-nineteenth century helped meet the political concerns of the democracy.
- Contrast Northern and Southern schools during the post–Civil War period.
- Discuss the history of education of blacks and women.

T he past is never totally past. It invariably informs the present. Thus whatever educational problems and issues exist in today's society can be said to be a product of both the recent and distant past. We study the history of education to learn from our past, to learn of our origins. Knowing from where we have come enables us to understand who we are and where we are going.

HISTORY OF EDUCATION

According to educational historian Sol Cohen, "We think and behave the way we do because we have traversed this road and not some other" (1978, 1:1). Understanding the history of education helps us think about the course of action we choose and evaluate it in terms of past performance. (See appendix 1, p. 541 for a historical timeline of the history of education.)

Greek and Roman Roots

An early form of education was provided by the Athenian **Sophists** (490–480 B.C.), who taught grammar, logic, and rhetoric with a view to educating the citizens to become effective legislators. Protagoras used a teaching method of debate by which the students could learn to confound any opponent by taking ideas the opponent had conceded and using them as a starting point for argument. Protagoras was probably the first to teach the possibility of arguing for or against any position. Plato (427–347 B.C.) learned by sitting at the feet of Socrates (469–399 B.C.). Aristotle (384–322 B.C.) learned from Plato. Their methods are still part of our teaching vocabulary. The **Socratic method** involves the use of systematic doubt and questioning to get at underlying, universal meaning. Socrates believed that knowledge was the search for the ideal that already existed in latent form within the individual. It was the job of the teacher to ask the kinds of questions that would lead the students to discover the truth within themselves. Even today, highly regarded scholars and critics of education, like Mortimer Adler in *Paideia Problems and Possibilities*, (1983) espouse Socrates' method as the best way to produce an educated society.

Plato continued the pursuit of the ideal, as did Socrates, believing it was inherent in the universal concepts of truth, goodness, justice, and beauty, the philosophical basis of idealism. These ideals could not be reached through the imperfect senses but rather had to be attained through the intellect. Because these ideals were universal and permanent, education had to be universal.

In contrast to Socrates, Aristotle believed that reality is physical and exists in objects—the philosophical foundation of realism. Thinking and knowing begin with the sensate perception of objects in the environment, but concepts are formed by the process of deducing pattern and order from specific observation. Teaching and learning are thus based on a body of knowledge and disciplined inquiry into the nature of things. This philosophy was stressed in the eighteenth and nineteenth centuries by such educators as John Locke and Johann Pestalozzi.

An early attempt at formal education occurred in ancient Rome. The philosopher and orator Quintilian (A.D. 35–95) trained orators so they could persuade the citizenry to agree with the empirical point of view. In *De Institutione Oratoria* (A.D. 96/1970), which became a manual for teachers, he recognized that education should be based on individual stages of human growth and development. Thus he established four stages of learning: from birth until age seven the child should have as a nurse and pedagogue someone who used correct speech patterns; from seven to fourteen the child formed ideas and learned to read and write; from fourteen to seventeen the student studied the liberal arts such as literature, mythology, music, and grammar; and finally, from seventeen to twenty-one the prospective orator began rhetorical studies such as drama, poetry, history, law, philosophy, and rhetoric. Quintilian's influence extends to the modern teacher's concern for individual differences and the quest to make learning interesting.

However, by the end of the Roman Empire, formalized instruction had become lifeless. Christians such as Saint Augustine (A.D. 354–430) attempted to revitalize learning by placing greater emphasis on deeds rather than words. Hence, instead of focusing on rules of rhetoric and grammar, Saint Augustine advocated the study of great orations. He claimed that nothing could be learned under compulsion and suggested that students should ask questions to further their own comprehension rather than merely accept the answers provided by scholars. Few followed Saint Augustine's teachings as the Roman Empire declined along with its education, politics, economics, and culture when barbarians invaded from northern Europe. The main thrust of the limited education that existed during the final years of the empire and the early Middle Ages was to preserve the culture. Thus, memorization and imitation were the basic educational methods of this time.

Medieval Period

It was not until the end of the Middle Ages and the rise of the medieval university that the systematic development of the educational method continued. Pierre Abelard (1079–1142), a monk known as one of the **Schoolmen**, argued issues related to Greek and Christian viewpoints. Abelard broke from his contemporaries by suggesting the use of open-ended questions that he published without their proper answers.

Abelard's technique of open questioning influenced Saint Thomas Aquinas (1225–1274), a Christian philosopher and author of the *Summa Theologica*, still the standard work on Catholic theology. Aquinas rejected the Platonic concept of innate ideas because he believed that they did not exist in actuality but in potentiality. Learning was an actualization of this potential based on the intellect's capacity to form universal concepts from the perception of objects through the senses.

THE RENAISSANCE

By the Renaissance (1330–1500), younger students required teaching methods other than the lecture and disputation approach suggested by early scholars. Dutch philosopher Desiderius Erasmus (1466–1536) was the first of the humanistic scholars, those advocating a return to classical studies of Greece and Rome, who were interested in how to make the educative process an attractive one. He differentiated between innate capacity, those abilities with which we are born, and what could be accomplished through instruction. He realized that no student was endowed with aptitudes in all areas; therefore, it was important to develop individual methods of instruction. He realized that students learned in stages and so encouraged teachers to move slowly and not expect students to learn that for which they were not ready.

Historians credit German religious reformer Martin Luther (1483–1546) with the development of a universal educational system for all people without regard to class or "special life work." He believed that schools should be established by the state, not the church, and students should be trained not only in religion but also in science, mathematics, logic, and rhetoric. This change of focus from the church to the individual and secular learning was a major turning point in educational history.

John Calvin (1509–1564), another Protestant reformer, like Luther, affirmed that education was the combined responsibility of the church, the state, and the home. According to Calvin, all three must follow the same strict moral code in teaching, discipline, and training. He placed more emphasis on what we today think of as secondary education (the gymnasium, where older boys were taught Greek, Hebrew, physics, mathematics, oratory, and rhetoric), than on primary education.

John Amos Comenius (1592–1670) of Moldavia is frequently called the first modern educator because he devised specific instructional methods whereby the senses could be used to aid the intellect. In *Orbis Pictus* (*The Visible World in Pictures*), he employed the idea of using pictures as a teaching device (1659/1968). Comenius believed that students must learn not merely by seeing and hearing but also by doing. He claimed that schools were for all humanity, not merely for males and the aristocracy. "No reason can be shown why the female sex . . . should be kept from a knowledge of language and wisdom. For they are also human beings, an image of God, as we are. . ." (Comenius 1633/1956, 33).

Early European Educational Themes   Jean Jacques Rousseau (1712–1778) developed an educational philosophy that has become known as **naturalism**. Rousseau was the first to claim that environment plays a crucial role in the development of the individual and that it could be shaped through reason and science. He believed that the aim of education should be to return man to his "natural state" by developing knowledge based on sensations, natural feelings, and perceptions rather than on books and prescribed curriculums. Rousseau's ideas influenced Pestalozzi.

Although philosophers and scholars had discussed how children should be taught, the first schools devoted exclusively to teacher education were established in early eighteenth-century Prussia during the reign of Frederick the Great (1740–1786). After the Napoleonic Wars young Prussians traveled to

Johann Pestalozzi was a naturalist and a teacher who believed students learn best when they are emotionally secure, when they use their senses to observe the patterns and laws of their environment, and when they proceed in incremental steps to acquire knowledge. He was particularly sensitive to the poor and disadvantaged; in this engraving, he is teaching orphans.

Switzerland to study the work of Johann Pestalozzi (1746–1827) in preparation for establishing seminaries to train teachers in their country.

Pestalozzi's work was with poor and disadvantaged children. He was a naturalistic teacher who was influenced by Rousseau and believed that we learn primarily through our senses in observing nature. Thus, he used real, concrete objects to initiate learning before moving to abstract concepts. He urged that the teacher should move from the simple to the complex, the known to the unknown in gradual, cumulative steps respecting the individual differences of the child. He believed that children were born neither good nor evil but were shaped by their environments. He contended that providing children with healthy, supportive environments and a strong family life allowed them to develop their personalities and values to the fullest extent. Pestalozzi put his theory to work in schools based on the concepts of love, understanding, patience for children, a compassion for the poor, and teaching methods that depended on real objects and the senses.

Pestalozzi argued that the schoolmaster was one of the most important people in a community and, as such, must have integrity, understanding, and intelligence. He asserted that the state must assume the responsibility for educating teachers in order to invest the profession with importance.

Johann Friedrich Herbart (1776–1841), who studied under Goethe and Schiller and visited Pestalozzi in Switzerland, believed that education is a process. He asserted that teaching is not an inherent gift but, rather, a science that could be learned.

At Gottingen, Herbart started a pedagogical seminary and demonstration school to experiment with his educational methods, which he called *Vorstellung*, meaning "presentation." According to Herbart, there are five formal steps of teaching: preparation, in which the instructor reminds students of previously learned material; presentation, in which the new material is offered to students; association, in which the new material is systematically related to ideas or information learned previously; generalization, in which specific examples are used to illustrate the concept being taught; and application, in which students are tested to determine if they have understood the material.

Friedrich Wilhelm Froebel (1782–1852) was a philosopher and educator, the founder of the Kindergarten, the child's garden. According to Froebel, childhood was not just a transition toward adulthood, and a child's play was not merely preparation for adult life, but both were something complete and organic. He cultivated self-development, self-activity, and socialization in the child by songs, stories, games, "gifts," and "occupations." "Gifts" were objects whose form was fixed, such as balls, cubes, and cylinders, and that stimulated the child to make relationships between the object and its concept. "Occupations" consisted of manipulable materials such as clay, paper, or mud. His work led to the establishment of the first German Kindergarten in the United States in 1855 and the first English-speaking kindergarten in 1860.

These beginnings greatly influenced the development of schools in the United States. The work of philosophers, theologians, and educators influenced early colonial schools and continue to influence U.S. schools today.

THEMES OF U.S. EDUCATION

The study of the history of education in the United States illuminates not only the story of U.S. schools but also that of U.S. society. From descriptions of early schools, we learn about the culture that surrounded them. Furthermore, a comparative study of schools in the New England, Middle Atlantic, and Southern colonies helps us understand the schools of today.

We will use Lawrence Cremin's three themes of **popularization** (schooling for all), **multitudinousness** (breadth of opportunity), and **politicization** (schools as a force for political change) as the organizing focus for the remainder of this chapter, which deals primarily with the history of education from the colonial period through the nineteenth century, and for chapter 6, which deals with the twentieth century, a fascinating period of our history when all three themes of education came together in a unique fashion to characterize schools in the United States.

An Idealistic Interpretation of U.S. Education Before 1960

Prior to the 1960s, historical interpretation of U.S. education focused on the perfection of U.S. schools. History was "the story of [the schools'] foreordained, inevitable, and successive triumphs" (Button and Provenzo xiv). The father of this historical approach to the study of education was Ellwood P. Cubberley, whose pioneering book, *Public Education in the United States*, was published in 1919. Cubberley and educators influenced by his work viewed the schools as instruments of positive societal change.

A Sociological Interpretation of the History of U.S. Education After 1960

Since the 1960s and the work of historian Bernard Bailyn (*Education in the Forming of American Society*, 1960), the idealistic view has changed. From the 1960s through the 1980s, education was examined more realistically as the "sum of everything intended to enculturate child, youth, and adult—family, church, newspaper, and so on" (Button and Provenzo xiv). This view, of course, is consistent with that of sociologists, who define education as an enculturation process. Everything the child does under the guidance of an adult including formal schooling is **enculturation**. It occurs when a parent tells a child at the dinner table not to talk with her mouth full, a grocery store clerk gives a child change for a candy bar, or a lifeguard blows a whistle to warn that the water is too deep. Consequently, the sociological approach to a history of education does not look merely at the schools but at the role of society in the education of the young.

Educational historians and sociologists of the 1960s through the 1980s tended to agree that not all that has happened in formal education has happened for the best. Therefore, many historians have examined education in light of its social, racial, political, and cultural problems, believing that U.S. schools mirror society and at the same time are subject to societal pressures.

In the late 1980s and early 1990s, the approach to the history of U.S. education was again evolving. In the late 1980s historians began to examine themes that correlated education's history with the history of the United States. Historian Lawrence A. Cremin, for example, claimed in *Popular Education and Its Discontents* (1990) that education reflects society but also has the potential to change society. The characteristics of multitudinousness, popularization, and politicization are not "uniquely American—we can see them at work in any number of other countries—and yet the three in tandem have marked American education uniquely. . . . They have been associated with some of the formidable achievements of American education at the same time that they have created some of its most intractable problems" (vii–viii).

A Synergetic Interpretation of U.S. Education After 1980

This evolving view of the history of education illustrates how the institutions of education and U.S. society influence each other and work together. Education and society must continue to strive for egalitarianism and excellence.

5.1 POINTS TO REMEMBER

- Studying the history of education helps us understand why schools are as they are today.

- Greek and Roman philosophers provided education with its earliest discourse on teaching. Plato and Socrates developed a method involving systematic doubt and questioning. Aristotle developed the concept of understanding pattern and order through observation of objects in the environment. Quintilian recognized that education should be based on individual patterns of growth.

- In the medieval period, education was the province of the church. Augustine emphasized deeds rather than words. Aquinas believed that

students must be considered the primary agents of learning. Luther implemented the first universal educational system in Germany. Calvin, in Switzerland, claimed that education was the responsibility of the church, the state, and the home. Comenius, a Renaissance scholar, suggested students must perform a task in order to learn.

- Rousseau was the first to claim that environment plays a crucial role in the development of the individual. Pestalozzi was influenced by Rousseau's naturalism and maintained that children learn primarily through their senses. Herbart believed that teaching was a science and that students must learn to generalize knowledge and apply it to new information. Froebel developed the first Kindergarten

and believed in the importance of children's play.

- Popularization of education is the tendency to make the schools accessible to all. Multitudinousness describes the multiplication of institutions to provide accessibility. Politicization is the effort of schools to solve social problems indirectly. These three characteristics, in tandem, are found only in U.S. schools.

- Interpretations of the history of U.S. education have changed from the pre-1960s' view of the perfectability of U.S. schools to the post-1960s' view of the schools as the reflection of the best and worst in society. Contemporary historians look at the schools and society as influencing each other both positively and negatively.

ROOTS OF POPULARIZATION OF EDUCATION

Aristotle maintained that the popularization of education was vital for the maintenance of the state. Although we can see the adoption of some of Aristotle's concept of education for all in the general education adhered to by the New England colonists, it did not take root until the common schools movement of the nineteenth century (see p. 143). "And since the whole city has one end, it is manifest that education should be one and the same for all, and that it should be public, and not private . . ." (Aristotle 310 B.C./1984).

European Roots   Prior to the nineteenth century in Europe, the family was central to the education of the young. If the father was a shoemaker, the son usually became a shoemaker. If the family farmed, the children learned to work the farm. Daughters learned to make cloth, sew, cook, and clean. Parents had complete responsibility for the education of their children. Only the wealthy sent their children to private schools or hired someone to educate them in the home.

As industrialization began, however, families no longer were solely responsible for the education of their young. Communities began to train potential employees, often passing laws to prevent emigration from community to community.

By the nineteenth century in much of Europe, **general education** (education for all), not necessarily equal education, was available to most young people. In Great Britain the Education Act of 1870 provided a state-supported system with two types of schools: "board schools" attended by children of laborers and the lower class, and voluntary schools for middle- and upper-class students. This dual system of education had different curriculums, only one leading to higher education, and was administered by different governmental departments. It was the precursor of the dual track education system of the schools of colonial New England.

Schools in the Colonies   The educational system developed by the colonists was modeled on the schools
of New England   of Great Britain. Like the English, the colonists did not believe in total equality of educational opportunity. Children of workers and peasants received minimal training so that they could read the Bible but were not trained in the classics. Boys of the upper and middle classes were expected to attend colleges and universities, often in Europe. The English colonists upheld the tradition of the Old World that the woman's place was in the home, so girls were trained at home rather than at school to be mothers and homemakers. In spite of the fact that this system was inherently unequal, it planted the seed of general education for all children.

Religion

Since the colonists of New England were a homogeneous group, with primarily the same ethnic, linguistic, and religious background, they did not see their approach to education as inequitable. They were Puritans, an intensely religious group of people who believed that children were savage, primitive beings who had been conceived in sin and born into corruption and that the only way to be redeemed was through training, discipline, and religious

CROSS-CULTURAL PERSPECTIVE

Canadian Education

The Indians and Eskimos of what is now Canada had educational practices which contributed to the maintenance and modification of their respective cultures. The elders of these peoples ensured the transference of their ways of life to their young people, and did so both economically and efficiently. . . .

The educational practices of the native peoples of Canada were ignored in the course of the development of the formal educational systems introduced by church and state and it was not until after World War II that Indian and Eskimo language and culture began to find a place in formal schooling.

The religious orders were the first to establish formal schools in Canada, often in association with their church activities and their attempts to convert the natives to Christianity. The earliest such schools were established by the Recollects and Jesuits in Quebec in the first quarter of the seventeenth century. During the seventeenth and eighteenth centuries the westward flow of education also began with the religious orders. . . .

The French influence was matched by the British Society for the Propagation of the Gospel in Foreign Parts, whose members established schools in New Brunswick, Nova Scotia, and Newfoundland. In addition, there were schools conducted by itinerant schoolmasters, usually returned soldiers, and usually in remote areas where several families banded together to take turns in boarding the teachers for the benefit of their children.

The religious orders continue to play a part in education by maintaining separate or denominational schools in most provinces alongside the state school system. In the Northwest Territories, particularly, the schools maintained by the religious orders have played and still do play a most important part. However, here as elsewhere the economics of education and the decline in the numbers of lay and religious teachers available to these systems are contributing to their decline.

From: Katz, 1974

indoctrination. They regarded reading, writing, and mathematics as ways to gain an understanding of religious doctrines and avowed that a general education made all children equal in the eyes of God.

General Education

By 1642, the Massachusetts General Court enacted the first compulsory education law, which did not establish schools but required parents to be responsible for the education of their children.

Following the teachings of Calvin and in the tradition of Martin Luther (see pp. 128), in 1647 the Massachusetts General Court passed the Old Deluder Satan Law, by which the state was required to establish schools so that students would learn the teachings and the values of the church and of religion. Hence, they would be protected from their own evil tendencies, thereby defeating that "old deluder Satan."

The law of 1647 not only forced towns to provide schools but established ways to fund them. In addition, it established that elementary schools (for young children in towns of 50 or more families) and grammar or secondary schools (for older children in towns of over 100 families) would be for all students; that the curriculum would require religious and moral training; and that teaching methodology would acknowledge Calvin's belief that children were born in sin.

A In *Adam's* Fall
We Sinned all.

B Thy Life to Mend
This *Book* Attend.

C The *Cat* doth play
And after flay.

D A *Dog* will bite
A Thief at night.

E An *Eagles* flight
Is out of fight.

F The Idle *Fool*
Is whipt at School.

The New England Primer, only 2½ by 4½ inches in size, was used extensively in colonial schools until 1800. Based on religious and moral principles, as this page shows, it contained the alphabet, some syllables, and some rhymes.

Curriculum

Colonial schools followed the subject- or instructor-centered approach to curriculum. Children at the elementary level studied the alphabet, the Lord's Prayer, and elements of reading, writing, and counting. By the mid-to-late elementary levels, many boys, especially from less well-to-do families, were apprenticed to someone skilled in the trade of their choice.

Most elementary schools had no textbooks, and the teachers were not trained in methods of teaching. Therefore, the students were taught what the teacher knew through lecture and recitation. Those with the least formal education tended to teach in elementary schools populated with poor children whereas those who had more formal education taught in the grammar schools, the secondary schools of the wealthy. There were no formalized requirements for becoming a teacher. Some were unemployed tradesmen, some innkeepers, others members of the clergy. Many teachers in the rigorous secondary schools had achieved high levels of academic distinction. Elijah Corlett, for example, had degrees from the British universities of Oxford and Cambridge.

The **hornbook** was the first elementary "notebook" (1630s–1640s). It was not a book, however, but a board and handle covered with transparent paper made by flattening the horns of cattle. On the board appeared the alphabet with

Dame schools were an extension of the home education that most young people obtained in the early eighteenth century. Those women who became proficient at teaching children in their homes formalized their methods and organized instruction for the children in the community.

vowels listed separately, short meaningless syllables, and the Lord's Prayer, which students were expected to memorize.

The *New England Primer* (1687), the first actual textbook, replaced the Hornbook in most New England schools by the late seventeenth century. Its contents were entirely religious with moral verses and poems.

Latin Grammar Schools   In 1635 a **Latin grammar school**, a classical secondary school for young men, was established in Boston. It provided the principal means of college preparation for well-to-do young men. They memorized Latin grammar, a Latin-English phrase book, and Latin vocabulary, and read from Cicero, Virgil, Ovid, and Erasmus. During the last year of study, the boys were required to learn rhetoric and elementary Greek. Saturday afternoons were typically set aside for religious study.

Dame Schools, Town Schools, and District Schools   Most of the boys who attended the Latin grammar schools had been educated in their homes, in dame schools, or in town schools. **Dame schools** were private homes in which several children gathered to be taught by the woman of the household. This type of "public" school, however, was soon found to be impractical.

Town schools were established to provide elementary education to all the New England children. Most town schools received public support, although some charged fees and some received private donations.

As more and more families moved away from towns and established farms, churches, and villages, they petitioned to become a district parish or district with the rights of local government including the right to control education. Since many of these villages were long distances from towns, these families sought to establish **district schools**, which were legalized in Connecticut in 1766 and Massachusetts in 1789. These schools represented a democratic response to the educational needs of the dispersed population. Each district hired its own schoolmaster and set the length of its school term. The teachers rarely had training or educational background and provided only basic instruction in the alphabet, reading and writing, and religion.

ROOTS OF POLITICIZATION OF EDUCATION

The roots of politicization of education can be found in two aspects of the history of education in the colonial South, the education of blacks and of women. While Southern landowners passed laws forbidding the education of slaves in an attempt to keep them subservient, these laws, ironically, acknowledged the potential role of education for social change. Lawrence Cremin, in "Education and Politics" in *Popular Education and Its Discontents*, calls to mind the writings of Aristotle on the politics of education: "It is impossible to talk about education apart from some conception of the good life; people will differ in their conceptions of the good life, and hence they will inevitably disagree on matters of education; therefore the discussion of education falls squarely within the domain of politics" (1990, 85).

Schools in the Southern Colonies   The Southern colonies were sparsely populated. The plantations, which produced rice, tobacco, sugar, indigo, and cotton, were rigidly divided by class and race. Plantation owners, as a class, considered themselves to be descended from Cavaliers, the British landowners who supported the Stuart king in the English Civil War (1642–1649). As such, they reestablished an aristocratic way of life in the New World. They did not see education as a means to a new social order nor did they attempt to provide a general education for all children. Rather they believed that they were responsible for educating their own children, who were often taught by private tutors, while a few attended denominational schools. As in the New England colonies, the boys were taught subjects to prepare them to attend college later in England, while the girls were taught subjects to prepare them to manage the household. The Southern plantation owners' greatest need was to maintain the life of the gentleman planter rather than develop education for the masses.

Education of Women in the Southern Colonies

The young women of the Southern colonies fared less well in terms of education than their counterparts in New England. Although a few went to schools outside the home, such as the **parsons schools** (endowed free schools in the parishes or districts) of Virginia, and some were educated by tutors, most women of the Southern colonies were illiterate. One out of every three Southern women in the seventeenth century could sign her name, as compared to three out of five men. After the American Revolution, a few wealthy girls attended private schools but were taught reading, writing, dancing, and arithmetic rather than the Latin, Greek, and philosophy taught to wealthy boys (Spruill 1972). Consequently, college then was not an option for girls.

Training Black Slaves

The plantation economy thrived on cheap labor. By 1619, only twelve years after the settlement of the Jamestown colony, the first slaves were imported from Africa to work the plantations. Other sources of cheap labor included poor white Europeans who purchased their passage to the New World by agreeing to serve as indentured servants for a particular period of time.

Because wealthy landowners saw slaves as central to the maintenance of their life-style and believed education would make them less subservient and less useful, most blacks were denied an education. They were trained to perform the plantation's specific tasks, from fieldwork to household chores. Some received special training or were apprenticed as blacksmiths, wheelwrights, or mill hands. Few were taught to read or write. Fearing insurrection, many slave owners forbade blacks from becoming literate.

Missionary Societies and Black Slaves   In the eighteenth century French and Spanish missionaries organized the first attempt to educate blacks in colonial America primarily because they considered education a means of increasing the ranks of the Church. The Anglican Missionary Society followed their lead. The Anglican Society for the Propagation of the Gospel in Foreign Parts established charity schools in the 1750s and 1760s that taught Southern blacks to read and write.

But few blacks were educated despite the increasing number of schools where they could develop skills in reading, writing, and religion. By 1770, there were approximately seven hundred thousand blacks in the colonies. The number increased to over four million by 1860. Although black schools such as Samuel Thomas's enrolled sixty students in Goose Creek Parish, South Carolina, in 1705, and the Anglican Society's in New York City enrolled two hundred in 1714, the effort to educate blacks was negligible. Historians estimate that in 1863, at the time of the Emancipation Proclamation, the black literacy rate was 5 percent (Cohen 1974, 146).

Blacks Educated Through Informal Channels   However, some blacks were educated and spread their knowledge to other blacks primarily through informal channels. A common belief at the time, perhaps maintained to justify the denial of education to blacks, was that they were incapable of learning and could not achieve at the level of whites. The education of some blacks, in spite of incredible odds against them and the transmission of education among them, helped dispel this myth. John Chavis (1763–1838) provides an interesting example. He was sent to Princeton University as part of an experiment to see whether a Negro had the capacity for a college education. Chavis graduated from Princeton, became a preacher who ministered to both blacks and whites, and established a classical school teaching Greek and Latin. Ironically, however, this school trained only the sons of prominent white families for college. Hence, the formal education he received was transmitted only to a limited extent to other blacks.

Indentured Servants

White indentured servants in the Southern colonies were only slightly more likely than black slaves to gain an education. Education was largely informal and provided by parents who often were illiterate. Hence, the education of poor whites in the South rarely included reading and writing. Poor white boys learned to farm, hunt, and fish from their fathers. Poor white girls learned homemaking from their mothers. The Anglican Missionary Society for the Propagation of the Gospel in Foreign Parts conducted a few schools primarily designed to teach the students to read the Bible. Although these schools were an early attempt to improve the lot of the poor through education, the majority of poor white children had no access to them, so as an initial attempt at politicization, they rarely succeeded.

ROOTS OF MULTITUDINOUSNESS OF EDUCATION

Throughout the history of education in the United States, different themes predominate. During the colonial period we can find the roots of all three themes: popularization in New England, politicization in the South, and multitudinousness in the Middle Atlantic colonies. As with education that became popular in New England and the political attitude that denied education to some in order to promote particular social goals in the South, the development of a variety of educational institutions stems from the culture, language, and religion of the population of the Middle Atlantic colonies.

Schools in the Middle Atlantic Colonies

Unlike New England and the Southern colonies, the populations of the Middle Atlantic colonies of New York, New Jersey, Pennsylvania, and Delaware were heterogeneous in terms of ethnicity, language, and religion. The region was colonized by Dutch Calvinists, Anglicans, Lutherans, Quakers, Jews, Presbyterians, and Catholics. They included people of English, Scottish, Dutch, German, Swedish, Danish, and Irish origin. Cultural diversity flourished as these groups attempted to retain their heritage in the New World. These differences made it impossible to establish a single school system, and the density of the population compared to the Southern colonies made home tutoring impractical. Therefore, a multitude of educational options developed.

Parochial and Private Schools

The colonies originated **parochial schools**, supported by religious organizations, and **private schools**, supported by individuals rather than by public funds. In fact, it has been said that if the roots of public education are in New England, then the roots of private education are in the Middle Atlantic region.

The Dutch settlers, mainly members of the Dutch Reformed Church, established **vernacular schools** to teach reading and writing in their native language in New Amsterdam, which later became New York. After taking control of New York in 1664, the English set up Anglican charity schools to teach reading, writing, arithmetic, religion, and catechism to poor children.

Quaker Schools

Unlike the Puritans of New England and the Dutch Calvinists of New York, the Quakers rejected corporal punishment as inhuman and cruel; they viewed children as individuals with individual needs and interests.

Quaker elementary schools stressed religion, reading, writing, and arithmetic and were open to all children without restriction. Some black youngsters were actually housed in Quaker homes while they attended the schools, which were a model of equality for the time. By 1869, there were 47 Quaker schools throughout the colonies, including one established specifically for blacks in 1700 in Philadelphia.

By 1880, there were 25 Quaker secondary schools that were open to all students. Tuition was charged to those who could afford it; the poor attended free. However, despite the equality of the education offered in these schools, they were not funded by public monies and remained private and parochial.

Vocational Education

By the late seventeenth century the demand for skilled workers such as navigators, surveyors, accountants, and printers was growing in the busy commercial colonies of the Middle Atlantic states. There, lacking a common school system, a number of informal **private venture training schools** were developed by businesses and trades to meet this demand. These private schools met the needs both of those who did not intend to go to college, and of new businesses and industries for a trained work force. These schools taught such practical courses as writing, arithmetic, geometry, trigonometry, astronomy, and surveying. Frequently, they lasted only as long as the need for workers existed.

5.2 POINTS TO REMEMBER

- Colonial New Englanders believed in a general education for all white children so that they could learn to read the Bible and develop discipline. Early schools taught reading and basic mathematical skills. Wealthy boys were educated in the classics in Latin grammar schools so that they could attend Harvard or college in Europe. Education in colonial New England thus popularized education in the United States.

- In the South the children of landowners were educated at home. Schools were few and far apart and few children attended them. Blacks and the children of indentured white servants were usually uneducated. However, the seeds of politicization of education were planted by the landowners who passed laws against educating slaves and by the missionary societies that attempted to educate them.

- The Middle Atlantic colonies had a heterogeneous population. Various ethnic groups developed their own parochial and private schools. Industries also developed private venture schools to train students in the trades required in those industries. Consequently, the concept of multitudinousness of education developed in the Middle Atlantic colonies.

POLITICIZATION OF EDUCATION PREDOMINATES

As discussed earlier, one of the three historical themes of U.S. education is politicization. According to Lawrence Cremin, politicization is the assumption that one of the roles of education is to change society indirectly through the schools rather than directly through politics. This means that rather than making laws or passing bills to alter some aspect of society, we look toward the schools to implement reform through education. Throughout the history of education we will see examples of this politicization. Education had been used for political aims in the colonial South, but it was not until the postrevolutionary period that schools were used extensively to educate the young in the skills and knowledge necessary to be active citizens of a common culture.

Education of the Postrevolutionary Period

During the postrevolutionary war period (1776–1830) it became necessary to find a means of developing a single nation from the various backgrounds and beliefs of the colonists. To many early scholars and politicians, the schools were an avenue through which young people could be trained in the rudiments of democracy. Just as the colonists of New England recognized the power of the schools to indoctrinate the young in their religious theory, the thinkers of the new nation recognized the schools' potential in the indoctrination of the young into citizenship in the new republic. Hence the politicization of the schools.

Changes in Curriculum

Although the curriculum changed little in the elementary schools after the Revolution, especially in rural America, new textbooks made the task of teaching reading and arithmetic easier. The *McGuffey Reader* (1836) and *Ray's Arithmetic* (1834) were the common subject-oriented texts used by almost all students through the mid-nineteenth century. Teachers could rely on these texts to set forth the curriculum; they had to provide only the instruction.

In the secondary curriculum, classical studies were replaced by more practical classes related to everyday life. By the mid-eighteenth century, middle-class settlers, believing that education could effect social change, were advocating a curriculum that would help the country deal with everyday problems.

Educational Thought of the Postrevolutionary Period

Various political leaders such as Benjamin Franklin, Thomas Jefferson, and Noah Webster proposed new educational strategies and institutions to educate people in the new republicanism. **Republicanism**, based on the political theories of the Englishman John Locke (1632–1704), was founded on the principle that government arises from the consent of the governed. In this case, the governed needed education to cultivate the skills, knowledge, and values that would be necessary for participating in the new political order, thus giving rise to the concept of education as a means of addressing the country's political needs.

Benjamin Franklin Benjamin Franklin (1706–1790), a highly respected statesman, politician, and philosopher whose own schooling was minimal, developed a prototype for the contemporary secondary school. He considered Latin grammar schools impractical for life in a democracy. His **English language academy**, established in Philadelphia in 1751, included courses in English, oratory, commerce and politics, mathematics as an applied subject, history, and foreign languages as needed for professional training and vocational courses. It introduced into the secondary school curriculum many practical and vocational courses that had previously been part of only private venture schools. Franklin's English language academy served as the precursor to vocational education in contemporary high schools.

Thomas Jefferson   Thomas Jefferson (1743–1826) was one of the most influential early American statesmen to profess the importance of equality of educational opportunity. Jefferson, echoing the words of Aristotle, advocated passage of "A Bill for the More General Diffusion of Knowledge" (1779), a law that would provide an education "adapted to years, the capacity, and the condition of everyone, and directed to their freedom and happiness" (Jefferson 1779/1954, 134).

Jefferson advocated three years of free education for all white children in Virginia. For those gifted males who could not afford grammar school, a scholarship for an additional three years was provided. Jefferson was the first influential American spokesman for free public education for the masses.

Noah Webster   Noah Webster (1758–1843) has been called the "schoolmaster of the Republic." He believed that the development of an American language, separated from British English and without regional usage, was essential if a unified nation were to develop. Toward this end he established a system of phonics to differentiate American from British English and wrote *American Spelling* (1783), later editions of which were to become famous as the *Blue-Backed Speller*, and *American Dictionary of the English Language* (1828). Webster's speller reportedly sold over 24 million copies and, for the most part, replaced the *New England Primer* in the classroom. The popularity and wide use of his speller made his name commonly known in educational circles, and his system of phonics is still an important element in reading instruction today.

Schooling, the Prerogative of the States

Schooling was firmly established as the states' prerogative during the postrevolutionary period. In 1787, Congress enacted the *Northwest Ordinance*, by which the lower Great Lakes Region, then known as the Northwest territory, was divided into townships. The newly formed federal government showed its commitment to the principles of education in the Northwest Ordinance, which stated that education is "necessary to good government and happiness of mankind."

The U.S. Constitution, ratified in 1788, failed to mention education. However, under the "reserved powers clause" of the Tenth Amendment to the Constitution, ratified in 1791, educational prerogatives remained with the individual states. Therefore, from the very beginning of the Republic, the legal roles of the states and the federal government in education were firmly established (see also chapter 15).

POPULARIZATION OF EDUCATION PREDOMINATES

Although many state legislative bodies of the late eighteenth and early nineteenth centuries continued to take a laissez-faire view of education, the American public was beginning to demand that the states take action to ensure wider educational opportunities. Some states moved a few steps toward public education by subsidizing some private and philanthropic schools. In some cases, states allotted to the schools revenues from excises, lotteries, and the sale of public lands. In other cases legislation was passed allowing local agencies to tax themselves for schools.

During this period the concept of the common school was developed in which all children would get an education for their own good and the good of society (see also p. 143). Education in the United States was moving irrevocably toward popularization. The road, however, was not always smooth.

Jackson's Presidency Enhances the Status of the Common Man

The transition was hastened by a new political, social, and economic spirit in the country. The years between 1812 and 1865 became known as the **age of the common man**, partly due to Andrew Jackson's presidency (1829–1837). Jackson was the first president from a frontier state where vast tracts of land were free and open to all, resulting in equality of economic and political opportunity. Jackson was elected by the common man—farmers, trappers, and laborers.

It is no surprise that the rise of the common man, which took place during Jackson's administration, coincided with what has become referred to as the great American revival in education. During this time, state education offices were established, and the public school system as we know it today was born. It was not long afterward that compulsory attendance laws were passed and high schools were opened. **Normal schools** expressly for the education of teachers were also started during this period.

Compulsory Attendance Laws

Massachusetts enacted the first compulsory attendance statute. Passed in 1852, this law required that all children between eight and fourteen attend school for at least twelve weeks per year, six of which had to be consecutive, and carried penalties for violators.

Throughout the nineteenth and early twentieth centuries, such laws were strengthened by extending age limits, lengthening the school term, and tightening enforcement. However, they did not address equality of educational opportunity and tended to interpret "all children" as meaning all white males of economic means. Compulsory attendance laws moved the ideal of common education closer to reality.

The Child Labor Law

During the age of the common man, a new, unlikely political alliance was formed between the old middle class and those with philanthropic interests who viewed the industrialists as brutalizing their work force, particularly children. Articles about the horrors of child labor began to appear in the press.

As a response to the concerns of a vocal public and press, Massachusetts passed the Child Labor Law in 1866. It required that no child under ten be

Prior to the Child Labor Law of 1866, children sometimes worked seventy-two hours a week in factories. This law required that no boys under the age of fourteen could be employed unless they had first attended public or private school for six months.

employed and that no child under fourteen be employed unless he had attended a public or private day school, approved by the school committee, for six months in the year prior to his employment. This law made it possible and, indeed, necessary for boys under the age of fourteen to attend school. Articles in the newspapers, the leadership of the middle class, and the votes of the laborers put pressure on the government to change its laissez-faire approach to education and hastened the movement toward public schools.

The Common School

By the early nineteenth century, as industry became more and more mechanized, it was obvious that workers needed to develop the skills required to operate the increasingly complex machinery. Voluntary philanthropic schools, sponsored by businesses and industries, were inaugurated. Individual workers saw the schools as a way to educate themselves and improve their position in the workplace. The schools, therefore, met the needs of both worker and employer.

Consequently, educators and businessmen began discussing the need for publicly supported education for all children. This ideal was called the **common school**. Of course, to many, the common school was far more than a means of educating the masses for the work force. It was an egalitarian and democratic ideal: a means of preserving and strengthening the culture and conveying and reinforcing American values.

The District School

The years immediately after the Revolution until about 1840 have become known as "the period of the district school." Following a New England practice, many states delegated authority over school districts to municipalities. Control of education remained a state function, but much of its power and support derived from local governments and boards such as selectmen (an elected board of officials). In each division of the town the control of the school was delegated to a prudential committeeman, elected by the people of the district. Money needed to support the school was assessed with other taxes and determined by the town.

The early district schools were rather primitive and often overcrowded. Most were heated by fireplaces. Students sat on backless benches placed against the walls. At times as many as one hundred students, between the ages of six and sixteen, attended a school no bigger than thirty feet square taught by one teacher. Supplies were limited. Above the students' benches were a few shelves for books. There were rarely maps or pictures. Blackboards were uncommon until about 1820, and it was not until 1840 that large stoves replaced fireplaces. Children were often required to bring their own firewood to school.

In the earliest district schools, the masters were male. However, after 1820, more young, unskilled women took over the task. The period of the common man also opened up some jobs to women since it was assumed that any citizen of the community had the qualifications to fill any public office as long as he or she was a loyal American. The employment of women also helped the communities support the district school; women of the nineteenth century earned considerably less than men. The average weekly salary for male teachers in 1841 was $4.15; for women it was $2.51. Therefore, during the period of the district school the tradition of women as teachers was forged, and by the beginning of the U.S. Civil War, the majority of American teachers were women.

Sunday Schools

Many young children were unable to attend school because they worked at low-paying jobs during the week and on Saturday. Around 1830, the **Sunday school** emerged as a philanthropic endeavor sponsored by the church to help educate these children in the basics of reading, writing, religion, and character development. By 1870, Sunday schools were well-established in Protestant churches. However, the focus was moving from teaching basic skills to teaching the Bible.

Infant Schools

In the early 1800s, **infant schools** for children from the ages of two to six whose mothers worked in factories were developed by Welsh educator Robert Owen (1771–1858) in Scotland and later were established in New Harmony, Indiana. These antecedents of modern day care were instituted primarily in the industrial areas of the Northeast to give children, three years and older, moral, intellectual, and physical training.

Monitorial Schools

At about the same time that these philanthropic schools were developing, Joseph Lancaster (1778–1838) believed that it was possible to educate large numbers of children effectively, efficiently, and inexpensively. To do so, he developed the concept of **monitorial schools**. In this system, a small number of master teachers trained advanced students to teach beginning students. Lessons were reduced to small elements of basic skills, and each advanced student taught a single phase of each skill. **Ability grouping**, assigning students to groups based on their ability to learn the skill, was established in order to make teaching easier for the advanced students. The first monitorial school in the United States was established in New York City in 1805.

The High School

During the nineteenth century statesmen and educators began to question the value of the classical grammar school curriculum for the growing number of children of immigrants. Likewise, they began to look critically at the needs of the burgeoning industrial economy. Clearly, Latin grammar schools met the needs of neither immigrants nor industry.

In the early part of the nineteenth century, the Latin grammar school was replaced by the **academy**, based on the concept of vernacular (in this case, English language) education for the middle class. The academy, following the model provided by Benjamin Franklin, offered a wide range of subjects for college preparatory students as well as others. Although academies often received some funding from cities and states, most were private. Consequently, they failed to reach the large, growing class of immigrant workers.

By the 1870s, high schools began to replace academies. The development of the high school was aided by a series of court cases such as *Charles E. Stuart et*

The public high school began to replace the academies in the 1870s primarily because states were allowed to support their schools by taxes. In addition, the urbanization and industrialization of the United States in the mid-nineteenth century and the specialization of professions required an educated populace. These socioeconomic forces contributed to the growth of the public high school.

al. v. School District No. 1 of the Village of Kalamazoo (1874), in which the court ruled that school districts could establish and support public high schools with tax funds. Urbanization and industrialization stimulated the need for training at the same time as specialization in industry increased, so these schools developed quite rapidly. In 1889–1890 there were 2,526 public high schools with a total of 202,063 students.

Ironically, the high school's curriculum remained elite in character. Even though only 5 percent of the students in high school went on to college, the curriculum was primarily for the college-bound.

Expanding Access for Female Students

In the early years of the twentieth century, an increasing number of female students wanted to attend secondary schools, forcing many educators to debate the value of education for females. Most of the debate, however, focused on practical, economic considerations of female attendance rather than on their potential educational benefits. In 1902, E. E. White, Ohio State commissioner of common schools, sent a report to the United States commissioner of education regarding the need for coeducation in the secondary schools.

> More high schools are needed for both boys and girls; and this immediately presents the question of the uniting or the separating of the sexes in the new high schools. Shall we put up two distinct buildings with two distinct principals and faculties, thus doubling the expense; or shall we erect one building in which the boys and girls shall be educated together, with one principal and faculty for such a school? (Report of United States Commissioner of Education, 1902, cited in Foy 1968, 178–179)

As White's 1902 argument for coeducation shows, it was won on financial grounds rather than on the basis of equality or educational opportunity. However, when it was decided that girls and boys should be educated in one building, the differentiation of curriculum became an important question. Again, equal opportunity was not the determining factor. In fact, although boys would be allowed to take courses designed primarily for girls, there was no mention of girls being permitted to take courses offered for boys.

Nevertheless, the arguments for coeducation opened the doors of public education to most white females of school age and were another move toward the popularization of U.S. education.

Educational Leadership and the Common School

Between 1820 and 1850, Horace Mann and Henry Barnard, two influential statesmen, did a great deal through their writings to influence the ideal of the common school and eventual implementation of publicly supported schools.

Horace Mann

Horace Mann (1796–1859), a lawyer and politician, became secretary of the Massachusetts State Board of Education in 1837. During his twelve-year tenure, he produced yearly reports to the board in which he addressed the needs of many different groups and individuals, always emphasizing that common schools met these needs.

Among the many issues he discussed were the development of better school buildings and responsible local boards of education (1837) and the students' need for intellectual development (1838). He advocated the establishment of free circulating libraries in every school district (1839) and argued that the schools should promote a morality that would ensure the protection of the individual's right to property (1841). He discussed the employment of women and the necessity of developing effective teacher-training institutions (1842). Mann asked, "But why should a woman receive less than two-fifths as much as a man, for services which in no respect are of inferior value?" In the tenth (1846) and eleventh (1847) reports he discussed the state's role in education and the power of education to redeem the state. Mann so strongly believed in the common school that he asserted that it "may become the most effective and benignant of all the forces of civilization" (1848).

Mann wrote not only about the popularization but the politicization of education. He was idealistic in his belief in education as a reformer of society, the "great equalizer of the conditions of men." Through education, each individual could become independent and resist the selfishness of others, feelings of social responsibility would expand, and distinction between classes would diminish.

Henry Barnard

Henry Barnard (1811–1900) was secretary of the Connecticut Board of Education, commissioner of public schools in Rhode Island, first U.S. commissioner of education, and chancellor of the University of Wisconsin. Whereas Mann's writing was primarily for legislative use, Barnard's was much more accessible to educators and the public through two journals he established: *Connecticut Common School Journal* (1839) and *American Journal of Education* (1848).

Barnard supported Mann's idea that training in civic values and health and diet was as valuable as training in basic skills. He believed that the most important subject to an informed citizenry was the English language. He supported improved teacher education and increased teacher salaries. Barnard's efforts led to the establishment of the first federal office of education in 1867, now called the Department of Education.

Point/Counterpoint

FOR FREE SCHOOLS

How valuable soever high seminaries of learning may be, we cannot rely upon them for instructing the great body of the people, because they are to be found only in the primary schools. They ought to be the foundation of our whole system of public instruction, as they are indeed the chief support of all our free institutions. . . . It is . . . of the first importance that this foundation be laid deep and firm, not only in the constitution and laws of the country, but also in the warmest affections of our people.

. . . Children of every name and age must be taught the qualifications and duties of American citizens, and learn in early life the art of self-control—they must be educated. And to accomplish this object, our chief dependence must necessarily be the free school system. . . .

Let free schools be established and maintained in perpetuity, and there can be no such thing as a permanent aristocracy in our land; for the monopoly of wealth is powerless, when mind is allowed freely to come in contact with mind. It is only by erecting a barrier between the rich and the poor, which can be done only by allowing the rich a monopoly of learning as well as wealth, that such an aristocracy can be established. But the operation of the free school system has a powerful tendency to prevent the erection of this barrier.

. . . The primary schools should be on the first order, the academies of the highest grade, and the universities assume and maintain a commanding position; and each and all of them be so ably conducted as to give entire satisfaction to all reasonable, unprejudiced minds. With such schools, the rising generation would be thoroughly taught, and the wants of the state adequately supplied.

From: Pierce, 1837, in Cohen 1978, vol. 2:1025–1026

AGAINST FREE SCHOOLS

I am . . . in the full sense of the word "a self-made man." I have paid large sums for the education of my children in private seminaries, both in Europe and America. I have paid heavily to have them taught the ornamental branches—ever so many 'ologies and ever so many languages. But what do I find? I find that I am taxed to have the sons and daughters of my tailor, my shoemaker, my plumber and my very coachman educated in these self-same ornamental branches, the 'ologies and the languages, in the public common school. . . .

I think it very unjust to tax me to educate the common people. It is all nonsense to say that education will make them better citizens. I maintain it will make them worse citizens. I don't believe one word of the statement made by certain editors that in educating the people we diminish the cost of prisons and alms-houses: and suppose it did, I would much prefer to pay my money to punish criminals and feed paupers. In every enlightened country, when there are a great many rich people, there must be a great many poor people and a great many criminals. It is only in the savage state that there is equality. Down, therefore, with the ornamental branches in the common schools, with the history and the geography and the drawing and the grammar; and restrict them to the three R's, to the reading, the writing and the arithmetic that enabled me to become a millionaire.

From: McSordad, 1883 in Foy 1968, 344

POSTSCRIPT

Today, the public school system is so much a part of our lives and our heritage that it is hard to believe that resistance to the concept of a common school was so prevalent among much of the population. However, in spite of the arguments against the common school, the seeds for a public school system to educate all students had been planted.

The argument here is not simply whether the public should pay for common education for all, but whether the concept of equality in education, the concept inherent in the common school movement, should be pursued. Superintendent Pierce clearly believed it should, whereas Mr. McSordad clearly believed it should not. This argument continued for many years.

Today, few would contend that any citizens should be denied an equal education based on their social and economic status. Rather, we discuss how to implement this equality in a large and diverse school population.

POLITICIZATION OF SCHOOLS REALIZED: EDUCATION OF THE POST–CIVIL WAR PERIOD

In the post–Civil War period, education expanded to meet the needs of society primarily in the Northeast and Midwest. In the South it was a time of reconstruction after a war that was disastrous to the region's economy and society.

By the late nineteenth century, educators in the urban areas of the Northeast and Midwest recognized the economic and social need to educate the large secondary school-aged population, who did not plan to attend college, in vocational subjects and democratic values. At the same time, popularization of schooling became the rallying cry of the people.

Schools to Meet the Needs of the Democracy

One important example of the politicization of schools to meet society's democratic needs can be seen in the St. Louis public schools of the mid-nineteenth century. Superintendent William Torrey Harris recognized that 46 percent of the students were children of German immigrants. He counted at least ten distinct languages spoken by the expanding European population of the city. In addition, he recognized their differences in manners, customs, and values. His goal was to limit these differences and "ascend into a new homogeneous nationality . . ." (Harris 1898, 35).

In order to accomplish this, Harris believed that the common national language must be English. However, he realized that a period of transition was necessary when bilingual traditions should be maintained. Gradually students would take all courses in English, although German language courses would remain in the curriculum.

Consequently, children of immigrants enrolled in the schools in large numbers, up from 1,300 in 1860 to more than 20,000 in 1880. Harris believed that in order to assimilate the children of immigrants into U.S. culture, the curriculum must be sequential and structured. For example, students would study U.S. history in German. Moreover, German would be integrated into courses in grammar, literature, art, mathematics, and geography. Harris called these subjects the "six windows of the soul." He believed that their study would allow students to master the mystery and nature of the human mind. At the same time, students would be developing skills in English and learning about the United States. Thereby, the school not only would help students assimilate U.S. culture but also would help them become functioning citizens in the democracy.

Curriculum for the Democracy

If schools were to educate an increasingly diverse population and help all these students become participating citizens in the democracy, the classical curriculum of the Latin grammar school and teaching by recitation would no longer be appropriate. In an unprecedented manner, educators of the late nineteenth century examined the school curriculum and teaching methodology.

Although the National Education Association (NEA) had clearly asserted in two reports in 1893 and 1895 that the subject-centered approach to curriculum was appropriate in elementary and secondary schools, the educators' commitment to these approaches was diminishing. By 1918, the NEA challenged its earlier convictions by issuing the *Seven Cardinal Principles*. This report recommended a new nonclassical curriculum for the large influx of non-college-bound students. According to this report, all students should be prepared by the schools to be successful in seven endeavors: health, command of fundamental processes, worthy home membership, vocation, civics, worthy use of leisure, and ethical character. These represented a significant departure from the classical approach of the curriculum of earlier times. The NEA commission that published this report claimed that previous curriculums had served the minority rather than the majority.

The report represented the first attempt to examine curriculum in terms of needs of individual students by offering them a variety of different educational options, including several occupational choices in secondary school.

The commission also advocated a significant change in how equality of educational opportunity was viewed. It maintained that there was greater equality of educational opportunity for a boy who was not going to attend college if he had a specially designed curriculum than if he had to take a curriculum designed for college entrance. It ushered in an age in which the idea that same education means equal education was disputed. However, the report did not address the specific needs of lower-class students, minorities, or women. The beginning of World War I (1914) kept the recommendations from being implemented in the schools.

In spite of the limited immediate impact of the *Seven Cardinal Principles*, curriculum theory and design slowly evolved away from complete subject dominance toward some concern for the needs of the population, including a commitment to different educational options for different students.

Progressivism

Notwithstanding the common school movement of the nineteenth century, the needs of large portions of American society, particularly the poor and immigrant classes, were not being met by the schools. The **progressive movement** was an attempt to improve society by bringing the disenfranchised into the schools. Progressive educators believed that through schooling the poor could rise above their lot and societal problems could be mitigated.

The best-known educator to be associated with the progressive movement was John Dewey (1859–1952), who maintained that the experiences of children should be related to the subject matter that made up the student's course of study. According to Dewey, schools must reflect society and must actively seek to improve it by allowing students to become effective participants in the democratic process while in school (see also chapter 7, p. 211 and chapter 9, p. 273).

Most contemporary historians see the progressive movement in education as part of the larger reform movement that began in the 1890s. A new, articulated middle class was emerging and began to address the problems of poverty. Jane Addams, for example, believed that she could improve the conditions of immigrant slums by developing a sense of community through settlement houses, places of refuge for the urban poor. To prove her theory she established Hull House in Chicago in the 1890s where, for example, if the community needed instruction in care of childhood diseases, it was provided. Through education, the people who operated Hull House attempted nothing less than a renewal of society.

Progressive Education

Although for some children, Hull House provided an alternative to the public schools, the movement toward politicization of the schools was occurring in the schools simultaneously. According to Lawrence Cremin, "To look back to the nineties is to sense an awakening of social conscience, a growing belief that this incredible suffering was neither the fault nor the inevitable lot of the sufferers, that it could certainly be alleviated, and that road to alleviation was neither charity nor revolution, but in the last analysis education" (1957, 59).

The Gary Plan   Although progressive curriculums such as Dewey's, based on the need of the child and on activity, influenced numerous experimental educational programs, their impact on the public school curriculum was limited, at least initially. Probably the most comprehensive application of Dewey's curriculum can be seen in the Gary Plan. Under this plan, each school in Gary, Indiana, was organized as an "embryonic community" (Bourne 1916, 144). Work and study were done in a practical, as well as intellectual, setting. Physics laboratories, for example, adjoined machine shops to allow students to apply scientific principles to practical situations. Learning by doing was practically implemented as the children operated the school: The lunchroom was run by students, supplies were ordered and distributed by students, students did accounting for the administration, and younger children became assistants of older children.

To make this program administratively feasible, the school day was departmentalized into what was called the "platoon" system, which allowed for complete use of the facility. While one group of students was studying the basic subjects, another group was studying other disciplines. Ironically, this organizational approach, the one aspect of the plan widely adopted by other public schools, was what defeated it in the end. Departmentalization makes integration between subjects almost impossible (Flexner and Bachman 1918, 77).

Schooling in the South During Reconstruction

Infrequently in U.S. society, conditions make one section of the country different from another in terms of educational history. The Civil War and the period immediately following it was such a period.

The economic and social climate of the South after the Civil War was very different from that in the North and caused the development of schools in the South to suffer. The plantation economy was in ruins, factories were destroyed, families were separated, banks were insolvent, and civil authority was limited. There was a great deal of poverty, crime, and starvation. Education was of limited concern to Southerners.

The government established in the South by the victorious federal government in Washington, D.C., tended to be corrupt and poorly administered. Over $5 million in federal funds were provided for education from 1865 through 1871. However, because this money was administered by Northerners who did not understand local conditions, most Southerners were indifferent or resisted these attempts to educate their children.

George Peabody and Other Philanthropists

In 1887 George Peabody gave $2 million for the education of the poor in the South and Southwest. The funds were used to (1) improve state school systems,

(2) develop state normal schools, (3) train black teachers, and (4) strengthen the professional activities of teachers. In 1905 the George Peabody College for Teachers, a model for teacher training in the South, opened in Nashville, Tennessee.

Other philanthropists assisted the cause of education in the South. In 1882 John Slater donated $1 million to provide teacher training and industrial education for blacks. Anna T. Jeannes created a fund in 1907 to raise the quality of black education. In 1917 Julius Rosenwald established a fund to assist all areas of Southern education for 30 years.

In 1901 Southern educational leaders formed the Southern Education Board to guide education in the South. However, by 1918 the South was still far behind the rest of the United States in enrollment, attendance, and funding, especially in the high schools. Teachers in the South were poorly trained and paid compared to teachers in other regions of the country.

Education of Southern Blacks Following the Civil War

In addition to the philanthropic support of education for blacks in the Reconstruction South, black educators developed schools and provided inspiration for the education of black children. Booker T. Washington (1856–1915) established Tuskegee Normal and Industrial Institute in Tuskegee, Alabama, in 1875. It was designed to offer industrial education for black students and stressed hard work, vocational skills, and economic advancement. Washington contended that it was the kind of education needed for both races, particularly because of the undeveloped material resources of the South. He, however, supported the concept of separate schools for black students. At the Cotton States Exposition in Atlanta in 1895 he said, "In all things that are purely social we can be as separate as the fingers, yet one as the hand in all things essential to mutual progress" (Harlan, 1972).

Frederick Douglass (1817–1895), an orator who spoke for abolitionist groups, supported education for blacks and contended that the Fourteenth Amendment to the U.S. Constitution, the rights of citizens, and the Fifteenth, the right to vote, were a mockery if they did not ensure equal rights to black citizens. Douglass devoted his efforts to improving the education of blacks, especially vocational education. He believed, as did Washington, that through vocational education blacks could advance economically and socially.

William E. Burghardt Du Bois (1868–1963), the first U.S. black to receive a Ph.D. degree, attended Fiske University, Harvard University, and the University of Berlin. Du Bois spoke eloquently of the right of black citizens to play an equal role with whites in U.S. society. He argued that blacks should become prepared for positions of leadership not only in the black community but in society as a whole, and that this required a good education. Du Bois, a sociologist by education, founded the National Association for the Advancement of Colored People (NAACP) to help develop black leadership. His goal was to develop an African-American culture that would blend blacks' African backgrounds with American culture. He declared that in order to bring about change, blacks needed to be educated to be discontented with the social system of the South.

Mary McLeod Bethune (1875–1955) was educated at Scotia Seminary in Concord, North Carolina, and Moody Institute in Chicago. In 1904 she founded Daytona Normal School (now Bethune-Cookman College) in Daytona, Florida. The college was developed to provide religious, academic, and vocational

Tuskegee Institute was established for the education of black students in Alabama in 1875. Booker T. Washington believed that blacks should be educated in agricultural and occupational skills so as not to compete with and cause conflicts with whites in the professions. While Washington fought for the education and advancement of blacks, he is, nevertheless, sometimes seen as a controversial figure who compromised the position of blacks in society.

programs for black students. Bethune was a strong advocate for the rights of women and of blacks and later became an adviser in the Franklin D. Roosevelt and Harry S. Truman administrations.

Freedmen's Bureau

In 1865 the U.S. Congress established the **Freedmen's Bureau** to work with voluntary organizations to provide basic education to blacks who had been slaves. Although many blacks did learn to read and write as a result of the Freedmen's Bureau, it did not do much to improve their social or economic life, which had been its original goal.

By the end of the nineteenth century, the themes of education in the United States were firmly established. Popularization, the concept of schooling for all, was introduced by the New England colonists and developed by those who began the common school movement. The politicization of the schools to solve the problems of society through education rather than through politics was a predominant concern of the mid- to late-nineteenth century as the nation attempted to deal with the new industrialization and waves of immigrants. Multitudinousness, the establishment of a variety of educational approaches to meet the needs of a diverse society, was begun in the urban and multiethnic Middle Atlantic colonies and continued as politicians, activists, and educators of the nineteenth century recognized that vast social, economic, and cultural differences required different kinds of schooling if all citizens were to participate in democracy. It was not, however, until the twentieth century that all three themes became integrated in U.S. education. We will examine this unique synergy in chapter 6.

5.3 POINTS TO REMEMBER

- Benjamin Franklin developed the first English language academy for young men in Philadelphia. Thomas Jefferson proposed public education for all males through elementary school and for the ablest students through secondary school. Noah Webster's speller and dictionary were widely circulated, and he developed a system of phonics for American English.

- Horace Mann advocated a system of free education for all students. Henry Barnard edited two journals that further developed the concept of the common school.

- The common school movement provided the framework for publicly supported education for all children.

- After the Civil War schools in the Northeast and Midwest educated more and more children of immigrants in the English language and the manners, customs, and values of the U.S. society. The *Seven Cardinal Principles* broadened the purpose of schooling to include vocational and civic education. The progressive movement encouraged student involvement in their own learning to help them become active citizens of the democracy.

- Schools in the Northern United States in the period following the Civil War helped integrate immigrants into U.S. society, prepare them for civic duty, and train them for work in industry. The thrust of education during this period was to meet society's democratic needs. Many Southern schools, developed by philanthropists, became models for redevelopment. Black educators, such as Frederick Douglass and Mary McLeod Bethune, developed schools for blacks in the South.

- During the colonial period, women and blacks were frequently excluded, particularly from secondary schools and universities. Although some blacks proved that they were as intellectually capable as whites, the predominant view was that they, and women too, were less able than white males to learn.

"Don't you recognize us, Bob? We're Dick and Jane!"

FOR THOUGHT/DISCUSSION

1. Which aspects of the concept of naturalism are expressed in the educational theory of progressivism?

2. What part did the church play in popularizing education?

3. What role did black slaves play in the politicization of education?

4. How did the report *Seven Cardinal Principles* affect the development of diversity of education?

5. Do you believe that education is primarily a tool for developing a democratic society or a means of accumulating individual knowledge? Explain.

FOR FURTHER READING/REFERENCE

Douglass, F. 1855. *My bondage and my freedom.* New York: Miller, Orton, and Mulligan. Douglass describes the Southern slave community of the mid- to late-1800s with particular attention to slave oppression, his education, and the education of other slaves.

Downs, R. B. 1974. *Horace Mann: Champion of public schools.* New York: Twayne Publishers. This well-documented biography describes Mann's personal life and his mission to establish common schools. The book catalogs his work with legislators and educators in the 1830s and 1840s.

Kaufman, P. W. 1984. *Women teachers on the frontier.* New Haven, CT: Yale University Press. This account describes the work of women teachers in many one-room schools on the western frontier of the late 1800s.

Schlesinger, A. M. 1981. *The birth of a nation: A portrait of the American people on the eve of independence.* Boston, MA: Houghton Mifflin. This work portrays the everyday concerns of Americans during the mid- to late-eighteenth century including the role of the family, education of youth, education of girls and blacks, and the social conscience of that period.

Winslow, A. G. 1974. *Diary of Anna Green Winslow: A Boston school girl of 1771,* ed. A. M. Earle. Williamstown, MA: Corner House. This book provides a description of the education and schooling of Anna Green Winslow, who lived in the late eighteenth century.

6

Twentieth-Century U.S. Education

The education of women is one of the many changes that occurred during the 20th century. In the first excerpt, Maryjane Meaker, a well-known author of books for young adults who writes under the pen name M. E. Kerr, tells of her experience at a junior college in the mid-1940s. In the second, Faith O'Brien writes to her daughter, who is about to begin college in 1990.

Vermont Junior College had decided to take a chance on me. That was the way the dean put it. She was a woman named Ruth Kingsley, whose personality was as far removed from Ape's as Athene's is from Hecate's.

"I know my grades weren't very good," I told Dean Kingsley.

"Your grades were the least of it," she answered. "Listen to this evaluation of you from your boarding school. 'If you tell her to walk, she'll run. If you tell her to run, she'll walk. If you ask her to whistle, she'll sing; to sing, she'll whistle. She delights in stirring up the student body against any/all authority, and at best, her personality might be described as refractory.' " The dean put down my file and said, "You didn't come highly recommended."

"Refractory?" I said.

"Hard to manage," she said.

"How come I got in here?"

"Part of it was my curiosity. Part of it was my interest in psychology. I teach psychology. Some of it was your stated interest in being a writer. I wanted to be a writer once, myself."

"My first choice was the University of Missouri, for journalism," I said.

"You could still make it," she said. "And meanwhile, we're very interested in starting a school newspaper. How would you like to work on the project?"

I knew I was going to like Vermont Junior College. That very first day, down in the basement "smoker," I puffed on cigarettes with my new classmates and heard an old, familiar song:

We are the girls from V.J.C., you see,
There's not a man in this damn nunnery,
And every night at eight they lock the door . . .

I felt like someone who'd been let out of prison. I was finally going to school again with Yankees who talked like me, knew what deep snow was, and owned skis, skates, and toboggans. (Winters you could take skiing for gym, go off on skis before breakfast with the class, and come in to a feast of pancakes with real Vermont maple syrup poured over them.)

From: Kerr, 1983, pp. 147–150, 154–155

This letter was written to Margaret O'Brien by her mother, Faith, on September 5, 1990, from Asheville, North Carolina. It expresses a parent's hope that education will open new doors and provide intellectual stimulation and growth for her daughter. When compared to Jefferson's letter to his daughter Martha, at the beginning of chapter 5, and with the excerpt above, this letter provides an excellent example of how, through history, people have changed their attitudes toward education for women.

Dear Molly,

Tomorrow the doors of the world begin to open to you. Your father and I have only one request as you begin your college years: Don't close the doors.

You will meet people who are very different from your family and friends. They will look different, have different values, express different ideas, talk differently. . . . Although we do not suggest that you embrace either the person or her ideas, we want you to listen and to think. What does she believe? Where does he come from? How has her life been different from yours? What does he know that you do not know? Listen and learn, Molly.

It's funny how I can remember things from my first day of college. Sometime during that day President Graham spoke to us and our parents. He said something like, "This great and grand college and her esteemed faculty have one responsibility to you and that is to force you to change your minds; to question your values." At the time I wondered what he meant. But, when he asked us at our senior banquet if they, the faculty and the administration, had forced us to rethink our values and if we had changed our minds, we all agreed that they had and that we had.

Your father and I believe we have provided for you a foundation on which to build your own life. We know that the decisions you make will be built on that foundation. We will not always agree with your decisions. But, if each opens a new door, we will support your right to make it.

Molly, you can learn, grow, and change knowing that you have our love and respect. We will always love you. And, more importantly, as you become the person only you can be, you will come to love and respect yourself.

We look forward to watching you open doors, and we pledge to help you in any way we can. We will try to remember to give you the opportunity to ask for our help.

Please allow us our tears as we leave you to your new life, friends, and experiences. We will miss the daily opportunity to share them with you. But, we know you will call and write. We will look forward to discussing with you what you are feeling, experiencing, and learning. We are anxious to get to know you as a friend as well as a daughter.

With love and respect,
Mom

P.S. Sometimes it's better to let a door slam on your toe than to lock it behind you.   Daddy

157

CHAPTER OBJECTIVES

After studying this chapter, you should be able to:

- Define popularization, expansion, and politicization of U.S. education in the twentieth century.
- Explain how World War I affected U.S. schools.
- Discuss the impact of the Great Depression on U.S. schools.
- Understand how World War II affected U.S. schools.
- Discuss the impact on U.S. schools of the Soviet Union's launching of Sputnik.
- Explain how the civil rights period affected U.S. schools.
- Discuss the influence of *Brown v. the Board of Education of Topeka* on the public schools.
- Define equal educational opportunities after integration.
- Discuss the reasons for the implementation of Head Start.
- Understand the Elementary and Secondary Education Act (1965).
- Discuss changes in schooling for multicultural and bilingual students.
- Discuss changes in schooling for those with disabilities following P.L. 94–142.
- Compare equal educational opportunities in the 1970s and 1980s.
- Discuss the reform movement of the 1980s.

T o people of the eighteenth and nineteenth centuries, education was the fire that burned under the melting pot to create a unified democratic nation. It is clear from the opening excerpts that education is still, in the twentieth century, a great force for growth, change, and opportunity.

THE TWENTIETH CENTURY'S EDUCATIONAL THEMES

There are no easy solutions to the problems created by the growth of democracy and the concept of equal education for all. As society changes, the system of education must find ways of dealing with a complex and burgeoning student population. How one interprets the historical developments of education, and the suggested proposals for reform, influences what changes will ultimately be implemented. Three such interpretations follow.

Lawrence Cremin   Lawrence A. Cremin's interpretation of U.S. educational history focuses on the development of democratic trends that combined to make American education unique. He determined that by the twentieth century, popularization, "the tendency to make education widely available in forms that are increasingly accessible to diverse peoples," was close to complete. However, one overriding question was yet to be answered. If the schools or educational programs provided to these diverse students are unequal, is quality education accessible to all? The debate over this question continues today.

Attempts to answer this question have also led to concerns about "the proliferation and multiplication of [educational] institutions to provide that wide availability and that increasing accessibility" (1990, vii–viii), what Cremin called multitudinousness. In the twentieth century it became increasingly clear that children's educational needs differ and that not all of them will benefit equally from the same curriculum. Therefore, a growing variety of educational opportunities was offered to the diverse U.S. school population. The schools of today continue this trend but not without inconsistencies and controversies around the country.

Concerns about the equality of educational opportunity and the diversity of that opportunity to meet the needs of different populations have increased the politicization of American schools. Cremin defines politicization as "the effort to solve certain social problems indirectly through education instead of directly through politics" (1990, viii). Increasingly, twentieth-century schools were expected to solve many social problems. And, when they were unable to, they were repeatedly criticized.

Of course, there are interpretations of education in the twentieth century other than Cremin's democratic approach. The work of neo-Marxist revisionist historian Joel Spring is most notable. In two important books, *The American School: 1642–1985* (1986) and *Education and the Rise of the Corporate State* (1972), Spring relates the history of nineteenth- and twentieth-century U.S. education to the capitalistic system. According to Spring, schools will not provide equal opportunities to all until the capitalistic system is changed. Spring believes that the purpose of the U.S. school system is what Ivan Illich calls in the foreword to Spring's 1972 book "social control for a corporate state, and for an economy which has as its goal the efficient production and the disciplined consumption of growing amounts of goods and services" (p. x). According to Spring, it was the progressive educators of the early twentieth century (see chapter 5, pp. 150–152) who promoted the rhetoric of schools as a cure for social and economic problems. However, these progressivists, says Spring, were "labor leaders, corporation heads, financiers, politicians, political philosophers, and educators" (1972, xii). They saw the "good society" as "a highly organized and smoothly working corporate structure" (p. xi). This image of society, affirms Spring, shaped and formed the image of twentieth-century public education.

Joel Spring—A Revisionist View

Some of Spring's work is based on the revisionist work of historian Michael Katz in *The Irony of Early School Reform* (1968). He claimed that historians had helped to perpetuate a "noble story" of an enlightened working class led by idealistic humanitarian intellectuals "wresting free public education from . . . selfish, wealthy elite and from the bigoted proponents of orthodox religions" (1968, 1), and he asserted that this interpretation was false. Katz arrived at this conclusion by examining the 1860 conflict of Beverly, Massachusetts, voters involving the establishment of a high school. He found that working-class groups voted against it while the well-to-do of the community worked actively for it. He also found that those who lived outside the town opposed a high school serving the entire district. He used his analysis of this 1860 decision to produce a new examination of the common school reforms (see chapter 5) and claimed that the impetus for the common school movement had to do with social and economic conditions of the time: the rise of factories, increase in immigration, and growth of cities. According to Katz, upper-class educational reformers benefited from the development of a common school system that was designed to train workers for factories and inculcate immigrants with the values of the ruling elite. Thus, the factory-like schools that Katz claimed existed in the late nineteenth century were such by design.

Michael Katz

The interpretations of U.S. educational history by Cremin, Spring, and Katz serve as a backdrop for the numerous studies and proposals for educational reform that have characterized much of the twentieth century. This chapter will examine the major influences on education in the twentieth century and some of the major suggestions for reform.

(continued on p. 162)

VIEWPOINTS

The 6-Lesson Schoolteacher

Call me Mr. Gatto, please. Twenty-six years ago, having nothing better to do, I tried my hand at schoolteaching. My license certifies me as an instructor of English language and literature, but that isn't what I do at all. What I teach is school, and I win awards doing it.

Teaching means many different things, but six lessons are common to school-teaching from Harlem to Hollywood. You pay for these lessons in more ways than you can imagine, so you might as well know what they are:

The first lesson I teach is: "Stay in the class where you belong." I don't know who decides that my kids belong there but that's not my business. The children are numbered so that if any get away they can be returned to the right class. Over the years the variety of ways children are numbered has increased dramatically, until it is hard to see the human being under the burden of numbers he carries. Numbering children is a big and very profitable business, though what the business is designed to accomplish is elusive. . . .

The lesson of numbered classes is that there is no way out of your class except by magic. Until that happens you must stay where you are put.

The second lesson I teach kids is to turn on and off like a light switch. I demand that they become totally involved in my lessons, jumping up and down in their seats with anticipation, competing vigorously with each other for my favor. But when the bell rings I insist that they drop the work at once and proceed quickly to the next work station. Nothing important is ever finished in my class, nor in any other class I know of.

The lesson of bells is that no work is worth finishing, so why care too deeply about anything? Bells are the secret logic of schooltime; their argument is inexorable; bells destroy the past and future, converting every interval into a same-ness, as an abstract map makes every living mountain and river the same even though they are not. Bells inoculate each undertaking with indifference.

The third lesson I teach you is to surrender your will to a predestined chain of command. Rights may be granted or withheld, by authority, without appeal. As a schoolteacher I intervene in many personal decisions, issuing a Pass for those I deem legitimate, or initiating a disciplinary confrontation for behavior that threatens my control. My judgments come thick and fast, because individuality is trying constantly to assert itself in my classroom. Individuality is a curse to all systems of classification, a contradiction of class theory.

Here are some common ways it shows up: children sneak away for a private moment in the toilet on the pretext of moving their bowels; they trick me out of a private instant in the hallway on the grounds that they need water. Sometimes free will appears right in front of me in children angry, depressed or exhilarated by things outside my ken. . . .

The fourth lesson I teach is that only *I* determine what curriculum you will study (rather, I enforce decisions transmitted by the people who pay me). This power lets me separate good kids from bad kids instantly. Good kids do the tasks I appoint with a minimum of conflict and a decent show of enthusiasm. Of the millions of things of value to learn, I decide what few we have time for. The choices are mine. Curiosity has no important place in my work, only conformity. . . .

This is another way I teach the lesson of dependency. *Good people wait for a teacher to tell them what to do.* This is the most important lesson of all, that we must wait for other people, better trained than ourselves, to make the meanings of our lives. It is no exaggeration to say that our entire economy depends upon this lesson being learned. Think of what would fall apart if kids weren't trained in the dependency lesson: The social-service businesses could hardly survive, including the fast-growing counseling industry; commercial entertainment of all sorts, along with television, would wither if people remembered how to make their own fun; the food services, restaurants and prepared-food warehouses would shrink if people returned to making their own meals rather than depending on strangers to cook for them. Much of modern law, medicine, and engineering would go, too—unless a guaranteed supply of helpless people poured out of our schools each year. We've built a way of life that depends on people doing what they are told because they don't know any other way. For God's sake, let's not rock *that* boat!

In lesson five I teach that your self-respect should depend on an observer's measure of your worth. My kids are constantly evaluated and judged. A monthly report, impressive in its precision, is sent into students' homes to spread approval or to mark exactly—down to a single percentage point—how dissatisfied with their children parents should be. Although some people might be surprised how little time or reflection goes into making up these records, the cumulative weight of the objective-seeming documents establishes a profile of defect which compels a child to arrive at certain decisions about himself and his future based on the casual judgment of strangers. . . .

In lesson six I teach children that they are being watched. I keep each student under constant surveillance and so do my colleagues. There are no private spaces for children; there is no private time. Class change lasts 300 seconds to keep promiscuous fraternization at low levels. . . .

The lesson of constant surveillance is that no one can be trusted, that privacy is not legitimate. Surveillance is an ancient urgency among certain influential thinkers; it was a central prescription set down by Calvin in the *Institutes*, by Plato in the *Republic*, by Hobbes, by Comte, by Francis Bacon. . . .

None of this is inevitable, you know. None of it is impregnable to change. We do have a choice in how we bring up young people—there is no one right way. There is no "international competition" that compels our existence, difficult as that is to even think about in the face of a constant media barrage of myth to the contrary. In every important material respect our nation is self-sufficient. If we gained a non-material philosophy that found meaning where it is genuinely located—in families, friends, the passage of seasons, in nature, in simple ceremonies and rituals, in curiosity, generosity, compassion, and service to others, in a decent independence and privacy—then we would be truly self-sufficient.

How did these awful places, these "schools," come about? As we know them, they are a by-product of the two "Red Scares" of 1848 and 1919, when powerful interests feared a revolution among our industrial poor, and partly they are the result of the revulsion with which old-line families regarded the waves of Celtic, Slavic, and Latin immigration—and the Catholic religion—after 1845. And certainly a third contributing cause can be found in the revulsion with which these same families regarded the free movement of Africans through the society after the Civil War.

Look again at the six lessons of school. This is training for permanent underclasses, people who are to be deprived forever of finding the center of their own special genius. And it is training shaken loose from even its own original logic—to regulate the poor. Since the 1920s the growth of the well-articulated school bureaucracy, and the less visible growth of a horde of industries that profit from schooling exactly as it is, have enlarged schooling's original grasp to seize the sons and daughters of the middle class.

From: Gatto, 1991

POLITICIZATION OF SCHOOLS IN THE EARLY TWENTIETH CENTURY

There is no doubt that the schools of the late nineteenth century provided the impetus for social change. During that period educators and politicians believed that education could have a positive impact on society. From this belief came social programs such as Hull House (see chapter 5, p. 150), the progressive education movement (see chapter 5, pp. 150–152), and the NEA's seven cardinal principles (see chapter 5, p. 149).

The belief in the school as a tool for social change continued in the early twentieth century. However, the needs of society were changing. It was time to see how the schools could help the nation recover from World War I (1914–1918) and later help the country survive the Great Depression.

Curriculum of the Post–World War I Period

In order to facilitate these social goals, educators made many changes in the high school curriculum early in the twentieth century. In *An Introduction to the Study of Education* (1925), Elwood P. Cubberley points out that it was crowded with new courses designed to prepare students for college and/or for jobs. As an increasingly diverse population attended both elementary and high schools for the first time in the history of U.S. education, the curriculum adapted its aims and purposes to the needs of this population.

Emphasis was placed on the development of citizenship, guidance services, school health services, and vocational education. During this period, the schools developed programs in which nurses and teachers visited the homes of pupils experiencing problems in school. In addition to curricular changes, extracurricular opportunities were developed and parents became more involved in the schools through organizations such as the Parent-Teacher Association.

PROVIDING EDUCATIONAL INSTITUTIONS FOR A GROWING POPULATION

The Great Depression of the 1930s was very hard on the public school system. Many schools, particularly in rural areas, were closed. Those that remained open did so with fewer teachers, larger classes, decreased support staff, limited curriculums, and outdated materials. While many young males were forced to leave school and get jobs to help support their families, school enrollment during the Great Depression generally increased as adolescents who could not find jobs entered the schools in greater numbers. (From 1929 to 1934, the number of secondary school students grew from 3,911,000 to 5,669,000. The number of high school graduates per one hundred jumped from 26.2 to 39.2.)

Schools were severely handicapped by economic conditions forcing cutbacks in every area. (During the depression, the gross national product dropped by almost half, from $103.1 billion to $55.6 billion in the three years from 1929 to 1932. Personal income fell from $85.9 billion to $47.0 billion; unemployment increased from 3.2 percent to 24.9 percent. Average teachers' salaries fell from $1,420 to $1,227, a decrease of 13.6 percent.) Because the reform of society was an impossible task for a school system barely able to continue operation itself, progressivism, the concept that schools could reform society through a child-centered, experiential approach that focused on the needs of the individual child and the society, was severely criticized.

George Counts, in *Dare the School Build a New Social Order?* (1932), for example, agreed with progressive educators that the schools should take on the task of social reconstruction. However, he contended that progressive education had a class bias according to which only the liberal-minded, upper middle-class parents sent their children to progressive schools. He claimed that if education was to become genuinely progressive, it had to free itself from class bias, take on a more realistic view of every social issue, and establish a total relationship with the community. He challenged the schools to use creative efforts to put "real content" into such terms as democracy, citizenship, and ethical character (1932, 3–7, 9–10).

On the other hand, Robert Hutchins in *No Friendly Voice* (1936) and *Higher Learning in America* (1936) criticized the schools for putting too much emphasis on preparation for the future. He proposed general schooling for all based on the classic disciplines of grammar, rhetoric, logic, mathematics, and the great books of the Western world. He took issue with the progressive educator's contention that education must be adapted to the needs of society at a particular time.

Curriculum Moves Toward Multitudinousness

World War I and the Great Depression had convinced the public of the need for more practical courses in the schools to prepare students for jobs. In 1917 the Smith-Hughes Vocational Education Act (P.L. 64–347) provided funding for states to create agricultural and vocational education programs. These courses helped retain many students who would have previously found the college-bound curriculum of the high schools impractical for their career needs.

Ironically, during the Great Depression of the 1930s, more students, particularly young women, remained in school than ever before because jobs were unavailable. However, most of these students needed to obtain jobs upon graduation. Consequently, the secondary curriculum, although still content oriented and primarily designed for college-bound students, shifted its emphasis away from the strictly intellectual to the practical. This was the first actual move of the schools toward multitudinousness, an attempt to develop school programs that were appropriate for various segments of society.

The schools still hadn't established accessibility for all students, however. There was a great deal of difference in the educational opportunities available to poor and rich students. High school students of the 1930s had limited diversification of secondary curriculums. They allowed either for occupational training or for college preparation. Lower socioeconomic students spent less time in school, participated in fewer extracurricular activities, and took fewer college preparatory courses. According to a series of studies by W. Lloyd Warner, Robert J. Havighurst, and Martin B. Loeb, repeated in *Who Shall Be Educated?* (1944), "The lower class is almost immediately brushed off into a bin labeled 'nonreaders,' 'first grade repeaters,' or 'opportunity class,' where they stay for eight years and then are released through a chute to the outside world to become 'hewers of wood and drawers of water' " (p. 38). The issue of accessibility of education for rich and poor alike continues to be a problem.

Post–World War I School Populations

With few exceptions, students who went to high school prior to and immediately following World War I had been carefully selected by their elementary school teachers, who had firm standards of achievement. Admission to U.S. high schools was selective and retention depended on the students' scholastic records.

After World War I this situation began to change. The child labor laws, which removed children from the work force, and compulsory attendance laws, which required children to attend school, were enforced for the first time, increasing elementary school enrollment. This new heterogeneous school population, in which only a minority of students would attend college, forced the schools toward a more diverse curriculum.

EDUCATION OF THE POST–WORLD WAR II PERIOD

World War II paved the road to economic recovery after the Depression; it instilled a belief in the technological superiority of the United States and it brought newfound economic prosperity to the population as industry retooled after the war. Politicians and the public depended on the schools to educate students to develop a new technologically and scientifically superior society.

New Scientific Impetus The needs of a society at war magnified the necessity for an educational system that equipped students for scientific research. The gigantic leaps made in scientific knowledge, such as the development of the atomic bomb, led to further discoveries in the fields of mathematics and physics and changed the industrial emphasis of the postwar economy. A greater value was placed on scientific research, and more and more industries needed employees trained in the hard sciences and mathematics.

Soviet Sputnik

With the launching of the world's first Earth-orbiting satellite, Sputnik, by the Soviet Union in 1957, the feeling of U.S. scientific superiority vanished almost overnight. Criticism of U.S. schools, especially of the progressive philosophy, gained new momentum. It centered on the fact that inadequate numbers of people were being trained to meet the technological needs of an increasingly specialized industrial nation. A direct result of this realization and a fear that the United States would lose its superiority over the Soviet Union in the cold war was the passage of the National Defense Education Act (NDEA), P.L. 85–864, in 1958. It expanded the federal government's role in education by providing categorical aid to improve instruction in science, mathematics, and foreign languages. The federal funds were to be used to develop new curriculums, improve teacher training, purchase equipment for the target subject areas, and supply fellowships and low-interest loans to needy college students. The act was based on the assumption that the defense of the United States depended upon the population's mastery of modern scientific techniques, scientific principles, and new scientific knowledge, and that more adequate educational opportunities must be provided to talented students.

Child labor laws of the early twentieth century brought more children into the public schools who previously would have worked in the factories. Not only greater numbers, but greater heterogeneity caused the schools to provide a diverse curriculum.

Criticisms of the schools were heard in Senate hearings of the late 1950s. Werner von Braun, a German-educated missile expert, testified in 1958 urging the elimination of such courses as "family life" and "human relations," developed during the early years of the twentieth century to meet the needs of students and society, and adoption of the European system of education which, according to von Braun, emphasized technical and scientific subjects and academic excellence. Lee DuBridge, president of California Institute of Technology, testifying before the same Senate committee, recommended that science and mathematics courses be given federal support.

University academicians were the most powerful critics of the curriculum. Arthur Bestor, a University of Illinois historian and author of *The Restoration of Learning* (1956), was particularly critical of a curriculum that attempted to meet the social needs of students. He proposed a systematic study within individual disciplines with history as the central discipline. According to Bestor, it was not the job of the school to meet the needs of its students; that was the responsibility of the home.

Columbia University's historian Richard Hofstadter was an even more verbal critic. In *Anti-Intellectualism in American Life* (1963) he decried the availability of public education to all youth. Hofstadter was criticizing the popularization of education that had been the predominant theme throughout most of U.S. education's history. According to Hofstadter, the only aim of secondary education should be development of the mind, not the education of the masses.

Critical Commissions and Reports

6.1   POINTS TO REMEMBER

- During the twentieth century, U.S. schools were increasingly moving toward popularization. The diverse school population was beginning to require a multitude of offerings. Educators believed that the schools had the ability to affect society through politicization.

- World War I led to a greater need for students to enter the work force. Consequently, the curriculum of the high schools became more and more practical.
- The Great Depression depleted many resources of the public schools. However, since students could not find jobs, the enrollment in schools increased.

- During World War II, industry relied increasingly on science. Consequently, the schools were called upon to improve the teaching of science and mathematics.
- The launching of Sputnik resulted in increased demands on the public schools to train students in mathematics and science.

THE CIVIL RIGHTS PERIOD

The changes in the school population and the developing emphasis in society on equal rights for all citizens led to what Cremin called multitudinousness in the public schools. Although the trend toward providing unique opportunities for different students could be seen as early as the NEA's seven cardinal principles of 1918, the beginnings of coeducation in the high schools, and the addition of courses in agriculture and industrial arts following World War I, it was not until the civil rights period, narrowly defined as occurring between 1955 and 1968, that broad-based opportunities for a heterogeneous population became the central theme of public education.

Synergy of Educational Themes

Although multitudinousness dominates this period of educational history, all the characteristics of education identified by Lawrence Cremin occurred simultaneously for the first time. The schools were increasingly popularized, thereby making education widely available to diverse people. To meet their needs, the schools developed many options and to bring the disenfranchised minorities into the mainstream of society, the schools were increasingly politicized, thereby encouraging social change indirectly through education.

The Education of Minorities: Inequalities

While schools were gradually embracing the democratic ideal of equal education for all citizens, in practice many inequities still existed. In *Plessy v. Ferguson*, 163 U.S. 537 (1896), for example, the Supreme Court ruled in favor of the principle of "separate but equal," implying that students in equal educational facilities were able to attain equal opportunities even if they were separated by race. However, studies of schools from the late nineteenth through the mid-twentieth century show that they were not equal.

In 1945, for example, South Carolina spent three times as much on education for white students as it spent on black students, even though blacks outnumbered whites. Facilities were unequal; educational levels of teachers were unequal; materials were unequal.

Table 6.1 on page 168 clearly shows that the percentage of white students completing four years of high school has always been higher than the percentage of black students, and the difference was particularly great prior to the integration of schools in the 1960s and 1970s. Since the early 1980s the gap has narrowed, but statistics like these make it evident that separate was not necessarily equal.

Funding

All these inequalities can be attributed, in part, to the amount of money spent. In the area of transportation, for example, in 1945 South Carolina spent one-one-hundredth as much to transport blacks as it spent to transport whites, even though the distances from black homes to schools were longer than the distances from white homes to schools. It was not unusual to find that black schools were supplied with discarded textbooks, furniture, and equipment from white schools. If separate meant unequal funding, how could schools be considered equal?

The U.S. Supreme Court recognized inequalities of educational opportunities in the landmark *Brown v. Board of Education of Topeka, Kansas*, 347 U.S. 483 (1954) case, in which it ruled that "separate is not equal." The Court said in its majority opinion: "Separate but equal has no place. . . . Separate educational facilities are inherently unequal and violate the equal protection clause of the Fourteenth Amendment." Perhaps the most vital issue in the decision, according to Chief Justice Earl Warren, was the psychological effect that racial separation had on minority children. It "generates a feeling of inferiority as to their status in the community that may affect their hearts and minds in a way unlikely to be undone." At the time of the *Brown* decision, approximately 40 percent of public school students were enrolled in segregated systems.

Academic Opportunity

After the *Brown* decision, the problem became how to enforce integration. On May 31, 1955, the Supreme Court ruled in a second *Brown* decision that the implementation of desegregation of these schools was to be left to local school authorities, subject to the supervision of federal district judges. This ushered in a period of unrest and confusion, with many local authorities and district judges opposed to the rulings of the Court and unwilling to enforce them. Those students who attended the newly integrated schools frequently found that even they did not necessarily ensure equal educational opportunity.

In 1966 James Coleman conducted a study of schools ordered by the U.S. Congress to determine what recommendations could be made for improving minority education. The study consisted of 645,000 students in grades 1, 3, 6, 9, and 12 in 4,000 schools from five geographic regions. He found that in 1965, 65 percent of all black students in grade 1 attended schools that were 90–100 percent black, and 66 percent in grade 12 attended schools that were 50 percent black. Almost 80 percent of all white students in grades 1–12 attended schools that were 90–100 percent white. He found that blacks in the rural South and whites in the urban Northeast began school much further apart intellectually than blacks and whites in the urban Northeast. Not only did the gap not change during the school years, but in many instances, it widened.

After studying the test results, Coleman concluded that the foremost contributing factor to this eventual gap, and to initial student achievement, was the educational and social background of their families. The second most important factor was the educational and social background of the other

(continued on p. 170)

TABLE 6-1

Years of School Completed by Persons Age 25 and Over and 25 to 29, by Race: 1910 to 1989

Race, age, and date	Percent, by years of school completed			Median school years completed
	Less than 5 years of elementary school	4 years of high school or more	4 or more years of college	
1	*2*	*3*	*4*	*5*
ALL RACES				
25 and over				
1910[1]	23.8	13.5	2.7	8.1
1920[1]	22.0	16.4	3.3	8.2
1930[1]	17.5	19.1	3.9	8.4
April 1940	13.7	24.5	4.6	8.6
April 1950	11.1	34.3	6.2	9.3
April 1960	8.3	41.1	7.7	10.5
March 1970	5.3	55.2	11.0	12.2
March 1975	4.2	62.5	13.9	12.3
March 1980	3.4	68.6	17.0	12.5
March 1982	3.0	71.0	17.7	12.6
March 1985	2.7	73.9	19.4	12.6
March 1986	2.7	74.7	19.4	12.6
March 1987	2.4	75.6	19.9	12.7
March 1988	2.4	76.2	20.3	12.7
March 1989	2.5	76.8	21.1	12.7
25 to 29				
April 1940	5.9	38.1	5.9	10.3
April 1950	4.6	52.8	7.7	12.1
April 1960	2.8	60.7	11.0	12.3
March 1970	1.1	75.4	16.4	12.6
March 1975	1.0	83.1	21.9	12.8
March 1980	0.8	85.4	22.5	12.9
March 1982	0.8	86.2	21.7	12.8
March 1985	0.7	86.1	22.2	12.9
March 1986	0.9	86.1	22.4	12.9
March 1987	0.9	86.0	22.0	12.8
March 1988	1.0	85.9	22.7	12.8
WHITE[2]				
25 and over				
April 1940	10.9	26.1	4.9	8.7
April 1950	8.9	36.4	6.6	9.7
April 1960	6.7	43.2	8.1	10.8
March 1970	4.2	57.4	11.6	12.2
March 1975	3.3	64.5	14.5	12.4
March 1980	2.6	70.5	17.8	12.5
March 1982	2.4	72.8	18.5	12.6
March 1985	2.2	75.5	20.0	12.7
March 1986	2.2	76.2	20.1	12.7
March 1987	2.0	77.0	20.5	12.7
March 1988	2.0	77.7	20.9	12.7
March 1989	2.0	78.3	21.7	12.7

Race, age, and date	Percent, by years of school completed			Median school years completed
	Less than 5 years of elementary school	4 years of high school or more	4 or more years of college	
1	*2*	*3*	*4*	*5*
WHITE[2] (continued)				
25 to 29				
1920[1]	12.9	22.0	4.5	8.5
April 1940	3.4	41.2	6.4	10.7
April 1950	3.3	56.3	8.2	12.2
April 1960	2.2	63.7	11.8	12.3
March 1970	0.9	77.8	17.3	12.6
March 1975	1.0	84.4	22.8	12.8
March 1980	0.8	86.9	23.7	12.9
March 1982	0.8	86.9	22.7	12.9
March 1985	0.8	86.8	23.2	12.9
March 1986	0.9	86.5	23.5	12.9
March 1987	0.8	86.3	23.0	12.9
March 1988	1.0	86.6	23.5	12.9
BLACK AND OTHER RACES[2]				
25 and over				
April 1940	41.8	7.7	1.3	5.7
April 1950	32.6	13.7	2.2	6.9
April 1960	23.5	21.7	3.5	8.2
March 1970	14.7	36.1	6.1	10.1
March 1975	11.7	46.4	9.2	11.4
March 1980	8.8	54.6	11.1	12.2
March 1982	7.4	58.1	12.4	12.3
March 1985	6.0	63.2	15.4	12.4
March 1986	5.5	65.3	15.2	12.4
March 1987	5.1	66.7	15.7	12.4
March 1988	5.1	66.7	16.4	12.5
March 1989	5.6	67.0	16.8	12.5
25 to 29				
1920[1]	44.6	6.3	1.2	5.4
April 1940	27.0	12.3	1.6	7.1
April 1950	16.1	23.6	2.8	8.7
April 1960	7.2	38.6	5.4	10.8
March 1970	2.2	58.4	10.0	12.2
March 1975	0.7	73.8	15.4	12.6
March 1980	1.0	77.0	15.2	12.7
March 1982	0.7	82.2	15.8	12.8
March 1985	0.5	82.4	16.7	12.8
March 1986	0.9	84.3	16.3	12.8
March 1987	1.1	84.1	16.9	12.8
March 1988	1.2	82.0	18.1	12.6

[1]Estimates based on retrojection, by the Bureau of Census, of the 1940 census data on education by age.

[2]Persons of Hispanic origin are included as appropriate in the "White" or in the "Black and other races" category.

Note—Data for 1975 and subsequent years are for noninstitutional populations. Some data have been revised from previously published figures.

From: National Center for Education Statistics, *Digest of Education Statistics* (Washington, DC: U.S. Department of Education, 1990), (NCES) 91–660, p. 17.

This table graphically compares the years of schooling achieved by whites and blacks and other races. While the percentage of all races completing four years of high school has risen dramatically over the years, there is still a wide gap between the percentage of whites and blacks and other races who do.

children in their school. These two factors were greater contributors to achievement, according to Coleman, than the school, facilities, curriculum, or teachers. He declared that to overcome the disadvantages of a poorer educational and social background, schools must be integrated.

De Facto Segregation

Integration did not necessarily ensure equal educational opportunities. In fact, many researchers contended that opportunities were at least as unequal as they had been before segregation. In its 1967 and 1969 decisions, *Hobson v. Hansen* (269 F. Supp. 401 CDDC, 1967) and *Smuck v. Hobson* (408 F. 2d 175 CDC Cir., 1969) and its reconsideration of *Hobson v. Hansen* (327 F. Supp. 844 CDDC, 1971) in 1971, the U.S. Supreme Court found that the Washington, D.C., schools used tracking as a way to ensure **de facto segregation**. This was a subtle though legal means of ensuring that segregation was continued in a school or a district. The Court found, for example, that minority students were usually placed in a low ability track as early as kindergarten, and few students moved from that track by high school graduation, if they graduated at all. The judges found that the education offered to students in the low track was inferior to education offered to students in average and upper tracks; it did not push them to higher levels of achievement. As a matter of fact, students in the lower track received little stimulation or curricular enrichment and counseling was ineffective in directing them to appropriate tracks.

EQUALIZING EDUCATIONAL OPPORTUNITY

Despite the failure of the schools to provide a completely equal education for all children, the attitude of Americans toward minorities had begun to change in the late 1950s and early 1960s. It was primarily through a series of legislative acts that some changes were instituted in the educational system.

Economic Opportunity Act and Head Start

As part of President Lyndon B. Johnson's War on Poverty, Congress passed the Economic Opportunity Act (EOA) (P.L. 88–452) in 1964. It was designed to help bridge the gap between poverty and prosperity by giving everyone the opportunity for education and training for work, and the chance to live in decency and dignity. This antipoverty bill authorized the creation of the Job Corps, whereby men and women, ages sixteen through twenty-one, could work in conservation camps and training centers. EOA also authorized funding for work-training programs and Volunteers in Service to America (VISTA). Modeled after the Peace Corps, VISTA was designed to provide community service projects for economically poor communities. Also funded under EOA were work-study programs for college students; community action programs to allow state and local governments to develop employment opportunities; adult education grants for those who could not read or write; and loans for low-income families, migrant worker programs, and business incentives.

Head Start, which evolved as a result of the Community Action Programs of EOA, was a comprehensive child development program for four- and five-

(continued on p. 172)

V I E W P O I N T S

Savage Inequalities

I visit P.S. 79, another elementary school in the same district [the North Bronx]. "We work under difficult circumstances," says the principal, James Carter, who is black. "The school was built to hold one thousand students. We have 1,550. We are badly overcrowded. We need smaller classes but, to do this, we would need more space. I can't add five teachers. I would have no place to put them."

Some experts, I observe, believe that class size isn't a real issue. He dismisses this abruptly. "It doesn't take a genius to discover that you learn more in a smaller class. I have to bus some 60 kindergarten children elsewhere, since I have no space for them. When they return next year, where do I put them?

"I can't set up a computer lab. I have no room. I had to put a class into the library. I have no librarian. There are two gymnasiums upstairs but they cannot be used for sports. We hold more classes there. It's unfair to measure us against the suburbs. They have 17 to 20 children in a class. Average class size in this school is 30.

"The school is 29 percent black, 70 percent Hispanic. Few of these kids get Head Start. There is no space in the district. Of 200 kindergarten children, 50 maybe get some kind of preschool.". . .

The school tracks children by ability, he says. "There are five to seven levels in each grade. The highest level is equivalent to 'gifted' but it's not a full-scale gifted program. We don't have the funds. We have no science room. The science teachers carry their equipment with them."

We sit and talk within the nurse's room. The window is broken. There are two holes in the ceiling. About a quarter of the ceiling has been patched and covered with a plastic garbage bag.

"Ideal class size for these kids would be 15 to 20. Will these children ever get what white kids in the suburbs take for granted? I don't think so. If you ask me why, I'd have to speak of race and social class. I don't think the powers that be in New York City understand, or want to understand, that if they do not give these children a sufficient education to lead healthy and productive lives, we will be their victims later on. We'll pay the price someday—in violence, in economic costs. I despair of making this appeal in any terms but these. You cannot issue an appeal to conscience in New York today. . . .

While we talk, three children who look six or seven years old come to the door and ask to see the nurse, who isn't in the school today. One of the children, a Puerto Rican girl, looks haggard. "I have a pain in my tooth," she says. The principal says, "The nurse is out. Why don't you call your mother?" The child says, "My mother doesn't have a phone." The principal sighs. "Then go back to your class." When she leaves, the principal is angry. "It's amazing to me that these children ever make it with the obstacles they face. Many *do* care and they *do* try, but there's a feeling of despair. The parents of these children want the same things for their children that the parents in the suburbs want. Drugs are not the cause of this. They are the symptom. Nonetheless, they're used by people in the suburbs and rich people in Manhattan as another reason to keep children of poor people at a distance."

I ask him, "Will white children and black children ever go to school together in New York?"

"I don't see it," he replies. "I just don't think it's going to happen. It's a dream. I simply do not see white folks in Riverdale agreeing to cross-bus with kids like these. A few, maybe. Very few. I don't think I'll live to see it happen."

From: Kozol, 1991, 88–90

Head Start was developed under the Economic Opportunity Act of 1964 to help bridge the educational gap that developed between children of poverty and children of comfortable or prosperous means even before they started school.

year-olds from low-income homes. It addressed the mental and physical health and intellectual development of children in poverty. Half a million children were initially enrolled in Head Start preschool programs during the summer of 1965, and from 1966 through 1970 an additional 200,000–300,000 were enrolled annually.

Studies of Head Start children drew conflicting results. A 1968 Westinghouse Learning Corporation and Ohio University study compared differences in intellectual and social-personal development between first, second, and third graders who had and had not participated in Head Start programs. The study concluded that summer-only Head Start programs were ineffective in producing lasting gains in either **affective** (value) or **cognitive** (intellectual) **development** and that year-long programs were ineffective in aiding affective development and only marginally effective in producing cognitive gains. Head Start children were still below national norms on language development tests, but school readiness at grade one did approach the national norms. Another study conducted by Burt S. Barnow for the National Institute of Education of the U.S. Department of Education (1973) revealed different results. This study found that Head Start programs do benefit the cognitive development of minority and white children from mother-headed families.

Studies conducted in the 1970s and 1980s by David Weikart and his colleagues at High/Scope Educational Research Foundation revealed significant results in terms of success of Head Start students in later schooling and ability to obtain and hold employment. In 1984, a study conducted by Raymond Collins reviewed the Head Start research from 1964 through 1984. According to

Collins, a synthesis of all the research convincingly demonstrated that Head Start programs significantly improved the educational attainments and life circumstances of low-income and minority children, especially in cognitive and socioemotional development, child health, and community involvement.

Congress passed the **Elementary and Secondary Education Act (ESEA)** in 1965 (P.L. 89-10). This act and its corollary sections, identified by Titles, may have done more to improve the educational opportunities of all children than any before or since. Long-standing social and economic disadvantages had resulted in great disparities between the educational development of the poor and minorities and those in the middle and upper classes. ESEA helped bring more students into the schools, which in turn created a need for additional facilities to serve the growing student population.

The Elementary and Secondary Education Act: 1965

Title I: Enforcement

Title I of ESEA (1965) mandated a formula by which states and districts, although entitled to a certain amount of money, must make application to receive it. As interpreted by Francis Keppel, then U.S. commissioner of education, it required that schools spend more money for educationally disadvantaged students than for others in order to receive federal funds. Initially, Title I of ESEA received almost 80 percent of the $1.25 billion allocated. Money was provided to local education agencies (school districts) with high concentrations of poverty-level children in the form of basic grants and special incentive grants for programs, projects, equipment, and facilities intended to narrow the intellectual and developmental gap between those who were economically disadvantaged and those who were not. Today, Title I (now Chapter I) is the largest single program of federal aid to education, accounting for approximately 22 percent of the entire Department of Education budget. During 1990-1991, Chapter I provided $5.4 billion to serve approximately 5 million children with special needs. In 1991-1992, there was a 16 percent increase in funding to $6.2 billion (LeTendre 1991, 578).

Title VII: Race and Ethnic Discrimination

Title VII (1974) of ESEA (P.L. 93-517) gave to the Department of Health, Education, and Welfare (HEW) and to the Office of Civil Rights (OCR) the power to reshape aspects of the educational program such as classification practices, testing procedures, guidance and counseling programs, extracurricular activities, disciplinary procedures, special education, instructional methodology, and the curriculum in general in order to balance the schools racially. The basis for this power was the belief that the federal government has the responsibility to ensure that no student be discriminated against because of race or ethnicity.

Title IX: Sex Discrimination

Title IX (1975) of ESEA did for sexual discrimination what Title VII did for racial discrimination. It prohibited schools from discriminating against both women and men in their admission policies and in their classes. Physical education classes had to be integrated by sex but could be segregated for contact sports such as football or wrestling. Schools had to establish women's

Title IX of the Elementary and Secondary Education Act (ESEA) in 1975 provided athletic opportunities for women equal to those that had been provided for men. Title IX was the first instance of equal opportunity for women being addressed by the federal government. One result is that both boys and girls are allowed to play on this junior high school basketball team.

athletic teams in interscholastic, intercollegiate, or intramural sports, but expenditures for women's and men's sports did not have to be equal. The bill barred discrimination on the basis of sex in all aspects of employment in schools including recruitment; leaves of absence; rates of pay and other compensation; fringe benefits; and tuition, training, and sabbatical assistance. Schools were prohibited from barring pregnant women from school or placing them in separate classes unless they specifically requested separation. Schools were required to treat childbirth, termination of pregnancy, and recovery as any other disability. Pregnant women who left school had to be reinstated to the status they held before they left.

For the first time, federal legislation was directly related to the education of women. Part C of Title IX (P.L. 95–561) is known as the Women's Educational Equity Act, passed in 1978:

> The Congress finds and declares that educational programs in the United States, as presently conducted, are frequently inequitable as such programs relate to women and frequently limit the full participation of all individuals in American society. The Congress finds and declares that excellence in education cannot be achieved without equity for women and girls.

Education of the Disadvantaged

The Civil Rights Act of 1964 was the first federal legislation to extend equal educational opportunity to all Americans. In the early 1970s the definition of disadvantaged was broadened by researchers and bureaucrats to include

CROSS-CULTURAL PERSPECTIVE

Australia and Equality of Educational Opportunity

Frequently we think of the schools of Australia as having a similar historic foundation to schools in the United States. However, the underlying themes that have affected U.S. education are quite different from those that have influenced the development of schools in Australia. In *Society, Schools and Progress in Australia*, P. H. Partridge writes,

Now, in spite of what was said . . . about the influence of the idea of equality in the founding of the public school system, Australian social thinking has not on the whole conceived the character and function of the school quite in this way. For one thing, this wider social function of the school has not been so explicitly stated and reiterated in Australian as it has been in American thinking. It might be said, perhaps, that Australian public schools have been traditionally thought of more in terms of what they offer to the individual child, and of the opportunities they open up for him, rather then in terms of the quality of social life—with its implication for the wider life of the community—to which they introduce and habituate him. The notion of the school as being itself a kind of society [as per John Dewey and the progressive movement], impregnated with particular social ideologies and moralities derived from objectives and ideals operative throughout the national society, has not been very conspicuous in modes of educational thought in Australia. This difference perhaps reflects a more general difference between the two nations: American political and social life has been more saturated with ideology, by explicit social ideals, principles, and dogmas, than has Australian, which has been in thought as well as deed more opportunistic, pragmatic, and non-theoretical. It is not surprising that throughout their history Americans have tried more persistently than Australians have done to weave their educational thinking and institutions into the pattern of their wider social ideologies—their attempts to capture in abstract conceptions and principles the essence of the "American way of life."

From: Partridge, 1968

multicultural, bilingual, and disabled students. This resulted in an increase in the number of students defined as having special needs.

Funds for Multicultural Students

The Bilingual Education Act (P.L. 94–247) of 1968 began the trend to expand bilingual programs in schools. This act provided federal funding to those states with large numbers of non–English-speaking students to develop and maintain bilingual programs, provide needed materials and equipment, and develop preservice teacher training. The trend continued in the Supreme Court ruling, *Lau v. Nichols* (483 F 2d 9th Cir., 1973), which stated that schools must help students who "are certain to find their classroom experiences wholly incomprehensible" because they do not understand English. And in the same year, the Denver school system was required by the court in *Keyes v. School District No. 1, Denver* (414 US 883, 1973) to develop a pilot bilingual-bicultural program.

The capstone to providing equal educational opportunities for bilingual students is Title VI (P.L. 93–380) of the 1974 Civil Rights Act, which called for instruction in two languages for children whose native tongue is not English.

> Where inability to speak and understand the English language excludes national origin minority group children from effective participation in the educational program offered by a school district, [it] must take affirmative steps to rectify the language deficiency to open instructional programs to these students.

School districts that did not meet this provision could not be granted federal aid.

Both the Bilingual Acts of 1968 and 1974 caused controversies about the purposes and effects of bilingual education. Should educators help students make transitions to English-speaking classrooms or should they help students develop more fully in their native language and culture? Do bilingual education programs enhance or retard student achievement if and when students enter English-speaking programs?

In spite of these questions, in 1976 California passed legislation requiring all school districts to provide bilingual education for all grades. During the 1970s, Congressional appropriations for bilingual education increased from $7.5 million in 1969 to $158 million in 1979. In 1990, federal funding for bilingual education had increased to over $188 million (see also chapter 13, p. 448).

The Handicapped and P.L. 94–142

The cornerstone of federal policies dealing with students who are mentally and physically disabled as well as those who are learning-disabled is the 1975 Education for All Handicapped Children Act (P.L. 94–142). This act defines disabled students as those who are mentally retarded, hard of hearing or deaf, orthopedically or otherwise health impaired, visually impaired, or emotionally disturbed. It mandates that the schools provide free and appropriate education for these children and those with special learning disabilities.

"Appropriate" programs as defined by P.L. 94–142 required that schools provide specially designed instruction, at no cost to parents or guardians, in the classroom, in the home, or in hospitals and institutions. In addition, schools must offer related services such as transportation, psychological testing, physical and occupational therapy, speech pathology, and medical counseling. An **Individual Education Program (IEP)** is required for each handicapped student. The program must be written and developed by representatives of the local education agency that supervises the special program, the child's teachers, parents or guardians, and, when appropriate, the child.

As often as possible, schools must allow for handicapped students' participation in the regular educational program. This is called **mainstreaming**. Often it requires the removal of barriers such as stairways and narrow hallways. Furthermore, mainstreaming may stipulate that a special teacher attend the regular classes with the disabled student. For example, a teacher who is trained in sign language may attend the class with a deaf student.

Changes in Curriculum To meet the social goal of equal educational opportunity, curricular changes in the 1960s and 1970s moved away from subject orientation toward more emphasis on the needs of the students and society. Many of these changes were affected by federal funding for disenfranchised students, particularly through ESEA and its Titles, P.L. 94–142, and the Civil Rights Act. Some of the curricular revisions that can be indirectly and directly traced to this legislation include

Federal District Judge Jackson L. Kiser ruled in 1991 that the Virginia Military Institute's refusal to admit females does not violate antibias laws. He based his decision on the idea that a military school would, of necessity, have to change its program for females and thus would lose its identity and jeopardize its purpose. The Justice Department, which sued the Institute in 1990 on behalf of a Virginia woman who wanted to apply, is expected to appeal the case.

> (1) adding to existing courses, topics such as environmental protection, drug addiction, black-white inequality, urban problems, aggression and violence, and the meaning of the law; (2) providing educational "alternatives" as a response to the demand for freedom of choice (ranging from the choice of a school with a given curricular focus, to a smorgasbord of electives at the secondary school level, to allowing elementary school pupils to study what interests them); and (3) including out-of-school activities of a social-service nature. (Tanner and Tanner 1975, 365)

These curricular changes occurred at all levels and in all areas of education. One response concerned school architecture, which changed in many schools from self-contained classroom space to more open, flexible space with room for individual study, small and large group work. Frequently, classrooms, especially in elementary schools, had no walls or movable walls. Schools were more open, not only in terms of physical space and student choice, but also in terms of bringing the community to the school or the student to the community. High school students participated in work-release programs, field trips became increasingly common, and parents and a variety of community resource people were frequently seen in classrooms.

It is important to note that many educators believed that many of these changes were counterproductive. The criticisms can be seen in many of the reform reports of the late 1970s and 1980s, which will be discussed later in this chapter.

Point/Counterpoint

SEPARATE INSTITUTIONS ARE EQUAL

In this case the plaintiffs, all males, sued to enjoin the enforcement of a South Carolina state statute that limited admissions to Winthrop College, a state-supported school, to girls. In his opinion, District Court Judge Russell ruled in favor of Winthrop College.

It is clear from the stipulated facts that the state of South Carolina has established a wide range of educational institutions at the college and university level. . . . With two exceptions, such institutions are coeducational. Two, by law, however, limit their student admissions to members of one sex. Thus the Citadel restricts its student admission to males and Winthrop . . . may not admit as a regular degree candidate males. . . . [T]he Citadel . . . is designated a military school. . . . Winthrop, on the other hand, was designed as a school for young ladies, which, though offering a liberal arts program, gave special attention to many courses thought to be specially helpful to female students.

The equal protection clause of the Fourteenth Amendment does not require "identity of treatment" for all citizens, or preclude a state, by legislation, from making classifications and creating differences in the rights of different groups.

From: *William v. McNair* (316 F.Supp. 134 DSC, 1970).

SEPARATE INSTITUTIONS ARE NOT EQUAL

Suppose that South Carolina, in addition to operating one or more racially mixed institutions, should maintain two other colleges. One, Dred Scott Institute, would offer degrees in agriculture, music, dance and physical education; it would accept only black students. The other, Calhoun College, would offer degrees in nuclear physics, medicine, law, engineering and business administration; only whites need apply. Assuming that all of these studies were available at a biracial institution, would such a scheme survive constitutional scrutiny?

It is difficult to see how; indeed, any other answer is unthinkable. And yet, the maintenance of two institutions for the sexes in South Carolina, one for male warriors and the other for female domestics, is different only in that the assumptions it reflects about individual capabilities and aspirations are more widely shared.

From: Johnston, Jr., and Knapp, 1971

POSTSCRIPT

The issue of equal educational opportunity for all will not be easily resolved. In 1991, for example, a federal judge ruled that Virginia Military Institute does not violate antibias laws by refusing to admit women. The decision was based on the fact that admitting women would necessarily change the physical and emotional atmosphere of the institution; it would become inherently different. Officials at the Citadel, a South Carolina military institution for men, concurred with the decision, but many women's groups, and politicians of both sexes, disagreed.

The real difficulty in defining equality of education lies in the difficulty of defining equality itself. What does it mean to be equal? Does equal mean that all individuals must have the right to attend the same educational institution if another one of equal quality is available to them? If institutions are separate, can they be equal? Or are they inherently unequal because the separateness leads to different expectations and opportunities? Does equality of opportunity necessarily guarantee equality of educational excellence?

These questions apply also to separate activities within single institutions. For example, do we limit the potential of especially talented students if we place them in classes with academically weak students? Does total integration provide for equality of opportunity? Or are the opportunities of the able diminished by the increased opportunities of the disabled? Is it equal if sports activities are segregated by sex, if an equal number of sports activities are available to both sexes?

EDUCATION IN THE 1970s AND 1980s: A PERIOD OF CONFLICTS

Education reform in the 1970s and 1980s was marked by struggle and conflict. On the one hand, there was the attempt to ensure equalization of educational opportunities for all students; on the other, there was decreased federal funding for elementary and secondary schools, making impossible an increase in educational programs for the diverse school population. Richard M. Nixon's election in 1969 followed on the heels of violent protests against the war in Vietnam that spilled over into student protests against all forms of authority. In the resulting social confusion, Nixon's administration questioned whether the War on Poverty's legislation, enacted during the administration of Lyndon B. Johnson (1963–1969), had resulted in improved educational conditions for the poor. Thus, Nixon vetoed three compensatory education and desegregation programs, reducing the total budget for public education reform. President Ronald W. Reagan's (1981–1988) conservative approach to federal spending resulted in a further shift of funding from the federal government to the states. Reagan contended that since the schools were controlled by the states, the states should be responsible for funding public education. They, however, did not always have the funding necessary to implement the various stipulations of the Elementary and Secondary Education Act and the Civil Rights Act.

Equal Access

In an attempt to determine if ESEA had made an early impact on equalizing educational opportunities, a study ("A Reassessment of the Effect of Family and Schooling in America") was conducted by Christopher Jencks and seven associates from 1968 to 1971. The results compared test scores, educational attainment, occupational status, and income level in different schools. They found that "qualitative differences between schools had relatively little impact on students' test scores, especially at the high school level" (Jencks 1972, 146). Likewise, they found that differences among schools had little to do with a student's eventual educational attainment. Rather, the most important determinants of level of educational attainment were a family's socioeconomic background and cognitive skill, the ability to think, reason, and solve problems.

Their study also found that access to education was far more equal for children between the ages of six and sixteen than for older or younger children. If the results of their study are accurate, they confirm the conclusion of an earlier study by James Coleman (1966) that differences in the school had little impact on student achievement. However, he did find that for average white students, achievement was less influenced by the strengths and weaknesses of the school than for average minority students. Coleman, like Jencks, contended that inequality of educational opportunity was more pronounced before age six, when the child enters school, and after age sixteen, when the child leaves or continues school.

John Goodlad, in his 1984 study of thirty-eight elementary, middle, and junior and senior high schools, stated that the central issue of equality of educational opportunity in the 1980s was no longer access to schools but access to knowledge. His studies found, for example, that **tracking**, or ability grouping, which separates students by academic ability, often in early elementary school, limits equal access to knowledge. In other words, according to Goodlad, students of the mid-1980s may have had approximately equal opportunity to attend school but not equal access to knowledge in that school.

Minorities and The Handicapped

The question of equal access to knowledge also involved programs for those with disabilities. Many studies of the 1980s called into question whether P.L. 94–142 was giving equal access to knowledge to all students or was actually limiting it for some disabled students. On the one hand, studies by Mary Moore, L. Walker, and R. Holland (1982) and Margaret Wang, Maynard Reynolds, and Herbert Walberg (1986) concluded that the implementation of P.L. 94–142 had resulted in more equal and appropriate access to education for all disabled students. However, other studies, such as one in 1982 by Kurt Heller, Wayne Holtzman, and Susan Messick, found that there was a disproportionate number of minority and male children in special education programs. This study posed some difficult questions: Are minority males more likely to be emotionally or mentally disabled than any other group of students? Or is placement based on some other factor, such as behavior? Does this placement limit their access to regular academic programs and knowledge? Barbara K. Keogh (1983) determined that classification of students for special education programs was often influenced by factors other than the children's needs, such as availability of staff; availability of space; and federal, state, and local guidelines and pressures.

Comparisons of students in special education programs across the states call into question whether the placement of minorities in these programs may limit their access to regular academic programs. Since P.L. 94–142, states with greater minority populations have tended to have more students placed in special education programs. In Utah, a state with a relatively homogeneous population, for example, there was a 1.5 percent increase in students classified as learning disabled between 1977 and 1981, while in Washington, D.C., a city with a very large minority population, there was a 40 percent increase (Moore, Walker, and Holland 1982). In Washington state there was a 5 percent decrease in students enrolled in emotionally disabled programs from 1977–1978 through 1980–1981, while in Mississippi during the same period, there was a 49 percent increase. If these studies are correct, and if the educators and researchers who claim special education students do not have equal access to knowledge are also correct, it may be that P.L. 94–142, which was designed to provide equal access to all those with disabilities regardless of severity, may be, in fact, limiting access for some of those who are only mildly disabled.

In addition, Mara Shevin (1989) reported that the proliferation of new categories in special education, such as mildly disabled and mildly retarded, may keep many students out of the regular classroom from which they could profit more. Researchers suggest that the criteria for success in programs for disabled students should be: How many master the competencies of required high school course work? How many leave school as independent, well-educated young adults? How many find jobs to match their talents (Gloeckler and Cianca 1986, 30)?

Funding Other studies indicated an inequality of resources within and among states (Keppel 1966; Stern 1987; Bastian et al. 1986) and questioned if education can be equal if resources for education are not. In 1963 the average real expenditure per pupil per state was between $317 and $867 a year; in 1969 between $1,402 and $3,715 a year; in 1984 between $2,220 and $7,482 a year; and in 1987 between $2,718 and $7,971 a year. The more prosperous the state, the more spent on education.

Francis Keppel in *The Necessary Revolution in American Education* (1966) reported that the way schools are funded has meant that richer school districts get richer, while poorer school districts get poorer. This, according to Keppel, is due to a funding system, called "foundation," in which the states are required to spend equal amounts of money for each student. Local school districts are then required to levy property taxes for their share of the foundation amount. Thus, the poorer the district, the poorer the property values, and the lower the revenue produced for schools. The foundation system of funding, although challenged by the courts in several states, remains firmly in place.

There is significant debate about whether dollars spent per pupil have anything to do with educational equality. The debate revolves around the definition of educational equality. On the one hand, those who claim that equality can be measured by the attainments of students assert that dollars spent have little to do with educational equality. On the other, those who contend that equality relates to the distribution of democratic opportunity believe that dollars spent do relate to educational equality (see also chapter 15).

Amy Gutman, a Princeton University researcher, in *Democratic Education* (1987), and Jean Allen, editor of *Business/Education Insider* (1991), exemplify the two sides of the issue. Allen refutes the claim of the Louisiana League of Women Voters in its call for higher spending to improve education in the state, which in 1991 was forty-third in state spending for education with test scores well below national norms: "Studies on school spending conducted within the past two years find no correlation between student achievement and higher spending to reduce class sizes, raise teacher salaries, or construct new buildings" (1991, 2).

Gutman states that the Coleman study, *Report on Equality of Educational Opportunity* (1966), and the Jencks study, *Inequality* (1972)—on which most subsequent studies on financing and school equality have been based—found that differences in spending among schools could not account for differences in average attainment of students. But they failed to look at how these school districts distributed funding among the children. For example, she claimed that the findings "cannot be used to conclude that significant changes in the internal organization of schools—for example, assigning the most experienced and highly paid teachers to the least advantaged children—would make no difference" (1987, 152). Rather, funding makes a great deal of difference to the attainment of equal opportunity. Funding provides access to the most recent, most up-to-date textbooks, adequate libraries, and the best teachers. Hence, according to this argument, equality should be measured by whether the students' educational opportunities are equal rather than by standardized tests and subsequent income attainment.

Entry Into the Work Force   In 1988 the William T. Grant Foundation Commission on Work, Family, and Citizenship found that public schools were not helping non-college-bound high school students move into the work force.

Therefore, the commission concluded, these students did not receive the same educational opportunity as their college-bound counterparts. It concluded that the schools must do much more to prepare students for work, beginning with preschool education through retraining of already employed adults.

The commission recommended that the federal government invest $5 billion annually for ten years in the following: (1) Head Start, with state and local help, so that the 81 percent of eligible youngsters currently not being served could be included, (2) extension of Chapter I (previously Title I of ESEA) programs into the middle and secondary schools so that earlier educational gains are maintained; (3) expansion of the Job Corps, which was designed to move sixteen-to-eighteen-year-olds into the work force; (4) redirection of vocational education with hands-on methods to help students acquire basic skills; and (5) provision for monitored work experience such as internships, apprenticeships, reemployment training, and school/industry cooperatives.

Potential Solutions

During the 1970s and 1980s educators tended to agree that not all students had equal educational opportunities despite the increased popularization of the schools for all groups. Frequently, this inequality stemmed not from unequal access but unequal opportunities. Finding solutions to this problem is a complicated and ongoing task.

Compensatory Education

One solution to providing equal educational opportunities for all students suggested by Edmund Gordon is for schools to compensate for the unequal learning and experiences that students bring to the classroom. **Compensatory education** needs to be individualized based on the student's unique learning characteristics. In the middle 1970s, when Gordon did his work, there was no evidence that compensatory education was in use or effective.

In *A Place Called School*, a study of thirty-eight elementary, middle, and junior and senior high schools conducted in 1984 by John Goodlad, he concluded that some schools were providing more equal educational opportunities than other schools and, in some, compensatory education was working. According to Goodlad, earlier studies, such as Gordon's, failed to examine classroom practices within individual schools.

In studying more than one thousand classrooms, Goodlad found similarities in methods, materials, tests, content of curriculum, grouping, modes of learning, and arrangement of classrooms. He found differences, however, in how teachers teach, distribution of resources, how curriculum is designed, and how equality of access to knowledge is regarded by individuals within the schools. Differences in the curricular content for racial and socioeconomic groups included such factors as whether the school emphasized learning facts rather than solving problems, encouraged active rather than passive learning, and working alone rather than in groups. Schools that had more resources, better teachers, and a more flexible curriculum tended to provide more adequate compensatory education than schools that were not adequately funded or flexibly organized.

Title I/Chapter I, for example, was designed to bridge the gap between advantaged and disadvantaged students by supplying the disadvantaged compensatory programs with additional federal and state funds. In a 1986 report, "The Effectiveness of Chapter I Services," Kennedy, Birman, and Demaline reported that the achievement of disadvantaged students relative to the general population had improved since 1965, particularly in reading. The study further concluded that Chapter I had been effective in raising the standardized achievement test scores of the disadvantaged children it served, but had not substantially moved them toward the achievement levels of more advantaged students. It also found that students participating in Chapter I mathematics programs gained more than those participating in Chapter I reading programs, and that students in early elementary programs gained more than students in later programs. In 1988, Congress mandated, under the Hawkins-Stafford Amendments, a review of Chapter I programs, including a study of their effectiveness. Because, by statute, Chapter I students are to receive more funds and more services than non-Chapter I students, Congress assumed that the performance of these students should improve. By statute, each district receiving Chapter I funds must set realistic goals that can be measured to demonstrate the program's effectiveness. These goals must relate, in part, to student aggregate achievement on nationally normed tests. However, the federal regulations set minimal standards requiring that Chapter I students should show improvement "beyond what a student of a particular age or grade level . . . would be expected to make during the period being measured if the child had no additional help" (Hawkins and Stafford Elementary and Secondary School Improvement Amendment of 1988—P.L. 297–20). Hence, Chapter I programs have tended to set very conservative goals so as not to be found needing improvement. Therefore, Thomas W. Fagan and Camilla A. Heid report that it is difficult to determine whether Chapter I programs are compensating for the disadvantages of some students over other students (1991).

Preschool

In 1988 the Carnegie Foundation for the Advancement of Teaching reported a "disturbing gap between reform rhetoric and results" (p. xi) for black and Hispanic children in urban schools. They recommended that (1) all eligible poverty-level preschoolers be served by Head Start by the year 2000, (2) nutritional programs be increased, (3) poverty parents be given a choice between summer and afternoon programs for their children, and (4) a 5 percent increase be made in Chapter I/Title I to focus on teaching of basic skills. The conclusion of the Carnegie Foundation report was that if the gap between advantaged and disadvantaged children were narrowed before the children entered school, the disadvantaged would have a better chance of success in school. In 1988, Congress allocated $50 million under the Hawkins-Stafford Elementary and Secondary School Improvement Amendments for each fiscal year to the states for a program called Even Start (P.L. 100–297, Title I, Part B). Even Start is for disadvantaged children, including children of migrant workers, and their parents. It is designed to improve child care and education for both children and parents "by integrating early childhood education and adult education for parents into a unified program" (P.L. 100–297, 20 USC 2741). Local education agencies are eligible to apply to the states for grants through this bill. Programs that "assist parents in becoming full partners in the education of their children and assist children in reaching their full potential as learners" (20 USC 2744) include such elements as:

1. Identification and recruitment of eligible children (eligible children in this program are between the ages of one and seven with educationally disadvantaged parents with a basic skills equivalent of no higher than fifth grade).
2. Screening and preparation of parents and children (testing and referral for counseling and related services).
3. Programs and support services appropriate to work and other responsibilities (locations that allow joint participation, transportation, and child care).
4. Instructional programs that promote adult literacy, train parents to support the educational growth of their children, and prepare the children for school.
5. Special training for staff.
6. Home-based programs that provide for and monitor integrated instructional services to parents and children.
7. Coordination of Even Start programs with other federally funded programs such as the Adult Education Act, the Education of the Handicapped Act, the Job Training Partnership Act, and Head Start.

Magnet Schools

One possible solution to the problem of unequal access to knowledge is the **magnet school**. It allows parents to select among different schools with different educational programs for their children. One magnet school, for example, might stress the theme of multiculturalism; another might be a basic school emphasizing reading, writing, arithmetic, and discipline. Still another might focus on the arts or the sciences and mathematics. In this way, according

Magnet schools are one method of improving education for all students by appealing to their specific interests. Allowing students to attend a school of their choice gives them a sense of purpose and direction lacking in other schools.

to proponents, the needs of all children can be met, complete integration can be achieved, and only the best schools will survive since parents will not select inferior schools.

However, reports seem to indicate that new forms of discrimination of poor and minorities are arising as a result of magnet schools. In four urban districts (New York City, Boston, Chicago, and Philadelphia) a 1988 study found that selective admission criteria were employed by many magnet schools, thereby providing opportunities for high achievers but not those who are disadvantaged. According to the study, these districts had "created a five-tiered school system that offers unequal opportunities to students from different backgrounds." These five tiers were: selective schools based on exams, selective magnet schools, selective vocational schools, nonselective schools drawing students from families with moderate income levels, and nonselective schools drawing students from poor neighborhoods. "Many schools in upper tiers operate as separate, virtually private schools" (Snider 8). The study found that selective schools were given extra resources, had limited enrollments, and sent students who did not do well back to their neighborhood schools (see also chapter 13, p. 437–440).

The 1980s saw more than a dozen major commission reports focusing on the problem of the U.S. high school, claiming that it was no longer encouraging academic excellence. The second wave of reports focused on elementary and middle school education. The reports seemed to suggest a move away from the popularization, multitudinousness, and politicization of the most recent decades. However, careful reading shows that they merely suggest other means for reaching the goals of U.S. education.

A Renewed Search for Academic Excellence

Reports Focusing on Secondary Schools

The titles of the high school reports—*A Nation at Risk* (1983) and *Action for Excellence* (1983)—were indicative of their findings. They emphasized a need to strengthen the curriculum in the core subjects of English, mathematics, science, foreign languages, and social studies. They commonly mentioned a need for courses in the new technologies, such as computers, and they stressed the need for high-level cognitive skills, along with higher standards and more difficult course work.

Several of the reports emphasized that students needed increased homework, more time for learning, more time in school, and more rigorous grading, testing, and discipline. They discussed upgrading teacher education programs by requiring more work in academic disciplines. Although these reports emphasized the secondary school, the commissions believed that their work would spill over into the primary schools, private schools, and colleges. Most of the reports placed the responsibility for implementing these so-called reforms on the states and the local boards of education. Table 6.2, overleaf, briefly describes the key reports. See appendix 5, p. 553 for a description of these and other major reports in greater detail.

Reports Focusing on Elementary Schools

The first of the elementary school reports, *First Lesson* (1986), was written by William Bennett, then U.S. secretary of education. Although this report

(continued on p. 188)

TABLE 6-2

Summary of Major Reports on Education, 1982–1990

The Report	Source	Recommendations	Implementers
A Nation at Risk (1983)	National Commission Excellence in Education, a group of educators and legislators assembled by Terrell Bell, U.S. Secretary of Education.	1. Schools, colleges, and universities should adopt more rigorous measurable standards and higher expectations for academic performance and student conduct. 2. The high school curriculum for all students should include 4 years of English and math, 3 years of science and social studies, 5 years of computer science, 2 years of foreign language for college-bound students. 3. Teaching should be improved by attracting better teachers and paying them more. 4. More time should be spent on teaching and learning. The present school day should be used more effectively, the day and year lengthened, and more homework required.	1. Federal government. 2. State and local officials. 3. School boards, principals, superintendents. 4. Citizens, educators, parents, students.
Report of the Task Force on Federal Elementary and Secondary Education Policy (1983)	The Twentieth Century Fund Task Force on Education, a report to the U.S. House of Representatives Budget Committee	1. The federal government should stress better schooling for *all* students. 2. A national master teacher program should be instituted to improve the quality of teachers. 3. Federal "impact" aid should be sent to school systems with large enrollments of immigrant students. 4. The primary language taught in schools should be English; all students should be offered a second language. 5. Schools should offer advanced courses in math and science. 6. School districts should be awarded federal moneys to create small, individual programs for students who are failing.	1. Elementary and secondary schools. 2. Federal government.
A Nation Prepared (1986)	Carnegie Forum on Education & the Economy	1. Create schools that provide a professional environment for teaching. 2. A national board for professional teaching standards should be formed. 3. Licensing authority should remain with the states. 4. States should abolish undergraduate degrees in education. 5. Undergraduate programs in the arts & sciences should be evaluated to ensure adequate preparation of teachers. 6. Ensure an increasing number of minority teachers. 7. Salaries should be linked to performance. 8. Salaries should be increased.	1. State and local policy makers. 2. Education Commission of the States. 3. Colleges and universities. 4. Federal and state governments. 5. Corporate leaders and local communities.

The Report	Source	Recommendations	Implementers
Tomorrow's Teachers (1986)	The Holmes Group	1. Establish a 3-tier system of teacher education: the professional and career with tenure and the instructor with a temporary certificate. 2. Develop a graduate professional teacher education program. 3. Connect schools and colleges. 4. Make schools better places for teachers to work. 5. Create standards for entry to the profession.	1. Colleges and universities. 2. Elementary and secondary schools. 3. State and local policy makers.
Time for Results: The Governors' 1991 Report on Education (1986)	National Governors Association: Center for Policy Research and Analysis	1. Teaching, Leadership and Management, Parent Involvement and Choice Readiness, Technology, School Facilities, and College Quality.	1. State governments. 2. State and local policy makers. 3. Corporate leaders. 4. Parents, local communities. 5. Colleges and universities. 6. Elementary and secondary schools. 7. Preschools.
Report of the Task Force on Education: State Strategies for Achieving the National Education Goals (America 2000) (1990)	National Governors' Association: Center for Policy Research and Analysis	1. By the year 2000, all children in America will start school ready to learn. 2. By the year 2000, the high school graduation rate will increase to at least 90 percent. 3. By the year 2000, American students will leave grades four, eight, and twelve having demonstrated competency over challenging subject matter including English, mathematics, science, history, and geography. 4. By the year 2000, American students will be first in the world in mathematics and science achievement. 5. By the year 2000, every adult American will be literate and will possess the knowledge and skills necessary to compete in a global economy. 6. By the year 2000, every school in America will be free of drugs and violence and will offer a disciplined environment conducive to learning.	1. State governments. 2. State and local policy makers. 3. Corporate leaders. 4. Parents, local communities. 5. Colleges and universities. 6. Elementary and secondary schools. 7. Preschools.

Adapted and updated by the authors from B. Loman, "Improving Public Education: Recommendations From Recent Study Commissions," *Popular Government* (Winter 1985), 14–16.

Concern for the quality of education in the United States has risen dramatically in the past few years, resulting in a series of reports suggesting various types of reforms. This table summarizes the major reports; a complete list will be found in appendix 5 on p. 553.

claimed elementary education was in "pretty good shape," it maintained that increased parental involvement was "the single best way" to bring about much needed improvement.

In addition, the Bennett report suggested that teacher certification "depend on demonstrated knowledge and skills, not on paper credentials," and that the "chronological lockstep" of students through grades be "loosened" to allow for individual progress.

According to Bennett's report, the elementary school curriculum must first teach children to read. The report also said that children should learn that "writing is more than filling in blanks," science should include "hands-on" experiments, social studies should be broadened to teach the academic disciplines in early grades, mathematics should emphasize problem solving, and instruction in the arts should be an integral part of every elementary school curriculum. Students should gain a grasp of the uses and limitations of computers, health and physical education should be taught, and every school should have a library (p. 2).

In August 1988 Bennett issued a second report on elementary education, *James Madison Elementary School*. Besides referring to the usual elementary school academic subjects, the report suggested a new emphasis on foreign languages, fine arts, physical education, and health. The report also recommended that more emphasis be placed on mathematics and science, beginning in the fourth grade.

Report Focusing on Middle Schools

The Carnegie Council on Adolescent Development in the report *Turning Points* (1989) called for a restructuring of middle schools wherein students and teachers would be grouped together as teams with emphasis on intellectual and personal growth. The council suggested a core academic program (integrating English, fine arts, foreign languages, history, literature and grammar, mathematics, science, and social studies); the promotion of cooperative learning (students of varying abilities working together as a team) rather than placement by academic achievement level; staffing middle schools with teachers who are experts at teaching young adolescents; emphasizing the health of the adolescent; and connecting the schools with the community.

Political Response to the Call for Reforms

In August 1986 the National Governors' Association conference, chaired by Lamar Alexander, then governor of Tennessee, released a report on education that attempted to deal with some of the demands of the earlier commission studies. *Time for Results: The Governors' 1991 Report on Education* suggested, among other things, that public schools reexamine their organizational structures and provide a choice for parents and students by developing public alternative schools and allowing parents to select the school best suited to their children. According to Richard D. Lamm, then governor of Colorado, author of the "choice" section of the report, "Our task force believes that public education cannot, as presently structured, deal effectively with the nation's diversity and its demand for compulsory education. . . . We propose something in the great American tradition: that you increase excellence by increasing the choices" (*Wall Street Journal* staff 1986, 14). Governor Lamm's task force believed that choice would produce competition, a more responsive system, and a "distinct shared philosophy, mission, and faculty agreement called for in literature on effective schools" (*Time for Results*, 69). The issue of choice continues to be an important method of reform in the 1990s (see also chapter 13, p. 441).

These reforms also addressed issues related to the teaching profession. They set standards for initial certification of teachers, testing requirements for permanent teacher certification, teacher evaluation systems, eligibility require-

FIGURE 6-1

The Common Core Curriculum of William Bennett's
James Madison High School

THE PROGRAM IN BRIEF: A Four-Year Plan

Subject	1st Year	2nd Year	3rd Year	4th Year
ENGLISH	Introduction to Literature	American Literature	British Literature	Introduction to World Literature
SOCIAL STUDIES	Western Civilization	American History	Principles of American Democracy (1 sem.) and American Democracy & the World (1 sem)	
MATHE-MATICS	Three Years Required From Among the Following Courses: Algebra I, Plane & Solid Geometry, Algebra II & Trigonometry, Statistics & Probability (1 sem.), Pre-Calculus (1 sem.), and Calculus AB or BC			
SCIENCE	Three Years Required From Among the Following Courses: Astronomy/Geology, Biology, Chemistry, and Physics or Principles of Technology			
FOREIGN LAN-GUAGE	Two Years Required in a Single Language From Among Offerings Determined by Local Jurisdictions			
PHYSICAL EDUCA-TION/ HEALTH	Physical Education/ Health 9	Physical Education/ Health 10		
FINE ARTS	Art History (1 sem.) Music History (1 sem.)			

From: W. J. Bennett, *James Madison High School: A Curriculum for American Students* (Washington, DC: U.S. Department of Education, 1988), 11.

As a response to the reform movement in the 1980s, curriculum became subject centered and less responsive to students' individual needs. In the core curriculum of *James Madison High School*, the emphasis was on basic language and mathematical skills.

ments for merit pay (salary increments based on evaluation of teaching performance), and requirements for career ladder programs (staffing patterns that award salary levels based on differing responsibilities and levels of success in classroom teaching evaluations).

The goal of these reforms was to improve the quality of schooling. Most of the reformers suggested that this improvement could be measured through student achievement test scores, but the outcome has as yet not been categorically determined. Owing to the cries for reform in the 1980s, the curriculum became increasingly subject centered and less responsive to individual student needs. An example of that curriculum can be seen in William Bennett's *James Madison High School* (see figure 6.1 on p. 189). Changes in the academic programs included more attention to the gaining of basic language and mathematics skills in the elementary school, increased promotion and graduation standards, development of objectives, measurement of student progress, increased college admission standards, additional academic requirements for high school graduation, and evaluation of teachers based on a set of criteria.

As a result of the work on the Education Commission of the States, the National Governors' Association outlined six major goals for education in 1990:

> Goal 1: By the year 2000, all children in America will start school ready to learn.
> Goal 2: By the year 2000, the high school graduation rate will increase to 90 percent.
> Goal 3: By the year 2000, American students will leave grades 4, 8, and 12 having demonstrated competency in challenging subject matter including English, mathematics, science, history, and geography, and every school in America will ensure that all students learn to use their minds well, so they may be prepared for responsible citizenship, further learning, and productive employment in our modern economy.
> Goal 4: By the year 2000, U.S. students will be first in the world in mathematics and science achievement.
> Goal 5: By the year 2000, every adult American will be literate and will possess the skills necessary to compete in a global economy and exercise the rights and responsibilities of citizenship.
> Goal 6: By the year 2000, every school in America will be free of drugs and violence and will offer a disciplined environment conducive to learning. (National Governors' Association, *Educating America: State Strategies for Achieving the National Education Goals* [Report of the Task Force on Education], 1990, pp. 10–11.)

America 2000

In 1991, President George Bush outlined his agenda for reforming the schools. The plan was designed by Secretary of Education Lamar Alexander only two months after his appointment to the post, and Assistant Secretary of Education David Kerns, former executive director of the Xerox Corporation. The program, America 2000, utilizing the proposals of the National Governors' Association, called for several reform strategies. They included:

- A voluntary national system of examinations in mathematics, science, English, history, and geography.
- Incentives to states and communities that develop school choice for parents and teachers.

- Differentiated pay for teachers who teach well, teach core subjects, teach in dangerous or challenging settings, and who serve as mentors for new teachers.
- Certification of nontraditionally trained teachers and administrators.
- Involvement of business and industry in setting job-related skill standards and providing money for new schools.

TABLE 6-3

Falling Short of the Goals—America 2000

Goals	What the panel said
That all children will start school ready to learn	No clear way to measure progress, although many indicators are discouraging, like the number of children who attend pre-school programs, the number who see a doctor regularly and the number who get adequate nutrition.
That 90 percent of all high school students graduate	White students are approaching this goal now; black students have shown progress, up to a 78 percent rate in 1990, but Hispanic students have shown little or no progress, with about a 60 percent graduation rate.
That students achieve competence in core subjects in grades 4, 8 and 12	This goal is almost impossible to achieve by the year 2000, given the low rates of competence shown in the most recent nationwide tests.
That American students be "first in the world" in math and science achievement	New studies comparing Americans with students in other countries are still under way, but recent studies indicate this goal, too, is virtually impossible to reach by the year 2000.
That every adult American be literate and have the skills to function as a citizen and a worker	Recent studies provide mixed results, and there is not enough information to state progress accurately.
That all schools will be free of drugs and violence and "offer a disciplined environment conducive to learning"	Drug and alcohol abuse seems to be down, but school violence remains a problem.

From: *New York Times* (October 1, 1991), A17.

This table summarizes the results of the National Governor's Association September 1991 study of the progress being made to accomplish the six major goals of President Bush's America 2000 program intended to reform the schools.

Martha F. Campbell in *Phi Delta Kappan.*

"When he said Klondike, *I thought he meant bars. When he said* Quaker, *I thought he meant* oats. *When he said* Philadelphia, *I thought he meant cheese. I would've done better if the test had been after lunch."*

Even before the official announcement of Bush's reform package was made, criticisms were heard. Albert Shanker, president of the American Federation of Teachers, expressed concern about the involvement of business and industry in the plan. According to Shanker, if government officials thought the plan was important, they would pay for it. He expressed concern that the school choice initiative involved private and religious schools as well as public schools. He further suggested that any new plan should involve the continued funding of successful programs such as Head Start and Chapter I rather than developing new, untested initiatives (April 21, 1991, E7).

Concerns were also voiced in Congress. Senator Edward M. Kennedy of Massachusetts maintained that school choice involving private schools could become a "death sentence for public schools struggling to serve disadvantaged students" (Chira, April 19, 1991, A1). According to Michael Casserly, associate director of the Council of Great City Schools, which represents the nation's largest school districts, Bush's proposed school choice plan, which would allow Chapter I money to follow underprivileged students to private and parochial schools, is probably "unworkable" and "unconstitutional" because poor school districts would be likely to lose Chapter I money. Others objected to the proposal for nationwide tests. Deborah Meier, who runs a school-of-choice that has been cited as a model by Bush, claims that the tests would hamper efforts to create innovative schools and innovative curriculum because they would dictate what must be taught (Chira, April 20, 1991, 1). These are serious criticisms of a wide-ranging, complicated proposal to reform the schools.

In September 1991 the National Governor's Association issued its first report card on the progress being made to reach the goals of America 2000. It conceded that little has been achieved in most areas and insisted that more data was necessary in order to make more accurate assessments. Its findings are summarized in table 6.3 on page 191.

6.2 POINTS TO REMEMBER

- As more and more previously disenfranchised students entered the public schools during the civil rights period, the schools offered many educational opportunities to meet their needs.
- The U.S. Supreme Court decision *Brown v. the Board of Education of Topeka, Kansas,* which ruled that separate schools were not equal schools, resulted in integration of the public schools.
- After integration many studies revealed that educational opportunities for minorities were still unequal. The students were frequently placed in schools where they were not welcome; funding in poor districts was not equal to funding in prosperous districts; minorities were frequently tracked into lower level classes.
- Head Start, a preschool program, was developed to bridge the educational gap between impoverished and prosperous children. The Elementary and Secondary Education Act of 1965 provided increased opportunities and funding for special programs for minorities, bilingual and multicultural students, and women.
- Public schools were required to educate bilingual and multicultural students in their own language.
- P.L. 94–142 provided funding for public schools to develop equal access and special programs for all those with disabilities.
- Educational opportunities of the 1970s and 1980s were increasingly multitudinous but were still not equal. Federal funding cuts meant that many of the programs for the disenfranchised were eliminated.
- Critics of education in the 1980s contended that more had to be done to ensure excellence in education.

FOR THOUGHT/DISCUSSION

1. Describe the effect on American education of the launching of the Soviet Sputnik in 1957. Do you believe that the scientific achievements of students in the 1990s has kept pace with the achievements of students in the late 1950s? Why or why not?

2. Do you believe that the landmark *Brown v. Board of Education of Topeka, Kansas* decision has had a net positive or negative effect on equality of American education? Explain.

3. Which aspect of President Bush's *America 2000* proposal do you feel is most viable? Why?

4. If you had to choose a school for your child, what specific aspects of the school would influence your decision?

FOR FURTHER READING/REFERENCE

National Commission on Excellence in Education. 1983. *A nation at risk: The imperatives for educational reform.* Washington, DC: U.S. Government Printing Office. An examination of the problems of education in the 1980s and recommendations for attacking the problems in the 1990s.

Ravitch, D. 1983. *The troubled crusade: American education 1945–1980.* New York: Basic Books. A discussion of the concerns and problems of educational opportunity, beginning with progressive education in the 1940s and extending to the growth of the schools in the 1950s and 1960s and finally to the bureaucracy of the schools in the 1980s.

Record, W., and Record, J. S. (Eds.). 1960. *Little Rock, U.S.A.* San Francisco, CA: Chandler Publishing Company. A collection of newspaper accounts, court records, and other documents related to the Little Rock incident of September 1957, when nine black teenagers tried to enroll at an all-white school.

Reisman, F. 1962. *The culturally deprived child.* New York: Harper Brothers. Presents characteristics of the culturally deprived child and explains how the verbally loaded curriculum of the 1950s and 1960s failed to meet the needs of this child.

Tuyack, D., Lowe, R., and Hansot, E. 1984. *Public schools in hard times: The Great Depression and recent years.* Cambridge, MA: Harvard University Press. A discussion of how economic conditions in the 1930s caused cutbacks in education and how these cutbacks led to growing tensions between professional educators and business and industry; also compares education of the 1930s to that of the 1980s.

7

The Philosophical Foundations of Education

This is a classic evaluation of Socrates as a teacher done in a twentieth-century style with twentieth-century attitudes. Intended to be humorous, at the same time it focuses on how philosophies of teaching may change with the times. The ratings go from high to low with 1 being high.

A. Personal Qualifications

1. Personal appearance

   Rating: 1   2   3   4   ⑤

   Comment: Dresses in an old sheet draped about his body

2. Self-confidence

   Rating: 1   2   3   4   ⑤

   Comment: Not sure of himself—always asking questions . . .

3. Adaptability

   Rating: 1   2   3   4   ⑤

   Comment: Prone to suicide by poison when under duress

B. Class Management

1. Organization

   Rating: 1   2   3   4   ⑤

   Comment: Does not keep a seating chart

2. Room appearance

   Rating: 1   2   3   ④   5

   Comment: Does not have eye-catching bulletin boards

3. Utilization of supplies

   Rating: ①   2   3   4   5

   Comment: Does not use supplies

C. Teacher-Pupil Relations

1. Tact and Consideration

   Rating: 1   2   3   4   ⑤

   Comment: Places students in embarrassing situations by asking questions

2. Attitude of class

   Rating: 1   ②   3   4   5

   Comment: Class is friendly

D.   Professional Attitude

   1. Professional ethics

      Rating: 1   2   3   4   ⑤

      Comment: Does not belong to professional association
                or PTA

   2. In-service training

      Rating: 1   2   3   4   ⑤

      Comment: Complete failure here—has not even both-
                ered to attend college

   3. Parent relationships

      Rating: 1   2   3   4   ⑤

      Comment: Needs to improve in this area—parents are
                trying to get rid of him

**Recommendation: DOES NOT HAVE A PLACE IN EDUCA-
TION—SHOULD NOT BE REHIRED.**

From: J. Gauss, "Evaluation of Socrates as a Teacher," *Phi Delta
Kappan* (1962).

**Socrates (469–399 B.C.), a great teacher, believed in teaching by a
method of questioning his students, known as the Socratic Method.**

CHAPTER OBJECTIVES

After studying this chapter, you should be able to:

- Define philosophy.
- Discuss metaphysics, epistemology, axiology, and logic.
- Explain why it is important for educators to study philosophy.
- Explain how the categories of philosophy (metaphysics, epistemology, axiology, and logic) relate to the schools of philosophy.
- Discuss the five schools of philosophy: idealism, realism, pragmatism, existentialism, and philosophical analysis.
- Explain how the five schools of philosophy relate to the five theories of education.
- Define the five theories of education: perennialism, essentialism, progressivism, social reconstructionism, and behaviorism.
- Explain how each of the five theories of education relate to educational practice.
- Discuss how philosophy affects education in terms of goal setting, curricular emphasis, and the role of the teacher.
- Develop a personal philosophy of education.

In the current climate of educational reform, teachers need to look back to the philosophies that have informed their educational thinking and forward to ways that thinking might be used to creatively restructure what goes on in the classroom and in schools. As Roland Barth says in a recent issue of *Phi Delta Kappan*, "Let go of the trapeze. Think otherwise. Become an independent variable. Lick the envelope. Bell the cat. Fly the cage. Leave your mark" (1991, p. 128).

WHAT IS A PHILOSOPHY OF EDUCATION?

Philosophy and education are closely related fields. Both are vitally concerned with humankind, the nature of humankind, knowledge, relationships, and behavior. But whereas philosophy seeks to understand the fundamental theoretical basis of existence, education seeks to understand the more practical answers. Where philosophy would ask, Where are we going? education would ask, How can we get there? Where philosophy would ask, How do we define ourselves as humans? education would ask, How do I become self-reliant? Where philosophy would ask, Is there life on other planets? education would ask, How do we get there? The various belief systems or schools of philosophy are the foundations on which educational theory is built.

The word *philosophy* comes from the Greek **philos**, which means "love," and **sophos**, which means "wisdom." Hence, philosophy literally means love of wisdom. Philosophy is, therefore, the inquiry into the principles of knowledge, reality, and values that constitute wisdom.

Organizing Knowledge   Philosophy seeks to organize and systematize all fields of knowledge as a means of understanding and interpreting the totality of reality. Or put another way, it is a search for truth. Philosophy is comprised of the following general categories: metaphysics, epistemology, axiology, and logic. They provide philosophers with questions and specific approaches to examine truth.

Metaphysics

The philosopher uses **metaphysics** to speculate on the nature of ultimate reality. Literally, metaphysics means "beyond the physical." Hence it deals with the comparison of "other worldly" to "this worldly" (Brameld 1971, 47). Metaphysical questions include those such as: "Is the universe as a whole rationally designed or is it ultimately meaningless? Is what we call mind or spirit nothing more than an illusion bred by the present inadequacy of scientific

196

knowledge, or does it possess a reality of its own? Are all organisms determined [life preordained by the 'other worldly'], or are some, such as man, free?" (Kneller, 1964, 5–6).

According to Everett W. Hall, metaphysics affects how humankind acts by shaping people's views of what nature is and how it can and should be controlled. Educational philosopher Theodore Brameld states that metaphysics searches for the principles of human existence, whether physical or spiritual; it does not prejudge what they are.

We can see how metaphysical questions shape action by examining a problem in education. George F. Kneller writes about practical aspects of metaphysics in *Introduction to the Philosophy of Education.*

> Take . . . [a] practical problem in education, which is basically metaphysical. One hears a great deal about teaching the child and not the subject. What does this statement mean to a teacher? Even if the teacher replies, "I prefer just to teach my subject," the question still remains, "Why?" What is the *ultimate* purpose of teaching the subject? (1964, 24)

The answers to these questions are likely to be based on the teacher's metaphysical beliefs. If, for example, the teacher believes that very specific basic knowledge is crucial to the child's intellectual development, it is likely that this teacher will focus on the subject matter. If, on the other hand, the teacher holds that the child is more important than any specific subject matter, it is likely that this teacher will focus on the child and allow the child to provide clues as to how he or she should be instructed. The action that the teacher takes will depend on his or her answer to the metaphysical question, What is the ultimate purpose of teaching the subject?

Epistemology

The category that deals with the nature and universality of knowledge is **epistemology**. It attempts to discover what is involved in the process of knowing. "It asks such questions as: Is there something common to all the different activities to which we apply the term 'knowing'? Is knowing a special sort of mental act? If so, what is the difference between knowledge and belief? Can we know anything beyond the objects with which our senses acquaint us? Does knowing make any difference to the object known?" (Kneller 8).

The epistemologist neither attempts to gather and classify facts nor attempts to explain how people think scientifically. Rather, the goal of the epistemologist is to understand how we define, and thus acquire, knowledge.

Because epistemological questions deal with the essence of knowledge, they are central to education. Teachers must be able to assess "what is knowledge" in order to determine if a particular thing or idea should be included in the curriculum, and they should be able to distinguish this knowledge from opinion and belief.

A teacher must determine, for example, if a commonly held belief (**maxim**) is knowledge. Does it meet the standards of reliable knowledge? Is the statement that "all men are created equal" an example of knowledge or a belief? Obviously, this question revolves around the issues of whether all people are created equal in the first place and whether equality in any human endeavor is possible. How one answers the question determines what is included in the curriculum and how one teaches this knowledge.

Axiology

The category of philosophy that deals with the nature of values is **axiology**. It is divided into the study of **ethics** (moral values and conduct) and **aesthetics** (values in the realm of beauty and art).

Ethics deals with such questions as: "What is the good life for all men?" and "How ought we to behave?" (Kneller 15). An ethical system may be secular, or it may be based on the absolutism of some religions that have fixed rules of conduct that people are expected to obey. In the United States, for example, the separation of church and state has tended to divorce the country's ethical code from religion, in spite of the fact that it is grounded in Judeo-Christian traditions.

Aesthetics deals with the theory of beauty and art in its broad sense. A major question aesthetics asks is: "Should art be imitative and representative, or should it be the product of the private creative imagination?" (Kneller 16). In other words, What are the proper subject matter and scope of art? Should an autumn sunset always be depicted in tones of orange and yellow, or could it be portrayed in black and brown? Is human elimination an appropriate subject for artistic works? In recent decades these questions have occupied a prominent place in the news media as the U.S. Congress has debated whether it is appropriate to provide public funds, such as the National Endowment for the Arts, to artists if some of their works are considered inappropriate or distasteful by many people.

Both ethics and aesthetics are important issues in education. Should a system of ethics be taught in the public school? If so, which system of ethics should be taught? Should the system be based on religion or should it be totally secular? (Ethics as related to teaching is discussed in chapter 13, p. 462).

One of the most divisive questions of ethics in public education has been the issue of Bible reading and prayer in the classroom. Should public school children be allowed to participate in exercises during the school day in which the Bible is read and/or a prayer is delivered or recited?

The issue was debated in the Supreme Court case *Abingdon School District v. Schempp* (374 U.S. 203, 1963), in which two Schempp children participated in readings of verses from the Bible and recitation of the Lord's Prayer that were conducted daily over the school intercom. Although participation was voluntary by statute of the Commonwealth of Pennsylvania, the children remained in the classroom during the exercises because their father believed that their relationships with teachers and other students would be adversely affected if they did not. According to the plaintiffs, a literal reading of the Bible was "contrary to the religious beliefs which they held and to their familial teaching." The Schempps were practicing Unitarians.

The Supreme Court ruled in the Schempp case as follows: "Such study of the Bible or of religion, when presented objectively as part of a secular program of education, may not be effected consistently with the First Amendment. But the exercises here do not fall into those categories. They are religious exercises, required by the states in violation of the command of the First Amendment that the government maintain strict neutrality, neither aiding or opposing religion." Thus, the prayers and Bible readings were judged against the law. Others, including a dissenting opinion of the justices of the Supreme Court, disagreed with the ruling, claiming that not permitting prayer and Bible reading in the school impedes the right of free exercise of religion and violates the foundations

Mike Luckovich ATLANTA CONSTITUTION

Nice touch, Michaelangelo. I've decided to grant you an arts endowment...

Congress

of the nation. While many of the arguments in favor of prayer and Bible reading are based on questions of ethics rather than law, the Court's decision in this case was based on the Constitution, as it is required to be.

Aesthetic questions in education involve deciding which works by which artists should be included or not included in the curriculum and what kind of subject matter should be allowed or encouraged in a writing, drawing, or painting class. Are nude figures by Michaelangelo more acceptable than those by the photographer Robert Mapplethorpe? At what age should children be exposed to art that some might consider pornographic? Or does the mere process of selecting pieces of art encourage a liberal or conservative attitude in students? Should teachers compromise their own attitude toward a piece of artwork if it disagrees with that of a parent or a school board? One example occurred recently in a local independent school in North Carolina. An exhibit was displayed in the art gallery, which students also used as classroom space. Because the works dealt with the topic of feminism, several of the pieces used symbols of female genitalia. The artist was asked to remove the exhibit since, according to the headmaster's aesthetic values, it was not appropriate material for the students.

Logic

The philosophical category that deals with the nature of reasoning is **logic**. It examines the principles that allow us to move from one argument to the next. There are many types of logic, but the two most commonly used and studied are deductive and inductive. **Deduction** is a type of reasoning that moves from a general statement to a specific instance. For example, the statement "All people are mammals" is a general statement of fact, or a **major premise**. "Jane is a person" is a particular fact, or a **minor premise**, that no one disputes. The **conclusion**, therefore, is obvious. "Jane is a mammal." Thus the conclusion is logically inferred from the general statements made.

Induction is a type of reasoning that moves in the opposite direction, from particular instances to a general conclusion. Certain observations are categorized, and then generalizations are made based on these particulars. One of the dangers of inductive reasoning is jumping to conclusions with too few particular observations. For example, a teacher might reason, "Sammy is having difficulty learning to read. Sammy's mother works. Therefore, Sammy is having difficulty learning to read because his mother works." This generalization is based on the assumption that mothers who work do not devote sufficient time to their children and, therefore, the children are likely to do poorly in school. This reasoning is clearly flawed and dangerous.

Logical reasoning is used all the time in making educational decisions. We use logic when we determine how to order the curriculum. Does it make sense to teach correct spelling before we teach students to compose a story? Does it make more sense to teach history chronologically than thematically? We use logic when we determine how to place students in homogeneous groups. We use logic when we make emergency decisions. Should school be canceled because of the weather? All these are educational questions that use the principles of logic, but it is easy to see how some decisions may be flawed if the basic logical foundation is invalid or flawed.

Thinking Clearly

Philosophy provides us with the tools we need to think clearly. Let's go back to the aesthetic question of the headmaster and the art show to see how philosophy might help us to think clearly about an educational issue.

The headmaster used questions of aesthetics to make his decision to remove the art show. However, if he had asked other philosophical questions earlier, he might have avoided the whole conflict. For example, if he had asked the metaphysical question "What is the purpose of education?" he might have answered, "The purpose of education is to teach students to make ethical and aesthetic decisions for themselves." If he had determined this ahead of time, he would have displayed the show, left it up, and developed curriculums and teaching strategies to help the students make a decision for themselves. On the other hand, he might have answered, "The purpose of education is to teach students what is aesthetically acceptable in polite society." If this had been his answer, it is likely that the show would not have been displayed in the first place.

He also might have asked epistemological questions. For example, going beyond his own subjective judgment, he might ask "Can we know anything beyond the objects with which our senses acquaint us?" If he had answered affirmatively, he might have decided to exhibit the paintings to determine what else they might teach him and his students. He then would have needed to work with his faculty to develop a curriculum to help the students get beyond their own sensory impressions.

We've already dealt with this incident in terms of its aesthetic questions, but what of its ethical questions? Suppose the headmaster had asked "How should I behave?" Would he have removed the show after the commitment had been made to the artist? Or would he have allowed it to be displayed prior to carefully reviewing it in terms of other philosophical questions? How would he answer any complaints of parents or school board members?

Finally, he might have dealt with the issue through logic. Deductively he might have concluded, "Painting on canvas is art. This is painting on canvas. Therefore, it is art." It appears that he did deal with the issue inductively, reasoning in this way: "Some of the paintings in this show will be offensive to some people. Therefore, this show is offensive and should be removed." Did he use good logic in his decision-making process? Using the questioning techniques of philosophy, the headmaster would have been helped to arrive at a satisfactory decision.

WHY STUDY THE PHILOSOPHY OF EDUCATION?

Having a philosophy of education is important if educators are going to develop the ability to think clearly about what they do on a day-to-day basis and to see how these things extend beyond the classroom to the whole of humankind and society. Philosophy does not provide us with answers but, instead, gives us a means of inquiry so that we can gain insight into contemporary problems. People who use the tools of philosophy are more concerned with appropriate questions than with finding the correct answers. By using the tools of philosophy we can analyze who we are, what we do, and how we do it. Philosophy not only helps us analyze problems, but supplies us with the means for seeking alternative solutions to them. For example, an English teacher is faced with the decision of teaching either the great works of Western literature in the eleventh-grade curriculum or literature that provides a global perspective. He asks many philosophical questions as he ponders his decision: Many of my students come from non-Western cultures. Should they be taught the literature from their cultures or a common core of literature? Is there a common literary terminology that my students can apply to various works of literature? Can we examine both Western and non-Western literature in terms of that terminology? What values should I be teaching my students? Is it more important that they examine how different cultures deal with values in literature, or that they understand how Western culture deals with them? Do I intend to encourage the value of reading for pleasure? Or do I hope to help them develop a love of great writing? As the teacher explores the many possible answers, he discovers a variety of approaches to the teaching of literature.

Studying the philosophy of education enables you to recognize the philosophical perspectives of educational theory and practice. Education is both changing to adapt to the needs of society and attempting to change it. As you develop your own philosophy of education, you can weigh these changes against your own beliefs and can also determine their likely educational outcomes.

For example, the reform movements of the 1980s suggested a return to a subject-centered curriculum in which students would learn the accumulated knowledge of society. What is the philosophical basis for this reform? What metaphysical questions have been asked and how have they been answered? What is the nature of knowledge according to these reformers? How would these reforms deal with questions of ethics and aesthetics? How do these reforms fit with your own philosophical leaning? Do you agree or disagree with the reformers' contentions? How can you justify your opinions based on a philosophical point of view? Knowing how to ask and interpret philosophical questions will not only help you better understand the reforms, but it will help you reevaluate and defend your own philosophical points of view.

THE SCHOOLS OF PHILOSOPHICAL THOUGHT

The categories of philosophical thought (metaphysics, epistemology, axiology, and logic) yield the questions by which we can derive a system of thought or a school of philosophy. Each of the philosophical schools deals with reality in a different way. The traditional schools of philosophy include idealism, realism, pragmatism, and existentialism. Philosophical analysis is a modern school with a methodological approach. We will discuss how each deals with reality. See table 7.1, p. 216, for a comparison of how each school of philosophy deals with the questions of metaphysics, epistemology, axiology, and logic.

Idealism   According to the traditional philosophical school of **idealism**, ultimate reality consists of an idea, a nonphysical essence, that is the foundation of all things. According to the Greek philosopher Plato (427–347 B.C.), the originator of idealism, ideas alone, because they transcend the physical, are genuinely real. The idealist contends, "I think, therefore I am." Plato assumed that the world was made up of "eternal verities," which consisted of the True, the Good, and the Beautiful, and that the universe, which is an expression of will and intelligence, is ordered by this eternal, spiritual reality.

The idealist claims that individuals originated within the mind of a deity, a first cause, or a creator, thus people are finite and limited beings, microcosms of the greater cosmic mind, which is infinite.

According to the idealist, an individual can transcend the physical world and can have knowledge of the spiritual world simply by intuition. The development of the mind and self is primary to the idealist; the development of the physical being is secondary. Since people are the only educable organisms, only humans, along with God, have self-controlled minds.

Founders and Proponents

Idealism has numerous proponents. The Greek philosopher Plato (see chapter 5, p. 126) is considered to be the father of idealism. René Descartes (1596–1650), a French Catholic, was influenced by Plato and the works of Saint Augustine (see chapter 5, p. 127). The two main idealistic concepts developed by Descartes are that the self is the most immediate reality in the individual's experience and that the existence of God is proved in that we have an idea of a perfect being. Baruch Spinoza (1632–1677), a Spanish Jew who lived in Holland, was also an idealist. According to Spinoza, there is an enduring substance that exists now, always has existed, and always will exist. He contended that this substance is correctly called God.

George Berkeley (1685–1753), an Irishman, wrote extensively on idealism. His best-known work is *A Treatise Concerning the Principles of Human Knowledge* (1710). Berkeley, who based some of his beliefs on the work of physicist Sir Isaac Newton, claimed that the key to solving problems in philosophy was in solving problems of knowledge. If, according to Berkeley, we successfully understand the character of knowledge, we have taken an important step in understanding the character of reality. According to Berkeley, things cannot exist without some mind to know or perceive them. The argument about whether a tree that falls in a forest makes a noise if no man hears it is appropriate in discussing Berkeley. Berkeley would say, "No, the falling tree does not make a noise unless it is heard because there is no mind to interpret the noise."

The German philosopher Immanuel Kant (1724–1804), in *Metaphysics of Morals* and *Critique of Practical Reason*, spelled out his idealistic philosophy. He believed in freedom, the immortality of the soul, and the existence of God. He believed that there are universal moral laws and man has an obligation to obey them. Kant wrote extensively on human reason. We see the world, the "thing-in-itself," through our senses. Each sensation is an infinitesimal representation of a microscopic part of the physical world. At higher levels of reasoning, the world takes on unity through these sensations. We see objects that are external to us as related to other objects in an orderly way. Reason fits perceived objects into classes according to similarities and differences. Thus, it is through reason that we acquire knowledge of the world.

Georg Wilhelm Friedrich Hegel (1770–1831), another German idealist, enjoyed paradoxes that emerged in his philosophical pattern. Hegel formalized dialectical logic into three stages: thesis, the Idea; antithesis, Nature; and synthesis, Mind, or Spirit. The thesis and antithesis, as Hegel sees them, are contradictory. The synthesis unifies the positive aspects of each.

Idealism and Education

Although there are few classical idealists (those who believe the ideal rooted in God is central to all things) among contemporary philosophers, idealism has been a major influence in the foundation of Western educational thought. Idealistic educational philosophy centers on epistemology, the theory of knowledge. According to the classical idealist, because the Creator makes Himself evident in the universe, when we understand the nature of knowledge, we will understand the nature of reality and of God.

The classical idealist believes that thinking is an active process of a rational and substantive mind and that values are genuine, absolute, and permanent. The goal of learning is to understand universal ultimate reality.

The educational philosophy of the idealist is ideal—or idea-centered rather than either subject-centered or child-centered—because the ideal, or idea, is the foundation of all things. This knowledge is directed toward "self-hood, self-consciousness, and self-direction" (Bigge 1982, 30) and is centered on the growth of rational mental processes of the individual. One of the major tenets of idealism is that the individual who is created in God's image has free will, thus making learning possible.

The idealist believes that learning comes from within the individual rather than from without. Hence, real mental growth and spiritual growth do not occur until they are self-initiated.

(continued on p. 206)

CROSS-CULTURAL PERSPECTIVE

Shakespeare in the Bush

Laura Bohannan is an anthropologist who on a trip to West Africa attempted to prove the universality of knowledge by telling the story of Hamlet *to a group of African tribal leaders. What she found is that truth and wisdom are related to human experience, and the concept of "eternal verities" applies only if individuals exist within the same culture.*

Just before I left Oxford for the Tiv in West Africa, conversation turned to the season at Stratford. "You Americans," said a friend, "often have difficulty with Shakespeare. He was, after all, a very English poet, and one can easily misinterpret the universal by misunderstanding the particular."

I protested that human nature is pretty much the same the whole world over; at least the general plot and motivation of the greater tragedies would always be clear—everywhere—although some details of custom might have to be explained and difficulties of translation might produce other slight changes. To end an argument we could not conclude, my friend gave me a copy of *Hamlet* to study in the African bush: it would, he hoped, lift my mind above its primitive surroundings, and possibly I might, by prolonged meditation, achieve the grace of correct interpretation. . . .

[Bohannan is invited to tell a story of "things a long time ago" to the elders of the tribe.]

Realizing that here was my chance to prove *Hamlet* universally intelligible, I agreed [to tell a story].

The old man handed me some more beer to help me on with my storytelling. Men filled their long wooden pipes and knocked coals from the fire to place in the pipe bowls; then, puffing contentedly, they sat back to listen. I began in the proper style, "Not yesterday, not yesterday, but long ago, a thing occurred. One night three men were keeping watch outside the homestead of the great chief, when suddenly they saw the former chief approach them."

"Why was he no longer their chief?"

"He was dead," I explained. "That is why they were troubled and afraid when they saw him."

"Impossible, began one of the elders, handing his pipe on to his neighbor, who interrupted, "Of course it wasn't the dead chief. It was an omen sent by a witch. Go on."

Slightly shaken, I continued. "One of these three was a man who knew things"—the closest translation for scholar, but unfortunately it also meant witch. The second elder looked triumphantly at the first. "So he spoke to the dead chief saying, 'Tell us what we must do so you may rest in your grave,' but the dead chief did not answer. He vanished, and they could see him no more. Then the man who knew things—his name was Horatio—said this event was the affair of the dead chief's son, Hamlet."

There was a general shaking of heads round the circle. "Had the dead chief no living brothers? Or was this son the chief?"

"No," I replied. "That is, he had one living brother who became the chief when the elder brother died."

The old men muttered: such omens were matters for chiefs and elders, not for youngsters; no good could come of going behind a chief's back; clearly Horatio was not a man who knew things.

"Yes, he was," I insisted, shooing a chicken away from my beer. "In our country the son is next to the father. The dead chief's younger brother had become the great chief. He had also married his elder brother's widow only about a month after the funeral."

"He did well," the old man beamed and announced to the others, "I told you that if we knew more about Europeans, we would find they really were very like us. In our country also," he added to me, "the younger brother marries the elder brother's widow and becomes the father of his children. Now, if your uncle, who married your widowed mother, is your father's full brother, then he will be a real father to you. Did Hamlet's father and uncle have one mother?"

His question barely penetrated my mind; I was too upset and thrown too far off balance by having one of the most important elements of *Hamlet* knocked straight out of the picture. Rather uncertainly I said that I thought they had the same mother, but I wasn't sure—the story didn't say. The old man told me severely that these genealogical details made all the difference and that when I got home I must ask the elders about it. He shouted out the door to one of his younger wives to bring his goatskin bag.

Determined to save what I could of the mother motif, I took a deep breath and began again. "The son Hamlet was very sad because his mother had married again so quickly. There was no need for her to do so, and it is our custom for a widow not to go to her next husband until she has mourned for two years."

"Two years is too long," objected the wife, who had appeared with the old man's battered goatskin bag. "Who will hoe your farms for you while you have no husband?"

"Hamlet," I retorted without thinking, "was old enough to hoe his mother's farms himself. There was no need for her to remarry." No one looked convinced. I gave up. "His mother and the great chief told Hamlet not to be sad, for the great chief himself would be a father to Hamlet. Furthermore, Hamlet would be the next chief: therefore he must stay to learn the things of a chief. Hamlet agreed to remain, and all the rest went off to drink beer."

While I paused, perplexed at how to render Hamlet's disgusted soliloquy to an audience convinced that Claudius and Gertrude had behaved in the best possible manner, one of the younger men asked me who had married the other wives of the dead chief.

"He had no other wives," I told him.

"But a chief must have many wives! How else can he brew beer and prepare food for all his guests?"

I said firmly that in our country even chiefs had only one wife, that they had servants to do their work, and that they paid them from tax money.

It was better, they returned, for a chief to have many wives and sons who would help him hoe his farms and feed his people; then everyone loved the chief who gave much and took nothing—taxes were a bad thing.

I agreed with the last comment, but for the rest fell back on their favorite way of fobbing off my questions: "That is the way it is done, so that is how we do it."

I decided to skip the soliloquy. Even if Claudius was here thought quite right to marry his brother's widow, there remained the poison motif, and I knew they would disapprove of fratricide. More hopefully I resumed, "That night Hamlet kept watch with the three who had seen his dead father. The dead chief again appeared, and although the others were afraid, Hamlet followed his dead father off to one side. When they were alone, Hamlet's dead father spoke."

"Omens can't talk!" The old man was emphatic.

"Hamlet's dead father wasn't an omen. Seeing him might have been an omen, but he was not." My audience looked as confused as I sounded. "It *was* Hamlet's dead father. It was a thing we call a 'ghost.' " I had to use the English word, for unlike many of the neighboring tribes, these people didn't believe in the survival after death of any individuating part of the personality.

"What is a 'ghost?' An omen?"

"No, a 'ghost' is someone who is dead but who walks around and can talk, and people can hear him and see him but not touch him."

They objected. "One can touch zombis."

"No, no! It was not a dead body the witches had animated to sacrifice and eat. No one else made Hamlet's dead father walk. He did it himself."

"Dead men can't walk," protested my audience as one man.

I was quite willing to compromise. "A 'ghost' is the dead man's shadow."

But again they objected. "Dead men cast no shadows."

"They do in my country," I snapped.

The old man quelled the babble of disbelief that arose immediately and told me with that insincere, but courteous, agreement one extends to the fancies of the young, ignorant, and superstitious, "No doubt in your country the dead can also walk without being zombis." From the depths of his bag he produced a withered fragment of kola nut, bit off one end to show it wasn't poisoned, and handed me the rest as a peace offering.

"Anyhow," I resumed, "Hamlet's dead father said that his own brother, the one who became chief, had poisoned him. He wanted Hamlet to avenge him. Hamlet believed this in his heart, for he did not like his father's brother." I took another swallow of beer. "In the country of the great chief, living in the same homestead, for it was a very large one, was an important elder who was often with the chief to advise and help him. His name was Polonius. Hamlet was courting his daughter, but her father and her brother . . . [I cast hastily about for some tribal analogy] warned her not to let Hamlet visit her when she was alone on her farm, for he would be a great chief and so could not marry her."

"Why not?" asked the wife, who had settled down on the edge of the old man's chair. He frowned at her for asking stupid questions and growled, "They lived in the same homestead."

"That was not the reason," I informed them. "Polonius was a stranger who lived in the homestead because he helped the chief, not because he was a relative."

"Then why couldn't Hamlet marry her?"

"He could have," I explained, "but Polonius didn't think he would. After all, Hamlet was a man of great importance who ought to marry a chief's daughter, for in his country a man could have only one wife. Polonius was afraid that if Hamlet made love to his daughter, then no one else would give a high price for her."

"That might be true," remarked one of the shrewder elders, "but a chief's son would give his mistress's father enough presents and patronage to more than make up the difference. Polonius sounds like a fool to me."

"Many people think he was," I agreed. "Meanwhile Polonius sent his son Laertes off to Paris to learn the things of that country, for it was the homestead of a very great chief indeed. Because he was afraid that Laertes might waste a lot of money on beer and women and gambling, or get into trouble by fighting, he sent one of his servants to Paris secretly, to spy out what Laertes was doing. One day Hamlet came upon Polonius's daughter Ophelia. He behaved so oddly he frightened her. Indeed"—I was fumbling for words to express the dubious quality of Hamlet's madness—"the chief and many others had also noticed that when Hamlet talked one could understand the words but not what they meant. Many people thought that he had become mad." My audience suddenly became much more attentive. "The great chief wanted to know what was wrong with Hamlet, so he sent for two of Hamlet's age mates [school friends would have taken long explanation] to talk to Hamlet and find out what troubled his heart. Hamlet, seeing that they had been bribed by the chief to betray him, told them nothing. Polonius, however, insisted that Hamlet was mad because he had been forbidden to see Ophelia, whom he loved."

"Why," inquired a bewildered voice, "should anyone bewitch Hamlet on that account?"

"Bewitch him?"

"Yes, only witchcraft can make anyone mad, unless, of course, one sees the beings that lurk in the forest."

I stopped being a storyteller, took out my notebook and demanded to be told more about these two causes of madness. Even while they spoke and I jotted notes, I tried to calculate the effect of this new factor on the plot. Hamlet had not been exposed to the beings that lurk in the forests. Only his relatives in the male line could bewitch him. Barring relatives not mentioned by Shakespeare, it had to be Claudius who was attempting to harm him. And, of course, it was. . . .

[The story of Hamlet went on at some length with the tribesmen interjecting their own interpretation of the events.]

"Sometime," concluded the old man, gathering his ragged toga about him, "you must tell us some more stories of your country. We, who are elders, will instruct you in their true meaning, so that when you return to your own land your elders will see that you have not been sitting in the bush, but among those who know things and who have taught you wisdom."

From: Bohannan, 1966

Realism   Modern classical realists derive their system of formal reasoning from Aristotle (384–322 B.C.). **Realism** seeks knowledge about the nature of reality and humankind and attempts to interpret people's destiny based on that nature. Aristotle believed that reason was the ability to know the unchanging form of objects through sense experience and then to deduce from these forms the characteristics of the objects themselves.

Realism asserts that we live in a world in which many things, including people and objects, take their form independently of human reason or imagina-

While Plato based his philosophy on the theory that reality exists in ideas, Aristotle based his on the theory that reality exists in forms, an objective world that we can know only through our senses. This is a detail of the fresco *School of Athens* by Raphael that depicts Plato and Aristotle. The fresco is in the Camera della Segnatura, the Vatican, Rome.

tion; they exist in their own right and we experience them through our senses. Our most reliable guide to human behavior is knowledge of the objects, the laws that govern them, and their relationships, since all things behave according to rational, natural laws.

In order to understand an object, we must understand its absolute form, which is unchanging. To the realist, the trees of the forest exist whether or not there is a human mind to perceive them, an example of an independent reality.

Aristotle believed that ideas (or forms), such as the idea of God or the idea of a flower, can exist without matter. However, matter cannot exist without form. Matter has both universal and particular properties. Hence each rose shares universal properties with every other rose and every other flower. However, the particular properties of a rose differentiate it from all other flowers. The same is true of humans, all of whom have properties that distinguish them from other animals but who also have different shapes, heights, and hair colors. Forms (ideas) are nonmaterial representations of universal properties of the material objects. Humans arrive at these forms (ideas) through an examination of material objects that exist apart from themselves.

Founders and Proponents

Plato first developed the doctrine of ideas, while Aristotle developed the doctrine of forms. According to Plato, ideas are independent of both the mind by which they may be known and the world of particulars in which they may take place. Aristotle, the realist, amended this, claiming that forms have an existence only in things (*in rebus*).

Classical realists maintained that each truth had a First Cause or an Unmoved Mover. The major development of modern realism, which developed from classical realism in the sixteenth century, was a method of inductive thinking, which previously had not been adequately addressed.

Francis Bacon (1561–1626) condemned Aristotelian realism for its theological, nonscientific method of thought, which began with dogma and *à priori* assumptions and then deduced conclusions. Bacon claimed that science must be based on inquiry without preconceived assumptions. We must begin with observable, verifiable instances and then, through reason, arrive at general statements or laws. This approach differed significantly from the theological methods of Thomas Aquinas, in which an axiomatic belief about God's power led to deductions about the use of God's power in the universe and in human affairs.

Bacon pointed to errors caused by this theological approach. A historical example of such an error can be seen in the dispute between Galileo and the Catholic church, in which the church had maintained that the Earth was the center of the universe. The church's position was based on the *à priori* assumption that God created the Earth, and, since God created it, it must be the center of the universe. Galileo, however, argued the position of Nicolaus Copernicus that the sun is the center of the universe, and he employed a telescope to provide empirical proof. Based on this proof, Bacon argued for a new method of inquiry that would not begin with previously assumed knowledge.

John Locke (1632–1704) supported Bacon's contentions and attempted to explain how we develop knowledge. His major contribution to realism was to dismiss preconceived ideas in human thought. At birth, according to Locke, the mind is a *tabula rasa*, a blank slate, upon which ideas are imprinted. Hence, all knowledge is acquired from sources independent of the individual's mind and from experience by way of sensation and reflection. Locke claimed that some primary qualities of objects were objective or directly connected with the object whereas others were subjective or dependent upon an individual's experiencing them. Many scholars believe that the work of Francis Bacon and John Locke opened the door for the scientific revolution.

Alfred North Whitehead (1861–1947) attempted to reconcile some aspects of idealism and realism. As a mathematician, he is typically thought of as a realist. He was the coauthor of *Principia Mathematica* (1903) with another realist, Bertrand Russell (1872–1970). Process is the central aspect of Whitehead's concept of realism. Unlike Locke, he did not see objective reality and subjective mind as separate; he saw them as an organic unity that operates by its own principles in process.

Russell agreed with Whitehead that the universe was characterized by patterns, but he believed that these patterns could be verified and analyzed through mathematics. Russell contended that philosophy is both analytical, based in science because science has the only genuine claim to knowledge, and synthetic, because it must provide hypotheses that science has not yet determined. Russell did not necessarily accept the results of science, but he did accept its methods.

Realism differs from idealism in that the idealist believes that the only genuine reality comes from the nature of the mind, whereas the realist contends that physical entities exist in their own right.

Realism and Education

According to the classical realist, the ultimate goal of education is advancing human rationality. Aristotle held that the goal of education is to aid human beings in attaining happiness through the cultivation of their potential for excellence. Schools, according to contemporary realists, can do this by requiring students to study organized bodies of knowledge, by teaching methods of arriving at this knowledge, and by assisting students to reason critically through observation and experimentation.

According to the realist, the objects that comprise reality can be classified into categories based on their structure or form. Consequently, contemporary advocates of classical realism contend that the logical ordering of the curriculum is by disciplines or subjects, which, according to Gerald L. Gutek, "consist of clusters of related concepts and of generalizations that interpret and explain interactions between the objects which these concepts represent" (p. 47).

Teachers, therefore, must have specific knowledge about a subject so that they can order it in such a way as to teach it rationally and must also have a broad liberal arts background in order to show clearly and logically the correlations that exist in all fields of knowledge. Therefore, teachers must know and use a variety of methods to communicate the subject to the student. Students, according to the realist, are expected to be ready and willing to learn what is being taught.

Pragmatism

Coming from the Greek word *pragma*, meaning "work," **pragmatism** encourages processes that allow individuals to do those things that lead to desired ends. It is primarily a twentieth-century American philosophy that examines traditional ways of thinking and doing and reconstructs them to fit modern life.

Pragmatists agree with realists that a physical world exists in its own right, not as merely a projection of the mind. However, unlike the realist, they believe that this world is neither permanent nor exists independent of humans. Instead, the pragmatist contends that humans and their environment interact and that both are equally responsible for that which is real. If humans cannot experience something, according to the pragmatist, it can't have reality for humankind. Thus, the mind is active and exploratory rather than passive and receptive; humans do not simply receive knowledge, they make it.

Problem solving is the primary methodology of the pragmatist. Human intelligence proposes hypotheses in order to explain or solve problems, then collects data to support each hypothesis. The hypothesis that solves the problem most successfully is regarded as true. However, the resolution to problems may change as new methods emerge and data are collected. Hence, truth is relative and subject to change.

Founders and Proponents

The pre–twentieth-century European background of pragmatism can be found in the work of Francis Bacon, John Locke, Jean-Jacques Rousseau, and Charles Darwin. Bacon's influence on pragmatism is primarily his method of induction, which serves as the basis of the scientific method. The pragmatists extended Bacon's scientific approach beyond simple material things to include problems in economics, politics, psychology, education, and ethics. Locke influenced pragmatism through his concept of experience as the source of knowledge. He emphasized the idea of placing children in the most desirable environment for their education. Further, he described the ideal education as being exposed to many experiences. However, his concept of the *tabula rasa* was rejected by the pragmatists because it implied that the mind is passive.

Rousseau's major contribution to pragmatism was a belief that knowledge was based on the sense experience of the natural world. He thought of individuals as basically good but corrupted by civilization, including art and science. He argued not that humans should give up technology but that its corrupting influences should be controlled. He used as his model for the "noble savage" Emile, in a novel of the same name, Daniel Defoe's Robinson Crusoe, who returned to his shipwrecked vessel many times to remove only what he needed for survival in his natural life. Rousseau did not see children as miniature adults but as humans passing through various stages of development. His work led to questions about what was natural for children and opened the door for modern psychological studies of childhood and contemporary child-centered education.

Charles Darwin (1809–1882) had the greatest scientific impact on pragmatism. Reasoning from scientific evidence, Darwin argued that species evolve naturally through a universal struggle for existence. Through the interaction of organism and environment based on available food supply, absence of predators, and geographic conditions, the strongest of the species survives. Favorable characteristics of the species are maintained and unfavorable characteristics are eliminated. Darwin's view helped foster the concept that humans are in the process of developing and becoming, as is the universe. This led to the pragmatists' belief that reality is an open-ended process.

The work of these individuals set the stage for the development of pragmatism, which was formalized in the United States in the early part of the twentieth century. Charles S. Peirce (1839–1914), although little known in his day, influenced other pragmatists such as William James (1842–1910) and John Dewey (1859–1952). Peirce accepted Aristotle's idea that the mind is different from material reality. However, he also declared that what we know about objective reality resides in the ideas we give objects and that true knowledge depends upon verification of ideas in experience. Therefore, it is essential that our ideas be as clear as possible.

Peirce's friend and contemporary William James had a much greater impact on pragmatism. James used Peirce's concept of reality as a consequence of ideas to form his theory of truth. He saw the truth of an idea in terms of its "workability." He did not view truth as an absolute but rather as a variable based on real-life events. Truth lies in individual experiences and cannot be verified objectively by someone else.

John Dewey was the most notable pragmatist in education because he applied his theory in the schools. Because Dewey considered nature and human affairs changeable, he viewed education as a constant "reorganizing and reconstruction of experience" (1928, 89).

Dewey agreed with Rousseau that nature in education is essential but he differed from Rousseau in that he believed that the child should not be removed from the social environment in order to be educated. Dewey maintained that nature includes not only physical objects but also social relationships.

Pragmatism and Education

At Dewey's Laboratory School at the University of Chicago, he put his theory into practice. By solving personal, social, and intellectual problems, children exercised their intelligence and used the accumulated knowledge of science and the humanities. He put into operation three levels of learning he based on his philosophy: development of the senses and physical coordination; use of materials and tools found in the environment; and use of intelligence to discover, examine, and use ideas. In this way students observed, planned, and prepared for the consequences of their actions. He abandoned the idea of a fixed subject matter outside the children's experience. Rather, he believed that the curriculum should be continuously restructured so that it moved from the child's experience into what he called "the organized bodies of truth" (1902, 11).

Since pragmatists believe that change is the essence of reality, the curriculum must be flexible. Likewise, since reality is defined as the interaction of humans with their environment, the curriculum must assist students in learning how the world affects humankind and how people affect one another. Because the mind is actively engaged with experience, the curriculum and teaching methodologies should encourage activity, exploration, and problem solving.

The school, as a social institution, should not be viewed as separate from life itself. According to the pragmatist, education is part of life, not a preparation for it. Schools should use real situations, not just formal academic subjects, to help students learn how to interact with their biological and social environments.

Existentialism

Those who believe in **existentialism** believe that reality is lived existence, and final reality resides within the individual. Reality begins with being aware of one's own existence; it is, therefore, human-made. It is not a state of being, but a process of becoming.

The existentialist believes that people live on earth for a short time, are born by chance in a chance place, and are affected by situations beyond their control. According to existentialist philosopher Jean-Paul Sartre (1905–1980), "Existence precedes essence." He means by this that things exist before we may give any definition to them. Thus, knowledge, like all things, exists only in light of human consciousness.

Similarly, the universe is without meaning or purpose. Humans are not part of a great cosmic "design," because design is merely a concept of the mind.

The purposes humans think they detect in the universe are merely projections of humans' desire for order. We are placed in an alien universe in which we will sooner or later die. The existentialist talks about *Angst*, the German word for dread, which comes from people's awareness of the absurdity of the human condition—we are free and yet finite; we are in the world and yet apart from it; we are condemned to death. According to the existentialists, humans transcend the world through their freedom and submit to it through their death.

According to the existentialist, humans have free choice. They can choose to either conform and accept society's norms or revolt against and reject them. As individuals make various choices, they engage in defining who they are, their reality. A person is what a person does. According to Van Cleve Morris in *Existentialism in Education: What It Means* (1966), the existentialist says:

1. I am a *choosing* agent, unable to avoid choosing my way through life.
2. I am a *free* agent, absolutely free to set the goals of my own life.
3. I am a *responsible* agent, personally accountable for my free choices as they are revealed in how I live my life. (p. 135)

Founders and Proponents

Existentialists claim ancient roots extending back to some Greek philosophers of the fifth and fourth centuries B.C. However, existentialism is basically a philosophy of nineteenth-century thought that allowed humans the freedom to define their own essence based on their existence in a moment in time. It was explored in the philosophical writings of such men as Søren Kierkegaard (1813–1855) and Jean-Paul Sartre and the literature of such writers as Albert Camus (1913–1960).

Kierkegaard, a Danish theologian, examined the life of the lonely individual against the objective, scientific world. He criticized science, contending that its objectivity was an attempt to drive society away from the Christian faith. He described three stages of life: the aesthetic stage, in which humans live in sensuous enjoyment and emotions dominate; the ethical stage, in which humans achieve understanding of their place and function in life; and the religious stage, for Kierkegaard the highest, in which humans stand alone before God. It is only through faith that humans can bridge the gap between man and God. He believed that individuals must come to understand their souls, their destinies, and the reality of God through education. Kierkegaard also maintained that individuals must accept responsibility for their choices, which they alone can make.

Sartre published *L'Etre et le Néant* (*Being and Nothingness*) in 1943 in France. In it he spelled out his existentialist philosophy, which differed significantly from Kierkegaard's because it was basically secular rather than religious. Sartre believed that objects exist prior to any essence or definition humans may give them. The world exists, is concrete and particular, and any interpretation humans give to it is less real than the data from which the interpretation is abstracted. By itself the universe is meaningless, human interpretation of meaning is nothing more than a desire for order.

Sartre affirmed that man possesses absolute freedom. Since man is free, he "makes himself." Freedom is merely potential until man acts; man is "nothing" until he acts. In Sartre's words, "If man, as the existentialist sees him, is indefinable, it is because at first he is nothing. Only afterwards will he be something and he himself will have made what he will be" (1957, 18). Because man is free, he is always potentially in conflict with others. This is because humans must either dominate or be dominated by the other. In the first case, he treats the other as an object by denying the other's freedom. In the second, he denies his own freedom, thereby "objectifying" himself.

Existentialism and Education

Existentialism has been translated into educational thought by the humanistic psychologists Carl Rogers (see chapter 9, p. 273) and Abraham Maslow (see chapter 10, p. 335). Rogers believed that teachers should seek the potentiality and wisdom of their students by helping them work for self-directed change. The teacher must trust the learner and serve as a facilitator for learning. Maslow contended that individuals have a hierarchy of needs beginning with basic needs and culminating in what he called "metaneeds." Basic survival needs include such things as food, health, shelter, and protection. Metaneeds are the individual's strivings to transcend basic needs. They include such things as acceptance, understanding, and aesthetics. According to Maslow, meeting these needs is essential if an individual is to become self-actualized and reach his or her full potential. The work of these psychologists has been implemented in the schools through counseling and instructional methodologies that strive to help students reach their full potential.

The existentialist believes that most schools, like other larger corporate symbols, deemphasize the individual and the relationship between the teacher and the student. Existentialists claim that as educators attempt to predict the behavior of students, they turn individuals into objects to be measured quantitatively. They feel that grouping, measurement, standardization, and scheduling all work against creating opportunities for self-direction and personal choice.

According to the existentialist, education is a process of developing a free, self-actualizing person, centering on the feelings of the student. Therefore, education does not start with the nature of the world and with humankind but with the human, moral self.

Since the final goal of existentialism is a completely autonomous person, the existentialist suggests education without coercion or prescription. Students should be active and encouraged to make their own choices. According to Morris L. Bigge, "There is no existential learning *system*. Instead, existentialists have an ever-shifting vision of what transpires in conscious minds; human mentalities are always in process. As long as one lives, one's unfinished experience is always shifting and changing" (1982, 140).

The teacher who follows existentialist educational philosophy emphasizes learning situations in which each student makes choices. According to Van Cleve Morris, "The environment of the child should be one of complete and absolute freedom . . . where selfhood can operate without hindrance. We should not impose upon a youngster any environments whatever—neither Mind, nor things, nor God, nor Truth, nor Experience lived with and among other human beings" (pp. 80–81). With this statement the existentialist educator rejects the philosophical schools of idealism, realism, and pragmatism. The existentialist approach, never widely accepted in its more extreme forms, has lost favor in contemporary schools. However, its several legacies include the practice of basing instruction on an assessment of student interests, abilities, and needs; counseling with students about academic and/or discipline problems; allowing students to make choices about books to read or exercises to complete; developing a variety of learning centers from which students can select activities; and contract grading.

Philosophical Analysis

Philosophical analysis classifies and verifies phenomena in order to define reality. Unlike existentialists, philosophical analysts attempt to remove the personal and the subjective from the search for truth and therefore base their information on whatever can be confirmed through the senses; knowledge gained in this way takes the form of empirically verified propositions, grounded in experiment and observation. Truths about the universe, reality, and humankind are thus empirical, not philosophical matters. The branch of philosophical analysis based on experiment and observation is known as **logical empiricism**.

Knowledge founded on empirical evidence satisfies the **theory of verification**, which states that empirical propositions may be verified either directly or indirectly. Direct verification is tested through sense perception. "I feel the rain." But logical empiricists rely most often on indirect verification. This is the scientific method in which tests can be developed to determine whether something is true. George F. Kneller provides this description of indirect verification.

> Proposition P1: This book is made of paper. Such a proposition is not *directly* verifiable, but we may set up the following premises in order to test it:
> P2: "If fire is placed under paper, it burns." This is a physical law, already directly verified.
> P3: "This flame is fire." This proposition is also directly verified; that is, we can see flame or feel it.
> P4: "The fire is placed under the book." This proposition is *now* directly verified by observation.
> We may now deduce the conclusion from our premises:
> P5: The book will now burn. (1964, 74)

According to Kneller, the final proposition is a hypothesis that may be tested by observation. If observation and further tests support the hypothesis, we can be more certain that the book is made of paper. But we can never be absolutely certain. According to the empiricist, statements about the material world can carry only a "very high degree of probability" (p. 75). For example, the book also will burn if it's made of plastic or cloth.

Unlike the major schools of philosophy, analytical philosophers attempt to clarify language and thought rather than develop new theories or, in other words, to verify that which is already believed to be true. The analysts' tools are language, particularly grammar and structural linguistics, and logic. This branch of philosophical analysis is known as **linguistic analysis.**

Founders and Proponents

The historical roots of philosophical analysis can be traced to ancient Greek philosophers Anaximander and Anaximines and the ancient atomists, who believed the universe was made of tiny, simple particles that could not be destroyed or divided. In the eighteenth century Auguste Comte was one of the first to assert that philosophy could be used to clarify the concepts of science, which are both testable and universal. However, modern analytical philosophy was developed in the early and mid-twentieth century. The proponents of this philosophy included George Edward Moore, the architect of linguistic analysis, and Bertrand Russell, a proponent of the use of mathematical logic for scientific analysis and meaning.

George Edward Moore (1873–1958) in "The Defence of Common Sense" in *Main Problems of Philosophy* (1953) focused on common speech as the most logical extension of common sense. Moore claimed that in both philosophy and ordinary language there are things that cannot be proved or disproved; therefore, it made sense to analyze commonly used terminology to assess what is meant by words such as *good, know,* and *real.* Moore believed that knowing the concept of the word and analyzing the meaning of the word are two different things. Analysis would help the user determine what Moore called the "goodness of fit" of the word.

Bertrand Russell developed a logical system of philosophical analysis incorporating a precise vocabulary. In *Principia Mathematica* mathematics was reduced to a logical language. Russell's logic dealt with the relationship of propositions to each other. For example, "If the temperature is below freezing, the water on the road will freeze." This statement consists of two propositions, each with a relationship to the other. According to Russell, language has a basic logical structure similar to mathematics, which can be used to clarify the meaning of language.

Philosophical Analysis and Education

Philosophical analysis teaches students two different sets of skills to verify propositions. The first is the scientific method of logical empiricism and the second is the critical examination of language, or linguistic analysis.

The goal of education is to teach students to think empirically by seeking evidence to confirm propositions. The logical empiricist directs students to find true knowledge by observing and doing. According to analytical philosopher Gilbert Ryle (1900–1976), educators often confuse "knowing that" and "knowing how to." "Knowing that" may simply mean filling the student's head with information. This, according to Ryle, is not "knowing." "Knowing" requires "knowing how to," or being able to perform tasks using available data. An individual may know, for example, that driving a car requires turning the key in the ignition, shifting gears, putting the foot on the accelerator, and steering. However, this individual does not know how to drive a car until he or she has had the experience of driving. This is the basis for liberal arts education, in which students are taught not only specific facts but also how to think and question within disciplines.

Linguistic analysts encourage the critical examination of language. Students are taught to establish meaning in language and clarify assumptions of different points of view. They attempt to defuse propaganda and examine the substance of slogans to clarify ambiguous terms and phrases.

Analysts try to develop a scientific language that orders and evaluates propositions. To this end, they study language games, symbolic language, metaphorical language, and other forms of expression in order to establish

(continued on p. 217)

TABLE 7-1

Schools of Philosophical Thought

	Idealism	Realism	Pragmatism	Existentialism	Philsophical analysis
Metaphysics (Reality)	Reality consists of ideas, thoughts, minds, and selves. It is essentially spritual.	Reality is the absolute form or idea of physical objects, experienced through our senses. It is permanent, unchanging.	Reality is the total of the individual's experience; the interaction with his/her surroundings; it is forever changing.	Reality is a process of becoming; an awareness from within one's self; from his/her own existence.	Reality is common sense; it is classifying and verifying much as in a scientific analysis.
Epistemology (Knowledge)	Knowledge is an active process of a rational and substantive mind	Knowledge is direct contact with objects and the laws that govern them; their relationships.	Knowledge comes from actively exploring, solving problems, and from interaction with others.	Knowledge results from free choices made in the process of becoming, and from accountability for choices made.	Knowledge results from observations, experiments, and analysis.
Axiology (Values)	Values are genuine, absolute, rooted in deity, and permanent.	Values are permanent, objective.	Values change as situations change; they are relative.	Values are individual decisions; selective.	Values are based on reasoning.
Logic	People come from an existing infinite God, having a mind and soul: i.e., people grow in the image of God.	People are biological existing organisms in a real world: i.e., all people have power to acquire and use knowledge.	People are biological and social beings, interacting with their environment: i.e., people continually discover knowledge.	People are born by chance in a chance place; they have free choice to accept or reject: i.e., people gain knowledge of self.	Analysis involves classifying and verifying: i.e., people can reason, solve problems, and think empirically.
Educational Implications	Education is idea centered. Learning leads to self-initiated mental and spiritual growth. Based on intuition and recall.	Education's goal is to develop potential for excellence through organized sequencing of subjects/disciplines. Teachers must know both subject and student. Students must be receptive to learning/achievement.	Education involves real-life problem-solving activities. Teachers should be knowledgable in child/adolescent development and in the group process. Students must interact, solve problems, creating knowledge.	Education should emphasize development of self-hood—of an autonomous person. Students should have an environment where they are free to make choices and to be active.	Education should emphasize the scientific method and analysis of language. Students should be taught to observe, experiment, think critically, and observe rules of formal logic.

Philosophical theories derive their concepts of reality from basic approaches to philosophical inquiry. These approaches are listed in the left-hand column along with their educational implications. Listed horizontally are the philosophical interpretations of each of these approaches and their practical application to education.

veracity based on a common understanding of terminology. For example, middle school students might examine television advertisements to find overstatements such as "an extra large quart size"; "lite dinners are lower in calories" (what the ad doesn't tell us is they are also smaller in size); and "the best steak dinner east of the Mississippi."

7.1 POINTS TO REMEMBER

- Philosophy is the love of wisdom. It is an inquiry into the principles of knowledge.
- Metaphysical questions deal with the nature of reality. Epistemological questions deal with the nature and source of knowledge. Axiological questions deal with the nature of values and aesthetics. Logic deals with the nature of reasoning.

- It is important for educators to study philosophy because it helps us think clearly about educational issues and gives an educator a theory with which to back up practice.
- The categories of philosophy (metaphysics, epistemology, axiology, and logic) provide philosophers with questions to ask about reality, knowledge, values, aesthetics, and reasoning.
- Idealists contend that reality con-

sists of ideas, thoughts, minds, and selves. Realists believe that we live in a world in which many things, including people, exist without benefit of human knowledge. Pragmatists contend that reality is constantly changing. Existentialists believe that reality is defined by lived existence, and final reality exists within the self. Philosophical analysts hold that things are not real unless they can be classified and verified.

PHILOSOPHICAL THEORIES OF EDUCATION

Theories of education are based on the schools of philosophy: idealism, realism, pragmatism, existentialism, and philosophical analysis. The anecdote at the beginning of this chapter represents a satirical glimpse at the difference between a school of philosophy and a theory of education. The young teacher Socrates is not rehired. Of course, John Gauss, the author of this anecdote, was poking fun at systems of evaluation that would keep a teacher like Socrates from being hired by the schools. However, the anecdote can be used to illustrate another point: schools of philosophy are NOT theories of education but are instead the foundations for theories of education. Philosophers ask questions about knowledge, truth, and education, whereas educators develop the ideas of philosophers into specific theories of teaching and learning.

Theory guides action; it is a hypothesis or set of hypotheses that have been verified by observation and experiment. Philosophy, on the other hand, does not guide action; it asks questions. Therefore, attempting to develop teaching methodology from a specific school of philosophy is likely to be as successful as making soup from stones and nails. Unless, of course, educators, like the soldiers in the French folktale *Stone Soup*, add ingredients to the recipe other than just stones.

The theories of education based on the schools of philosophy include perennialism, essentialism, progressivism, social reconstructionism, and behaviorism. See table 7.2 (p. 225) for a comparative illustration of how each theory of education deals with curricular focus, methodology, and the role of the teacher.

Perennialism

Perennialism is based on the philosophical schools of classical idealism and realism. Perennialists stress the permanence of time-honored ideas, the great works of the intellectual past, and the human ability to reason. They attempt to develop both the intellectual and spiritual in students through study of the traditional disciplines of history, language, mathematics, logic, and literature, which survive from one generation to the next and provide insights into the true, the good, and the beautiful and develop the intellect.

Perennialism, according to George F. Kneller, has six basic principles: (1) Human nature is constant; therefore the nature of education is constant. (2) Humans' distinguishing characteristic is reason; therefore education should help students develop rationality. (3) Education should lead students to the truth, which is eternal, rather than to an understanding of the contemporary world, which is temporal. (4) Education is a preparation for life rather than an imitation of life. (5) Students should be taught basic subjects that will lead them to an understanding of the world's permanence. (6) Students should be introduced to the universal concerns of humankind through the study of great works of literature, philosophy, history, and science.

Perennialists most often cite the classical realist philosophies of Aristotle and Saint Thomas Aquinas. Recent educational proponents include Robert Maynard Hutchins, former president of the University of Chicago who wrote scathing attacks on progressive education, and Mortimer J. Adler, who developed his own perennial philosophy and teaching methodologies based on great books and questioning techniques. Adler's best-known educational work is *The Paideia Proposal: An Educational Manifesto* (1982), in which he asserts that all students should be taught to deal with great literary works through well-developed questioning techniques.

Perennialists expect teachers to use Socratic methods of questioning and well-organized lectures. Students are coached to recite information correctly. Therefore, teachers are the most essential element in perennialism. According to Hutchins in *The Higher Learning In America* (1936), "Education implies teaching. Teaching implies knowledge. Knowledge is truth. The truth is everywhere the same. Hence education is everywhere the same" (p. 66).

Essentialism

The educational theory of **essentialism** is, like perennialism, based in the philosophical schools of idealism and realism. Unlike perennialism, however, essentialism began as an educational rather than a philosophical movement. The essentialist believes that there are certain basic facts, which have permanent value, that all students must know, and that the school's role is the transmission of these essential facts and, thus, of a common culture. The primary function of the school is academic in providing broad general knowledge, and it therefore does not take on any nonessential functions such as preparing students for careers.

There are four basic principles of the essentialist: (1) Learning, by its very nature, requires hard work and often unwilling application. (2) The initiative toward education lies with the teacher, not with the student. (3) The student's absorption of the prescribed subject matter is the heart of the educational process. (4) The school should employ traditional methods of mental discipline. Therefore, the teacher must be the central classroom authority in terms of discipline, motivation, and curriculum. She or he must know what is to be learned and administer discipline to ensure that it is.

Like perennialism, the philosophical foundation of essentialism lies in the classical philosophies of idealism and realism. The principles are those of Plato and Aristotle, and the teaching methodologies are consistent with those of Socrates. The best-known contemporary proponent is E. D. Hirsch, Jr., who spelled out his essentialist theory in *Cultural Literacy: What Every American Needs to Know* (1987). According to Hirsch in the preface to the 1988 edition of the book: "This book focuses on the background knowledge necessary for functional literacy and effective national communication. . . . American literacy has been declining at a time when our changed economy requires that our literacy should rise" (xi). In part, Hirsch maintains that in order to have effective communication, we must have a national language and a national culture. He states that since our culture changes slowly, students should learn the works on which it is based. His alphabetical list of authors who must be taught includes Aristophanes, Aristotle, Bacon, Cicero, Dryden, Homer, Locke, Milton, Pope, Rousseau, Shakespeare, and Virgil.

Hirsch's work is one example of the neoessentialist or essentialist revival movement of the 1980s. In addition to Hirsch's book, this movement included many of the reform reports of the decade, including *A Nation at Risk* (National Commission on Excellence in Education, 1983) and *Action for Excellence* (Task Force on Education for Economic Growth, 1983). (See chapter 6 for a discussion of these and other neoessentialist reports and books.)

Progressivism, rooted in the philosophical school of pragmatism, is the counterpoint to both essentialism and perennialism. According to the progressive educator, the child should be the focal point of the school, and therefore the curriculum and teaching methodology should relate to the students' interests and needs. Moreover, progressivism contends that children want to learn if they are not frustrated by adults; therefore, teachers should act merely as guides to student learning and, in order to respond to different requests for knowledge, must possess significant knowledge and experience.

Progressivism

The school, according to the progressive movement, is a microcosm of society, and learning experiences should occur in the school as they do in society; they should not be artificially divided into time, space, and content. English and social studies, for example, should be integrated and focus on problem solving rather than simple memorization of content. According to the progressivist, education is part of life itself, not a preparation for life; this is the exact opposite of the perennialist's point of view. Thus, learning should be cooperative as it is in a democratic environment. Teachers and students should be involved in the operation of the school. Teachers should participate in such things as curriculum planning and assignment of students to groups.

According to George F. Kneller, the basic principles of progressivism include the following: (1) Learning should be active and related to the interests of the child. (2) Individuals handle the complexity of life more effectively if they break experiences down into specific problems. Therefore, learning should involve the solving of problems rather than memorization of subject matter. (3) Since education is a reconstruction of experience, education is synonymous with living. So education should be like life itself rather than a preparation for life. (4) Because interests of the child are central to what is taught, the teacher should act as a guide rather than a figure of authority. (5) Individuals achieve

Progressivists believe that education is a part of life itself, not a preparation for life. Thus, children learn more quickly if the classroom is structured in such a way as to resemble the real world. These students are learning math and reading by pretending they are in a grocery store.

more when they work with others than when they compete. Therefore, the schools should encourage cooperative learning practices. (6) In order to grow, individuals need the interplay of ideas and personalities. Since this is best achieved in a democratic system, the school must operate within the principles of a democracy.

Progressivism was an attempt to reform the essentialist and perennialist views of schooling in the late nineteenth and early twentieth centuries. In the 1870s educator Colonel Francis W. Parker was one of the first to argue that schools were too authoritarian, relied too heavily on textbooks and passive learning, and isolated learning from social reality. In *Schools of Tomorrow* (1915) John Dewey spelled out his pragmatic philosophy by explaining how progressive methodology functioned in the classroom. In 1919 the Progressive Education Association was founded. But its rise corresponded with World War I and, as a result, its influence on the schools was not as great as it might have been. However, its influence has been far-reaching, particularly in elementary education. Some of the legacies passed down to contemporary schools from progressive education include manipulatives in science and mathematics, field trips, projects related to study of community issues, and classroom stores and kitchens.

During the years of the Great Depression and those immediately following it, progressivists moved away from emphasis on the individual child toward emphasis on education for the good of society. They advocated that schools be heavily immersed in solving society's problems and issues. Progressivists take the pragmatic view that change is the essence of reality, and, therefore, education is always in the process of changing; it is a positive, continual reconstruction of experience. The more radical wing of the progressive movement became known as reconstructionists.

Point/Counterpoint

LITERATURE TOWARD A COMMON CULTURE

According to a survey of 325 scholars, journalists, teachers, and government and cultural leaders sponsored by the National Endowment for the Humanities (NEH) in 1984, there are certain works that every student in the country "might reasonably be expected to have studied before he or she graduates from high school."

This list is topped by the works of Shakespeare, *Huckleberry Finn* (Mark Twain), the Declaration of Independence, and the Bible. It includes such authors as Homer, Dickens, Plato, Steinbeck, Sophocles, Melville, Thoreau, Frost, Whitman, Fitzgerald, Chaucer, Marx, Aristotle, Dickinson, Dostoevski, Faulkner, Salinger, de Tocqueville, Austin, Emerson, Machiavelli, Milton, Tolstoy, and Virgil.

From: Reed, ed., Fall 1984 and Winter 1985

LIMITATIONS IN DEFINING COMMON CULTURE

Readers of the educational journal The ALAN Review, *published by the Assembly on Literature for Adolescents of the National Council of Teachers of English, were asked in the Fall 1984 issue of the journal to respond to this report.*

Request for response:

It is interesting to note that the most recent work included on the [NEH] list is J. D. Salinger's *Catcher in the Rye* [1951], the only female writers on the list are Jane Austin and Emily Dickinson, and no minority writers are included. I can't help but wonder what kind of a world view this "common literary heritage" gives our students.

The questions I pose to readers are: Should our students have a common literary heritage? If so, is this the heritage [the one proposed by NEH] we want them to have?

Responses from readers:

I consider the publication of the list, and implications that the best high school minds (168) were applied to the questions, a misuse of the National Endowment's considerable (and merited) prestige.

It was a temptation to interrupt my fellow NEH seminarians in the Patsy Scales [a well-known librarian who has written widely about literature for adolescents] tradition (just after she asked her audience to do the same thing): "Only put down titles of books YOU read all the way through, AND enjoyed as a high school student."

Helen Fairbanks
Asheville, NC

"There are certain foods that every healthy person should reasonably be expected to eat" . . . and yet so many pout over a plate of fresh calves liver! So much for the survey of 325 "scholars, journalists, teachers, and government and cultural leaders" who would continue the great American tradition of forcing children to read what they are not yet emotionally or intellectually ready to read.

I remember having lunch one summer with a group of English teachers. The conversation turned to this very topic, and all agreed (with the exception of me) that, yes, there certainly were works of literature that every educated person should have read. Yet, I was the only one to have read *The Scarlet Letter* (and several other prominent pieces of literature, for that matter). It occurred to me then that when most people speak of what should be, it is just that—a Utopia that is best left to the realm of idle wishes and after-lunch conversation.

Kay Gore
Tempe, AZ

Traditions die hard and traditional approaches to a "Common Literary Heritage" will not be challenged lightly.

What distresses me is that the particular group of books missing from this "perfect list" includes many female authors and authors who describe lifestyles of many minorities, both in our country and abroad.

As in the textbooks so often used to teach the historical and political perspectives of the world, the voices of these writers are seldom, if ever, heard. This, to me, is the ugliest form of censorship, since it teaches a subtle form of tunnel vision.

Sherrill Osgood
Presque Isle, ME

From: Reed, ed., Fall 1984 and Winter 1985

POSTSCRIPT

As with most arguments in education, this one is not easily resolved. On one hand, the NEH is arguing for an academic base of permanent knowledge and values with which all students should be familiar. The great difficulty with this argument is in deciding what specific knowledge and values should be common to all students. How can any one institution or group of people decide what is best for everyone? On the other hand, the editor and teachers are suggesting that knowledge and values should change to keep up with changing perspectives and ideals in society. The problem with this point of view is that then, all standards become arbitrary. The NEH point of view is idealistic and perennialist, while the editor's and teachers' is pragmatic and progressive or, perhaps, social reconstructionist. Where does your point of view fit into this argument?

Social Reconstructionism   Those who follow the ideas of **reconstructionism** believe that the purpose of education is to reconstruct society. As such, it is built upon the foundation of progressivism and, like progressivism, derives from the philosophical school of pragmatism. Reconstructionists view the educational theories of perennialism and essentialism as mere reflections of societal patterns and values and urge educators to originate policies and programs to reform society.

George S. Counts is considered to be the first and foremost proponent of reconstructionism. Counts, a professor at Columbia University, stated, in *Dare the School Build a New Social Order?* (1932), that the great crises of the twentieth century (World War I and the Great Depression) were a result of profound transition and rapid change. According to Counts, it is not change itself but, rather, the inability of humans to deal with change that promotes crisis. Hence, Counts believed, the educational system must prepare students to deal cognitively and attitudinally with change that occurs multilaterally (changes in one arena of society affect changes in other arenas).

V I E W P O I N T S

Excerpt from *A Tale of Two Cities*

It was the best of times, it was the worst of times, it was the age of wisdom, it was the age of foolishness, it was the epoch of belief, it was the epoch of incredulity, it was the season of Light, it was the season of Darkness, it was the spring of hope, it was the winter of despair, we had everything before us, we had nothing before us, we were all going direct to Heaven, we were all going direct the other way—in short, the period was so far like the present period, that some of its noisiest authorities insisted on its being received, for good or for evil, in the superlative degree of comparison only.

From: Charles Dickens, 1859

Social reconstructionists believe that a society's culture does not keep pace with its dynamic technology. Students should be taught, therefore, to reconstruct and reform society so that, for example, it can efficiently use the products of technology without endangering the environment.

According to Gerald L. Gutek, social reconstructionism is founded on the following principles: (1) All philosophies, ideologies, and theories are culturally based. Each culture is influenced by the living conditions of a specific time and place. (2) Culture is dynamic, continually changing and growing. (3) Humans can change the culture so that it reflects their growth and development. Therefore, educational theories, according to reconstructionists, are a product of the particular historic period and culture at the time in which they existed.

Social reconstructionists believe that society itself must be reformed since it is in severe crisis caused by the unwillingness of humans to reconstruct institutions and values to meet the changing needs and demands of contemporary life. Modern technological society still clings to the values of an agrarian, preindustrial society, leading not only to problems in adapting to change but also to what the reconstructionist calls **social disintegration**. Consequently, humans need to reexamine their institutions and values in order to adapt them to the new society.

Thus, the task of education is twofold. First, educators must reconstruct the theoretical base of the United States' cultural heritage. Second, they must develop school programs with a clearly thought-out curriculum of social reform to deal with extreme cultural crisis and social disintegration. The new social order of the school must be democratic yet the teacher must persuade students of the importance of the reconstructionist point of view. Theodore Brameld, in

Patterns of Educational Philosophy: Divergence and Convergence in Culturological Perspective (1971), says "The teacher of reconstructionist inclination, being an important member of cooperative learning, is subject to the same guiding principles of practice as is any other group member. His [or her] classroom (whether enclosed by walls or embraced by a community) affords continuous opportunity for unrestricted, impartial study just because he [or she] and [the] students cannot otherwise reach effective agreements that are themselves partial" (p. 474).

Behaviorism

Behaviorism is rooted in the philosophical schools of realism and philosophical analysis. It was developed by psychologists in the mid-twentieth century who believed in the scientific method, objectivity, immediate results, efficiency and economy, and positiveness.

Behaviorists contend that only those things that can be examined and validated in a laboratory are part of psychology. Therefore, behavior must be observable; there is no time for philosophizing or speculating about human nature. John B. Watson was the first to elaborate on behaviorism. Its major contemporary proponent, until his death in 1990, was B. F. Skinner.

Skinner maintained that applying science to human nature should lead to advances equivalent to those in other scientific fields. He believed that scientific knowledge could lead to teaching improvements as educators and psychologists developed what he called a "technology of teaching." Skinner based much of his work on the assumption of Locke that the newborn's mind is a blank slate and that all that is learned is acquired through experience. Therefore, he concluded that those who arrange experiences control behavior and shape personality, primarily by means of reinforcement. In a series of laboratory experiments with animals, he showed how repeated rewards affected the animal's behavior. He applied the results of these experiments to children, saying that the child's tendency to repeat certain acts is a function of which acts have been rewarded. Skinner wrote in *The Technology of Teaching* (1968):

> Some promising advances have recently been made in the field of learning. Special techniques have been designed to arrange what are called contingencies of reinforcement—the relations which prevail between behavior on the one hand and the consequences of the behavior on the other—with the result that a much more effective control of behavior has been achieved. It has long been argued that an organism learns mainly by producing changes in its environment, but it is only recently that these changes have been carefully manipulated. (p. 9)

Humans need to learn the laws of behavior, to be taught to act in specific ways through either reward or punishment. In simple terms, those behaviors that are rewarded are increased, those that receive no rewards diminish, and those that are punished are more rapidly lessened. The task of education is to develop learning environments that lead to desired behaviors in students for which they are rewarded so that they are motivated to continue to learn.

Behaviorists believe that the school environment must be highly organized and the curriculum based on behavioral objectives. They strongly contend that empirical evidence is essential if students are to learn and that the scientific method must be employed to arrive at knowledge. Student progress must be observed so that it can be verified.

(continued on p. 226)

TABLE 7-2

Theories of Education

	Perennialism	Essentialism	Progressivism	Social reconstructionism	Behaviorism
Origins	Idealism	Idealism/Realism	Pragmatism/ Science	Pragmatism/ Events of History/ The Great Depression	Realism/ Philosophical Analysis/ Science
Goals	Development of intellectual and spiritual potential.	Preserve and transmit the basic elements of human culture.	Reconstruct experiences related to needs and interests of students and society.	Reconstruction of existing society.	Provide experiences that develop intellectual and moral dispositions in the form of desired behavioral patterns.
Curriculum	A curriculum based on great works of literature, history, science, philosophy. Basic skills that are constant and a preparation for life.	Subject-centered curriculum. Basic skills of literacy and math (elementary), content of history, English, math, science, literature, foreign language (secondary).	Child-centered curriculum, emphasizing problem solving, activities, projects related to child's interests, integration of subject areas, and social issues.	A curriculum based on social reform. Emphasis on social sciences and process.	A curriculum based on problem areas in life situations rather than on subjects. Most conventional courses taught but through the problems to be solved. (Communication, city planning)
Methods and Teachers	Didactic methods developing rationality. Teacher is knowledgeable and asks probing questions and has directed discussions.	Directed teaching for mastery of essential skills. Teacher must be competent in subject matter and method.	Problem solving, active group-learning activities. Teachers should be stimulators, consultants to students, and active in the curriculum planning and operation of the school.	Democratic cooperative learning. Teachers should identify major social problems and direct students to study them impartially.	Use behavioral objectives to direct teaching and learning programmed materials. Teachers encourage objectivity, inquiry, and stimulate each student's participation for desired behavioral outcomes.

Goals, curriculums, and methods of instruction are based on a specific theory of education which is, in turn, derived from a philosophical school of thought. This table compares the approaches of the major theories of education.

Behaviorists have these eight educational goals:

1. To develop a world view devoid of all dualisms that separate humankind from nature, spirit from flesh, purpose from mechanism, and morals from the conditions of living.
2. To promote the integration of the development of human values and intelligence through furthering a rich appreciation of the forms and qualities of things in their connection with one another as a positive resource for the development of intellectual powers.
3. To promote the primary mode of experiencing, which involves feeling, doing, and undergoing; and learning from that which is done, suffered, and enjoyed.
4. To emphasize dealing with both things and words. An educational program that emphasizes things and not words is as defective as one that emphasizes words and not things.
5. To give students a balance of primary experience and learning through the use of literary materials.
6. To develop in students the ability to preserve a characteristic pattern of activity through a process of continuous adjustment with surroundings.
7. To help biological organisms become selves, which are inherently social in nature, through their participation in the ways of life and thought of a community that include language, history, knowledge, and practical and fine arts.
8. To develop the kinds of persons who will be responsible citizens in a democratic society, not obedient, submissive subjects of an autocratic leadership who carry out the functions that are imposed upon them. (Bigge, p. 158)

In order to fulfill these goals, behaviorists contend that the classrooms should represent the world of problems, and teachers should serve as directors of the students' social and intellectual learning. The behaviorists agree with the progressivists that education is life itself rather than a preparation for life. Instead of teaching formal subjects, the curriculum should revolve around problem areas such as the environment or housing. Students and teachers should analyze and evaluate how communities evolve and change. Thereby, education takes an active role in social change, and students learn the "intrinsic connection between freedom of thought and inquiry and the maintenance of a society that is cooperatively controlled in the interest of the good life of all its members" (Bigge, p. 159).

HOW DOES PHILOSOPHY AFFECT EDUCATION?

As we discussed earlier, philosophy cannot be directly translated into teaching. Philosophy is the love of wisdom seeking answers about knowledge and reality, humankind's relationship to nature and the deity, and morals and beauty. Philosophy does, however, provide the basis for theories of learning that address such issues as how best to teach a subject area, problem solving, and values. Unlike theories of learning that are based on psychology, those based on philosophy do not attempt to explain systematically how students learn but, instead, direct educators toward goals and methodologies that explore the nature of knowing.

According to George R. Knight in *Issues and Alternatives in Educational Philosophy* (1982), how individuals view reality, knowledge, and values will determine the educational goals they set for their students. The goals in turn will determine the curricular emphasis.

Goal Setting

 For example, if an individual believes that the universe exists independently of humankind and humans have limited control over it (realism), then it is likely that the goals will emphasize teaching the students about the existing universe. On the other hand, if an individual believes that reality is continuously changing and that humans can affect how it changes (pragmatism), then it is likely that these goals will involve teaching the students to deal with the changing universe and assisting them in becoming agents of change. See figure 7.1 for a graphic representation of how philosophy affects education.

 Knight points out that in addition to philosophy, politics, economic conditions, and social factors influence education. He suggests that differing philo-

FIGURE 7-1

The Relationship of Philosophy to Educational Practice

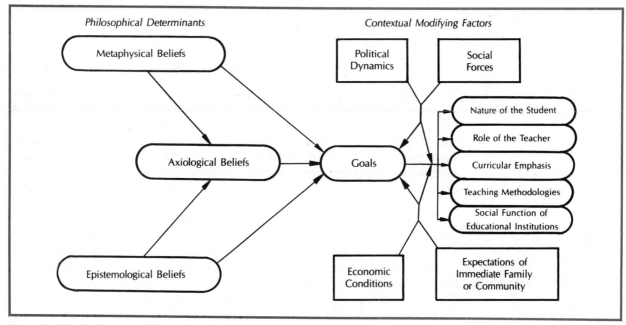

From: G. Knight, *Issues and Alternatives in Educational Philosophy* (1982), 33.

A teacher's view of reality (metaphysics), knowledge (axiology), and values (epistemology) leads to the setting of educational goals which in turn leads to a curricular emphasis. This curriculum, however, is also influenced by outside forces such as political dynamics and expectations of families and communities.

sophical beliefs do not always lead to different goals and hence different educational practices. Some people arrive at the same destination from different starting points. In other words, in spite of differing educational philosophies, two teachers might employ the same teaching methodology. Conversely, people with similar philosophical orientations will not always have the same goals or teach in the same way.

Curriculum   Based on a teacher's philosophical beliefs, he or she establishes educational goals and designs the curriculum. For example, if a teacher believes that it is essential for the students to learn universal and unchanging truths (idealism) that must be communicated to them through the study of the great works of humankind (perennialism), she or he may adopt the curricular focus of Mortimer Adler's *Paideia Proposal*.

Paideia is the Greek term for the "upbringing of children." Adler's proposal states that all humans should have a similar general educational background. According to Adler, schooling has three major goals: "(1) it should provide the means by which people can grow and develop mentally, morally, and spiritually; (2) it should cultivate the civic knowledge and virtues needed for responsible and participatory citizenship; (3) it should provide the basic skills that are common to and which are needed for work rather than a particular job training that limits a person to a single occupation" (Adler 1982, 10–12). The *paideia* proposal attempts to accomplish this through a common curriculum of twelve years of basic schooling. In this curriculum students acquire knowledge, develop learning and intellectual skills, and enlarge their understanding of ideas and values.

Philosophy Affects the Role of the Teacher   Just as individuals' philosophical beliefs affect their goals and curricular emphases, they also influence how these individuals view themselves as teachers. Those who believe in the classical philosophies of realism and idealism are likely to view themselves as authoritarian figures giving the students the skills and the information they need to succeed. The educational theories of essentialism and perennialism, based on these philosophies, see teachers as central to the educational process, which cannot proceed without their knowledge, instruction, and modeling.

On the other hand, teachers who believe in the philosophies of pragmatism, existentialism, and philosophical analysis contend that students should work together, have the ability to direct change, and must observe and experiment in order to determine what is real. These teachers believe that it is their responsibility to guide rather than to direct the students' learning. They therefore lean toward the educational theories of progressivism, social reconstructionism, and behaviorism. They tend to believe that much of learning comes from student interaction, discovery, and experimentation. Education in this scenario can, in part, proceed without a teacher's direct intervention. In fact, educators who profess these beliefs frequently describe their role as a facilitator who designs an environment in which students can learn. Their most important role is observation of student progress.

HOW TO DEVELOP A PHILOSOPHY OF EDUCATION

Earlier in the chapter we discussed that it is important to have a philosophy of education so that teachers can have a means of logically inquiring into educational issues. We examined how asking the philosophical questions of metaphysics, epistemology, and axiology (values and aesthetics) can assist educators in avoiding potential problems and pitfalls. We discussed how the use of logic can lead teachers to making critical educational decisions. We discussed how a philosophy can help an individual think rationally, clarify ambiguity, and interpret others' beliefs. We discussed what happens when teachers do not have the time to think about what they do, and do not take the time to reflect. And we talked about how philosophy can provide an additional perspective on teaching. If developing a philosophy of education is so important, how can you develop one?

According to George F. Kneller, the best way to begin developing a personal philosophy of education is by examining the schools of philosophy. The five schools of philosophy discussed in this chapter are idealism, realism, pragmatism, existentialism, and philosophical analysis. As you read about these schools of philosophy, which one comes closest to your beliefs? Perhaps you agree with more than one. In fact, you may be attracted in different ways to all of them.

Examine the Schools of Philosophy

Next, you must examine the theories of education discussed in this chapter. The five theories of education are perennialism, essentialism, progressivism, social reconstructionism, and behaviorism. Which of their elements come nearest to your philosophy? You may find that the concept of the great books as proposed by perennialists fits your idea of the value of accumulated knowledge and spirituality, whereas the concept of the classroom as a community of students working together to gain knowledge expressed by the progressivist is compatible with your beliefs about how students learn. Can you make these two elements compatible? You must, if you are going to develop a workable philosophy of education.

Examine the Theories of Education

Here's one way in which the two might be compatible. You select a series of six books that relate to the theme of lack of compassion toward others, a universal theme of literature. All these are important works; some, however, are contemporary and some are not. They also span a wide range of reading levels and interests. Perhaps the books are by authors as diverse as Ernest Hemingway, Robert Cormier, Lois Duncan, Herman Wouk, Ernest Gaines, and Daniel Defoe. You tell the students about each of the books and let each student select the book he or she would like to read. If necessary, you guide the students in their selections. Once the students have selected a book, you form small discussion groups based on their selections. You prepare questions that each group must answer about the book they are reading. You develop class activities that relate to the theme. As a final project, each group presents the theme of the book to the class by performing a dramatic presentation, conducting a debate, developing a panel discussion, videotaping a student-made documentary, or interviewing guest speakers. In this way the students are sharing a universal theme through great works of literature at the same time as they are working together to discover how individual authors deal with this theme. You have, in practice, united the philosophies of idealism and pragmatism and the theories of perennialism and progressivism.

Examine Your Own Philosophical Beliefs

Once you have developed a personal philosophy of education, examine it in terms of your own beliefs. Is it compatible? Are you comfortable with the elements of the philosophies and theories of education you have selected? If you are, it would be helpful to write down your educational philosophy and periodically reexamine it. If you are not, you need to return to step one.

Once you have an educational philosophy, you are likely to be a more effective teacher. George F. Kneller says of the teacher with an educational philosophy:

> Philosophy frees the teacher's imagination and at the same time controls his intellect. By tracing the problems of education to their roots in philosophy, the teacher sees these problems in ampler perspective. By thinking philosophically, he applies his mind systematically to issues of importance which have been clarified and refined. (p. 128)

Kneller claims, on the other hand, that:

> The teacher without a personal educational philosophy is less likely to be effective. An educator who does not use philosophy is inevitably superficial. A superficial educator may be good or bad—but, if good, less good than he could be, and, if bad, worse than he need be. (p. 128)

7.2 POINTS TO REMEMBER

- The theories of education discussed in this chapter are based on the schools of philosophy. They attempt to describe educational practice, whereas the schools of philosophy attempt to categorize and systematize reality, knowledge, values, aesthetics, and reasoning by asking metaphysical, epistemological, axiological, and logical questions.

- The five theories of education are perennialism, which emphasizes great works; essentialism, which emphasizes bodies of knowledge; progressivism, which emphasizes the changing nature of knowledge and the child as the curricular focal point; social reconstruction-ism, which emphasizes the need to help children become social change agents; and behaviorism, which emphasizes the importance of the scientific method, objectivity, immediate results, efficiency and economy, and positiveness.

- Each theory relates to educational practice. Perennialism and essentialism focus on an unchanging curriculum based on great books and content determined by scholars. Teaching methodology is instructor centered. Progressivists and social reconstructionists contend that the curriculum must change continually to meet the needs of the child. Teaching methodology focuses on the needs and interests of the students and society. Behaviorists believe that students must be actively involved in their own learning through observation and experimentation and must be rewarded for appropriate behavior. Teaching methodology focuses on the students, with the teacher setting behavioral objectives.

- Personal educational philosophies are essential to effective teaching. They affect the teacher's goals, curricular focus, and perceived role.

- Personal educational philosophies can be developed by reviewing the schools of philosophy and the theories of learning and determining which are congruent with the individual's beliefs. The various elements of the individual's philosophy must complement one another. It must be carefully examined in light of the individual's personal philosophy and reviewed now and then.

FOR THOUGHT/DISCUSSION

1. How did existentialism affect modern educational methods?
2. Is it possible to teach without a philosophy of education? Why or why not?
3. The high school you attended had an educational philosophy even if you weren't aware of it. Can you determine now, what it was? Do you think it was effective? Why or why not?
4. Which educational theory do you think will have the most influence on education in the future?

FOR FURTHER READING/REFERENCE

Counts, G. S. 1932. *Dare the school build a new social order?* New York: John Day. A description of the transition from a rural, agrarian society to an industrialized, technological society and a call for schools to prepare students to resolve the social crisis by reconstructing ideas and beliefs in light of changing conditions; an example of social reconstruction educational theory.

Dewey, J. 1900. *The school and society.* Chicago: University of Chicago Press. A description of the author's earliest revolutionary emphasis on education as a child-centered process; an example of the educational theory of progressivism.

Hirsch, E. D. 1987. *Cultural literacy: What every American needs to know.* Boston: Houghton Mifflin. A treatise that suggests that in order for America to produce a literate, skilled population, schools must emphasize teaching of basic skills and classical content; an example of the essentialist theory of education.

Hutchins, R. M. 1968. *The learning society.* New York: Praeger. A treatise that suggests that liberal education will prepare students for manhood rather than manpower. According to the author, the aims of education should be the development of a capacity to think; an example of a perennialist theory of education.

Rogers, C. 1983. *Freedom to learn for the 80s.* Columbus, OH: Charles E. Merrill. A presentation of several case studies of the relationships between teachers and students, which the author defines as the facilitation of learning based on the philosophy of existentialism.

8 An Effective School

Since the school is the institution in which most people are educated and which has a profound influence on the individual and ultimately on society, it is important to define a school in which the vast majority of students succeed. Researchers have begun to identify the attributes of effective schools by observation, testing, and comments of students. In this chapter we will examine the results of the research—part science, part art—and identify what makes some schools more effective than others.

9 The Curriculum

In this chapter we will define curriculum from a variety of points of view. We will attempt to illustrate how the individual's definition of curriculum helps determine its organization. We also will examine the philosophical basis of a curriculum and discuss its major organizational structures. Finally, we will examine the social and economic forces that have affected how curriculum is defined, developed, and implemented.

For moments then, the room was still. From the bilingual class next door to the south came the baritone of the teacher Victor Guevara, singing to his students in Spanish. Through the small casement windows behind Chris came the sounds of the city—Holyoke, Massachusetts—trailer truck brakes releasing giant sighs now and then, occasional screeches of freight trains, and, always in the background, the mechanical hum of ventilators from the school and from Dinn Bros. Trophies and Autron, from Leduc Corp. Metal Fabricators and Laminated Papers. It was so quiet inside the room during those moments that little sounds were loud: the rustle of a book's pages being turned and the tiny clanks of metal-legged chairs being shifted slightly. Bending over forms and the children's records, Chris watched the class from the corner of her eye.

From: Kidder 1989, pp. 6–7, 12–13.

PART III

Schools and Curriculum

8
Effective Schools

*ifth-grade teacher Chris Zajac prepares for the opening of school
long before the students arrive and begins the year with a new
group of students and a student teacher. Here's how Tracy Kidder
describes the scene.*

When Chris had first walked into her room—Room 205—back
in late August, it felt like an attic. The chalkboards and
bulletins boards were covered up with newspaper, and the
bright colors of the plastic chairs seemed calculated to force
cheerfulness upon her. On the side of one of the empty
children's desks there was a faded sticker that read, OFFICIAL
PACE CAR. A child from some other year must have put it there;
he'd moved on, but she'd come back to the same place. There
was always something a little mournful about coming back to
an empty classroom at the end of summer, a childhood feeling,
like being put to bed when it is light outside.

She spent her summer days with children, her own and
those of friends. While her daughter splashed around in the
wading pool and her son and his six-year-old buddies climbed
the wooden fort her husband had built in their back yard, she
sat at the picnic table and there was time to read—this summer,
a few popular novels and then, as August wore on, a book
called *The Art of Teaching Writing*, which she read with a
marking pencil in hand, underlining the tips that seemed most
useful. There was time for adult conversation, around the
swimming pool at her best friend's house, while their children
swam. In August she left Holyoke and spent a couple of weeks
near the ocean with her husband and children, on Cape Cod.
She liked the pace of summer, and of all the parts of summer
she liked the mornings best, the unhurried, slowly unfolding
mornings, which once again this year went by much too fast.

Chris looked around her empty classroom. It was fairly
small as classrooms go, about twenty-five by thirty-six feet. The
room repossessed her. She said to herself, "I can't believe the
summer's over. I feel like I never left this place." And then she
got to work.

She put up her bulletin board displays, scouted up pencils
and many kinds of paper—crayons hadn't yet arrived; she'd
borrow some of her son's—made a red paper apple for her
door, and moved the desks around into the layout she had
settled on in her first years of teaching. She didn't use the truly
ancient arrangement, with the teacher's desk up front and the
children's in even rows before it. Her desk was already where
she wanted it, in a corner by the window. She had to be on her
feet and moving in order to teach. Over there in the corner, her
desk wouldn't get in her way. And she could retire to it in
between lessons, at a little distance from the children, and still
see down the hallway between her door and the boys' room—a

strategic piece of real estate—and also keep an eye on all the children at their desks. She pushed most of the children's small, beige-topped desks side by side, in a continuous perimeter describing three-quarters of a square, open at the front. She put four desks in the middle of the square, so that each of those four had space between it and any other desk. These were Chris's "middle-person desks," where it was especially hard to hide, although even the pack row of the perimeter was more exposed than back rows usually are.

When the room was arranged to her liking, she went home to the last days of summer. . . .

There was a lot of prettiness in the room, and all the children looked cute to Chris.

So did the student teacher, Miss Hunt, a very young woman in a dress with a bow at the throat who sat at a table in the back of the room. Miss Hunt had a sweet smile, which she turned on the children, hunching her shoulders when they looked at her. At times the first days, while watching Chris in action, Miss Hunt seemed to gulp. Sometimes she looked as frightened as the children. For Chris, looking at Miss Hunt was like looking at herself fourteen years ago.

The smell of construction paper, slightly sweet and forest-like, mingled with the fading, acrid smell of roach and rodent spray. The squawk box on the wall above the closets, beside the clock with its jerky minute hand, erupted almost constantly, adult voices paging adults by their surnames and reminding staff of deadlines for the census forms, attendance calendars, and United Way contributions. Other teachers poked their heads inside the door to say hello to Chris or to ask advice about how to fill out forms or to confer with her on schedules for math and reading. In between interruptions, amid the usual commotion of the first day, Chris taught a short lesson, assigned the children seat work, and attended to paperwork at her large gray metal desk over by the window.

For moments then, the room was still. From the bilingual class next door to the south came the baritone of the teacher Victor Guevara, singing to his students in Spanish. Through the small casement windows behind Chris came the sounds of the city—Holyoke, Massachusetts—trailer truck brakes releasing giant sighs now and then, occasional screeches of freight trains, and, always in the background, the mechanical hum of ventilators from the school and from Dinn Bros. Trophies and Autron, from Leduc Corp. Metal Fabricators and Laminated Papers. It was so quiet inside the room during those moments that little sounds were loud: the rustle of a book's pages being turned and the tiny clanks of metal-legged chairs being shifted slightly. Bending over forms and the children's records, Chris watched the class from the corner of her eye.

From: Kidder 1989, pp. 6–7, 12–13.

CHAPTER OBJECTIVES

After studying this chapter, you should be able to:

- Define effective schools research.
- Describe what is meant by the social organization of the school.
- Explain what is meant by a school's positive ethos.
- Identify those things that make a classroom climate conducive to learning.
- Define the role of the leader in a good school.
- Discuss student involvement in a good school.
- List those elements that make schools ineffective.
- Discuss how students' definitions of school relate to their experiences in school.
- Explain how classroom organization is affected by the teacher's definition of school.
- Explain why most adults define school in terms of students and learning.
- Discuss how examining another culture's definition of school helps us better understand U.S. schools.

S ince the school is the institution in which most people are educated and which has a profound influence on the individual and ultimately on society, it is important to define a school in which the vast majority of students succeed. Researchers have begun to identify the attributes of effective schools by observation, testing, and comments of students. In this chapter we will examine the results of the research—part science, part art—and identify what makes some schools more effective than others.

WHAT IS A GOOD SCHOOL?

In 1936 scientist Albert Einstein defined the school by focusing on its most important goals in an address given in Albany, New York.

> Sometimes one sees in the school simply the instrument for transferring a certain maximum quantity of knowledge to the growing generation. But that is not right. Knowledge is dead; the school, however, serves the living. It should develop in the young individuals those qualities and capabilities which are of value for the welfare of the commonwealth. But that does not mean that individuality should be destroyed and the individual become a mere tool of the community, like a bee or an ant. For a community of standardized individuals without personal originality and personal aims would be a poor community without possibilities for development. On the contrary, the aim must be the training of independently acting and thinking individuals, who, however, see in the service of the community their highest life problem. (Einstein 1954, 60)

Therefore, according to Einstein, the good school serves two essential and interrelated functions. First, the development of an acting and thinking individual. And, second, service to the community by these individuals. Einstein, like most people who attempted to define a good school prior to the 1980s, defined it based on what the school should do. Also, like most writers, Einstein had difficulty determining how the school should accomplish its lofty goals.

> But how shall one try to attain this ideal? Should one perhaps try to realize this aim by moralizing? Not at all. Words are and remain an empty sound, and the road to perdition has ever been accompanied by lip service to an ideal. But personalities are not formed by what is heard and said, but by labor and activity. (Einstein 1954)

In other words, we can develop a good school by implementing what makes the school good. But what is it that makes a school good? Einstein goes on to say that it is "actual performance" based on personal motivation to succeed rather than on "fear and compulsion." He claims that the good school cannot work with "methods of fear, force, and artificial authority" (p. 61).

Einstein spends a great deal of time explaining what he means by a personal motivation to succeed. In the end he has brought his definition of school back full circle to the individual. He concludes that "the most important motive for work in the school and in life is the pleasure of work, pleasure in its result, and the knowledge of the value of the result to the community" (p. 62). He never makes it clear how the good school develops motivation based on pleasure in its students. After reading Einstein's definition, one might conclude that a good school is simply one that is populated with good students who are motivated to do good work.

Most attempts to define a good school prior to the 1980s resulted in descriptions like the one above. And, like Einstein's definition, they tended to be what Einstein warned against, "moralizing . . . lip service to an ideal." However, in the 1980s educators developed a body of research that began to describe the specific attributes of effective schools. This research was carried out through careful observation of schools and classrooms judged to be effective.

Effective Schools Research

A variety of measures was used to determine effectiveness: test scores, other measures of student achievement, perceptions of students and parents, and panels of experts. Of course, the means used to select the effective schools often dictated the results of the study. For example, if researchers used test scores as a measure of the schools' effectiveness, the schools found to be effective exhibited high test scores, high academic achievement of students, a curriculum emphasizing skills required on the tests, and, many educators argued, a population that tended to be successful taking standardized tests, largely white and middle or upper class.

From this body of research, no specific definition of a good school was developed; however, educators and researchers identified many attributes that identify an effective school. See table 8.1, overleaf, for a summary of this research.

Most studies of effective schools found that there is little difference in instructional patterns between schools that are considered good and those that are not. Instead, the difference seems to come from things such as goals, high expectations, reward systems, and leadership.

Social Organization of a Good School

A Positive Ethos

Gerald Grant, a professor of sociology and education at Syracuse University, defined quality in terms of a school's positive ethos: the school teaches both intellectual and moral development (1985). Academic achievement as evidenced by high test scores is only one of the aims of "schools that make an imprint." Also needed is the development of character, or ethos, evident in the high expectations teachers have for students and reflected as much in what people *do* as in what they say.

The school's ethos, to be adequately developed, must be shared by the community, a situation more commonly found in private schools in which, in this largely homogeneous population, parents share intellectual and moral values with the faculty and staff. In public schools a shared ethos is more

(continued on p. 239)

TABLE 8-1

Summary of Effective Schools Research and Opinions, 1979–1991

Findings	Practice
Effective schools have:	
1. *A positive ethos* Edmonds (1979), Goodlad (1984), Brown (1984), Grant (1985), Stedman (1988), Feinberg (1990), Banks (1991)	Students and teachers are expected to achieve and are told they can Standards for achievement are related to individual differences Lines of communication among administrators, teachers, students, and parents are kept open Students from varied backgrounds and cultures study and socialize together Required subjects, varied curriculum, and choices are available Teachers and administrators are role models for developing honesty and respect Literature is used to nurture qualities of good character
2. *A classroom climate conducive to learning* Brown (1984), Goodlad (1984), Ravitch (1984), Bennett (1987)	Teachers are involved in decision making Students are more interested in learning than in sports and socializing Teachers spend more time on instruction than on controlling behavior Parents volunteer or keep in close contact with teachers Attendance is high Classrooms have few interruptions
3. *Clearly understood goals* Wynne (1981), Persell and Cookson (1982), Goodlad (1984), Carnegie Foundation for the Advancement of Teaching (1988)	Students, teachers, parents, and administrators agree on goals for academic achievement and broad goals for the school Administrators and teachers monitor progress toward goals Students and teachers can verbalize the goals of the school
4. *Effective teachers* Wynne (1981), Ravitch (1984), Bennett (1987), National Governors' Association (1990), Shanker (1990), Banks (1991)	Schools recruit and keep knowledgeable and talented teachers Schools recruit and keep talented minority teachers Teachers use time wisely Teachers set objectives and learning strategies related to student needs Teachers use materials in addition to textbooks Teachers are firm but friendly
5. *Clear and effective leadership* Edmonds (1979), Wynne (1981), Brown (1984), Ravitch (1984), Carnegie Foundation for the Advancement of Teaching (1988)	Goals are established, agreed upon, and followed through on Policies and procedures are initiated and carried out A climate of high expectations for students and teachers is developed The staff members work hard and cooperate with one another Academic achievement is monitored
6. *Good communication* Wynne (1981), Brown (1984), Stedman (1988), National Governors' Association (1990)	Principals visit classrooms Teachers have time during school day to communicate with one another Parents are informed of student life and growth in school Teachers respond to students' personal problems
7. *Active student involvement* Wynne (1981), Goodlad (1984)	Students participate in special interest clubs, sports, honor societies, student government, and the performing arts Students tutor one another Students are assistants to teachers and administrators
8. *Positive incentives and awards* Brookover et al. (1977), Bennett (1987), National Governors' Association (1990), Shanker (1990)	Students receive honor awards and badges for academic achievement and other accomplishments Teachers of the year are recognized Students are given remedial attention if needed Parents recognize all teachers during Education Week Professional development days are provided for teachers Schools have flexible semesters that provide academic incentives

9. *Order and discipline* Edmonds (1979), Wynne (1981), Brown (1984), Bennett (1987), National Governors' Association (1990)	Rules that are a happy medium between strong discipline and the growing student are established Rules are clearly stated to students and parents so that standards, rewards, and punishments are clearly understood There is follow-through on agreed-upon rules There are goals and programs to remove drugs and violence from the school
10. *Focus on instruction and curriculum* Edmonds (1979), Brown (1984), Ravitch (1984), Bennett (1987), Carnegie Foundation for the Advancement of Teaching (1988), National Governors' Association (1990), Banks (1991), Committee for Economic Development (1991)	Schools have large media centers that students use More time is spent on instruction than on keeping an orderly classroom There is an emphasis on basic skills and academic subjects Technological innovations are implemented, particularly for the disadvantaged There is a multicultural emphasis to the curriculum

In an effort to define an effective school, many studies have been conducted on those schools that have already proven to be effective in one area or another. Rather than arrive at one specific definition of an effective school, research has instead identified qualities that cumulatively result in an effective school.

difficult to achieve because teachers and students are, by definition, diverse and possess different values. However, according to Grant, these differences can be overcome through the common core of a democratic society's beliefs. He observed that a positive ethos does not necessarily require a particular moral content. He cited examples of the common positive ethos in the United States: "Decency, fairness, the minimal order required for dialogue, the willingness to listen to others, the rejection of racism, honesty, respect for truth, recognition of merit and excellence . . . a sense of altruism and service to others and respect for personal effort and hard work" (1985, 143). William J. Bennett, former U.S. secretary of education, suggests in *What Works: Research about Teaching and Learning* (1987) that the kind of moral character that Grant examines "is encouraged by surrounding students with good adult examples and by building upon natural occasions for learning and practicing good character" (p. 59).

Bennett also suggests that high expectations for both students and teachers are required if schools are to develop a positive ethos. Arthur W. Steller in *Effective Schools Research: Practice and Promise* (1988) agrees with Bennett's contention that teachers' expectations for good or poor student performances are self-fulfilling prophecies. Steller quotes George Bernard Shaw's *Pygmalion*: "The difference between a lady and a flower girl is not how she behaves but how she's treated." He cites Robert Rosenthal and Lenore Jacobson in *Pygmalion in the Classroom* (1968), saying that teachers' expectations of achievement influence students' levels of achievement. According to Bruce R. Joyce, Richard H. Hersh, and Michael McKibbin in *The Structure of School Improvement* (1983), "High expectations carry several messages. First, they symbolize the demand for excellence and tell the student, 'I think you ought to and can achieve.' . . .

V I E W P O I N T S

Billy Paris

Mel Glenn teaches high school English in Brooklyn, New York. He writes poems about his students who he says are often misunderstood. This poem is about Billy Paris. The Spanish classroom of which Glenn writes is one that displays a positive ethos.

> This term I don't have a lunch period.
> Too many subjects to make up.
> So while I learn new nouns in Mr. Brewer's Spanish class,
> I munch on some potato chips.
> Two days ago he laid down the law:
> "No snacking while speaking Spanish."
> Yesterday I got even.
> I pulled out from my bag
> A checkered tablecloth,
> Two candlesticks,
> One bowl,
> One spoon,
> And a thermos full of soup.
> I slowly set the table,
> Said a blessing (in Spanish) over the food,
> And named every object with perfect accent.
> Mr. Brewer stood there, dumbstruck.
> Then he began to laugh.
> The class joined in.
> You know, school doesn't have to be so grim.

From: Glenn, 1982

Second, they communicate to the student that the teacher *cares* by saying, in effect, 'The reason I have high expectations for you is that I believe in you.' Third, high expectations serve as the adult world's professional judgment which is translated to the student as, 'I am really more capable than even I at times think I am' " (p. 26). According to Grant, schools that achieve these positive goals provide quality education for their students.

A Classroom Climate Conducive to Learning

John Goodlad (1984) in his observation of over one thousand classrooms found that differences in the quality of schools have little to do with teaching practices. Differences come instead from what he called classroom climate. The most satisfying schools are ones with favorable conditions for learning; parent interest in, and knowledge of, the schools; and positive relationships between principals and teachers, and teachers and students.

In a National Institute of Education publication, *Reaching for Excellence: An Effective Schools Sourcebook* (1985), Steven Bossert claimed that 1,750 school districts identified as promoting effective practices at the building and district levels had in common "a school climate conducive to learning—one free from disciplinary problems and vandalism; the expectation among teachers that all students can achieve; an emphasis on basic skills instruction and high levels of student **time-on-task**; a system of clear instructional objectives for monitoring and assessing students' performance" (p. 7). In "A Good School" (1984), Diane Ravitch further defines positive school climate as "relaxed and tension-free. Teachers and students alike know that they are in a good school, and this sense of being special contributes to high morale" (p. 493).

Clearly Understood Goals

Edward Wynne, in a survey of schools considered "good," found that their principals, teachers, and parents had developed, knew, and could articulate the school's academic and social behavior goals. Likewise, he found that "the staff— especially the teachers/administrators and even the students and parents evolved a clear idea of what constitutes good performance" and knew what was expected of them. He also found that good schools are generally small and have highly visible staffs (1981, 377). John Goodlad further stated in *A Place Called School* (1984) that when parents and teachers reported congruence between their preferred goals for the school and its actual goals, they were largely satisfied with the school's program.

Effective Teachers

According to Joyce, Hersh, and McKibbin, effective schools have a strong sense of teacher efficacy, which arises from the conviction that " 'I *know* I can teach any and all of these kids.' Efficacy is a sense of potency, and it is what provides a teacher with the psychic energy to maintain a high task orientation by the students" (1983, 26).

Wynne's study also determined that teachers who are rated as good care about teaching and their students in observable ways. They have regular and timely attendance, well-organized lesson plans, reasonably orderly classes, routinely assigned and appropriately graded homework, friendly but authoritative relations with students, purposeful use of class time, and supportive relations with colleagues (p. 378). According to Wynne, good teachers are more frequently found in schools in which they are required to set performance goals for their students and translate these goals into objectives. He found that the principals in these schools also set goals. According to William Bennett, good teachers are enthusiastic and confident, have high standards, demand mastery of materials from all students, have instructional management skills that give students maximum time for instructional tasks (time-on-task), and enforce discipline consistently and fairly. Teacher effectiveness is discussed in depth in chapter 2.

Clear and Effective Leadership

Wynne's study also found that, in good schools, staffing roles are clear; staff members and volunteers, including parents, know their jobs and work hard at them. He found that administrators are able to conceptualize goals; are tactful, tough, and ambitious; believe in education; and are determined to get things under control.

Ron Edmonds found in a 1979 study, "Effective Schools for the Urban Poor," that even in schools populated by economically disadvantaged youngsters, students can achieve at levels equal to middle class students if there is "strong leadership and a climate of expectation that students will learn" (p. 15). According to Edmonds, "There has never been a time in the life of the American public school when we have not known all we needed to in order to

Effective schools have principals who provide clear direction to their staff, involve them in decision making where appropriate, and encourage creativity.

teach all those whom we chose to teach" (p. 16). Edmonds asserts that leaders of ineffective urban schools often chose not to teach poor students. Edmonds cites a 1974 State of New York Office of Education Performance Review study of the academic performance of students in two inner-city schools, both with a predominantly poor pupil population, but one with high-achieving students and the other with low-achieving students. Edmonds found that student performance in these two schools could be "attributed to factors under the schools' control," which included administrative behavior, policies, and practices. In the school where students had achieved at high levels, the administrative team "provided a good balance between both management and instructional skills; developed a plan for dealing with the reading problem and had implemented the plan throughout the school"; and created an environment in which the students were expected to succeed (pp. 16–17).

Bennett's study found that successful schools have "successful principals [who] establish policies that create an orderly environment and support effective instruction" (1987, 64). Good administrators keep teachers' instructional time from being interrupted, supply necessary materials, create opportunities for faculty/staff development, encourage new ideas, involve teachers in formulation of school policies and selection of materials, and provide aides or volunteers for routine work.

Good Communication

Wynne's study further showed that in schools rated as good there is a constant information flow among principals, teachers, students, and parents. Principals frequently visit classrooms, usually unannounced, and monitor teacher performance in other areas such as hall duty, attendance records, report cards, lesson plans, records, and test scores. Principals communicate the results of their evaluations to the teachers and allow teachers to respond. Similarly, principals and teachers in good schools encourage family involvement in such things as homework by suggesting nightly supervision of students' work.

According to B. Frank Brown in *Crisis in Secondary Education: Rebuilding America's High Schools* (1984), communication between parents and schools is needed today more than ever before. He claims that schools must recognize that American families are in transition and that the two-parent family no longer represents the norm. Effective schools "must revise their calendars to make certain that working single parents have regular access to school personnel and activities after working hours" (p. 140). The National Governors' Association in its report, *Educating America: State Strategies for Achieving the National Education Goals* (1990), agrees. Parents must become equal partners in their children's learning and schooling if schools are to be effective, beginning during early childhood with programs such as Head Start and continuing as children progress through the public schools (see also chapters 12 and 13).

Active Student Involvement

In good secondary schools, Wynne's study found that students are actively involved in the school's governance. Many activities focus on the achievements of students: award assemblies, pep rallies, athletic events, arts events, science fairs. Extracurricular activities, such as fund-raising, hall or crossing guards, chorus, band, teachers' aides, tutors, and newspaper and yearbook staffs allow students to function in leadership capacities.

According to Goodlad's 1984 study, involvement in student activities is important in effective schools, particularly sports and games in junior and senior high schools. Goodlad's study pointed to a slight decline in participation in sports at the senior high level at effective schools because of the intensity of the performance required and an increase in the number of students working. He also found a greater involvement of students in special interest clubs in secondary schools than in junior high schools; nearly 33 percent of the students report involvement in service activities related to either the school or the community; approximately 14 percent of students participate in student government; and about 19 percent in honors organizations.

Positive Incentives and Awards

In effective schools incentives and rewards are given to students and staff in the form of honor societies, honor rolls, mentioning accomplishments in daily announcements and school newspapers, displaying photographs of successful students, and awarding them pins, badges, and ribbons in special assemblies. Good schools retain rather than automatically promote students with learning problems, preferring to work with them to achieve promotion. In a 1977 study, *Schools Can Make a Difference*, Brookover et al. suggest that effective schools display excellent student work, have honor rolls and convocations to honor

When students feel they have an important voice in the government of the school, they are likely to view their school experience as positive. This attitude contributes to high morale and positive school spirit.

student excellence, and communicate with parents. Effective schools also use positive feedback and smiles to motivate student achievement.

Staff incentives include, according to the National Governors' Association, increased involvement for teachers in school governance. This, according to the governors' task force study, requires helping teachers gain the knowledge they need to participate in school decision making and then giving them the time to do it. Other staff incentives that have been investigated in studies of effective schools include incentive pay and differentiated staffing and pay for differing responsibilities (see chapter 4, pp. 94–99).

Order and Discipline

According to Wynne's study, good schools develop discipline by "maintaining effective physical boundaries [creating a sense of safe haven], especially in disorderly urban areas" (p. 381). Students remain in the buildings and recognize their rights and obligations. Symbolic boundaries such as uniforms are also found in many good schools. According to Wynne's study, good schools have well-enforced dress codes and use mottoes, school songs, colors, ceremonies, parades, assemblies, athletic events, faculty and student social events, and dances to develop this safe haven for students.

According to Brown, the measures of a well-disciplined school include good student behavior, high attendance rates, minimal delinquency, and achievement as confirmed by examination. Good discipline and safe schools, according to Steward C. Purkey and Marshall S. Smith in *Review of Effective Schools* (1983), comes from effective school governance. The Carnegie Foundation for the Advancement of Teaching report *An Imperiled Generation: Saving Urban Schools* (1988) agrees, and further states that effective governance of urban schools requires that principals are not "crippled by mindless regulations" (p. xv). Schools must be decentralized in terms of decision making and they must be accountable for the decisions they make. In addition, the National Governors' Association task force report asserts that schools must make a commitment to eliminate drugs and violence. This may require significant school reorganization, including a curriculum to motivate students to learn and calendar revisions to help keep students in school throughout the year. Many students, particularly those who are not college bound, are shortchanged by the schools, according to the report, and many quit school in order to work. If schools are to become safe havens of academic achievement, they must recognize the needs of all students, not just those who are college bound (pp. 15–16).

Although most of the studies that identified common characteristics of effective schools focused on the social organization of the schools, some attempted to examine common features of instruction and curriculum. Frank Brown in *Crisis in Secondary Education* found that highly effective schools differ from less effective schools in several ways: they have a balanced blend of classroom instruction, discipline, and sound administration; they have better teacher salaries, smaller class size, and larger libraries with greater student use; they effectively manage time spent on instruction, determine who makes decisions about learning, and have positive relationships with the school district authorities. Attributes of curriculum and instruction in schools found to be effective will be more specifically examined in chapter 9.

Instruction and Curriculum in Good Schools

Because determining what makes schools good is so difficult and subjective, many educators have reverted to examining why schools are not as effective as they could be. We will look at the results of some of these studies below.

Some Reasons for Ineffective Schools

Lack of Innovation

John Goodlad (1983) contends that most people teach as they were taught, modeling their practices on what they observed for sixteen or more years. Teacher training, he says, is of short duration and students discuss innovations but rarely get to observe them. Once on the job, teachers conform to social pressures that support inadequate teaching. The cards are stacked against innovation, he says, because the pressures teachers face to maintain control over a large group in a small room pushes them into methods that seemed to work for their teachers. According to Goodlad, teachers are torn between professional beliefs and on-the-job realities; they need more incentives and support to be innovative.

Teachers in urban schools, according to the findings of the Carnegie Foundation for the Advancement of Teaching (1988), soon learned that conformity, not creativity, was rewarded. Seventy percent said that the teachers lacked family support and that the students' culture involved cutting class and

(continued on p. 247)

Point/Counterpoint

RESEARCH CAN IDENTIFY QUALITIES OF EFFECTIVE SCHOOLS

For the past two years we have been reviewing research to determine what, if anything, makes some schools and teachers more effective than others. Happily, there emerges from such research a variety of clues, which when put together into a coherent whole, make a great deal of intuitive sense. What is particularly pleasing is that different researchers in a variety of studies are reaching similar conclusions about teachers and administrators who bring to research programs the critical eyes of experience. Because of the conjunction of researchers' knowledge and professional educators' wisdom we optimistically believe that we can improve education in America both on its current terms and by using technology and fresh curriculum alternatives more extensively. . . .

What is important is that [beliefs about effective schools] are shared by educators who otherwise espouse and have developed very different approaches to the creation of an effective education.

From: Joyce, Hersh, and McKibbin, 1983

RESEARCH IS LIMITED IN IDENTIFYING EFFECTIVE SCHOOLS

School effects data are limited in several respects. First, most effective schools research has been conducted in urban schools, so its application to suburban schools is unknown. Second, the description of effective schools is based largely on their effectiveness in obtaining high student performance on standardized achievement tests. This is a narrow definition of school effectiveness. Although there is some evidence that schools can simultaneously achieve several goals (e.g., high attendance rates, high student engagement rates, high achievement), for the most part the question of school success on cognitive criteria other than standardized achievement (e.g., decision-making skills) has been ignored. There is no evidence that schools that teach the basic skills relatively well can also teach computer skills, science, and writing relatively well. Furthermore, process measures usually have been limited to a few global dimensions of schooling, and these examine *form* more than *quality*. Often, data are collected on only a few teachers per school, and the information about what even these teachers do is sketchy. . . .

Another major constraint on effective schools research is that existing evidence is largely correlational. Whether active leadership precedes or follows the development of high expectations or whether student achievement precedes or follows high expectations for performance is uncertain. . . .

Although certain aspects of the school effects literature may help practitioners to identify their problems and alternatives and thus allow them to think more systematically about their instructional programs, this research does not yet yield answers. . . . The research completed to date shows that individual school variance is an important dimension that can be influenced by selected actions and resources. Despite this progress, the next step does not involve application. Rather, it requires further extending the basic knowledge in this field by completing new studies that help us to understand more the fully qualitative aspects of schooling.

From: Good and Brophy, 1986

POSTSCRIPT

Joyce, Hersh, and McKibbin believe that the cumulative and interactive effects of research and practice confirm the importance of effective schools research. They point to a parallel from the 1960s, when federal educational programs for economically poor children were developed based on specific beliefs about early childhood education. And, they say, in spite of extreme programmatic differences, the programs adopted shared a number of common beliefs. These included: "That education should begin where children are ready to learn. . . . Instruction should be individualized to a large extent.

Instruction, materials, and other conditions of learning can ensure success for all children. . . . Goals should be clear to all. . . . All children need to learn how to learn. . . . Emotional development must be enhanced" (p. 31). When this cumulative and interactive effect of research and practice occurs, they contend, we should use the research as the basis for the improvement of education.

On the other hand, Good and Brophy suggest caution in implementing effective schools research before researchers have had time to examine areas that have not yet been sufficiently studied. Should we proceed with the information we have, despite the fact that it might not be complete? Or should we seek additional information to further confirm what we have found? These authors do not disagree on the importance of the effective schools research, but merely on how soon it should be implemented.

We agree with Joyce, Hersh, and McKibbin that the research is broad based enough and has such potential for improving education that it should be implemented. On the other hand, we also agree with Good and Brophy that many important aspects of what makes a school effective have yet to be examined. Therefore, we suggest the middle road. Use what you know about effective schools to examine the schools in which you observe, to develop your own definition of the word *school*, and to think about how your classroom will be organized.

---

school. On one day in one high school in New York City, for example, eleven of twenty-eight students came to math class and seven of eighteen to biology. Attendance problems were also evident in middle schools. In a Boston middle school, the annual absence rate increased from 14 to 22 percent in one year (p. xiii).

Inadequate Funding

The Carnegie Foundation also pointed to another roadblock in making all schools effective: inadequate funding. "We strongly urge that states fulfill their legal and moral obligations by achieving equity in the financing of urban schools. Once a standard of expenditures for effective schools is determined, the goal should be at least to meet the standard for all schools. Unless big city schools are given more support, much of what we propose will remain a hollow promise" (1988, 51). (See chapter 15 for an in-depth discussion of funding.)

Mindless Regulations

John Goodlad also found that states set broad educational goals for schools but do not articulate them to the schools or to the public vigorously or clearly. Similarly, the Carnegie Foundation found that urban school principals were crippled by mindless regulations; schools were viewed as one more administrative unit to be controlled rather than inspired. According to the Carnegie Foundation report, here is how one New York City principal described her situation:

As I stare at the piles of memos and forms that confront me as a school principal, the job appears somewhere between a joke and an impossibility. The staff and I are directed instantly to implement new programs to resolve current crises, to use the latest research on teaching, to tighten supervision, increase consultation, and to report back in detail on all the above. There are pages of new rules and regulations to study: It would take a few months to make sense of the Regents plan alone. Responding to it would take a lifetime. Meanwhile, finding the funds to buy paper, repair our single rented typewriter, fix a computer, or tune the piano requires most of my time and imagination. (p. 6)

The foundation learned that purchasing, from pencils to textbooks, was centralized in district offices, giving individual schools little discretion in how to spend tax dollars to best meet the needs of their students.

8.1 POINTS TO REMEMBER

- Effective schools research involves the observation of schools using a variety of measures such as standardized tests and public opinion in order to establish the elements of a school that make it effective.
- The social organization of the school includes such things as goals, levels of expectations, reward systems, and leadership. Social organization differs more between effective and ineffective schools than do curriculum and instruction.
- A positive ethos in a school requires the teaching of both intellectual and moral development.
- A classroom climate that is conducive to learning is fostered by a family's interest in the school and positive relationships among teachers, administrators, parents, and students.
- Good school leaders develop clear roles for all school employees.
- They establish an orderly environment and communicate effectively with teachers and students.
- Students in a good school are actively involved in the governance of the school and in various school activities.
- Schools are ineffective when teachers are not innovative, funding is inadequate, and regulations get in the way of effective administration.

SCHOOLS FROM DIFFERENT PERSPECTIVES

Notwithstanding the research on effective schools, educators frequently do not agree on what schools should do to be more effective. These differences can be seen in various definitions of school. "Schools should be a place where children learn what they most want to know, instead of what we think they ought to know" (Holt, 1964, 175). Martin Carnoy and Henry M. Levin express a different point of view in *Schooling and Work in the Democratic State* (1985). "The school . . . contributes to the making of competent adults. . . . Schools are . . . functional institutions that satisfy the needs of adult society" (pp. 19, 20).

Holt, and Carnoy and Levin each define school in terms of its function. However, Holt emphasizes that school is "a place where children learn," whereas Carnoy and Levin believe that schools *make* competent adults. In other words, Holt defines school as a place for students and learning, and Carnoy and Levin define school as a place of instruction and subject matter. The distinction between school as a locus for learning and school as a locus of instruction is a critical one in terms of how schools are defined and organized. Holt's school, for example, would be organized with the student as its focus; Carnoy and

Levin's school would be organized with instruction and content as its focus. In practice, however, most schools generally focus on both the student *and* instruction, depending on a given situation.

The authors interviewed students, educators, and adults from a variety of walks of life, from various geographic regions of the United States, in a range of communities from urban to rural to obtain definitions of a school. We also examined various studies of schools to achieve a balance to these definitions. We selected the following as a representative group.

The students' perspective on school depends largely on their experiences there. Ryan Eller, age seven, from a suburban southern community, says that "school is a place where you learn things, like how to read." His eight-year-old brother, Justin, says, "In a way, school is fun. It's a place where you learn science, math, English and geography." Ryan's definition is of the place, as is Justin's, but Justin adds that school is fun, "in a way." Justin is commenting on the social, as well as the instructional, organization of the school. Ryan is still learning to read, but Justin is already moving into subjects such as science, math, and geography.

Nine-year-old Sharon Elliman from a small New England community thinks of school as "a place where you learn about science, social studies,

The Contemporary Student's Perspective

A student's perception of school may range from sheer joy to sheer disaster, depending on her or his experiences there, both in the classroom and out of it. These students enjoy working on a project together, making learning meaningful and happy.

geography, and much more. In school they also teach you math, spelling, and how to read. I like school a lot." Her best friend, nine-year-old Christina Marie Caviello, says, "I think school is great. Because the teachers make the work fun. . . . At the end of the year I feel sad because I had so much fun during the year." Sharon and Christina think more about the curriculum when they think about school. To them school is working and learning and having fun. Being with their peers is yet to become a primary purpose of going to school.

Eight-year-old Ellen Stanley, who attends school in a small rural community, says of school, "It's where there's kids and teachers and you learn stuff." Alicia Hall, age seven, who lives in a small southern town, also recognizes that school is more than a place; it is a place with people. "It's a building where we work and people go there to play with things and go on field trips." Her thirteen-year-old brother, Eric, has a slightly more sophisticated view of school based on his experiences. "It's a place to learn from books and about basketball, and there are lots of friends there, but you don't get to see them often." To Eric, as to most thirteen-year-olds, learning is important only if it relates to current interests, and school is a place where you meet your friends.

Jason Whitaker, a sixteen-year-old high school sophomore in a consolidated rural high school, describes school as "a place where you and your friends go to learn what you will use later on." Sixteen-year-old sophomore Mary Russell, also a student in a rural high school, says, "School is a place where you work, get an education, have friends. It's like a family to me, where there are teachers, and you have fun, but sometimes it's boring." To these high school students, learning, in terms of future directions, begins to take on importance, but peers and social interaction remain an essential part of the school experience.

Not all students find school a positive experience, however. In fact, in New York City, at a high school geared to prepare students for college, one student reported to the Carnegie Foundation for the Advancement of Teaching in *An Imperiled Generation: Saving Urban Schools*, "I made guest appearances when I was enrolled." Another student said, "The environment there was not one in which the kids wanted to learn. They just wanted to hang out on the streets." The Carnegie Foundation refers to this as the school's "culture of cutting" (p. xiii).

Other students depict the school experience as mixed. Caroline Owens, a twelve-year-old seventh grader in an urban middle school, said, "Some of the students have bad attitudes—like wanting to fight. They are school bullies. It's just the way they learned. They can't help it." However, Caroline says that for her, the "classes are great . . . I like the teachers because they are understanding, funny, and treat you like a person." David Smith, another twelve-year-old urban middle schooler, confirms Caroline's concern about the students. "Lots of kids pick on other kids—put them down. They're mean; they don't want to be social." He also finds school less satisfying than Caroline. "I like the social part of school, like the thirty minute breaks so we can visit. . . . The health classes are good, but you need teachers you can talk to and ask questions—teachers have to be open so you can ask questions about sex and drugs and alcohol—not just read it in the books."

The Carnegie Foundation for the Advancement of Teaching found that a student's experience in school depended, at least in part, on the curriculum. According to the commission the school's curriculum tends to put students in boxes: academic, vocational, and general. The North Carolina Task Force on

Excellence in Secondary Education reported in an unpublished series of research reports that students in general tracks are caught in an educational wasteland; they are less likely to succeed than their peers in more goal-oriented academic and vocational tracks. The Carnegie Foundation for the Advancement of Teaching says in the prologue to its report that "a reform movement launched to upgrade the education of *all* students is irrelevant to many children—largely black and Hispanic—in our urban schools" (p. xi).

Fifteen-year-old Aisha Washburn, a student in an urban high school, confirms their view. "I don't see much point in going to school. The teachers don't care whether I'm there or not. It's a waste of time; I learn more watching TV. What good is reading Shakespeare gonna' do me? I gotta' kid to take care of. As soon as I'm sixteen, I'm gonna quit."

By the time most students are ready to graduate from high school, they define school primarily in terms of preparation for college or life. Peers, of course, do not diminish in importance, but, rather, the students' definitions of school focus on how it prepares them for the future. According to Marc Bart, an eighteen-year-old senior in a city high school, who was taking a Scholastic Aptitude Test (SAT) preparation course when he wrote this definition, "School is a place that either prepares you for life directly outside of high school or prepares you for further education, and it also gives you the basic skills to get along in the world." Mary Quigley, a seventeen-year-old junior in a city high school, says that school is "a place where you go to learn different things so when you go out into the workforce you'll be prepared."

However, those students who do not see school as leading them toward their future careers or education tend to define and describe school as a waste of time. The Carnegie Foundation for the Advancement of Teaching concludes in its 1988 report that although most "Americans talk of providing a quality education for all children, we found that many people, both in and out of schools, simply do not believe this objective can be reached" (p. xv). Rather, many believe that urban students from underprivileged economic and social backgrounds cannot succeed. Hence, the report begins with the following declaration: "An urban school will be successful only as teachers, administrators, and community leaders have confidence that all students can succeed" (p. 1).

As students develop, their definitions of school evolve. Younger students think in terms of the activities of the classroom. Their friends are important, but they rarely define school in terms of relationships.

Older students, particularly in middle school and early high school, tend to define school in terms of both relationships and school activities. However, relationships take on primary importance, and activities are described in terms of what the student did or how the learning relates to the student's current interests.

As students mature, the importance of school to their future jobs or education takes precedence, but peer interactions remain a central focus of how they view schools. By the time students are completing their secondary education, their educational focus moves from peer interaction to preparation for jobs or college—life beyond school.

Note that all the students view school from the perspective of the learner. None of them talks about school as a place of instruction but rather as a place where learning happens.

In some classrooms, students freely interact with the teacher and are allowed to develop their natural curiosity in an unconventional manner. The teacher must always, however, balance the needs of the individual child with those of the group.

The Educator's Perspective

Although teachers and administrators spend much of their lives inside school buildings, they are rarely asked to define school. What they believe about schooling, their philosophy of education, is the basis for the organizational structure of their schools and classrooms.

Alice Evans, a retired early childhood teacher from Los Alamos, New Mexico, answers her own question.

> What is a school? A school is the raveling and unraveling of life. It is not confined to four walls. It is ever present from the day we are born to the day we die.
>
> What is a school? A school is a place where students and teachers meet to interact, to learn and grow together, to experience the excitement of curiosity and knowledge.

It is likely none of us were in Ms. Evans's classroom. However, we can imagine what it was like. Ms. Evans claims that school is a place that is "not confined to four walls," and the interactions between students and teachers takes precedence over the specifics of the content. Ms. Evans's classroom had walls, but the walls didn't keep the outside out or the inside in. The classroom was filled with critters in boxes and cages; in one corner was a microenvironment of a stream. Every spring the ant colony revisited the room. The children observed the activities of the animals and kept a class journal. They wrote books for the classroom library about their animal friends and life along the stream. The children freely wandered out the classroom door to fetch samples of grass or dirt. On fine days they frequently sat in circles on the lawn and wrote poems about the sounds of spring or the tastes of winter. Parents and other adults often visited the classroom. A trip to the local fire station, accompanied by the station dalmation, was the highlight of one walking field trip; another was to a corner grocery store, to reinforce addition and subtraction skills.

Lee Fowler has taught high school social studies and Latin for twenty-four years in Du Page County, Illinois. She says of school:

> A school is a place to instill WONDER—about the student's own life, the community, and the whole world. If the school sees itself *only* as a training place so that the students can make a living, the children are diminished.
>
> A child starts out life with such a tremendous amount of curiosity, and school should take that motivation to develop an awareness of self-importance as well as the individual's relationship to others and the world—both the physical world and the world of ideas and feelings.
>
> I've seen children begin school with such anticipation and eagerness. Why do those two marvelous traits seem to so often get killed off?

Ms. Fowler's definition tells us a great deal about the structure of her classroom. As a social studies teacher, she believes that individuals grow in self-importance through their interaction with one another. Her classroom is an active place. Groups of students work on projects. The group project is planned by Ms. Fowler, but the students' interaction is frequently unplanned. Ms. Fowler has an objective in mind for the group work; however, she is never sure of the exact direction the students will take. Will their study of "The Aging of America" lead a group of students to conduct interviews with residents of a local retirement home? Will their study of the Civil War lead to a reenactment of the Battle of Gettysburg? You never know where students will go when you give them a direction and send them on their way.

Cleveland Smith, a high school science teacher in Asheville, North Carolina, believes that "a school is a place where students learn academically, as well as through extracurricular activities and socially, a place where learning is nurtured in many different ways." Mr. Smith places a high value on both the knowledge his students gain in his science classroom and the time he spends working with them outside class. His choice of the word *nurture* shows how he views the role of the teacher—he or she is one who works closely with the students, continuously encouraging them, helping them feel good about themselves.

Marjorie Parker Jones is an assistant professor of education at St. Martin's College in Olympia, Washington. According to Ms. Jones, "Schooling is a dynamic that awakens the individual to self, spiritual, and material awareness through books (appropriately taught 'great books' and those self-chosen) and reflection on personal experience." Ms. Jones's definition indicates that her students read widely. Together, they discuss what they have read, and, through Ms. Jones's questioning, they relate their reading to their own experiences. Her classroom is an active place, pursuing knowledge through reading, reflection, writing, and discussion.

Ron Eller is an associate professor of history at the University of Kentucky in Lexington. According to Mr. Eller, "School is a place where the values of the community are passed on to the next generation." Mr. Eller is a scholar who researches the past and examines the values that have created communities. His classes reflect his beliefs. He encourages his students to become scholars of their cultures, to investigate their communities, to learn about their past, and thereby understand their present and future.

IN THE CLASSROOM

The work of Eliot Wigginton, a high school English teacher from Rabun Gap, Georgia, has been well documented in his students' *Foxfire* books. However, Mr. Wigginton's teaching did not begin with the production of these international best-sellers but in a small, conservative, rural classroom in the northwestern Georgia mountains.

Wigginton began his teaching career attempting to teach his students great literature. He soon learned, after the students nearly destroyed the classroom, that he would either have to change the teaching methods he had experienced as a student at Cornell or move to a different community and school. Luckily, he decided on the former. First, however, he almost made the error of assuming that his methods were correct and that he needed to force the students to comply and learn.

> It frightens me to think how close I came to making another stupid mistake. First, I had bored them unmercifully. Now I was about to impose a welcome punishment. Two weeks out of that class would have been more pleasure than pain. . . .
> I am not sure what that magic formula [for teaching] is or whether I have it pegged yet, but it involves a chemistry that allows us to believe we may have worth after all. Someone says, "You've done well," and we hunger to make that happen again and again. Too often we, as teachers, slip, and that first flush of success our students get comes after they've survived a night of drinking Colt 45, stuck up the local gas station, or taken two tabs of acid and made it out the other side alive.
> We could catch some of those if we would.
> The next day I walked into the class and said, "How would you like to throw away the text and start a magazine?" And that's how *Foxfire* began. (Wigginton 1972, 10)

Today *Foxfire* is a series of internationally known books that catalog the oral history and traditions of the people of the southern Appalachians. The students interview the people of the mountains armed with questions and tape recorders. They learn the old traditions and write them into profiles for their newsletters and books. They also do layout, makeup, design, do art work, select manuscripts from outside poets and writers, and produce the newsletters and books. The students are involved in the entire process, with Mr. Wigginton acting as editor in chief and publisher.

Some worry that an approach such as this ignores the basics of English. Mr. Wigginton argues that this is not the case. "English, in its simplest definition, is communication—reaching out and touching people with words, sounds, and visual images. We are in the business of improving students' prowess in these areas" (Wigginton, 13).

Mr. Wigginton started small. It wasn't until after his program received national recognition and several grants that it moved to the major publishing operation it is today. Although most teachers do not aspire to such an enterprise for their students, an oral history publication on a smaller scale is possible in most schools and allows students to realize their potential.

Eliot Wigginton is a master teacher. He has allowed his students' learning to be the primary goal of his English program. "An article of faith here is that pupils need a voice in what and how they learn" (Ansberry, R24). Today students can elect to take one of fifteen Foxfire classes at Rabun Gap High School taught by Eliot Wigginton and three others; one-third of Rabun Gap's 900 students are enrolled in the classes. The Foxfire project has produced twelve best-selling books, a Broadway play, a TV special, and a number of albums and videotapes. Mr. Wigginton now conducts workshops to help teachers from around the country create programs modeled after Foxfire. Clare Ansberry, a reporter for the *Wall Street Journal*, recently visited Rabun Gap High School to observe firsthand the Foxfire program 23 years after its inception. Here are some of her impressions.

> On a recent afternoon, four eighth-graders huddled around a TV screen in a classroom at the high school, editing tapes that will become a video on how to teach storytelling. Down the hall in tiny studios, aspiring folk and rock musicians critique their recent performances at an Atlanta high school and a local hospital. On the wall hangs a framed album by the Foxfire String Band, one of six Foxfire recordings. . . .
>
> [According to senior Darion Marcus], "If you make a mistake, they let you go back and correct it. They don't do it for you." He adds, "I'm working harder than ever before, but I'm having fun." (p. R24)

The teachers quoted above have largely positive definitions of school. Some, however, are negative in their descriptions. In the Carnegie Foundation for the Advancement of Teaching report on urban schools, the task force members discovered that many educators described school in terms of "failures." They talked about students who were merely "marking time" in school. "A social studies teacher in a Los Angeles high school confided somewhat sheepishly that her students were using a book written on a third-grade level because it was 'all they could handle.' 'It's a game we play,' said a teacher in Houston. 'If we held them all back, the system would get clogged up. So we water down the curriculum and move them along' " (1988, p. 1).

Teachers in urban schools further reported to the Carnegie Commission task force that school is "paper work." As one urban teacher said to the task force:

> Paper work is one of the things that competes for my time. You have to check roll in homeroom and then you have to see if anyone is tardy. In second period, you have to fill out an attendance report that is audited for average daily attendance.

"Sorry, Bigley, but it's all the budget will allow for research."

You have to keep those records in your grade book. Then, if a student is absent three times you have to list him on a special form that goes to the principal with your lesson plans. And you have to call the student. On the fourth day, you have to send a letter to the student's parents, and send another form into the office when the student is absent the sixth time. I think that is a lot of time that surely could come from some other source, like from the attendance office. It is an every period activity. (1988, 6–7)

Another problem urban teachers related to the task force was lack of materials and supplies. Here is how one urban teacher described the problem:

I sometimes wonder how we're able to teach at all. A lot of times there aren't enough textbooks to go around; the library here is totally inadequate; and the science teachers complain that the labs aren't equipped and are out-of-date. We're always running short on supplies. Last year we were out of mimeograph paper for a month, and once we even ran out of chalk. After a while you learn to be resourceful. But it's still frustrating to try to teach under these conditions. I mean, talk about teaching the basics! We don't even have the basics to teach with. (1988, 7)

It is not only in urban schools in which teachers define schooling negatively. Paul Houts, director of the Carnegie Foundation's Study of the American High School, summarized the study's findings in a conference in Racine, Wisconsin, in 1982.

They [high school teachers] have little time to prepare for what they do each day, no authority to make decisions, frequent interruptions by disruptive students and by principals with nearly incessant public address announcements, and pay so low that moonlighting on second jobs is often necessary. In many places, teachers also lack the support and respect of the community in which they work. And after the school year ends, many must take jobs as clerks, waitresses, house painters, or other non-professional work in order to make ends meet. There is considerable demoralization out there.

Recently we asked students who had just finished their student teaching at an urban high school to define school. One of them summarized his impressions.

It is like there are two (or maybe more) schools. There is a school for the good students. These kids are largely economically advantaged and white. They get a good education in my school. They take advanced classes; some of them take Advanced Placement courses [classes that provide college credit depending on the results of a national test]. These kids could compete anywhere. Then, there is the other school, the school of the disenfranchised kids. These kids are largely economically disadvantaged and nonwhite. They get a poor education in my school. They take low-level classes. They study a curriculum which helps prove to them that there are no people of color who do work that is worth studying. Do you know, that in spite of the fact that my school is over forty percent black, the English curriculum has no black writers—even in the classes which are largely black? In history, the students do not study great African or native Americans. Many of these kids drop out, and those that don't are prepared for little when they graduate. There are at least two schools in my school, one very good and one very poor.

A report funded by the William T. Grant Foundation Commission on Work, Family and Citizenship, *The Forgotten Half: Pathways to Success for America's Youth and Young Families* (1988) states, "Educators have become so preoccupied with those who go on to college that they have lost sight of those who do not. And more and more of the non-college-bound now fall between the cracks when they are in school, drop out, or graduate inadequately prepared for the requirements of the society and the workplace" (p. 3). Hence, the report tends to confirm the student teacher's impression: school must be defined from the perspective of the background of the students.

As the leader of the school, the principal affects the school's organization by his or her definition of school. Larry Liggett has been a principal of a small city high school for fourteen years. According to Mr. Liggett, "A school is a family of people, gathered together to learn." Mr. Liggett's high school is large, but students and teachers are encouraged to think of themselves as part of a family.

Nevertheless, he makes it clear that what the school family does together is learn. The students in Mr. Liggett's school are highly rewarded for their academic achievements. Students in the Latin classes annually win the state Junior Classical League competition and place highly in the national competition. The ROTC unit has been judged the best in the nation. Mr. Liggett's definition makes it clear that no student achieves this alone because each is a part of a family of learners.

The superintendent's definition of school affects not only a single school but potentially the entire school district. According to Culver R. Dale, retired superintendent of a small-town school district, "A school is an institution of formal instruction where a person learns in order to grow into a happy, productive, self-supporting, reliable, contributing individual. A school enables a person to develop to the fullest extent whatever talents and abilities he or she possesses. Thus, leaves this world a better place than he or she found it."

Sam Haywood, area superintendent in the Charlotte/Mecklenburg, North Carolina, schools, defines schools in a way that reflects the altruistic goals of the schools and the realistic problems of the schools.

Schools are places where knowledgeable and committed administrators and teachers help great kids learn how to think about important and even less

The Administrator's Perspective

important issues and problems. Schools are places where students learn basic skills.

Schools are places where students from many different economic and ethnic backgrounds come together. The school is a melting pot of the world and students are exposed to many things their parents had not taught them—like inappropriate sexual behavior, profanity, fighting, drugs, and using guns. The parents try to help, but sometimes it's too late.

Schools are places where kids have fun playing in sports, participating in band and chorus, experimenting in labs and just plain socializing together.

All these educators have different definitions of school; however, all of them agree that it is a place in which students learn. How that learning is to be carried out, the activities of the classroom, vary according to their personal definition.

The Contemporary Adult's Perspective

None of the people whose interviews follow is an educator. The one thing they have in common is that they all attended school. Some of them are parents of children currently in school; some of them have children who have completed school; some work inside the home; others pursue careers outside the home. Their definitions of school reflect their own experiences and the experiences of their children. In addition, their definitions express their adult concerns about what schools should do.

Anne Coviello is a mother and homemaker from a small town in Massachusetts. She says of school:

A school is one of the greatest influences in an individual's life. For those who are receptive, school acts as a foundation for the many paths we choose to follow as adults.

In talking with many friends, we all agree that "school" is the main thing that we wish we could "do again" and, somehow, "make right."

We, the homemakers and mothers, who for the most part work a minimal amount of time outside of the home, have a real thirst for knowledge at this stage of our lives. School takes on a new and much more valuable meaning for us now, perhaps because we're so caught up in the education of our children. The same "school" that we, as children, trudged through (all too often reluctantly and with little appreciation) has become a primary focus in our lives in terms of wanting the best in education for our children. We would love to be in the position to "learn it all," again. Consequently, we become frustrated when our children don't approach the learning process with the same enthusiasm that we would now were we given the opportunity.

Ms. Coviello, like most parents, wants more from school for her children than she got from it. In fact, she longs for the opportunity to go to school again, and, this time around, take all that it has to offer. She worries that her children are not eager to learn, perhaps no more eager than she was as a young student. Ms. Coviello places the greatest importance on what the students learn in school, calling that learning the "foundation" for life's choices. She does not say what should be included in that foundation, but she believes that it involves the gaining of knowledge. To Ms. Coviello, the instructional organization of the school takes precedence over the social. However, it is likely if we had asked her what she remembers most from her own schooling, she would recall those aspects that involve interaction with her peers.

Foster Evans, a theoretical physicist from New Mexico, says school is "a place where a person may go to learn. A successful school is one that provides an environment conducive to learning. [A school is a group of teachers that provides such an environment.]" Mr. Evans recognizes that a school is a place where a person "may" go to learn. He makes it clear, through the use of the word *may*, that learning is not the only reason why people go to school, and that not all people who go to school will learn. In addition, Mr. Evans acknowledges that a school is successful only if the environment is conducive to learning.

Doris Phillips Loomis, an attorney and mother from North Carolina, says that "a school is an arena is which the inquisitive can thrive and the complacent can absorb. It sets those two groups apart. In order for this definition to be accurate, however, a school must be construed to be not only an educational institution but also the world in general." Ms. Loomis's definition looks at school as more than a place with four walls. She refers to school as an "arena" and acknowledges that if school is to allow the "inquisitive to thrive" it must be viewed as more than an institution; it must be viewed as the "world in general." In Ms. Loomis's ideal school, the world will be brought into the classroom, and the students will be taken into the world.

Although all these adults, who at one time were students, have different definitions of a school, all of them recognize the centrality of the learner to the learning process. None of them places instruction at the forefront but each recognizes that some interaction between student and teacher must occur. All these adults speak from their own experiences, the experiences of their children, and what their lives have taught them school should be. For all of them, schools in the United States are far more than "buildings where instruction takes place."

Schools from a Cross-Cultural Perspective

To help us better understand the contemporary view of schools in the United States, we asked Japanese, Argentinean, and Chinese high school exchange or immigrant students to discuss the schools in their home countries and compare them to the American public schools they were attending. Through these cross-cultural comparisons we can see how *all* the definitions above differ from those of these students.

Ayumi Moro, a nineteen-year-old high school graduate visiting an American high school, says of schools in Japan:

School [one term] begins in April. There are three terms. Most of the Japanese students wear school uniforms. They go to school by train, bus, or bicycle. Some walk. There is no school bus. People under eighteen years of age cannot drive cars. In addition, they cannot go by car to school.

School usually begins at eight thirty and finishes at three o'clock. There is a ten minute break between classes for the teacher to change rooms. The students don't change rooms, but they have different schedules everyday. They have five big exams a year. This decides the grades on the report card.

Summer vacation lasts about forty days. School [another term] begins in September. In autumn, there are many school events—a culture festival, an athletic meet, and a school excursion for seniors only. This is a very big event.

The winter vacation starts at Christmas and lasts about two weeks. In March seniors graduate from school.

According to Chikako Yokogawa, an eighteen-year-old senior visiting an American high school as an exchange student:

> I go to a public school in Japan. After students finish compulsory education through junior high school, most go on to complete high school so that they can get a good job. This is because the Japanese society puts so much emphasis on one's educational background, and most Japanese companies demand people to have a high educational background. To attend a high school, each student must pass an entrance examination; however, the number of applicants for admission is far greater than the number actually accepted. This makes it very difficult.
>
> The students must study very hard, since the school has major exams often. Over half the students go to a private tutoring school in the afternoons after regular school. This is especially true for seniors, as they have to study even harder than anyone else to get into a university. It is referred to as "Examination Hell."

Kyoko Shogetsu frankly says of her experience as a Japanese public school student, "I like school, but there are so many programs, I have to study very hard. Japanese schools are boring. I come here to an American high school so I won't be so bored in school. I have many friends in school [in America], then it's not so boring."

Claudio Bottero, a seventeen-year-old exchange student from Argentina, compares schools in Argentina to the one he is visiting in the United States.

> School is a place to learn many things. There are more possibilities to learn in America—like many science labs and electronic labs. There is a lot of opportunity to practice. Practice is better here. In Argentina, I had to study very hard, like five hours to study for a calculus test. Here I study about thirty minutes and can get B's and A's. Theory is much harder there.
>
> Students here waste a lot of time. Many don't do their homework. They like to have parties and drink to get drunk. In Argentina, we like to drink because we enjoy it, but not to get drunk. Every day when I go into the bathrooms [in the school] I can smell the pot, but I don't see any of that in classrooms or the halls.

Quingfei Zhang is an eighteen-year-old high school senior who came to the United States two years ago with his parents. He compares U.S. schools to those in mainland China.

> Schools in America have lots of free choices of subjects to take. In China, in my first two years of high school, I had to take just those classes that I need to have to get into an engineering college. Here I can take those classes but other ones too, like swimming and advanced English. There is more leisure time here—lots of activities and clubs. The clubs are good if you do something, but some students join clubs that meet during the school day to get out of going to class, and in the clubs they sit there and just talk. I guess that's o.k. It depends on what your career aspirations are. I want to be an engineer, so I don't want to waste my time that way.

It is interesting to compare the exchange and immigrant students' descriptions of school with the American secondary school students' definitions. School, to the foreign students, is an academic endeavor filled with studying, tutoring, long hours of work, and tests, "Examination Hell," as one student calls it. None of these students mentions what he or she learns in school but rather what is required. The distinction is important. In every definition provided by U.S. students, educators, and non-educator adults, what the student learns is the most important element of the school. However, in the exchange and immigrant students' descriptions of schools in their home countries, what the student learns is not mentioned. Instead, whether or not the student meets the demands of the educational system and/or business appears to be the central element of schooling.

The Japanese and Chinese definitions of school center on instruction and content to be taught. In fact, it appears from the Japanese definition that what the student learns is more important for business and industry than for the student. Likewise, it appears that the approach to school described by all five students is almost totally instructional rather than social.

Sheppard Ranbom, a reporter visiting Japanese schools for *Education Week* (1985), quotes Riyoichi Matsumura, the chief geography instructor in Yamaguchi province: "Japan's resources are human resources. Schools cultivate the human talent that provides the ability and productivity that allows the nation to survive" (p. 12). According to Ranbom, Japanese education has been great for building a competitive economy, but now "there is a strong national capacity for research and innovation, demanding traits and abilities not presently rewarded in Japanese schools—like originality, diversity, creativity, risk-taking and inventiveness" (p. 14). According to Ranbom, schools in Japan emphasize

> the same level of instruction for all, without regard to individual ability or development, stress on memorization and facts, rather than on thinking and problem solving, heavy reliance on tests and measurement of achievement and potential. . . . The standardization that has served Japan so well in the past, producing a uniformly well-educated work force, may not be the medium through which creative genius can be nurtured. (p. 14)

However, Merry White points out in *The Japanese Educational Challenge: A Commitment to Children* (1987) that most Japanese children report "liking school" (p. 136). She cites a study in which Japanese children scored highest among students in several countries in finding school "a good place to be" (p. 136).

White also found that not all students in Japan are academic achievers. As in the United States, many students do not want to attend school, what the Japanese call the "school refusal syndrome." She confirms other problems in Japanese schools, many that parallel problems in U.S. schools, such as violence against teachers, but, as in the United States, its statistical incidence is very small. Suicide, particularly among students who fail college entrance exams, has also received much publicity. However, White points out that the suicide rate among fifteen- to twenty-year-olds in Japan declined from 1980 to 1987, and since 1980 was lower than in the United States (12.5 suicides per 100,000 fifteen- to twenty-year-olds in the United States compared to 10.8 per 100,000 in Japan) (p. 137).

White also asserts that Japanese schools can be considered creative by Japanese standards. The conclusion that they are not is at "least partly the result of ethnocentric assumptions about the source and meaning of creativity" (p. 81). She claims that "Americans . . . confuse self-expression with creativity, placing the greatest value on spontaneity rather than on taking pains" (p. 79). White discusses the crafts and arts of Japan, which tend to emphasize what she calls the "old-style" creativity of traditional forms. On the other hand, a "new kind of creativity can be fostered. Japanese schools are, like most of ours,

(continued on p. 264)

CROSS-CULTURAL PERSPECTIVE

The Chinese School

To look around a typical urban Chinese elementary school classroom might remind an American visitor of the "good old days" of no-frills education. Here's what you might expect to see:

- Lots of desks arranged in tight rows with narrow aisles and no space for small-group instruction
- A raised podium for the teacher at the front of the room
- Walls dominated by pictures of government leaders, but rarely displaying student work or curricular material
- A neat, clean, but poorly lit room equipped with well-worn furniture and hardly any of the gadgetry found in most American classrooms
- No basic reference materials available for easy student access.

What goes on in this seemingly Spartan environment? Let's observe the daily routine of a typical Chinese elementary school student.

Our student walks or bicycles to a neighborhood school unless ability, good luck, and connections have combined to permit attendance at a special school for the academically talented.

On the playground, our student greets friends or plays games until the morning bell rings. The academic day then begins with the entire student body participating in a 15- to 20-minute playground exercise period. The routinized program, done to music, is memorized by all the students.

Once students enter their classrooms, the morning is divided into four classes. First graders stay with the same teacher all day, but above the first grade level, instruction is departmentalized. The students remain in their homerooms while the teachers rotate through the various grade levels, teaching their subjects to between 40 to 55 students in each classroom.

The primary curriculum includes Chinese, math, physical education, music, drawing, painting, and moral (political) education. The difficult Chinese language requires one-third to one-half of the instructional time.

Foreign language instruction in English, Japanese, or Russian begins in the third grade in some schools. In addition to the primary curriculum, instruction in grades 4, 5, and 6 includes general history, geography, natural science—and physical labor.

The physical labor component, designed to demonstrate the value of work, varies from school to school. Our student might be required to work on projects around the school for a two-week period.

Our student remains attentive (or at least not disruptive) for the entire length of each 50-minute period, which is followed by a veritable explosion of children fleeing to the playground to unwind from the long lesson.

In most classes, our student participates in whole-class oral recitation lessons. He stands when called on to recite, and is accustomed to receiving minimal positive feedback. Teachers are sparing in their pronouncements of *hao* (good).

After the morning classes, everyone goes home for lunch and *xiuxi* (rest) for about two hours. The students then return for three afternoon periods that are usually not as rigorous as the morning sessions. When classes end, at about 4:00 P.M., some children go home while others stay at school to do their homework or to receive special help from the teachers, whose day ends at about 5:30 P.M.

School is also in session on Saturday, when classes are held in the morning. Saturday afternoons are devoted to school-sponsored organized sports or occasional field trips.

Chinese schoolchildren have been stereotyped as paradigmatic Boy and Girl Scouts: courteous, kind, obedient, thrifty, and highly intelligent (Rosemont, 1985). This would seem to attest to the success of a curriculum that is aimed at developing these characteristics. Moral, physical, and intellectual development is emphasized in Chinese schools.

Moral education, which deals with the role of government and Communist philosophy, is also an important focus of the Young Pioneers, the youth organization of the Chinese Communist Party. Elementary schoolchildren proudly wear the red neckerchief that symbolizes membership in the

Students in Chinese schools face a more structured curriculum and environment than their counterparts in the United States. These primary school students are performing gymnastics in a school in Beijing.

Young Pioneers. Almost all children who are diligent in school (level of achievement is not as important) and who possess qualities of good citizenship are nominated for membership by their teachers. Young Pioneers, who are led by teachers, undertake community service projects and also have excursions and other special activities.

Enrichment of intellectual development is the focus of the Children's Palaces, after-school centers whose membership is more selective than the Young Pioneers. Only a small percentage of students are recommended to attend programs that provide creative opportunities in art, music, dance, and science.

The themes of moral, physical, and intellectual development in elementary school education are in keeping with the stated purpose of education in China, which is "to cultivate in the pupils the moral character of loving the Motherland, the people, physical labor, science, and public property, cherishing socialism and supporting the Communist Party; to help them acquire reading, writing, and arithmetic; knowledge in natural sciences; and good study habits, to enable them to enjoy good health and acquire fine habits in life and labor" (China Handbook Series, 1983).

From: Hauser, Fawson, and Latham, 1990

routinized. But because positive engagement and enthusiasm are emphasized, even what an American would call creativity is elicited in certain classes. The outcomes of *Japanese* routinization are, surprisingly, a high degree of analytical and creative problem-solving, as well as expressions of divergent points of view" (p. 80).

It can be said, then, that one's experience in school can influence not only one's definition of school but also one's perception of the school's effectiveness. As the student teacher in this chapter said, a school may be very good for some students and not good for others. Is it possible for a school to be effective for *all* students? Scholars and educators who have examined schools judged to be effective say that it is.

8.2 POINTS TO REMEMBER

- Students' definitions of school relate to their experiences in school. Elementary school students tend to define school in terms of what they are learning to do. By late elementary school, students frequently define school in terms of peer relationships. By late high school, students define school in terms of their future goals for employment or higher education.

- Teachers' definitions of school are reflected in the organization of their classrooms. If they think of school as a community in which students work together to learn, their classroom organizations will encourage student interaction and participation in learning.

- Most adults define school from their own personal experiences in school. Because they remember from the perspective of a learner, they define school in these terms.

- Examining how individuals in other cultures define schools helps us see how definitions of school relate to experience and school organization. In addition, these definitions help us better understand U.S. schools by knowing how they differ from schools in other cultures.

FOR THOUGHT/DISCUSSION

1. Do you think most U.S. schools teach a common positive ethos? If yes, what effect is it having on today's students? If no, why isn't it being implemented in all schools?

2. From your knowledge about schools and from information in this chapter, describe some elements that make schools ineffective.

3. What is your definition of a school from the perspective of a student and from the perspective of a teacher? How will this definition affect your classroom organization?

4. What qualities of a Japanese education do you feel could best be applied to the U.S. educational system?

FOR FURTHER READING/REFERENCE

Brandt, R. S. (Ed.). 1989. *Readings from educational leadership: Effective schools and school improvement*. Alexandria, VA: Association for Supervision and Curriculum Development. A collection of articles about effective schools that first appeared in *Educational Leadership*, the journal of ASCD. Articles by R. Edmonds and R. S. Brandt are particularly noteworthy.

Carnegie Foundation for the Advancement of Teaching. 1988. *An imperiled generation: Saving urban schools*. Princeton, NJ: The Carnegie Foundation. A report about the condition of urban schools, resulting from on-site visits to several urban schools throughout the country with emphasis on school units within the six largest cities in the United States. Conditions of school buildings, resources, and impressions of teachers, principals, and students are related. Recommendations for improvement are presented.

Fiske, B. 1991. *Smart schools, smart kids: Why do some schools work?* New York: Simon and Schuster. A description of on-site visits to public school classrooms that have made recent innovative structural changes. The author suggests that smart schools blend elements of change that fit the school's particular circumstances.

Gilchrist, R. 1989. *Effective schools: Three case studies of excellence*. Bloomington, IN: National Education Service. Case studies of an elementary, a middle, and a high school in different areas of the United States. The case studies result from firsthand observations and interviews in the schools. The book concludes with a summary of seven similar broad characteristics of the schools.

Goodlad, J. I. 1984. *A place called school: Prospects for the future*. New York: McGraw-Hill. A description of the results of observations, interviews, and surveys in elementary, middle, and high school classrooms. The book compares the similarities and contrasts the differences between the schools that Goodlad classifies as most and least satisfactory.

Houlihan, G. T. 1988. *School effectiveness: The key ingredients of schools with heart*. Springfield, IL: Charles C. Thomas. The author, a superintendent of a North Carolina county school district, describes how parents, teachers, administrators, and students interacted in the everyday world of the classroom and school. Calling these interactions the key ingredients of school effectiveness, he suggests techniques for how to implement interactive systems elsewhere.

9

The Curriculum

Henry is a high school English teacher who has been teaching for more than twenty years. A friend asked him to appear on a panel at a professional meeting to discuss how teaching English has changed during that period. In reflecting upon his topic, Henry realized that there had been many changes in the students, the way the school is administered, how teachers are treated, and requirements for certification. But, most of all, Henry thought, the curriculum had come full circle. That's what Henry decided to talk about.

When I began teaching in the mid-1960s, I was assigned to three sections of average 11th-graders, one section of remedial students, and one section of advanced students. By the late-1960s I had been "promoted" to three sections of advanced and two sections of average. The better I became as a teacher, the better the students I was given to teach.

However, I taught to all three levels the same 11th grade material, using the same textbooks. The students read the same Shakespearean plays. The differences were in how quickly we got through the material, how frequently I lectured, and how many essays I asked each group to write. The better the students, the more we read, the more difficult the questions I asked, the more in depth their answers, and the longer their writing assignments and tests.

By the late-1960s the students began protesting. Was this material relevant? How did Shakespeare relate to the real world of Vietnam, segregation, and street riots? So, I tried to make the literature more relevant. In some of my classes we turned Hamlet into modern street dialect. That was fun; but was it more relevant? In response, we read more contemporary books like *Black Like Me* and *Catcher in the Rye*. The teachers began to talk about the students' concerns. Soon, the teachers decided to reorganize the curriculum into minicourses primarily in areas of personal interest with titles such as "Myth and Legend," and "Who 'Dun' It?" The students and teachers as well selected courses they were interested in. At first, nearly everyone was happy. I particularly enjoyed the humanities courses I was team teaching with the history, music, and art teachers. I think the best humanities course we taught was based on the theme of "War and Peace."

However, before a generation of high school students had passed through the minicourses, concerns were voiced: Were the students selecting courses that would teach them to write? Were the students selecting only "gut" courses? How was reading adolescent literature going to help them understand great literature? Were advanced students penalized by having remedial students in the same class? What about spelling and grammar; where did they fit in?

The teachers began to make changes. All students were required to take one quarter of composition and grammar each year. Advanced students were required to take one quarter of "the classics" each year. Within a few years, minicourse electives had become no more than required quarter courses. Allowing students to select among the required courses was an administrative headache. We decided then to go back to full-year courses. At first, they were similar to the minicourses. Most teachers organized the year into units based on themes or types of literature; most still taught one quarter of grammar and composition.

But, then, along came competency tests and concern that advanced students were not doing well on college entrance exams. So, we added more grammar, composition, and vocabulary to each class. More often than not, these were isolated lessons, not related to the literature the students were reading. In advanced classes teachers were required to teach specific "classics." Student choice was limited to free reading time. And, now, national studies seem to indicate that all students should be aware of a common "classical" body of literature. Consequently, the curriculum in my classes today looks remarkably like the curriculum I taught in the mid-1960s. The only difference is that now the state provides me with thirty or forty pages of competencies which the students must meet. At our last meeting of English teachers I heard a rumor that we need to begin reexamining our "classical" curriculum in light of the whole language approach in the elementary schools. Some of my colleagues were complaining that our curriculum is too exclusive and too fragmented.

CHAPTER OBJECTIVES

After studying this chapter, you should be able to:

- Define curriculum from the point of view of the essentialist.
- Define curriculum from the point of view of the progressivist.
- Describe how curriculum of the twentieth century has evolved.
- Compare how the schools of philosophy and the theories of education relate to curricular organization.
- Describe the subject-centered curriculum.
- Explain the competency-based curriculum.
- Define mastery learning.
- Describe the broad fields curriculum.
- Define core curriculum.
- Describe the child-centered or activity curriculum.
- Discuss the humanistic curriculum.
- Explain how society's economic needs affect the curriculum.
- Discuss how women and minorities affect the curriculum.
- Describe how textbooks and tests affect the curriculum.
- Discuss how technology affects the curriculum.

Henry wonders. "What is curriculum, anyway?" Is it simply a set of courses to be taught? Is it a response to social demands? Is it in any way related to the students' needs? Who defines students' needs? In this chapter we will define curriculum from a variety of points of view. We will attempt to illustrate how the individual's definition of curriculum helps determine its organization. We also will examine the philosophical basis of a curriculum and discuss its major organizational structures. Finally, we will examine the social and economic forces that have affected how curriculum is defined, developed, and implemented.

WHAT IS A CURRICULUM?

Literally, by definition, curriculum is what is taught in an educational institution, usually a series of courses. However, since learning is the presumed product of teaching, curriculum is also used to describe what is learned. Herein lies the difficulty in defining curriculum. It is easy to describe what is planned to be taught. It is far more difficult to determine what is actually taught, and even more difficult to assess what has been learned.

An Essentialist Definition

The word *curriculum* is derived from the Latin word *currere* meaning "the course to be run." Its derivation implies that curriculum is like a track with a beginning, a series of steps, and an end. The school sets the order of these steps, the essential building blocks of learning, making them increasingly difficult to achieve. Students must successfully complete each stage before being allowed to tackle the next. This definition is based on the essentialist theory of learning, which focuses on the basic, or essential, courses such as reading, writing, and arithmetic at the elementary level, and subject-matter disciplines such as mathematics and language at the secondary level.

A recent essentialist interpretation of curriculum can be seen in David P. Gardner's recommendations in his 1983 reform report, *A Nation at Risk: The Imperative for Educational Reform.*

> We recommend that State and local high school graduation requirements be strengthened and that, at a minimum, all students seeking a diploma be required to lay the foundations in the Five New Basics by taking the following curriculum during their 4 years of high school: (a) 4 years of English; (b) 3 years of

mathematics; (c) 3 years of science; (d) 3 years of social studies; and (e) one-half year of computer science. For the college bound, 2 years of foreign language in high school are strongly recommended in addition to those taken earlier. (p. 24)

However, the essentialist definition limits curriculum to what is taught and/or what is planned to be taught. Learners, and even teachers, are left out of this interpretation of curriculum. John Dewey in *Democracy and Education* (1928) criticizes the essentialist definition of curriculum.

> The notion that the "essentials" of elementary education are the three R's mechanically treated, is based upon ignorance of the essentials needed for realization of democratic ideals. Unconsciously it assumes that these ideals are unrealizable; it assumes that in the future, as in the past, getting a livelihood, "making a living," must signify for most men and women doing things which are not significant, freely chosen, and ennobling to those who do them; doing things which serve ends unrecognized by those engaged in them, carried on under the direction of others for the sake of pecuniary reward. (p. 226)

Many educators believe that curriculum is far more than the development of a course to be run. Instead, curriculum includes, according to Elliot W. Eisner, "all the experiences the child has under the aegis of the school" (1985, 40).

This definition became popular during the progressive education movement of the 1920s. (For a discussion of progressivism, see chapter 7, pp. 219–221.) According to progressive educators, the "real" curriculum includes not only what goes on in the classroom within the planned lesson but also what goes on in the hallways and on the playground. Dewey and other progressive educators define curriculum as "continuous reconstruction of experience, an idea which is marked off from education as preparation for a remote future, as unfolding, as external formation, and as recapitulation of the past" (Dewey 1928, 93). The progressive definition of curriculum assumes that every student has his or her own curriculum because every student has different experiences.

A Progressive Definition

The essentialist and progressivist definitions of curriculum can be viewed as two extremes between which are definitions that attempt to combine specific areas of curriculum with individual teaching styles and the learner's experiences. For example, B. Othaniel Smith believes curriculum is "a sequence of potential experiences . . . set up in the school for the purpose of disciplining children and youth in group ways of thinking and acting. . . . It is a reflection of the way people think, feel, believe, and do" (1957, 3). Or, John P. Miller and Wayne Seller state that "curriculum is an explicitly [written curriculum or course of study] and implicitly [hidden curriculum, including interactions between students and teachers, other students, subject matter, computers, communities . . .] intentional set of interactions designed to facilitate learning and development and to impose meaning on experience" (1985, 3).

Other Definitions of Curriculum

The "Hidden Curriculum"

The "hidden curriculum" is that which occurs in the school but is not a part of the formal curriculum or course of study. John D. McNeil defines the hidden curriculum as including the "unofficial instructional influences [of schooling], which may either support or weaken the attainment of manifest goals" (1977, 209). Observers who gathered data in 129 elementary, 362 junior high, and 525 senior high classes for John I. Goodlad's study *A Place Called School: Prospects for the Future,* defined the hidden curriculum as the many informal aspects of life in the school environment such as student-to-student interaction, student-to-teacher interaction, the lunchroom environment, the aesthetics of the school building, the use of technological equipment, students' involvement in decision making about their own learning, percentage of class time in which students talk and teachers talk, the use of small groups in the classroom, use of praise and laughter, and hands-on activity and physical movements (pp. 226–230).

Both the neo-Marxists and humanists have critically examined the hidden curriculum. Neo-Marxists such as Michael Apple, Henry Giroux, Nancy R. King, and David Purpel analyzed it in terms of its economic and social context. (See chapter 6, p. 159, for a discussion of the neo-Marxist view of the history of education.) Humanists, such as Philip W. Jackson and Arthur Combs, analyzed it in terms of the students' life in the school.

Apple and King, in "What Do Schools Teach?" (1977), believe the hidden curriculum is the tacit teaching of social and economic norms and expectations. They claim that it is not as hidden or "mindless" as many educators believe since much of what the school does is to "certify adult competence" for involvement in an advanced industrial society.

Therefore, educational knowledge dispensed by the schools must be considered in light of the larger distribution of goods and services in society. Neo-Marxists such as Michael F. D. Young state there is not only an unequal distribution of economic capital in society but also an unequal distribution of cultural capital. The school plays a critical role in dispensing this capital because school personnel make decisions about what is to be included in the curriculum and which students are to study which topics. "Principles of selection, organization, and evaluation of this knowledge are valuative selections from a much larger universe of possible knowledge and collection principles" (Young 1971, 31). Therefore, deciding that college-bound students will study Shakespeare, physics, foreign language, and world civilization and non-college-bound students will not, is part of the hidden curriculum in that these decisions determine to whom specific cultural capital will be given.

Neo-Marxists also discuss "access to power" as part of the hidden curriculum. There are numerous ways that this access to power can be seen in the school curriculum: Who develops the curriculum? Who has access to aspects of the curriculum that encourage development of power? Which students can make curricular choices? Do students work in small groups in some classes while being lectured to in other classes? Which students have access to positions of power in the school? Which students participate in important extracurricular activities such as interscholastic sports?

Philip W. Jackson in *Life in Classrooms* (1968), on the other hand, describes the hidden curriculum differently. "School is a place . . . in which people sit, and listen, and wait, and raise their hands, and pass out paper, and sharpen pencils. School is where we encounter both friends and foes, where imagination is unleashed and misunderstanding brought to ground" (p. 4). All these things are part of the hidden curriculum.

Jackson says that we can examine the hidden curriculum in terms of the amount of time students spend in school, the settings in which they perform,

The hidden curriculum influences a student's education almost as much as does the obvious selection and organization of subject matter. Such things as time spent in class, the physical structure of the school building, student-to-teacher interaction, and classroom atmosphere can all be considered a part of the hidden curriculum.

and the fact that they are in school whether they want to be or not. He maintains that in most classrooms "the social composition is not only stable, it is also physically arranged with considerable regularity" (1968, 7). Students typically have assigned seats and usually can be found in them. He further claims that despite diversity of subject matter content, "the identifiable activities are not great in number. The labels: 'seat work,' 'group discussion,' 'teacher demonstration,' and 'question-and-answer-period' (which would include work 'at the board'), are sufficient to categorize most of the things that happen when class is in session" (p. 8).

What then is the hidden curriculum if schools are so similar? Jackson's definition includes such things as how time is spent by the student in the classroom, how the environment of the classroom affects the students' roles, and how the instructional techniques employed by the teacher involve the students.

The curriculum in U.S. schools has been influenced by several psychologists. In this section of the chapter, we will examine some of their theories.

Influence of U.S. Psychologists

G. Stanley Hall

G. Stanley Hall (1846–1924), considered by many to be the father of educational psychology, developed a field that has come to be called **child-centered psychology**. Significantly influenced by the work of biologist Charles Darwin, the premise of his theory, which he called **paidocentric** (from Greek

pais, paidas meaning "the upbringing of the child"), was that various stages in the history of organic evolution are repeated in the gestatory period of the human embryo. He expanded this theory further to the social stages in history, claiming that each stage of man's progress from savagery to civilization is mirrored in the child's development.

Although the research he conducted is considered today to be handicapped by serious inaccuracies, his work forced educators to examine the stages of children's physical, intellectual, and behavioral development. In addition, Hall was the first to describe the characteristics of adolescence with any scientific accuracy. He noted the rapid physiological and psychological growth during this period, especially sexual differentiation and maturation. Hall's research led to examination of how children develop and eventually to curriculum and teaching strategies designed for the developmental stages of the child. Hall's major contribution to modern curriculum development can be seen in the child-centered or activity curriculum (see pp. 287–289).

William James

William James (1842–1910), a pragmatist from the United States, was also influenced by the theories of Charles Darwin, particularly the theory of evolution. James believed that the human mind was a latecomer in the evolutionary stages of development. He contended that the mind biologically adjusts to the environment; the learner is not a passive receptacle but rather one who reacts to what is received in an instinctive order, the first based on repetitive physical movements. The student is then ready to acquire the ability for rationally conceptualizing material. James's major contribution to curriculum is the idea that teaching requires a specific sequence of skills. Consequently, the teacher must know the student well enough to be aware of his or her previously learned skills. His major contribution to teaching can be seen in the child-centered or activity curriculum.

Edward L. Thorndike

Edward Lee Thorndike (1874–1949), through studies of animals, theorized that learning is connecting the correct stimulus to the correct response, and that the correct response is to a large degree accidental, a matter of trial and error. His theory has come to be known as *stimulus-response (S-R)* and *conditioning*. Another contribution of Thorndike was in the area of measurement. Because progress in learning is a series of decreases in errors and increases in successes, Thorndike was able to plot, mathematically, a *learning curve*. At the turn of the century, he offered the first university course in the application of statistics to education. For the first time educators examined how teaching and learning could be measured through the use of concepts such as averages, means, probable errors, and correlations. Thorndike's major contribution to modern curriculum development can be seen in the competency-based curriculum (see pp. 279–281).

William H. Kilpatrick

William H. Kilpatrick (1871–1965) believed that education required a social emphasis that included all the formative influences and agencies that help induct the person into the life and culture of the group. Instructing students to work with groups "becomes even the more necessary because for some two decades now the dominant stress in study and research has been laid upon the scientific and impersonal aspects of education, with a resulting accumulation of techniques and procedures that largely ignore any social outlook and bearing" (Kilpatrick 1933, 257). Kilpatrick's major contribution to modern curriculum development can be seen in the project method. This curriculum included such things as the development of school newspapers, student gardens, and student construction of buildings.

During the twentieth century the definition of curriculum has fluctuated between the two positions of essentialism and progressivism, as illustrated by Henry in the opening chapter anecdote. Many educators contend that today's definition of curriculum is as close to the essentialist view as it has been any time since before the 1920s, when progressive education was developed. This contention can be illustrated by such 1980s reform reports as *The Nation At Risk* (1983) and *American Education: Making It Work* (1988a). In the latter William J. Bennett, secretary of education in the Reagan cabinet, talks about curriculum in essentialist terms.

Twentieth-Century U.S. Definition

> Providing a strong curriculum is a requirement even of the earliest school grades; too often our schools delay the introduction of serious academic material for too long. Children should leave elementary school able to read and write, and possessing a solid foundation in history, geography, civics, mathematics, science, and the arts. . . .
>
> We want our students—whatever their plans for the future—to take from high school a shared body of knowledge and skills, a common language of ideas, and a common moral and intellectual discipline. We want them to know math and science, history and literature. We want them to know how to think for themselves, to respond to important questions, to solve problems, to pursue an argument, to defend a point of view, to understand its opposite, and to weigh alternatives. We want them to develop, through example and experience, those habits of mind and traits of character properly prized by our society. And we want them to be prepared for entry into the community of responsible adults. (1988a, 24)

The *competency-based education* (CBE) movement, popular in the late 1970s and early 1980s, also illustrates the essentialist approach to curricular organization. CBE assumes that there is a series of increasingly complex skills, or competencies, which students must meet as they progress through the content of each discipline. Curriculum developers decide on these competencies. Although CBE is based on the learning theory of behaviorism (see chapter 7, pp. 224–226), many educators argue that CBE emphasizes only what is to be learned, ignoring the needs of the students and the skills of teachers in the process. It approaches the essentialist view of curriculum and the "course to be run" definition.

On the other hand, many educators contend that *open education*, an approach to curricular organization made popular by Carl Rogers and others during the 1960s and early 1970s, pushed the definition of curriculum beyond progressivism. Rogers, who changed the term *teacher* to *facilitator*, believed students should be asked, What do you want to learn? not told what they should learn (1983, 35). Hence, the term *curriculum* became obsolete because, as many critics of open education maintain, Rogers's approach removed not only the content but the professional from the teaching and learning process.

9.1 POINTS TO REMEMBER

- The essentialist definition of curriculum derives from the Latin word *currere*, meaning "the course to be run." Hence, this definition represents a subject-centered approach to curriculum.

- The progressivist definition of curriculum contends that it includes all the experiences of the child that come under the aegis of the school.
- Curriculum in U.S. schools in the twentieth century has moved between the two positions of essentialism and progressivism. Today's

definition of curriculum comes closer to the essentialist definition.
- Schools of philosophy are the basis for theories of education and curricular organizations.

THE ORGANIZATION OF CURRICULUM

Since philosophy organizes and systematizes all fields of knowledge as a means of interpreting this knowledge, curricular organization itself is a philosophical process. Throughout this chapter we will identify a variety of different curricular organizations and show how they are based on a particular school of philosophy, which was discussed in chapter 7 (see table 9.1).

Subject-Centered Curriculum Organization

The type of curricular organization of which Henry, in the opening anecdote, was a part in the 1960s and again in the 1980s is the *separate subject*, or *subject-centered*, curriculum. This organizational approach has its roots in the philosophical schools of idealism and realism and the educational theories of perennialism and essentialism.

Separate subject, or subject-centered, is the most widely used form of curricular organization. Its roots are in ancient Greece and Rome, where learning was divided into the seven liberal arts: the *trivium* (grammar, rhetoric, and logic) and the *quadrivium* (arithmetic, geometry, astronomy, and music). Although the subjects have changed somewhat, the concept of separation of the subjects has remained. In colonial America the typical division of subjects was reading, writing, religion, and arithmetic at the primary level; classics, language, trigonometry, geometry, and botany at the secondary level. In the subject-centered form of curricular organization, the material is compartmentalized into bodies of knowledge taught in isolation from other material based on the belief that each subject has a separate series of essential skills and concepts that must be learned.

The curriculum within each subject is sequentially organized from the simple to the complex and based on previous learning. Typically, this curricular organization divides subjects into two groups: required courses and electives. The assumption is that certain subjects are so important that all students must study them to acquire a common body of knowledge and a common set of skills, hence the terms *essential* and *perennial*, which are the foundation of the essentialist and perennialist theories of learning.

Typically, core or required courses include reading, language, composition, literature, arithmetic or mathematics, computer science (beginning in the

TABLE 9-1

Curricular Organizations Influenced by Schools of Philosophy and Theories of Education

Curricular organization	School of philosophy	Theory of education
Subject Centered/ Separate Subjects	Idealism/Realism	Perennialism/Essentialism
Competency Based	Realism/Analysis	Essentialism/Behaviorism
Mastery Learning	Realism/Analysis	Essentialism/Behaviorism
Broad Fields	Pragmatism	Progressivism/ Reconstructionism
Core	Pragmatism	Progressivism/ Reconstructionism
Activity/ Child-Centered	Pragmatism	Progressivism
Humanistic	Existentialism	Progressivism

The organization of curriculum is influenced both by a school of philosophy and a theory of education. The educational theory and the philosophy from which it is derived are discussed in chapter 7.

1980s), science (at the secondary level divided into separate sciences), social studies (usually divided into separate disciplines such as history, economics, civics or government, geography, and less frequently sociology and psychology), foreign language (historically in the secondary school but during the late 1950s, early 1960s, and late 1980s in the elementary school as well), and health and physical education.

Other subjects are less important. Therefore, they can be elected by students who are interested in them. Electives include the arts (divided into separate disciplines), home economics, and industrial arts and other vocational courses at the secondary level.

Attributes of the Subject-Centered Curriculum

Subject-centered organization has many attributes. It is a logical, effective way to organize new knowledge and allows logical progression from one level of education to the next. With this rather simplified organization of material, all students should meet basic, minimal levels of achievement and possess a common knowledge. With this type of organization, teachers can be trained in various subject areas.

Problems of the Subject-Centered Curriculum

Of course, many questions arise when educators attempt to determine which are the core courses and what is essential within these courses. New

(continued on p. 277)

VIEWPOINTS

The Poor Scholar's Soliloquy

No I'm not very good in school. This is my second year in the seventh grade and I'm bigger and taller than the other kids. They like me all right, though, even if I don't say much in the school-room, because outside I can tell them how to do a lot of things. They tag me around and that sort of makes up for what goes on in school.

I don't know why the teachers don't like me. They never have very much. Seems like they don't think you know anything unless they can name the book it comes out of. I've got a lot of books in my own room at home—books like *Popular Science Mechanical Encyclopedia,* and the Sears' and Ward's catalogues, but I don't very often just sit down and read them through like they make us in school. I use my books when I want to find something out, like whenever Mom buys anything secondhand I look it up in Sears' or Ward's first and tell her if she's getting stung or not. I can use the index in a hurry to find the things I want.

In school, though, we've got to learn whatever is in the book and I just can't memorize the stuff. Last year I stayed after school every night for two weeks trying to learn the names of the Presidents. Of course I knew some of them like Washington and Jefferson and Lincoln, but there must have been thirty altogether and I never did get them straight.

I'm not too sorry though because the kids who learned the Presidents had to turn right around and learn all the Vice Presidents. I am taking the seventh grade over but our teacher this year isn't so interested in the names of the Presidents. She has us trying to learn the names of all the great American inventors. . . .

I guess I can't remember names in history. Anyway, this year I've been try-ing to learn about trucks because my uncle owns three and he says I can drive one when I'm sixteen. I already know the horsepower and number of forward and backwards speeds of twenty-six American trucks, some of them Diesels, and I can spot each make a long way off. It's funny how that Diesel works. I start-ed to tell my teacher about it last Wednesday in science class when the pump we were using to make a vacuum in a bell jar got hot, but she said she didn't see what a Diesel engine had to do with our experiment on air pressure so I just kept still. The kids seemed interested though. I took four of them around to my uncle's garage after school and we saw the mechanic, Gus, tearing a big Diesel down. Boy, does he know his stuff!

I'm not very good in geography ei-ther. They call it economic geography this year. We've been studying the im-ports and exports of Chile all week but I couldn't tell you what they are. Maybe the reason is I had to miss school yester-day because my uncle took me and his big trailer down state about two hun-dred miles and we brought almost ten tons of stock to the Chicago market.

He had told me where we were going and I had to figure out the highways to take and also the mileage. He didn't do anything but drive and turn where I told him to. Was that fun! I sat with a map in my lap and told him to turn south or southeast or some other direc-tion. We made seven stops and drove over five hundred miles round trip. I'm figuring now what his oil cost and also the wear and tear on the truck—he calls it depreciation—so we'll know how much we made.

I even write out all the bills and send letters to farmers about what their pigs and beef cattle brought at the stock-yards. I only made three mistakes in 17 letters last time, my aunt said—all commas. She's been through high school and reads them over. I wish I could write school themes that way. The last one I had to write was on "What a Daffodil Thinks of Spring," and I just couldn't get going.

I don't do very well in school in arithmetic either. Seems I just can't keep my mind on the problems. We had one the other day like this:

If a 57 foot telephone pole falls across a cement highway so that 17³/₆ feet extend from one side and 14⁹/₁₇ feet from the other, how wide is the highway?

That seemed to me like an awfully silly way to get the width of a highway. I didn't even try to answer it because it didn't say whether the pole had fallen straight across or not. . . .

Even in shop I don't get very good grades. All of us kids made a broom holder and a bookend this term and mine were sloppy. I just couldn't get

interested. Mom doesn't use a broom anymore with her new vacuum cleaner and all our books are in a bookcase with glass doors in the parlor. Anyway, I wanted to make an end gate for my uncle's trailer but the shop teacher said that meant using metal and wood both and I'd have to learn how to work with wood first. I didn't see why but I kept still and made a tie rack at school and the tail gate after school at my uncle's garage. He said I saved him $10. . . .

Dad says I can quit school when I'm fifteen and I'm sort of anxious to because there are a lot to things I want to learn how to do and, as my uncle says, I'm not getting any younger.

From: Corey, 1944

---

knowledge has increased the problem of what to include within the core. William J. Bennett states:

> Elementary education is basic education, and no academic subject is more basic than English. All American children must learn to read, write, and speak our common language well. And helping them to do it is our school's paramount responsibility. (1988b, 13)
>
> Educational expectations must be high, attainable, and worthwhile. . . . The National Commission's central recommendation was that course requirements in basic academic subjects be strengthened. No American student, the Commission concluded, should graduate from high school without first completing at least four years of English and three years each of social studies, mathematics, and science. (*James Madison High School: A Curriculum for American Students*, 1987, 2)

Competency-based education is a fairly recent curricular pattern, common during the 1970s and 1980s. Its philosophical foundations are in the schools of realism and philosophical analysis and the educational theories of essentialism and behaviorism. It differs from subject-centered curriculum in that CBE's approach is to help students develop competencies, bits of knowledge related to a particular subject. It is similar to subject-centered curriculum in that subjects tend to be isolated from one another, and students move from the simple to the complex within the material. The underlying assumption of CBE is that there are certain identifiable, measurable skills and concepts within each subject that students must learn in order to master the discipline.

Development of a CBE curriculum begins with the identification of competencies, usually by professional educators. A **competency** is an element of knowledge that is essential if the student is to master the content of the discipline. For example, word recognition is a competency required if the

Competency-Based Education

student is to learn to read. Once the competencies have been identified, teaching methodologies are devised to help students achieve them. Finally, students are tested using *criterion-referenced tests* to determine if the competencies have been reached. Tests typically are given several times during elementary and junior high school and at the end of high school. Most often, these criterion-referenced, standardized tests are divided into specific subject areas, such as reading, language, spelling, vocabulary, arithmetic, science, and social studies.

Competency-based education has as its foundation the behavioral philosophy of B. F. Skinner. It assumes that competencies can be expressed in terms of student behavior and, thereby, can be observed and measured. Using this form of curricular organization, schools and teachers, as well as students themselves, can be held accountable for the students' reaching predetermined levels of competence. Herein lies the major difference in the CBE approach and the subject-centered approach. CBE emphasizes student outcomes, whereas the subject-centered approach emphasizes teacher input.

Attributes of the Competency-Based Curriculum

Hildreth H. McAshan in *Competency-based Education and Behavioral Objectives* (1979) has outlined some of the attributes of competency-based curriculum.

> CBE, in its purest form, has been designed to overcome perennial problems that have plagued experience-based programs prior to the behavioral objective era. [A *behavioral objective* is a goal that can be measured by behavioral change in the students.] These problems were based upon the following needs:
>
> 1. To avoid duplication of content within a program
> 2. To establish and maintain consistency of competencies taught with courses, regardless of the instructor teaching the course
> 3. To revise and implement appropriate systems of evaluation and reporting of student achievement
> 4. To better communicate to the students the learning tasks that they are expected to achieve and how their success will be determined
> 5. To better provide students with ongoing information regarding their personal progress
> 6. To be better accountable to the general public for the educational program standards accepted by educational institutions
> 7. To better determine student achievement through more systematic procedures of evaluation. (pp. 31–35)

Proponents of CBE contend that it is a real-life orientation to curriculum development as expressed in life roles (Parnell 1978). Frequently, students are asked to read newspapers, balance checkbooks, make out budgets, design menus, and seek employment as a way to perform identified competencies. By breaking down the curriculum into small instructional modules, according to proponents of CBE, educators and students can address skills and concepts with increasing complexity.

Problems of Competency-Based Curriculum

In an anecdote in *Good Work* (1980), E. F. Schumacher illustrates some of the problems of competency-based curriculums.

It was during the War and I was a farm laborer and my task was before breakfast to go to yonder hill and to a field there and count the cattle—there were always thirty-two—and then I went back to the bailiff, touched my cap, and said, "Thirty-two, sir," and went and had my breakfast. One day when I arrived at the field an old farmer was standing at the gate, and he said, "Young man, what do you do here every morning?" I said, "Nothing much. I just count the cattle." He shook his head and said, "If you count them every day they won't flourish." . . . One day I went back, I counted and counted again, there were only thirty-one. Well, I didn't want to spend all day there so I went back and reported the thirty-one. The bailiff was very angry. He said, "Have your breakfast and then we'll go up there together." And we went together and we searched the place and indeed, under a bush, was a dead beast. I thought to myself, Why have I been counting them all the time? I haven't prevented this beast's dying. Perhaps that's what the farmer meant. They won't flourish if you don't look and watch the quality of each individual beast. Look him in the eye. Study the sheen on his coat. Then I might have gone back and said, "I don't know how many I saw but one looked mimsey." Then they would have saved the life of this beast. (pp. 144–145)

Critics of CBE contend that it is not possible to break all disciplines into small instructional modules; students can miss seeing the forest if all they are required to do is look at the trees. Or, as in Schumacher's anecdote, the cow died while the laborer was competently counting them. According to critics of CBE, many things, such as appreciation of art or creativity in writing, cannot be measured or stated in a behavioral manner. Frequently, only easy-to-teach, easy-to-test bits of knowledge are tested, and a student's understanding of a larger whole is ignored. For example, a standardized test can measure if a student has memorized the presidents of the United States, but it can't determine if the student understands the democratic process.

Likewise, critics maintain that making schools and teachers accountable for student learning is a dangerous practice. They point to the differences among students from class to class and district to district. They contend that basic competencies are not the same for all children. That, for example, in an urban district an important competency may be street sense; whereas in a rural district a basic competency might be water conservation. These critics also worry about the tendency to teach for the test so that students score well and so that, thereby, teachers and schools appear to be doing their jobs successfully. And, finally, critics of CBE ask such questions as, What is a minimum competency, anyway, and, how can we avoid making the minimums become maximums if the tests test minimums?

An outgrowth of CBE is *mastery learning*. Like CBE, it is based on the philosophical schools of realism and philosophical analysis and the educational theories of essentialism and behaviorism. Its major proponent is Benjamin Bloom.

Mastery Learning

Like CBE, the mastery approach to curriculum development is based on the belief that objectives can be predetermined. However, it contends that each student will move toward mastery of specific skills and concepts in different ways and according to different timetables.

Mastery learning differs from CBE in that it places more emphasis on instruction than on objectives and assessment. In fact, it assumes that what is

Mastery learning is a concept that assumes all students can learn any subject matter or any skill if given enough time and individual instruction. One way of implementing mastery learning successfully is to provide one-on-one instruction in the form of tutors or teacher aides where appropriate or necessary.

an objective for one student may not be an objective for other students. Consequently, mastery learning requires that students be treated individually and that teachers avoid preoccupation with the group. Like CBE and subject-centered curriculum, mastery learning groups skills and concepts by subject. However, it also assumes that the vast majority of students "can learn selected subjects up to as high a level as the most able students in the group" (Bloom 1976, 223).

Attributes of Mastery Learning

The most important attribute of mastery learning is the belief that the vast majority of students can succeed on any given task if given enough time and appropriate instruction. Benjamin Bloom believes it is essential that schools in the United States require mastery learning.

John Miller in *The Educational Spectrum* (1983) delineates the major characteristics of mastery learning.

1. Mastery of any subject is defined in terms of sets of major objectives which represent the purposes of the course or unit.
2. The substance of the subject matter is then divided into a larger set of relatively small learning units, each one accompanied by its own objectives, which are part of the larger ones or thought essential to their mastery.

3. Learning materials are then identified and the instructional strategy selected.

4. Each unit is accompanied by brief diagnostic tests to measure the student's developing progress (the formative evaluation) and identify the particular problems each student is having.

5. The data obtained from administering the tests are used to provide supplementary instruction to the student to help him overcome his problem. (p. 26)

According to studies conducted by Bloom, more than 90 percent of all students could learn a skill or concept if given instruction that takes into account individual differences and gives the student enough time to learn. Bloom claimed that the common use of the bell curve to illustrate the distribution of student performance assumed that only a small percentage could master a skill or concept at a high level, and that this was erroneous. The **bell curve** is a bell-shaped symmetrical distribution in which most scores or human attributes

FIGURE 9-1

Achievement Distribution for Students Under Conventional, Mastery Learning, and Tutorial Instruction

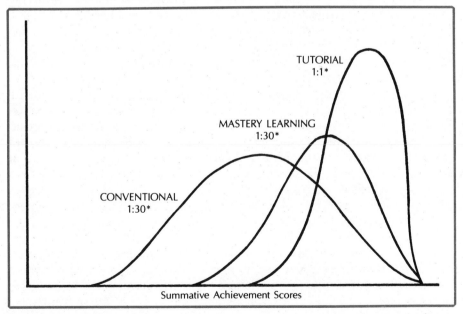

*Teacher:Student Ratio

From: B. Bloom, "The Search for Methods of Group Instruction as Effective as One-to-One Tutoring," *Educational Leadership* (May 1984), 5.

Bloom's research indicates that a large percentage of students can reach mastery of a skill and concept when appropriate instructional methods are employed and can achieve at even higher levels when the ratio of student to teacher is one-to-one, as it would be in a tutorial situation.

(for example, height and weight) fall near the mean (arithmetic average), with only a small percentage of scores or attributes extending well above or below the mean. A bell-curve distribution does not account for individual differences in learning style and time needed to master a skill or concept. Mastery learning individualizes large group instruction so that appropriate instructional methods are selected for individuals or small groups of students. See figure 9.1 for achievement distribution of students under conventional (bell curve), mastery learning, and tutorial (one-on-one) instruction. Bloom and his associates have spent nearly three decades studying teaching methodologies that are most likely to produce mastery. As late as the early 1990s, the results of Bloom's research have had little impact on the schools. Although some elementary schools have utilized limited aspects of the mastery learning approach, most still use large group conventional instruction as the primary mode and assume that student performance will distribute along a normal bell curve.

Problems of Mastery Learning

Critics of the mastery approach maintain that although its goals are laudable and that probably every child can achieve mastery in a given subject, its procedures are cumbersome and likely to be inconsistent. For example, how is it possible to give students unlimited time to master a skill when there is not unlimited time in the school day or school year? They also express concern about the articulation among classes, levels, and schools. For example, a typical student may change schools a minimum of three times during his or her educational career. How is the middle school to know what has been mastered by each child at each level? If individual teachers are setting the goals, won't goals change with each teacher? Isn't this likely to produce confusion? What about record keeping; how is it possible to communicate each student's progress to another school or another teacher?

Robert E. Slavin, in *Mastery Learning Reconsidered* (1987), found no evidence to support the claim that mastery learning improved student performance. Students did not achieve at higher levels on standardized tests after participating in group-based mastery learning programs, and improvement on experimenter-made tests was moderate and not maintained over a long period of time. Slavin pointed to the problem of allowing students to take as much time as needed to master an objective. "If some students take much longer than others to learn a particular objective, then one of two things must happen. Either corrective instruction must be given outside of regular class time, or students who achieve mastery early on will have to waste considerable amounts of time waiting for their classmates to catch up" (p. 6). In addition, spending significant time mastering an objective means that students must select content mastery over content coverage. Slavin also found that the amount of time spent on remediation was not sufficient for students needing it. These conditions, Slavin suggested, might negatively influence scores on standardized tests.

Broad Fields Curriculum   The *broad fields* approach to curricular organization combines several related subjects into larger fields of study. It is based on the philosophical school of pragmatism and employs the educational theories of progressivism and social reconstructionism. For example, language arts might include reading, literature, composition, grammar, spelling, penmanship, vocabulary, speaking, and

(continued on p. 284)

Point/Counterpoint

MASTERY LEARNING REDUCES VARIABILITY IN LEARNING

A modern approach to the notion that most students can learn what the schools have to teach has been developed under the rubric of mastery learning. There are many versions of mastery learning in existence at present. All begin with the notion that most students can attain a high level of learning capability if instruction is approached sensitively and systematically, if students are helped when and where they have learning difficulties, if they are given sufficient time to achieve mastery, and if there is some clear criterion of what constitutes mastery. . . .

If students are normally distributed with respect to aptitude, but the kind and quality of instruction and learning time allowed are made appropriate to the characteristics and needs of *each* learner, the majority of students will achieve mastery of the subject. And, the correlation between aptitude measured at the beginning of instruction and achievement measured at the end of the instruction should approach zero. . . .

There is little question that mastery learning strategies have been effective in many classroom situations at all levels of learning from the elementary school level through the graduate and professional school levels. . . .

The main conclusion to be drawn . . . is that rate of learning or amount of time needed to learn to some criterion of achievement is an *alterable characteristic*. That is, when students are provided with the time and help they need to learn and when this produces positive entry characteristics (cognitive and affective) [the prerequisite learning held to be necessary as a basis for learning new tasks], students not only become better able to learn, they also become able to learn with less and less time. Finally, the evidence . . . suggests that the differentiation between good and poor learners, or fast and slow learners, tends to be reduced to a point where it is difficult to measure in hours or minutes. In other words, the terms fast learner and slow learner, under the favorable learning conditions indicated in these studies, have little to recommend them as practicable distinctions. Who is fast and who is slow changes from learning task to learning task, and the final differences between fast and slow are exceedingly small and can only be measured if the units of time measurement are exceedingly fine. (pp. 3–6, 191)

From: Bloom, 1976

MASTERY LEARNING RESULTS IN VARIABILITY IN LEARNING RATES

[Benjamin] Bloom makes a potentially radical claim. Everyone, he asserts, can learn everything the schools have to teach. Furthermore, individual differences in learning can be reduced to zero. . . .

While Bloom may be overly enthusiastic in his inference, the evidence does support his first claim that mastery learning procedures can make it possible for most students to learn what is in the curriculum. But with his second claim, that variability in learning rates can and should reach negligible levels under mastery instruction, I disagree. Mastery learning strategies shift school organizations from allowing equal amounts of time for all students for any particular topic to allowing as much time as each individual needs to master that topic. Unless variability in time actually does reduce to zero, the very possibilities of mastery learning raise important questions for educational goals and priorities which must be considered. The students who learn fastest have a cumulating amount of "extra" time as the

course proceeds. Educators must consider what these faster learners will do. . . .

. . . The individualized instruction tradition [a basic assumption of mastery learning], which relies heavily on self-instruction, has developed instructional programs that are designed both to assure mastery of prerequisites for successive units of instruction and to allow individual students to proceed at their own "optimal" rates. . . .

As a result, students spread out through the curriculum increasingly over time, with faster students moving further and further ahead as the slower ones carefully master the earlier units. If students are allowed to proceed onward in the curriculum rather than waiting for slower classmates to catch up, variability increases instead of decreases.

The implication of this is that mastery learning results in decreased variability in learning outcomes only when the material to be learned is defined in a limited way. Does Bloom's claim that mastery-learning procedures can make it possible for virtually everyone to learn everything that the schools have to teach depend upon our accepting a minimum definition of "what the schools have to teach"? If he means that virtually everyone can be effectively taught a limited set of basic skills and knowledge, his hypothesis seems reasonable. . . .

Yet there are many . . . who are not content to see the school's role limited to these "fundamentals." (pp. 445, 451–452)

From: Resnick, 1977

POSTSCRIPT

The argument about whether mastery learning will reach its primary goal of all students successfully learning and mastering content is typical of many arguments about the organization of curriculum. How can we best meet the common goal of student learning? What should be included within the curriculum? Should the content taught in the curriculum be central to its organization? Or should the students' activities be central to its organization? How much should be taught in how much time to whom? Should the curriculum be the same for all students? Should some students be taught differently than other students? Who decides? All these questions are central to the development of curriculum, yet neither Resnick nor Bloom gives completely satisfying answers.

listening. Similarly, geography, history, civics, economics, sociology, and psychology are taught within the general subject matter of social studies. At times the number of disciplines included within a broad field can be even greater. Broad field curriculum is multidisciplinary (many) rather than interdisciplinary (interrelated and integrated).

In this approach, which is used more frequently in elementary and middle schools than in high schools, students may spend two hours per day dealing with the language arts. During that time they may read or have read to them a story. Then they might write about it or produce an informal skit related to it. During their study of the story they might examine vocabulary words, develop spelling lists, and participate in other activities related to the story.

Attributes of Broad Fields Curriculum

Proponents of the broad fields approach claim that it is more natural than separating the various components of the discipline. They claim, for example, that writers do not simply write a book. They research the material, talk to others about what they plan to write, write letters to publishers, check words in dictionaries, and participate in numerous other activities which eventually, through a long process, may result in a book. Therefore, the natural approach of the writer and most other professionals is dealing with broad fields of learning rather than single subjects in isolation.

Problems of Broad Fields Curriculum

Opponents of the broad fields approach contend that it can be chaotic. Students do not know what they are supposed to learn from the activities. Frequently the products of their efforts lose significance. Students do not know whether a paper or an art project is well done or poorly done. For example, in the writing process approach mentioned above, students may spend so much time researching, talking to others, developing topics, and illustrating their writing that they might lose sight of the importance of a grammatically correct final paper.

Critics also claim that the approach is too general. There is not a careful study of any aspect of the discipline and, consequently, the student's learning is hit or miss. Depending on the teacher, students may or may not be taught specific skills and concepts. Those using this approach do not believe that there are some things so important that everyone must learn them.

Core Curriculum

An even broader approach to curriculum than the broad fields is the *core curriculum*. A core or **integrated** approach, unifies a number of subjects or fields of study into one topic. In the 1970s, for example, Henry, of the opening anecdote, participated in a curricular organizational pattern known as the core curriculum. Henry's program taught minicourses in English and the humanities related to specific themes.

Core, as it relates to curriculum, is used in two ways. It can be used to describe a required set of subjects, or core courses, to be taken in common by all students. This approach is single subject centered, not integrated. When core is used in this way it is based on the philosophical school of realism and the

The core curriculum organizes a number of subjects into an integrated study of a theme or problem. These high school students on the HWS *Explorer,* a research vessel owned by Hobart and William Smith Colleges, are studying the effects of pollutants on the Finger Lakes in upstate New York. Here they use an anemometer to gauge wind velocity as part of an experiment.

educational theory of essentialism. However, this is not how the term *core* is being employed here.

The core curriculum, as it is used here, is the integration of a variety of disciplines around a single core, often a theme or a problem. The core curriculum is based on the philosophical school of pragmatism and the educational theories of progressivism or social reconstructionism. This approach to curriculum is student centered because it focuses on a topic of interest to the learner. For example, if the topic being studied is pollution, the students might study ecology, biology, statistics, mathematics, political science, history, psychology, reading, writing, and literature. In other words, all subjects are studied simultaneously to better understand the theme or solve the problem. The possibilities are limited only by the imagination of the teacher or teachers involved in the planning process. Cores usually involve broad, preplanned problem areas. However, it is also possible to develop a core curriculum around a theme, such as "People Against People," wherein students might read fiction (perhaps a work such as John Hersey's *The Wall* and nonfiction (perhaps a work such as Milton Meltzer's *Never to Forget: The Jews of the Holocaust*); they might pursue research projects on various aspects of the theme; they might study the history of political movements that pitted people against each other; they might examine the psychology that allowed a Hitler to gain power. The key to the success of the core curriculum, say its proponents, is that it must relate to the interests of the students.

Attributes of the Core Curriculum

Although the core approach to curricular organization has many influential proponents, it has not been widely employed by the schools. As early as the mid-nineteenth century, German philosopher and psychologist Johann Friedrich Herbart, basing much of his work on that of Johann Heinrich Pestalozzi, "favored the unification and correlation of all school subjects around a central core" (Reinhardt 1960, 253). Herbart's approach was practiced in the United States in the 1890s at the laboratory school of what is now Illinois State University by brothers Charles and Frank McMurry. They used the culture epoch as the unifying core for teaching history, geography, science, arithmetic, and language.

> [They] would teach an epoch only one time and then it would be done thoroughly. For example, in the fifth grade . . . the story of Captain John Smith would be read in history. At the same time, in geography the class would investigate the Chesapeake area, its climate, soil and products, such as clams, oysters, fruit, and tobacco. In science the tobacco plant, oysters, and other products would be studied. In arithmetic there would be statistics on amount of tobacco produced, exported, and consumed. The findings in these various areas would be carefully recorded and thus serve the purposes of language composition in narration, description, and exposition. To McMurry and his fellow Herbartians, history was very important in the elementary curriculum. (Reinhardt, 1960, 253)

The idea of a core curriculum was also very important to John Dewey at the University of Chicago in the early twentieth century. The core that Dewey suggested related to the problems of democratic life. "A curriculum which acknowledges the social responsibilities of education must present situations where problems are relevant to the problems of living together, and where observation and information are calculated to develop social insight and interest" (1928, 226).

In the 1980s John Goodlad advocated the idea of a core curriculum. In a study done in 1984 of 38 schools, 1,000 classrooms, and 1,350 teachers, he concluded that the "major shortcomings of the schools' subject offerings is the common failure of the learning activities to connect the student with the 'structure and ways of thinking' " (1984, 291). According to Goodlad, in many schools, topics such as magnets and batteries are unrelated to the concept of energy. He suggests that all students study a common set of concepts, principles, skills, and ways of knowing, rather than a common group of subjects (1984, p. 284).

Problems of the Core Curriculum

The core approach has many critics. Many find the integrated core approach too broad and not likely to produce specific knowledge, complaints similar to those raised against the broad fields or multidisciplinary approach. Many are concerned that students will know "how to," but they will not know "what." Critics claim that the core curriculum does not provide a systematic approach to gaining knowledge, that the outcomes of such an approach cannot be measured, and that it requires teachers who are specifically trained in integrating subjects.

According to opponents of multidisciplinary approaches such as the broad fields approach, and integrated approaches such as the core curriculum, these approaches fail to delineate what is essential for all students to learn. These critics advocate subject-centered curricular organizations in the belief that they ensure that all students have a common core or base of knowledge.

Child-Centered or Activity Curriculum

The *activity,* or *child-centered,* curriculum is rooted in the philosophical school of pragmatism. Progressivism, the theory of education rooted in pragmatism, was based on the work of John Dewey. The child-centered or activity curriculum differs from the broad fields and core curriculums in that the experience of the student is central to its development. As proponent Hilda Taba states, "People learn only what they experience" (1962, 401).

By the early twentieth century Dewey was working to counteract what he saw as passivity in the subject-centered curriculum. The approach he developed at the University of Chicago Laboratory School saw children as active problem solvers, envisioned the interrelationship of subjects, believed that children gained skills as they needed them, and contended that they learn best what they experience. As early as 1902 Dewey wrote about the need to "abandon the notion of subject matter as something fixed and ready-made in itself, outside the child's experience; cease thinking of the child's experience as also something hard and fast; see it as something fluent, embryonic, vital; and . . . realize that the child and the curriculum are simply two limits which define a single process" (1902, 16).

Dewey pointed out that because the child is a beginner, he or she is not able to approach learning with the completed experiences of adulthood. Thus, the teacher must organize the curriculum to capitalize on the child's experiences.

It is essential that teachers assess what the needs and interests of the students are rather than trying to determine what they should be. This requires that the teacher have a thorough knowledge of the theories of childhood and adolescent growth and development. The curriculum should not be preplanned by the teacher, but rather cooperatively planned by both students and teacher. Since problem solving is its central focus, subjects are viewed as resources instead of as bodies of knowledge that are ends in themselves. Thus, the structure of the child-centered or activity curriculum is determined by the needs and interests of the students.

Attributes of the Child-Centered or Activity Curriculum

Proponents of the child-centered or activity curriculum are many. In fact, this curriculum has been reinstated in many forms since Dewey's earliest writings. The impact of his work, particularly on the elementary curriculum, cannot be overemphasized. Dewey's philosophy and child-centered approach are frequently considered to be at the opposite end of the spectrum from the subject-centered approaches to curriculum. His influence changed the direction of elementary education, which even today, through several generations of subject-centered reform, remains largely child centered; elementary teachers usually base instructional strategies on the developmental stage of the students (see chapter 7, pp. 209–211).

Problems of the Child-Centered or Activity Curriculum

According to many opponents of the child-centered or activity curriculum, the complexity of Dewey's theories makes them impractical in most school settings. The teacher must be an expert not in a single subject but in all subjects and able to subdivide them into their component parts. She or he must be able to deal with all subjects or themes in a problem-solving approach. In addition, the teacher must be thoroughly grounded in developmental psychology, knowing what children can and should be able to do at any given time, and he or she must know the interests, needs, and abilities of each student. Finally, the teacher must continually restructure the curriculum based on the changing child. Consequently, most programs that have emulated Dewey's curricular approach have either turned his definition of experience into overt activity and focused on physical contact with objects (Taba 1962, 404), reverted to the logical organization of the subject-matter curriculum (Brubacher 1966, 293), or romanticized Dewey's philosophy as a "sentimental regard for the child's interests and needs" (Brubacher, 294).

IN THE CLASSROOM

Peggy Allan, who teaches in Greenville Junior High School, Greenville, Illinois, believes in the "rippling" effect of teaching and learning. She encourages each student to imagine that s/he is a rock, specially chosen by that student, tossed in the "great pond of life" (Allan 1989, 4). She demonstrates how the resulting ripples extend outward over the pond's surface. This, according to Peggy, helps the students realize how they can send out their own "ripples" that affect the world.

She reinforces the rippling technique by encouraging students to share things learned in school with their parents. When they do, they record it on a "ripple card," which is signed by the parent. According to Peggy, both parents and students enjoy this technique, and students attempt to "out-ripple" each other.

Rippling also applies to the teaching methods she employs. She related one prime example of how rippling worked in her classroom. Her students became concerned about the nuclear disaster at Chernobyl during a discussion in a current events class. The students wondered if the nuclear waste from Three Mile Island that was passing by rail through Greenville, or the Clinton Nuclear Power Plant, located ninety miles from Greenville, could cause a similar tragedy in their town.

As always, Peggy took the lead from her students. The class began small group investigations that extended their ripples statewide. Peggy first contacted officials from the Illinois Power Company to come talk to her class. They did, and because of the students' questions, the company mailed them volumes of material, which the students sorted.

The students gathered information from a variety of sources including newspapers, magazines, and the Greenville College library. They wrote the American Nuclear Society, the Nuclear Regulatory Commission, and other government agencies. When that didn't turn up all the information they needed, they made phone calls. When each group felt they knew enough, they gave an oral report to the class. Of course, the students' learning rippled through many subject areas: reading and language arts, social studies, science, and mathematics.

A survey the students conducted and rippling conversations with their parents showed that most of the public was opposed to nuclear power but didn't know why. So the students decided to conduct a nuclear power seminar. The seminar was attended not only by parents and others from the community, but also by representatives from the Illinois Power Company and the Clinton Nuclear Power Plant. The students did a presentation with representatives from the power company, displayed their projects, did skits, and answered questions. Power company officials were so impressed that they displayed the students' projects at local and regional offices around the state.

Humanistic Curriculum

The *humanistic curriculum* is based on the philosophical school of existentialism and the educational theory of progressivism. Like the activity curriculum, the humanistic curriculum is student centered. The teacher's primary task is to permit students to learn how to learn. Teachers in the humanistic curriculum are what psychologist Carl Rogers calls "facilitators." Although the general material of the course and some requirements may be defined by the facilitator, most of the curriculum emerges through interaction among the students, teacher, and content in a climate of trust "in which curiosity and the natural desire to learn can be nourished and enhanced" (Rogers 1983, 31, 33).

The humanistic curriculum is based on Gestalt psychology and therapy, whose principles are openness, uniqueness, awareness, and personal responsibility. Hence, curriculums that are consistent with this theory of psychology deemphasize competition and emphasize personal responsibility. In the humanistic curriculum there are no right or wrong answers; its goal is personal development and change. Because Gestalt psychology contends that discrete elements are meaningful only in relationship to the whole, humanistic curriculums attempt to integrate the student's behavior with course content.

Implementation of the curriculum requires an emotional relationship between the students and the teacher. The teacher must be warm and nurturing to facilitate each student's learning. Students are motivated through mutual trust. Humanistic teachers do not require students to do anything they do not want to do; they simply provide materials and opportunities for learning.

V I E W P O I N T S

The Real-Tiger School

In "The Real Tiger School," Professor J. Abner Peddiwell (pseudonym of Harold Benjamin) gives five lectures presumably during the Paleolithic period about education in that day—hence the references to fish-grabbing, one of the "basic" subjects of the era. This is an excerpt from one of the lectures.

Many of the education professors were intelligent and sensitive men. . . . [A]nd some of them actually began to think about the purpose of education, and a few even went to the length of observing the schools critically. They were struck at once by the artificial character of school learning, by its dissociation from educational objectives, and they set about remedying the situation in various ways.

One group of observers concluded that the chief mistakes in the current educational methods came simply from the circumstance of having too much direction of the learning. "Let the child grow naturally into his learning activities," they advised the teachers. "Let all his purposes and procedures be self-impelled. Without teacher interference or domination, let him always decide what he wants to do, plan what he purposed, carry out what he has planned, and judge the worth of what he has done."

The teachers were disturbed. "But where, then, do we come in?" they inquired. "If the children are going to do it all, they don't need any teachers."

"Oh, no!" assured the experts. "The teacher is a very necessary guide. He will lead the child in the direction of wise choices of right activities and show him how to engage more intelligently and effectively in those activities in which he would have engaged anyway."

"And suppose," said one teacher guardedly, "that the child wants to engage in cutting up fishnets. Shall I show him how to do it better than he could without my guidance?"

"You are being facetious," smiled the experts. "Get the real progressive spirit and such questions will not occur to you."

Whereupon the teachers withdrew and consulted among themselves. "It is very clear," suggested one, "that we are still supposed to teach fish-grabbing."

"Yes," agreed another, "but we must not tell the children they *have* to learn fish-grabbing. We must just arrange everything so they themselves will think of learning to grab fish and ask us if they can't do it."

"Ah, I see," said a third, "and then we give them permission and guide—guide—"

The teachers then went back to their classes and proceeded enthusiastically upon this new basis.

"Now, children, what would you like to learn today?" one of them began to a class of twelve-year-olds.

The children stared in astonishment. "We're supposed to learn fish-grabbing, aren't we?" they asked.

"Well—er—not unless you *want* to. What do you really *want* to do?"

"I want to leave school and go to work," announced one of the duller boys.

"Ah but you *have* to go to school," explained the teacher. "Our compulsory education laws, you know—"

"Who is going to decide whether we pass into the next grade in June?"

"Why—I am, of course," admitted the teacher.

The members of the class looked at one another a little dubiously, drew a deep collective breath, and then chanted in polite unison, "We want to learn fish-grabbing!"

From: Peddiwell, 1939, 58–61

Attributes of the Humanistic Curriculum

The humanistic curriculum, according to its advocates, helps all children succeed in school by not setting objectively defined criteria for achievement. Because the humanistic curriculum is interested in personal growth no matter how it is measured or defined, all children are considered successful. Evaluation of the activities in which students are engaged, process, is at least as important as evaluation of the student's achievement, product. Teachers examine activities in terms of whether they lead to student openness and independence. Success of the curriculum is based on subjective assessments by both teachers and students.

From the late 1960s through the middle 1970s, dozens of critics of subject-centered education supported the concepts of the humanistic curriculum. They include Herbert Kohl (*On Teaching* and *The Open Classroom*), James Herndon (*How to Survive in Your Native Land* and *The Way It Spozed To Be*), Neil Postman and Charles Weingartner (*Teaching as a Subversive Activity*), and John Holt (*How Children Learn, How Children Fail,* and *What Do I Do Monday?*). According to John Holt in *How Children Fail* (1963):

> Nobody starts off stupid. You have only to watch babies and infants, and think seriously about what all of them learn and do, to see that, except for the most grossly retarded, they show a style of life, and a desire and ability to learn that in an older person we might well call genius. . . . But what happens, as we get older, to this extraordinary capacity for learning and intellectual growth?
>
> What happens is that it is destroyed, and more than by any other one thing, by the process we misname education. (p. 167)

Problems of the Humanistic Curriculum

By the beginning of the 1980s few proponents of the humanistic curriculum remained, primarily because its implementation was impractical and disorganized. How could teachers develop a curriculum based on the needs of all the children in the classroom? How could teachers ensure that students learned what they needed to, if the students themselves determined the curriculum? Would students know what was best for them? On the preceding page is a satirical look at the humanistic curriculum from *The Saber-Tooth Curriculum,* a book that satirizes a variety of curricular organizations.

9.2 POINTS TO REMEMBER

- The separate subject, or subject-centered, curriculum contends that each subject should be taught separately and its components organized sequentially from the simple to the complex.
- The competency-based curriculum believes that each subject can be divided into essential elements of knowledge and students can be evaluated on what they learned.
- Mastery learning assumes that all students can master concepts if provided with appropriate instruction and an adequate amount of time.
- The broad fields, or multidisciplinary, curriculum combines several related subjects into larger fields of study such as language arts (reading, literature, writing, speaking, and listening) or social studies (history, sociology, political science, economics, and geography).
- The core curriculum, or integrated approach, arranges various subjects or fields into a related, unifying topic.
- The activity, or child-centered, curriculum contends that children learn best through experience.
- The humanistic curriculum believes that the role of the teacher is to permit students to satisfy their own curiosity.

SOCIAL FORCES THAT INFLUENCE CURRICULUM

Numerous social forces influence the development of curriculum in the schools. Among these are the economic and business needs of society, disenfranchised groups such as women and minorities, textbooks and tests, and technological developments. This section of the chapter will deal with these curricular influences.

Economy   Perhaps the primary influence on the curriculum of schools in the United States is the economy. During the colonial period, when the needs of society were agrarian, the schools prepared students for a life on the land and in the home. As industry grew in the mid-nineteenth and early twentieth centuries, the schools prepared students to work on the assembly lines.

By the middle of the twentieth century the U.S. work force was again changing. More workers were needed at middle levels of management. In addition, an increasing number of skilled laborers were required as assembly lines became computerized, using fewer and fewer unskilled workers. The schools again responded to this change, adding more courses in science, mathematics, and technology. More and more students attended institutions of higher education as the needs of the workplace could no longer be met in four years of high school.

Many argue that in this final decade of the twentieth century the needs of business and industry are again changing. Large numbers of workers are at upper and middle levels of management. They must be able to work cooperatively with others in order to make decisions and solve problems, many of which are increasingly technical in nature. How the curriculum will meet the demands of the contemporary workplace is not completely clear, but the ubiquitous computer in the schools is one way.

Schools respond not only to business and economic needs of the U.S. society but also to other social changes and demands such as the changing role of women and the influence of minorities.

Women   During World War II as U.S. men went off to war, women replaced them on the assembly lines and at the cash registers. As men returned from the war, they took their original places in the work force and women returned to maintaining home and family (Sleeter and Grant 1988, 153). In fact, as recently as the 1950s most middle class men considered themselves failures if their wives worked. However, many sociologists believe that although women were replaced in the workplace by returning soldiers, they never totally moved back into the home.

The women's movement of the late 1960s and 1970s is a result, at least in part, of women discovering their potential as workers. Women also found new rewards, including increased family income and autonomy, through the roles they played in business and industry. By 1987, 83 percent of all U.S. women worked outside the home (The U.S. Department of Commerce, Bureau of Census, *Statistical Abstract of the United States*, 1990). However, although women's salaries had increased, they did not equal those of their male counterparts. A large proportion of women managers, for example, are in professions that have been traditionally low paying, such as education and nursing, rather than in business, industry, and medicine, where the pay is generally higher. This seems to be confirmed by statistics. Of all registered nurses, 94.6 percent are women, whereas of all physicians, only 20 percent are women. In teaching, excluding the college and university level, 72.9 percent are women. According to the American Association of School Administrators' 1988 report, *Women and Minorities in School Administration*, only 30 percent of all school administrative positions, only 3.7 percent of superintendencies, and only 24 percent of principalships were occupied by women.

The schools have only partially responded to the needs of women workers. Today, more female students take academic courses to prepare them for college; fewer take courses such as home economics. However, high school secretarial courses are still primarily populated by women students. This, too, is supported by statistics. In 1990, the National Center for Education Statistics, *Digest of Education Statistics*, reported that female high school graduates completed slightly more **Carnegie Units** in 1987 in vocational education (3.67) than their male counterparts (3.64). (Carnegie Units represent the amount of course time spent in each subject; credit for high school graduation, in some school districts, is based on Carnegie Units.) However, most of the units earned in vocational education by female students were in traditionally female-dominated programs such as business or secretarial studies (1.01 Carnegie Units for females as compared to 0.34 for males) and occupational home economics (0.15 Carnegie Units for females as compared to 0.05 for males).

It is true that there has been a decrease in the number of Carnegie Units earned by women in vocational programs that are traditionally female dominated. This change appears to be a result of an overall decline in the number of Carnegie Units earned by all students in vocational education rather than a significant change in the ratio of men to women. Similarly, in academic fields, the number of Carnegie Units earned by female students in 1987 decreased from the number earned by females in 1982. But the same decrease is evidenced by male students. For example, in 1982, males earned an average of 3.09 Carnegie Units in mathematics whereas females earned 3.12 Carnegie Units. In 1987, males earned 3.03 Carnegie Units in mathematics and females earned 2.92. Therefore, although the curriculum has responded to the vocational, professional, and educational needs of both male and female students, it has done little to help women move into traditionally male vocations and professions.

Minorities

There have been only minimal changes in the schools to meet the needs of minorities. Although the schools of the 1980s were more culturally heterogeneous than ever before, the curriculum only minimally reflected these changes. Some schools added bilingual studies and some offered courses in black history; however, the role of minorities in U.S. society was scarcely included in existing courses such as history, science, and English. In addition, the curriculum of such subjects as English required an increased number of prescribed classic works, which tended to limit the number of works by minorities and women that were included.

Although more minority students attended college in the 1980s than in the middle years of the twentieth century, they still did not attend at the rate of their white counterparts. In 1982, 53.9 percent of college-age whites enrolled in college, whereas only 39.2 percent of blacks and 49.3 percent of Hispanics did. In 1987, enrollments of blacks had increased to 44.1 percent and whites to 57.7 percent. However, the percentage of Hispanics decreased to 45 percent (U.S. Department of Education, *The Condition of Education*, 1990). In spite of increases in enrollment, black and other minority students did not achieve at the level of their white counterparts. In 1988, for example, only 16.4 percent of blacks over the age of twenty-five had completed four or more years of college, whereas 20.9 percent of whites had. Similarly, 66.7 percent of blacks over the age of twenty-five had completed four years of high school in 1988, whereas 77.7 percent of whites had (National Center for Education Statistics 1990). Why? Has contemporary U.S. education responded to the needs of the heterogeneous school population? Many educators contend that the poor records of most minority students indicate that public education has not changed sufficiently to meet their needs.

James Banks, in *Teaching Strategies for Ethnic Studies* (1991), states that while the United States has always "held tightly to the idea that ethnic cultures would melt or vanish" (p. 3), this has not been the case. "Discrimination prevents many individuals and groups with particular ethnic, racial, and or cultural characteristics from attaining full structural inclusion into U.S. society" (pp. 3–4). Banks claims that the schools have attempted to *Americanize* or *Anglicize* the curriculum. He suggests that until the schools recognize the important accomplishments of individuals from various racial, cultural, and ethnic groups and incorporate these into the curriculum, minority students will not achieve at levels equal to white students. He suggests that simply adding a lesson about minorities here and there in the curriculum will not help. Instead, schools must "reconceptualize how [they] view American society and history in the school curriculum" (p. 15).

Textbooks Textbooks are the single most important instructional tool in the classroom. Through them subject matter is organized for instruction. Many teachers refer to the textbook, the teacher's guide, workbooks, and other instructional materials as a "curriculum package," acknowledging its impact.

In addition, as educator Michael W. Apple points out in "Making Knowledge Legitimate: Power, Profit, and the Textbook," the textbook also influences the social climate of the classroom. According to Apple, "The impact of textbooks on the social relations of the classroom is also immense." It is estimated, for example, that 75 percent of classroom time and 90 percent of homework time are spent with text materials (1985, 75). Hence, Apple concludes that social interaction between students and students, and teachers and students is limited.

Benefits of Textbooks

While some may decry the text as the basis of the curriculum, many educators point to its benefits. These include organized and sequential instruction of the material, articulation between grade levels and schools about the curriculum, benefits of the latest knowledge and research, assistance provided to teachers who cannot know everything about a subject, and teachers working together to utilize the material in curriculum packages.

Daniel and Laurel Tanner point out in *Curriculum Development: Theory into Practice* (1980) that a book can be a very personal learning tool. Students can

In many schools, teachers select the curriculum package that best meets the needs of their students and most nearly matches their own teaching approach and focus. In some schools, a committee of teachers may make a selection of texts for an entire department or grade level.

make their own analysis and synthesis while reading a book, allowing for divergent thinking. Benjamin Bloom suggests in *All Our Children Learning: A Primer for Parents, Teachers and Other Educators* (1981) that in most schools teachers have the freedom to determine which of several textbooks or curriculum packages best meets the needs of their curriculum and students, and what to utilize from the textbook in the classroom.

Problems of Textbooks

On the other hand, critics of statewide textbook adoption systems claim that the quality of the books is not as good as it could or should be. Bloom claims that his examination of textbooks revealed that many of them were as alike as "peas in a pod" (p. 144). Many educators suggest that this lack of diversity in textbooks is a result of marketplace demands: teachers and parents will purchase books that are more alike than they are different.

Another problem cited by critics of the curriculum's reliance on textbooks is the role of special interest groups in textbook adoption. For example, in several court cases in the 1980s, Christian fundamentalist groups attacked books for including the theory of evolution, and humanistic literature and for not including information about Christianity. Other groups condemned texts for being too simplistic and not scientific enough in their approach.

John Goodlad, in his study of effective schools *A Place Called School: Prospects for the Future* (1984), evaluated texts and found that many emphasized the rudiments of reading and computation at the expense of skills such as comprehension, analysis, problem solving, and drawing conclusions (pp. 205–209). According to Goodlad, some leave out enrichment activities in the arts and humanities; many simply repeat and extend material rather than teaching new material (1984, 206). Other researchers found that texts presented only shallow knowledge in order to appeal to a wider audience (Newman in Rothman 1988a, 1). Many of these researchers condemned texts for prejudice and misinformation, especially when reporting on other cultures, and others claimed that texts were written at very low reading levels in order to appeal to the widest range of students.

These textbook problems were summarized by correspondent Paul Solman in the Public Broadcasting System's 1989 three-part series "Learning in America."

> We live in a global market with global competition, and yet, for most American kids, it's out of state, out of mind. Part of the problem lies with our curriculum. Most of the curriculum depends on textbooks and textbooks just aren't doing the job, because in the words of one educator, Harriet Tyson Burnstein, there's a conspiracy of good intentions. The conspirators include the watchdogs with their deeply held political beliefs, the educators with their ingrained habits and limited resources, and the publishers with their need to sell a product. All are well meaning but too many cooks can spoil the book.

What Can be Done to Improve Textbooks?

David Gardner in *A Nation at Risk* says that texts should be (1) upgraded and updated to assure more "rigorous content," (2) available in "thin markets" for groups such as disadvantaged and gifted, (3) based on results of field trials and creditable evaluation, (4) reflective of the most current application, the best scholarship, the best teaching and learning in each discipline, and (5) evaluated by state and school districts on the above criteria (1983, 25–26).

Whatever is included in the textbooks has an undeniable impact on the public school curriculum. How to balance the criticism of groups who want less scientific inquiry in texts and groups who demand more is a difficult problem, but one that textbook publishers will continue to attempt to solve.

Tests   Tests also have a huge impact on the public school curriculum, and, like textbooks, their production is a very profitable business. According to Elliot Eisner in *The Education Imagination: On the Design and Evaluation of School Programs* (1985), since the late 1970s, testing has become the most powerful control on educational practice in U.S. public schools. College admission tests, particularly the Scholastic Aptitude Test (SAT), are one example. In recent years the SAT has become the benchmark for how the secondary schools are performing. If scores fall, it is assumed the schools are doing poorly. Consequently, most schools, school districts, and states take seriously the performance of their students as compared to those in other schools, districts, and states.

The "Big Books" program in New Zealand has contributed to one of the world's highest literacy rates. The schools emphasize sharing the delight of reading both in school and out, involving the parents at every level. The Ministry of Education contracted for books to be written that were appropriate to this island nation. These New Zealand children enjoy reading the books written especially for them.

Attributes of Tests

Standardized tests designed to examine levels of knowledge in specific content areas also have an impact on curriculum. The largest of these testing programs, designed more as an evaluation of schools than of students, is the National Assessment of Educational Progress (NAEP). It is a program in which third-, seventh-, and eleventh-grade students have been tested every two years since 1969 on a rotating basis in reading, writing, mathematics, science, and other subjects. The NAEP, administered by the National Assessment Governing Board, which was established by Congress in 1988, is the only regular national assessment of what U.S. students know in various subject areas. The results of these tests are used to examine areas of student weakness and recommend curricular change (see chapter 11).

For example, the 1986 NAEP tests showed that "relatively few students were knowledgeable about computer programming" (Rothman 1988b, 1), a finding which seemed to contradict earlier industry studies. Also, the 1986 test seemed to indicate that students knew little about American history. As a result, many states adopted new requirements in computer education at all levels and emphasized history content beginning in the early grades, a direct shift from the previous sociological approach of studying the individual, the family unit, and the community before dealing with specific historical content.

CROSS-CULTURAL PERSPECTIVE

New Zealand's Student-Centered Language Curriculum

New Zealand is an island nation in the South Pacific with a population of 3.3 million people. The first settlers were Maori from Polynesia; in present-day New Zealand they make up about 12 percent of the population. People of British, Yugoslav, European, Asian, and Pacific Island descent have also settled here, bringing with them a rich diversity of cultures and perspectives on life.

New Zealanders—and 85 percent of us were born here—grow up in small neighborhood schools that serve all the children in the community. Well over half the primary (elementary) schools have fewer than 120 children, so mixed-level teaching is the norm. These community schools have always had parents involved in various ways: in home-school associations, helping with class outings, and the inevitable fund-raising. In recent years parents have become even more involved with class programs, particularly those in reading, language, and art.

New Zealand mandated free compulsory schooling in 1877. Our national curriculum is delineated in syllabuses that describe the aims and objectives for each subject, some ideas for various teaching approaches, and suggestions for evaluation and assessment.

We have never had basal texts for any subject in New Zealand; teachers decide on resources that suit their children's needs and on the teaching methods that work for them based on the syllabus. There has always been this strong element of teacher choice. The Department of Education publishes and provides all schools with a number of exemplary materials. In addition, schools have grants that enable them to choose a variety of books and other resources.

The last 20 years have seen important developments. Exciting work was done in the '60s by Don Holdaway (1972, 1979), Warwick Elley (1981, 1985, 1987), and Marie Clay (1972, 1985) among many, many people who combined research and practical application. Holdaway saw the way we liked reading to children, so he elaborated on the "Big Book" idea. He emphasized the importance of sharing reading, both in school and out. Elley, in his investigations of the development of facility in language, documented the need for a good rich diet of books with diversity and choice. Clay, known especially well in the United States for her work in reading recovery, refined techniques for observing and monitoring children as they read. Her work led to the development of the "running record" as a diagnostic teaching tool. I could name many others.

By the '70s we were ready to offer some key principles involved in learning to read. Our friends in the United States will recognize the influence of

In addition, most educators realize that when test scores are appropriately used they allow teachers to make sound decisions about students and the curriculum. For example, careful analysis of answers permits reading teachers to determine if a student's reading problem is in word recognition or comprehension. Similarly, if a teacher compares the results of a standardized reading test to the results of an oral IQ test and discovers that a student has a very high IQ and a low reading test score, this may influence the type of reading material the teacher assigns. It may also lead the teacher to ask important questions: Are the results of the tests accurate? Should the student be retested? Does the student have a physical problem that is affecting his or her test score? Is a learning disability negatively affecting test results? When did the student's scores begin to decline? Is the student experiencing social or emotional stress that might be affecting achievement? The importance of tests to assist teachers in asking and answering these questions cannot be overemphasized.

the work of Frank Smith (1978) and Ken Goodman (1986) in these. We learned from their work and from that of other fine researchers around the world. Some of those principles include:

- Reading, talking, and writing are inseparably interrelated
- The foundations of literacy are laid in the early years
- Reading for meaning is paramount
- Books for children learning to read should use natural idiomatic language that is appropriate to the subject
- There is no one way in which people learn to read. A combination of approaches is needed. . . .

We've learned to be very attentive to what children do in classrooms. We've become more and more observant, watchful, and responsive, ready to stand back at the right moment and to move forward when the child needs a little extra help. Our teachers let the children explore and try out ideas and are skillful in encouraging classroom discussion. They help children to express themselves fully.

Our appreciation for the vital role that parents play has grown, and we recognize the importance of interaction between home and school. A reform of 1989 placed a majority of parents on every school governing body. Twenty years ago we were not so much at ease in having parents fully involved with classroom programs.

We have the very best of materials! I have a special interest in this, because I work in the Ministry of Education, which is responsible for our Ready to Read books. These are the 65 or so books that form the framework for our early reading program. They're "real books" that can take their place alongside the best children's books on any market. They were written in response to a nationwide invitation for scripts, and a selection was made of titles to try out in classrooms. Afterwards, we discarded, revised, edited, and developed them, until finally we had a group which met all the criteria for production. Now these books are used in all our schools, and we are continuing to add to their numbers. The teachers augment them with a huge variety of other titles from publishers around the world, ensuring that children have access to the best of writing from a diversity of sources. But Ready to Read is the heart of the early reading program. . . .

We delight in watching our children talk, read, write, paint, and model, and we love to see their colorful work going up on the classroom walls, even hanging from ceilings. I recently negotiated my way around a 6-foot-high dragon that occupied the center of a "sole charge" (one teacher) school. The 25 5- to 12-year-old children there were all talking, writing, and reading about beasts of myth and legend. Lately I've read the opening chapter of *Bleak House* [Charles Dickens] to 17-year-olds and then read their vivid accounts of 19th century Chancery Lane. Our children talk and write and write and laugh, and read . . . and read . . . and read.

From: Mabbett, 1990

Many educators also believe that tests such as the NAEP are leading the United States closer to a national test of achievement and, hence, a national curriculum. In April 1991, President George Bush and Secretary of Education Lamar Alexander proposed a national system of achievement testing. Proponents of nationwide testing, including Ernest L. Boyer, president of the Carnegie Foundation for the Advancement of Teaching, suggest that it will allow schools to assess the progress of their students and the strength and coherence of their curriculum.

Problems of Tests

Opponents of President Bush's call for national achievement tests suggest that nationwide testing would lead to centralized control over what children learn, and they fear that all children, no matter what their ethnic or racial background, will be required to learn the same content so that they can successfully pass the tests. They also worry that the tests will be unfair to children from widely diverse backgrounds.

Critics, such as Elliot Eisner, maintained that the emphasis on testing removed from the curriculum that which could not be measured: appreciation, self-worth, motivation, commitment, problem solving, and creativity, for example. Many educators, including Philip Jackson, Michael Apple, and Vincent Rogers, voiced concern that the teaching, testing, teaching process was a meaningless series of steps in which only easy-to-teach and easy-to-test material was included in the curriculum, and that frequently teachers taught to the test rather than to the student's development.

Many educators wondered if standardized tests were statistically valid and reliable. A widely publicized 1988 study by the psychologist John Jacob Cannell reported that most students performed above the norm on many standardized tests, a statistically impossible occurrence (Watters 1988). Cannell's survey, in *How Public Educators Cheat on Standardized Achievement Tests: The "Lake Wobegon" Report* (1989), reported that the standards used by many test companies to establish "averages" were outdated and misleading. Critics of many standardized tests maintained that since the test results were so important to the schools' reputation and standing in the community, administrators would not buy a test on which they could be reasonably sure that their students would not perform well. Therefore, as in Garrison Keillor's comedy routines about Lake Wobegon, all the children would be above average. Many claimed that this apparent misrepresentation of results allowed the public and schools to believe that the current competency-based approach was working, when, in fact, it was not.

Further criticism came from a three-year (1987–1990) study on the testing practices in schools and workplaces funded by the Ford Foundation and chaired by George F. Madaus, director of testing and evaluation at Boston College. The study charged that in terms of minorities and women, the U.S. testing system had become a "hostile gatekeeper," that is, yet another method of keeping them out of opportunities for advancement, and called for a new system that would "open the gates of opportunity for America's diverse population" (Rothman 1990, 1). One article reporting on the study claimed that schools and businesses increasingly rely on standardized, multiple-choice tests to make judgments about individuals and institutions, and that these tests tend to be biased in terms of race and gender.

The study claimed that each year elementary and secondary school students take 127 million separate tests as part of test batteries mandated by states and school districts. This testing costs over $1 billion annually. "The opportunity costs of missed instructional time used to drill students in the narrow skills measured by standardized tests are even greater than financial costs. Such time could be better used to develop students' higher order skills" (Rothman, 12).

The Association for Childhood Education International (ACEI) published an international position paper on standardized tests in the spring of 1991. It stressed the inappropriateness of standardized tests to make any judgment about a child. It set forth unequivocally the belief that all testing of young children in preschool and grades K–2 and the practice of testing every child in elementary school should cease. According to ACEI, standardized testing:

- Results in increased pressure on children, setting too many of them up for devastating failure and, consequently, lowered self-esteem.
- Does not provide useful information about individual children, yet often becomes the basis for decisions about children's entry into kindergarten, promotion and retention in the grades, and placement in special classes.
- Leads to harmful tracking and labeling of children.
- Compels teachers to spend precious time preparing children to take the tests, undermining their efforts to provide developmentally sound programs responsive to children's interests and needs.
- Limits educational possibilities for children, resulting in distortion of curriculum, teaching and learning, as well as lowered expectations.
- Fails to set the conditions for cooperative learning and problem solving. (Perrone 1991, 141)

It is impossible to overemphasize the impact of technology on the curriculum. Ask someone who has been teaching for more than a decade how the use of technology in the classroom has changed, and you might hear something like the following:

Technology

> When I began teaching in the late 1960s the extent of the technology we used was motion pictures and filmstrips. Within a decade we had moved to videotapes and sound-slide shows. Today, almost every classroom in my school has a computer; a computer lab is usually available to students most periods of the school day; and many students are not only able to play games on the computer but can create their own computer programs. I use the computer to keep track of student assignments, to average grades, and to keep attendance records. I do all of my lesson planning on the computer. All of my handouts are typed and duplicated on the computer. This year, with the help of a college class, I developed a system for having my students write essays on the computer. I use the computer to check for spelling and grammatical errors. This allows me to read the essays for content only. I can't begin to tell you how much technology has changed my teaching.

Of course, this scenario does not exist in all schools, but the computer is playing an important role in more and more of today's classrooms.

Benefits of Technology

The benefits of technology are obvious in the teacher's statement above. In addition, Henry Jay Becker, in "The Computer in the Elementary School," states that the microcomputer in the classroom has had more effect on the social organization of the classroom than on learning. In a 1983 survey of 2,209 elementary and secondary schools, teachers reported that microcomputers led to increased student enthusiasm toward school, improved academic learning for above-average students, more students working independently, helping other students with questions, and working at their own ability levels.

In 1989, the U.S. Census Bureau determined that 46 percent of three- to seventeen-year-olds enrolled in schools used computers there. According to the 1990 *Digest of Education Statistics*, in 1986, 95.6 percent of all schools used computers as compared to 18.2 percent in 1981 (see table 9.2, overleaf).

© 1990 by Sidney Harris–*Phi Delta Kappan.*

"Remember, all these life experiences will someday count as college credit."

TABLE 9-2

Microcomputer Use by Elementary and Secondary Schools, 1981 to 1986

| Year | Percent of schools using microcomputers | | | |
	All schools	Elementary	Junior high	High school
1981	18.2	11.1	25.6	42.7
1982	30.0	20.2	39.8	57.8
1983	68.4	62.4	80.5	86.1
1984	85.1	82.2	93.1	94.6
1985	92.2	91.0	97.3	97.4
1986	95.6	94.9	98.5	98.7

Adapted from: National Center for Education Statistics, *Digest of Education Statistics* (Washington, U.S. Government Printing Office, 1990), 402.

From: Market Data Retrieval, Inc., *Microcomputers in Schools*, 1984, 1985, 1987; and unpublished tabulations.

The use of computers in the classroom not only facilitates learning and builds skills, but also leads to increased enthusiasm for school, independent study, and cooperative learning.

Problems of Technology

There are numerous potential problems with technology in the schools. One of the most difficult is how best to use technology in the curriculum. Should there be separate courses for students in how to use computers? Should programming languages be taught in high schools? When in the curriculum should these things be added? Who should have access to computers? Should calculators be used in mathematics classrooms? If they are used, how and when should they be used?

Studies show that the students with high academic achievement have greater access to computers in their homes than poorer achieving students (Becker 1985, 32–33). Does this further separate opportunities for able and less able students? Moreover, how should computers and other technologies be purchased for the schools? Are children in rich districts likely to have more access to technology than children in poor districts?

There is no doubt that curriculum is influenced by changes in the society. Likewise, it is clear that there are many definitions of the word *curriculum* and a variety of ways in which curriculum is organized. The importance of the school's curriculum cannot be overemphasized. It affects what is taught, how it is taught, and to whom it is taught.

9.3 POINTS TO REMEMBER

- When the economy of the United States needs a particular set of skills, such as computer literacy, or concepts, the schools generally include these within the curriculum.
- As women entered the U.S. workforce in greater numbers, the curriculum adapted by preparing them in specific skills and by increasing the courses needed for entry into college. The role of minorities was introduced into such courses as history, English, and science, and the college entrance curriculum expanded to allow them access to the courses they would need. Many critics still contend that the U.S. public school curriculum has not successfully met the needs of either women or minorities.
- In periods when the curriculum is primarily subject-centered, the textbook is the main source of curricular design. Since schools want their students to be successful on standardized achievement tests, the curriculum is strongly influenced by skills and concepts students need to do well on the tests.
- Technology, primarily in the form of computers, has had a major impact on the curriculum and on teaching methodology.

FOR THOUGHT/DISCUSSION

1. Is there any way curriculum can combine the best attributes of essentialism and progressivism? How?

2. One might assume, according to Bloom's theory on mastery learning, that anyone can learn to be a neurosurgeon given enough time. Do you believe that is true? If mastery learning is viable in theory, what are its practical drawbacks?

3. Devise a method of testing that would allow the teacher to assess his or her student's progress without causing the student undue stress and that would be fair to all students.

4. Must all students be educated by a similar curriculum to ensure that our nation will be able to compete in the international arena? Why or why not?

FOR FURTHER READING/REFERENCE

Bennett, W. J. 1987. *James Madison High School: A curriculum for American students*. Washington, DC: U.S. Department of Education. A description of a subject-centered curriculum and profiles of exemplary high schools that implement subject-centered curriculums.

Bloom, B. S. 1981. *All our children learning: A primer for parents, teachers, and other educators*. New York: McGraw-Hill. A discussion of how children can learn at home and at school when mastery learning techniques are implemented.

Holt, J. 1967. *How children learn*. New York: Delacorte. A description of a humanistic approach to learning, relating how easily children learn to read, do mathematics, draw, and paint when those experiences are not forced and are pleasurable.

Jackson, P. W. 1968. *Life in classrooms*. New York: Holt, Rinehart, & Winston. A description of the school's hidden curriculum from firsthand observations in elementary school classrooms.

Molnar, A. 1985. *Current thought on curriculum*. Alexandria, VA: Association for Supervision and Curriculum Development. Eight articles discussing issues in curriculum including curriculum and technology, gaps between curriculum theory and practice, and psychological theory and curriculum.

10 The Students

It is an unusual public school classroom in which most children are the same race, same religion, and same socioeconomic status. In fact, court rulings and federal and state mandates have required heterogeneity in the public schools since the 1960s. The nature of the students and their numbers have a great impact on the school environment, the teacher and method of instruction, the curriculum, and other students. In this chapter, we will examine the nature of some of the special groups that constitute the population in American classrooms.

11 Learning

Our understanding of the concept of learning involves the idea that people will gain new skills, insights, concepts, values, and ideas through some process that may or may not involve a teacher, may or may not require a specialized setting and materials, and may or may not find the learner proceeding through a series of prescribed steps. The assumption that learning has taken place, however, is based on the observation that, in some way, behavior has been changed. This chapter will explore many ways in which researchers from various academic disciplines have attempted to define learning. We will focus on how students learn, what they learn, and what they do not learn.

Lupe is not waiting for the future to make a difference. Every week, she travels to a housing project to tutor a young Hispanic grade-school student. "I don't think I should have had to go through what I went through," she says. "It isn't right for kids to be exposed to that kind of situation. There's so much potential in them, but they don't show it because of the obstacles they face."

Each week, Lupe teaches her student math and English and tries to let the young girl know that she too can break out of poverty. "I guess I had an internal drive not everyone has," Lupe says. "But many people can do it if you give them a little push. I try to tell her that she is someone, that she has value. You can make a difference in kids' lives if you tell them that."

From: M. Ryan, "I Needed to Show Them Who I Was," *Parade* (August 19, 1990), 12–13.

PART IV

Students and Learning

10

The Students

It is not enough to say that all students are different. It is not enough to try and understand what makes them different. Teachers must somehow reach students from all kinds of backgrounds with varying degrees of limitations and potentials. A few of these students are represented here.

Manolo. A recent immigrant to the United States, 4-year-old Manolo was immediately enrolled in a comprehensive nursery school. Fortunately, his teacher spoke some Spanish and they were able to communicate. But Manolo, who had previously been popular with peers, suddenly felt excluded. When he proudly wore a pair of red leather sandals to school and was taunted on the playground about wearing "girl's shoes," Manolo responded by pelting his tormentors with sand. To make matters worse, this rejection was followed by the disapproval of his admired teacher. (Jalengo 1985, 53)

Jacob. Three days ago Jacob came to our Open Classroom orientation meeting with nine other new kindergartners and their parents. We all sat together in a circle and began the process of getting to know one another. Except for a brace on his leg and a funny way of walking, Jacob did not seem to be too different from the other children. He was comfortable about sharing his new watch, and he and his mom sang a funny song together that the other children enjoyed. He made comments in response to things the other children said. . . .

Jacob has minimal cerebral palsy and *is* different from the other children. He has difficulty standing up and sitting down, and difficulty walking. His balance is poor, and if a child bumps into him, he topples over. The process of getting up again takes time and effort and involves a kind of struggle that seems strange to the other children. (Heitz 1989, 11)

Bianca. Bianca feels safe when she is at home in front of the television. When Jem, a shapely, superstar rock singer who is the title character of her favorite cartoon show, shakes her radiant pink hair and makes her magical red earrings sparkle, Bianca is transported into another world. Jem embodies what Bianca would like to be as an adult: sexy, a singer, and a success. "I don't want to be a maid at hotels when I grow up," says Bianca. "That's what my auntie is. . . ."

For Bianca, Jem is something of an obsession. When Bianca was seven, she watched the show once a week on Sundays. Now, two years later, she watches it at 7:30 each weekday morning and again at 4:30 every afternoon. The escape into television extends beyond Jem. . . .

Until last year, Sherri [Bianca's mother] and Bianca lived in another predominantly black area of New Orleans with Sherri's mother, Maurine Belonga, who raised five children by herself after she and her husband were divorced. Sherri is the youngest. Six weeks after she met Leonard, 29, a soft-spoken, neatly dressed mail clerk, on a blind date, Sherri and her daughter moved in. (Morrow 1988A, 50)

Josh. At 14, Josh is astute enough to understand that his bar mitzvah was more a ceremonial aspiration than a sudden transformation. Between childhood and adulthood lies the ridiculous and treacherous territory of adolescence. It is a region full of dangers, brainless impulses, hormonal furies. And it must be crossed.

Josh has just successfully passed one milestone in the process: his freshman year of high school. . . . Josh has always been small for his age. That bothers him but does not slow him down. Barely 5 ft. tall, he competes in a sport of giants: his ambidextrous dribbling helped him become a starting point guard on the ninth grade basketball team at Belmont High School in suburban Boston. (Morrow 1988B, 55)

Katie. Katie clearly does not like day care. "A lot of times it gets really boring just going there," she says. "It's the same setting and usually the same things to do. I wish every day they would have a different setting, one day have a jungle look and the next day have a different look because it really gets boring." At day care, there are no Disney tapes to push into the VCR, as there are at home, no video games to play. She cannot invite friends over to her house, nor can she go to theirs. Worst of all, she cannot disappear by herself into her bedroom and play with her toys or work on her next book. "I would love if I could just stay in the attic," she says. . . . There's this little door to get in. It is really fun in there. They have all these old literature books and poetry books and drawing books. It is like a big library, and I could just sit there and read all day." (*Time*, August 8, 1988, 35)

CHAPTER OBJECTIVES

After studying this chapter, you should be able to:

- Discuss the heterogeneity of today's students.
- Describe the various types of students likely to be in your classroom: children with disabilities, children in poverty, and minority children.
- Discuss students' poor motivation toward school.
- Understand students' interests, values, and worries.
- Discuss the problems of low graduation rates.
- Explain the likely differences among students you might find in a homogeneously grouped class.
- Define human cognitive development.
- Define developmental needs.
- Explain how psychosocial needs develop.
- Define moral development.
- Discuss how a student's perception of school changes from first grade to high school.
- Understand how a student's skills develop from first grade through high school.

It is an unusual public school classroom in which most children are the same race, same religion, and same socioeconomic status. In fact, court rulings and federal and state mandates have required heterogeneity in the public schools since the 1960s (see chapter 6). The nature of the students and their numbers have a great impact on the school environment, the teacher and method of instruction, the curriculum, and other students. In this chapter, we will examine the nature of some of the special groups that constitute the population in American classrooms.

WHO ARE TODAY'S STUDENTS?

Public school enrollment in the United States peaked in 1970, when 45,909,000 attended public elementary and secondary schools. By 1984 the number had decreased to 39,295,000. However, public school enrollment in the 1990s is again increasing (see table 10.1). Students in the United States come from a wide variety of backgrounds, have a broad range of beliefs, are raised under different ethical and religious codes, possess various cultural imperatives, and are taught different approaches to education. The classrooms of the 1990s reflect these differences.

Students With Disabilities

In 1988–1989 there were 40,192,000 public and private school (K–12) students in the United States. Over 10 percent (4.5 million) were classified either as needing special education or having disabilities. They are served under the federally sponsored Chapter I and Education of the Handicapped Act (EHA) programs (amended in 1988) (see chapter 6, p. 176). The number has increased by nearly 20 percent since the late 1970s, from 3.7 million in 1977 to 4.4 million in 1990. In the 1990–1991 school year, programs for the disabled spent $2 billion, or roughly $8,800 per student. The biggest proportion of that money went to students classified as learning disabled, a group which has grown by 142 percent in ten years, simply because the classifications keep expanding. A **learning disability** is "a disorder in one or more of the basic psychological processes involved in understanding or in using language, spoken or written, which may manifest itself in an imperfect ability to listen, think, speak, read, write, spell, or to do mathematical calculations." The percentage of emotionally disturbed students is up 36 percent since 1980. **Emotional disturbance** is a condition with one or more of the following characteristics over a period of time that adversely affects educational performance: inability to learn that cannot be explained by intellectual, sensory, or health factors; inability to build or maintain interpersonal relationships; inappropriate types of behavior or feelings; a tendency to

TABLE 10-1

Public Elementary and Secondary Schools—Enrollment, 1960 to 1988, and Projections, 1990 and 1995

Item	Public		
	Total	Elementary	Secondary
Enrollment: 1960	36,281	24,350	11,931
1965	42,173	26,670	15,504
1970	45,909	27,501	18,408
1975	44,791	25,640	19,151
1980	40,987	24,156	16,831
1985	39,509	24,290	15,219
1986	39,837	24,201	15,636
1987	40,024	24,315	15,709
1988, est.	40,196	25,206	14,990
1990, proj.	40,772	26,027	14,745
1995, proj.	43,453	27,022	16,431

Note: Numbers listed in thousands

From: U.S. Department of Commerce. Bureau of the Census, *Statistical Abstract of the United States* (1990), 138.

Student population in public elementary and secondary schools peaked in 1970, and then declined. It is rising again in the 1990s due not only to a rise in births, but also to a growing number of immigrants, and, to some extent, to the mainstreaming of those with disabilities.

develop physical symptoms or fears associated with personal or school problems; and schizophrenia. The percentage of students with mental disabilities is down 32 percent from 1980. A **mental disability** is defined as "significantly subaverage general intellectual functioning existing concurrently with deficits in adaptive behavior and manifested during the developmental period, which adversely affects a child's educational performance" (Office of the Federal Register 1990, 13).

Because more than 40 percent of special education students ages six to eleven and nearly 20 percent of special education students ages twelve to seventeen are mainstreamed into the regular classroom for some part of the school day, it is imperative that classroom teachers learn to work with students with a variety of disabilities (U.S. Department of Education 1991, A-80, A-102). In addition, mainstreaming these students into the regular classroom may require that special education teachers, such as those who can use sign language, attend class with their students. Having a special teacher signing for a deaf student may mean that the regular classroom teacher has to make some adjustment in his or her teaching methodology. Assume, for instance, that some of the terminology is difficult to translate exactly into sign language; it may be necessary for the teacher to write complicated terminology on the chalkboard or overhead transparency so that the student and the special teacher can see the terminology in print. (For additional information about the disabled in school, see chapter 6, p. 176.)

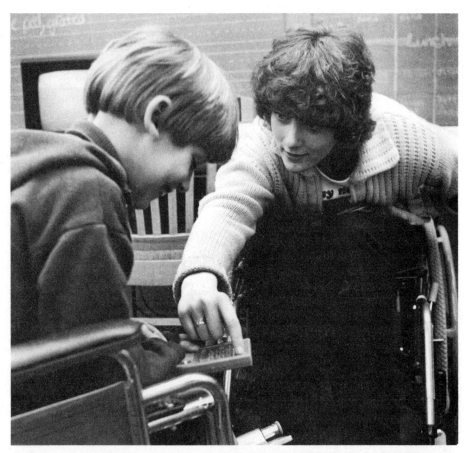

Students with disabilities of all kinds are being mainstreamed wherever possible into a regular classroom. Teachers must be prepared to deal with these students in a sensitive and meaningful way at the same time that they must meet the needs of all other students in the class.

IN THE CLASSROOM

Andy is a 15-year-old speech and language impaired student in rural Mississippi. He is so severely disabled that mainstreaming into regular classrooms has not been possible. However, because of an event and a sensitive teacher, that will soon change.

His teacher says, "Something really great happened to Andy this year, and I just know he will continue to improve." Although Andy's hearing and vision are within normal range, his speech is severely retarded. He is the youngest of six children from a low income and environmentally deprived family. He exhibits evidence of both physical and emotional abuse. He is very withdrawn and afraid of people, particularly adults.

In the fall of 1988, Andy rarely communicated with his teacher or classmates. But, one day his teacher happened to overhear Andy talking to a pet rabbit in the classroom; shortly thereafter she heard him talking to a young girl. Andy was communicating. How could she get him to communicate with students his age and with adults?

Suddenly, an opportunity presented itself. A teacher from a school for the deaf visited Andy's class to teach the students sign language. His teacher reports, "I noticed a smile on Andy's face and saw how quickly he learned the signs." So his teacher arranged for Andy to take signing three times a week for thirty minutes each time. She also took the lessons so that she could sign with Andy. "I have never seen a student so excited about learning!" remarks his teacher. After six weeks, Andy started talking and signing together [at the same time]. Soon he was talking and signing everywhere— in the lunchroom, on the playground, at the store, in church—even to strangers. Since this time his grades have improved and he has become increasingly communicative. Because of Andy's success, he was mainstreamed for the first time in the fall of 1989. And he now plans to graduate from high school.

An observant, caring teacher made Andy's breakthrough possible. As she says, "I know that Andy needed . . . to break through that terrible barrier of years of fear and neglect. I'm sure we don't know it all. I gave him all the support and caring I could muster, but it was the signing that met his need. He learned so fast, because his need to communicate was so great." *(Note: The names in this profile have been changed to protect the student's right to privacy.)*

In 1980, 15.3 percent of all five- to seventeen-year-olds were in poverty. By 1991 that number had grown to 26 percent. Between 1985 and 1989 Mississippi had the highest poverty level at 34.3 percent of all children, followed by Louisiana (32.4 percent), Alabama (30.9 percent), Arkansas (29.2 percent), the District of Columbia (28.5 percent), West Virginia (28 percent), New Mexico (27.8 percent), Tennessee (25.7 percent), and Texas (24.5 percent) (The Center for Study of Social Policy 1991).

According to the National Center for Educational Statistics, in 1987 the percentage of black children living in poverty was 3 times that of white children, and Hispanic children, 2.6 times. In addition, children from female-headed households were much more likely to live in poverty than children with two parents (see figures 10.1 and 10.2).

Children who live in poverty are more likely to experience problems related to low birth weight, inadequate diet, inadequate health care, limited parental education, limited parental supervision, and poor living conditions than children who do not live in poverty. What do these problems mean to the classroom teacher? Take for example Derek, a ten-year-old child of a single parent. Derek comes to school without breakfast; he is provided breakfast by the school cafeteria. His lunch is also provided by federal free and reduced-cost lunch programs. All these programs require that Derek's teacher complete extensive paperwork. Derek rarely has school supplies such as paper, crayons, and pencils. His teacher tries to provide them when she can, but reduced budgets may make it necessary for her to buy some supplies for needy students out of her own money if she so desires. When the class goes on field trips,

Children in Poverty

FIGURE 10-1

Percent of Children Under 18 in Poverty by Race/Ethnicity: 1960–1987

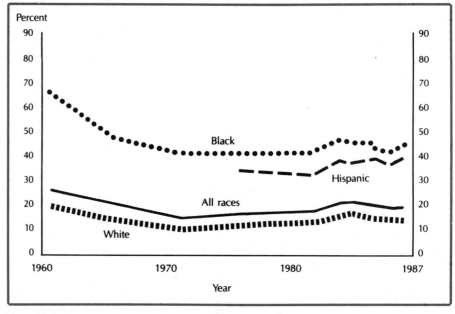

Note: Plotted points are 1960, 1965, 1970, 1975, 1980–1987

From: National Center for Education Statistics, *The Condition of Education. Vol. 1: Elementary and Secondary Education* (1990), 65.

Children who live in poverty have a difficult time succeeding in school primarily because their basic needs are not being met. Children who come to school hungry or sick or without supplies can't be expected to perform at high levels. Blacks and Hispanics are two to three times as likely as whites to live in poverty.

Derek can rarely go. Even if the money is available from another source, his mother does not return the required permission slips. Derek misses school often or comes to school sick. He seems to get more colds and ear infections than his classmates and usually comes to school with them. This fall Derek had head lice. His mother could not afford the expensive shampoo, so Derek's teacher arranged for her to pick it up from the community health service. However, since Derek's family does not have a phone, the teacher had to go to his home to give them this information. But Derek's mother had no way to get to the health service and no one to take care of her children when she went. Therefore, Derek's teacher helped arrange transportation through a local church group. Furthermore, Derek rarely does his homework. When his teacher visited his home she better understood why. There is no place for Derek to do his homework; no place for him to escape from his brothers and sisters. All five children sleep in one room, and the only other room in the house is a combination living room, kitchen, and bedroom for his mother. Derek's mother does not encourage him to do school work; instead, she needs him to help with the other children. When the school has activities, Derek's mother cannot attend. Because she herself has problems with reading and mathematics, she is

FIGURE 10-2

Percent of All Children in Female-Headed Households in Poverty by Race/Ethnicity: 1960–1987

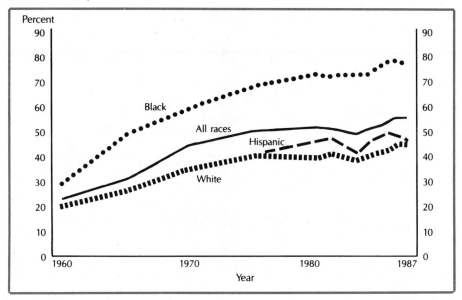

Note: Plotted points are 1960, 1965, 1970, 1975, 1980–1987

From: National Center for Education Statistics, *The Condition of Education. Vol. 1: Elementary and Secondary Education* (1990), 65.

Children of all races who live in families headed only by a female are more likely to live in poverty than those who live in families with two parents. Not only do females generally earn less than their male counterparts, they also must provide for child care.

unable to help her own children. Derek has both academic and behavioral problems in school. He is easily distracted from his work, has difficulty reading and computing, and often disturbs the other children. His teacher finds that when she works with Derek individually he can do the work, but as soon as she leaves him to work with other children he is off-task. Derek's teacher understands and sympathizes with his problems and is very concerned about him. However, she has twenty-eight children in her classroom and nearly half of them come from homes as poor as Derek's. Thus, subsidizing the poor students from a teacher's modest salary is not a sustainable solution to a chronic social problem.

In 1987, 30 percent of the school population was classified as minority (non-white). The largest concentrations of minority school populations were in the District of Columbia, 96 percent; Hawaii, 57 percent; New Mexico, 57 percent; Mississippi, 56 percent; Texas, 49 percent; California, 46 percent; and South Carolina, 45 percent. The smallest concentrations of minorities in the school population were in Vermont, New Hampshire, and Maine, 2 percent; West

Minority Students

FIGURE 10-3

E Pluribus Unum: Racial Makeup of Population

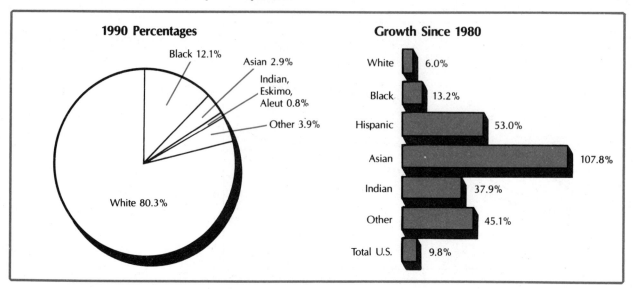

Note: Hispanics can be of any race
From: *Education Week* (March 20, 1991), 16.

The public school population is becoming increasingly diverse as the nonwhite population of the United States continues to grow. Unless the numbers of ethnic and minority teachers keep pace with the numbers of ethnic and minority students, a disjunction will occur between a teacher's perceived reality and that of her or his students.

Virginia, 4 percent; Iowa, 5 percent; Minnesota, 6 percent; and Montana, 7 percent.

As the nonwhite population of the United States increases, the definition of the word *minority* is changing. According to Vance Grant, a specialist from the National Center for Education Statistics of the U.S. Department of Education, the federal government's definition of minority now includes all racial and ethnic groups except whites and Hispanics (telephone conversation with the authors, May 20, 1991). Hispanics are an ethnic rather than a racial group and are not, in fact, all members of the same racial group. James Banks suggests that new demographic realities call into question the definition of minority as all nonwhites. According to Banks, by the year 2020, 46 percent of the nation's school children will be children of color (speech given at the University of North Carolina at Asheville, March 1, 1991). In addition, in many of the largest cities and school districts in the United States, minorities (nonwhites) today represent the majority of the population.

The minority population of the public schools is growing because the minority population of the United States is growing (see figure 10.3). By 2020, the number of whites in the United States is expected to account for 70 percent of the total population and by 2050, 60 percent. The greatest increase in minorities will probably be in the Hispanic population, which is expected to more than double from 6.4 to 15 percent, and Asians, from 1.6 to 10 percent (Bouvier and Agresta 1987).

Coupled with the growing minority student population is a decreasing population of minority teachers. Although, according to James Banks, students of color made up the majority of students in twenty-five of the nation's fifty largest school districts in 1991, teachers of color will decline from 12.5 percent of all teachers in 1980 to only 5 percent by the year 2000. According to Martin Haberman in *Preparing Teachers for Urban Schools* (1988), this should not be surprising because by 2000 only 5 percent of college students will be minorities. What are the implications of the growing minority school population and the decreasing percentage of minority teachers? Again, according to Banks, teachers will be working with children who are ethnically different than they are. Students and teachers will be challenged to "construct their own view of reality" from the "multiple voices" they hear. Teachers will have to decide which view of reality should be presented to students through books and classroom materials. Which authors will appear in literature anthologies? Whose view of history will be presented? Will students learn about the lives of the slaves as well as the slave owners on the plantations of the pre–Civil War South? According to Banks, schools should eliminate "Eurocentrism" from the curriculum and its language. Schools and teachers must establish a clear commitment to provide a diversified school population with what Banks calls "a multicultural literacy" (speech given at the University of North Carolina at Asheville, March 1, 1991). Of course, not everyone agrees with Banks's position on multicultural literacy. E. D. Hirsch, the author of *Cultural Literacy: What Every American Needs to Know*, believes in an "essential, uniform, literate education" for every student and that, regardless of racial or ethnic background, each student should be given similar information so that we can develop a national culture and language (1987).

Another implication of the increase in minority students may be declining standardized test scores, since minority students do not score as well on standardized tests (see chapter 11, pp. 365–371). The reasons for this result are complicated, but Asa Hilliard (1989) contends that many teachers "teach down" to minority students by making the material much simpler and more superficial than it needs to be. Many teachers mistake the differing learning styles of minority students for lack of intellectual potential. Hilliard, in citing research summarized by Jere Brophy, lists teaching strategies used in teaching down to minorities as:

- less wait time for students to answer questions
- calling on students less often
- criticizing students more frequently
- praising them less frequently
- interacting with them less frequently
- seating them farther away from the teacher
- accepting lower quality work

However, when minority and underprivileged children are treated as if they can achieve, they generally do.

(continued on p. 318)

VIEWPOINTS

Slow Readers Sparkling With a Handful of Words

Eleven-year-old Erik Rotger likes to say 13 words out loud as he walks down the street in his north Bronx neighborhood: outstanding, frolicsome, comprehensive, impressionable, Walt Disney, Poconos, Leonardo, oneiromancy, coruscation, conclusions, discombobulate and, his favorite, hierophant.

"I like the sound of it—hierophant," said Erik, a fifth grader at Public School 94 with a dreamy look in his brown eyes. "One who champions a cause."

Those are Erik's words, and he says them with enormous pride. Erik has had to work much harder than most of his classmates to learn to read. Last year, he was still struggling with the first-grade primer. He had to attend summer school to make it to fifth grade. Now, though, he is reading almost at a fourth-grade level. His words are one measure of how far he has come this year at P.S. 94.

Erik discovered his words in the cramped room on the fourth floor that belongs to Louise Warren, one of the school's two resource, or remedial math and reading, teachers. Erik is one of 17 students who leave their classrooms for one or two periods a day to work with Mrs. Warren. She wants them to love words, and each day they choose a new word, any word, they want to learn.

Some of her students have serious learning disabilities, like dyslexia. Others, like Erik, are two or more grade levels behind in math or reading. Most have trouble concentrating, a problem made worse by the severe overcrowding at P.S. 94. Erik spent first grade in the noisy gymnasium, which has been turned into four makeshift classrooms.

In Mrs. Warren's room, the ceiling leaks, and the plaster is peeling so persistently that the children's work keeps falling off the walls. But it is a room filled with books in a school without a library. And there, with Mrs. Warren, and with 5 students instead of 30, children who feel scared and stupid in their own classrooms can begin to learn.

Most New York City schools have resource teachers, part of a federally mandated program that provides extra help for children without segregating them in special education classrooms. The experts call it "mainstreaming." Judith Markowitz, a guidance counselor at P.S. 94, says it works. "We could use 10 resource rooms," she said.

Mrs. Warren started P.S. 94's resource program 10 years ago. "You have to prove to these children that they can learn," she said. "Telling them is not enough. Believing in them is not enough. You have to get them to succeed at something. The words convince them they're smart. . . ."

Mrs. Warren says her methods have been influenced by Sylvia Ashton-Warner, who taught Maori children in New Zealand. She never rejects a word a child asks to learn.

"You have to respect their words," Mrs. Warren said. "It's an affirmation of what they think is important. If you can get children to love words, for whatever reason, you've got it made."

Her students search for words in the 365 New-Words-A-Year Calendar that is displayed on the wall. Hierophant was the word for Jan. 16, 1989. ("One who champions a cause or proposal" was one of two definitions listed.)

Each child's words, and the definitions, are printed on index cards, and filed under their names in a metal box. Superman belongs to a fourth grader named Damon Howlett. Melitza Ruiz, another fourth grader, likes paraphernalia. Jennifer Cruz, a third-grader, recently added suede to her vocabulary, like her new shoes. Henry Alamo, a second grader, took on discrimination last week.

"I like big words," Henry explained.

The other morning, Desmond Howell, a sixth grader who could not read when he came from Jamaica two years ago, read his words aloud. Mrs. Warren beamed. Desmond's classroom teacher, Ellie Diaz, had just nominated him as most improved student.

"Customary," Desmond began shyly, holding tightly to his cards. "Spectacular. I like the sound of it—spectacular. Like something is real, real great. Magnifying. Adverse. Permissive. Friendly. Knowledge. You have to have knowledge to do something in life. Fourberie. That means trickery. I'll never forget that word—fourberie."

Mrs. Warren, a passionate reader who enjoys histories of the civil rights movement, grew up in the Bronx in an apartment filled with books. Many of her students are not as fortunate.

"The experts say you can't use socioeconomics as an excuse," she said. "The hell you can't. If you come from a house without books, you're at a disadvantage." . . .

"These children can do the work if you give them the time," she said. "A teacher might say, 'But I gave him 10 minutes.' But they might need 20 or 30 minutes." . . .

Erik's mother, Migdalio Ledesma, talked the other afternoon about how she had fought to get help for her son.

"He would tell me, 'Mommy, I try hard, I try hard,' " she said. "He was sick when he got left back. I got a tutor. It was expensive—$10 an hour. I went to the principal. I said, 'My son needs help.' "

Erik, seated across from his mother in their living room, was listening intently. Suddenly, his face lit up with understanding.

Looking at his mother, he declared: "She's a hierophant!"

From: Rimer, 1990

Louise Warren is a resource teacher at P.S. 94 in the Bronx. Resoure teachers provide students with specific learning activities that focus on their individual needs, and with the kind of encouragement and support students couldn't get in a large classroom. Here she has kind words for Erik Rotger, who, under her tutelage, has gone from a first- to almost fourth-grade reading level in a year. Jillian Velez, another student in the class, looks on.

Immigrants   In 1987 between 2.1 and 2.7 million students were immigrants, with the highest concentrations occurring in California, New York, Texas, Florida, Illinois, New Jersey, Massachusetts, New Mexico, and Pennsylvania (Haney 1987).

The National Coalition of Advocates for Children illustrated the impact of new immigration on school districts by reporting testimony from public hearings sponsored by the Immigrant Student Project, *New Voices: Immigrant Students in U.S. Public Schools* (1988). Some excerpts from this testimony follow.

> More than a third of San Francisco United School District's student population's primary language is other than English. . . . The immigrant students coming to the district represent 20 or more different language groups. Roughly one-third of [the district's] population of 65,000 has immigrated here within the last five years, the two largest groups being Asian and Hispanic. . . . The school district's ethnic distribution has changed dramatically over the past twenty years. . . . The Spanish surname population has increased from 11.5% to 18.3%. . . . The White population has decreased from 45.3% to 15.6%. . . . The Black population has decreased from 25.6% to 20.6%. . . . The Chinese population has increased from 13.3% to 25.5%. . . . [and the Filipino population from 2.5% to 8.9%]. (Ramon Cortines, superintendent of San Francisco United School District)

Similar reports come from other urban centers around the United States. In Lowell, Massachusetts, for example, Prem Suksawat, a bilingual school psychologist, reports, "Right now there are about 2,000 Southeast Asian students. . . . In 1980, there were 98." Reine Leroy, an intergroup relations specialist with the Dade County Public Schools in Miami, Florida, reports: "At this point in Dade County [FL], we have approximately 8,000 Haitian kids." In a number of schools in the Miami area, Haitian children now make up the majority of the schools' population. According to Elizabeth Bogan, director, New York City Office of Immigrant Affairs:

> In 1980, there were almost 2.8 million households total in New York City, of which 781,000 or 28% were headed by an immigrant. . . . When we look at the schools themselves, we find a little more than a quarter of the city's public school children—27.2%—came from households headed by an immigrant. . . . In addition to the 273,000 children of immigrant families in the public schools, the schools are also educating 174,000 children whose parents were born in Puerto Rico, bringing [to] nearly 450,000 the number of children whose parents' native language and culture was not English. . . . That was, in 1980, almost half the school's total enrollment.

Urban vs. Rural   The percentage of children under the age of fifteen who live in the nation's major urban centers has changed little in the last two decades. However, the number of rural children has declined by 10 percent, while the urban population has increased by 1 percent and the suburban by 8 percent (U.S. Department of Commerce 1986, 32).

Minority school populations tend to be centered in the nation's major urban areas. In the fifteen largest school systems in the United States, the minority population ranges from 70 to 96 percent (National Coalition of Advocates for Children 1988). A study by the National School Boards Association confirms that the largest percentage of students in urban school districts

(continued on p. 322)

Point/Counterpoint

IN DEFENSE OF TRACKING

A variety of . . . reasons explains why tracking has become a tradition. It is one method of trying to improve the instructional setting for selected students, or what one researcher refers to as a "search for a better match between learner and instructional environment" [Strather 1985, 309]. Tracking becomes a very common way of attempting to provide for individual differences. Unless everyone is going to be taught everything simultaneously, grouping is necessary. . . .

Tracking is not an attempt to create differences, but to accommodate them. Not all differences are created by the schools; most differences are inherited. . . . Students vary widely. . . .

. . . An approach that treats all students the same and ignores the real differences among them can guarantee unequal experiences for all. Treating all students the same is not a formula for equity or excellence.
From: Nevi, 1987

IN DEFENSE OF HETEROGENEITY

Despite the fact that the first assumption—that students learn more or better in homogeneous groups—is almost universally held, it is simply not true. Or, at least, we have virtually mountains of research evidence indicating that homogeneous grouping doesn't consistently help *anyone* learn better. Over the past sixty years hundreds of studies have been conducted on the effects of ability grouping and tracking on student learning. These studies have looked at various kinds of groupings, measured different kinds of learning, and considered students at different ages and grades. The studies vary in their size and in their methodology. . . . But, one conclusion emerges clearly: *no group of students has been found to benefit consistently from being in a homogeneous group.* A few of the studies show that students identified as the brightest learn more when they are taught in a group of their peers, and provided an enriched curriculum. However, most do not. Some studies have found that the

learning of students identified as being average or low has not been harmed by their placement in homogeneous groups. However, many studies have found the learning of average and slow students to be negatively affected by homogeneous placements.

The net result of all these studies of the relationship of tracking and academic outcomes for students is a conclusion contrary to the widely held assumptions about it. We can be fairly confident that bright students are *not* held back when they are in mixed classrooms. And we can be quite certain that the deficiencies of slower students are *not* more easily remediated when they are grouped together. And, given the evidence, we are unable to support the general belief that students learn best when they are grouped together with others like themselves.

From: Oakes, 1985

POSTSCRIPT

The changing face of the U.S. school population brings to the forefront the issue of **tracking**, or grouping by likeness, usually ability. Tracking is a common practice in public schools in the 1990s. The questions are: Does tracking work? Do students achieve more or less if they are placed with students of like ability? It is clear that Nevi and Oakes disagree.

In April 1991 the issue of tracking was brought before the Committee on Labor and Human Resources of the United States Senate. The committee attempted to determine whether Title VI was being adequately implemented and enforced by the Office for Civil Rights of the Department of Education, but was unable to come to a conclusion and determined only to improve their monitoring practices. A major question has to do with the possibility that tracking leads to "with-in school discrimination" in that a disproportionate number of minority students are in low-ability tracks. This issue is a complicated and continuing one as we attempt to educate all students in the U.S. melting pot.

CROSS-CULTURAL PERSPECTIVE

Immigrant Diversity

A widely divergent immigrant school population across the United States has led to an astonishing array of social and cultural problems in the classroom. The solutions to these problems have been equally varied. The following excerpt illustrates just a few.

Celebrating Diversity: Brookline, Massachusetts

An interesting mix of immigrant students has long given the Brookline school system an international character. Last year, for example, Joan Tieman's third-grade class included children from Japan, China, the Soviet Union, Iran, Bangladesh, Korea, and Turkey.

Last year [1989] also marked the beginning of a major trend in Brookline classrooms: a wave of immigrant Soviet children, here now as a result of *glasnost* and the continued persecution of Jews in the Soviet Union. "This year, we're expecting as many, if not more, as we had last year," explains teacher Sima Kirsztajn, an English as a Second Language (ESL) teacher at Brookline's K–8 Edith Baker School. This immigration of people from the countries of the former USSR is likely to continue as they face economic strife.

How do Brookline teachers welcome these new students?

"First, you have to understand why they came," explains Tieman, who teaches at the Amos Lawrence School. "These families have come here to be free, and for their children to be safe from persecution. Most of them had no idea until just before they came that they were going to leave their homes and friends. Some children had toys confiscated at the airport; some were strip searched.

"Many of the Russian parents are educated professionals who now must start over from scratch, often in a new occupation," adds Kirsztajn. "It's very hard for many of them. All their hopes are in their children. And most families have just one child. So all those hopes are on that child."

Bambie Goode, an ESL teacher from the Driscoll School in Brookline, notes that while they receive some support from community groups, most Soviet families come with nothing. "The first thing many parents do is learn English or improve their English. Others are already fluent," says Goode. "The children range in their adaptation. Older kids who speak some English tend to sparkle; younger kids are less comfortable. For the younger students, the move [to America] may be even more difficult, more inexplicable."

ESL pullout and bilingual classes offer the Soviet children a "safe place where they can come—nobody expects them to understand language that's above their heads," Goode adds.

"Compared with the schools in Russia, classes here are small," explains Kirsztajn. "And older kids are no longer being teased, taunted, and poked by anti-Semitic classmates." But the adjustment to a new school culture is not always smooth, the teachers note. Schools in the Soviet Union tend to be more formal with set seating patterns and an emphasis on whole-group instruction and participation.

One strategy Goode finds successful with her ESL classes is storytelling. A child tells a native folktale first in his or her own language, then in English. The first telling allows kids to concentrate on fluency and dramatic effects, giving Goode an opportunity to see a different side of the child—a more confident, more animated side. It also "celebrates the notion that we do have this diversity of languages here, so let's hear how the language sounds. The more language diversity in the class, the more fun it is," she says. "It's such a feast for the ears."

Kirsztajn starts the day by writing letters to the children and exchanging responses in class. "It begins a dialogue with the child and gets him or her writing." She also uses ESL "jazz chants"—rap-like, content-rich, rhythmic sayings.

Joan Tieman advocates journal writing to get kids to express themselves and relate their experiences. "Some children are afraid to risk writing something or saying something unless it's perfect. That's why I like journals. Children are not as fearful because I haven't marked up their writing." She also tries to find a book in the child's native language—even if that means borrowing one from a parent—so the child has something familiar in the classroom. In addition, Tieman does not discourage kids from speaking their native languages at home.

"The most important thing for classroom teachers is to really respect the child's culture," she says. "I'm not so sure that we all understood that several years ago. It's also very important for the other children to learn why and where and how the child has come, and how hard it is to be new. All the children come anxious, especially the non-English speakers, so I allow all children, when they first come, to write in their native languages—even though I don't understand them—to help ease their fear.

"The kids really learn so much from each other," Tieman continues. "Children will applaud when a classmate achieves a goal." Tieman also encourages flexible and voluntary groupings for review and practice in her regular classroom. "Children are much more likely to join a group if they know they're not stuck in it," she explains.

And what do the immigrant families think of American education? "The parents have said to me that here in the United States their children have learned to think, analyze, and discuss—that's interesting," says Kirsztajn.

Creating a Safe Learning Environment: Dearborn, Michigan

Of the 2,700 students in bilingual classes in the Dearborn public school system, 1,800 speak Arabic, according to Wageh Saad, head of the district's bilingual program. New students arrive each year, the majority of whom are Lebanese, Palestinian, Saudi, and Yemeni. But children from Romania, Italy, Greece, Albania, and Spain are also arriving in Dearborn.

The unrest in Lebanon has had an effect on many of the children, notes preschool teacher Maria Ali: "I work with parents a lot, giving them make-and-takes [projects that they can take with them] and showing them techniques for playing with their children. A lot of these parents really don't know how to play. They grew up in war-torn areas and were pressed into adult roles. Everything in this country is so foreign to them—even going to the grocery store, things we take for granted."

Ali recalls one girl who had been in the United States only a short while when school pictures were taken. When the camera flashed, the girl started screaming. The flash seemed like the bombs she remembered from Lebanon.

It's especially important to consider the soul healing involved with kids who are refugees, notes ESL teacher Maura Sedgeman. "You can do that just by giving them the opportunity to talk, to paint, to draw in a safe environment, maybe in their own language. You have to be ready for unexpected triggers, too." The camera flash was such a trigger. "A lot of it is just letting kids talk it out, just listening," she says.

Because many of the immigrant children are Shiite Moslems, cultural adjustments can be especially complex. Dearborn educators who are not Moslems often work with mosques to find solutions when traditional American school practices conflict with religious beliefs, notes Sedgeman. For example, in some schools, girls and boys have separate physical-education classes, pork is not served in the cafeteria, and school activities adjust to kids' low energy levels during *Ramadan*, a month when many Moslems fast from sun up to sun down.

Other adjustments are more individual. Some families' religious beliefs forbid the making of human images, so those children may not have their photos taken; some religions ban singing when there has been a death in the family. Teachers must then find other ways for those children to participate in a class activity.

"You have to take your cues from the child," notes Sedgeman, "and not insist on something until you've found out if the reluctance has a cultural foundation."

From: Harbaugh, 1990, 45–47

(those with between 7,500 and 937,000 students) were black (40 percent), followed by white (34 percent), Hispanic (21 percent), and Asian (5 percent) (1990).

The primary implication for schools and teachers of the decline in rural school-aged population is that there will be fewer jobs for new teachers in many rural school districts, and more in urban schools. Because more than half of all urban schoolchildren are minority students (if we define minority as non-white), a large percentage of new teachers, most of whom will be white (94 percent in 1988), will be teaching students with whom they don't share an identity. Since new urban teachers must learn to successfully interact with the students they will teach, Martin Haberman in *Preparing Teachers for Urban Schools* (1988) suggests that colleges must provide a minimum of at least 200 pre-student-teaching hours in the schools and that at least part of this time should be spent working with minority students who need extra help in regular school subjects. He also suggests that pre-student teachers should conduct after-school activities with urban youngsters. According to Haberman, 95 percent of students entering teaching cite a desire to help students build self-esteem as a reason for teaching; 81 percent say they love children. Haberman suggests that these are not sufficient reasons for teaching in an urban setting.

> Successful urban teachers are able to teach effectively whether their pupils are lovable or not; and they are able to teach students who may not demonstrate gratitude or affection in return. Preservice students and beginning teachers must be disabused of the notion that love is the basis of instruction. . . . [T]here is an extremely strong case to support the contention that how people feel about themselves is a function of the situations in which they find themselves and not in some persisting inner state called the "self-concept." Finally, the cumulated craft wisdom of successful urban teachers supports the premise that how pupils feel about themselves is a *consequence* of successful school experience, not a *prerequisite* condition for learning. . . . Urban schools will chew up and spit out novice teachers who begin with the notion of love as the basis for relating to pupils or who believe that students' lack of achievement or misbehavior is a function of low self-concept. (1988, 29–30)

MOTIVATION TOWARD SCHOOL

According to a survey done by Harris and Associates of 1,208 teachers and 2,700 students in grades four through twelve, *How Teachers and Students View Their Schools, the Learning Process, and Each Other,* 92 percent of the students report they want to do as well as they can in school and 58 percent are enthusiastic about what they learn (Metropolitan Life Insurance Company, 1988). John Goodlad (1984) found that students in grades four through high school were most interested in the arts, physical education, and vocational education because they had the largest decision-making role in these subjects; "they liked to do activities that involved them actively and in which they worked with others" (p. 115). Students conversely indicated less interest in English, mathematics, social studies, and science. Perhaps this is because when Goodlad visited classrooms he found a great deal of telling, explaining, and questioning as well as a great deal of passive seatwork in these classes. In the arts, physical education, and vocational education, on the other hand, Goodlad observed demonstrations, showing, modeling, acting, constructing, and carrying out of projects (p. 115). He suggests that the students' level of activity may be one reason why they do or do not respond positively to a subject. Allowing them to be more actively involved in all subjects may improve motivation.

Susan Mernit, in *Instructor*, states that "today's kids find themselves with more unsupervised time on their hands than their counterparts did a generation ago" (1990, 41). They spend much of this time, like Bianca in the opening anecdote, watching television. Children between the ages of five and twelve watch an average of four to six hours of television per day and actually spend less time doing homework than watching television. According to the 1990 National Assessment of Educational Progress, 34 percent of all fourth graders say they spend 30 minutes or less on homework each day; 41 percent of eighth graders spend one hour or less on homework per day.

Interests of Today's Students

The 1990 NAEP survey also found that most students under the age of twelve like to read. The majority of fourth graders surveyed say they read at home, own at least twenty books, take books out of the library each week, and tell their friends about books they enjoy.

Although more and more students compete in sports, most nonathletes do little to remain physically fit, according to a 1985 fitness study conducted for the President's Council on Physical Fitness by Guy Reiff of the University of Michigan. In the study, more than 18,000 students, ages six to seventeen, were tested in nine different fitness tasks. It found that 50 percent of girls and 30 percent of boys between the ages of six and twelve could not run a mile in less than 10 minutes; 55 percent of girls between six and twelve could not do a single pullup and 40 percent of boys could do only one. The study also found that 40 percent of boys could not touch their toes.

These results reveal potential health hazards for young people. Forty percent of five- to eight-year-olds have at least one risk factor for heart disease, according to the President's Council on Physical Fitness. One-third of children over the age of twelve have elevated blood cholesterol levels, according to the American Academy of Pediatrics. The American Heart Association reports that today's children have more fatty streaks in their heart arteries than did their counterparts in the 1960s. The results of these and other fitness studies suggest that secondary physical education programs should develop a curriculum of physical fitness and lifetime sports skills rather than focus on competitive sports (Hill, Leslie, and Snider 1991).

Increasingly, students seem to be concerned with money. Children between the ages of four and twelve together saved a total of $2.6 billion in 1988, 30 percent of it from earnings and allowance. This is a marked increase from the $500 million children of the same age group saved in 1984. However, these children also spend more than they save; in 1989, they spent an average of $6.2 billion of their own money to buy snacks, candy, and toys. (Mernit 1990).

In 1988, it was estimated that one-third, or 7.7 million, of fourteen- to nineteen-year-olds worked at jobs as diverse as cooks, janitors, and typists. The implications of the large number of secondary school students who have jobs are both positive and negative. Teachers worry that many students who work

Some teenagers who work may find motivation to succeed in their school work through their jobs. They learn what skills are necessary to compete in the marketplace, how to be responsible, and how to organize their time. Other teens may find too many work hours interfere with their completion of homework and their concentration in school. This student is a cashier at McDonald's in the Minneapolis/St. Paul International Airport.

put a greater value on their jobs than on their educations. Teachers point out that jobs provide immediate gratification, a paycheck. And, since many adolescents have difficulty thinking about long-term goals, the immediate gratification displaces the long-term goals of educational achievement. Moreover, students who work, often long hours after school, have difficulty staying awake and focusing on the content of the subject and have difficulty completing homework because of the number of hours they spend on the job.

On the other hand, many students find a motivation to succeed in school through their work. They see firsthand the kinds of education they need to be successful on the job. They see how adults deal with the problems of the workplace—juggling families and work, negotiating with the boss, and dealing with customers. They learn to deal with people and are trained in the use of equipment. They learn the importance of being on time and doing a good job. They develop a commitment to something beyond themselves. For some students, it's the job that keeps them in school. Others discover new educational and vocational aspirations through the job. Some employers require students to remain in school and get good grades; some even provide scholarships for students who worked during high school and continue on during college or technical school.

Teachers who can use the world of work to enliven and supplement the world of the classroom can help students realize the positive long-term values of their jobs. For example, a social studies teacher in Ohio did a unit on values and ethics in the workplace. She had employers of her students come into the classroom and discuss work-related ethical issues and values they expect to see in employees. The students who worked kept a journal about ethical issues that arose on the job. One student wrote about finding a $20 bill on the floor in the restaurant in which she worked. She gave the money to the manager in case the customer who lost it returned. Several days later she asked the manager if the customer had returned, and he denied that she had ever given him the $20. Should she tell her employer? Would he believe her or the manager? If the manager found out she told the employer, would he make her life unbearable? What would she do if she found something else of value in the restaurant? Did she want to work for a manager who was a liar and a thief? She decided to tell her employer, quit her job, and seek another one. Many valuable lessons were learned by these students through sharing and discussing ethical issues such as this one in the classroom.

Values of Today's Students

A survey of 410 elementary students conducted by the American Student Council Association in Alexandria, Virginia, revealed that despite America's many social problems, most of today's children have traditional values. They are concerned about social issues; 80 percent think it's important to volunteer for community service, 43 percent of their schools' student councils work on community projects. Forty-five percent of the students believe that crime and drugs will be the major problems they will face when they grow up, and 32 percent claim that good health will be most important to them as adults.

Eighty-two percent of the elementary students surveyed say they believe in God. Forty percent pray daily, and 33 percent say they have had a significant religious experience.

A 1990 Girl Scouts Survey on the Beliefs and Moral Values of America's Children indicated that the vast majority of children have special adults in their lives. Most, 95 percent, report that the special adults are their parents. Sixty-five percent have extended family members who serve the role of adult mentor; 42 percent have a teacher or coach who fills this role. Thirty percent have an adult neighbor who is special in their lives, 22 percent a minister or rabbi; and 19 percent a social worker.

Worries of Today's Students

Despite the adult perception that young people are carefree and have no worries, several studies have proved otherwise. In the 1990 Girl Scouts survey, five thousand boys and girls between the fourth and twelfth grades were asked which social expectations create the most pressure for them, and in a study of high school seniors by social psychologist Lloyd Johnston of the University of Michigan (1986), students reported that they have many worries.

An examination of the results of these two studies shows that most student concerns relate to personal achievements and success. However, both groups have concerns about social problems such as abuse of drugs and contracting AIDS.

TABLE 10-2

Pressures of Today's Students

4th–12th grade students	High school seniors
Obedience to parents/teachers	Having a good marriage and family life
Getting good grades	Choosing a career/finding steady work
Not taking drugs	Doing well in school
Preparing for the future	Being successful in line of work
Earning money	Having strong friendships
Fitting in	Paying for college
	The country going down hill
	Making a lot of money
	Finding a purpose, a meaning to life
	Contracting AIDS

From: Girl Scouts of the United States of America, *Girl Scouts Survey on the Beliefs and Moral Values of America's Children* (1990); Reprinted by permission of Girl Scouts of America.

Adults generally perceive youth as a carefree time and school to be the best years of one's life. Students, however, have many concerns, not the least of which is succeeding in school.

It is also interesting to compare the overall concerns of U.S. students with those of a specific ethnic group. For example, Valerie Ooka Pang has studied the concerns of Asian American immigrants. These students represent highly diverse ethnic groups: Cambodian, Chinese, East Indian, Filipino, Guamanian, Hawaiian, Hmong, Indonesian, Japanese, Korean, Laotian, Samoan, Vietnamese, Bangladeshi, Bhutanese, Bornean, Burmese, Celebesian, Cernan, Indochinese, Iwo-Jiman, Javanese, Malayan, Maldivian, Nepali, Okinawan, Sikkimese, Singaporean, and Sri Lankan. These Asian immigrants make up the fastest growing minority group in the United States. From 1970 to 1980, the Asian population in the United States grew by 143 percent. The concerns of Asian American students focus on conflicts between parental expectations of success and their own desires (see table 10.3).

Teachers need to understand the problems of immigrant students and to acquire a global view of the U.S. society so that myths about ethnic cultures and false generalizations about them are eliminated. Non-minority students should understand that even within an ethnic group there are many differences—such as language, culture, tradition, religion, education, aspirations—which result in differing needs. They must recognize the ethnic students' frustration, depression, and desperation and should consider instituting programs to help Asian American students and their parents deal with conflicting academic values. At the same time, schools should work with students to help them become a part of the U.S. school community.

TABLE 10-3

Worries of Asian Immigrant Students

Parental expectations for high academic achievement

"Model minority" myth/myth of homogeneity of ethnic
   population

Participation in peer group conversations

Conflict between parental academic values and participation in
   sports and other extracurricular activities

Ethnic prejudice (name-calling)

Examinations/Tests

Note: not rank ordered

From: V. Ooka Pang, *Asian American Children: A Diverse Population* (1990).

Asian immigrant students are just as concerned as American students are about fitting in and succeeding academically, but have the added concern that their parents have high expectations of academic achievement that might be in conflict with the emphasis on sports and other activities in the culture of the United States.

In 1988, 71.1 percent of the school population who had entered ninth grade four years earlier graduated with their class. This was a 1.4 percent increase from the graduation rate in 1982. The highest graduation rates were in Minnesota, 90.9 percent; Wyoming, 88.3 percent; North Dakota, 88.3 percent; Montana, 87.3 percent; Iowa, 85.8 percent; and Nebraska, 85.4 percent. The states with the lowest graduation rates were Florida, 58 percent; Georgia, 61 percent; Louisiana, 61.4 percent; New York, 62.3 percent; South Carolina, 64.6 percent; Texas, 65.3 percent; Alaska, 65.5 percent; California, 65.9 percent; North Carolina, 66.7 percent; and Mississippi, 66.9 percent (National Governors Association 1990, 35).

> **Graduation Rates**

According to the National Center for Education Statistics, the black male dropout rate, although still higher than the white male dropout rate, had declined significantly since 1969, when 11 percent of black males dropped out of school. In 1987, 6.2 percent of black males dropped out of school compared to 4.6 percent of all white students and 9.5 percent of all Hispanic students.

One of the reasons for decreases in the dropout rate is that many programs designed to work with at-risk students have been implemented. According to the National School Boards Association report *A Survey of Public Education in the Nation's Urban School Districts* (1989), half of the urban school districts have programs for at-risk students. At-risk students are defined as those who may be classified as or who are involved with one or more of the following:

• Substance abuse
• Suicide attempt/depression/low self-esteem
• Child abuse (physical, emotional, verbal, or sexual)
• Poverty

FIGURE 10-4

Dropout Rates From Grades 10–12 by Race/Ethnicity, and Sex: 1968–1987 (3-Year Average)

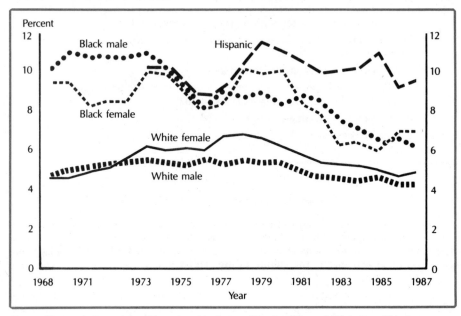

From: National Center for Education Statistics, *The Condition of Education. Vol. I: Elementary and Secondary Education* (1990), 21.

There are many reasons why students drop out of school or finish their education late. Minorities, those living in poverty, and substance abusers are the students most at risk for dropping out of school. Since special programs have been implemented in many schools, particularly for black males, their dropout rates have declined significantly.

- Child of alcohol or substance abuser
- Illiteracy
- A migrant life-style
- School dropout
- Sexual activity/pregnancy
- Crime
- Minority
- Student with disability

(Helge 1990)

Indications that the dropout rate is declining also can be found in the encouraging statistic that, although 17 percent of sophomores dropped out of school in 1980, almost half returned to receive a high school diploma or equivalency certificate by 1986. See figure 10.4 for a graph of the event dropout rates from grades ten through twelve. An event dropout rate measures the proportion of students who drop out during a twelve-month period (see chapter 13).

One major challenge for schools and teachers is to prevent students from dropping out of school. Special programs for at-risk students may be one potential solution to the problem. Ernest Boyer in *High School* (1983) states that dropout prevention must begin as early as the third grade. He suggests giving remedial help to students who are deficient, organizing alternative schools for at-risk students, putting at-risk students into small and highly structured groups with close student-teacher relationships, providing them with regular access to a counselor, and getting them in touch with community colleges. Other options, suggests N. L. Gage in his summary of programs that work, *Dealing with the Dropout Problem* (1990), include vocational programs that remove potential dropouts from traditional school settings, place them in new environments, and allow them to apply their academic learning to real-life situations. Connecting these programs with paid employment is also helpful. Gage also suggests that low student-teacher ratios are needed so that a bond between teacher and student can form. With this mutual trust it is more likely that at-risk students will stay in school and graduate.

10.1 POINTS TO REMEMBER

- The typical public school is heterogeneous in terms of its student population. The demographic reality of the U.S. population is that it is increasingly minority and immigrant.
- Nearly 10 percent of all students in public and private schools are classified as special education, meaning they are learning or physically disabled, emotionally disturbed, or mentally retarded. Students from numerous ethnic and racial groups, many of them speaking English as a second language and living in poverty, bring a multiplicity of problems into the classroom.
- Although most students are motivated to do well in elementary school, they lose much motivation as they enter high school. Students are more motivated in classes in which they are actively involved.
- Students at the same age levels have similar interests based on their development. Today's students watch more television than students of previous generations. They also read less and do less homework than their counterparts from earlier decades. Students' values tend to be rather traditional. Most report a belief in God and value the importance of adults in their lives. Today's students also have many worries about getting good grades, avoiding drugs, and making money.
- Dropout rates are a problem in many states. The District of Columbia, for example, graduates barely half of its high school students.

PROFILE OF A CLASS

Even in classrooms in which ethnic and racial homogeneity are the norm, the differences among individual students are extensive. The profile of the sixth-grade class in table 10.4 is from a middle school in a racially and economically homogeneous, middle class neighborhood near a small city. Less than 1 percent are minorities and at least 50 percent have attended local schools since kindergarten. All students, except transfers, come to this school from the local K–5 schools and are placed in homerooms, using random selection. Students spend approximately three hours of the school day with the homeroom teacher who, in addition to teaching, records attendance, issues report cards, records standardized test scores, and makes parental contacts. They represent an academically high group as measured on achievement tests. There are twenty-eight students in this class, including four who transferred in, one from a local

(continued on p. 332)

TABLE 10-4

Profile of a Middle School Class

I. BACKGROUND

Special students

Identified as gifted	Females	0
	Males	3
	Total	3
Resource students (learning disabled)	Females	0
	Males	0
	Total	0
Students receiving services	Female	1
	Males	0
	Total	1
	TOTAL	4

Average daily attendance in days absent[1]

0–5 days	Females	4
	Males	6
	Total	10
6–10 days	Females	5
	Males	5
	Total	10
11–15 days	Females	1
	Males	2
	Total	3
16–20 days	Females	1
	Males	0
	Total	1
Over 20 days	Females	1
	Males	0
	Total	1
	TOTAL	25

Activities, concerns, attitudes

Extracurricular	Females	3
	Males	5
	Total	8
Poor health	Females	3
	Males	2
	Total	5
Behavior problems	Females	0
	Males	2
	Total	2
Like school	Females	7
	Males	10
	Total	17
Dislike school	Females	6
	Males	10
	Total	16

II. PARENTAL INFORMATION

Occupation

Blue-collar	20
White collar	5
Unemployed	2
Unknown	1
Total	28

Family dynamics

Single parent	Females	5
	Males	5
	Total	10
Living with non-parent family member	Females	2
	Males	0
	Total	2
Two parents (including step-parents)	Females	6
	Males	10
	Total	16

Involvement in school functions (PTA, open house, visiting days, volunteering)

Uninvolved	14
Very little involvement	9
Some involvement	4
Very involved	1
Total	28

Involvement in academic/ behavioral program[4]

Uninvolved	6
Very little involvement	13
Some involvement	4
Very involved	5
Total	28

III. STUDENT ACADEMIC ACHIEVEMENT

Standardized test results (California Achievement Test—national percentile scores—math, reading, language, spelling)[2]

Below 25th % (repeating 6th grade)	Females	0
	Males	1
	Total	1
26th–50th %	Females	3
	Males	3
	Total	6
51st–75th %	Females	1
	Males	4
	Total	5
76th–90th %	Females	2
	Males	2
	Total	4
91st–99th %	Females	5
	Males	3
	Total	8
	TOTAL	24

Mathematics grouping[3]

Below average	Females	0
	Males	4
	Total	4
Average	Females	3
	Males	6
	Total	9
Above average	Females	8
	Males	5
	Total	13
	TOTAL	26

Reading levels

Below grade level	Females	1
	Males	0
	Total	1
Low/on grade level	Females	1
	Males	5
	Total	6
Average/on grade level	Females	6
	Males	2
	Total	8
High/on grade level	Females	8
	Males	5
	Total	13
	TOTAL	28

Retention status

Students retained previous years	Females	0
	Males	2
	Total	2
Students retained current year	Females	0
	Males	0
	Total	0
Students required to attend summer school	Females	1
	Males	0
	Total	1
	TOTAL	3

Overall student achievement (yearly grades on standardized tests and teacher observation)

Below average	Females	3
	Males	3
	Total	6
Average	Females	5
	Males	9
	Total	14
Above average	Females	5
	Males	3
	Total	8
	TOTAL	28

[1]No record for three transfers

[2]No scores available for four students

[3]Information unavailable on two students who transferred

[4]Attending conferences, requesting make-up work, monitoring school progress, contacting teacher by letter/phone

From: Kim Wave, Enka Middle School, Buncombe County Schools, Asheville, North Carolina.

Every class assumes a personality of its own based on the background and performance of its members. For example, in this class, many students are above average in both reading and mathematics; about the same number like school or dislike it; most parents are uninvolved in school functions.

independent school, and three from out of state. As you read Table 10.4 (p. 330), notice the differences in such things as the students' grades, reading levels, mathematical abilities, standardized test scores, health, attitudes toward school, and family dynamics. How are these differences likely to affect the classroom?

In spite of the relative homogeneity of this middle school class, it is obvious that the students' diversity will affect instruction in the classroom. For example, in general academic achievement, eight of the students score above the 91st percentile on a standardized achievement test, whereas six students score below the 50th percentile. Similarly, in specific academic areas, seven students are either below grade level or just at grade level in reading; whereas thirteen students are at the high grade level in reading. In mathematics achievement, thirteen students are average or below average, and thirteen are above average. These differences in academic achievement and performance require classroom teachers to adjust instruction to meet the needs of individual students.

The involvement of the parents also affects life in the classroom. Some volunteer to work as tutors and special classroom assistants. Others help with special projects and evening activities. Some parents, however, never attend school events, and a few do not even respond to special requests from the teacher. It is important that the classroom teacher understand which parents are willing and able to be involved in the school and which are willing but have limitations that keep them from becoming involved. The teacher can continue to encourage parental involvement and interest through newsletters, personal letters of communication about the students, invitations to special events, phone calls, and even home visits.

THE LIFE OF A STUDENT

During a single day in the life of a teacher as many as 150 students may pass through the classroom door. Even though it may be difficult, teachers should know as much about their students as possible.

They can do this by reflecting on what it was like to be a child, a preteen, or a teenager. However, this perspective is limited by time, place, and individual experiences. What it was like to be a child growing up in suburban Connecticut may be different from what it was like growing up in the rural South or the ghettos of a large midwestern city. Although most teachers can empathize with students who are disabled or who do not speak English, they would, of course, find it difficult to understand another's experiences completely.

Similarities of Agemates

Teachers frequently comment that despite significant individual differences, students seem similar in many respects. It's not unusual, for example, to hear a teacher say, "If one more student asks how to do that assignment, I'll scream." Frequently, similarities in how students think and act are a result of their age and developmental characteristics. The physical, intellectual, emotional, social, and moral characteristics of early adolescents and later teens have been studied and common developmental patterns seem to emerge.

In fact, a special issue cover story in *Newsweek*, "The New Teens: What Makes Them Different" (1990), contends, in a somewhat humorous classification, that teenagers can be divided into four groups: malljammers, house hoppers, video vogues, and neonormals. Although there are differences in terms of the activities and interests of these distinct groups, there are far more similarities. For example, almost all today's teens like movies and television, but the types of programs they select differ. All teens are consumers, buying clothes, records, and videos. However, what they choose to purchase within these categories differs. For example, in 1990, according to *Newsweek*, malljammers favored Paula Abdul, the movie *Pretty Woman*, the television show "America's Funniest Home Videos," cruising, and Dick Tracy T-shirts. The house hoppers selected Technotronic, the movie *House Party*, the television show "The Simpsons," line dancing, and suede Fila hightops. The video vogues liked Madonna, the film *Blue Velvet*, the television show "Twin Peaks," thrift shopping, and nose rings, and the neonormals selected the Grateful Dead, the movie *Driving Miss Daisy*, the television program "Doogie Howser, M.D.," volleyball, and Gap pocket T-shirts (Gelman, 11–17).

Teachers also recognize significant differences in how students of the same age behave and learn. "I can't believe these kids are the same age and the same ability level. The second period students are so enthusiastic, so eager to learn. I hate it when the bell rings and third period arrives. Third period students are so impressed with themselves, so cruel to each other." Differences occur because each group of students is made up of individuals, and, even if the classroom, teacher, and subject are the same, there are subtle variations in the physical and social environment from one class hour to the next. The personalities of the students are affected by the differing environments, each class acquiring its own individual personality much as each family does.

Differences of Agemates

HOW STUDENTS DEVELOP

Psychologists have documented the developmental characteristics of human beings that help explain both why agemates are similar and why they are different. First we will discuss the cognitive, needs, psychosocial, and moral development of humans as outlined by Piaget, Maslow, Erikson, and Kohlberg and then present several student diaries. In reading the diaries, see if you can determine which stage of development the student is manifesting.

Jean Piaget, a Swiss psychologist, was the first to document the cognitive growth of humans. He believed that children learn because their developing mental structures are challenged by what they observe and experience in the environment, which in turn results in the development of a more complex mental structure or scheme. He defined **scheme** as an organized pattern of behavior or thought that children formulate as they attempt to interact with their environments, parents, teachers, and agemates. By relating new experiences to an existing scheme through assimilation, a child develops a sense of **equilibrium,** or balance. Or, a child may accommodate for a lack of equilibrium by modifying an existing scheme or developing a new one.

    Piaget believed that there are two processes required in cognitive development. The first, **assimilation,** allows the child to integrate a new stimulus into

Cognitive Development: Piaget

existing schemes. For example, a child learns that there are dogs that look different from his dog but are still dogs. He has assimilated the concept of different breeds of dogs into his scheme of dog.

However, if a new concept cannot be assimilated, a scheme must be changed or a new scheme must be developed. Piaget calls this **accommodation**. For example, a child has learned that dogs and cats are pets. He has a pet dog and plays with him regularly; when he pets the dog, it wags its tail. One day when the child is walking with his mother they see a dog across the street. The child says, "Doggy, doggy," and moves toward the dog. The dog runs to the child, jumps up on him, and knocks him to the ground. The child begins to cry. There is a need to reestablish equilibrium in his cognitive structure; his existing scheme has been challenged, and, therefore, he must accommodate the new experience by developing a new scheme.

Piaget postulated several recognizable stages of development that follow a sequential but uneven or zigzag pattern. These stages begin at birth and continue through adulthood.

Sensorimotor Period

According to Piaget, the earliest period in the child's development, between the ages of birth and two years, is the **sensorimotor period**. Marked by the development of reflexes and responses, it involves the practicing and experimentation of motor responses which are increasingly complex. Perception patterns usually begin between eight and twelve months. By the end of this period, the child recognizes that an object may exist even if he can't see it, a skill called **object permanence**.

Preoperational Period

The second stage of cognitive development is the **preoperational period**, which occurs between two and seven years of age. At this stage, children acquire language and learn to represent the environment with objects and symbols. At the earliest period of this stage, children infuse their inanimate world with conscious attributes, behavior that Piaget referred to as **animism**. For example, the child plays with dolls and stuffed animals and gives them human characteristics, or talks about "the man in the moon." Some children develop imaginary playmates and create an entire world around these imaginary friends. Children at this stage are **egocentric**; they see the world as revolving around themselves. They focus on their own pleasures and pains and are unaware of others around them. By the latter period of this stage, children can group objects into classes according to their similarities. However, they are frequently unable to discuss the features common to a given class of objects. Hence, they can think intuitively and solve problems, but often they cannot explain the steps they used in solving the problem.

Concrete Operational Period

The **concrete operational period**, ages seven to eleven, is characterized by an ability to solve problems through reasoning and thinking symbolically with words and numbers and by grouping into hierarchies by similarities. For example, Piaget suggests in *The Child's Conception of Number* (1952) that if a child at the preoperational stage is given twenty brown and two white wooden beads, the child will agree that all the beads are wooden and that twenty are brown and two are white. If the child is asked, "Are there more wooden beads or more brown beads?" the child is likely to answer that there are more brown beads. This is because the child can compare the classes of brown and white but cannot compare the subclass of brown beads to the larger class of wooden beads. However, at the concrete operational stage, the child will demonstrate the **principle of inclusion** and will respond that the class of brown beads is of necessity smaller than the class of wooden beads. Children at this stage are able to consider differences (nonbrown beads) as well as similarities and can reason about the relationships between classes and subclasses.

Children at the concrete operational stage can also order objects in a series. For example, they can group beads from large to small or small to large. Children at this stage also demonstrate the principle of **conservation**, the ability to recognize the difference between volume and size. If, for example, during the preoperational period you show a child a glass of water in a short, wide glass and pour that water into a tall, narrow glass, it is likely that the child will say that there is more water in the tall glass because she or he does not see the two containers as equivalent in volume. By the concrete operational period, the child recognizes that the amount of water is the same no matter what size container it is in. At this stage, children also show **reversal**, the ability to work a problem backward. In addition, concrete operational children **decenter**; they learn that their perspective is only one of many perspectives. They begin to understand the viewpoints of others.

Formal Operational Period

Finally, according to Piaget, humans enter the **formal operational period** between the age of eleven and adulthood. This stage is characterized by abstract, logical, hypothetical reasoning and systematic experimentation. They can think through the implications and complex relationships of ideas; they can approach problems by thinking through several possible solutions.

In spite of the importance of Piaget's work in cognitive development, he is the object of much criticism, primarily that cognitive development is more gradual than he had suggested (Flavel 1982) and that the age levels Piaget placed on the stages tend to be too high (Gelman and Gallistel 1978).

Development of Needs: Maslow

Psychologist Abraham Maslow developed a hierarchy to show graphically how a human meets individual needs; he or she must first meet one level of needs before achieving the next.

The lowest levels of needs are the **physiological** and **safety** needs. The individual must have food, health, warmth, and shelter before working toward the second level, which is represented by the **belonging or love** needs. The individual must feel wanted and loved before achieving the next level, the **esteem** needs, self-respect, achievement, and status. Once the individual feels personally confident, he or she can begin to seek the higher levels of needs called by Maslow **knowledge or understanding** and **aesthetics**. The need for knowledge is the need to understand one's environment while the need for aesthetics is the need for beauty. Once all these needs have been met, an individual may be able to attain the highest human need of **self-actualization**, reaching one's full human potential.

Generally an individual progresses upward on the needs hierarchy but it is also possible to progress downward. For example, if a child's parents divorce, she or he may feel alone and unwanted, causing the child to withdraw and/or seek attention from others rather than focus on learning.

It is also possible that striving to meet one set of needs may get in the way of meeting a higher set of needs. The adolescent who strives to be part of a peer group, even if that group violates the values the adolescent has been taught, may find it impossible to meet the higher level, esteem needs. It is difficult to feel good about one's self if behaviors are counter to personal beliefs.

Psychosocial Development: Erikson

Psychologist Erik Erikson became interested in the relationship between child-rearing and culture as a result of his interest in the work of psychologist Sigmund Freud. Erikson studied child-rearing practices in several societies and concluded that there were recurrent themes in emotional/social development even when the cultures differed. Erikson identified goals, concerns, accomplishments, and dangers which mark each stage from infancy to adulthood. According to Erikson, the stages are interdependent; accomplishments at any stage depend on how conflicts were resolved at earlier stages. If individuals successfully deal with a crisis at one stage, they have the foundation for dealing with a similar crisis at a subsequent stage (see table 10.5). Thus, an infant should learn trust in others in the first stage. If he or she is not loved adequately or cared for appropriately, then mistrust will develop instead and may be a problem for the individual throughout life.

Moral Development: Kohlberg

Psychologist Lawrence Kohlberg examined the moral development of the individual. He based his theory, in part, on Piaget's stages of cognitive development. Kohlberg believed that individuals develop moral reasoning in a pattern, passing through three levels of development, each with two stages.

The first level, **preconventional moral reasoning**, is characteristic of very young children. At this level, moral judgments are based on expectation of rewards or punishments. In stage I, rules are obeyed to avoid punishment; in stage II, compliance with rules is based on the expectation of reward.

Older children typically employ the second level of moral reasoning, **conventional moral reasoning**, basing their judgments on others' approval, family expectations, traditional values, the laws of society, and loyalty to country. At the first stage, behavior is predicated on the approval of others. At the second stage of this level, moral behavior is based on law and authority in an attempt to avoid guilt and formal censure. It is important to note that many people never move beyond this stage of moral reasoning.

The final level of the development of moral reasoning, is that of **postconventional moral reasoning**. In the first stage of postconventional moral reasoning, good is determined by socially agreed-upon standards of individual rights and democratically determined laws. In the final stage of postconventional reasoning, the individual possesses a universal ethical principle. "Good and right are matters of individual conscience and involve abstract concepts of justice, human dignity, and equality" (Kohlberg 1981, 409–412). This is a stage of moral development reached by few people.

It is important to note that the work of both Erikson and Kohlberg has been criticized because their research centered on the psychosocial and moral

TABLE 10-5

Erikson's Theory: Stages of Psychosocial Development

Psychosocial stage	Approximate age	Elements for positive outcomes
Trust v. mistrust	0–1 yr.	Infant's needs for nourishment, care, familiarity are met; parental responsiveness and consistency
Autonomy v. shame and doubt	Toddler period (1–2 yrs.)	Greater control of self in environment—self-feeding, toileting, dressing; parental reassurance, availability, avoidance of overprotection
Initiative v. guilt	Early childhood (2–6 yrs.)	Pursuing activity for its own sake; learning to accept without guilt that certain things are not allowed; imagination, play-acting adult roles
Industry v. inferiority	Elementary–Middle school (6–12 yrs.)	Discovery of pleasure in perseverance and productivity; neighborhood, school, and peer interaction becomes increasingly important
Identity v. role confusion	Adolescence	Conscious search for identity, built upon outcomes of previous crises
Intimacy v. isolation	Young adulthood	Openness and commitment to others in deepening relationships
Generativity v. stagnation	Young and middle adulthood	Having and nurturing children and/or involvement with future generations; productivity; creativity
Integrity v. despair	Later adulthood; old age	Consolidation of identity; sense of fulfillment; acceptance of death

From: Erikson, *Childhood and Society* (1963), 272, 273.

Erikson believed that human emotional and social development occurred in stages and that conflicts must be resolved for positive relationships to develop. Thus, if adolescents don't successfully find their identity in their teens, they are likely to be confused about their roles throughout their lives.

development of males. In "Adolescent Development Reconsidered" (1988), Carol Gilligan attempts to show "an alternative world view . . . [which] called attention to moral judgments that did not fit the definition of 'moral' and to self-descriptions at odds with the concept of 'self' " [in studies of moral development of male subjects only]. Gilligan found "two moral voices [male and female] signaled different ways of thinking about what constitutes a moral problem and how such problems can be addressed or solved" (p. xvii). The males focused primarily on justice and the females on justice and care and concern for others. She also suggests that these two modes of moral judgment might be related to modes of self-definition (p. 23).

SCHOOL FROM THE PERSPECTIVE OF STUDENTS

Although teachers can know a great deal about their students, they rarely have the opportunity to see the school day from the students' perspective. To give you some insight into the lives of students, we asked several, at various grade levels from different geographic regions, to keep diaries.

A First Grader: Sarah

Sarah Bachinski is a first grader in a small Vermont city. Sarah's account of each school day is primarily factual. She provides us with few details, particularly in the earlier entries. This may be because Sarah's written vocabulary is limited. Sarah wrote the diary entries herself; the "creative" spelling has not been changed.

> Jan. 16: Monring—We wrote to are pen pels in North Carolina today. We wrote in our fun book. Thaey are books waht you wraht in and dare dare in.
> Affotarnon—We went to Sing a long. My clas Sang the Soing WaSh WaSh WaSh your handS. We did manth waht mrss. mory.
> Jan. 20: Friday—I red to radenise Conagrdn. Wan I got bake I wark on our garnd. Aftrnoon—Mr. Schwarz red a book to us. We did the math Bard.

By May, Sarah's descriptions give us a lot more information. Sarah is developing, growing intellectually, socially, and emotionally. She is learning many things and writing more fluently. It's also interesting to note that, with the exception of Mr. Schwarz's oral reading, all Sarah's comments relate to activities in which she is actively engaged.

> May 25: We fond a letter from Mr. Schwarz it siad I wold liKe you to write story problems. We Sang Down By the Bay. Mr. Schwarz riad The Trip by Ezra Jack Keats. Sh word. We made shadow boxs. We hade SSR Silent reading. One grop The Monster Pals Shared their flannel board Stories. 2nd graade came in to read to us. We hade library. We hade Gim. We had Math adding Two numbers. We used the blacklight and the numbers glowed.
> May 31: We made cards for Mrs. Dodd becass She is on crcs. We read books by Ezra Jack Keats and collages. We hade SSr. Mr. Schwarz did reading tests. We got ready for the field trip. We had storyproblems written by the class.
> June 1: We went to our filed trip. We hade fun. We huged trees. We went on trals. We hade lanh ther too. We iesprmt woder. We want on a nahtr hike togatter. We saw tepes. Thay were neht. We sow a Indin boat.

A Second Grader: Julie

Second-grader Julie Harvell kept her own diary. Julie goes to school in a suburban community in North Carolina. The details that Julie writes about school and how she reacts to it, compared to the lack of details and limited reactions in the early entries of Sarah's diary, show some interesting developmental changes that usually occur during the early elementary grades. In addition, note how much more concerned Julie is about her relationship to her friends than is Sarah, who never mentions a friend. This, too, is developmentally appropriate. Julie's "creative" spelling has been left as she wrote it. Notice how her spelling develops throughout the diary.

> Sept. 12: Today was a good day because we hade art. We leard a bought secondary colors. We had Math and did problems. In reading we sumerrized. In social studies we leard abought maps.

Elementary school students, for the most part, enjoy school, are enthusiastic about learning, and want to impress teachers and parents. These third graders wait patiently to enter another room.

Sept. 13: Today was sort of sort of day. Becaus at playtime me an Rachel wanted to talk privtley. And Rebecc and Amee wien't leave us alone. We hade music today. With therd grdrs. Brodon and Mike gote ther nams on the bord. You are nice Techs Ms. Galeason and Mrs. Denon.

Sept. 14: I was sapos to read today but Kean took to long I do not mind. We hade putis made. We hade math abought ghfsi bacly. We sarted a studd of dnoaisors. Today was a good day. Becas of picis. [The class had school pictures taken.]

Feb. 13: Today we sewed up harts. Tomorrow is Valentine's Day. In writing we learned how to make the captil D and S. At lunch I sat next to John and Brooke. After math the people that brought their valentines delivered them. Today is great.

Feb. 14: Today was great! We have no homework. In math all we had to do was eight problems. I got alot of valentines. It's my sisters birthday. In handwriting we learned the cusive captil S and G. [Julie wrote her "S" and "G" in cursive lettering.]

May 22: Today was an O.K. day. I wore some sandles to school and people kept stepping on my feet! What was good is that we got our year books and I got to go to the computer.

Jessica Condits is a fifth-grade student in a growing community on the east coast of Florida. Jessica's diary is filled with details, a concern about time, and the things she likes about school. Jessica, like Sarah and Julie, responds most favorably to learning in which she is actively involved. Her exact, vivid

A Fifth Grader: Jessica

description of the fifth grade field trip is particularly revealing. It is interesting to compare her report to Sarah's description of her first grade field trip. Also, notice that Jessica is concerned about her friends and how they are feeling. However, when one gets hurt, she is more concerned about celebrating her own birthday than about her friend's injury. This, of course, is developmentally appropriate for a ten-year-old.

Jan. 23: Everyday before school I work in the Library as an aide. I put books away and straighten them. At 8:40 the bell rings and I go to class. At 8:55 we listen to announcements on the intercom. Then at 9:00 we go to a special class (on Monday we have music). We played the sticks and the two tambourines. Music was fun.

After Music we go to the Computer Lab from 9:40 to 10:00. When we get back to class we work on spelling.

At 10:15–11:05 we change classes for reading. Then my class goes to science from 11:05–11:35. The other two classes—one goes to English and the other goes to Social Studies.

From 11:35–12:05 my class goes to English. Then we go back to class. I think it's fun to change classes because in reading I can see my other friends.

When we go back to the classroom we put our books down and get ready for lunch. We have lunch from 12:20–12:45. I like lunch because it's one of the times I can talk to my friends in my class.

On Monday we go to art from 12:50–1:25. Then we go back to our class to work on Social Studies and Math.

At 2:50 the bell rings and I go to the Library and put my books away. I can't wait until tomorrow because we will get our pen pal letters.

Jan. 26: Today was my birthday and we went to P.E. and my best friend hurt her ankle and she had to go home. My mom made a cake and I brought it to school and it was delicious. I had a fun day.

In social studies we did a play.

Jan. 27: Today our class didn't have a special class at 9:00.

After Computer Lab we went to an assembly on lungs. He had a laryngectomy. I got to use the devise they use to talk. I thought the assembly was interesting.

May 24: On Wednesday the whole fifth grade went on a river trip. There were 6 different stations. The first station my group went to was canoeing. We Canoed on part of the Indian River. At station 2 we tried to catch different creatures with a net. Next at station 3 we dug up sand and put it through a sifter to see what different creatures live in the sand. Then we went to station 4. We walked up into some water to see the 3 different kinds of mangroves. Some parts of the sand were squishy and we almost lost our shoes! At station 5 we went out on boats and saw different islands. At station 6 we learned how to clean fish and got to try crab. I didn't try any.

It was a fun day but my best friend and I were split up so one was in one group and one in the other.

That afternoon I didn't feel good so my mom took me to the doctor and I had a strep infection.

A Sixth Grader: Karen

Karen Hueber is in the sixth grade in a small city in upstate New York. In her diary she devotes a good bit of space to how she and others react to the school day. Notice how she contradicts herself about schoolwork: sometimes asking for more difficult work, frequently complaining about too much work. Karen is more concerned than the younger students about the feelings of others, including how her teachers feel about her, and about how others are reacting toward her and her peers. She, too, responds most favorably to schoolwork in which she is actively involved. She also writes at some length about her own academic success. In addition to worrying about whether the teachers will approve of her work, she is much more likely to speak positively about subjects in which she is successful. All these concerns are developmentally appropriate for the preadolescent student. The teachers' names have been changed in Karen's diary.

Oct. 31: I'm so excited about our class halloween party. I hope I have a good day. Cause I think the teachers are mad. Boy! I just handed in my reading. I didn't know we had to hand it in. We usually don't.

This social studies class is boring because everybody is slow at answering the questions. I'm sort of bored because my work is done. I hope Mrs. Lee doesn't give a big assignment in math, so I don't have a lot of homework. I'm nervous about the halloween party. But then again I'm excited. I wonder if Miss Cleaver is dressing up.

I wish Robbie would shut up.

Why does Mrs. Lee give such easy assignments. Yeah no homework. We don't have any more classes. Not even reading. I'm glad because I have computer club.

Nov. 2: I can't believe that almost all of the girls in the sixth grade are going to gym for activity day.

I hope Chris stays away from me.

Gym was great today. Oh no science.

I hope we don't have a lot of work today.

Oh great a sub. She is nice. I've had her before.

I wish everybody would be quiet.

I wish this class would move on.

I wish everybody would just sit down and shut up. Because I don't like it when teachers are mad because then they don't talk or explain anything and that is real hard to understand anything. I like it when teachers are friendly.

Uh oh math.

Boy that math was easy. I just hope that we don't have more.

I guess I have homework. I don't want to but I have to.

May 3: Today is probably going to be a bad day too. My stomach hurts too. Good start, huh.

I have never seen Mrs. Lee yell so loud. But she should not have yelled at Jake. But at least she apologized. Mrs. Lee must feel awful.

Mrs. Lee must be having a bad day. Or, the class is having a bad day. I'm confused.

Mr. Blue just came in with something that looked like PEP tests.

Maybe I was wrong, today wasn't so bad after all. But it wasn't so good either. Tomorrow will be better.

May 4: My science project looks really good.

I hope Mrs. Lee likes my project.

All right, she liked it.

That test was not too bad.

I was wrong today has been a good day. I said yesterday that it wasn't going to be a good day. I guess I don't know anything, do I?

That was the best math class we've had all year.

So far, not a lot of homework. But, if I have reading assignment then I might have a lot of homework. It all depends on the assignment.

Yeah! No homework! All right! Phew!

An Eighth Grader: Sandee

Sandee Cramer is an eighth grader in an independent school in Massachusetts. According to Sandee's homeroom teacher, she is a good, not outstanding, but enthusiastic student. Sandee writes only about her science class in this diary. Notice the reasons that she does not enjoy the class. She shows more discontent with school than the younger students. She is less accepting of what the teacher asks her to do. She tends to be more negative about school and places the blame for her lack of interest on her teacher. This is not only because the inactivity in the class bores her, but also because young adolescents are not yet developmentally aware of how their own behavior affects them and others. However, she is beginning to recognize that errors she makes are a result of her own effort. Sandee is developmentally typical. The names in this diary have been changed.

Feb. 13: Science Class 1:40–2:18

I am so bored, why doesn't Mr. Bridgers actually try to do something exciting. I am sick of the regular note taking and lectures. This class is so boring. I could fall asleep any time. Abby is sitting next to me, she looks as bored as I do. 2:10 only 8 more minutes. I'm starting to fall asleep. I hate Mr. Bridgers, he is so boring.

Feb. 14: Science—2:10–2:42

It is the last class of the day, thank God. I can't wait until it is over. Mr. Bridgers is so boring. This class might actually be fun if we did something. All we ever do is sit and build up our finger muscles by taking notes. Genes how exciting can they be, more than this. Finally the bell. I hate this class.

Feb. 16: Science, 8:55–9:36

First period, what a way to start the day, a test. We have our genetics test today, wonderful, just what I need. It isn't that long but each question counts for 20 points. I think I got a 60 or 80, mostly because of stupid mistakes. At least tests make the day go by faster.

A Ninth Grader: Darius

Darius Baker is a ninth-grade student in a magnet school in South Miami, Florida. He is more concerned with what he is doing in school than Sandee is. He tells us that he is "task person" and is going on a field trip to a T.V. station. Although he seems to be interested in much of what is going on in school, particularly as it relates to his magnet program, he, like the other early adolescents, is bored with traditional subjects such as geography. It is interesting to compare how much he writes about the field trip and how little he writes about geography and math. Darius is proud of his accomplishments. He takes his job as "task person" seriously and tells us that their broadcast is on now, "5–4–3–2–1 !!!!" He uses the slang of his generation, but is able to write quite well. However, at times he becomes careless and writes "to" for two and "there" for they are. This is typical of students of Darius's age.

Class 1, October 1, 1991

8:45 class started. I am task person for the week. They think I'm playing but I'm serious! I told them to be quiet, they keep talking, their names go down. The day's going by smooth, It seems as if it'll be a perfect day.

Class 2, October 1, 1991

9:40 class started second half of class one. I have to work on my group project. I like doing it because it contains music videos, I like rap videos.

Class 3, October 1, 1991

10:45 the 3rd class has started. Its a little dull now. Were about to color a map—of Egypt.—Mr. Parker's telling us the four directions N.S.E.W.

Class One/Two, Oct. 2-91

Its another beautiful day first period. I'm in broadcastin' now—It's quiet that's cool.
Class Three, Oct 2-91
Its alright today, better than yesterday. I think I'll go to the Afro Club meeting or library, if he let's me go — I know he will! He's nice!
Class 4, Oct 2
I'm chillin' in math—I had to assignment that cool there easy. Becide I'm workin' with someone I can associate with.
Class 1, Oct. 3
8:45 I'm still task person. Were doing newsroom, setting up for our broadcast. We are eating lunch, at ten thirty today. Due to a field trip. What kind of trip? To channel 23, its a spanish station. I don't know too much spanish— I dont know any spanish. We're gonna be an audience anyway—They're going to do a broadcast for us. Their camera, computers and newsrooms are busting! They make our school, want to do undercover work! We're back!!!!! Its sixth period now—Im in science our broadcast goes on now! 5 4 3 2 1 !!!!

Are These Students Typical?

If you look back at the earlier developmental characteristics of today's students, (pp. 333–337), you will see many of them reflected in these diaries. These students want to do well in school and are, for the most part, enthusiastic about what they do. They enjoy participating in schoolwork and are less enthusiastic about subjects in which they must sit and listen.

The students are not particularly interested in doing homework. Second-grader Julie says, "Today was great! We have no homework." However, several of the students, including Julie, mention specific books they are reading. In addition, the adults in their lives are important; the students are concerned about what their parents and teachers think of them. They are concerned about doing well in school and getting good grades.

Are the Students Developing?

It is clear that the students whose diaries appear above are learning and developing in ways representative of students their age.

First-grader Sarah's language makes remarkable gains in five months. By May she doesn't just tell us that Mr. Schwarz read us a book today, as she did in January, she tells us the book is by Ezra Jack Keats. Although Sarah may have hugged a tree in September, she wouldn't have told us so. However, by May she is telling us that she "huged trees" and made a card for Mrs. Dodd because she is on crutches. In spite of the fact that Sarah spells crutches "crcs," she is willing to attempt the word in order to put more detail into her writing. She is gaining confidence in herself. Sarah is also learning how to tell stories. Her May entries frequently cover an entire page and tell things like what the children did after Mr. Schwarz read to them.

We can also see Sarah's growth and development exhibited through her diary. For example, Sarah's success in learning how to use language allows her to write a word even when she knows she cannot spell it. Her language learning is helping her become more confident and independent. Sarah is growing developmentally as the first-grade year progresses.

Julie Harvell, who is in the second grade, is also learning what she has been taught. In September she spells "had" "hade" and "learned" "leard," but she knows how to spell "social studies" and "secondary colors." She has been taught to spell these words. And she has also been taught to spell words the way they sound. That's why she spells "summarized" "sumerrized," a very intelligent misspelling. By May she has learned to spell "had" and "learned." Julie is learning the conventions of the English language.

By second grade, Julie's diary is more descriptive. She, like Sarah, still enjoys school most when she can be active. She is concerned about her relationships with her friends. She talks frequently of her friends and comments on her classmates who get their names on the "bord," presumably because they have misbehaved. She talks about school in terms of good or bad days. Good days are when learning is active, when there is no homework, and when she can be with her friends. Children of Julie's age frequently see situations as good or bad, black or white.

Fifth-grader Jessica is learning how she learns. She tells us in detail about the assembly on lungs and the field trip to the river. Jessica doesn't tell us much about what she is learning in English, but we observe what she has learned as we compare her January diary entries, where she mostly lists, to her May entries, where she describes in detail.

In the fifth grade Jessica is increasingly concerned with her friends. She has a best friend who hurts her ankle on Jessica's birthday and is in a different group than Jessica on the field trip. The idea of a best friend is very important to Jessica, and she looks forward to times when she can talk to her friends at school. In fact, she is more concerned with her friends than she is with what she is doing in school. Jessica, too, is meeting the developmental tasks of her age group. By the time students reach the age of ten, they are increasingly concerned with having friends and becoming part of a peer group. Preteenagers are also becoming increasingly concerned with helping others and are willing to accept more responsibility than the younger students. Jessica, for example, works in the school library each morning as a volunteer. However, although students of Jessica's age have a broader world view than students of Julie's age, they are still more concerned about their own social needs than the welfare of a friend. Although Jessica expresses concern that her friend hurt her ankle, her primary thoughts center on her own birthday party.

Karen in grade six is experiencing the first conflicts of early adolescence. She is not sure whether the problems in the classroom are because the teacher is having a bad day or the class is having a bad day. She expresses her confusion in her diary. She feels sorry for a classmate when he is yelled at by the teacher but also sympathizes with the teacher: "Mrs. Lee must feel awful." She gets angry with her classmates for talking too much in class, is upset when the teacher reprimands them, complains when they are given too much homework, and wonders why the teacher doesn't make the work more difficult. She worries about whether the teacher will like her work, and has a great day when she's told she's done something well. Karen is learning to perform as part of a group at the same time that she feels rewarded by her individual achievements. Although during early adolescence it sometimes appears as if the developmental tasks interfere with learning, they do not. If Karen feels rewarded because the teacher likes her science project, she is experiencing acceptance and developing self-esteem, which eventually will translate into a desire to learn for the sake of learning.

Sandee is in the eighth grade and in the midst of adolescence. Like most students her age, she is less satisfied with school than younger students.

Although she is still concerned with how her teachers perceive her, she blames her lack of success on her teachers. She is egocentric. However, toward the end of the eighth-grade year, Sandee is beginning to realize that her mistakes may be her own. She complains about how boring her science class is, how dull the teacher makes it, but, after the test, she acknowledges, "I think I got a 60 or 80, mostly because of stupid mistakes." Sandee, like most students her age, is beginning to accept some responsibility for her own actions. If she continues to develop normally, what her teachers do will matter less and less. She will learn because she knows that only she is responsible for her own learning.

Darius, who is in ninth grade, is more contented with school than Sandee is. He is maturing and displays an interest in broadcasting and in his accomplishments. He uses the slang of his peers, but doesn't focus on his interaction with them. Like the other adolescents, he finds some of his academic subjects boring and likes it when he finds them easy. He does not yet focus on the world beyond high school; he is still consumed with his day-to-day activities.

Today's student population represents numerous ethnic and racial groups and comes from a wide range of economic and social backgrounds. A large percentage have disabilities. Although their values tend to be traditional, students today have additional concerns about social problems such as drugs and AIDS. Differences in background and gender may affect cognitive and psychosocial development in ways that were not imagined by early theorists. Even in classrooms in which students are more similar than they are different, the differences are vast. Some children read well above grade level; others read below grade level. Some children have parents who are actively involved in the schools; other parents never cross the school threshold.

The teachers of today must learn to work with all these children. Teaching them a common set of skills and concepts is no longer possible. Helping a diverse group of children develop a global, multicultural view of their world is the challenge and may be the reward of teaching in the twenty-first century.

10.2 POINTS TO REMEMBER

- Even in homogeneously grouped classrooms, there are numerous differences: ability levels, parental background, home environment, behavior, or health problems.

- Humans develop cognitively, from the sensorimotor period of reflexes and responses, to the preoperational period of egocentric thinking, to the concrete operational period of thought and logic, and, finally, to the formal observational period of logic and reasoning. (Piaget)

- Needs are developed, in hierarchical order, from the basic human physiological and safety needs to those of belonging and esteem, understanding and knowledge, and, finally, self-actualization. (Maslow)

- Early psychosocial development is marked by trust or mistrust. By the time the student is an adolescent, psychosocial development is marked by identity or role confusion. (Erikson)

- Humans also develop morals through stages. The preconventional stage of moral reasoning is based on the rules of others, the conventional stage on expectations and approval, and the postconventional stage on socially agreed standards and individual rights. (Kohlberg)

- Students' perceptions of school change. In the early years, students tend to like school and teachers. By the middle of elementary school, students are beginning to be more interested in their relationships with their peers than schoolwork. By junior high school, students are likely to blame their lack of success on others. They discuss school in terms of what they do not like about it. However, by the time students enter high school, they are more able to see how their own actions affect their performance in school.

- Students' skills develop throughout their school years. In the early years they have limited language skills. As language skills develop, the student's expression of thoughts becomes more complete, including the ability to analyze and interpret.

Martha F. Campbell in *Phi Delta Kappan.*

"First grade would be all right if it weren't for the 11 sequels."

FOR THOUGHT/DISCUSSION

1. How can understanding a student's interests, values, and worries help a teacher prepare a class that will be meaningful and interesting to students?

2. If Maslow's development of needs theory is correct, how can children of poverty be expected to learn if they come to school hungry and tired? What would you do, if such children appeared in your class, to help them learn effectively?

3. If you have a homogeneously grouped classroom, is it reasonable to expect that everyone will achieve at the same level? Why or why not?

4. The biggest complaint of most students in the diaries in this chapter is boredom. As a teacher, what would you do to counteract this attitude?

FOR FURTHER READING/REFERENCE

Gay, G. 1990. Ethnic minorities and educational equality. In *Multicultural education: Issues and perspectives,* ed. J. A. Banks and C. A. M. Banks, 167–188. Boston, MA: Allyn and Bacon. A discussion of educational inequality and comparison of access of blacks, Hispanics, Asians, and Native Americans in the same school and instructional programs to that of middle class white students.

Oakes, J. 1985. *Keeping track.* New Haven, CT: Yale University Press. Firsthand information regarding tracking practices taken from observation and surveys; results of tracking and grouping; grouping recommendations for school personnel.

Reed, S., and Sautter, R. C. 1990. Children of poverty: The status of 12 million young Americans [special report]. *Phi Delta Kappan*, 71 (10), K1–K12. Discussions of the children of poverty, what child advocates say should be done about them, and whether schools can realistically improve their lives.

Sachar, E. 1991. *Shut up and let the lady teach*. New York: Random House. Experiences of a journalist/author who spent a year teaching in an urban middle school. Discussed are physical facilities, racism, urbanism, tracking, and literacy.

Wirths, C. G., and Bowman-Kruhm, M. 1987. *I hate school: How to hang in and when to drop out*. New York: Thomas Y. Crowell. A discussion of how it is possible for students to take control of their school life rather than dropping out; suggestions for helping with social problems.

Sources of current demographic data

Because the demographics of schools and society change so rapidly, we are including in this list of further readings two sources that provide periodic updating of statistical information.

National Center for Education Statistics, U.S. Department of Education (annual). *Digest of education statistics*. Washington, DC: Author. An annual publication providing a compilation of statistical information covering the broad fields of American education, including enrollment, graduates, dropouts, the disabled, teacher salaries, and educational achievements.

U.S. Department of Commerce, Bureau of the Census (annual). *Statistical abstract of the United States*. Washington, DC: Author. Published since 1878, this annual statistical abstract is the standard summary of statistics on the social, political, and economic organization of the United States. Presents demographics such as population trends, education statistics, poverty, racial and ethnic population, employment, and families.

11
Learning

For any freshman at Stanford, experiencing for the first time dormitory life on one of the most exclusive and beautiful campuses in the nation, life is a pleasant change from doing the dishes and taking out the garbage at home. But for Maria Guadalupe Vasquez, it was an even bigger contrast: Before she came to Stanford, Lupe Vasquez was homeless.

"We never really had a permanent home when I was growing up," the 18-year-old explains. "We moved seven times when I was in junior high school. Then, in my junior year in high school, we were evicted again. Before, when we were evicted, we had people to go to. But this time we knew no one, we had no relatives to stay with. It was scary."

Lupe's family consisted of herself, her teenage sister, her mother and stepfather, and their three small children. After a few frightening days, they were taken in by a shelter for the homeless in Oxnard, Calif. "When I was at school, I just didn't mention where I lived," Lupe says. "I didn't want anyone to know that I lived in a shelter and that I was real poor. Now I know that I couldn't do anything about it. It wasn't my fault that I was homeless. And I don't mind talking about it today."

A social scientist who looked at Lupe's history would have predicted a future filled with despair, little education, menial work, possibly drugs and crime. What had made the difference in her life? "I suppose it would be my mother," Lupe says. "She came from Mexico, and she only had a sixth-grade education. She came to Arizona as a single parent, because she wanted a better life for me and my sister. I was 2 and my sister was 8 months. When we came here, she was a live-in, a maid. They treated her very badly and paid her nothing, so she moved us out and went to work in the fields."

Lupe's face takes on a pained expression. "Every day, I saw my mom breaking her back," she says. "She'd leave at 5 or 6 in the morning and work until 3 or 4 or 5 in the afternoon. She always told me to do well in school. She said, 'You don't want to work in the fields or clean houses. You deserve something better.' "

Children of migrant workers, constantly on the move, often enter grade school unprepared and rapidly fall behind. "My mother didn't speak a word of English," Lupe says, "but she would come home and teach me in Spanish. Before I got to kindergarten, she taught me the ABCs and numbers and colors in Spanish."

When Lupe was enrolled in first grade, she spoke no English. No bilingual classes were available, so she learned the language by listening to her classmates. Her teachers say that, although she is very bright, she is no genius: Hard work got her where she is today.

"Every time I went to a new school, I wanted to get to the top of the class and be No. 1," Lupe says. "I needed to compete against the other kids and show them who I was." Usually, she *was* No. 1—even though she had to deal with frequent moves and four younger siblings. And, for the last two years of high school, she had to study in the noisy television room of a shelter for the homeless.

"It probably would have been easier if I didn't have all those disruptions," Lupe concedes. "They just created another obstacle I had to overcome. I didn't say, 'I'll never do this,' or 'I'm not going to try to do well.' I'd say, 'It's put before me, and I have to do it.' "

Early in life, Lupe decided to go to college. "I thought that, with a college education, I'd be able to get a good job and help my mother out," she says. Her plan was to apply for Army ROTC until, two years ago, friends told her she might be eligible for financial aid. Stanford accepted her application, gave her $10,000 in aid, and—with additional aid from the federal government and private scholarships—she began school last September.

In her first quarter, she got two B-pluses and one B; in her second quarter, she decided to tackle physics and calculus simultaneously. "I'm thinking of becoming an environmental engineer," she reports. "There'll be a big need for them in the future, and I might be able to make a difference—and help my family too."

But Lupe is not waiting for the future to make a difference. Every week, she travels to a housing project to tutor a young Hispanic grade-school student. "I don't think I should have had to go through what I went through," she says. "It isn't right for kids to be exposed to that kind of situation. There's so much potential in them, but they don't show it because of the obstacles they face."

Each week, Lupe teaches her student math and English and tries to let the young girl know that she too can break out of poverty. "I guess I had an internal drive not everyone has," Lupe says. "But many people can do it if you give them a little push. I try to tell her that she is someone, that she has value. You can make a difference in kids' lives if you tell them that."

From: M. Ryan, "I Needed to Show Them Who I Was," *Parade* (August 19, 1990), 12–13.

CHAPTER OBJECTIVES

After studying this chapter, you should be able to:

- Define learning.
- Define the behavioral view of learning.
- Explain how the neobehaviorist view of learning is built on the behaviorist view.
- Discuss the cognitive view of learning.
- Understand the neurological concept of hemisphericity.
- Explain how sociologists examine learning.
- Discuss how learning styles differ.
- Identify the results of the National Assessment of Educational Progress in reference to the reading and writing progress of U.S. students.
- Identify the results of the National Assessment of Educational Progress in reference to the mathematics and science performance of U.S. students.
- Identify the results of the National Assessment of Educational Progress in reference to the history performance of U.S. students.
- Compare the achievement of U.S. students with that of students in other countries.
- Assess SAT and ACT scores over the last three decades.
- Explain why U.S. students do not do well on standardized tests.

Our understanding of the concept of learning involves the idea that people, like Lupe, will gain new skills, insights, concepts, values, and ideas through some process that may or may not involve a teacher, may or may not require a specialized setting and materials, and may or may not find the learner proceeding through a series of prescribed steps. The assumption that learning has taken place, however, is based on the observation that, in some way, behavior has been changed. This chapter will explore many ways in which researchers from various academic disciplines have attempted to define learning. We will focus on how students learn, what they learn, and what they do not learn.

WHAT IS LEARNING?

Psychologists, neurologists, sociologists, and educators have attempted to describe how and why human learning occurs and, thereby, define learning. They have established that there is no single way in which all humans learn, but many ways, perhaps as many as there are human beings. In addition, since researchers bring to their observations their own individual perceptions of learning, there are nearly as many different definitions as there are researchers. The one common denominator, however, is a change in behavior.

Definitions of learning and descriptions of how learners learn differ, in part, because researchers from different academic disciplines attempt to examine the process using different research methodologies. Psychologists, for example, observe behavior, frequently in a laboratory setting, sometimes in the actual learning environment, attempting to determine how the organism's actions, traits, attitudes, and thoughts develop.

Neurologists study ways in which the brain functions. Recent neurological studies of the hemispheres of the brain have produced new interpretations of learning and new descriptions of how we learn.

Sociologists examine the learning environment. Sociological research on effective schools has given us descriptions of common environmental factors that appear to contribute to learning.

Educators attempt to translate how humans learn into teaching strategies. Educational researchers have described various "learning styles" in an attempt to determine if specific students learn best in specific ways and if these individual learning styles require that students be paired with teachers who have compatible teaching styles.

Maria Guadalupe Vasquez, homeless throughout high school, succeeded at Stanford University largely through the encouragement of her mother and her own internalized drive to overcome adversity. She helps other Hispanic poor by tutoring them in mathematics and English and, by her own example, inspires them to work hard at their studies.

Within a single academic discipline there are various ways of examining how students learn. In psychology, for example, there are two major schools of learning theories: behavioral and cognitive. In addition, a neobehaviorist theory, also referred to as the social cognitive theory, has expanded the behavioral view of learning.

Learning: A Psychological Perspective

Behavioral View

Behavioral psychologists define learning as "a change in behavior, in the way a person acts in a particular situation" (Woolfolk 1987, 165).

Four of the most important proponents of the behavioral point of view were Ivan Pavlov, J. B. Watson, Edward L. Thorndike, and B. F. Skinner. These men focused their research on observable behavior and behavioral change in learners. Consequently, they rarely discussed thinking or emotions as part of learning. Behavioral learning studies are usually conducted in laboratories using animals to identify some general laws of learning that are then applied to humans.

Ivan Pavlov In the late nineteenth and early twentieth centuries Ivan Pavlov (1849–1936) developed the concept of classical conditioning while studying the digestive process of dogs. Pavlov and his colleagues recognized that if a piece of meat were placed near a dog, the dog would salivate. Because the meat

---

V I E W P O I N T S

Learning—Second Graders' Perspective

When Sue Morrison, a second-grade teacher, asked her class, "What is learning?," this is what they told her. Ms. Morrison wrote down their responses on chart paper for all to read.

—If you didn't learn your friend would have to help you all through life and you couldn't help yourself or anyone else.

—When you learn you think about things . . . lots of things.

—Learning is like when you go to school and find out what something is.

—If you had no education you would have a hard time surviving.

—You wouldn't know anything if you didn't learn.

—If our country wasn't as well educated as another country then that country might make fun of our country and might even try to challenge our country and take all we had. Then we'd lose.

—A person needs an education to apply for a job.

—It would be horrid not to learn . . . maybe even harmful. I mean . . . if I had a baby and couldn't read or learn then I couldn't feed my baby and we would both die.

—If you want to be educated and learn, you have to put your mind on it and really try to learn to live.

—If you don't know anything you get all mixed up and you feel like you want to learn but you don't know how to express what you want to know. . . .

From: Sue Morrison, Ira B. Jones Elementary School, Asheville, North Carolina

---

automatically provoked the salivation, Pavlov called it an **unconditioned stimulus**. Likewise, because the salivation response was not taught, he called it an **unconditioned response**.

Pavlov experimented by introducing the dog to the stimulus of a bell. The dog did not respond. Therefore, he called the bell a **neutral stimulus** because it had no effect on the dog. However, when he paired the neutral stimulus (the bell) with the unconditioned stimulus (the meat), the dog salivated. When the meat was removed, the dog still salivated when the bell was rung. Hence, the neutral stimulus became what Pavlov called a **conditioned stimulus**. He referred to this process as **classical conditioning**. Pavlov further learned that from time to time it was necessary to **reinforce** the conditioned response by presenting the dog with meat after the bell had been rung or the response would disappear or **extinguish**.

J. B. Watson   John B. Watson (1878–1959) believed that scientists should base their conclusions exclusively on the observation of behavior and coined the term **behaviorist** to emphasize this point. Believing that Pavlov's experiments provided the key to behavior manipulation in humans, he continued investigating behavior by experimenting with an eleven-month-old boy and a white rat. As the boy began to enjoy the activity of playing with the white rat, Watson introduced a sudden, loud sound that he had observed frightened most children. When the boy began to associate the rat with the frightening stimulus,

The behavioral psychologist B. F. Skinner stressed that behavior can be reinforced positively by rewards such as food, praise, or gifts. Among the positive reinforcements for learning is the diploma or the degree earned upon graduation.

he responded with fear and later generalized his fear to anything white and fuzzy.

E. L. Thorndike Edward L. Thorndike (1874–1949) believed that stimuli in the environment could prompt behavioral responses. His theory was the forerunner of what has come to be known as stimulus-response, or S-R, theory. Thorndike linked behavior to certain physical reflexes that occur without conscious or unconscious thought, such as the reflexive jerking of the tapped knee. Thorndike experimented by placing cats in boxes from which they had to escape in order to get food. He found that over time the cats escaped from the boxes more and more rapidly by repeating those behaviors that led to escape and eliminating those that did not. He named this the **law of effect**, which states that if an act leads to a satisfying change in the environment, the likelihood that the act will be repeated in similar situations increases. However, if the act does not lead to a satisfying change, the likelihood that the act will be repeated decreases.

B. F. Skinner Burrhus F. Skinner (1904–1990), the best-known of the behavioral psychologists, coined the term **operant conditioning** to stress that an organism "operates" on the environment when it learns. He also referred to this as **instrumental learning** because the organism is "instrumental" in securing a response that may be repeated if the organism receives **reinforcement**, a

V I E W P O I N T S

Learning—High School Students' Perspective

"Learning is reaching a destination and knowing why and how you got there, and where you'll go from there."

Bryan Dover, 17, eleventh grade

"Learning is understanding what you didn't understand before, from either a mistake you made or from someone telling you."

Michael Berry, 16, tenth grade

---

reward of some type such as food, money, or praise. Skinner believed human behavior is caused by experiences over which the individual has incomplete control. Therefore, students can learn if they are presented with stimuli designed to produce a predetermined, desired result. To this end, teachers should construct a methodology providing either positive or negative reinforcement so that students will actively learn.

For example, if the student does well on a quiz, using positive reinforcements such as praise, a high grade, or a sticker, would likely cause the behavior to continue.

Negative reinforcement strengthens a behavior if an unpleasant situation or incident is removed. For example, if a student has done well on a quiz, he or she may be exempt from taking the next quiz. This should then reinforce behavior that produced learning, for subsequent quizzes.

In 1968 Skinner outlined four behavioral learning principles based on his research: (1) Students will learn better if they know exactly what they are expected to learn—in other words, what learning will be reinforced. (2) Students must master basic/simpler skills before they can master complex skills. (3) All students do not learn at the same rate. (4) Subject matter should be programmed into small bits, with immediate positive feedback. Based on Skinner's principles, computer-programmed instruction was developed. **Computer-assisted instruction** allows students to progress at their own rate by completing a series of complex tasks, each of which receives immediate feedback in the form of a corrected response.

Neobehaviorist View

Neobehaviorists, such as Albert Bandura, expanded the behaviorists' view of learning into a social cognitive theory that includes such internal, unobservable behaviors as intentions, expectations, beliefs, and thoughts. Bandura determined, as well, that children learned as much by imitation and observation as they did by reinforcement of specific behaviors. In one famous experiment with a punching toy, called Bobo, he determined that children were more aggressive after watching an adult punch the toy or after viewing an aggressive film or cartoon than after viewing a nonaggressive one. This theory became known as **modeling**. According to Bandura, there are four elements to observational learning: (1) The learner must pay attention. (2) The learner needs clear explanations. (3) The learner produces the desired behavior with practice and receives feedback. (4) The learner needs incentives and reinforcement in order to continue the behavior.

The concept of modeling is still a very important one for teachers. Teachers model behavior for students in many ways: through their own actions, through demonstrations, through guided practice leading the student step-by-step through a process, and through the selection of materials and activities.

Cognitive View

The cognitive psychologists view learning as an internal process that cannot be observed directly and involves such complex tasks as problem solving, concept learning, perception, and remembering. Cognitive psychologists, such as Jean Piaget, Jerome Bruner, David Ausubel, and Robert Gagne usually conduct their research in schools with human learners. Although all cognitive theorists define learning in similar ways, they do not agree upon a learning model in which all people learn in a similar way, as the behaviorists do. These theorists agree that "learning is the result of our attempts to make sense out of the world" (Woolfolk, p. 234). To do this, according to the cognitive theorists, learners use the various mental tools at their disposal. The learners' thoughts about the situation, along with beliefs, expectations, and feelings, make them actively seek out information to solve problems and reorganize what they know in order to achieve new learning (Woolfolk, p. 235). Piaget, discussed in chapter 10 (pp. 333–335), developed a hierarchy of how learners learn. The theories of Bruner, Ausubel, and Gagne will be introduced here.

Jerome Bruner Jerome Bruner (b. 1915) contends that we learn by actively being involved in problem solving through the use of inductive reasoning and intuitive thinking—making guesses, confirming, disproving, and discovering solutions.

Bruner believes that the best way for students to learn is for teachers to confront them with problems so that they can seek solutions. According to Bruner, this is important because "conceptions that children arrive at on their own are usually more meaningful than those proposed by others and . . . students do not need to be motivated or rewarded when they seek to make sense of things that puzzle them" (Biehler and Snowman 1986, 254). In addition, according to Bruner, when children are given practice finding solutions to problems they acquire the skills necessary to solve other problems.

Bruner's instructional model has become known as **discovery learning**. In this model, teachers create learning situations where children learn through discovery rather than through prepared and teacher-presented information. For example, children can discover phonetic coding skills by noting similarities and differences in consonant/vowel sequences rather than by memorizing phonetic rules. And by using concrete rectangles and squares, students can discover differences in length, width, and weight.

David Ausubel David Ausubel (b. 1918) contends that children learn through reception and listening rather than through discovery. The key to this theory, however, is that all new learning must be linked to what the student already knows and that facts, principles, and concepts should be presented in meaningful ways and in a sequential and organized manner.

Cognitive psychologist Jerome Bruner contended that the best way to encourage learning is to confront students with an important problem to solve and give them the opportunity to do it. These students at a Catholic girls' school are working on a chemistry problem.

Since Ausubel believed that children learn deductively, from the general to the specific, from rule to example, he developed a concept of expository teaching, where the teacher provides external motivation for learning by beginning a lesson with overall aims, giving examples, relating the learning to past learning and experiences (what he called **advanced organizers**), and presenting the lesson in an organized sequence from the general to the specific. His theory has come to be called **expository learning**, or **deductive teaching**.

Ausubel's theory has many applications in the classroom. For example, a teacher might begin a unit on the Civil War by telling students that the goal of the unit is to help them better understand how that war affected various groups of people. Using Ausubel's approach, the teacher would use a series of increasingly specific advanced organizers. The teacher might begin with a film such as *Gone With The Wind* to help students tie the Civil War to their own experience. Next, the students and teacher might discuss how the Civil War affected plantation owners in general and the South specifically. This might lead to readings on the causes and effects of the war. The teacher might then provide another advanced organizer to examine the Civil War through the eyes of slaves. For example, the teacher might read aloud selections from Toni Morrison's *Beloved* and Julius Lester's *To Be a Slave*, which focus on the life of slaves and the implications of slavery. Irene Hunt's *Across Five Aprils*, about a family in which one son fights for the Union and the other for the Confederacy, might then be read. The students might then investigate how different individuals reacted to the causes of the war. Perhaps, after several more advanced organizers, the students would work in groups to develop class presentations related to how different populations reacted to and were affected by the war. As a culminating activity, the students and the teacher might develop an interconnected learning web, diagrammed on the chalkboard, in an attempt to connect the various populations of the Civil War to its effects. The unit would continue in this manner until the original aims were reached. Expository teaching, such as that described by Ausubel, requires a great deal of interaction between students and teacher.

Robert Gagne   According to Robert Gagne (b. 1916), learning skills, which he calls **learning outcomes**, can be categorized into five types: (1) attitudes—learned through positive/negative experiences and modeling, (2) motor skills—learned through observation and practice, (3) verbal data—learned in almost every lesson, (4) intellectual skills—learned as symbols for communicating and solving problems, and (5) cognitive strategies—learned to assist in selecting, processing, and retrieving information. The more complicated skills are discussed below.

An attitude (a reaction toward or against a solution, person, or thing learned through positive or negative experiences and modeling) intensifies a person's reaction toward something. For example, if a person has a positive attitude toward music, she or he will frequently choose to listen to it. The more positive the attitude, the greater the frequency with which the individual chooses to pursue the activity. The opposite is also true: a negative attitude decreases the frequency with which the activity is pursued. The relationship between attitude and performance is very strong. Hence, a positive attitude toward music, for example, may result in playing an instrument.

Intellectual skills are those capabilities that make individuals competent. They enable people to respond successfully to their environment and range from simple skills, such as arranging a sentence, to technical ones involved in the sciences and mathematics. They allow students to think, analyze, and create at high levels. For example, those who possess intellectual skills not only know the meaning of the term *metaphor* but can also think metaphorically and use metaphorical language in speech and writing. This intellectual skill then becomes the basis for future learning—developing more sophisticated writing techniques; comparing unlike elements such as an individual in history to a mountain; or conducting sophisticated scientific experiments such as determining how a specific insect might affect a specific plant were it to be introduced to the plant's environment.

Cognitive strategies govern the individual's learning, remembering, and thinking abilities. They allow students to read a passage and determine what is most important, to analyze information that is learned, and to solve problems. These skills are gained over a long period of time through active studying, learning, and thinking.

To assist students in developing these capabilities, Gagne suggested that there are eight essential **events of instruction** that directly influence the process of learning. These include the following:

- motivation (teacher provided stimulus and lesson objective)
- apprehending (directing student's attention/focusing on particulars)
- acquisition (recalling past, related information/presenting new material/ giving examples)
- retention (practicing new skill)
- recall (review over several days)

- generalization (transfer of new information to other situations)
- performance (demonstration of knowledge: tests, written papers, experiments)
- feedback (grades, praise, and correction)

These events are external to the learner and can be structured by either the learner or the teacher. In an authoritarian or subject-centered classroom, for example, the teacher will organize the events of instruction, and in a student-centered classroom, the students will largely determine the method or pattern of learning.

Learning: A Neurological Perspective

In the late 1970s, studies by neurologists who had researched the function of each of the brain's hemispheres began to appear. They have determined that each hemisphere has a specialized, but not exclusive, function. Both hemispheres in normal individuals receive the same information but process it differently. There is a combination of specialization and integration of functions between and within the hemispheres, both of which are necessary to learning (Fadely and Hosler 1983).

Each hemisphere controls the opposite side of the body, and each has specialized functions. Researchers believe that the left hemisphere is the more logical, analytical, and verbal; it controls manual dexterity, reading, language, and understanding speech. The right hemisphere processes nonverbal information and organizes a human's artistic aptitudes and emotions. The primary functions of each hemisphere have been studied and outlined by such researchers as Roger Sperry, Ronald Myers, and Michael Gazzaniga in the 1950s (see table 11.1).

We can understand how the hemispheres work, both together and separately, primarily because of the work of Roger Sperry, who studied epileptic individuals in whom the corpus callosum, the nerve bundle connecting the two hemispheres, had been cut to attempt to reduce the frequency of seizures. He found subtle dysfunctions in these individuals. In a normal individual without a split brain, the eye's left field of vision is initially received only by the right hemisphere, and the right field of vision is received only by the left hemisphere. The information is quickly transmitted to both hemispheres, and the left hemisphere, the center of language production, names it. Sperry found that this was not true in split-brained patients. If an object was placed in the right hand of a split-brained patient, the information was received by the left hemisphere and the patient named the object. However, if it was placed in the left hand and received by the right hemisphere, the patient could not name the object. Why? According to Sperry, the right hemisphere, which had received the information, could not transfer it to the left, the center for language production.

Researchers contend that some people are whole brained; others have dominant left or right hemispheres. Most, according to researchers, have dominant left hemispheres. However, no matter which hemisphere is dominant, all individuals use both sides of the brain. As Bernice McCarthy (1980) states, "The goal of education should be to help develop a whole brain . . . intellectual and intuitive, mind and heart, content-centered and student-centered" (p. 77). Constant use of one hemisphere over the other can lead to either

(continued on p. 360)

TABLE 11-1

Summary of Hemisphericity: Left- and Right-Brained Functions

Left hemisphere	Right hemisphere
• Has Intellectual Focus • Recognizes and Controls Speech; Relies on Language; Prefers Talking and Writing • Rarely Uses Metaphors and Analogies • Receives, Stores and Syntheszes Verbal-Auditory Data • Responds Best to Auditory, Visual Stimuli • Serializes and Sequentially Organizes Verbal Data • Remembers Names • Responds to Verbal Instructions and Explanations • Focuses on Temporal (Time) Memory and Behavior • Has Logical, Rational Problem-Solving Behavior • Plans and Structures • Analyzes Reading • Prefers Multiple-Choice Tests and Research with Single Variable • Socializes Values; Establishes Information • Prefers Hierarchical Authority Structures; Likes Structured Environment • Makes Objective Judgments • Is Not Facile in Interpreting Body Language • Controls Feelings • Prefers Higher Math Skills Involving Formulation and Time-Space Concepts • Systematically Controls Experimentation	• Is Intuitive; Insightful • Is Fluid and Spontaneous • Relies on Images in Thinking and Remembering • Frequently Uses Metaphors and Analogies • Prefers Nonverbal Auditory Information; Minor Comprehension of Language • Is Creative and Artistic • Recognizes and Synthesizes Musical Perception, Rhythm, and Movement Patterns in Music • Prefers Drawing and Manipulating Objects • Easily Manipulates Forms, Shapes, Form-Space Relationships • Develops Complex and Fine Motor Skills • Responds Best to Kinetic Stimuli • Remembers Faces • Interprets Nonverbal Information; Good at Interpreting Body Language • Responds to Demonstrated, Illustrated, Symbolic Instructions • Synthesizes Reading • Prefers Open-Ended Questions, Work and Study, and Multivariable Research • Prefers Collegial (Participative) Authority Structures • Is Self-Acting • Sees the Whole; Solves Problems Intuitively by Examining the Whole • Makes Subjective Judgments • Experiments Randomly With Little Restraint • Is Free With Feeling • Prefers Concrete Math Functions; Simple Calculations

Adapted from: J. L. Fadely and V. N. Hosler, *Case Studies in Left and Right Hemispheric Functioning,* (Charles C. Thomas, 1983) and B. McCarthy, *The 4 MAT System: Teaching to Learning Styles With the Right/Left Mode Techniques,* (EXCEL, 1980).

Researchers have found that both hemispheres of the brain have different but not mutually exclusive functions. The left side is primarily verbal, logical, and analytical; the right side is primarily nonverbal and emotional. This table summarizes the functions of each hemisphere.

habitual right- or left-brained thinking. Researchers agree that both are important, but schools generally tend to emphasize the left, limiting students with right-brain dominance.

Learning: A Sociological Perspective

Sociological research on effective schools examines those elements of the instructional environment that promote academic achievement (see chapter 8 for more information about effective schools research). It is important to note that effective schools research does not attempt to define learning, nor does it attempt to determine why and how the best students learn. Instead, it attempts to describe which specific environments help children learn most effectively. The results of this research are summarized below.

Reading

- Children get more out of a reading assignment when the teacher precedes the lesson with background information and follows it with discussion.
- Students in cooperative learning teams work toward a common goal, help one another learn, gain self-esteem, take more responsibility for their own learning, and come to respect and like their classmates.
- Telling young children stories can motivate them to read. Storytelling also introduces them to cultural values and literacy traditions before they can read, write, and talk about stories by themselves.
- Hearing good readers read and encouraging students repeatedly to read a passage aloud helps them become good readers.

Science and Mathematics

- Children learn science best when they are able to do experiments, so they can witness "science in action."
- Although students need to learn how to find exact answers to arithmetic problems, good math students also learn how to estimate answers.
- Children in early grades learn mathematics more effectively when they use physical objects in their lessons.
- Students will become more adept at solving math problems if teachers encourage them to think through a problem before they begin working on it, guide them through the thinking process, and give them regular and frequent practice in solving problems.

Writing

- The most effective way to teach writing is to teach it as a process of brainstorming, composing, revising, and editing.
- Students become more interested in writing and the quality of their writing improves when there are significant learning goals and a clear sense of purpose for the assignments.
- Children learn vocabulary better when the words they study are related to familiar experiences and to knowledge they already possess.

Understanding Student Development

- Children's understanding of the relationship between being smart and hard work changes as they grow.

- As students acquire knowledge and skill, their thinking and reasoning take on distinct characteristics. Teachers who are alert to these changes can determine how well their students are progressing toward becoming competent thinkers and problem solvers.

Classroom Management

- How much time students are actively engaged in learning contributes strongly to their achievement. The amount of time available for learning is determined by the instructional and management skills of the teacher and the priorities set by the school administration.
- Good classroom management is essential for teachers to deal with students who chronically misbehave.
- Specific suggestions from teachers on how to cope with their conflicts and frustrations help students gain insights about their behavior and learn control.

Motivation of Students

- When teachers explain exactly what students are expected to learn and demonstrate the steps needed to accomplish a particular academic task, students learn more.
- Constructive feedback from teachers, including deserved praise and specific suggestions, helps students learn, as well as develop positive self-esteem.
- Teachers who set and communicate high expectations to all their students obtain greater academic performance from those students than teachers who set low expectations.
- Students tutoring other students can lead to improved academic achievement for both student and tutor, and to positive attitudes toward coursework.
- Memorizing can help students absorb and retain the factual information on which understanding and critical thought are based.
- Frequent and systematic monitoring of students' progress helps students, parents, teachers, administrators, and policymakers identify strengths and weaknesses in learning and instruction.
- When teachers introduce new subject matter, they need to help students grasp its relationship to facts and concepts they have previously learned.
- Student achievement rises when teachers ask questions that require students to apply, analyze, synthesize, and evaluate information in addition to simply recalling facts.
- Well-chosen diagrams, graphs, photos, and illustrations can enhance students' learning.

Homework

- The ways in which children study influence strongly how much they learn. Teachers can often help children develop better study skills.
- Student achievement rises significantly when teachers regularly assign homework and students conscientiously do it.
- Well-designed homework assignments relate directly to classroom work and extend students' learning beyond the classroom. Homework is most useful when teachers carefully prepare the assignment, thoroughly explain it, and give prompt comments and criticism when the work is completed. (U.S. Department of Education, 1987)

Learning: An Educational Perspective

In spite of research that attempts to identify common elements of learning, many educators contend that everyone learns differently. Rita Dunn and Kenneth Dunn in *Learning Styles/Teaching Styles: Should They . . . Can They . . . Be Matched?* (1979) claim that **learning style** is the manner in which various elements in one's environment affect learning. Barbara Bree Fischer and Louis Fischer in *Styles in Teaching and Learning* (1979) say that "style" refers to a "pervasive quality in the behavior of an individual, *a quality that persists though the content may change*" (1979, 245). They illustrate this point by discussing speaking styles. According to Fischer and Fischer, John F. Kennedy and Martin Luther King, Jr., each had persistent, identifiable speaking styles that did not change even when the content of the speech changed. They suggest the same is true of artists such as Monet and Picasso. And, they conclude, the same is true in learning.

A ten-year study on how individuals learn resulted in the identification of four stimuli and eighteen environmental variables that affect an individual's

TABLE 11-2

Learning Styles: Research Findings

Fischer and Fischer	Good and Stipek	Grasha
Incremental Learner: step-by-step	Field-Dependent: group interaction with teacher, motivated by praise, needs explicit instruction, defined outcomes, prefers humanities	Dependent: little intellectual curiosity, needs structure and support, looks to authority
Intuitive Learner: unsystematic		Independent: self-thinking, works on own, listens to others, self-confident
Sensory Specialist: relies on one sense	Field-Independent: independent, individualized, prefers to structure own tasks, prefers math/science	Participant: wants to learn course content, likes school, works with others, responsible, does little beyond what is required
Sensory Generalist: all or many senses		
Emotionally Involved		Avoidant: doesn't want to learn, doesn't participate, uninterested, overwhelmed
Emotionally Neutral		
Explicitly Structured: unambiguous structure		Collaborative: learns most by sharing, sees class as social interaction
Open-Ended Structure: open environment		
Damaged Learner: negative learning style		Competitive: learns to perform better than others, sees class as win-lose situation, must always win
Eclectic Learner: shifting style		

Each researcher listed in this table has identified individual learning styles. While the terminology might be different for each researcher, all learning styles are influenced by four major stimuli: environmental, emotional, sociological, and physical-perceptual.

learning. Dunn and Dunn point out that individuals respond differently to each of these stimuli and variables. "Regardless of their age, ability, socioeconomic status, or achievement level, individuals respond uniquely to their immediate environment. Some require absolute silence when they are concentrating, while others can 'block out' sound. In addition, there is a segment of the population who actually *require* sound when they are trying to learn" (1979, 239). The stimuli and variables they identified are (1) environmental—sound, light, temperature, and design of room; (2) emotional—motivation, persistence, responsibility, and structure; (3) sociological—working with peers, alone, in pairs, in teams, with adults, or in varied combinations, and (4) physical-perceptual-strength, intake, time of day, and mobility (pp. 238–240). Table 11.2 identifies how several researchers described differences in individuals' learning styles.

Dunn and Dunn and Fischer and Fischer suggest that not only do individuals have specific learning styles, but teachers have different teaching styles that are related to their own individual learning styles. Dunn and Dunn feel it is accurate to say, "Teachers teach the way they learned" (1979, 241). Just as learners can expand their dominant learning styles, however, teachers can modify and expand their teaching styles. No single teaching style is effective with all learners; hence, it is important for teachers to adapt their teaching styles to the various learning styles of their students.

Fischer and Fischer suggest that there may not be sufficient research in learning styles to adequately guide the teacher (1979, 246). They also caution that not all teaching styles are acceptable in the classroom. Fischer and Fischer believe that "Well, that's my style" is not an excuse for poor teaching. In addition, some educators worry that focusing on individual learning style may encourage the same kind of self-indulgence in students as observed in some teachers. There is a danger, they contend, that students may begin to think they can do everything just the way they want to in the name of "style."

11.1 POINTS TO REMEMBER

- Learning is defined differently by different disciplines but always indicates a change in behavior.
- The behaviorists define learning as an observable change in a student's behavior. They study how laboratory animals learn and apply their results to humans.
- Neobehaviorists examine internal and unobservable behaviors as well as those that can be observed. They examine such aspects of learning as attitudes and beliefs.
- Cognitive psychologists look at learning as an internal process that cannot be directly observed. They examine problem solving, concept learning, perception, and remembering.
- According to many neurologists, the brain has two hemispheres, which receive stimuli at the same time but process them differently. The left hemisphere processes verbal stimuli; the right, spatial stimuli. Each has an integrative learning relationship with the other.
- Sociologists observe learning environments and conduct teacher effectiveness research to determine successful learning.
- Students have different learning styles. Some learn better in groups, others individually. Scholars are attempting to define learning styles.

CROSS-CULTURAL PER·SPECTIVE

Learning Styles of Students in Other Cultures

If we assume that learning styles do not necessarily reflect some biological or genetic characteristic, we can reasonably assume the cultural experience of youngsters does shape their style. . . . Afro-American students tend to learn more effectively in situations marked by high activity, rhythmic patterns of stimulation, and structure. . . . In the socialization experience of middle-class, white students, they are likely learning to create structures for themselves. The lower-class, black students don't learn to generate structure themselves, so they need structure from an external source.

[When studying how Hispanic students perceive standardized tests, researchers determined that]

Hispanic students tended to view the testing situation as a game and were relaxed about it; whereas, the middle-class, white students tended to be challenged, sometimes even threatened, and were much more serious, even anxious. . . .

[Researchers] found that the Hispanic mothers seldom make precise intellectual demands on the youngsters; instead, they encourage their offspring to explore words, songs, or experiences in a playful manner rather than a work-related manner. Hispanic youngsters don't need to produce a reaction to outside stimulus as long as they can produce a response to their own stimulus. Therefore, to the extent that response to demand could be called a learning style, the Hispanic population tends to demonstrate that tendency much less frequently than a middle-class, white group that is socialized almost from early childhood to produce on demand as is expected in school.

From: an interview with Edmund W. Gordon by Rabianski-Carriuolo, 1989

HOW WELL ARE STUDENTS LEARNING?

The only measures we have of students' learning are scores on standardized tests based only on easy-to-test bits of information in any given subject area. Test results tell us little about whether students have developed the ability to solve sophisticated problems. Neither do they tell us about students' appreciation of art or reading or mathematics. Tests tell us, instead, the level at which the students can succeed on the particular tests.

National Assessment of Educational Progress

In an attempt to determine the level of student learning, the **National Assessment of Educational Progress (NAEP)** was begun in 1969. Since that date, this test has been given periodically to nine-, thirteen-, and seventeen-year-old students across the United States to sample educational progress by race, ethnicity, gender, and geographic region. This congressionally mandated test is a project of the National Center for Educational Statistics of the U.S. Department of Education. The results have been called *The Nation's Report Card*.

Reading Assessment

From 1971 to 1990, NAEP reading test results indicate improvement at all three age levels, nine-, thirteen-, and seventeen-year-olds, for whites, blacks, and Hispanics, particularly for those students at the lower end of the scale.

TABLE 11-3

Trends in Percentages of Students At or Above Five Reading Proficiency Levels, 1971 to 1990

Skills and strategies	Age	Assessment years					
		1971	1975	1980	1984	1988	1990
Level 350 Learn from Specialized Reading Materials [Advanced]	9	0 (0.0)	0 (0.0)	0 (0.0)	0 (0.0)	0 (0.0)	0 (0.1)
	13	0 (0.0)	0 (0.0)	0 (0.0)	0 (0.1)	0 (0.1)	0 (0.1)
	17	7 (0.4)	6 (0.3)	5 (0.4)	6 (0.3)	5 (0.6)	7 (0.5)
Level 300 Understand Complicated Information [Adept]	9	1 (0.1)	1 (0.1)	1 (0.1)	1 (0.1)	1 (0.3)	2 (0.3)
	13	10 (0.5)	10 (0.5)	11 (0.5)	11 (0.4)	11 (0.8)	11 (0.6)
	17	39 (1.0)	39 (0.8)	38 (1.1)	40 (0.8)	41 (1.5)	41 (1.0)
Level 250 Interrelate Ideas and Make Generalizations [Intermediate]	9	16 (0.6)	15 (0.6)*	18 (0.8)	17 (0.6)	18 (1.1)	18 (1.0)
	13	58 (1.1)	59 (1.0)	61 (1.1)	59 (0.6)	59 (1.3)	59 (1.0)
	17	79 (0.9)*	80 (0.7)*	81 (0.9)	83 (0.5)	86 (0.8)	84 (1.0)
Level 200 Partially Developed Skills and Understanding [Basic]	9	59 (1.0)	62 (0.8)	68 (1.0)*	62 (0.7)	63 (1.3)	59 (1.3)
	13	93 (0.5)	93 (0.4)	95 (0.4)	94 (0.3)	95 (0.6)	94 (0.6)
	17	96 (0.3)	96 (0.3)	97 (0.3)	98 (0.1)	99 (0.3)	98 (0.3)
Level 150 Simple, Discrete Reading Tasks [Rudimentary]	9	91 (0.5)	93 (0.4)*	95 (0.4)*	92 (0.3)	93 (0.7)	90 (0.9)
	13	100 (0.0)	100 (0.1)	100 (0.0)	100 (0.0)	100 (0.1)	100 (0.1)
	17	100 (0.1)	100 (0.1)	100 (0.1)	100 (0.0)	100 (0.0)	100 (0.1)

*Statistically significant difference from 1990. The standard errors of the estimated percentages and proficiencies appear in parentheses. It can be said with 95 percent certainty that for each population of interest, the value for the whole population is within plus or minus two standard errors of the estimate for the sample. When the proportion of students is either 0 or 100 percent, the standard error is inestimable. However, percentages 99.5 percent and greater were rounded to 100 percent, and percentages less than .5 percent were rounded to 0 percent.

From: Educational Testing Service under contract with National Center for Educational Statistics, U. S. Department of Education. *Trends in Academic Progress* (NCES 91–1264). (Washington, DC: U.S. Government Printing Office, September 1991), 15.

The National Assessment of Educational Progress (NAEP) has tested students at ages nine, thirteen, and seventeen in reading proficiency. The levels range from rudimentary (level 150) to advanced (level 350). Progress has been steady at all age levels at all levels of reading except for those characterized as adept (level 300) and advanced.

Testing levels for whites were higher than for either blacks or Hispanics on each of the five tests. However, reading scores of blacks have risen significantly, while scores for whites have shown limited improvement since 1971, tending to decrease the performance gaps at all three age levels. Females outperformed males at all three age levels. Reading achievement changed little in the Northeast for nine- and thirteen-year-olds from 1971 to 1990, but fell initially and then improved significantly for seventeen-year-olds. Students in the Southeast scored markedly better at all three age levels in 1988 than in 1971, but dropped in 1990. In the Central region of the country, the reading performance for nine- and seventeen-year-olds remained relatively constant from 1971 to 1990. However, the proficiency of thirteen-year-olds in the central region rose from 1971 until 1980 and then dropped significantly from 1980 to 1990. See table 11.3 for a summary of the percentage of students above the five levels of reading proficiency from 1971 to 1990.

Although it appears that progress has been made in raising the number of students who acquire rudimentary, basic, and intermediate reading skills and strategies, no gains are evident at the higher levels of reading ability characterized by NAEP as adept and advanced skills and strategies. The percentage of seventeen-year-olds performing at the advanced level declined from 6.6 in 1971 to 4.8 in 1988, but advanced to 7.0 in 1990. The instructional and curricular interventions of recent years may have succeeded in strengthening students' rudimentary, basic, and intermediate reading proficiencies, but these efforts must continue to be pursued, reevaluated, and redirected in the years ahead to provide for more substantial gains, especially at the advanced level where test reading passages contain "challenging syntactic and rhetorical elements" and test questions are more open-ended, "asking students to articulate their views and ideas based on the selection presented" (Educational Testing Service 1990, 33–35).

Lack of Homework   The NAEP found that students who spend more time on homework test at a higher level of reading proficiency than those who spend less time.

The National Assessment of Educational Progress (NAEP) found in its research that the more time a student spends on homework, the higher will be her level of reading proficiency. Homework that is effectively assigned and conscientiously done can help students become independent thinkers and learners.

Of course, it is not only the amount, but the kind of homework that is important. William J. Bennett in *What Works: Research About Teaching and Learning* (1987) suggested that homework is most useful when teachers carefully prepare and explain assignments, discuss them with students after they have been completed, and give prompt feedback and criticism (p. 53). In addition, research suggests that assignments that encourage students to think are more effective in motivating them to want to learn. Effective homework does not merely supplement classroom work but helps students become independent learners. This may help explain why students with more homework tend to score at higher levels on standardized tests that require high-level thinking skills.

It is also interesting to note that the amount of homework completed by students may not equal the amount assigned. According to Bennett, high school teachers report giving an average of ten hours of homework per week, and high school seniors report doing only four to five hours per week (p. 51). This may be because the students complete the homework more quickly than the teachers expect, do it incompletely or poorly, or do not do it at all. In any case, it may help explain why students who do more homework generally do better on standardized tests.

A similar positive relationship between the amount read per day and achievement as measured by the NAEP was found. Students who read more per day tended to score at a higher level of proficiency than students who read less. A negative relationship was found at all age levels for the amount of time watching television and achievement on the NAEP.

IN THE CLASSROOM

Michael Brownstein teaches third grade at the John Farren Elementary School in inner-city Chicago. It didn't take him long to discover that his third graders could not read, did not know the alphabet.

He set out to change this, not believing that his students couldn't learn but that no one had let them. He began by visiting every parent in the Robert Taylor Housing Project, across from the school, and getting them to allow him to tutor the children in their homes. Within three weeks he had established an after-school tutoring program.

During a Chicago teachers' strike, he became concerned that his students would fall even further behind. So he started a program in an old storefront called RAMP (Reading and Math Program). Today, the program not only reaches schoolchildren but anyone in the community. The students who participate in the RAMP program have boosted their reading scores by 1.5 months for every week's participation.

The instruction the students receive in the RAMP program is based on their individual needs. "I want the children to see other ways of thinking, to use a part of their brains they may not realize they have" (Foltz 1989, 16). He also wants his students to learn to work together, so he encourages them to be coaches, tutors, and role models.

Students who attend RAMP first complete their homework and then tackle special projects. In addition, RAMP has developed its own special programs: a chess club, a literary magazine, Junior Achievement, and preparation for the Chicago Department of Human Services' Reading Olympics.

Besides the school year program, RAMP has a summer program in which students start their day by writing. After they write about unusual pictures, the students do "motor-eye" work. Michael draws elaborate pictures on the board and has the students copy his drawings on individual slates. This is to improve their perceptual ability, which is important if they are to learn to read. The students also participate in brainstorming sessions in which they work together to determine a variety of ways to solve a single problem. Finally, the children read both silently and aloud. They answer questions and write about what they have read.

Furthermore, the RAMP summer students take weekly field trips. Michael explains, "Inner-city kids grow up really isolated" (p. 18). So the students travel through the city each Thursday seeing things they have never seen. This gives them a background from which to learn.

Brownstein believes that the most important element of RAMP's program is that it helps students learn to believe in themselves. "I tell my students, 'If you try, there's no way you can fail.' If they try, I'll really go to bat for them—no matter what it takes." And, he means it. In his sixteen years of teaching, he has "shut down a dope house, confronted a gun-carrying fourteen-year-old, defused a young teen who called at 2 A.M. with murder on his mind, and negotiated a truce between two rival gangs" (p. 18). He did all these things so that his students could keep learning. (Foltz, 1989)

Writing Assessment

Levels of writing performance, based on two national assessments of writing proficiency conducted by the NAEP, changed little from 1984 to 1990. In fact, they have remained relatively constant since 1974. Whites continued to outscore blacks and Hispanics at all three age levels. However, at all three levels, black and Hispanic students appear to show consistent, if not statistically significant, improvement.

Females at all grade levels scored noticeably higher than males in overall writing proficiency between 1984 and 1990. The NAEP analyzed scores using the average response method, which estimates how well students in each grade would have done if they had taken eleven of the twelve writing tasks tested. Fourth-grade girls' writing scores on a scale of 0–400, for example, increased significantly, from 184.0 in 1984 to 193.0 in 1990, whereas boys' scores remained essentially the same. At grade eight, boys' writing proficiency decreased from 199.0 in 1984 to 187.0 in 1990, whereas girls' scores increased slightly. As with reading scores, in 1990 "many students continued to perform at minimal levels on the NAEP writing assessment tasks, and relatively few performed at adequate or better levels" (Educational Testing Service 1990c, 6). At the "minimal" level on writing samples, students "recognized some or all of the elements needed to complete the task but did not manage these elements well enough to assure that the purpose of the task would be achieved," whereas students scoring at what NAEP calls the "adequate" level provided "adequate responses [including] the information and ideas necessary to accomplish the underlying task and were considered likely to be effective in achieving the desired purpose" and, at the "elaborated" level of writing proficiency, students "elaborated responses [that] went beyond the essential, reflecting a higher level of coherence and providing more detail to support the points made" (p. 7). According to an NAEP summary of the results of the writing assessments, students scored best on "informative writing tasks that required straightforward reports or letters" (p. 8). We must ask ourselves why students are able to perform at basic, rudimentary levels in both reading and writing but rarely achieve higher levels of performance. Are U.S. schools adequately challenging students? Are schools spending too much time emphasizing basic skills and not enough time requiring students to think and perform at the higher cognitive levels of analysis, synthesis, and evaluation?

Mathematics and Science Assessment

In 1990, mathematics proficiency, measured by the NAEP, improved for nine- to thirteen-year-olds, but stayed the same as it was in 1973 for seventeen-year-olds. Science proficiency for thirteen- and seventeen-year-olds, however, was lower in 1986 than it had been in 1970, and levels of mathematics and science proficiency remain low. Most U.S. students, even at age seventeen, are unable to perform at the upper levels of the NAEP mathematics and science proficiency scale.

As in reading and writing, results of NAEP tests in mathematics showed that students' performance on basic skills improved between 1978 and 1990; however, performance on more advanced operations remained the same or declined. The proportion of thirteen-year-olds who could perform basic numerical operations rose from 65 percent in 1978 to 75 percent in 1990, but the proportion of students who could perform moderately complex mathematical procedures declined from 18 percent in 1978 to 17 percent in 1990. The proportion of seventeen-year-olds who could perform basic numerical operations rose from 92 percent in 1978 to 96 percent in 1990, but the proportion of those who could perform multistep problems remained at the same 7 percent level for the same time period.

According to the NAEP's assessment of test results, performance improved especially among black and Hispanic students and students in the Southeast. However, these positive changes must be tempered with a concern about the fact that the improvement is at low levels of skill performance. According to NAEP, this suggests that schools are more concerned with "students' rote use of procedures than with their understanding of concepts and development of higher-order thinking skills" (Educational Testing Service 1988a, 12).

Similar results are seen on the NAEP science assessment. Students' achievement scores in science rose between 1977–1990 for nine- and thirteen-year-olds but showed no significant change for seventeen-year-olds. In fact, from 1969 to 1990 there was a significant decline in science achievement scores. Although blacks and Hispanics have made substantial gains in recent years, the average proficiency for thirteen- and seventeen-year-old blacks and Hispanics is considerably lower than their white peers. NAEP's analysis of scores suggested that the differential in scores between races may relate to parents' socio-economic status and level of education. They cite a study by Donald Rock et al., *Excellence in High School Education: Cross-Sectional Study, 1972–1980, Final Report*

TABLE 11-4

Trends in Percentages of Students At or Above Five Mathematics Proficiency Levels, 1978 to 1990

Proficiency levels	Age	Assessment years			
		1978	1982	1986	1990
Level 350	9	0 (0.0)	0 (0.0)	0 (0.0)	0 (0.0)
Multi-Step Problem	13	1 (0.2)	1 (0.1)	0 (0.1)	0 (0.1)
Solving and Algebra	17	7 (0.4)	6 (0.4)	7 (0.5)	7 (0.6)
Level 300	9	1 (0.1)	1 (0.1)	1 (0.2)	1 (0.3)
Moderately Complex	13	18 (0.7)	17 (0.9)	16 (1.0)	17 (1.0)
Procedures and	17	52 (1.1)*	49 (1.3)*	52 (1.4)	56 (1.4)
Reasoning					
Level 250	9	20 (0.7)*	19 (1.0)*	21 (0.9)*	28 (0.9)
Numerical Operations	13	65 (1.2)*	71 (1.2)	73 (1.6)	75 (1.0)
and Beginning Problem	17	92 (0.5)	93 (0.5)	96 (0.5)	96 (0.5)
Solving					
Level 200	9	70 (0.9)*	71 (1.2)*	74 (1.2)*	82 (1.0)
Beginning Skills and	13	95 (0.5)	98 (0.4)	99 (0.2)	99 (0.2)
Understandings	17	100 (0.1)	100 (0.0)	100 (0.1)	100 (0.1)
Level 150	9	97 (0.3)	97 (0.3)	98 (0.3)	99 (0.2)
Simple Arithmetic	13	100 (0.1)	100 (0.1)	100 (0.0)	100 (0.0)
Facts	17	100 (0.0)	100 (0.0)	100 (0.0)	100 (0.0)

*Shows statistically significant difference from 1990. The standards errors of the estimated percentages appear in parentheses. It can be said with 95 percent certainty that for each population of interest, the value for the whole population is within plus or minus two standard errors of the estimate for the sample. When the percentage of students is either 0 percent or 100 percent, the standard error is inestimable. However, percentages 99.5 percent and greater were rounded to 100 percent and percentages less than 0.5 percent were rounded to 0 percent.

From: Educational Testing Service under contract with National Center for Educational Statistics, U.S. Department of Education. *Trends in Academic Progress* (NCES 91–1264). (Washington, DC: U.S. Government Printing Office, September 1991), 13.

As measured on the NAEP (National Assessment of Educational Progress), students have improved mathematical skills from 1978 to 1990, but only at the low skill levels. At moderately complex levels (level 300), little more than half of all seventeen-year-olds were able to perform adequately, and at the highest level (level 350), only 7 percent of all seventeen-year-olds were able to solve the problems.

(1984), which concludes that, when other school and home factors are controlled, the students' socioeconomic status accounts for gaps in mathematics and science.

The greatest improvement in science achievement is of nine-year-olds, to the levels they had achieved in 1969. In 1990, 76 percent, up from 68 percent in 1977, could understand simple scientific principles. At age nine, the proficiency of boys and girls was relatively the same, but by ages thirteen and seventeen,

TABLE 11-5

Trends in Percentages of Students At or Above Five Science Proficiency Levels, 1977 to 1990

| Proficiency levels | Age | Assessment years | | | |
		1977	1982	1986	1990
Level 350	9	0 (0.0)	0 (0.1)	0 (0.1)	0 (0.0)
Integrates Specialized	13	1 (0.1)	0 (0.1)	0 (0.1)	0 (0.1)
Scientific Information	17	9 (0.4)	7 (0.4)*	8 (0.7)	9 (0.5)
Level 300	9	3 (0.3)	2 (0.7)	3 (0.5)	3 (0.3)
Analyzes Scientific	13	11 (0.5)	10 (0.7)	9 (0.9)	11 (0.6)
Procedures and Data	17	42 (0.9)	37 (0.9)*	41 (1.4)	43 (1.3)
Level 250	9	26 (0.7)*	24 (1.8)*	28 (1.4)	31 (0.8)
Applies General Scientific	13	49 (1.1)*	51 (1.6)*	53 (1.6)	57 (1.0)
Information	17	82 (0.7)	77 (1.0)*	81 (1.3)	81 (0.9)
Level 200	9	68 (1.1)*	71 (1.9)*	72 (1.1)*	76 (0.9)
Understands Simple	13	86 (0.7)*	90 (0.8)*	92 (1.0)	92 (0.7)
Scientific Principles	17	97 (0.2)	96 (0.5)	97 (0.5)	97 (0.3)
Level 150	9	94 (0.6)	95 (0.7)	96 (0.3)	97 (0.3)
Knows Everyday	13	99 (0.2)	100 (0.1)	100 (0.1)	100 (0.1)
Science Facts	17	100 (0.0)	100 (0.1)	100 (0.1)	100 (0.2)

*Statistically significant difference from 1990. The standard errors of the estimated percentages appear in parentheses. It can be said with 95 percent certainty that for each population of interest, the value for the whole population is within plus or minus two standard errors of the estimate for the sample. When the percentage of students is either 0 or 100, the standard error is inestimable. However, percentages 99.5 percent and greater were rounded to 100 percent and percentages less than 0.5 percent were rounded to 0 percent.

From: Educational Testing Service under contract with National Center for Educational Statistics, U.S. Department of Education. *Trends in Academic Progress* (NCES 91-1264). (Washington, DC: U.S. Government Printing Office, September 1991), 11.

Analysis of the NAEP (National Assessment of Educational Progress) tests of science proficiency indicates that at lower levels of factual knowledge, most students perform very well, but that at higher levels of analysis and interpretation very few do.

roughly one-half of the boys and only one-third of the girls could analyze scientific procedures and data. According to the NAEP, the difference in scientific achievement by gender cannot be explained by course-taking patterns. Citing a study by Marsha Matyas and Jane Kahle, *Equitable Precollege Science and Mathematics: A Discrepancy Model* (1986), NAEP suggested that the differential may stem from teachers' higher expectations of boys than girls: asking boys higher-level questions than girls and providing different treatment and opportunities in science instruction. In addition, NAEP suggested that textbooks that show that most scientific accomplishments are made by white males might contribute subtly to this gender discrepancy (Educational Testing Service 1988b, 8).

More than in any other content areas, U.S. students' achievement in mathematics and science has been compared with students' achievement in other countries. In both disciplines, the achievement of U.S. students is relatively low when considering the scientific contributions of U.S. scientists. In mathematics, students ranked last when compared to students in five other developed nations; in science they ranked second to last. In the United States, thirteen-year-olds, for example, could compute only at the basic operational and problem-solving level in mathematics, whereas Korean students could operate at the intermediate level and solve two-step problems. The same contrast can be seen in science, where thirteen-year-olds in the United States could work only marginally at the basic level, understanding simple scientific information. Korean students, operating a level above U.S. students, could use scientific procedures and analyze scientific data.

Again, we must question why this is so. According to the NAEP assessment, Americans are relatively unscientific. Use of scientific equipment by third graders and seventh graders is relatively low. Only 68.1 percent of U.S. third graders, for instance, had used a yardstick. Similarly, only 25.1 percent of U.S. seventh graders had used a barometer. However, 91 percent had used a microscope. The NAEP also asked students about their independent science activities. According to the study, only 39 percent of high school students read books or articles about science, and fewer engaged in scientific discussions with friends, took trips to museums, or had science hobbies. A surprisingly small percentage of U.S. eleventh graders report applying scientific knowledge to practical situations. Only 27 percent reported fixing anything mechanical, and only 10 percent reported figuring out what was wrong with an unhealthy plant. Likewise, a low percentage reported participation in conservation efforts. Only 8 percent of seventeen-year-olds said they had helped in a litter cleanup project and only 15 percent had separated trash for recycling (Educational Testing Service 1988b, 103–116).

Denis P. Doyle, former director of Education Policy Studies and Human Capital Studies at the American Enterprise Institute, in a special issue of *Business Week* (1989), says there are other reasons why U.S. students do not do as well in science and mathematics. For a variety of reasons—all cultural—most Americans are willing to admit they have no "aptitude" for science and math. By this they mean to excuse and justify their ignorance without embarrassment; to most it is apparently the intellectual equivalent of admitting to not being a gifted athlete. Not being a world-class athlete, while a source of disappointment, is not a source of embarrassment. Fair enough. And shouldn't it be the same for science and math?

As long as most people think it is, American performance in science and math will continue to be dismal. Although it is true that few of us have the natural talent of Einstein or Newton, all normal children can learn math and science to a high level of complexity and proficiency. Look at the Japanese, who consistently score among the top students in the world in math and science. How do they do it?

It is not due to diet, climate, innate superiority, or some cultural predisposition to mathematics and science; nor, as some observers speculate, is it plausible to believe that the use of *kanji*, the symbolic characters that comprise Japanese writing, set the stage for math and science. To what is it due then? That old-fashioned virtue, hard work. The Japanese don't believe they have any

TABLE 11-6

Levels of U.S. History Proficiency for the Nation, 1988

	Percentage of students at or above each level		
	Grade 4	Grade 8	Grade 12
Level 200 Knows Simple Historical Facts	76.0 (1.0)	96.0 (0.3)	99.4 (0.1)
Level 250 Knows Beginning Historical Information and Has Rudimentary Interpretive Skills	15.9 (0.9)	67.7 (0.9)	88.9 (0.6)
Level 300 Understands Basic Historical Terms and Relationships	0.2 (0.1)	12.7 (0.5)	45.9 (1.3)
Level 350 Interprets Historical Information and Ideas	0.0 (0.0)	0.1 (0.0)	4.6 (0.5)

Standard errors are presented in parentheses. Standard errors of less than 0.05 are rounded to 0.0. It can be said with 95 percent certainty that for each population of interest, the percentage of students at or above each level is within ± 2 standard errors.

From: Educational Testing Service under a grant from the National Center for Education Statistics, U.S. Department of Education (1990). *The U.S. History Report Card* (NAEP 19-H-01). (Princeton, N.J.: Author), 16.

Given for the first time in 1988, the National Assessment of Educational Progress in History revealed results similar to those in reading, mathematics, and science. While most students were able to identify simple historical events, very few were capable of analyzing historical information and interpreting policies.

special aptitude for math or science either; as a consequence, they try harder. They believe that math and science are difficult, that study is demanding, and that the path to mastery is application and diligence. They are probably right.

When an American parent is asked what accounts for academic success, the answer is invariably "ability." When a Japanese parent is asked the same question, the answer—just as invariably—is "effort." It pays (Doyle, p. E121).

History Assessment

In 1988, the NAEP assessed student progress in history for the first time. Students were tested in the fourth, eighth and twelfth grades. According to the test results, most students, at all three grade levels, have a limited grasp of U.S. history (see table 11.6).

Because this was the first history assessment of U.S. students, it is not possible to make comparisons across years. It is possible, however, to examine the results of this test. NAEP concludes that "a large percentage of students approaching high school graduation—and a disproportionally large percentage of minority students—lack a sense of the national heritage" (Educational Testing

(continued on p. 376)

Point/Counterpoint

JAPANESE EDUCATION FOCUSES ON CHARACTER BUILDING

I am staying with an architect and his family for a few days while commuting to Tokyo to do my business. Today, the weather is hot and humid. At 8:30 A.M., it is an un-air-conditioned 90 degrees.

My host, Seiji Kawazu, a Buddhist to the bone, does not believe in air conditioning. "I like nature," he says. "I like to feel the cold in winter and the heat in the summer. Weather is a part of life."

As we walk along the winding path through the pear orchards and tomato fields to the commuter station, he tells me how good the humid weather is for the tomatoes (although I notice that the pear trees must be protected from the heat and insects with heavy nets of gauze).

He is teaching his children also to observe nature. It is summer vacation for his oldest boy, Koichi, 6 years old. He has given Koichi an assignment. Every day he must look out the window at the weather. The boy must observe closely the signs of weather—the force of wind, the shapes and color of clouds, the amount of sun. Koichi has a worksheet that he works on every day. It is the drawing of a window. Koichi must draw in the window what he sees, describe it in words, and write down the time of the observation and a general summary of the weather.

When the father comes home from work, if it is a reasonable hour, he first asks to see his son's worksheet and sits with him asking questions about his assignment. He has high expectations for Koichi. Not only does he expect neat penmanship and clear answers to his questions, but he demands that Koichi pay close attention to what he has to say and show the proper respect—not merely out of a sense of duty to the father but out of a concern for learning.

From: Ranbom, 1985

AMERICAN EDUCATION FOCUSES ON INTELLECTUAL GROWTH

By American standards Japanese junior highs and high schools are needlessly onerous. Yes, Japan makes nearly all its people literate; yes, sheer memory work is the only way for students to master the written Japanese language. Nonetheless, the schools often seem to be harassing students for the sake of building character. In her book about the Japanese school system, Merry White, of the Harvard School of Education, quoted this statement of purpose for Japanese public schools: "It is desirable that, in the lower grades, one should learn to bear hardship, and in the middle grades to persist to the end with patience, and in the upper grades, to be steadfast and accomplish goals undaunted by obstacles or failure." It is hard to imagine an American public school that could issue such a document. When my older son was in sixth grade in a Japanese public school, his teacher would make the class of usually squirming boys and girls sit perfectly still for five or ten minutes during "concentration" exercises every few days. The teacher would prowl between the desks with a cane in his hand, rapping the knuckles or necks of students who let their attention wander.

The standardized tests that are so famous a part of Japanese education also reflect the emphasis on duty for its own sake. The Japanese tests differ from American IQ-style tests in their consequences: the major companies hire strictly according to where job applicants went to college, and colleges admit students mainly on the basis of test scores. But they also differ in their content. Few people in Japan contend that the tests are primarily measures of "ability" or "intelligence." Instead, the tests are straightforward measures of memorized information. No one seems interested in discussing whether the knowledge measured on the tests is related to skills that will later prove valuable on the job. That's not what the tests are about; they are measures of determination and effort, pure and simple, so the pointlessness of their content actually enhances their value as tests of will. The most common encouragement for students in "exam hell," cramming for the tests, is *Gambette!* In context it means, Keep trying! Never give up! It reflects something deep in the Japanese scheme of values.

From: Fallows, 1989

POSTSCRIPT

In recent years many critics of U.S. education have compared the progress made by U.S. students to that of students in other countries. As in figure 11.3, the comparisons are frequently unfavorable. Why? Does it matter?

Along with the NAEP discussion of the unscientific American (p. 372), James Fallows in *More Like Us: Making America Great Again* may give another partial answer to the question why. Contemporary U.S. schools typically have not designed curriculum and instructional strategies with the goal of preparing students for tests; U.S. education is devoted to teaching students how to learn. Ironically, as shown in NAEP's own assessments of test results, in all subjects students' scores indicate that the majority are functioning at a barely basic level, and rarely functioning on an advanced level. It appears that U.S. schools are failing to do what Fallows suggests they are devoting much of their time to, teaching students how to learn.

In the United States, tests are most frequently a means to an end rather than an end in themselves. For example, standardized achievement tests given in elementary schools are used to assess students' skills and knowledge in order to determine how best to instruct them. Similarly, college entrance examinations are used to determine if students are likely to succeed in specific institutions. In Japan, the tests are an end unto themselves; they determine the future of the student.

Many U.S. educators worry that today's new emphasis on measuring student achievement by such standardized tests as the NAEP will lead to test taking for the sake of the test rather than for the sake of the student. Since so much of what is taught in U.S. schools cannot be measured on standardized tests, many fear that the emphasis of curriculum will shift from learning how to learn, to memorizing easy-to-test, easy-to-teach bits of information. Perhaps, as even the NAEP suggests in its analysis of test results, much teaching is done at the barely basic level in all subjects. The irony of these educators' concerns is that the results of tests such as the NAEP and the Educational Testing Service's interpretation of test results in each volume of *The U.S. Report Card* indicate that students in U.S. public schools are not being challenged with high-level information and problems and are not achieving at advanced levels, but rather are being asked to function on minimal levels and are achieving at minimal levels in all subjects. It further suggests that schools must challenge students by presenting them with sophisticated, multistep problems.

Another reason that U.S. students may not do as well as their counterparts around the world on standardized tests is the multicultural nature of U.S. schools. A report in *Educational Leadership,* "U.S.–Japan Comparisons Called Misleading," cites Frank Betts's analysis, based on a visit to Japan, that "sociological factors such as Japanese parents' universally high expectations, family structure and roles, homogeneity of the population (racially, culturally, and economically), obedience to authority, and group behavior norms" have more to do with Japanese students' success on tests than school-related factors. Betts suggests that in order to improve U.S. students' performance on standardized tests as compared to their Japanese counterparts, "we would have to restructure a whole system of beliefs we hold about the values of independence, the rights of individuals, and the virtues of competition." He claims that although there are elements of the Japanese system worth considering, such as high expectations and effective time on task, we do not want to limit the U.S. "strengths" and "vulnerabilities" that are found in "our diversity, our sense of rugged individualism, and our competitive spirit" (Betts 1991, 5).

TABLE 11-7

College Entrance Examination Scores

SAT scores and percent taking SAT: Selected school years ending 1973–1990

School year ending	SAT total	Verbal	Mathematics	Percent taking SAT[1]
1973	926	445	481	33.4
1974	924	444	480	32.1
1976	903	431	472	31.8
1978	897	429	468	31.6
1980	890	424	466	32.6
1982	893	426	467	33.0
1984	897	426	471	34.9
1986	906	431	475	37.9
1988	904	428	476	40.5
1990	900	424	476	38.5

ACT scores and percent taking ACT: Selected school years ending 1986–1990

School year ending	ACT Composite	English	Mathematics	Percent taking ACT[1]
1986[2]	20.8	—	—	27.6
1988[2]	20.8	—	—	30.1
1990[2]	20.6	20.5	19.9	30.7

— Not available.

[1] The percent taking the SAT or ACT is the ratio of the number of individuals taking the SAT or ACT in the year to the number of high school graduates in the same year.

[2] The 1990 ACT assessment was significantly different from previous assessments. ACT has established links between scores earned on the ACT tests administered before October 1989 and scores on the enhanced test. The data for 1986 and 1988 are estimated average ACT scores.

From: College Entrance Examination Board, *National Report: College Bound Seniors,* various years; The American College Testing Program, *The High School Profile Report, Normative Data,* various years; U.S. Department of Education, National Center for Education Statistics, Common Core of Data survey.

The Scholastic Aptitude Test (SAT) and the American College Testing Program Assessment (ACT) are the tests taken most frequently by college-bound students. Both are designed to predict success in the freshman year in college. After years of decline, SAT total scores began increasing slightly in 1982, and continued increasing until 1987. From 1987 to 1990, SAT mathematics scores remained constant, and verbal scores fell 6 points.

Service 1990b, 6). At grade four, approximately three-quarters of students tested performed at or above level 200, the lowest proficiency level. Approximately two-thirds of eighth graders performed at or above level 250 and could identify more events and personalities of U.S. history. However, only 13 percent scored at level 300 and could understand historical terms and relationships. Eighty-nine percent of high school students displayed an understanding of beginning historical information, and 46 percent understood historical terms, texts, and relationships. However, only 5 percent of high school seniors performed at the highest level and could interpret historical information and ideas. Only 38 percent of high school seniors, for example, recognized the opening statement of the Declaration of Independence and had more than a rudimentary understanding of U.S. historical policies on civil rights. Hence, this assessment, like the other NAEP assessments, seems to reveal that U.S. students have basic and rudimentary knowledge of a subject, but few possess knowledge at advanced levels (Educational Testing Service 1990b).

The single most quoted measure of student progress through high school is the Scholastic Aptitude Test (SAT), used primarily to assess students' likely success in college. The American College Testing Program (ACT) is also used by college admissions staffs to predict student success in college.

College Entrance Exams

From 1982 until 1986, SAT and ACT scores increased after a nearly twenty-year decline. However, from 1986 through 1990, the scores again fell. From 1976 to 1990, average SAT verbal and mathematics scores of black students increased by 20 and 31 points respectively, on an 800-point scale (see table 11.7). Although minority students are making progress, the gap between minority and white students is still large. In 1991, white students had a composite (combined verbal and mathematics) score of 930 on the SAT and black students had a composite score of 736. The only minority students who score higher than white students are Asian Americans, who had a composite score of 941 in 1991.

Since the SAT does not test specific knowledge, the decline in its scores may be related to the minimal knowledge held by the majority of high school students in all subjects, as revealed by the NAEP. The SAT tests a student's ability to analyze, synthesize, evaluate, and solve multistep problems. NAEP results indicate that the vast majority of U.S. students do not function well on these high-level skills. If, as many educators suggest and NAEP results seem to confirm, most school time is used obtaining basic skills, it may be that students are not prepared to perform successfully on the SAT. Of course, as suggested in the postscript of the Point-Counterpoint (pp. 374–375), there are a number of explanations as to why students do not score well on tests; these apply to college entrance examinations as well as to other tests.

Although most students in U.S. schools are learning, many are not. As the test results show, many of the students who do not progress at expected levels as measured by standardized tests are nonwhite, poor, urban, and male. Is the public school system failing these students? In addition, test results reveal that few students are performing successfully at high cognitive levels. Are the public schools failing to challenge students to reach their highest level of potential? And what of society? Are the values of society militating against the academic achievement of U.S. students? We will deal with these questions in chapters 12 and 13.

11.2 POINTS TO REMEMBER

- The NAEP indicates that most students in the United States are not doing as well on standardized achievement tests as might be hoped. In both reading and writing, students score better in areas of basic skills than on test items that require critical and creative thinking.

- In mathematics and science, students function more successfully in areas of rudimentary knowledge and basic, simple functions. In mathematics, most U.S. students are unable to complete multistep problems. In science, students cannot relate basic scientific principles to other scientific concepts or to experimentation. There is a significant gap between the achievement of male and female students in both science and mathematics, particularly at the higher levels.

- In history, students are able to identify important historical personalities and events but are unable to relate these to each other. Students are unable to think at the higher levels of synthesis, analysis, and evaluation.

- Students in the United States score lower on standardized tests than students in many other developed nations. In one study, U.S. students scored fifth out of six developed countries in science and sixth in mathematics.

- SAT and ACT scores declined significantly from the early 1960s through the early 1980s, when there was a slight increase. However, the scores declined again in the late 1980s and early 1990s.

- Theories about why U.S. students do not do well on standardized tests include: U.S. schools aim to teach students to think rather than to take tests; U.S. values do not encourage students to do well on standardized tests; U.S. students do not do as much homework as students in other countries; U.S. students are not as willing to work as hard as students in other countries.

"But isn't it more important to learn how to be a decent human being?"

H. L. Schwadron in *Phi Delta Kappan*

FOR THOUGHT/DISCUSSION

1. What are the differences between the behaviorist and neobehaviorist definitions of learning? How can these differences be reconciled in a practical way in the classroom?

2. From the sociological perspective of learning environment, what are some things teachers can do to motivate students to learn?

3. What are the relationships among television, homework, and students' test scores? If you were a parent, how would you balance the time your child spends watching television, reading, and doing homework without causing negative psychological attitudes?

4. If the Japanese attitude toward test taking is that it is intended primarily to build character, how do you account for the fact that the Japanese seem to be outscoring American students in almost every test area?

FOR FURTHER READING/REFERENCE

Brown, R. C. 1991. *Schools of thought.* San Francisco: Jossey-Bass. A discussion of the definition of literacy as the ability to think critically and creatively and to become a lifetime learner. The author contends that many of the methods used in today's schools discourage critical and creative thinking.

Crow, G. 1978. *Children at risk.* New York: Schocken. Identification of psychological, emotional, and environmental factors affecting academic learning in the early years, probable causes of learning problems, and possible solutions.

Educational Leadership. 1990. 48 (2), complete issue. "Learning styles and the brain." Discussions by various authors on learning styles. Articles include student awareness of learning styles, left brain/right brain, how learning styles should influence teaching and curriculum, and a private school that implements learning styles research.

Gazzaniga, M. 1988. *Mind matters: How the mind works together to create our conscious lives.* Boston, MA: Houghton Mifflin. A nontechnical introduction to basic brain and mind questions that affect how teachers relate to the learning styles of students.

Holt, J. 1989. *Learning all the time.* Reading, MA: Addison-Wesley. A discussion of how children learn from those things that are significant for them in the real world rather than from special learning materials.

McCarthy, Bernice 1987. *The 4MAT® System: Teaching To Learning Styles With Right/Left Mode Techniques.* Barrington, IL: EXCEL, Inc. Those desiring a copy of the complete work for furhter reading may acquire it from the publisher, EXCEL, Inc., 200 W. Station St., Barrington, IL 60010.

White, M. 1987. *The Japanese educational challenge.* New York: Macmillan. An analysis of how differences in the Japanese and American cultures affect learning and achievement in Japan and the United States.

12 Society's Effect on the Schools

In this chapter we discuss some of the major issues facing U.S. society and how they affect children and the school. These include the changing family, teenage sexual activity, chemical abuse, crime, and suicide. Many of the statistics presented in this chapter are grim. However, because society's problems have such a major impact on today's children, teachers must be aware of them. Here and in chapter 13 we will talk about some of the ways in which contemporary schools are attempting to meet the needs of children and, thereby, help solve some of society's problems.

13 Schools Respond to Social Change

Although schools do not change rapidly and many argue that they should conserve rather than change society, they do attempt to deal with social changes and to meet the needs of society through direct and indirect measures. This chapter will examine some of the ways in which schools are affected by social change and how schools attempt to meet the needs of today's children and families.

Robbie—My first impression of Robbie was of the dull appearance of his hair and eyes. Somehow this was even more striking than the odor emanating from his corner desk. Sullen and quiet, Robbie drifted through my first grade lessons, barely able to find a pencil in his disorganized desk. His lunch usually consisted of Twinkies, which he said he bought on his walk to school. Later I learned that he more frequently stole them from the corner store. He eyed the other children's lunches covetously, and once I saw him steal an apple when a classmate turned her back. Quickly, like a furtive animal, he thrust the apple into the pocket of his dirty, faded, tattered pants.

Notes and phone calls to his parents met with no response. Robbie was a sad little nomad, drifting into school and listlessly returning home, reportedly to take care of his younger brother and sister.

From: C. C. Tower, *How Schools Can Help Combat Child Abuse and Neglect* (1987), 29.

PART V

Society and Schools

12

Society's Effect on the Schools

Barbara Jordan-Browne—8:00 A.M. on a Monday morning in 1988: Barbara Jordan-Browne, age 40, calls "good-bye" to her husband as he straightens up the breakfast dishes and she rushes out the door with 2-year-old Josh in tow. Next stop—the day care center. "It would be impossible," she thinks, "if he didn't do kitchen duty while I get Josh ready." Although Barbara feels rushed, she is confident that she's well prepared to represent her client in court and she feels attractive in her new maternity dress.

From: M. Fuller, "Delayed Parenting: Implications for Schools," *Childhood Education*, (Winter 1989), 75.

Rick—Divorced when his son Andrew was 3, Rick was determined from the beginning to stay involved in Andrew's life. Despite Rick's attempt to get joint custody, his son, like 90 percent of children of divorced parents, was placed in sole custody of his mother. Rick became a weekend visitor in his child's life.

Rick argues that his visitation time is too short to maintain a close relationship with his son. He turned down promotions that would have required him to move to other parts of the country so he could stay close to Andrew. While Rick is willing to make sacrifices, he is resentful that others continue to view him as an occasional parent, a checkbook.

Much of his anger is directed toward the school. Because he is not the primary caretaker, Rick is not given the same treatment as Andrew's mother. He says he is seldom informed of upcoming school events, his son's progress, parent-teacher conferences or other news. When Andrew was chosen "most artistic" student in his class, Rick was not informed until after the awards ceremony.

From: B. Lindner, *Drawing In the Family: Family Involvement in Schools,* (1988), 11.

Susan—Susan is a single mother, working full-time to support her two children, 3rd-grade Theresa and 3-year-old Jimmy. She must be at work by 8:00 A.M., so she leaves the house at 7:30 to drop Jimmy off at day care. Theresa's school bus doesn't pick her up until 8:15, meaning Susan must rely on a neighbor to take care of Theresa until then.

Susan missed a half day of work last week to attend Theresa's school conference. Today, the day care called to say Jimmy is sick. Because Susan has no one to care for him, she must leave work. She knows that she won't be able to take off time to attend Theresa's school play next week, which is only staged during school hours, and she fears her employer will be angry that she is leaving work again. In addition, her sick leave allows her to miss work only if *she* is ill, meaning she will lose pay if she takes off or will be forced to lie and say she is the one sick. Susan feels like she spends too much time juggling her work and family schedules. She lives in constant fear that one of the kids will get sick, or that she will lose one of her child-care arrangements. She feels guilty that she can't get involved in Theresa's school, and that Theresa can't get involved in extra activities like the swim team at the YWCA.

From: Lindner 1988, 13.

Teenage Mothers—"All I thought about was the good things . . . leaving home, getting out of school and receiving welfare. I never considered how much responsibility was involved. I really had no idea what motherhood was going to be like. I wish I could just run away and begin again—I really do. I would never have a kid until I was much older. . . ."

"I'm so jealous of my friends who aren't burdened with this responsibility. . . ."

"He won't even take care of her. He's afraid something will happen while I am gone. Somehow he thinks I just instinctively have the ability to care for her better. He hates listening to her cry and just leaves when he wants. . . ."

"My boyfriend was the one that wanted me to have the baby. I just assumed that he would share the responsibility both financially and in taking care of him. Not so, he just comes and goes as he pleases."

From: N. Compton, M. Duncan, and J. Hruska, *How Schools Can Help Combat Student Pregnancy* (1987), 113–114.

Robbie—My first impression of Robbie was of the dull appearance of his hair and eyes. Somehow this was even more striking than the odor emanating from his corner desk. Sullen and quiet, Robbie drifted through my first grade lessons, barely able to find a pencil in his disorganized desk. His lunch usually consisted of Twinkies, which he said he bought on his walk to school. Later I learned that he more frequently stole them from the corner store. He eyed the other children's lunches covetously, and once I saw him steal an apple when a classmate turned her back. Quickly, like a furtive animal, he thrust the apple into the pocket of his dirty, faded, tattered pants.

Notes and phone calls to his parents met with no response. Robbie was a sad little nomad, drifting into school and listlessly returning home, reportedly to take care of his younger brother and sister.

From: C. C. Tower, *How Schools Can Help Combat Child Abuse and Neglect* (1987), 29.

CHAPTER OBJECTIVES

After studying this chapter, you should be able to:

- Analyze the diversity of contemporary U.S. families.
- Discuss the single-parent family.
- Understand the problems of working mothers.
- Discuss the implications of homelessness for school-aged children.
- Discuss problems related to teenage parents.
- Compare and contrast characteristics of minority families with similarly configured white families.
- Discuss how schools can respond to the needs of families.
- Define and discuss child abuse and its impact on children and schools.
- Discuss the problems of children in poverty.
- Understand how crime affects the schools.
- Discuss how sexism affects students and the schools.
- Discuss how racism affects students and school personnel.
- Discuss how substance abuse education attempts to deal with society's needs.
- Analyze the problems of students who are chemically dependent.
- Discuss problems related to teenage sexual activity.
- Explain how sex education attempts to deal with students' needs.
- Define AIDS education.
- Define teenage suicide.

Carmen Ramos—Carmen Ramos is twenty-six and has five children, the eldest nine, the youngest an infant. She has lived in four or five New York City welfare hotels, including the infamous Martinique. Conditions there were crowded. There was a lot of thievery and drugs, she says, "lots of chaos, a lot of trouble." She says her children were "acting like savages because they had been living at the hotel for a long time."

Before the hotels, she had been living with the father of one of her children. He beat her. . . . She says her mother used to hit her with extension cords for coming home late from school. She once had a job for two months at a Jack-in-the-Box.

She plans to avoid living with any more men. . . .

"If I find the right job that pays more money than welfare," she says, "I might stop welfare. . . ."

Carmen was living in a hotel when she became pregnant with her last child. "I wanted another child," she says. "I planned for the pregnancy to take place. I love children."

From: C. Lockhead, "Homeless in America, All Alone With No Home," *Insight* (May 1988), 11.

I n this chapter we discuss some of the major issues facing U.S. society and how they affect children and the school. These include the changing family, teenage sexual activity, chemical abuse, crime, and suicide. Many of the statistics presented in this chapter are grim. However, because society's problems have such a major impact on today's children, teachers must be aware of them. Here and in chapter 13 we will talk about some of the ways in which contemporary schools are attempting to meet the needs of children and, thereby, help solve some of society's problems.

THE FAMILY AND THE SCHOOL

Families in the United States are diverse; they have different needs and problems. In fact, L. P. Howe, in *The Future and the Family*, wrote, "The first thing to remember about the American family is that it doesn't exist. Families exist. All kinds of families in all kinds of economic and marital situations. . . ." (1972, 11).

Barbara Lindner in *Drawing in the Family: Family Involvement in the Schools* identified eight basic family types: single-parent families, noncustodial parents, families with two wage earners, two-parent families with one wage earner, joined or blended families, homeless parents, teenage parents, and minority families. Within these groups there are numerous variations related to age, family size, culture, religion, socioeconomic level, education, and experience. There are almost as many variations as there are families, but we will discuss the eight basic types as one way of identifying and organizing them.

In 1989, more than 15 million (or 24.3 percent) of the 63 million children under the age of eighteen in the United States lived in **single-parent families** (see table 12.1). By 1990, 9.7 million of 34.7 million, or 28 percent of all family groups, were headed by a single parent, according to the 1990 U.S. Census.

Of children who lived with a single parent, 13.5 million lived with their mothers and 1.8 million with their fathers. In the past twenty-five years, the number of families headed by women has increased significantly. In 1960, only 8 percent of all families were headed by women; by 1990, the figure had grown to more than 24.2 percent.

Ninety percent of U.S. children whose parents divorce are placed in the sole custody of their mothers. Hence, most noncustodial parents are male. However, the number of children living with fathers almost doubled from 1960 through 1988.

Single-Parent Families

V I E W P O I N T S

A New Model for Single Parents

Some single parents have already established more informal models for the rest of us. One woman in Los Angeles, [a single parent for eighteen years and] a veteran of the women's movement . . . , suggested that new parent networks are a logical extension of feminism and the self-help movement. . . . "These groups are basically nonjudgmental, though there are a set of norms and values attached," she said. "People make fun of the self-help movement, but you don't solve problems by making fun of people. One woman in the group I attend . . . needed this group of other parents who were facing the same problem with their children because her family of origin just didn't know how to cope; if anything, their advice made the problem worse. . . . I'm a child of my times—I'm connected with both these movements. In the sixties I connected with other single parents through an alternative public school which we helped start. We could just as easily have linked through church or synagogue. . . . We were all single parents. We formed an informal extended family. With the exception of Dr. Spock, I've never read a how-to-parent book in my life; I have my friends. It's revealing, I think, that most of us who made these kinds of connections can truthfully say today that our kids are okay. The parents who didn't make those connections tend to be the ones with kids with severe problems. Those of us who connected with each other shared resources; it's the people without human resources who are so terribly lost, in part because human resources often lead to other resources." (p. 225)

From: Louv, 1990

TABLE 12-1

Living Arrangements of Children Under 18 Years, by Race and Hispanic Origin: 1989, 1980, 1970, and 1960
(Excludes persons under 18 years old who were maintaining households or family groups. Numbers in thousands)

Living arrangement	1989	1980	1970	1960	Percent distribution			
					1989	1980	1970	1960
ALL RACES								
Children under 18 years	63,637	63,427	69,162	63,727	100.0	100.0	100.0	100.0
Living with —								
Two parents	46,549	48,624	58,939	55,877	73.1	76.7	85.2	87.7
One parent	15,493	12,466	8,199	5,829	24.3	19.7	11.9	9.1
Mother only	13,700	11,406	7,452	5,105	21.5	18.0	10.8	8.0
Father only	1,793	1,060	748	724	2.8	1.7	1.1	1.1
Other relatives	1,341	1,949	1,547	1,601	2.1	3.1	2.2	2.5
Nonrelatives only	254	388	477	420	0.4	0.6	0.7	0.7
WHITE								
Children under 18 years	51,134	52,242	58,790	55,077	100.0	100.0	100.0	100.0
Living with —								
Two parents	40,706	43,200	52,624	50,082	79.6	82.7	89.5	90.9
One parent	9,626	7,901	5,109	3,932	18.8	15.1	8.7	7.1
Mother only	8,220	7,059	4,581	3,381	16.1	13.5	7.8	6.1
Father only	1,406	842	528	551	2.7	1.6	0.9	1.0
Other relatives	636	887	696	774	1.2	1.7	1.2	1.4
Nonrelatives only	166	254	362	288	0.3	0.5	0.6	0.5

The numbers of children living in families headed by a single parent has risen dramatically in recent years. This has serious implications for the students and the schools, which need to accommodate single working parents and noncustodial parents in their schedules.

Marriage and Divorce

The number of single adults increased from 16.2 percent in 1970 to 21.9 percent in 1988. The number of married adults decreased from 71.7 to 62.7 percent in the same period of time, while the number of divorced adults increased from 3.2 to 7.8 percent.

If predictions based on population demographics hold true, half of the newly married couples will eventually divorce. Therefore, one-third or more of all children will be living with a divorced parent at some point in their lives.

Problems of Single-Parent Families

This change in the structure of U.S. families puts significant pressure on the single parents, the children, and the school. In 1986, of the 15 million

Living arrangement	1989	1980	1970	1960	Percent distribution			
					1989	1980	1970	1960
BLACK[1]								
Children under 18 years	9,835	9,375	9,422	8,650	100.0	100.0	100.0	100.0
Living with —								
Two parents	3,738	3,956	5,508	5,795	38.0	42.2	58.5	67.0
One parent	5,362	4,297	2,996	1,897	54.5	45.8	31.8	21.9
Mother only	5,023	4,117	2,783	1,723	51.1	43.9	29.5	19.9
Father only	339	180	213	173	3.4	1.9	2.3	2.0
Other relatives	660	999	820	827	6.7	10.7	8.7	9.6
Nonrelatives only	75	123	97	132	0.8	1.3	1.0	1.5
HISPANIC[2]								
Children under 18 years	6,973	5,459	4,006[3]	(NA)	100.0	100.0	100.0	(NA)
Living with —								
Two parents	4,673	4,116	3,111	(NA)	67.0	75.4	77.7	(NA)
One parent	2,129	1,152	(NA)	(NA)	30.5	21.1	(NA)	(NA)
Mother only	1,940	1,069	(NA)	(NA)	27.8	19.6	(NA)	(NA)
Father only	189	83	(NA)	(NA)	2.7	1.5	(NA)	(NA)
Other relatives	142	183	(NA)	(NA)	2.0	3.4	(NA)	(NA)
Nonrelatives only	29	8	(NA)	(NA)	0.4	0.1	(NA)	(NA)

NA Not available
[1]Black and other races for 1960.
[2]Persons of Hispanic origin may be of any race.
[3]All persons under 18 years.
Source of 1970 Hispanic origin data: U.S. Bureau of the Census, 1970 Census of Population, PC(2)-1C, *Persons of Spanish Origin*.
Source of 1960 data: U.S. Bureau of the Census, 1960 Census of Population, PC(2)-4B, *Persons by Family Characteristics*, tables 1, 2, and 19.
(Excludes inmates of institutions and military in barracks.)

From: U.S. Department of Commerce, Bureau of Census (December 1990). *Marital Status and Living Arrangements: March 1989*, Population Statistics (Series P-20, No. 445) Washington, DC: U.S. Government Printing Office, p. 3.

children who lived in single-parent homes, 9.7 million had custodial parents who were in the labor force; nevertheless, of these, 1.4 million were unemployed. Over 5 million children lived in single-parent homes in which the custodial parent was neither employed nor in the labor force.

If the single parent works, child care is frequently a problem. Single parents, like Susan in the opening chapter anecdote, need to juggle work, family, social life, and school, frequently putting stress on all aspects of life. If Susan decides to leave work to go to Theresa's play, she risks losing her job, which she cannot afford to do. If she does not go to Theresa's play, she feels guilty and Theresa does not understand why her mother cannot be there. Not only does Susan not have much money left after she takes care of her family's basic needs and child care, but she has little time for her own social life.

Frequently, single parents who work are frustrated by the constraints and demands of the school, which functions during the same basic hours that most people work, thus preventing most of them from attending school meetings and events. In order to meet the needs of the child in single-parent homes, the school day might be structured to allow for varied activities before and after classtime so that children not only can be cared for but also can participate in motivational and enjoyable activities. With good after-school programs, Theresa might be able to participate on a swim team, for example. In addition, after-school programs should allow time for study and instruction (see also chapter 13).

Noncustodial Parents   **Noncustodial parents**, those who no longer live in the home, like Rick in the opening anecdote, also face problems. Most want to be considered more than a checkbook for their children; they want to be involved in their children's lives. But, like Rick, they frequently are not informed about activities, particularly at school. Schools need to be aware of the children's custodial arrangement and, whenever possible, inform both parents of school activities and arrange special functions for noncustodial parents and their children.

Families With Two Wage Earners   Although the percentage of children in two-parent households has decreased from 87.7 percent in 1960 to 73.1 percent in 1989, they are still in the majority. However, only 38 percent of black children in 1989 came from two-parent households, whereas 67 percent of Hispanic children did (see table 12.1 on p. 386).

Working Mothers

More and more children live in homes in which their mothers are in the labor force. In 1970, 29 percent of women with children under five and 43 percent of women with children between six and seventeen worked part or full-time. By 1988, those percentages had increased to 51 percent and 64 percent, respectively.

White married mothers with school-aged children are less likely to be working outside the home than white single-parent mothers. For black women, the reverse is true. The U.S. Department of Labor, Bureau of Labor Statistics, reports that the overall proportion of children with mothers working full-time for part of the year grew by more than half between 1975 and 1988, from 29 percent to 44 percent. Likewise, the proportion of children with mothers who work full-time throughout the year has nearly doubled since 1971, from 17 percent to 30 percent. As these percentages reveal, the majority of today's children (74 percent) have mothers who work outside the home at least part of the year.

Most women who work, generally work out of necessity rather than choice, mainly for economic reasons. The greatest growth in women workers in the past few years has been among the well-educated from families with moderate incomes that are insufficient to maintain established and expected patterns of consumption. Before World War II, those married women who worked were primarily from low-income families; today, they are just as commonly from middle-class families.

Problems of Families in Which Both Parents Work

Although families with two wage earners may avoid the financial problems of single-parent families, they frequently do not avoid many other problems. Like single-parent families, they are usually not available during the school day; therefore, parent-teacher conferences and other programs held during the day are difficult for working parents to attend. Like single parents, working parents are also concerned with child care. Many have to shuttle their children from a child-care facility to school and back to the child-care facility. Often the transportation has to be handled by someone other than the parent.

Because of the large number of parents who work, schools must attempt to accommodate the needs of these families. This might mean scheduling such things as parent-teacher conferences in the evenings, arranging for extended child care before, during, and after school hours and while parents attend special school events.

Two-Parent Families With One Wage Earner

Two-parent families with one wage earner were most common in the mid-1960s. Today only 7 percent of children come from such families. The increased number of single-parent families and mothers working have shifted family structures away from this model.

Problems of Two Parents, One Wage Earner

Many families with single wage earners experience financial difficulties. According to the U.S. Department of Labor, Bureau of Labor Statistics, the median family income where both parents were employed was nearly $40,000 in 1987; where only one parent was employed the income was $30,000. In those one-wage-earner homes in which the mother was looking for employment in 1987, the median income was $23,200.

In terms of accommodating school schedules, families of this type have fewer problems than families where both parents work. Volunteerism, daytime parent-teacher conferences, and parent involvement in school activities are relatively easy. In fact, in spite of the modest numbers of this type of family, most schools still operate as if it were the norm.

Joined or Blended Families

Within five years of their parents' divorce, four of every seven children become part of new **blended families**, in which one or both adults in a new marriage or living arrangement have children from a previous marriage.

Problems of Blended Families

Of course, the blended family can have many problems. The increased number of children may place demands on parents accustomed to having fewer children. Frequently, the children do not accept the authority of the new parent; they are confused about which parent makes the final decision. They are unsure of the role of the noncustodial parent in this new relationship, and if the noncustodial parent also lives in a blended household, the children may wonder, Who are my parents anyway? Visitation with these children can cause stress among the children who normally live in the household, and the noncustodial parent may experience anger or guilt because he or she spends more time with the children who live in his or her home than with his or her own children.

The blended household presents numerous difficulties for the school, which may have as many as four people to contact about an individual child. Frequently the school is unaware of which parent to contact for which purpose.

For children from blended families, sibling rivalries can also occur in school. For example, the Rosman family has six children: two are hers and two are his and two are theirs. All four oldest children are girls: two are named Jennifer and two Stephanie. Both Jennifers are in the same class at school. The Jennifers, one named Rosman and the other Smythe, have different biological parents but share a stepparent. They do not live in the same household. Jennifer Rosman lives with her biological mother and stepfather, whose name is Joe Smythe. Jennifer Smythe lives with her biological mother who is a single, custodial parent of Jennifer and Stephanie Smythe. The school did not realize when they placed the Jennifers in the same class that they were children of a blended family. Nor did they know that there were many conflicts between them. Each of the Jennifers complains that she is not treated equally by Joe. Jennifer Rosman complains that she gets none of the privileges of Jennifer Smythe but has to follow Joe's rules about bedtime and watching television. Jennifer Smythe complains that when she comes to visit she does not have her own bedroom and has to go places with Jennifer Rosman and her father. She also complains that Jennifer Rosman has nicer clothes and toys than she does. These conflicts carry over into the schoolroom and it is the teacher who must deal with the consequences.

Homeless Families

The image of the homeless as a collection of alcoholics, drug addicts, and those with mental disabilities is incorrect. In fact, fewer than half of the homeless fall into that group. More than half a million homeless people are children, with the fastest-growing group those under six years of age. Of homeless people, 22 percent of adults have jobs and one-third are families with children.

On any given night, nearly 68,000 children under the age of sixteen are sleeping in shelters, churches, abandoned buildings, or on the street, according to statistics compiled by the U.S. General Accounting Office (GAO) in a survey of shelters conducted in October 1988. The GAO acknowledges that these statistics are likely to be inaccurate since the survey came from only forty-two states, each of which used a different means of counting the homeless. In fact the GAO claims that there could be as many as 296,452 homeless children each night. According to the Urban Institute, because so many homeless persons do not use shelters or services, they are almost impossible to count (Burt and Cohen, 1989, 19).

Problems of the Homeless Family

The problems of the homeless family are numerous. Besides lacking security, homeless families are frequently in physical danger, have numerous health problems without appropriate care, are unable to obtain child care, often do not have enough to eat, are ostracized by the rest of society and thus have poor self-esteem. The children of the homeless are particularly vulnerable. Not only are they more likely to experience violence and illness than those who live in homes, but they also do not have appropriate resources for success in school: they have no place to study, cannot afford materials for studying, and cannot participate in school activities. Neither do their parents usually have the time, the ability, or the place to help them. However, 85 percent of these children attend school regularly.

For this reason, these children usually experience many problems in school. They frequently do not succeed and thus are often vulnerable to peer pressure that may encourage involvement in gangs, crime, and drugs. That is why Lupe Vasquez, the homeless child who is now a student at Stanford University (chapter 11, pp. 348–349), is so exceptional. Lupe did have the help and encouragement of her mother. In addition, she had the support and concern of her teachers and, despite her homelessness, was able to succeed academically. However, Lupe is the exception rather than the rule.

In 1987, 473,000 women under the age of twenty gave birth, representing 12.4 percent of all U.S. births (U.S. Department of Commerce 1990a). According to data reported by the National Education Association in *How Schools Can Help Combat Student Pregnancy* (Compton, Duncan, and Hruska 1987), approximately 12 percent of teenagers having babies have not yet completed ninth grade. Karen Pittman, in a 1985 Children's Defense Fund Study, *Preventing Children Having Children*, reports that three of four teenage pregnancies are unintended. By some reports, nearly twice as many teenagers become pregnant as give birth.

Teenage Parents

The younger the mother, the more likely the pregnancy, the birth, and the newborn will have complications, primarily because of the immaturity of the mother's young body and her lack of knowledge of prenatal and child care. Younger parents are also less emotionally prepared to nurture babies. According to the NEA study, "As a result, literally thousands of children each year enter life unhealthy, undernourished, and unwanted" (1987, 14).

About 90 percent of white teenage mothers and virtually all black teenage mothers keep their babies. Teenagers from higher socioeconomic and educational levels more frequently decide to abort their babies than their poorer and less-educated peers. A study conducted by the Alan Guttmacher Institute, *Teenage Pregnancy: The Problem That Hasn't Gone Away*, found that in 1981, among 600 fifteen- to seventeen-year-old white teenagers in the United States who became pregnant, 200 gave birth and 120 raised their children as single mothers. Of 1,400 black teenagers in the same age group who became pregnant, 700 gave birth and 660 raised their children as single parents. In 1989, approximately 40 percent of white babies and 90 percent of black babies of teenage parents were born and raised by their single parent (Natriello, G., McDill, E. L., Pallas, A. M., 1990). Since babies and children born to teenagers are more likely to experience health, social, and academic problems, teenagers, the least prepared group of parents, have more difficult problems with which to cope. This has an important implication for the schools not only in terms of educating the teenagers, many of whom have not yet completed high school, but also in terms of educating their children.

Teenage fathers have backgrounds similar to those of teenage mothers. Although there were 473,000 babies born in 1987 to teenage mothers, only 105,000 teenage males were reported as being fathers (U.S. Department of Commerce, 1990e). However, because many teenage mothers do not report the father on their child's birth certificate, the actual number is much higher. William Marsiglio in *Commitment to Social Fatherhood: Predicting Adolescent Males'*

Teenage parents not only have to continue their own education, but also have to care for their infants. Most schools do not have facilities for infant care, thus placing the teenage parent-student in a difficult situation. This sixteen-year-old nurses her seven-month-old son in a special class for young parents and pregnant teens in California.

Intention to Live With Their Child and Partner (1988) found that 7 percent of a nationally representative sample said they had fathered a child as a teenager: 15 percent were black, 12 percent economically disadvantaged whites, 11 percent Hispanic, and 5 percent middle-class whites. Teenage fathers, like teenage mothers, tend to be low academic achievers, naive, incorrectly informed about sex and parenthood, and want babies as an antidote for loneliness. In addition, they believe that getting a girl pregnant proves they have been successful.

One phenomenon that occurs in families headed by teenage parents is something sociologists call the **short-cycle family**. These are families that produce children approximately every fourteen years. It is not clear how many of these families exist; however, most of them live in extreme poverty. Harold L. Hodgkinson in *The Same Client: The Demographics of Education and Service Delivery Systems* (1989) gives a graphic example of the short-cycle family (see figure 12-1). This is a white family living in poverty in Los Angeles. The great-grandmother is only fifty-six years old; the youngest mother is fourteen.

Problems of Teenage Parents

Many of these children with children are unable to care appropriately for their infants. Those teenagers who keep their babies have few financial resources, limited emotional maturity and coping skills, and no support system to help raise their children (Compton, Duncan, and Hruska 1987). Teenage

FIGURE 12-1

Short-Cycle Family

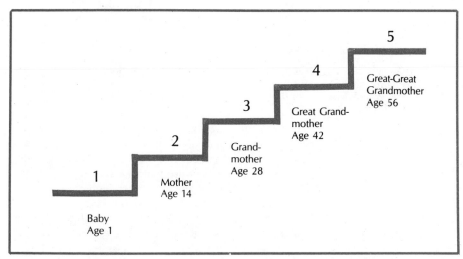

From: Harold L. Hodgkinson, *The Same Client: The Demographics of Education and Service Delivery Systems*, 1989, p. 5.

Sociologists have termed a phenomenon that frequently occurs in families headed by teenage parents, a short-cycle family. In these families, the age of the parents from generation to generation is much less than would normally be expected. Most short-cycle families live in poverty since their members have little time to acquire an education.

mothers who live with their own parents or other relatives generally are better parents themselves, frequently continue in school, and are more emotionally stable than those who live alone. In the long run, their children benefit from this stability and from social interaction with adults.

Teenage mothers, according to Compton, Duncan, and Hruska, are lonely, feel resentment toward the child's father, and are jealous of peers and friends not burdened with responsibility (p. 114). Teenage fathers frequently express concern for the teen mother but feel overwhelmed, burdened, angry, and confused. Counseling is rarely available to young fathers, and when it is, it is often not utilized. Few pregnant teenagers or teenagers with children marry, but those who do are likely, eventually, to separate and divorce. Seventy percent of children born to mothers seventeen and under have spent part of their childhood in a single-parent home.

The risk to children of teenage parents is also very high. Not only are they more likely to be born with birth defects and mental disabilities, but they are also more likely to be victims of childhood illness and more likely to die in infancy. Those who live beyond infancy are also at risk primarily because of the threat of abuse and neglect, the impairment of cognitive development because of limited interaction with caregivers, and social and emotional problems and subsequent low self-esteem. All these factors influence the children's school-work: they are more likely to have problems adapting to school, have lower test scores, achieve less in school, and repeat grades (Compton, Duncan, and Hruska 15–16).

V I E W P O I N T S

We Cannot Afford Education as Usual for Teenage Parents

The average family begun by a first birth to a teenager will cost the taxpayer $14,852 by the time the first baby reaches the age of twenty. This figure climbs to $18,913 if the teenage mother is under the age of fifteen, and to $37,500 if she receives welfare. (Center for Population Options 1986)

The National Governors' Association report *Making America Work: Bringing Down the Barriers* (1987) gives some options for dealing with the high cost, both financial and human, of teenage pregnancy. Here's one from Arkansas:

A school-based program for pregnant high school students in two Arkansas communities is operated by The Parent Center. The program is a cooperative, comprehensive effort between public and private agencies.

Services provided in the program include: a vocational skills course for credit toward high school graduation, which helps young women acquire skills to support themselves and their children; parenting education; assistance in goal setting; individual and group counseling; crisis intervention; advocacy for other needs; complete parental and postpartum health care; and ongoing education and support outside of school on a weekly basis in a program operated by the Parent Center, a cooperative comprehensive effort between public and private agencies and two Arkansas counties.

The Parent Center [which is funded by the Arkansas Department of Health, the Little Rock School District, United Way of Pulaski County, Winthrop Rockefeller Foundation, Title XX, and the Levi Strauss Foundation] is completing its third year, and 143 young women and about thirty teenage fathers have participated. Among participants, the school dropout rate is only 20 percent, compared to a much higher rate nationwide. There have only been two repeat pregnancies out of 143 mothers. Also, all six seniors eligible to graduate last year did so. Of these six, two went on to attend college, two found employment, and two went into the armed forces. All seven senior participants in the program this year are scheduled to graduate. There have been very few health problems with the babies or the mothers in the program.

The total cost of the program is about $100,000, which the executive director points out is less than it would cost to keep one premature baby in intensive care for the average two-month stay.

From: National Governor's Association, p. 61

Minority Families   If current **demographic patterns** (population trends due to births, deaths, marriages) continue, one-third of the United States population will be nonwhite by the year 2000. Of course, racial and ethnic minorities may fit into any of the previously discussed family types. However, minority families frequently exhibit characteristics different from similarly configured white families. Barbara Lindner states in *Drawing in the Family: Family Involvement in the Schools*, that minority families traditionally have less power, wealth, social status, and education than white U.S. families.

Black families, according to the U.S. Bureau of Census, are three times more likely to live in poverty than white families, Hispanic families twice as likely. In 1989, more than half of all black children and nearly 30 percent of Hispanic children were in households headed by single mothers. Only 38 percent of black children were in families with two parents (see table 12.1 on page 386). In 1990, over 50 percent of black children and nearly a third of all Hispanic children were born to mothers who had never married. Since families with mothers as heads of households tend to be poorer than families with two parents (61 percent, according to the Congressional Budget Office are poor compared to 13.8 percent in two-parent households), it follows that a larger percentage of minority families are likely to be poor. "In 1967 the income of white female-headed families averaged 57 percent of the income of white male-headed families; the income of black female-headed families averaged 52 percent of the income of black male-headed families. By 1973 the situation of female-headed families had worsened. The average income of white female-headed families was 49 percent, that of black female-headed families only 44 percent of the income of male-headed families" (Bane 1976, 119–120). In 1990, the average income of white female-headed households was down to 42 percent of white male-headed households, that of black female-headed households was down to 38 percent of black male-headed households.

Problems of Minority Families

In addition to the fact that minority families tend to be poorer and have less education than middle-class white families, they face other problems related to the schools. Minority students are not likely to do as well on standardized tests as their white peers (see also chapter 11). They are likely to be placed in low-ability tracks, to receive relatively low grades, and to drop out of school.

Why do these problems continue? As discussed in chapter 10 (p. 319), researchers such as Jeannie Oakes contend that tracking tends to categorize minority students, and teachers tend to teach down to them. Many educators also claim that the majority of teachers, who are predominantly white and middle class, may not be prepared to understand and deal effectively with minority students. If Edmund W. Gordon's studies on learning styles are correct, it may be that minority youngsters have different learning styles than white students and, hence, as Fischer and Fischer suggest, predominantly white teachers who tend to teach as they were taught may not use appropriate teaching styles for minority students (see chapter 11, pp. 362–363).

WHAT SCHOOLS CAN DO

Most schools have not changed how they interact with families since the early 1950s; however, family structures have changed significantly. If the schools are to involve parents in the education of their children, they must seek new ways to interact with the parents.

Instead of expecting parents to adapt completely to the school's agenda, teachers and administrators must respond to parents' changing circumstances by providing alternative schedules for meetings and conferences and designing programs that all parents can attend. They must consider spending more time in the neighborhoods and homes of the students they teach. They must find ways for parents to volunteer their services after school and in the evenings and

---

VIEWPOINTS

Programs That Help Combat the Effects of Poverty on Children

• The Center for Successful Child Development, known as the Beethoven Project, is a family-oriented early childhood intervention program at the Robert Taylor Homes, a public housing project on the south side of Chicago. Sponsored by the Chicago Urban League and the Ounce of Prevention Fund, the Beethoven Project opened in 1987. Some 155 families now benefit from a variety of educational, social, and medical services for young children who will ultimately enroll in the Beethoven Elementary School.

• In Missouri, Parents as Teachers combines an early childhood component with an education program for parents. It began as a pilot program in 1981, and today all 543 Missouri school districts are required to provide certain services to families, including parent education, periodic screening through age 4 to detect developmental problems, and educational programs for those 3- and 4-year-olds who are developmentally delayed. The program is not restricted to poor children, but it can catch their problems early, and the results have been encouraging.

• James Comer, director of the School Development Program at Yale University, is working with 100 inner-city schools across the country to create management teams made up of parents, teachers, and mental health professionals. The aims are to improve the teachers' knowledge of child development, to involve parents, and to provide children with community resources normally found outside the school.

• In California and Missouri a new approach, known as the Accelerated Schools Program, is trying to change parents' attitudes toward their children. The Accelerated Schools Program attempts to raise parents' expectations about what their children can do, while it also focuses on giving literacy training to the parents. The goal is to empower parents so that they can become involved in their children's education. The program currently operates in two schools in California and in seven schools in Missouri.

From: Reed and Sautter, 1990, K9

---

must hire additional support staff such as social service workers and counselors to assist in some of the programs conducted after regular hours.

Barbara Lindner states in *Family Diversity and School Policy* (1987) that "There is clearly a mismatch between family needs and school structures. Understanding the diversity of the family in American society prior to developing school policies and designing programs is essential. If this diversity is ignored, schools may be erecting yet another barrier to the education of youth and the family's ability to take part in that education" (p. 16).

In addition, schools must find ways to deal with the needs of minority families. Some of the solutions are obvious but not necessarily easy to achieve. More minority and/or bilingual teachers must be trained and hired. Educators must investigate the effects of tracking on minority students and must explore various teaching methodologies that would appeal to specific learning styles of minority students.

It is not only the teachers or the parents who must help reform the schools; business and industry must also become involved in the educational system as they have in several of the programs discussed above. Furthermore, business might provide day care for small children, personal leave for parents to attend important school functions, substitute employees on days in which important educational events occur at school, and some work that can be done at home.

IN THE CLASSROOM

Alan Goycochea, the principal at Sweetwater Union High School in National City, California, is called Mr. G, Mr. Goy, or El Pirata (the pirate) by his students. He is known as the pirate because of an eye patch where his left eye should be; he lost the eye to shrapnel in Vietnam.

His students know him as the disciplinarian who bolted all the lockers shut because of thievery and drug dealing from them. In spite of his harsh discipline, the students are fond of him. "He's a great guy. He's done a lot for this school," says Sweetwater student government leader Julio Juarez.

Goycochea makes it clear why his students like him so well; he cares about them. "To me, there are no such things as acceptable casualties in this business [education]. Every time a kid drops out of school, it diminishes all of us."

He talks about Sweetwater Union before he took over the reins. "Our test scores were low, and nobody gave a damn because this is a minority school [64 percent of the students are Hispanic; 20 percent are Filipino; 5 percent are black]. Nobody was that upset. It's expected. What we have done is turn this school around." Goycochea always uses the pronoun "we." He recognizes the success of the school as the joint effort of students, teachers, and administrators.

Goycochea believes that Sweetwater's students can achieve. However, he claims that students perform only as well as they're expected to. He points to the fact that students who are tracked into remedial classes in junior high school are still in remedial classes in high school, often performing worse and worse as time goes on. "If he's going to fail remedial math, why not have him fail basic algebra?" Not all his teachers agree with him, but even those who do not, recognize that his belief in the students has raised test scores, and his tightened discipline has changed the school environment.

Most of Sweetwater's students are underprivileged. One-third will drop out of school before graduation. Nearly one-third are not proficient in English. More than one-third have parents who did not graduate from high school. The average educational level attained by the Sweetwater students' mothers, their most influential parental role model, is fifth grade. More than 25 percent of the students' families live on financial aid from Families with Dependent Children.

According to Goycochea, "The kind of support they can get at home is limited. And if these kids are going to make it, by God, they're going to make it because we did something *extra*. It's not that they're not intelligent. It's not that they're not capable. It's that they have essentially been shot in the foot. What kids here die from is a lack of exposure." According to

Goycochea, showing up at school is a real act of courage for many of the students.

The staff at Sweetwater Union gives the students discipline, support, and exposure. Discipline comes from rules designed to protect the safety of the students. For example, the proms and other activities are canceled if the seniors participate in "Senior Ditch Day." This is because too many students get hurt or worse on days when they stay out of school en masse.

Support comes in the form of positive reinforcement and praise. Each week a snapshot is posted on the "Kid of the Week" bulletin board across from the principal's office. And each month a snapshot of a staff member is posted on the Staff Member of the Month bulletin board. Art work done by the students and photographs of school sports champs are prominently displayed on the walls of the principal's office.

The students are encouraged academically through a series of advanced courses, including classes in Spanish and Spanish literature, in which students can earn college credit. Sweetwater students are encouraged to go to college. In 1987, Sweetwater Union High School sent 86 students to San Diego State University, more than the total enrollment of Sweetwater alumni at SDSU at that time.

In 1989 Sweetwater Union High School was one of the few schools in California to pilot a year-round school calendar. Goycochea believes that the year-round school will help the students, particularly those who barely know English and tend to forget what they know over the long summer break.

Sweetwater Union High School is a school with a mission. Through strict discipline, encouragement and support, and increased academic requirements the students are succeeding. To Principal Goycochea he could ask no more: "I can't imagine not doing this [being a principal]. I really love the kids here in this school. They are an absolute inspiration to me." (McGrath 1988, D-2)

SOCIETAL CHANGES THAT AFFECT FAMILIES

Some of the other societal changes in the United States that affect families include the aging of the population, changes in the birth rate, and child abuse.

The Aging U.S. Family   From 1980 to 1987 the population of adults over the age of sixty-five increased by 4.3 million. During the same period the birth rate increased by only 1.9 million. In the 1990s it is expected that the birth rate will again decline as a smaller group of women enter the child-bearing years. By the year 2050, the U.S. Department of Health and Human Services predicts that the number of people over sixty-five years of age will exceed the number of people between the ages of birth and seventeen.

The aging of U.S. society will have a significant impact on the American family; longer life expectancy and more divorces will likely result in a great many extended families.

Long life expectancy plus more divorces yields the multiple-dependent family. Think of a married couple, the Smiths, 60 and 62 years old. The husband has had a stroke and cannot care for himself. The wife's 85-year-old mother has come to live with them. They have two daughters; the first has been divorced and has a child with partial paralysis who cannot go to school. The second daughter has two children; she and her husband live in the same house with all the others. The 60-year-old wife is responsible for the care of her mother, her husband, the partially paralyzed son of her first daughter when she is working, and the 4-year-old child of her second daughter, who is too young to go to school. This type of multiple-dependent family is rapidly becoming more common in the United States. (Hodgkinson 1989, 5)

This type of family will have a significant impact on the children when they reach school age. Who will go to the school to attend parent-teacher conferences and school events? Who will the school contact if one of the children becomes ill? Who is ultimately responsible for the education of the children?

Birth Rate

Since World War II the birth rate has dramatically dropped, especially among whites. In 1950 there were 47 million children under the age of eighteen. By 1970, as a result of the baby boom following World War II, there were 70 million. However, despite the increase in number of women of child-bearing age, the birth rate began to fall. By 1980, there were only 64 million children under the age of eighteen. It is expected that the birth rate will increase slightly in the next few decades, and by 2000 there will be approximately 67 million children in the United States.

On the other hand, the black and Hispanic birth rate has not declined. In 1970 there were 9.5 million black children under the age of eighteen. By 1985, the number had grown to 9.6 million and is expected to grow to 11.5 million by 2010. The number of Hispanic children has grown from 5.3 million in 1980 to 6.3 million in 1985. It is expected to grow to 9.7 million by 2010.

These fluctuations in birth rate affect the schools. The number of preschool children increased by more than 3 million from 1980 to 1989. It is, however, expected to decrease before the turn of the century. (The increase in preschool children relates not only to the birth rate but also to the fact that more mothers are working and leaving their children in preschool.) The number of elementary school children has remained relatively low when compared to 1970. Nevertheless, it is predicted that this number will increase through the year 2000 and then drop off again.

Because the birth rate affects school enrollment, the school must continually project changes in its structure. It is possible that one year a school's enrollment will be high, requiring new teachers and even new classrooms. But in two or three years the enrollment may decrease significantly, requiring the school to transfer teachers and close unused classrooms. Because schools recognize these demographic changes, they adapt by hiring district-wide teachers who move from school to school based on need, using temporary classrooms such as trailers rather than building new schools, and combining grade levels to make a complete class or sectioning grade levels to make several classes.

Child Abuse   Although child abuse and neglect are not new problems, they have been given increased attention in recent years. **Child abuse** by definition includes physical abuse, sexual abuse, physical neglect, and/or emotional maltreatment. Hence, cases of abuse or neglect are varied in terms of type and intensity and may be difficult to prove. However, there is no doubt that the number of reported cases of child abuse and neglect is increasing. In 1983, 828,417 child abuse and neglect cases were reported in the United States and in 1984, 958,590 cases. This represents an increase of 16 percent in one year.

By 1990, more than 2.5 million cases of child abuse and neglect were reported, a 4 percent increase over 1989. In 1990, more than 1,211 children died from abuse-related incidents. Why are reported cases of child abuse and neglect rising to such an alarming level? According to a study conducted by the National Committee for the Prevention of Child Abuse in 1989, this may be for two reasons: growing public awareness and an actual increase in abuse. More than half of the child welfare officials from all fifty states who were contacted for the 1989 study indicated that substance abuse was a primary cause for the increase in actual cases of child abuse and neglect.

It is difficult to tell how many cases of child abuse and neglect there actually are. Many cases still go unreported and of those that are, many may not actually be cases of abuse or neglect. Robert Emans reported in *Abuse in the Name of Protecting Children* (1987) that in 1985, 80 percent of reported sexual abuse cases were later believed to be unfounded (1987, 740).

Emans warns that publicity campaigns about child abuse and neglect must alert the public to what should, and should not, be reported. According to Emans, "Until this is done the system to protect kids from abuse will falter" (p. 743).

This is particularly important to teachers since they are legally responsible for reporting suspected child abuse and neglect cases to local protection agencies. However, many teachers and administrators are not aware of the magnitude of their responsibility, according to the National Education Association (NEA) publication, *How Schools Can Help Combat Child Abuse and Neglect*, written by C. C. Tower. The National Committee for the Prevention of Child Abuse completed a survey in 1988 which revealed that of the 2.1 million reports of child abuse in 1986, only 16.3 percent originated with school personnel. Ninety percent of the teachers responded that they had reported suspected child abuse cases to other school personnel, rather than to child protection agencies as mandated by state laws, primarily because they feared lawsuits if they were incorrect in their accusations. At the very least, teachers should avoid a situation in which the parents or the child are unnecessarily embarrassed. Only half of the teachers, according to the survey, reported that they had received training in detection and reporting of child abuse and neglect.

The National Committee for the Prevention of Child Abuse suggests that school districts should provide a good deal of information to teachers to help them recognize and report child abuse and neglect. In addition, the NEA recommends that each school develop a team consisting of a counselor or social worker, nurse, administrator, and teacher to discuss suspected child abuse or neglect cases. This team approach in the long run is the most efficient and most just method of deciding which cases should be reported to authorities (see table 12.2 on pp. 402–403).

Abused children, no matter the type or severity of mistreatment, do not achieve as well in school as those who are nurtured by caring parents. Cynthia Crosson Tower reports this incident in *How Schools Can Help Combat Child Abuse and Neglect:*

> Recently I had a workshop for teachers on preventing child sexual abuse. Amidst a flurry of questions, one frustrated teacher stood up and said, "Why can't we just forget about this stuff! My teachers never taught me anything about being abused and I'm fine." A hush fell over the audience as the man sat down, sure his point was well taken. All eyes turned to me expectantly, but before I could respond a woman in the back row stood up—unnoticed until then.
>
> "May I say something?" she asked quietly. "At six I was molested by my own father. I assumed all fathers treated their children that way. He beat me too, but no one seemed to notice the marks he left when I went to school. No one seemed to notice how unhappy I was. I especially liked my third grade teacher and I tried to tell her. I wrote notes and left them for her. I don't think it occurred to her that that kind of thing could happen. She was a good teacher and a concerned person, but she couldn't hear my cry for help. My mother wouldn't listen either. I knew after that it was useless to try to tell anyone. It never occurred to me that I could say no—that my body was my own. The abuse continued until I was married at 17—and it has hurt me in so many ways since. . . . I want my children to know they have choices. I want them to know they have rights and that no one can hurt them. I want them to know that there are knowledgeable people whom they can go to and who will believe them. I tell them that, but I want others to tell them too! . . . Now I'm a teacher and I want to be part of teaching children to protect themselves as well as learn." (1987, 17)

12.1 POINTS TO REMEMBER

- U.S. families are very diverse. They include eight basic family types: single-parent families, noncustodial parents, families with two wage earners, two-parent families with one wage earner, joined or blended families, homeless families, teenage parents, and minority families.

- Single-parent families, most often headed by women, are among the families most likely to be poor. Child care is often a problem, as is cooperating with schools.

- Nearly two-thirds of U.S. mothers work part- or full-time. These mothers must arrange for child care and before- and after-school care for their children.

- An increasing number of U.S. families are homeless. Homeless children face a lack of security, poor diet, health problems, and ostracism, all of which affect their ability to perform in school.

- Teenage parents are likely to be poor and poorly educated and their children are likely to experience health and other related problems.

- Minority families are more likely to be poor than white families. They traditionally have less power, social status, and education than similarly configured white families.

- Schools can respond to the needs of families by adapting their schedules to those of parents for such events as meetings and conferences.

- Physical, sexual, and emotional abuse or neglect of a child affects the child not only in the home but also at school. Teachers are responsible for reporting suspected cases of child abuse.

TABLE 12-2

Physical and Behavioral Indicators of Child Abuse and Neglect

Type of child abuse/neglect	Physical indicators	Behavioral indicators
Physical Abuse	Unexplained bruises and welts: —on face, lips, mouth —on torso, back, buttocks, thighs —in various stages of healing —clustered, forming regular patterns —reflecting shape of article used to inflict (electric cord, belt buckle) —on several different surface areas —regularly appear after absence, weekend, or vacation —human bite marks —bald spots Unexplained burns: —cigar, cigarette burns, especially on soles, palms, back, or buttocks —immersion burns (sock-like, glove-like, doughnut-shaped on buttocks or genitalia —patterned like electric burner, iron, etc. —rope burns on arms, legs, neck, or torso Unexplained fractures: —to skull, nose, facial structure —in various stages of healing —multiple or spiral fractures Unexplained lacerations or abrasions: —to mouth, lips, gums, eyes —to external genitalia	Wary of adult contacts Apprehensive when other children cry Behavioral extremes: —aggressiveness, or —withdrawal —overly compliant Afraid to go home Reports injury by parents Exhibits anxiety about normal activities, e.g., napping Complains of soreness and moves awkwardly Destructive to self and others Early to school or stays late as if afraid to go home Accident prone Wears clothing that covers body when not appropriate Chronic runaway (especially adolescents) Cannot tolerate physical contact or touch
Physical Neglect	Consistent hunger, poor hygiene, inappropriate dress Consistent lack of supervision, especially in dangerous activities or long periods Unattended physical problems or medical needs Abandonment Lice Distended stomach, emaciated	Begging, stealing food Constant fatigue, listlessness or falling asleep States there is no caretaker at home Frequent school absence or tardiness Destructive, pugnacious School dropout (adolescents) Early emancipation from family (adolescents)

Most teachers are not given training in recognizing child abuse and neglect. The school should ideally have a team of counselor, social worker, nurse, teacher, and administrator that can correctly evaluate a situation and report it to officials.

Type of child abuse/neglect	Physical indicators	Behavioral indicators
Sexual Abuse	Difficulty in walking or sitting Torn, stained or bloody underclothing Pain or itching in genital area Bruises or bleeding in external genitalia, vaginal, or anal areas Venereal disease Frequent urinary or yeast infections Frequent unexplained sore throats	Unwilling to participate in certain physical activities Sudden drop in school performance Withdrawal, fantasy or unusually infantile behavior Crying with no provocation Bizarre, sophisticated, or unusual sexual behavior or knowledge Anorexia (especially adolescents) Sexually provocative Poor peer relationships Reports sexual assault by caretaker Fear of or seductiveness toward males Suicide attempts (especially adolescents) Chronic runaway Early pregnancies
Emotional Maltreatment	Speech disorders Lags in physical development Failure to thrive (especially in infants) Asthma, severe allergies, or ulcers Substance abuse	Habit disorders (sucking, biting, rocking, etc.) Conduct disorders (antisocial, destructive, etc.) Neurotic traits (sleep disorders, inhibition of play) Behavioral extremes: —compliant, passive —aggressive, demanding Overly adaptive behavior: —inappropriately adult —inappropriately infantile Developmental lags (mental, emotional) Delinquent behavior (especially adolescents)

From: C. C. Tower, *How Schools Can Help Combat Child Abuse and Neglect*, 2nd ed. (Washington, DC: National Education Association, 1987), 162–163. Adapted from *Early Childhood Programs and the Prevention and Treatment of Child Abuse and Neglect*, by D. D. Broadhurst et al., The User Manual Series, 1979, Washington, DC: U.S. Department of Health, Education and Welfare.

Point/Counterpoint

THE MYTH OF THE FAMILY

First, what *is* the American family?

As parents, many of us dream about the past, about what families are supposed to be. But we cannot quite remember what we dreamed, as when lying half awake in the morning we catch and assemble the trails of mist from disappearing dreams. We attempt to remember our collective American childhood, the way it was, but what we often remember is a combination of the real past, pieces reshaped by bitterness and love, and, of course, the video past—the portrayals of family life on such television programs as "Leave It to Beaver" and "Father Knows Best" and all the rest. For many of the baby boomers I interviewed, the illusory Cleaver family came the closest to encapsulating what they felt they had lost, even if they had never had it. These television images drilled the myth of the American family into our minds and our culture even as the majority of families took on quite different shapes and characteristics. American family life has never been particularly idyllic. In the nineteenth century, nearly a quarter of all children experienced the death of one of their parents. (No wonder the plots of so many Disney tales, psychologically rooted in the nineteenth century and earlier, were centered on the death of a parent.) Not until the sixties did the chief cause of separation of parents shift from death to divorce. The twentieth-century trend toward a widening variety of family definitions was interrupted only by the post–World War II boom in large families and early marriage.

That period, however, may have been the real aberration. In the fifties, about 55 percent of American families were configured along the lines of the Cleavers. Today only three out of ten American families fit the "traditional" pattern of a homemaker mother and breadwinner father. Families today are more diverse and less stable. As Peter Morrison, director of the Rand Corporation's Population Research Center, told a congressional committee: "People think they are seeing departures from the norm, but departures now are the norm."[1]

Among the current realities of the American family:

- The family is shrinking. There are now fewer parents, children, and other members per family than ever before in our nation's history.[2]
- Younger couples divorce more readily and earlier in their marriages, which means that young children are more likely to be involved.
- The level and nature of divorce today foreshadow a future in which most first marriages will end in divorce.[3]
- Stepparents are entering the social mainstream. Many schools now publish directories cross-referenced to two sets of parents with different last names.
- More children are born and raised out of wedlock. According to the Census Bureau, nearly two out of ten of the women in the United States who gave birth in 1988 were unmarried.
- More families are headed by single parents—and children are spending more of their lives with single parents. Soon a quarter of white children and close to half of black children may lose regular contact with a parent at some point during their childhood.

1. Basia Hellwig, How Working Women Have Changed America: The Family, *Working Woman*, November 1986, pp. 134–137; Peter Morrison, *Changing Family Structure: Who Cares for America's Dependents?* December, 1986.
2. Randolph E. Schmid, Divorce Rate of 60% Seen for Over-30s, *San Diego Union*, April 5, 1986, sec. D.
3. Morrison, I, 3.

From: Louv, 1990

THE BREAKUP OF THE NUCLEAR FAMILY: CAN WE REVERSE THE TREND?

During the past 25 years, family decline in the U.S., as in other industrialized societies, has been both steeper and more alarming than during any other quarter-century in our history. . . .

In the 1960s . . . four major social trends emerged to signal widespread "flight" from both the ideal and the reality of the traditional nuclear family: rapid fertility decline, the sexual revolution, the movement of mothers into the labor force, and the upsurge in divorce. . . .

These trends signal a widespread retreat from the traditional nuclear family in its dimensions of a lifelong, sexually exclusive unit, focused on children, with a division of labor between husband and wife. Unlike most previous change, which reduced family functions and diminished the importance of the kin group, that of the past 25 years has tended to break up the nucleus of the family unit—the bond between husband and wife. Nuclear units, therefore, are losing ground to single-parent households, serial and stepfamilies, and unmarried and homosexual couples.

From: Popenoe, 1991

POSTSCRIPT

Both Louv and Popenoe use the same data, often provided by the same governmental sources. However, they reach different conclusions related to the assumptions they made when approaching the data.

Louv assumed that the American family is a myth; it never really existed except in our fantasies and on television. His conclusion is that the family is changing, evolving. On the other hand, Popenoe assumed that the nuclear family of two parents and children did exist and concludes that it is in the process of breaking up.

How important are their differing assumptions and conclusions? Louv, in the subtitle of his book, thinks of today's American family, whatever its makeup, as "new hope for the next generation." Popenoe, in the subtitle of his article, sees limited hope for today's families and poses the question: "Can we reverse the trend [of the breakup of the family]?" These differing conclusions could lead to differing approaches for dealing with families. For example, Louv suggests that today's families need to form new networks made up of friends and colleagues that can often provide superior support to old networks of extended family members. Popenoe, however, maintains that we must "reinvigorate the cultural ideals of family, parents, and children within the changed circumstances of our time." According to Popenoe, we can do this by bringing again "to the cultural forefront the old ideal of parents living together and sharing responsibility for their children and for each other" (p. 53). In the scope of his article he makes no specific recommendations for ways to reinvigorate these family ideals. Acceptance of one or the other of these conclusions by the schools could lead to very different educational programs.

THE COMMUNITY AND THE SCHOOL

In addition to changes in the structure of the U.S. family, other societal changes put pressure on the schools. This section of the chapter will discuss some of these community problems challenging the public schools.

It is 9 A.M. on a November morning, and Terrence Quinn, principal of Public School 225 in Rockaway, Queens, New York, is serving breakfast. But he's not in the school cafeteria. He's in the lobby of a ramshackle welfare hotel where homeless parents and their children come to seek shelter. With a social worker in tow, Quinn has cruised the hotel corridors, knocking on doors, inviting what is an ever-changing group of parents to share coffee and break bagels and doughnuts with him while he tries to persuade them to send their children to his elementary school six blocks—and a world—away. (Reed and Sautter 1990, K2)

This is a poignant example of how society affects the schools. Contemporary teachers and administrators can no longer simply teach and administer. In many communities, if they are to reach and educate the children, teachers and administrators must first reach out to them. The problems of poverty, crime, sexism, racism, and ethnocentricity paint a bleak picture. Although many schools are relatively free of overt examples of these problems, most are not. It is important that today's teachers understand these problems, so they are not shocked and surprised by the impact they have on their students and their classrooms.

- Every eight seconds of the school day, an American child drops out of school (552,000 during the 1987–1988 school year).
- Every 26 seconds of each day, an American child runs away from home (1.2 million a year).
- Every 47 seconds, an American child is abused or neglected (675,000 a year).
- Every seven minutes, an American child is arrested for a drug offense (76,986 a year).
- Every 30 minutes, an American child is arrested for drunken driving (17,674 a year).
- Every 36 minutes, an American child is killed or injured by guns (14,600 a year).
- Every 53 minutes, an American child dies because of poverty (10,000 a year).
- Every school day, 135,000 American children bring guns to school. A child is statistically safer in Northern Ireland than on the streets of America.
- Every day 10,000 American children become homeless. (Children's Defense Fund 1990, 3)

Poverty   We will begin by discussing poverty because it is the direct or indirect cause of many of the problems above. Children are more likely to live in poverty, as defined by the federal government, than any other age group. While the poverty rate for the nation as a whole was 13.1 percent in 1987, nearly 21 percent of all children under the age of eighteen and 22 percent of preschoolers lived in poverty.

Although the poverty rate increased in the 1970s and 1980s during periods of recession, it did not decrease significantly during the sustained period of economic growth of the late 1980s. Among families with children in the lowest 20 percent of income level the average income declined 14 percent during the 1980s, whereas for families in the highest 20 percent, average income increased 19 percent during the same period. By 1989, according to the Children's Defense Fund, 12.6 million children, or about one in five, were living in families with incomes below the poverty threshold.

In 1991, the Children's Defense Fund in their annual report on child poverty in the United States identified which children are poor, indicating that our stereotype of poor children is often misleading.

Poverty is a fact of life for many school-aged children in the United States. Children living in poverty are more likely to be malnourished, more often sick, and chronically tired than their well-off counterparts and, thus, have difficulty learning. This single mother and her three children entertain visitors in the hotel room they call home.

- In 1989 only one in ten poor children in America was black and living in a female-headed family on welfare in a central city.
- The youngest, most defenseless Americans suffer most of all. Younger children are more vulnerable to developmental delay and damage caused by inadequate nutrition or health care. One in four infants and toddlers is poor. The bulk of the growth in child poverty during the 1980s was among children younger than six.
- Two in three poor children are white, Latino, Asian, or Native American. One-third of poor children are black. A black child is more likely to be poor than is a white or Latino child. But because a relatively small share of the total population is black, blacks make up only a minority of poor children. During the 1980s Latino poverty rates grew fastest, and roughly half of all children who joined the ranks of the poor between 1979 and 1989 were Latino.
- Children in female-headed families are far more likely than others to be poor. Yet nearly one-half of poor children live in families where the father is present. Even if there were no families headed by women in this country, we still would have one of the highest child poverty rates among all industrialized societies.
- There are more poor American children living outside central cities (6.9 million in 1989) than inside them (5.7 million). The child poverty rate is

higher in rural areas than in the rest of the nation (22 percent versus 19 percent).

- Most poor families with children are working families. Nearly two out of three poor families with children had one or more workers in 1989. Nearly one in every five poor families with children had a household head who worked full-time throughout the year but still could not earn enough to lift the family out of poverty.
- Earnings from employment are the largest source of income for poor families with children. Total earned income for such families in 1989 was more than twice as great as the total amount of income they received through public assistance programs.
- The inflation-adjusted median income for young families (those headed by persons younger than 30) with children dropped by nearly one-fourth between 1973 and 1987. As a result, more than one in three children living in young families is poor. (Children's Defense Fund 1991, 2)

Crime

One of the results of poverty is crime. Violent crimes such as murders, rapes, and robberies and property crimes such as burglaries and larcencies continue to grow at an alarming rate across the United States. In a city such as New York, for example, it would have been difficult to imagine the amount of crime that occurs today as recently as forty years ago. In 1952, New York City had 8,757 robberies; in 1989, it had 93,387, one every six minutes. In the fifty-nine days of the Persian Gulf War in 1990 and 1991, for example, 281 Americans were killed in the war; during that same period, 295 were killed, as a result of crime, in New York City (ABC Morning News, June 10, 1991).

The U.S. Bureau of Justice Statistics estimates that 83 percent of children now twelve years old will become victims of actual or attempted violence, if crime continues to grow at current rates. The number of innocent bystanders, including many children, who have been gunned down in New York City, Boston, and Los Angeles tripled from 1985 to 1988 (Gest 1989).

How Crime Affects the Schools

In 1989, researchers Julius Menacker, Ward Weldon, and Emanuel Hurwitz studied teachers and sixth- and eighth-grade students in four Chicago inner-city schools that serve low-income and minority children in some of the most crime-ridden sections of the city. They reported that the following crimes occurred within the school:

- More than 50 percent of students reported that money, clothing, or property was stolen from them at least once during the school year, and 35 percent indicated that thefts occurred more than once
- 8 percent of students reported being threatened by someone with a gun or knife who wanted money or drugs, and 3 percent reported that they had been threatened more than once
- 4 percent of students reported being beaten so badly during the school year that they required medical attention
- 7 percent of students reported coming to school high on drugs or alcohol at least once during the year

- 32 percent reported that they had carried a weapon to school at least once, and 14 percent said that they had done so more than once. (p. 40)

Students in many inner-city schools have to deal with crime both in the school and outside of it. For example, 98 percent of teachers reported in the Menacker, Weldon, and Hurwitz survey that the neighborhoods surrounding the schools posed severe threats to the students. Thus, they concluded that "the public school is an island of relative safety in an ocean of danger that surrounds the school" (p. 39). Nevertheless, they suggest that school-based and community-based programs must be developed to solve the problems of lawlessness and fear in the inner city.

What Schools Are Doing About Crime

Menacker, Weldon, and Hurwitz suggest that the teachers and principals cannot be held responsible for all the discipline problems that occur within the school. Since the schools' safety, as bad as it is, is far better than the safety of the surrounding community, these researchers suggest that the schools and the community must work together to improve discipline in the schools by forming a discipline council, including members of the community, to deal with school safety, and dealing with students who commit crimes on school grounds as adult criminals.

Many schools and communities have developed programs designed to make students more aware of crime and to prevent it. For example, in Boston a program developed by Deborah Prothrow-Stith of the Harvard School of Public Health is designed to reduce the allure of violence by making students aware of the consequences and giving them alternative means for dealing with anger. In addition, every Boston public school student caught with a weapon is sent to the Barron Assessment and Counseling Center for a five- to ten-day stay. Students undergo psychological and educational assessments. A plan is developed for working with the student once he or she returns to school or an alternative setting. Students also participate in counseling, academic work, violence-prevention classes, and trips to detention facilities.

In Dade County, Florida, schools have initiated a gun-safety program in cooperation with the Center to Prevent Handgun Violence. Through books, videos, and role-playing, the program attempts to "deglamorize and deglorify the possession and use of guns" (*U.S. News and World Report*, April 8, 1991, 32). In Oakland, California, in a program called Teens on Target, student volunteers are trained as violence-prevention "advocates." As such they learn about guns, drugs, and family violence. They are then sent into schools to teach other teens about preventing violence.

Despite these efforts at controlling crime, because they are regional and limited in scope, the problem remains in many cities and their schools. Ultimately, schools and communities must work together to break the cycle of inadequate housing, poor-paying jobs, poverty, crime and substandard education.

Sexism

In spite of more than two decades of the women's movement in the United States, women still lag behind men in professional and economic status. This affects the schools in many direct and indirect ways.

Although an increasingly large percentage of women are in the labor force, the positions they hold are rarely positions of power. Women are vastly overrepresented in nonleadership positions with limited mobility. For example, 99.1 percent of secretaries are women, as are 97.1 percent of receptionists, 91 percent of bank tellers, 98.7 percent of dental assistants, and 94.6 percent of nurses (U.S. Department of Commerce 1990, 390–391).

Although legislation has been passed by Congress (1963 and 1972 Equal Pay Acts; the 1964 Civil Rights Act and 1972 amendment prohibiting discrimination in employment based on sex), local and state government salaries for men and women are unequal. Men in executive, administrative, and managerial positions, for example, made an average of $36,759 per year, and women made $23,356 per year in 1988. Even among office and clerical workers where women dominate, men are paid more. Male office workers are paid an average of $24,399 and women are paid an average of $16,676 (U.S. Department of Commerce 1990, 411).

Fully employed women in 1988 earned only about $70 dollars for every $100 earned by men. In 1985, an average woman with a college degree earned less than an average man who was a high school dropout (Golden 1985). The earning gap was also present among men and women with the same education and similar backgrounds. Whereas male executives earned an average of $682 per week in 1988, women earned $430 (U.S. Department of Commerce 1990, 409). According to a 1990 survey by *Working Woman,* male professors at public colleges and universities earned an average of $53,890 and women professors $48,490. The same was true at lower ranks; at the assistant professor rank, males earned $34,620 and women earned $31,830 (Russell 1991, 68). In fact, if a husband and wife are from the same social class and have the same educational background, the husband will generally earn more money than the wife (Oakley 1981). In 1988, according to the U.S. Bureau of Census, women full-time year-round workers earned $18,545 and men full-time year-round workers earned $27,342. Although this was an increase for both men and women, fully employed women in 1988 earned less than fully employed men in 1980.

Women in Education

Women make up the majority of professionals in education. In 1980, for example, 66 percent of the professionals in education were women. Since the early twentieth century women have held the majority of positions within the profession. Despite this, women teachers are paid less than their male counterparts. In 1987–1988, the base salary of male teachers was $28,244 and that of women teachers was $25,350 (U.S. Department of Commerce 1990, 82).

Moreover, women make up a declining percentage of the professionals in education as one ascends the professional ladder. The percentage of women at upper levels of the profession has begun to increase slowly, but this comes after a period of significant decline from the late 1960s through the mid-1980s. In 1973, 35 percent of public school administrators were women. In 1974, the number had declined to 14 percent, rising slowly to 20 percent in 1979, 25 percent in 1980, 26 percent in 1985, and 30 percent in 1988. In 1988, the percentage of women in administrative positions was lower than it had been in 1974. Why? The major shift in the percentage of women administrators occurred in the late 1960s, when black schools and white schools were inte-

While the majority of professionals in education are women, they have in the past filled very few administrative positions. In the early 1990s, however, their numbers have begun to increase on committees, school boards, as principals, assistant superintendents, and superintendents.

grated. Most black schools were headed by women principals. When the schools were integrated, most of the black principals lost their positions.

In the late 1980s, the number of women in high-level positions in education was beginning to increase. During the period from 1982 to 1987, women's school board membership increased from 28 to 39 percent. In 1988, five of the chief state officers of education and 3.7 percent of school district superintendents were women, up from 0.6 percent in 1971. However, in terms of numbers the 1988 figure translates to a total of 11,767 superintendents, 11,333 males and only 434 females. The percentage of assistant superintendents who are women is significantly larger, 22 percent in 1988. This compares to a meager 3 percent in 1971.

Although the percentage of minorities in positions of power has increased since the early 1960s, it is still relatively low. The higher up the socioeconomic and prestige ladder the position, the less likely minority members are to occupy it.

For example, in state and local governments in 1989 there were 961,000 blacks and 308,000 Hispanics out of 5,257,000 employed. In administrative positions in government in 1989 there were only 29,000 blacks and 9,000

Racism

Hispanics out of the total 292,000 administrators. Of the total 668,000 service and maintenance workers, 219,000 were black and 61,000 Hispanic (U.S. Department of Commerce 1990, 300).

Maxine B. Zinn and D. Stanley Eitzen in *Diversity in American Families* (1987) contend that blacks and Hispanics are clustered in service jobs such as cooks, dishwashers, cleaning service employees, nurses' aides, and child-care workers. In addition to low salaries, these positions have few fringe benefits and poor working conditions.

Minority Leadership in the Schools

Racial minorities have fared even less well than women in educational leadership positions. Between 1982 and 1987, the percentage of minority school board members remained at 5 percent across the nation. The percentage is slightly larger in the South, where 11 percent of school board members are black and 3 percent Hispanic.

In 1982, 12.9 percent of public school administrators were minorities. By 1988 that figure had increased to only 16.3 percent. In 1988, 83.5 percent were white, 10 percent black, 5.4 percent Hispanic, 0.7 percent Asian-Pacific, and 0.3 percent American Indian.

The percentage of minority superintendents has increased very slowly. In 1982, 2.2 percent of the superintendents in the thirty states reporting were minorities. By 1988, 3.1 percent were minorities. The percentage of assistant superintendents who are members of minority groups has risen equally slowly. In 1982, 10.8 percent of assistant superintendents were minorities in the twenty-three states reporting. In 1988, the number had grown to 12 percent. The percentage increase in minority principals has been equally slow. In 1982, 12.1 percent of principals in the twenty-three states reporting were minorities. In 1988, the figure had increased to 15 percent.

How Do Racism and Sexism Affect Students?

Racism and sexism affect students both directly and indirectly. The majority of students will be taught by female teachers and administered by male administrators; few students will have minority teachers or administrators. Similarly, few students will be in school districts with a large number of board of education members who are either women or minorities. Decisions thus made, in many cases, will not consider women or minorities as priorities. These are the direct results.

The indirect results lie in the message this gives to U.S. students. For example, are female and minority students likely to set goals to become school administrators and leaders in government and industry when they see few models in the schools? Are minority students likely to strive to become teachers when most of the teachers they know are white? Are male students likely to want to become teachers when all their teachers are female?

There may be another indirect result. If studies are correct and many white, middle-class teachers have difficulty dealing with minority students, these students may not be receiving the education they need in order to succeed. Similarly, if teachers tend to have lower expectations for minority students, these students may be given instruction that provides little challenge. (For what schools can do to improve the achievement and self-concept of minority students, see chapter 13, pp. 444–454).

THE INDIVIDUAL AND THE SCHOOL

While society and the family struggle with ethical, structural, and emotional changes thrust upon them, many students have problems of their own that interfere with their schooling. We will address three of these problems in this section: chemical dependency, sexual activity and AIDS, and suicide.

Chemical Dependency

In the 1990 Metropolitan Life Survey of the American Teacher, conducted by Lou Harris and his associates, 70 percent of teachers thought the use of drugs was a serious problem; this was up from 58 percent in 1985. Drinking was considered a problem by 81 percent of the teachers in 1989; this was up from 66 percent in 1985.

Educator Lloyd Johnston of the University of Michigan found that in 1990, 50.9 percent of the 17,000 high school seniors he surveyed indicated that they had used an illicit drug at least once. This was down from 53.9 percent in 1988. Fewer students reported using marijuana, cocaine, and alcohol, but the use of crack remained stable. Although there was an overall decline in drug use, these students reported that drugs were more available than ever (see figure 12.2).

Fewer students reported binge drinking in the 1990 survey, but one-third reported having at least five drinks in one sitting within the two weeks prior to the survey. Richard Towers indicates that teens drink and take drugs for many reasons: pleasure, peer pressure, life stress and pain, experimentation, rebellion, societal influence, low self-esteem, poor life attitude, family influences, and school factors.

According to a study by J. David Hawkins et al., in "Childhood Predictors and the Prevention of Adolescent Substance Abuse," family characteristics that are common among teens who take drugs include:

- parental drug-using behavior and attitudes toward drugs
- negative communication patterns, such as frequent criticism, blaming, and lack of praise
- inconsistent and unclear behavior limits
- parental denial of the child's drug abuse
- unrealistic parental expectations
- family self-medication
- miscarried expressions of anger (p. 82)

How Does Drug and Alcohol Abuse Affect the School?

"Teenage pregnancy, suicide, low self-esteem, poor nutrition, and drug abuse may indeed be different facets of the same set of problems [poverty, poor home life, home and school pressures] that are closely related to each other and to such other problems as class cutting, truancy, and disruptive behavior" (Towers, 51). Students who abuse drugs and alcohol are more likely to have academic, social, and behavioral problems in school. It is not clear whether these problems tend to cause chemical abuse, but it is clear that chemical abuse causes additional school-related problems. Similarly, drug and alcohol abuse can cause serious classroom problems for the teacher. Consider the difficulties in teaching a class if one or several of the students are drunk or high. Students

FIGURE 12-2

Drug Abuse Among High School Seniors

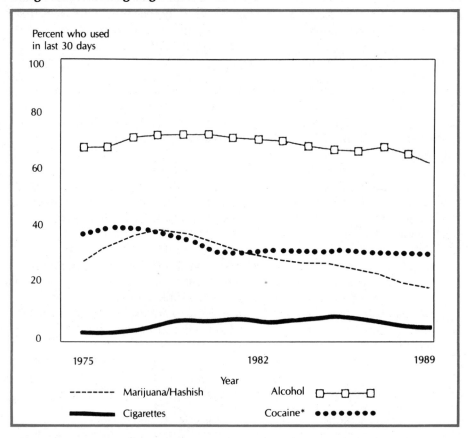

*Figures for "crack" cocaine appear in 1987–1989 as follows: 1.3% (1987), 1.6% (1988), 1.4% (1989).

From: National Institute on Drug Abuse, *Monitoring the Future Study.*

Teenagers abuse alcohol in greater numbers and greater quantities than any other substance. Teachers should be able to recognize some of the signs of substance abuse in their students: change in personality, work habits, appearance, and friends. Teachers should then express concern to the student, notify the parents, and work with the staff in the school to help the student.

who are unruly, sleepy, or boisterous will not be ready for learning and will adversely affect the learning of the other students in the classroom.

One of the educational goals outlined by President George Bush when he met with the nation's governors in 1989 was that "by the year 2000, every school in America will be free of drugs and violence and will offer a disciplined environment conducive to learning" (National Governors' Association, *Educating America: State Strategies for Achieving the National Education Goals*, 15).

In order to reach this goal, Towers suggests that teachers must know how to recognize the symptoms and signs of drug and alcohol abuse. The symptoms are many and varied but include such things as change in school achievement, lack of interest in anything related to school or home, change of friendships, change in personality, hostility, change in work habits, change in reputation, legal problems, change in appearance, wearing or using drug slogans or symbols, visible signs of drugs or alcohol, tiredness, deterioration in health, change in relationship with family, and appearance of being in a trance (Towers 63). He recommends that when confronted with a drug or alcohol problem, teachers do the following:

1. Express their concern to the student.
2. Notify the parents of their concerns.
3. Consult with and/or refer to appropriate staff.
4. Participate as appropriate in the intervention plan.

This, of course, means that each school must have a plan for dealing with drug and alcohol problems and an awareness of what resources are already available to help. In addition to developing educational programs to help students avoid drug and alcohol abuse, schools should be part of school-community action teams in which the entire school population and members of the community assume ownership of the problem, take part in the solutions, and help create a positive school climate.

V I E W P O I N T S

What One State Is Doing About Drug Abuse

New Jersey—The governor is calling for the creation of an Alliance for a Drug Free New Jersey. The alliance calls for business, law enforcement, religious, education, and community leaders to establish a statewide program against substance abuse. It plans to solicit New Jersey's 567 cities and towns in an effort to abolish drug abuse. The initiative will organize and coordinate the efforts of schools, police, business groups, and other community organizations to fight drug abuse; adopt comprehensive, effective drug abuse education programs in the schools, beginning in kindergarten and continuing through high school; adopt clear procedures for the intervention, treatment, and discipline of students abusing alcohol and drugs; provide a comprehensive drug abuse education and outreach program for parents as well as a comprehensive substance abuse community awareness program.

The program focuses heavily on the demand side and seeks to provide drug abuse education to every child in the New Jersey public school system. The program focuses on prevention, intervention, and treatment. Prevention programs are geared toward limiting the demand for drugs through increased public awareness, community activity and parental support. Intervention programs seek to identify drug abusers at the earliest point and encourage their participation in appropriate treatment. The most important aspect, however, is the education, treatment, and rehabilitation of the young people of New Jersey.

From: National Governors' Association, 1987

Drug and Alcohol Abuse Prevention Programs

Most middle and secondary schools are actively involved in helping students avoid the pressure to begin taking drugs or start drinking. The objectives of the National Institute on Alcohol Abuse and Alcoholism (NIAAA) kindergarten through 12th grade curriculum *Here's Looking At You, Two* are typical.

1. *Information*—to expose youth to the basic facts about the physiological, psychological, and sociological implications of drug and alcohol use, and to teach them how to gather information about alcohol and drugs; to distinguish between reliable and unreliable, and relevant and irrelevant information.
2. *Analysis*—to help youngsters identify and define problems; gather information; brainstorm alternatives; predict consequences associated with different choices and behaviors; identify analysis factors such as attitudes, values, feelings, emotions, pressures from peers and families, risk levels and habits; develop action plans on the basis of these analyses and evaluate the appropriateness of their actions.
3. *Coping skills*—to help students gain skills in identifying sources of stress in their lives; to recognize when they are stressed and its effects on them; to identify mechanisms for coping with the stress and determining consequences of the coping behaviors.

Many school programs have been instituted to help students become aware of the dangers of alcohol and drug abuse. Students are taught to analyze their own values toward drugs and alcohol and to cope with their problems in positive ways in order to develop self-confidence and a positive self-image.

4. *Self-concept*—to help young people increase their self-awareness by helping them identify what is important to them in their lives; to help them recognize their feelings and know how to express them by explaining how they feel about themselves and identifying their various roles and activities, as well as increasing positive self-concepts so that students can identify their own personal strengths and weaknesses and develop skills in selecting and practicing changed behaviors. (National Institute of Alcohol Abuse and Alcoholism, *Here's Looking at You, Two: A K–12 Drug and Alcohol Curriculum*, 1979)

According to the Center for Population Options, a large proportion of today's teenagers are sexually active. The Alan Guttmacher Institute, which studies questions related to reproductive issues, reports that the proportion of sexually active girls between the ages of fifteen and seventeen has jumped from 32 percent in 1982 to 38 percent in 1988. The 1988 National Survey of Adolescent Males reported that a third of the boys surveyed were sexually active at fifteen, half at sixteen, two-thirds at seventeen, and 86 percent at nineteen.

Sexual Activity

Of 29 million teenagers in the United States, 12 million, over 41 percent, have had sexual intercourse by age nineteen. This translates into 5 million females, 7 out of every 10 by age twenty, and 6.5 million males, 8 out of every 10 by age twenty. The average age for first sexual intercourse among females is 16.2, among males, 15.7.

The Planned Parenthood Federation reports that teenagers tend to begin sexual activity younger if they are from families of lower socioeconomic status, have below-average grades in school or do not go to school at all, are unemployed, and live with only one parent or have parents who are not college graduates. This group of teenagers is also less likely to use contraceptives.

According to the Planned Parenthood Federation, despite the fact that one-half of all U.S. teenagers are sexually active by their seventeenth year, only one-third use contraceptives consistently. The Center for Population Options claims that 27 percent of unmarried sexually active females have never used any method of birth control. Thirty-four percent used a method of birth control consistently, and 34 percent used birth control some of the time. Of those not using birth control, "forty-one percent of unmarried teens . . . say they did not use it because they thought they could not get pregnant at 'that time of the month' " (*Sexuality Today Newsletter*, March 9, 1987). The two major problems caused by teenage sexual activity that we will discuss are sexually transmitted diseases and teenage pregnancy.

Diseases Related to Teenage Sexual Activity

Pregnancy is not the only possible result of teenage sexual activity; sexually transmitted diseases such as syphilis, gonorrhea, and AIDS are also. According to the U.S. Centers for Disease Control, 3 million teens are infected by sexually transmitted diseases each year. Since 1956 the number of teens who contract syphilis and gonorrhea is up 300 percent. More than 1 percent of U.S. teenagers today report incidents of gonorrhea annually. The rate of syphilis has risen slightly during the 1980s, although the reported incidence, 24 per 100,000, is much lower than for gonorrhea.

TABLE 12-3

State Policy on the Teaching of Sex Education and Selected Topics, June 1988

| State | Sex education | Selected topics in sex education | | |
		Pregnancy prevention	AIDS	Sexually transmitted diseases
Alabama	E	D	R	E
Alaska	E	E	E	E
Arizona	NP	NP	E	NP
Arkansas	R	R	R	R
California	NP	E	E	E
Colorado	E	E	E	E
Connecticut	E	NP	R	NP
Delaware	R	R	R	R
Florida	E	E	E	E
Georgia	R	E	R	R
Hawaii	R	E	R	E
Idaho	E	E	E	E
Illinois	NP	NP	R	R
Indiana	E	NP	R	E
Iowa	R	R	R	R
Kansas	R	NP	R	R
Kentucky	R	E	R	R
Louisiana	NP	E	NP	E
Maine	E	E	E	E
Maryland	R	E	R	E
Massachusetts	NP	NP	NP	NP
Michigan	E	E	R	E
Minnesota	E	E	R	E
Mississippi	NP	NP	NP	NP
Missouri	E	NP	E	E
Montana	E	E	E	E
Nebraska	E	E	E	E
Nevada	R	E	R	R
New Hampshire	E	E	R	R
New Jersey	R	NP	E	E
New Mexico	R	R	R	R
New York	E	E	R	E
North Carolina	NP	NP	R	R
North Dakota	E	NP	E	E
Ohio	E	E	R	R
Oklahoma	E	E	R	E
Oregon	E	E	R	R
Pennsylvania	E	NP	R	E
Rhode Island	R	NP	R	R
South Carolina	R	R/E	E	R
South Dakota	NR	NR	R	NR
Tennessee	E	E	R	E
Texas	NP	E	E	R

		Selected topics in sex education		
State	Sex education	Pregnancy prevention	AIDS	Sexually transmitted diseases
Utah	R	P	R	R
Vermont	R	R	R	R
Virginia	R	R	R	R
Washington	E	NP	R	NP
West Virginia	R	E	E	R
Wisconsin	E	E	E	E
Wyoming	NP	NP	NP	NP

Notes: R = Required; E = Encouraged; D = Discouraged; P = Prohibited; NP = No Position; NR = No Response; and R/E = Required in grades 9–12/Encouraged in grades 7–8.

From: Kenney, Guardado, and Brown, "Sex Education and AIDS Education in the Schools: What States and Large Districts Are Doing," *Family Planning Perspectives* (March/April 1989).

From: National Governors' Association, *An Overview of State Policies Affecting Adolescent Pregnancy and Parenting*, 1990.

Because of the diverse attitudes about sex education across the country, not every state requires that information about sex be taught in the schools. This table indicates that seventeen states require sex education and twenty-three encourage it.

AIDS, which is caused by the human immunodeficiency virus (HIV), is the seventh leading cause of death among fifteen- to twenty-four-year-olds, according to a report in *Medical Clinics of North America*. Although adolescents represent only 1.2 percent of all AIDS cases, the number doubles every fourteen months (Hersch 1991). Approximately 21 percent of all AIDS cases in the United States fall within the twenty- to twenty-nine-year age group. However, the long incubation period of AIDS, up to seven years, indicates that many of these young adults were first infected as teenagers.

The two major causes of AIDS among young adults are sexual intercourse and drug abuse with shared needles contaminated with the AIDS virus. Sixteen percent of all teenage females who have had sexual intercourse report that they have had four or more partners. Over 12 million high school students used drugs such as heroin, cocaine, and other substances that can be injected intravenously. The large percentage of students who are sexually active and the problem of drug dependency among teenagers have both contributed to the increase in cases of AIDS among young adults.

Teenage Pregnancy

The U.S. teenage birth rate, at approximately 50 percent of the teenage pregnancy rate, is higher than in any other developed country. It cuts across all races and all classes. According to the Alan Guttmacher Institute, U.S. teenage pregnancy rates are seven times higher than those in the Netherlands and more than twice as high as those in Canada, Denmark, Finland, New Zealand, Sweden, England and Wales, and Scotland. Although the teenage birth rate is greatest among blacks and low-income youth, omitting blacks from teenage birth rate figures would still rank the United States first, according to the NEA publication *How Schools Can Help Combat Student Pregnancy* (see also pp. 391–392 of this chapter for more information on the teenage birth rate).

Each year 300,000 babies are born to teenage mothers who have not yet completed high school. Of these mothers, 36,000 have not yet completed ninth grade. Three out of four of the 1 million teenage pregnancies that occur each year are unintended. Most teenagers who decide to raise their children quit school and remain unmarried. These teenagers, therefore, become part of the female-headed household poverty statistics (see pp. 406–408).

How Does Teenage Sexual Activity Affect Education?

According to the Center for Population Options, only half of those teenagers who give birth before age eighteen ever complete high school, in comparison to 96 percent of those who don't. Of those women who have babies prior to age twenty, fewer than 2 percent complete college, compared to 20 percent of those who don't.

Of all the sexually transmitted diseases, AIDS has had the most devastating effect on American classrooms. Because of fear and misunderstanding, students with AIDS have been shunned, avoided, and in several instances have been banned from the classroom. The most celebrated case was that of Ryan White, a hemophiliac who contracted the disease during a blood transfusion (see also chapter 15).

Sexuality Education Programs

Sexuality education programs have objectives similar to those of drug and alcohol education programs. They were traditionally subsumed under health education and, therefore, had a biological and psychological focus. But they have become far more comprehensive and now cover the topics of: "family relations; gender identity/roles/socialization; dating and marriage; reproduction, pregnancy, and childbirth; parenthood; growth and development; family planning; sexual values; attitudes and behaviors; and rape and sexual abuse. . . . [S]exuality education . . . programs often extend the range of subject matter to include the historical, ethical, and cultural aspects of human sexuality, human sexual behaviors, and sexual functioning" (de Mauro, *SIECUS Report*, Dec. 1989/Jan. 1990, p. 2). And today, according to the 1989–1990 *SIECUS Report* (Sex Information and Education Council of the U.S.), most sexuality education programs also deal with AIDS and other sexually transmitted diseases.

Who Takes Sex Education?

Because teenage pregnancy, venereal disease, and AIDS have increasingly become problems, many school and governmental officials agree that the schools must assume responsibility for sex education. In addition, the grade level at which sex education is taught has moved from junior high school to late elementary school. Of those students who were twelve or thirteen years old in 1986, 13 percent had begun sex education as early as grades one through four; of those who were sixteen or seventeen years old, only 4 percent had begun sex education in grades one through four. The most common grade for younger students to begin sex education, according to this data, was grade five; for older students the most common grades were seven for fourteen- and fifteen-year-olds and nine for sixteen- and seventeen-year-olds.

The Controversy While sex education is being taught at younger and younger ages, the majority of the United States populace of the early 1990s is politically and socially conservative. Thus, many social and religious groups object to teaching sex education in the public schools, contending that it should be reserved for the home as it once was.

Only seventeen states require sex education in the public schools. However, twenty-three encourage it. Likewise, thirty states require some type of AIDS education, and sixteen encourage it (see table 12.3 for a summary of state policies on sex education).

AIDS Education

It is interesting to note that more states require AIDS education than require sex education. The 1986 federal *Objectives for the Nation* (U.S. Department of Health and Human Services, Division of HIV/AIDS, 1986) outlined preventative measures for the spread of AIDS including education about sexually transmitted diseases (STD) for all school children before and during high-risk periods (middle school through high school years). The Centers for Disease Control (CDC), the President's Domestic Policy Council, and the Institute of Medicine/National Academy of Sciences also support these educational programs.

The CDC has adopted specific guidelines for AIDS education, which have as their major goal the prevention of the transmission of the HIV virus. The guidelines suggest specific facts appropriate for different grade levels. For example, early elementary school children should be told that AIDS is a disease that cannot be transmitted by casual contact. By later elementary and middle school, students should be given information on viruses, transmission routes, and behavioral aspects of the disease. In junior and senior high school, students should receive explicit information about transmission, protective behaviors, testing, and where to get additional information. Although AIDS education programs differ, most schools today follow the CDC guidelines.

Suicide

According to Richard Towers in *How Schools Can Help Combat Student Drug and Alcohol Abuse* (1987) and Barry Garfinkle, chair of the Phi Delta Kappa Task Force on Adolescent Suicide, the percentage of young people who actually commit suicide has tripled in the last twenty to thirty years. Garfinkle further reports that suicide attempts have increased from 350 to 700 percent in the past thirty years. Teenage suicide is a problem related to drug dependency, pregnancy, parenthood, and other issues of adolescent development that cause depression and low self-esteem.

In the 1991 Gallup Teenage Suicide Study, teenagers were asked if they knew someone who had attempted to commit suicide. If they did, they were asked what signs there were prior to the suicide attempt. More than nine out of ten teens reported depression as the number one sign. Garfinkle claims that the number of severely depressed junior and senior high school students is between 6 and 8 percent of all students at any given time. Other signs of teenage suicide were problems that may have moved the teen toward depression. These included feeling worthless, not getting along with parents, trouble at school, dating problems, and alcohol and drugs (see figure 12.3 on p. 423). Suicide rates among teenagers are increasing at an alarming rate. In 1986, 2,100 teenagers between twelve and nineteen took their own lives. The largest number of these students, 1,896, were between the ages of fifteen and nineteen, an increase from 1,796 for the same age group in 1980. In the group between twelve and fourteen years of age, 130 committed suicide in 1980, 226 in 1986.

Males are much more likely to commit suicide than females, even though females are more likely than males to attempt it. According to Garfinkle, girls are more likely than boys to admit they are depressed and seek help for it. "Perhaps boys are culturally conditioned to view this as unmasculine, as an acknowledgment of weakness, but for every adolescent boy who seeks help, three girls do so" (Garfinkle interviewed by Frymier 1988, 292). Significantly more white than black teens will commit suicide; the rate of black teenage suicide is one-fifth that of white teenagers. Native American teenagers kill themselves ten times more often than whites. Suicide among teenagers is more of a problem in rural than in urban areas of the country, and although more males were likely to commit suicide than females, "the suicide rate for teen mothers is higher than that for other teens" (Compton, Duncan, and Hruska 1987, 16). The number of teenage mothers who attempt suicide is seven times the rate for all young teenagers.

Why Are Teenage Suicides Increasing?

Although a suicidal teenage personality has not been defined, numerous studies have been conducted to determine the causes of teenage suicide. Barry Garfinkle suggests that it can be correlated with family breakdown, youth unemployment, and decreasing religious observance. Compton, Duncan, and Hruska cite teenage parenthood and its overwhelming responsibilities, particularly among females. Richard Towers points to abuse of alcohol and drugs. Levine and Havighurst suggest that suicide relates to people's uncertainty about the future, lack of external rules and expectations on which they can depend, glorification of suicide by the media, the diminishing role of religion, family disruptions, failure in sports and in academics, and inability to find employment. When adolescents are unable to reach their goals or the goals of their families and schools, they may lose their sense of self-worth. Similarly, if they do not have supportive friends and family or if they attend large impersonal schools, they may become so depressed that suicide becomes an attractive alternative to coping with life's problems (Levine and Havighurst 1989, 187–188).

What Can Schools Do?

The primary role of the school must be in attempting to prevent teenage suicide. Superintendents must serve in a leadership role to raise the level of awareness of the staff and provide appropriate resources. Large schools should work toward becoming less impersonal and providing counselors and psychiatric services for students who are at risk. Students must be taught coping skills; they should understand that abuse of drugs, alcohol, and sexual promiscuity lead to school failure and more stress.

Teachers and students must be taught warning signs. These might include trouble complying with school rules, deteriorating academic performance, isolation from peer group, increased irritability, pushing others away who want to help, and increased aggression. Teens who are prone to suicide may become involved in crime, vandalism, drugs and alcohol, and sexual promiscuity in an attempt to solve their problems.

FIGURE 12-3

Signs Teenager Might Attempt Suicide

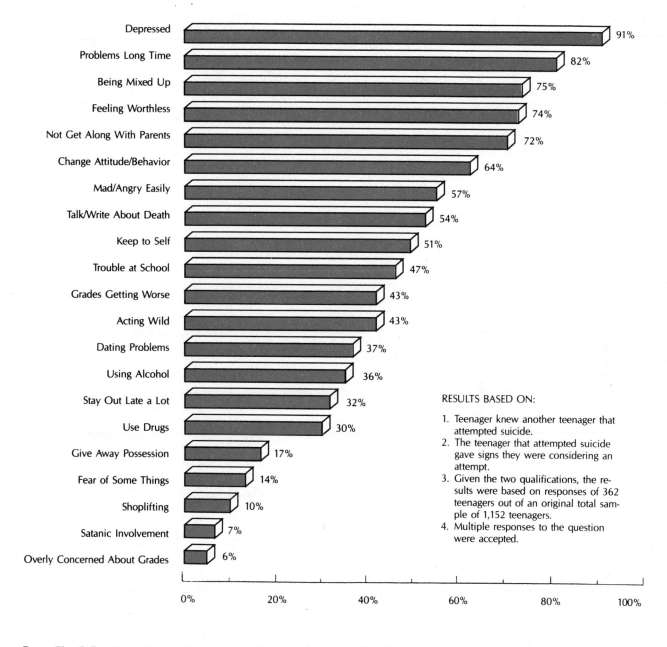

Depressed	91%
Problems Long Time	82%
Being Mixed Up	75%
Feeling Worthless	74%
Not Get Along With Parents	72%
Change Attitude/Behavior	64%
Mad/Angry Easily	57%
Talk/Write About Death	54%
Keep to Self	51%
Trouble at School	47%
Grades Getting Worse	43%
Acting Wild	43%
Dating Problems	37%
Using Alcohol	36%
Stay Out Late a Lot	32%
Use Drugs	30%
Give Away Possession	17%
Fear of Some Things	14%
Shoplifting	10%
Satanic Involvement	7%
Overly Concerned About Grades	6%

RESULTS BASED ON:

1. Teenager knew another teenager that attempted suicide.
2. The teenager that attempted suicide gave signs they were considering an attempt.
3. Given the two qualifications, the results were based on responses of 362 teenagers out of an original total sample of 1,152 teenagers.
4. Multiple responses to the question were accepted.

From: The Gallup Organization, Inc., *Narrative Summary Teenage Suicide Study*, January 1991, p. 57.

Teenagers are committing suicide at an alarming rate. Depression is the most common indicator in a suicidal personality, but feelings of worthlessness and confusion also contribute to the attitude that self-destruction is a viable alternative.

© Michael Streff in *Phi Delta Kappan.*

"Do you have a system designed to keep teenagers in?"

Although the percentage of teenagers committing suicide is relatively low, it is increasing. When a teenager dies for whatever reason, school is disrupted and students must be helped to understand and deal with the tragedy.

Many of society's problems affect children and the schools. In order to combat these problems, educators must reach out to parents to help them become involved in the education of their children; they must work with children and their families to help them overcome the problems of homelessness, poverty, child abuse, teenage sexuality, drug and alcohol abuse, sexism and racism, and suicide. Although the problems of society that affect children and the schools often seem overwhelming, school-based programs that involve other community agencies and business can often help children and families rise above these problems.

12.2 POINTS TO REMEMBER

- The number of children across all racial and ethnic groups who live in poverty is growing. Health and other poverty-related problems can affect a child's performance in school.
- Violence and crime infiltrate the schools and severely affect the learning environment.
- Women are less likely than men to attain high-prestige, high-paying positions in education. Therefore, female students have few role models of women in administrative positions.
- Minorities are even less likely than women to hold high-level administrative positions. Most minority students, therefore, do not have role models in the schools.

- Many middle and high school students abuse drugs and alcohol. Often the problems caused by this abuse directly affect the student's performance in the classroom and must be handled by the teacher.
- Substance abuse education is designed to help prevent students from abusing alcohol and drugs and to help them cope with the alcohol and drug abuse of the society.
- A large percentage of teenagers are sexually active, which can lead to pregnancy and sexually transmitted diseases, including AIDS. It is important for schools to recognize teenagers' sexuality and provide programs that help them deal with the potential results of their sexual activity, including pregnancy and STD.

- Sex education attempts to help students deal with problems related to sexuality on many levels. They deal with such issues as family relations, gender identity, dating and marriage, reproduction, family planning, sexual values, attitudes and behaviors, and rape and sexual abuse.
- AIDS education is required in more states than sex education and is designed to make students aware of how one can contract the AIDS virus, how to deal with AIDS victims, and how to prevent AIDS.
- The number of teenage suicides is increasing at an alarming rate. The most likely suicide victim is a white male. Schools need to develop programs that help vulnerable adolescents deal with depression, which can lead to suicide.

FOR THOUGHT/DISCUSSION

1. What specific things can schools do to accommodate the changing nature of the American family?

2. For what reasons are minority children more likely than whites to be poor and ineffectively educated?

3. What are some signs in the child of physical and/or emotional abuse? If such a child appeared in your classroom, what should you do?

4. Do you believe schools have a responsibility to teach sex education? If not, why not? If so, how would you deal first with a parent, and second with a school system, that opposed it?

FOR FURTHER READING/REFERENCE

Besharov, D. J. 1988. *Protecting children from abuse and neglect.* Springfield, IL: Charles C. Thomas. A collection of articles on physical, sexual, and emotional child abuse cases; problems related to reporting child abuse are discussed.

Blankenhorn, D., Bayme, S., and Elshtain, J. B. 1991. *Rebuilding the nest: A new commitment to the American family.* Milwaukee, WI: Family Services of America. A series of essays on the current state of the American family, including articles on the quality of life for children and family values.

Kirp, D. L. 1989. *Learning by heart: AIDS and school children in America's communities.* New Brunswick, NJ: Rutgers University Press. A discussion of how different communities throughout America have responded to schoolchildren with AIDS.

Mintz, S., and Kellogg, S. 1988. *Domestic revolutions: A social history of the American family.* New York: Free Press. American families in the seventeenth and twentieth centuries are compared and contrasted, with a focus on their diversity.

Weiss, L. (Ed.) 1988. *Class, race, and gender in American education.* Albany: State University of New York Press. Thirteen articles relating to race, gender, and social class in American schools, including such topics as Appalachian girls, black cultural norms in schools, and a rationale for integrating race, gender, and social class in the schools.

13

Schools Respond to Social Change

Choice in education? Can it happen? Would it be valuable? As parent and professional, I can't imagine another way.

When I sent my oldest child, now 21, off to kindergarten, the Minneapolis Public Schools' federally funded "Southeast Alternatives" program was in its fledgling years. I had the choice of four schools, each with a different philosophy. The school I chose fit with my philosophy of child development; my child's education complemented our family's values. At one point I had seriously considered moving out of the city, but, in the end, I just couldn't imagine buying into a suburban school system that believed there was only one way to educate all children. One system can't meet all of the diversity of our human interests and multi-intelligences.

As my last child prepares to enter high school, her choices are even broader—the Open Magnet, the International Baccalaureate, the Arts School, the Technology Magnet, the Liberal Arts Magnet—and, if none of these fully meets her needs, she has the right to enroll in classes at the University of Minnesota.

I am also an elementary teacher in a K–8 Minneapolis public alternative school, where parents, students, and teachers all have choices. Parents choose to send their children to our school and we have been overenrolled for years. Every spring parents visit our classrooms and give their input on choice of teacher for their child's next school year. For 10 years, we've held "Goal-Setting Conferences" each September, during which parents, teacher, and student discuss the student's strengths, interests, and needs, including academic, physical, interpersonal, and artistic goals. Together, they choose specific goals for the student, going beyond traditional curriculum. Our school's "whole child" emphasis includes interdisciplinary thematic curriculum, experiential curriculum, hands-on manipulatives, the direct teaching of social skills, and attention to each learner's distinct style.

In my multi-age classroom, students have many choices. They may elect to sit in the pillow corner or at the tables; they may decide to interact with peers for "teaching"; and they may choose what mini-courses to take or teach, how to organize their work time, what topics they believe are most meaningful to investigate within a theme, and when to eat a healthy snack. Our staff believes it is important for students to make choices and evaluate the results of their choices. We give students the opportunity to make many choices in order to help them learn how to make good choices.

As a teacher in this site-based managed school, I also make many choices each day. Some choices involve next year's budget, the staff development focus, and the day-to-day operations of our school. Most important, however, I choose how to facilitate the growth of my students. I determine the interdisciplinary themes that incorporate our district's curriculum guidelines, and I select the wide variety of materials for teaching each theme rather than relying on standard textbooks. I also choose the math manipulatives, the problem-solving situations, and the novels for my literature-based approach to reading. I am accountable for the success of each of my students; therefore, I choose the strategies that nurture each child's learning based on my understanding of his or her learning style, interests, skills, and deficits. I am the professional educator who determines—who chooses—how to help them focus their energies.

Over the years, my opportunity to make educational decisions has increased my commitment to excellence, to success for every student. Over time, increasing student choices has also significantly decreased my discipline problems. Maybe William Glasser has been right all along. After basic physical needs, we seek to have power, freedom, and fun. It certainly is a lot more fun to have the power and freedom to make choices than to have them made for us.

From: L. Ellison, 1990–91, "The Many Facets of School Choice," *Educational Leadership* 48 (4), 37.

I n the school district that is probably the most celebrated example of choice in the country, the students of the East Harlem Maritime School practice rowing and sea chanties. The students tug at the large oars under a hot sun, largely oblivious to the drama that has unfolded at their school over the last few years.

The Maritime School is one of 24 junior high schools that students in East Harlem's District 4 can choose as they leave sixth grade. Like many other schools in the district, in addition to regular course offerings the maritime school adopted a special theme to define its educational vision and appeal to students. . . .

The school now offers courses in navigation, oceanography and marine biology. Students took first and third prizes in a recent model boat regatta in Central Park. Once a week, they travel from East Harlem to the campus of the New York Maritime Academy at the base of the Throgs Neck Bridge in the Bronx. There they row, drill, and file into classrooms on a ship, the Ernestina. . . .

Fred Hornedo Jr., a dental technician and Navy veteran, visited several schools with his son, Freddy, who had done well at an alternative elementary school but was having trouble, as his father put it, "being able to sit down.". . .

"I was looking for a place where Fred could fit in," said Mr. Hornedo, an advocate of choice. "This is my first experience with this. I just went to school in my district. I find this to be great." Mr. Hornedo has been emboldened to send his son next year to a Staten Island high school with an even more extensive maritime program. . . .

From: S. Chira, June 12, 1991, "The Rules of the Marketplace Are Applied to the Classroom," *New York Times*, A1, B5.

CHAPTER OBJECTIVES

After studying this chapter, you should be able to:

- Identify how schools deal with society's problems.
- Discuss how preschools are attempting to meet the needs of society.
- Discuss how the middle school attempts to deal with the needs of early adolescents.
- Analyze the issue of school choice.
- Discuss different models for school choice.
- Understand how multicultural education programs attempt to deal with society's needs.
- Discuss how bilingual education programs are attempting to meet the needs of society.
- Assess the role of before- and after-school programs in the changing society.
- Understand the hurdles that students overcome with the help of dropout prevention programs.
- Understand programs for gifted and talented students.
- Define different approaches to discipline.
- Discuss the various roles of parents in education.
- Assess the ethical role of the teacher.

Although schools do not change rapidly and many argue that they should conserve rather than change society, they do attempt to deal with social changes and to meet the needs of society through direct and indirect measures. This chapter will examine some of the ways in which schools are affected by social change and how schools attempt to meet the needs of today's children and families.

SOCIETY AND THE CHANGING SCHOOL

We must first, however, understand the problems of society that affect children, families, and schools. Historian Lawrence A. Cremin in *Popular Education and Its Discontents* (1990) argued that "our recent assessments of how far [education has] come, especially as those assessments have been expressed in the policy literature of the 1980s, have been seriously flawed by a failure to understand the extraordinary complexity of education—a failure to grasp the impossibility of defining a good school apart from its societal and intellectual context" (p. viii). In other words, we really cannot understand schools unless we understand the society of which they are a part. And, according to Cremin, we have frequently failed to recognize the importance of the interrelatedness of society and the schools and how each affects the other. In chapter 12 we examined some of the problems that face today's children, families, and schools. In this chapter we will examine some of the ways in which the schools are attempting to deal with these problems.

PRESCHOOLS

One of the ways in which schools are meeting the needs of single-parent families, working parents, and underprivileged children is through the estab-lishment of preschools. Certainly, the concept of preschool is not new. You may have attended a preschool. Perhaps it was called a nursery school. What is new is the emphasis on early childhood education, including education for three- and four-year-olds in public schools.

Early childhood education differs from child care in that it prepares children for school. According to the Committee for Economic Development (CED), a research and policy organization of 250 corporate and university leaders, in *The Unfinished Agenda: A New Vision for Child Development and Education* (1991), child care is seen more as a benefit to parents than to children since it allows parents to work (p. 27). However, the CED suggests that

A preschool not only cares for the daily needs of children but also prepares them for school. Without any federal or state regulation in terms of teacher preparation or curriculum, preschools vary in their quality and effectiveness. Parents, therefore, need to select carefully the preschool that best meets the needs of their child.

attempting to separate the education and care of young children is counterproductive because all children need both.

In fact, child care has become even more important since the passage of the Family Support Act of 1988, which requires states to develop special education and employment/training programs for many, if not most, teenage parents on welfare. For these programs to succeed, child care must also be provided. According to the National Governors' Association, "Child care is an essential service for adolescent parents who are involved in educational, job training, and employment programs. . . . All states must supply child care to AFDC [Aid to Families with Dependent Children]-supported parents who are enrolled in education and/or employment training programs, as required under the Family Support Act" (1990, 19). This increasing emphasis on both early education and child care is related to society's changing needs, particularly the changing structure of the American family.

Preschool Enrollment

In the decade of the 1970s, preschool enrollment (three–five-year-olds) increased 19 percent. Between 1980 and 1989 preschool enrollment increased another 24 percent (U.S. Department of Education, National Center for Education Statistics 1990, 41). In 1970, 17 percent of preschool youngsters attended full-day school programs; in 1989, 37 percent did. These figures include only children enrolled in preschool programs that are monitored by governmental agencies; they do not include those who are cared for by unlicensed child-care givers.

This dramatic increase in the number of children enrolled in preschool programs illustrates a social need for more and better preschools. More are needed because more mothers are entering the work force rather than remaining home. Better preschools are required so that those underprivileged children who previously entered school developmentally behind their more privileged peers can improve their learning skills and function more successfully.

Funding of Preschools   By 1970, only seven states had appropriated funds for preschool programs in their public schools, and only four states had contributed funds to Head Start, a federally funded preschool program for underprivileged children (see chapter 6, pages 170–173). However, by 1989, thirty-one states had appropriated funds for state-initiated preschool programs and/or made direct contributions to Head Start (Mitchell 1989, 666). Most of the funded programs are all-day, year-round programs for at-risk children in local public school districts and are administered by state departments of education.

Many people, including those on the CED, believe that the funding of preschools must come from a combination of sources: foundations, corporations, and federal, state, and local governments. The CED estimates that $11.5 billion are needed during the first five years of the 1990s—7 percent of what was spent on all education in 1988.

The CED suggests that preschool programs, although expensive, are cost effective for dealing with long-term problems such as the dropout rate and helping at-risk students become more productive learners. "It has been shown that for every one dollar spent on a comprehensive and intensive preschool program for the disadvantaged, society saves up to six dollars in the long-term costs of welfare, remedial education, teen pregnancy, and crime" (1991, 28). They cite Project Giant Step, a preschool program in New York City, as an example.

Project Giant Step was begun in 1986 to provide a half-day, comprehensive public school program for underprivileged children. It is administered by the New York City Board of Education and the Agency for Child Development and takes place both in public schools and in other child care settings. It combines a preschool educational program for children with support services to parents. The children receive three hours of classroom experience five days per week, ten months per year. Eighty percent of the parents volunteered in the classroom and 70 percent attended classes or events organized by the program. The program also provided parents with information about health care, child care, employment services, and food assistance.

A study of 1,077 children and their parents who participated in Giant Step, by Abt Associates, revealed large student gains in both cognitive performance and social and emotional development. The turnover of personnel in the program was about half what it was in other preschool programs nationally primarily because staff members were pleased with the training they received and with the program itself and were committed to its success.

Head Start is another example of a preschool program that is successful in meeting the future educational needs of children. A review of the Head Start research from 1964 to 1984 reveals that the program has generally improved the cognitive and socioeconomic development of low-income and minority children. The program has also contributed to improved student health and increased involvement of parents in the child's education (see also chapter 6, pp. 170–173).

Point/Counterpoint

THE SCHOOLS CAN'T SOLVE ALL SOCIETY'S PROBLEMS

Critics [of the schools] ignore the fact that we have required our schools to become the largest and most comprehensive social service delivery system in the world! In *We the Teachers*, Terry Hernden [sic], a former Executive Director of The National Education Association remarks,

What is happening to our schools that we are obliged to run the largest juvenile delinquency program in town? To deliver the children to the school and, once there, to feed them if they haven't been fed at home? To provide psychological counseling and otherwise do what society once held to be the responsibility of the parents?

Our teachers should be capable and dedicated professionals, and our facilities and resources should be adequate for the educational tasks we wish to accomplish. However, we must understand that " our schools can't do it all." Using the schools to *achieve* racial balance, *eliminate* poverty, *fight* drug abuse, *prevent* pregnancy, and *reduce* youth suicide is simply too much! Our teachers and principals should be required to address *educational issues*, not unmet social needs.

From: Rittenmeyer, 1986

THE SCHOOLS MUST SOLVE SOME SOCIAL PROBLEMS

"Why is it that the school is expected to solve all of society's problems? Teenage pregnancy, suicide, drug abuse, poor nutrition, low self-esteem—you name it and we're supposed to cure it. Well, I don't know about you, but I was hired to teach algebra, not to play at being a psychiatrist." Sound familiar? It is a legitimate question. Why should teachers be expected to deal with these problems? What have such problems to do with teaching algebra or any other subject? The short answer to this question is they have everything to do with teaching.

First of all, teenage pregnancy, suicide, low self-esteem, poor nutrition, and drug abuse may indeed be different facets of the same set of problems that are closely related to each other and to such other problems as class cutting, truancy, and disruptive behavior. If students are unavailable for instruction, either physically or mentally, teachers cannot teach them.

From: Towers, 1987

POSTSCRIPT

Neither Towers nor Rittenmeyer would claim that schools do not respond to society's problems; nor would either say that they should not respond. Instead, they are arguing the extent of the schools' response and whether the schools should be charged with solving society's problems. Towers makes the point that schools should respond more to the needs of today's students, while Rittenmeyer suggests that schools have already responded too much. Where do you stand? Perhaps the rest of this chapter will help you answer this question.

Increased State Involvement

Anne Mitchell, dean of the Division of Research, Demonstration, and Policy at Bank Street College, says the increased state concern for preschool programs comes from five sources: (1) demand from working mothers in all income groups; (2) concern for present and future economic productivity, international competitiveness, and the changing nature of the work force; (3) efforts to get mothers with Aid to Families with Dependent Children (AFDC) funds into the work force; (4) desire to provide a better educational start for poor children; and (5) evidence that high quality early childhood programs have a long-term positive effect for disadvantaged children (p. 667). In addition, many groups, including the Carnegie Foundation for the Advancement of Teaching, the National Association for the Education of Young Children, the Task Force on Early Childhood Education for the National Association of State Boards of Education, the Committee for Economic Development, and the National Governors' Association, have taken an active role in promoting preschool funding initiatives.

Regulation of Preschools

Since nearly twice as many preschool programs in the late 1980s were private rather than public, regulation has been a problem. The vast majority of preschool teachers lack the training required of public school teachers. In fact, the majority of preschool teachers are care givers rather than educators. Will preschool teaching require state certification in the future? If it does, who will set and monitor the educational requirements? How much will certification of teachers increase the cost of the preschool? Will these requirements apply to private as well as public preschools? The answers to these questions are yet to be determined.

Preschool Curriculum

Arguments over the curriculum of preschool education must be resolved as well. On the one hand, many educators believe that the curriculum should develop socialization and readiness skills, which are required before a child can begin reading, writing, and computing. On the other hand, others argue that preschools should provide formal academic instruction in such areas as reading and mathematics. Not enough research has been done to justify any specific conclusion. Rather, parents generally select a preschool that fits the needs of their child.

MIDDLE SCHOOLS

The concept of middle school, a transitional institution between elementary and high schools, is not new. It is, however, evolving, with a new emphasis on what has been called the middle school philosophy, an approach that focuses on the early adolescent rather than on the subject matter. This emergence of the middle school concept is an attempt to meet the developmental needs of early adolescents. It creates a learning environment for early adolescents that bridges the gap between elementary school, where the child spends most of the day in a single classroom with a single teacher, and high school, where the adolescent moves from class to class and has as many as eight teachers per day. In addition, the middle school is intended to redefine not only the organizational structure of the school but also its educational methods. It not only meets the cognitive needs of the students but tries to meet their psychological and social developmental needs as well. Proponents of this student-centered middle school philosophy believe that it has the potential to deal with some of society's major problems, including drug abuse, teenage pregnancy, and dropping out of school, thereby improving the lives of adolescents.

By the late 1960s schools that had previously been called junior high schools were becoming middle schools. This restructuring involved a change in the ages within each school's population. Junior high schools usually house students from grades seven through nine; whereas middle schools house students from grades six through eight. But most middle schools that previously had been junior high schools did not change their organizational structure. Deborah L. Cohen found that most middle schools of the late 1980s still used the secondary school schedule of uniform periods. She also found that the majority of middle school teachers lacked special training to work with these students. Therefore, although the schools were restructured in terms of the ages of the students, their instructional approach did not change as rapidly (1989).

Adolescent Development

In June 1989, the Carnegie Council on Adolescent Development issued a report, *Turning Points: Preparing American Youth for the 21st Century*, in which it criticized middle-grade education as not focusing on the needs of early adolescents. This report, supported by developmental psychological research, stated that young adolescents ages ten to fifteen face more significant turning points—growth and changes—than any age group other than infants.

The report further contended that the conditions of early adolescence have changed dramatically from past generations. Although early adolescents today may have a better sense of self and more opportunities for intimate relationships, they also face unprecedented choices and pressures. They do not have the dependent needs of childhood but haven't found their own path to adulthood. They feel isolated while surrounded by peers. They are confused by all these changes and frequently make harmful decisions with harmful consequences. The report cited statistics about increased numbers of young adolescents who have alcohol and drug problems, who are pregnant, and who exhibit high risk behaviors and school failure (see chapter 12, pp. 413–424).

> Middle-grade schools—junior high, intermediate, and middle schools—are potentially society's most powerful force to recapture millions of youth adrift, and help every young person thrive during early adolescence. Yet all too often these schools exacerbate the problems of young adolescents. A volatile mismatch exists between the organization and curriculum of middle-grade schools and the intellectual and emotional needs of young adolescents. Caught in a vortex of changing demands, the engagement of many youth in learning diminishes, and their rates of alienation, substance abuse, absenteeism, and dropping out of school begin to rise. As the number of youth left behind grows, and opportunities in the economy for poorly educated workers diminish, we face the specter of a divided society: one affluent and well-educated, the other poorer and ill-educated. We face an America at odds with itself. (Carnegie Council on Adolescent Development 1989, 8–9)

Middle School Instruction

The difference between how students are taught in the traditional secondary school and the contemporary middle school is the difference between content-centered instruction and student-centered instruction (see chapter 9, pp. 274 and 287). This difference is made clear by Terry Weeks's experience.

> When Terry M. Weeks, former Teacher of the Year, set out in the mid-1970s to teach his Murfreesboro, Tennessee, 7th graders a lesson on the Middle East, the approach he chose was the lecture.
>
> He told his class the story of the Arab-Israeli conflict, hoping that they "would imagine it through my words."
>
> But last year when the topic came up, he let students offer their own solutions to the conflict. And when one suggested that the United States find a new homeland for Israelis, that became the inspiration for an exercise in which pupils assumed the roles of politicians, Jews, Arabs—and even American Indians.
>
> That lesson allowed the class to "see the solution through different eyes," Mr. Weeks says, to "play it through" to discover the problem's full complexity.
>
> He attributes the change in approach to his school's transition to the philosophy of what is known as the middle school movement. It was a shift, he says, that transformed "the heart and soul of what I do."
>
> "Students became my main focus," he explains, "rather than my subject." (Cohen 1989, 1, 20)

Improving Middle Schools

To help alleviate the problem of disenfranchised youth in the middle grades, the Carnegie Council on Adolescent Development proposed a series of recommendations intended to develop a teaching staff trained in the psychology of the middle-school student and a curriculum and approach to learning appropriate to that age level (see table 13.1).

In order best to implement these recommendations, the Carnegie Council on Adolescent Development suggested that the schools take some immediate steps: Change the focus of middle-grades education immediately, prepare teachers specifically for middle school, collaborating with middle schools in the process, and provide better access to health-care services. In addition the council suggested that: Statewide task forces should examine the implications for their schools, youth organizations should form partnerships with schools, the president and other national leaders should establish federal policy for funding youth development research, and parents should help their children define their goals, monitor their studies, and bring pressure on the schools for change.

The report of the Carnegie Council clearly intends to meet the special needs of the middle-school student rather than adapting materials for them from the lower grades and the higher grades. It is also clear that this middle level has its own developmental and emotional needs that must be met by trained professionals.

SCHOOL CHOICE

Perhaps the most controversial concept in public education in the United States is parental choice of educational institutions at the elementary and secondary levels. Many parents believe that they should have the right to determine the school that is most suited to the needs of their child.

TABLE 13-1

Summary of Carnegie Council on Adolescent Development Recommendations on Reforming Middle-Grades Education, 1989

1. Create small communities for learning.
2. Teach a core academic program (literacy, including in the sciences, ability to think critically, lead a healthy life, behave ethically, assume responsibilities of citizenship).
3. Ensure success for all students (eliminate tracking, promote cooperative learning, flexibility in arranging instructional time, and adequate resources for teachers).
4. Empower teachers and administrators to make decisions about the experiences of middle-grade students.
5. Staff middle-grade schools with teachers who are expert at teaching young adolescents.
6. Improve academic performance through fostering the health and fitness of young adolescents.
7. Reengage families in the education of young adolescents.
8. Connect schools with communities.

From: Carnegie Council on Adolescent Development, Carnegie Corporation of New York, *Turning Points: Preparing American Youth for the 21st Century* (Washington, DC: Author, 1989).

The middle school has begun to be viewed as an important developmental stage for adolescents rather than simply as a stepping stone from one phase to another. To this end, these recommendations have been proposed to improve the teaching, curriculum, and environment of the middle school.

There has always been some degree of choice in education; parents could elect to move or send their children to independent, private, or parochial schools. However, the degree of choice has been historically limited to people of means, either economic or educational. Many educators believe that allowing *all* parents to choose the educational institution to which they send their children will promote better education for all children.

Free Market System in Education

The concept of choice is built on the concept of competition in the free market system. Proponents of choice contend that if parents have the right to select their children's schools, they will select only the best schools; the others will have to close their doors or improve their methods of operation. Opponents, however, contend that "choice will not improve schools. If anything, it will take resources away from the schools that need it most" (Fiske 1989, 32).

Many educators warn that if school choice is widely employed, some schools will attract not only the better students but also the better teachers and, perhaps, more of the resources. What does this leave for other schools—poorer students and teachers, fewer resources? In fact, many critics contend that "open enrollment is elitist—at least in the sense that only those who have the means to do the driving will be able to choose. Choice will not be available to many low-

CROSS-CULTURAL PERSPECTIVE

Choice in the Dutch System

There is one distinctive feature of the Dutch educational system that U.S. visitors would notice (if they read a little Dutch). At certain times of the year, local newspapers are full of advertisements for schools; for example, "Come to our primary school, and see what good Christian education is like" and "A superior Catholic vocational school will hold a parent and student open house on. . . ." Are schools really competing with each other for pupils?

This market-like behavior derives from a critical feature of Dutch society: *verzuiling*. Roughly translated as "pillarization," the term refers to the tendency for Catholic, Protestant, and "neutral" organizations to exist in every sphere, from unions to libraries to hobby clubs (Schetter 1987). The role of pillarization in determining the jobs, friends, and political affiliations of Dutch citizens is rapidly diminishing. In the educational sector, however, it continues to be influential because it is supported by the Dutch Constitution. Article 23 states that "all persons shall be free to provide education" and that "private primary schools that satisfy the conditions laid down by Act of Parliament shall be financed from public funds according to the same standards as public-authority schools." This critical provision—passed in 1917 as a result of industrialists' concerns about the poor education offered in privately funded religious schools—obligates the government to fund all schools at an equal level (MOW [Ministry of Education and Science] 1988).

The basic implication of Article 23 is that any group of parents who share a set of values can establish a school without financial constraints. In practice, this means that more than 65 percent of all schools in the Netherlands are private (MOW 1988). Most of these are Catholic or Protestant (about equal numbers of each at the elementary level and a slightly larger number of Protestant schools at the secondary level), with a small number (slightly more than 5 percent) of "neutral" private schools (Montessori, Jena, Steiner, and so on). A foundation and a board of directors composed largely of parents and appropriate community members govern private schools; municipalities provide the administrative and policy-making authority for public schools. Parents may freely choose any school, and private schools may select among those children who apply.

Article 23 also ensures that schools (or municipalities) are free to develop their own curriculum. Current interpretations support government regulation of many aspects of educational quality standards: teacher qualifications, minimum number of basic subjects, use of finances, and so on. However, the government may not interfere with the right to determine how the "quasi-autonomous" schools will instruct students, the textbooks used, or the precise content of the curriculum. The government can only indirectly intervene in the curriculum through specific and narrow interpretations of the Constitution and by setting the final examinations for secondary schools.

Studies disagree about the importance of religious affiliation in determining parental school choice (Versloot 1990), but the principle of freedom of education is fiercely protected by the Center and Right political parties and is also privately valued by many Socialist and other Left party members.

From: Louis and Van Velzen, 1990

income or single-parent families. Distance and geography will also determine who can choose, especially when extracurricular activities are added to the schedule" (Pearson 1989, 821). Therefore, critics of school choice worry that it will do little to help meet the needs of society. In fact, it may exacerbate the situation further for those students who most need the best schools.

Despite these concerns, there is no doubt that some level of choice is the wave of the future. Fifty-eight percent of teachers surveyed in a 1989 poll favored choice for parents of public school students (Elam 1990). More than twenty states have passed or are considering bills that would permit student and parent choice. The state of Minnesota has an open enrollment plan that allows for parental choice in all districts with more than 1,000 students. According to Susan Tifft in *Time*, "Liberals like [choice] because it gives underprivileged children a chance for a better education. Conservatives like it because it's cheap, fosters competition among schools and transfers power from administrators to parents" (1989, 54). However, many educators remain wary.

The single most frequently proposed type of school for parental choice is the magnet school. Alternatives to traditionally structured schools, they are usually organized by academic or vocational theme and are generally open to all applicants based on availability. The term *magnet* assumes that the students will be attracted to the school because of the theme or special opportunities the school provides. Steuben Middle School in Milwaukee, Wisconsin, for example, has developed a computer specialty program. Students can become familiar with computer operation, robotics, and videodisc technology.

Magnet Schools

(continued on p. 439)

Magnet schools are organized around a particular theme or topic and attract those students who are motivated to study those subjects. These students of East Harlem Maritime School practice rowing and navigational skills. They also study such related topics as oceanography and marine biology.

V I E W P O I N T S

City Magnet School: A Microsociety

The Lowell Public Schools established the City Magnet School (K–8) in the downtown business district. The school was designed to engage students, parents, and teachers in the building of a miniature society. It was the first microsociety school in the nation.

The effort began with the introduction of money, markets, and property into the school. The students, advised by their teachers, used these ingredients to create a microeconomy. The microeconomy, in turn, has led to the creation of numerous organizations and jobs in them. Students fill these positions. Some of the work opportunities have arisen in the business sector; others have developed in government agencies, in the miniature society's fledgling legal system, and in a variety of cultural organizations. As these institutions evolve, so do markets for land, labor, and capital. Interacting with these markets has become a dynamic part of each student's school experience.

Beginning in kindergarten, children attending the microsociety school play with the fundamental building blocks of modern society. As they grow and mature, their miniature society matures with them. Apart from gaining insight into adult experience and adult society, there is no prescribed ideological path that the students must follow. With the assistance of parents and teachers, they fashion their own.

The Lowell microsociety school is a living experiment in applied moral development. Children and adults constantly face moral dilemmas that they must solve as they strive to build a "good" society. Do you want a microsociety with the extremes of poverty and wealth? Do you want a state based on law or one based on fear and violence? Should the microsociety's government assist or ignore children who may not be succeeding? Do you want a democracy or a totalitarian state? What liberties should students have? And what responsibilities should they shoulder? What kinds of activities should be taxed? When does one put the community's welfare ahead of the rights of the individual? What civil rights should children enjoy in their microsociety? When has justice been done? Children attending the City Magnet School face these dilemmas under the guidance of parents and teachers, many of whom may be struggling with similar issues in the real world.

The City Magnet School provides students with a strong, traditional program in the basic skills. Teaching the basic skills effectively is a goal of virtually every school in the nation. In this magnet school, however, the students learn basic skills as they legislate, adopt budgets, pass tax measures, administer justice, govern, or simply communicate with one another regarding commercial and legal matters. They read, write, and use mathematics with purpose. In other words, the basic skills have utility. In the tradition of John Dewey, *doing* reinforces *learning.* . . .

The microsociety school has produced dramatic changes in the curriculum. For example, publishing—generally known as "English" in the traditional curriculum—has evolved into the most important industry group. Children now write to be published, publish to be read, read to be informed, and use information to make intelligent decisions. The rewards for literacy are significant: recognition, influence, other writing opportunities, and payment in "mogans" (the microeconomic currency).

Arithmetic, once taught as a string of abstract concepts that might be useful in the future, now has immediate and practical application. Students bank, keep books, write checks, bill customers, prepare tax returns, prepare budgets, and perform financial audits. . . .

The microsociety has also produced subtle changes in students' status. A student's prominence in the classroom society now seems to be influenced by wealth, employment, intelligence, integrity, reliability, and loyalty. Muscle, appearance, and clothing still count—but not as much.

Because so many organizations arise in a microsociety, the students enjoy many opportunities to be both leaders and followers. A youngster can serve as a judge for six months, a business leader for a year or more, a legislator for a term of office. As the organizations evolve, students cooperatively define institutional purposes and desired outcomes. For example, they decide—often after intense debate—what public services their tax revenues will support, including welfare. Students pass budgets, levy taxes, and set tax rates. The government has its own internal revenue service and tax collectors. Every student files a tax return. Businesses are not taxed—at least, not yet.

The typical graduate of City Magnet School has had a host of socialization experiences and has been exposed to a variety of occupations. (One recent graduate wrote that she had served as a judge, a legislator, a lawyer, an entrepreneur, a writer, an editor, an accountant, and a tax collector—all in the same year.) Graduates leave, we hope, with a better sense of their own skills and interests and of the direction in which they are heading. They have also come to realize what organizations can and cannot accomplish and to understand the need for both cooperation and healthy competition.

From: Richmond, 1989

Since one of the goals of the magnet school concept is to attract students from all socioeconomic, ethnic, and racial backgrounds, a broad range of students is usually selected in an attempt to help integrate the public schools. LaGuardia High School of Music and the Arts in New York City and Thomas Jefferson High School for Science and Technology in Alexandria, Virginia, for example, have been able to balance their populations racially and socioeconomically by reattracting white students into urban schools that had been largely populated by black students. Proponents of school choice believe that this integration will lead to superior education for all students.

The graduates of a large proportion of magnet schools have been very successful. Average achievement scores at Thomas Jefferson High School, for example, were in the 98th percentile in science and mathematics and the 94th in reading. Fifty-nine of approximately four hundred seniors at Thomas Jefferson won National Merit Scholarships; fifteen were in the Westinghouse Talent Search.

However, opponents of magnet schools suggest that the only way to judge their success is by examining the success of other schools in that public school system. Are the students in the other schools achieving as much as or more than they did prior to the institution of the magnet school? If the answer is yes, the magnet school can be said to be a success in that it works to improve education for all. If the answer is no, the magnet school can be said to be a failure because it fails to improve education for all.

Funding of Magnet Schools

Magnet schools are funded like all public schools. Frequently, however, special state or federal grants are available for specialized programs in these schools. In 1991, President George Bush unveiled an education program in which he proposed a one-time grant for 535 new magnet schools, which would receive $1 million each. In addition, magnet schools have attracted significant private funding from business and industry. Thomas Jefferson High School, for

TABLE 13-2

A Comparison of School Choice Plans

California (Cupertino): The Cupertino Union School District near San Jose subsidizes home schooling. Parents who choose to educate their children at home can receive an annual $1,000 subsidy that can be used to purchase products or services available to public school students. It may not be used for private school tuition.

Massachusetts (Cambridge): The Cambridge School District has had a choice plan since 1981 that has served as a model for others in the state and around the nation. The district abolished school attendance zones, and parents may send their children to any of the district's 13 elementary schools. Assignments are made on a first-come, first-served basis, providing space is available and subject to desegregation constraints. According to the U.S. Department of Education, the proportion of students attending public schools in the district rose from 74 to 82 percent after the introduction of the choice plan.

Minnesota: Students in all parts of the state may attend public schools outside their district if the receiving district has space available and racial balance is not adversely affected. Parents may deduct from their taxable income up to $650 for elementary school students and up to $1,000 for secondary school expenses.

New Hampshire (Epsom): The small town of Epsom has enacted a controversial choice plan that allows parents who educate their children outside the public school system to receive a $1,000 property tax abatement.

New York (East Harlem): Students can choose among twenty-four public junior high schools offering spe-

cialties from maritime skills to performing arts. These magnet schools are available only to students in the district.

Vermont: Since 1969, Vermont has had a plan that allows parents in areas without public high schools to have the school district pay to send their children to public or private secondary schools (excluding parochial schools) in or out of the state. The plan covers the full tuition to a public high school and provides a capped tuition payment equal to the average tuition of the state's high schools to private schools. The plan was modified in 1990 to allow parents in areas that do have public high schools to participate. The 1990 law also extended the plan to elementary school students.

Washington: The legislature passed a new choice law during the 1990 session. It expanded the old choice law and widened the reasons a parent could give for requesting a transfer, such as proximity to day care or the parent's place of employment. It also provided that every school district have a policy on interdistrict transfers.

Wisconsin (Milwaukee): Initially, 24 of 144 schools were set aside as specialty schools, and the remainder were opened for students on the availability of space and racial guidelines in an attempt to desegregate the city schools. The Milwaukee Choice Plan, passed by the state legislature in 1990, allows parents to select private schools, to be funded by state aid reimbursements of $2,500 for each student accepted. Based on low-income guidelines, approximately 1 percent of students are eligible, making Milwaukee's plan the first voucher plan in the country.

From: R. Worsnop, "How Choice Plans Operate in the States," *CQ Researcher* (May 10, 1991), 269. Adapted, revised, and updated.

Parents have had the opportunity to select a school for their children for many years. Each plan is different and may involve private as well as public schools. This table describes some of the more common plans.

example, received over $4 million worth of high-tech equipment from four large companies in one year. Proponents of magnet schools contend that the increased involvement of business and industry in public education will not only provide needed funds, but also will lead to community awareness of social issues and, hence, involvement in helping to remedy these problems.

Tuition Tax Credits and Vouchers

To make a wide range of choice possible for all parents, some propose a system of tax credits and/or vouchers. A **tax credit** would allow parents to subtract from their state or federal income taxes an amount equal to a percentage of school tuition, up to a predetermined limit. In Minnesota, whose open enrollment program was upheld by the U.S. Supreme Court in 1983, parents can deduct up to $650 for elementary school tuition and school-related expenses and up to $1,000 for secondary school tuition from state income taxes whether their child attends public or private school.

Typically, **vouchers**, equal to the average per-pupil cost for educating a child in that specific area's public schools, are provided to all parents by their local governments. Parents then select their child's school, public or private, and the school redeems the voucher for cash from the government. The Wisconsin legislature passed the first voucher plan in the country in 1977. The Milwaukee Choice Plan allows parents to select private schools if their children meet low-income guidelines. These schools are then given $2,500 for each student admitted; up to 49 percent of the school's population may participate in this plan. Not all states agree, however, that these plans are legal. In the summer of 1990 the Dane County (Wisconsin) Circuit Court ruled that the Milwaukee Choice Plan did not violate the Wisconsin constitution, in a case brought by the Wisconsin Educators Association Council, the state's largest teachers union, and the National Association for the Advancement of Colored People and others. These organizations nevertheless have vowed to appeal the court's decision (see table 13.2).

How Will School Choice Affect Public Education?

If and how the school choice movement will change public education is still not clear. Initially, it has meant more variety in curricular and extracurricular programs. However, research shows that most parents are likely to select schools for their children like the schools they themselves attended. If this is true, increased variety may not be an ultimate outcome of school choice.

Whether increased parental choice will further integrate the schools is also uncertain. In fact, in some communities parents are selecting schools in which the children are most similar to their own. For example, in an elementary magnet school in Asheville, North Carolina, the percentage of minority students in the magnet school (18 percent) is only slightly higher than the percentage of minority children in a school in a predominately white neighborhood (13 percent), and is far below the percentage of minority students in the entire school population (42 percent). Although the ultimate educational and social outcomes of the choice movement are not clear, school choice will most likely be part of public education of the 1990s and beyond.

V I E W P O I N T S

Bottom-Line Education

Chicago—The turnout for the power breakfast was—as they say—gratifying. CEOs Vernon R. Loucks of Baxter International Inc., Edward A. Brennan of Sears, Roebuck & Co., and Stephen Wolf of UAL Corp. had packed a private hotel dining room with a few dozen of their cronies, the captains of Chicago's largest corporations.

Genially—if bluntly—Ed Brennan stated the agenda. "Frankly," he said, "we're here to put the arm on you." The cause? A fledgling inner-city elementary school. The featured speaker? Elaine C. Mosley, its demure black principal.

A few years back, such a meeting might have seemed improbable, even incongruous. But no longer. The schooling of poor urban children has become a priority for U.S. corporations hungry for skilled workers, and Ms. Mosley has emerged as a high-profile bridge between the converging worlds of business and education. As principal of the Corporate/Community School in Chicago, she presides over the nation's first corporate-financed and -managed elementary school.

"You and I have a lot in common," she told the breakfasting CEOs last summer. "You have chosen to provide services and make products to meet a select market demand. I'm in the business of developing minds to meet a market demand. . . . I'm developing people who will someday be able to participate in your businesses or own their own."

Schoolhouse and board room have merged at the Corporate/Community School. Dismayed by the faulty products being turned out by Chicago's troubled public schools, some 60 of the city's giant corporations have taken over the production line themselves. Their research-and-development laboratory is housed in a former parochial school in the impoverished, predominantly black neighborhood of North Lawndale on Chicago's West Side. Private, year-round and tuition-free, the school aims to prove that in the right setting poor children can learn as ably as suburban kids. It operates under the same constraints as Chicago public schools in terms of class size, and its pupils are selected by lottery to reflect a full range of abilities.

But there the similarities end. For the corporate school's founders are after something rarely seen in urban schools today: productivity. And they vow to solve the central dilemma of school reform: how to vastly improve educational quality for all children without a vast increase in costs.

Now well into its second year, the school has made an impressive beginning. Most students showed first-year gains in achievement-test scores, self-esteem and discipline. Staff and parent morale is high, and the 200-student school has been besieged with applicants—1,400 community children applied for 50 openings last fall. Although first-year operating costs were considerably higher than the Chicago average of $4,100 per pupil, they should be close to that target when full enrollment of 300 is reached in two years.

The key, the school's founders believe, is in a corporate management model. Why not, they reasoned, take the lessons learned by American industry during the past decade of restructuring and apply them to education? Their school would be small and nimble enough to stay responsive to its student customers. It would invest in teaching rather than tangled layers of administration. Its staff would be free to innovate, yet accountable to a board of directors for results.

These are radical ideas in most urban school districts, where teachers and administrators get their paychecks and tenure whether or not their students learn, and where school failure is usually blamed on such outside obstacles as underfinancing and ghetto pathology. If the corporate school works, the old excuses won't wash any longer. . . .

"You ask a typical class of 25 kids in this neighborhood if they've ever seen someone shot, and a third of the hands go up," says Mr. Mootry, who grew up in a Lawndale housing project. "They see things suburban kids might not see in a lifetime. Yet they still come to school ready to learn and be hugged."

This school doesn't disappoint: Hugs and praise envelop the children. More basically, teachers assume responsibility for their pupils' physical and emotional welfare outside school—a task that typically swamps inner-city schools with much larger enrollments. If a child needs housing, heat, glasses or a hearing aid, nurse Phyllis Pelt cuts red tape with the network of social agencies that the school has carefully cultivated. . . .

By design, the corporate school challenges most conventional notions of schooling. Classrooms are organized for discovery, teamwork and lively conversation, rather than numbing lectures by teachers standing at the blackboard. By admitting two-year-olds, it can provide optimal nurturing, stimulation and early remedial help. Its year-round schedule—and the fact that the building is open from 7 a.m. to 7 p.m.—assists working parents and reduces the negative distractions of the streets. Students progress through the curriculum at their own pace and, instead of report cards, receive four-page written evaluations four times a year.

Most important, teachers such as

Mary Kathleen Irwin don't put a ceiling on their expectations for these students. "A lot of our kids weren't sure if they knew anything," she says. "They had seen repeated failures. Adults here believed they could do it, and made them believe it, too. We've seen—I don't want to say miracles—but important, significant change." . . .

"It's worth our while to try to break the chain of poverty," says Warren L. Batts, chairman of Premark International, a Deerfield, Ill., maker of consumer and restaurant products. Premark has donated executive time and $50,000 a year for three years to the corporate school. Until recently, Premark's support of education was confined to colleges; now, like so many other corporations, it finds itself compelled to take a longer and broader view. One spur to action was a survey presented to Premark's board showing that 2% to 5% of its domestic assembly-line workers—mostly high-school graduates—were functional illiterates.

"There must be a reworking of the reward system that makes *not* educating kids so attractive," Mr. Batts says. "There's got to be measurable results—that's the corporate approach."

As he is acutely aware, a generation of children like nine-year-old Shanda Smith is waiting. Shanda, a pupil at the corporate school, has plans. Printed neatly in her lined school notebook, she has written: "I want to be something in life."

From: Graham, 1990

13.1 POINTS TO REMEMBER

- Schools deal with social problems in a variety of ways; there is disagreement about how involved schools should be.
- Preschools attempt to meet the needs of families and children

through child care and early childhood education. Proponents of public preschools point to the amount of money that may be saved in the long run.
- Middle schools meet the needs of early adolescents by designing instructional programs that focus on the developmental strengths of the middle-grade child.

- School choice is a controversial issue that allows parents to select the schools their children will attend.
- Some school choice programs allow parents to choose among a variety of public magnet schools or private schools. Tax credits or vouchers are two methods of financing school choice.

MULTICULTURAL EDUCATION

School choice by itself, however, will not solve all society's or education's problems. The increasing cultural diversity of the school population has caused problems of its own for students unfamiliar with both American customs and language. This has led to the call for multicultural education. **Multicultural education**, James A. Banks believes, is "at least three things: an idea or concept, an educational reform movement, and a process" (1989, 2). The guiding concept of multicultural education is that all students, no matter what race, gender, or social class, should have the same opportunity to learn in school. Some students have a better opportunity than others to learn in schools as they are currently structured. Banks points out as evidence of this that girls and boys achieve equally in mathematics and science in elementary school, but by high school boys achieve at a higher level than girls. He also cites evidence that in early grades ethnic minorities are close to parity with white students; however, the longer these ethnic students remain in school, the more their achievement lags behind their white peers (see chapter 11, pp. 364–366, and chapter 12, pp. 395–397). Hence, multicultural education is a movement to reform the structure of education so that all students regardless of ethnic background can have access to academic success.

The Multicultural Curriculum

In the 1970s the dominant approach to multicultural education was a "culturally disadvantaged model" which was predicated on the concept that "different is disadvantaged" (Puglisi and Hoffman 1978, 495). The authors (just cited) suggest that what is needed is a "culturally different model," based on "cultural variations [that] enrich a person's academic, intellectual and social experiences and contribute to the social and political qualities of a society" (p. 497).

James Banks suggests that the following curricular approaches can be used to develop a culturally different curriculum: contributions, additions, transformations, and decision making and social action (see table 13.3).

Banks believes these approaches form a hierarchy for integration of multiculturalism in the curriculum, the "contributions" approach being the least inclusive. It is often a first step in developing a multicultural curriculum by simply mentioning the contributions of specific ethnic people in a field. The "additive" approach, the second level in the hierarchy, simply adds ethnic content to the already existing curriculum without changing its basic structure. For example, students might study *The Color Purple* by Alice Walker in an American literature class. Or, in an elementary school, children might read literature that deals with various cultures, such as Isaac B. Singer's *The Power of Light: Eight Stories for Hannukah, Indian Tales and Legends* retold by J. E. B. Gray, *The Secret of Gumbo Grove* by Eleanora Tate, or *Three Stalks of Corn* by Leo Politi.

The "transformation" approach changes the structure of the curriculum by allowing students to view ideas from several ethnic perspectives. One example might be that rather than studying merely "standard English," students would study the regional, cultural, and ethnic influences on language.

The "social action" approach incorporates transformation but adds student action and decision making related to concepts, issues, or problems of ethnicity. For example, students might explore topics such as how to reduce prejudice in

(continued on p. 448)

V I E W P O I N T S

Teaching History So That Cultures Are More Than Footnotes

Rami Muth's eighth graders in Benicia, Calif., learn that George Washington was an American hero—and so were Mercy Otis Warren, Sacajawea, and Absalom Jones.

If those names sound unfamiliar, that is because they are only now being taught to American schoolchildren, as part of a fast-spreading and controversial movement known as multiculturalism. The idea is to change what children learn by including the contributions, perspectives, and sufferings of diverse ethnic and racial groups.

To some, multiculturalism is a long-overdue recognition that these groups' contributions have been unfairly excluded from American classrooms. Others fear that a new emphasis on diversity will stir up racial hatred, distort history, and undermine children's understanding of the values that hold Americans together. In many cases, the disagreements center on what should be emphasized: America's democratic ideals, or the times that the nation has failed to uphold them. . . .

Educators split over how America should be pictured: as an imperfect society that nonetheless offered opportunity and freedom to many people, or a society with a deep and enduring legacy of racism. One interpretation tends to view history as a way of justifying the status quo; another as a tool for changing society.

Bill Honig, California's superintendent of public instruction, said the state has tried to steer a middle course. "Shouldn't we tell the story of all different groups?" he asked. "Of course. Shouldn't we talk about our common ethical and democratic values? Of course. Either extreme is a disaster for this country."

In practice, the changes in California have meant substantial changes in what schoolchildren learn—and a lot of homework for teachers, who were never taught much of the new material themselves.

Mrs. Rocchio [a teacher] needed to research the San Gabrilieno Indians, the first people to inhabit what is now modern Newport Beach. Then she could teach her third graders about the tribe's customs, foods, and creation myths. One of the most important lessons she tries to impart, she said, is understanding different points of view.

"One little boy said to me, 'When I was researching the life of Martin Luther King, that book must have been written by a friend of his, but if that book had been written by the K.K.K., it would have been completely different,' " Mrs. Rocchio said. "That just made my year, to have a third grader understand that."

California substantially increased its requirement for world history because educators believe that children need to understand much more about other cultures in a world that no longer has Europe at the center.

So Jana Flores, a sixth-grade teacher in Santa Maria's Orcutt school district, headed for the library to learn about civilizations like Cush, the ancient African empire that briefly conquered Egypt, or about conditions in ancient Japan, India and China. . . .

Mr. Vigilante also prepared a special lesson on the Civil War's Port Royal experiment. Some Union military commanders who had seized land in South Carolina freed slaves, and others promised that if former slaves worked the land, they could later own it. Although many blacks flocked to the area and planted 40-acre plots, most found those promises betrayed after the war, when President Andrew Johnson returned much of the land to Southern planters.

From: Chira, July 10, 1991

TABLE 13-3

Approaches for the Integration of Ethnic Content

Approach	Description	Examples	Strengths	Problems
Contributions	Heroes, cultural components, holidays, and other discrete elements related to ethnic groups are added to the curriculum on special days, occasions, and celebrations.	Famous Mexican-Americans are studied only during the week of Cinco de Mayo (May 5). Black Americans are studied during Black History Month in February but rarely during the rest of the year. Ethnic foods are studied in the first grade with little attention devoted to the cultures in which the foods are embedded.	Provides a quick and relatively easy way to put ethnic content into the curriculum. Gives ethnic heroes visibility in the curriculum alongside mainstream heroes. Is a popular approach among teachers and educators.	Results in a superficial understanding of ethnic cultures. Focuses on the lifestyles and artifacts of ethnic groups and reinforces stereotypes and misconceptions. Mainstream criteria are used to select heroes and cultural elements for inclusion in the curriculum.
Additive	This approach consists of the addition of content, concepts, themes, and perspectives to the curriculum without changing its structure.	Adding the book *The Color Purple* to a literature unit without reconceptualizing the unit or giving the students the background knowledge to understand the book. Adding a unit on the Japanese-American internment to a U.S. history course without treating the Japanese in any other unit. Leaving the core curriculum intact but adding an ethnic studies course, as an elective, that focuses on a specific ethnic group.	Makes it possible to add ethnic content to the curriculum without changing its structure, which requires substantial curriculum changes and staff development. Can be implemented within the existing curriculum structure.	Reinforces the idea that ethnic history and culture are not integral parts of U.S. mainstream culture. Students view ethnic groups from Anglocentric and Eurocentric perspectives. Fails to help students understand how the dominant culture and ethnic cultures are interconnected and interrelated.
Transformation	The basic goals, structure, and nature of the curriculum is changed to enable students to view concepts, events, issues, problems, and themes from the perspectives of diverse cultural, ethnic, and racial groups.	A unit on the American Revolution describes the meaning of the revolution to Anglo revolutionaries, Anglo loyalists, Afro-Americans, Indians, and the British.	Enables students to understand the complex ways in which diverse racial and cultural groups participated in the formation of U.S. society and culture. Helps reduce racial and ethnic encapsulation.	The implementation of this approach requires substantial curriculum revision, in-service training, and the identification and development of materials written from the perspectives of various racial and cultural groups.

Approach	Description	Examples	Strengths	Problems
		A unit on 20th-century U.S. literature includes works by William Faulkner, Joyce Carol Oates, Langston Hughes, N. Scott Momoday, Carlos Bulosan, Saul Bellow, Maxine Hong Kingston, Rudolfo A. Anaya, and Piri Thomas.	Enables diverse ethnic, racial, and religious groups to see their cultures, ethos, and perspectives in the school curriculum. Gives students a balanced view of the nature and development of U.S. culture and society. Helps to empower victimized racial, ethnic, and cultural groups.	Staff development for the institutionalization of this approach must be continual and ongoing.
Decision Making and Social Action	In this approach, students identify important social problems and issues, gather pertinent data, clarify their values on the issue, make decisions, and take reflective actions to help resolve the issue or problem.	A class studies prejudice and discrimination in their school and decides to take actions to improve race relations in the school. A class studies the treatment of ethnic groups in a local newspaper and writes a letter to the newspaper publisher suggesting ways that the treatment of ethnic minority groups in the newspaper should be improved.	Enables students to improve their thinking, value analysis, decision-making, and social-action skills. Enables students to improve their data-gathering skills. Helps students develop a sense of political efficacy. Helps students improve their skills to work in groups.	Requires a considerable amount of curriculum planning and materials identification. May be longer in duration than more traditional teaching units. May focus on problems and issues considered controversial by some members of the school staff and citizens of the community. Students may be able to take few meaningful actions that contribute to the resolution of the social issue or problem.

From: A. Banks, "Integrating the Curriculum with Ethnic Content: Approaches and Guidelines," in J. A. Banks and C. A. M. Banks (Eds.), *Multicultural Education: Issues and Perspectives* (1989), 201.

In multicultural education, the teacher attempts to involve the students in a curriculum that includes materials from many cultures. The methods range from a simple mention of other cultures in an appropriate context to a complete integration of other cultures and ideas into their own perspectives and cultural ideas.

the school, how to ensure that women can participate equally in sports, or whether African-American students should sponsor a separate prom. Students would then not only suggest a plan of action but actually implement it.

Bilingual Education

Bilingual education is one form of multicultural education that is based on a paradigm that values diversity, "challenging melting pot assimilationist notions" (Garcia 1978). The 1968 Bilingual Education Act and the U.S. Supreme Court decision *Lau v. Nichols* (1973), which provides a legal basis for equitable treatment of limited-English-proficient (LEP) students in the United States, set the stage for bilingual education.

Carlos J. Ovando in "Language Diversity in Education" states that "about 206 Native American languages have survived the overwhelming powers of the English language" (1989, 211). These, along with non-native languages, make the United States what he calls a truly remarkable "language laboratory." Ovando points out that both Spanish and French are the "communicative and cultural instruments in various regions of the country" (p. 212). The range of languages still spoken in the United States today extends from Navajo to Hmong, the latter spoken by people from Laos and Cambodia. These do not include the numerous indigenous language varieties known as creole, pidgin, and dialect. According to Ovando, pidgin was the means of communication among slaves who came to the plantation speaking a variety of languages. When these slaves became free, pidgin was the only language they shared, and, consequently, it became the first language of the community. Creole is the adoption of pidgin as an accepted language of a community. He cites three examples of creole varieties: Gullah, an English- and West African-based creole spoken on the barrier islands from South Carolina to northern Florida; Louisiana French Creole, spoken in Louisiana and coexisting with two local variations of French and another variation of English; and Hawaiian Creole, which was influenced by the many languages of the islands (p. 212). Dialect is a variation of the English language. Black English is one example.

LEP students come from a wide range of backgrounds. Foreign-born students may enter U.S. schools speaking only their native languages; other students may have been born in the United States but do not speak English or speak some English and a native language. In 1987 it was estimated that students in the Los Angeles schools, for example, spoke seventy-nine different languages and those in the Anchorage, Alaska, schools spoke over one hundred languages.

The Bilingual Curriculum

Because of the wide variety of different languages spoken, even in a single school district, some believe there must be an equally wide variety of bilingual programs to meet the needs of LEP students and English-speaking students. Ricardo Garcia in *The Multiethnic Dimension of Bilingual-Bicultural Education* states that the purpose of bilingual education is to create an educational environment that is compatible with the student's home environment (1978, 492). He and many other proponents of bilingual education claim that placing Spanish-speaking children, for example, in an Anglo curriculum dominated by the English language creates an impossible stumbling block for the students.

Rudolph C. Troike in *Improving Conditions for Success in Bilingual Education Programs* suggests seven elements essential in a bilingual curriculum:

Bilingual education is an effort to reach all students regardless of their ethnic background. In classrooms where there is a diversity of languages spoken, however, it becomes difficult to balance the needs of all students. This small group of students in a northern California second grade are having a reading lesson in Spanish.

1. Emphasis must be given to the development of native language skills, including reading, and the overall amount of English used should not exceed 50 percent.
2. Teachers must be trained and able to teach fluently in the language of the students.
3. The program should extend over at least five grades, and preferably more.
4. The program must be integrated in the basic structure of the school administration and curriculum, and a supportive environment must exist.
5. Materials of quality comparable to those used in English should be available.
6. There should be support from the community and parents.
7. High standards for student achievement should be set and every effort made to maintain them.

Instruction for LEP students, often called English as Second Language (ESL), includes remedial instruction in either the native language or in English; linguistic enrichment by teaching in more than one language; teaching in both the native language and in English; and immersion, speaking the native (or target) language entirely.

The Bilingual Controversy

The road of bilingual education has not been smooth. It has been surrounded by controversy ever since the Supreme Court's 1974 *Lau* decision, that ruled a young San Francisco boy, Kinney Lau, who spoke only Chinese, had to receive special language attention. Cynthia Gorney in "The Bilingual Education Battle" (1985) suggests the controversy is as diverse as the languages spoken by the U.S. population. During the 1970s, proponents contended that bilingual education for Hispanics, for example, would improve their educational performance. However, the dropout rates for Hispanics changed little from the mid-1970s to the late 1980s. Therefore, many questioned whether bilingual education worked.

Others wonder how it is possible to provide adequate instruction in all the languages that are spoken by U.S. children. Gorney asks, "Where do you find a teacher who speaks Hmong?" And, if you find a teacher, how can the schools afford to pay for someone who may teach only one or two students? Opponents of bilingual education often cite its high cost as one of its problems.

Another concern, which has come to referendum in many states, is expressed by some English-speaking white parents who worry that their children are being short-changed. In Fillmore, California, for example, the city council adopted an English as the Official Language Resolution. Parents worry that the time children spend learning Spanish or any other language will take away from time spent learning English. In addition, some contend that bilingual education will eventually place non-English-speaking students at a disadvantage since they are less likely to learn English if they do not have to. Others are concerned that American patriotic values will be lost if schools emphasize the values of other cultures. It is likely that the controversy will continue since none of these questions have been answered satisfactorily.

BEFORE- AND AFTER-SCHOOL PROGRAMS

Another important development in American society is the proliferation of families in which both parents work outside the home. As a result of a growing need for affordable, accessible, supervised care for school-aged children, the length of the school day has been extended. Large numbers of children begin the school day in before-school programs, frequently beginning as early as 7 A.M., and end the day in after-school programs, frequently continuing to 6 P.M. Seventy percent of parents surveyed in a 1988 Gallup poll favored their local public schools offering before- and after-school programs for what are called **latchkey children**, those who come home from school to an empty house because their parents work (Gallup, 1988, 37).

Many such programs are currently in operation; they range from babysitting to formal activities for children and young adolescents. They are sponsored

Brian Watson, left, Steven Yow, center, and Charu Robinson of the Raging Rooks chess team from Adam Clayton Powell, Jr., Junior High School in Harlem have used the time before and after school to learn how to play chess and have become champions at it.

by public schools, social service agencies, libraries, YMCAs, YWCAs, Boys' and Girls' Clubs, churches, and a variety of independent groups. Although some states have regulations and the National Association for the Education of Young Children (NAEYC) has adopted guidelines, most of these programs are unregulated and rarely monitored. The care and services range from excellent to poor.

Many questions remain to be answered about before- and after-school programs:

- Is it the school's role to provide care, in addition to education, for the child?
- If it is, who will give the care and for how long?
- Will the care be supervised play or formal activity programs?
- Who will pay?
- Will there be academic/professional requirements for licensing of caregivers and programs?
- Who will license and who will monitor?
- How will the increased length of in-school time affect the curriculum during the regular school day?
- How will before- and after-school programs affect the giving of homework?
- Will the length of the teacher's and administrator's day change?
- How will discipline be handled? By whom?
- Will before- and after-school programs affect the extra-curricular program of the school?

There is little doubt that we will see a rapid increase in school-based before- and after-school programs; however, until the above questions are answered, their impact on the public schools remains unclear.

DROPOUT PREVENTION PROGRAMS

Many schools are developing programs with the specific goal of preventing students from dropping out. These programs are varied; but all of them attempt to make school a more hospitable place for students to learn and education more meaningful with a combination of course work, tutoring, and counseling. Many dropout prevention programs begin in late elementary school or in middle school.

Dropout Prevention Curriculum   Jerry Downing and Thomas C. Harrison, Jr., believe that dropout prevention programs must help students overcome specific hurdles that include completing high school graduation requirements, adapting to a teaching approach that is aimed at college-bound students, passing competency and proficiency examinations, understanding that it's a myth that a good job requires a college degree, following school rules, and fighting student isolation and bigotry (1990).

Although the goals of these curriculums are similar and all try to help the students overcome academic, social, and personal problems, the programs vary depending on the location. Some are "school-within-a-school" programs in which potential dropouts participate in activities that are parallel to the regular school curriculum but are designed specifically for them. For example, in Amityville, New York, teachers learn teaching styles compatible with the learning styles of their ninth graders who are potential dropouts.

Others are enrichment programs and occur outside school time. Keep Youth in School, a three-year research and demonstration project funded by the Children's Bureau, Administration for Children, Youth and Families, worked with twelve- to fifteen-year-old minority students in foster care in the Washington, D.C., schools. Besides pairing each potential dropout with a peer mentor, an undergraduate student at Catholic University, the program provided students with incentives to encourage them to stay in school, employment training, and guaranteed entry-level jobs at age sixteen. In addition, the programs offered guest speakers, camping trips, and mountain climbing expeditions. Students were recognized in a newsletter that was published several times a year and at an awards ceremony that was held twice a year.

Some programs feature tutoring as their primary objective. For example, a program in Asheville, North Carolina, matches each of approximately thirty-five University of North Carolina undergraduate students with two middle school students. The program emphasizes that each group learns from the other: the middle school students develop language and reading skills, and the university students develop teaching skills. The university students work with the two middle schoolers three times per week during school time. After school hours, the university students take the middle school children to athletic events, movies, and other events. During the school year several parties are held to establish a social camaraderie. Finally, the undergraduates publish a journal of writing completed during the school year by the middle school students.

IN THE CLASSROOM

Jorge (CoCo) Vazquez has taught students with special problems for fourteen years. He says that during most of those years he used traditional, behaviorally controlled environmental methods, and his students performed well in his classroom. However, he began to question what happened to them when they left the controlled environment. He decided he needed to prepare them for the outside world. But how?

Suddenly he saw a connection between his own work in the martial arts and his students' need for readiness skills—basic tools of learning and success. Now he helps his students gain these skills by teaching them the martial art of *shorinju kempo*, which the students call karate.

Shorinji kempo is different from some martial arts in that its basic purpose is self-management—training for life. It stresses cooperation rather than competitiveness. Only positive feedback is permitted in shorinji. This is critical for Vazquez's students who come from low-income or troubled families, who have been labeled behavioral problems, who have mental or physical disabilities, some severe, or who have learning disabilities. These students rarely experience success. CoCo's program is designed to give them this success.

CoCo, who teaches at Box Elder Junior High School in Brigham City, Utah, uses shorinji kempo to teach his students the essential learning tools of "listening and paying attention, compliance, following directions, concentration, stress management, visualization, self-discipline, and physical fitness."

According to CoCo, shorinji prepares his students in many ways. "For example, they're able to figure out for themselves the value of preparedness—both in learning and in self-defense." He uses the martial art's methods to help his students meet their academic requirements. Some of his students, for example, do "karate math." They put on their uniforms, do stretching and relaxing exercises, visualize the math they need, and break into groups to attack the math problems. The attention skills and relaxation techniques are especially useful for special students with behavioral or emotional problems.

During martial arts sessions, which are videotaped for the students to view afterwards, the students listen and watch their classmates. They talk about each student's efforts in positive terms and applaud all good effort. Although negative feedback is not a part of shorinji, CoCo teaches his students to take criticism, which, he says, is a part of life. "If you get chewed out for something, stand up straight. Put on a neutral facial expression. Nod your head. Listen. Say you're sorry, then move on. That's effective self-defense," he tells the students.

He teaches his students to be truthful with themselves by monitoring their own performance in other classes. Students fill out a daily sheet on which they rate themselves, from excellent to really rotten, in each class or special activity. CoCo monitors their truthfulness by talking to their teachers. Soon, he says, they learn to be truthful with themselves.

As the students progress through belt levels, they have specific requirements they must meet in the martial arts, citizenship, weight training, and academic classes. As they progress, the requirements get stiffer: a minimum GPA [grade point average] they negotiate with counselors for each belt level; letters of recommendation from a parent, teacher, or principal. This encourages the students to behave in their other classes since frequently CoCo requires that the letter be from a teacher with whom the student is having problems. Requirements are always possible to achieve, with effort. Vasquez has found a way to use his talent to help his special students find their own potential. (Foltz 1989, 10–12)

GIFTED AND TALENTED PROGRAMS

Programs for students classified as "gifted and talented" have increased in recent years in part as a response to declining Scholastic Aptitude Test (SAT) scores (see chapter 10, p. 315, and chapter 11, p. 377). In 1970, Section 806, Provisions Related to Gifted and Talented Children (P.L. 91-230), was added to the Elementary and Secondary Education Act (ESEA) Amendments of 1969. This law required the U.S. commissioner of education, Sidney P. Marland, Jr., to determine (1) the extent to which programs for the gifted and talented were necessary, (2) which federal assistance programs were used to meet the needs of the gifted, (3) how existing federal programs could be used to meet these needs, and (4) which new programs to recommend, if necessary.

In 1971, Marland reported his findings to Congress. Only 4 percent of an estimated 1.5–2.5 million gifted children were benefiting from existing programs and these were considered low priority. Guided by Marland's report, an increasing number of states funded programs for the gifted and talented. In 1977, Jeffrey Zettel determined that (1) nearly 75 percent of the states had identified gifted and talented students, (2) thirty-three states served 25 percent more gifted students than in the previous year, (3) thirty-one states increased appropriations to gifted and talented students by 50 percent, and (4) forty-two states reported sponsoring in-service training for teachers interested in working with gifted and talented students. By 1986–87, forty-four states had mandated programs for gifted and talented students (Council of State Directors of Programs for the Gifted 1987).

In 1988, Title IV, Part B, of the Hawkins-Stafford Elementary and Secondary Amendments to the ESEA (P.L. 100-197) was passed by Congress. This law, referred to as the Jacob K. Javits Gifted and Talented Students Act, provided financial assistance to each of the states, local education agencies, and institutions of higher education for research, demonstration model projects, and personnel training that helps to identify and meet the special needs of gifted and talented students.

Identifying the Gifted While it is obvious that some children are smarter than others, the idea of selecting some students for a gifted and talented school program has caused consternation among some parents, their children, and those who have been left out. Most schools rely on the I.Q. test to decide who should be included in the program. Some require a portfolio of work even from kindergarten children. At Hunter College Elementary School for the gifted in Manhattan, parents are required to write an evaluation of their child's strengths, and that, combined with an I.Q. score in the 98th percentile, may get the child invited to an interview with six or seven other youngsters. There they are evaluated for problem-solving ability, creativity, verbal and mathematical ability, and leadership before they are admitted to the program.

In Marland's 1971 report on the education of gifted and talented students, he suggested that students should be capable of high performance in general intellectual ability, specific academic aptitude, creative or productive thinking, leadership ability, visual and performing arts, and psychomotor ability. Joseph Renzulli finds that using extremely high I.Q. scores to identify the gifted is misguided, leaving out virtually all the poor and those who are late starters. He suggests that students with an above average I.Q. combined with creativity and persistence will ultimately benefit more from a gifted and talented program than those who have an extraordinary I.Q.

Curriculum for the Gifted and Talented

Most programs for the gifted are enrichment programs that can be described as a "grab-bag of extra goodies" (Tannenbaum 1983, 372). Tannenbaum believes that this isn't enough and that the programs should be instead "carefully selected to implement a comprehensive plan that has its own built-in rationale relating to the nature of the target population and the educational goals to be achieved" (pp. 372–373). Lynn H. Fox believes that gifted programs must include some common elements, such as an operational definition of giftedness and procedures for identification, multiple strategies for meeting the needs of this population, an outlined plan of action, and a mechanism for continual evaluation and monitoring (1979). Although many different approaches to gifted education exist, two of the most commonly employed ones will be discussed here.

In 1977, Joseph S. Renzulli suggested a curriculum consisting of an "enrichment triad" for the gifted that is still widely used. The basis of this triad is a self-designed and self-directed student learning program incorporating general exploratory activities, group training activities, and individual and small group investigations of problems.

Another enrichment approach to the education of gifted and talented students is **synectics**, which was first designed for industry by William J. Gordon in 1971. In education it is a process of thinking in which the strange is made to appear familiar and the familiar to appear strange by using metaphors to link various areas of substantive knowledge. For example, students might be asked to compare an automobile wheel to other things that rotate: the cutter on a can opener, the rotor of a helicopter, the orbit of Mars, a spinning seed pod, or a hoop snake (Joyce and Weil 1972, 238). Synectics also teaches problem solving because it requires creating something new or acquiring a new perspective of the familiar. The technique moves through several stages: phase one—the students describe the problem; phase two—the students state the problem and clearly define their task; phase three—the students then make direct analogies; phase four—the students make personal analogies; phase five—the students look for conflict; phase six—the conflict serves as the basis for the next analogies; and phase seven—the students examine the process and eventually return to the original problem.

<table>
<tr><td>

13.2 POINTS TO REMEMBER

* Multicultural education is based on the premise that differences in culture enrich the curriculum and tries to meet the needs of the diverse U.S. population.
* Bilingual programs are designed to meet the needs of students who do not speak English.

</td><td>

* Before- and after-school programs are designed to provide care for children who have come to be known as latchkey children because their parents work and are not home when the children arrive home from school.
* Dropout prevention programs are regular classroom programs, tutoring programs, or enrichment programs. They help potential drop-

</td><td>

outs deal with such problems as poor academic achievement, low test scores, myths about employment, social problems, and bigotry.
* Gifted and talented programs are designed to meet the needs of children who are academically, artistically, or physically gifted. Most provide enrichment beyond the regular curriculum.

</td></tr>
</table>

DISCIPLINE

Since schools are microcosms of the greater society, many of society's problems enter the classroom with the students. As the school population has become increasingly diverse and the roles of the home and church in the education of the child have diminished, teachers worry that their roles as models and symbols of authority will be diminished and that student peer groups will control the classroom.

Today, the most accepted definitions of discipline include the words training and self; **discipline** is the training that leads to the development of self-control, an internal conscience that acknowledges appropriate behavior. However, many of its earlier connotations are still accepted today: submission to authority and a system of rules and an acceptance of measures intended to correct or punish. Since neither self-discipline nor submission to authority seems to be widely practiced today, discipline in the classroom is a major concern of many teachers.

Approaches to Discipline   Because most educators recognize that a well-managed classroom leads to improved student and teacher performance, more positive relationships with and among students, and less misbehavior, effective methodologies have been developed for managing the classroom that range from those in which the teacher acts as the authority and imposes control from the outside, to those in which the student participates in the development of discipline techniques. The approaches described in the following section reflect a continuum from "external control" to "self-discipline."

Authoritarian Approaches

In the **authoritarian**, or teacher-dominant, approach the teacher sets rules and requires the students to submit to his or her authority. The teacher also sets consequences for rule infraction, contending that students can understand rules, accept their consequences, and more likely succeed academically using these models of classroom discipline. Likewise, the teacher must be fair-minded and consistent in fitting the consequences and punishments to the misbehavior. Authoritarian approaches to discipline have had many names; the most popular during the 1980s was the "Assertive Discipline Model" (Canter and Canter 1977). This approach assumes that teachers have the right to establish classroom structure and routine, to determine and request appropriate behavior, and to expect and get help from parents and the school administration.

Analytic Approaches

The teacher attempts, in the **analytic approach** to discipline, to identify the cause(s) of student misbehavior and then treats the cause(s) rather than the misbehavior. The underlying premise of this form of discipline is that the child's actions frequently do not reveal the underlying problem. For example, the child who is constantly disruptive in class may be insecure, unable to complete the work, or have a need for attention or a medical problem. In this approach various diagnostic tools are used: test results; social/psychological inventories; attendance records; medical records; cumulative school records; and interviews with student, parents, and previous teachers. Proponents claim that other forms of discipline do not deal with the causes of the misbehavior and, therefore, provide only temporary solutions; opponents say the approach is too time-consuming and does not deal with immediate problems.

Behavioristic Approach

Rooted in the work of psychologist B. F. Skinner, the **behavioristic approach** to classroom management rewards students for good behavior, which is then reinforced. In this behavior motification technique, specific misbehavior is identified, performance objectives are written to attain desired behavior, and positive behavior is reinforced through rewards appropriate to the child. Negative behavior may be ignored or the student may be removed from the situation that is its cause. Proponents contend that the approach is successful because it focuses on good behavior and deals with individual children. Opponents say that this approach renders the causes of misbehavior irrelevant and that frequently rewards are inappropriate.

Teacher-Student Interaction Approach

A combination of the analytical, the behavioral, and, to some extent, the authoritarian approach is the **teacher-student interaction approach**. In this technique, teacher and student develop a positive relationship that allows them to work together to find the causes of the misbehavior. They engage in structured discussions to help the student build confidence and a strong self-image.

Student-Centered Approaches

Students are given maximum freedom within limits in **student-centered approaches**. Teachers observe the students, determine their stages of development, provide work areas and materials appropriate for the students' stages of emotional and intellectual development, and act as resource persons. Proponents say that this approach allows students to develop naturally and that all students can succeed in this type of classroom, including those with physical or mental handicaps. Opponents contend that many children need limits and that this approach provides none.

PARENTS AND THE SCHOOLS

Recent educational initiatives for dealing with social problems have recognized that parents must be part of the solution. Today, most state and federally funded preschool programs require parental involvement and education. In *Educating America: State Strategies for Achieving the National Education Goals* (1990), a report of the National Governors' Association, the following ideas were suggested for encouraging parental involvement in the education of their children: (1) welcoming parents as equal partners in the learning and schooling of their children, (2) challenging parents to assume more responsibility for their children's learning, (3) helping parents and students to understand and take advantage of educational choices, and (4) engaging and supporting parents far more extensively in their children's learning at school (pp. 15–21).

Types of Parental Involvement

A study of over 3,700 teachers revealed that those who were "leaders in the use of parent involvement" encouraged parents from all kinds of backgrounds to be supportive of their children both in school and at home. Epstein identifies some of the areas in which parents need to work.

1. The basic obligations of parents include providing for children's health and safety, child-rearing to prepare children for school, and building positive home conditions that support school learning and behavior. Schools vary in how actively they assist parents with social services or provide programs to build positive parenting skills.
2. The basic obligations of schools include communicating with parents about school programs and children's progress. Schools vary the form and frequency of communications and greatly affect whether information sent home can be understood and used by parents.
3. Parent involvement at school includes parent volunteers who assist teachers, administrators, and children in classrooms or in other areas of the school. It also refers to parents who come to school to support student performances, sports, or other events, or to attend workshops or other programs for their own education or training. Schools vary in the extent to which they successfully recruit and maintain the involvement of many different parents at the school building.
4. Parent involvement in learning activities at home includes requests and instructions from teachers for parents to assist their own children at home on learning activities that are coordinated with the children's class work. Schools and teachers vary in how frequently and clearly they request parent-child interaction on homework and other learning activities at home.
5. Parent involvement in governance and advocacy includes parents in decision-making roles in the PTA/PTO, advisory councils, or other committees or groups at the school, district, or state level. It also refers to parents as activists in independent advocacy groups in the community. Schools vary in the extent to which parents have real influence in school policies, programs, and decision-making processes. (Epstein 1988, 2)

Low-Income Parents

As Epstein pointed out, all parents can be involved in the school. However, involving low-income parents has not been easy and may take additional effort. Because many low-income parents cannot come to the school, one way to involve these parents is in home-based programs, which, according to Mclaughlin and Shields (1988), yield academic gains for the students involved. To initiate home-based partnership programs, they suggest that teachers must be educated about the value of such programs and that administrators must realize the importance of making it possible for teachers to participate in them. Wolf and Stephens (1989) emphasize the value of teacher home visits, which can

(continued on p. 462)

V I E W P O I N T S

A New Road to Learning: Teaching the Whole Child

New Haven, [CT]—For more than 20 years in this city of scholars and elms, schoolchildren and their parents have been studying a basic axiom: students in troubled schools learn better when families and educators work together.

In the process, these children of troubled schools and their parents, most of them poor and black, are discovering that schools need not be rigid institutions concerned only with academic performance, but can also be places that tend to a child's psychological and social growth. And when those two sides of a child's life are entwined, the child feels better about himself and learns more.

This is the essence of a program developed by Dr. James P. Comer, a Yale University psychiatrist, and carried out in New Haven. The results have been higher attendance, fewer behavior problems and improved academic performance. School systems around the country are eager to replicate it, and the Rockefeller Foundation has committed $15 million to that end.

The process turns on a seemingly simple insight: that a child's home life affects his performance in school, and that if schools pay attention to all the influences on a child, most problems can be solved before they get out of control. The Comer process, as it is called, encourages a flexible, almost custom-tailored approach to each child.

Take the case of Ramon Cato. Ramon, a chubby, bright-eyed boy with a chipped front tooth, has known extreme family stress. For much of the last two years, Ramon has lived with his mother, described by relatives as a drug substance abuser, and her boyfriend in one room in a condemned house known as a haven for drug users. He struggled in school and behaved badly when he was there. He missed 57 of 180 days in the term that ended a year ago.

Educators at Grant Elementary School did not throw up their hands and write him off. When they could not get his mother involved, they found a great-uncle who cared. Now the uncle is a regular visitor to Ramon's classroom, and the boy is living with a foster family, doing well in school. He will graduate from fourth grade with his classmates. . . .

Not every child has problems as severe as Ramon's. But whatever the pressures on a family may be, a school using the Comer process will be alert to discovering those problems and helping solve them, supporters say.

This common-sense melding of home life, school life and social service aid is what attracted the Rockefeller Foundation's attention and led it earlier this year [1990] to make a five-year, $15 million commitment to replicate the methods of Dr. Comer, the coolly charismatic father of the approach.

The Comer process has already been adopted by more than 100 schools in

The method of instruction developed by Dr. Comer in the New Haven, Connecticut, school system combines a child's psychological, social, and intellectual needs. Its success hinges on the involvement of a parent or close relative in a child's education. Here, Jacqueline Lecraft helps her godson Jeffery Gilmore at Grant Elementary School.

nine districts in eight states. In the last three years, the New Haven school system has expanded it to include all 42 schools in the 18,000-pupil system.

"There's a difference one can see almost right away once his principles are applied," said Priscilla Hilliard of Howard University in Washington, D.C., who heads a partnership between the college and that city's public schools to carry out the program.

For low-income students in troubled inner cities, and especially for black and Hispanic students, whose achievement-test scores badly trail the national average, Dr. Comer's program offers one of the greatest hopes, many educators say. In an economy increasingly incapable of absorbing unskilled workers, undereducation may sentence much of a generation to join an underclass marked by joblessness and the pathologies of the forgotten.

The Comer process, which Dr. Comer himself calls the School Development Program, emphasizes building relationships based on sharing that bring school administrators, staff, teachers and parents together regularly—in many cases daily.

The approach concentrates on the emotional, social, and psychological needs. His clearly-structured programs establish three goals: to induce parents to participate in the school's life; to force school administration, teachers, and other staff to share authority in managing the school; and to bring guidance counselors, mental health professionals and teachers into a team that meets regularly to combat behavior problems.

Parents, for example, are encouraged to become classroom assistants, tutors or aides. Some are encouraged, as are some teachers, to join their school's governance committee, which meets biweekly and includes the principal. The mental health and guidance professionals are part of the process of school management.

According to Dr. Comer, most administrators and teachers are not trained to recognize that a student's academic and behavioral lapses may be linked to the cultural and social gap between home and school.

"Some of these children come from families that cannot give them often the elementary things they need, like how to say 'Good morning,' 'Thank you,' 'Sit still' and all kinds of stuff," said the 55-year-old psychiatrist. "On the other hand, you have staff that often doesn't understand that that is the problem."

The children, Dr. Comer said, "are in foreign territory."

When parents and educators work together in schools, social and psychological needs of students are not only better identified, but can be addressed to make students feel they are a welcome part of the school, say supporters of the Comer program. Their confidence is restored, and they are taught some of the things their families were unable to teach them. . . .

There are some, albeit only a few, detractors of the Comer program.

A professor of social work at a prestigious Southern university said Dr. Comer's program raises nearly as many questions as it answers. "A crucial question is whether Comer's model can be replicated in any school district," said the professor, who asked not to be identified. "Are there some school systems that are simply too large, such as New York City's?" The professor also wondered if Dr. Comer's program can cope with fragmenting families, whose members may be unable to participate in school life because of poverty.

Dr. Comer maintains that with careful application his program can be adapted to the needs of any school system, although neither he nor his Rockefeller Foundation supporters are yet prepared to tackle New York.

And Dr. Comer agrees with his critics to a degree in acknowledging that the social deterioration in many major cities will force educators and parents to work even harder.

"We are beginning to see the first of our crack babies in our schools," Dr. Comer said, adding that their behavioral problems will present his program with special challenges.

Nonetheless, he said he is not shaken in his long-held belief that child development should be the centerpiece of education. For many black and Hispanic children, whose parents, Dr. Comer says, have had a "traumatic social history," education must do more than teach the basics.

"Those families under stress are least able to give children the kinds of experiences they need to go to school and succeed," Dr. Comer said.

At Katherine Brennan School, one of the New Haven elementary schools where Dr. Comer introduced his approach early on, there is a climate of calm and caring. The sight of parents in the school is almost as commonplace as that of teachers. Halls are quiet and clean. Bulletin boards celebrate black history and achievement in brightly colored posters and hand-cut construction paper.

Outside, the school's double steel doors stand shut to a poverty-ravished neighborhood of public housing projects, graffiti-scarred streets and the ever-festering menace of drugs.

Brooke Rogers knows about the contrast. Recently, the fourth-grader said school represents her "inside world," one quite apart from the "outside world where people don't have anything in their heads but drugs and hurting people."

With that, she pushed away from the table, stood up, thrust out her chin and said: "I'm going to grow up and be somebody."

From: Marriott, 1990

build rapport between the parent and the teacher, through which the teacher can obtain information about the child, and through which the parent can obtain information about the school.

THE TEACHER'S ETHICAL ROLE

In dealing with social problems that affect students, the classroom, and the school, teachers are often required to make decisions they would rather not make. Often they require a great deal of thought and an understanding of the teacher's ethical role, including the principles that are the foundation of this role. The following situations, for example, require ethical decision making:

- Students in your social studies class have been studying democracy. They want to have a demonstration at the next school board meeting to change a requirement that nominations to the student council require the endorsement of at least two teachers. Students argue that this keeps those off the council who do not conform to school rules, and they think this is unfair. Although you understand the students' point of view, you also understand the history of the rule and are not convinced that a demonstration at the board meeting is a good idea. What do you do?

- You know that there is one child in your class who instigates the misbehavior of the rest of the children. However, you cannot determine who it is. You decide that the next time the misbehavior occurs you will punish the whole class and suggest that the punishment will be rescinded if they tell you who the culprit is. Before you even initiate this action, you begin to wonder if it is fair.

- You know that Sam has violated the team's rules by drinking on Saturday night. One of your students told you he saw Sam drunk, and when you confront Sam, he confirms it. You know that if you tell the coach, he will kick Sam off the team. He has been doing much better since he made the team; he's in school every day, does his homework, and participates in class. You know that if he is kicked off the team, he's likely to go back to his far less positive behavior. What do you do?

- You are planning a field trip for the children in your class. Two of your students have a physical disability. You learn that the location of your field trip is not equipped to handle those with disabilities, and you are asked to leave them in school. You believe that it is unfair to exclude these students, but you also believe the others will benefit from the field trip that is important to the unit you have been teaching. What should you do?

- You are in the hallway of your school and you notice Reggie walking down the hall scraping the eraser end of his pencil along the wall. Reggie never sits or walks quietly; he is always tapping on his desk or moving his feet. However, you know that Reggie needs to keep moving; he learns better when he is constantly active. You also know that Reggie is very musical. He always has a song in his head, and you've been encouraging him to develop his talent. One of the guidance counselors sees Reggie, calls him over, and begins to reprimand him loudly. You are upset because you believe that if Reggie had been white, the guidance counselor would not have confronted him. What should you do?

* Juan tells you confidentially that one of the coaches is sexually abusing some of his players. At first you don't believe it, but you overhear other students talking about it. You ask one of them about it, and he says, "It's a well-known fact that Coach is a pervert." You ask the student, "Why don't you report him?" The student replies, "Are you crazy? Not only would our asses get kicked off the team, but we'd be dead meat." What should you do?

It is the unusual teacher who is not faced with at least some ethical decisions. All these decisions are difficult. No matter what you do there will be consequences for you, the students, and others who are involved. In all these situations what is right and what is wrong is not obvious. How would you handle these very difficult situations?

Ethical Decision Making

Kenneth A. Strike in "The Ethics of Teaching" says "Ethical issues concern questions of right and wrong—our duties and obligations, our rights and responsibilities" (1988, 156). Strike suggests that ethical decision making has a unique vocabulary that includes such words as *ought, should, fair,* and *unfair.* He further suggests that, although facts are important in making ethical decisions, facts alone are not enough. Nor is knowing the consequences of our actions. For example, in the situation in which the teacher wants to punish the entire class for the behavior of one in order to find the culprit, the consequences might reveal the culprit. However, is the teacher's action an ethical one if all students are punished for the action of one student?

Ethical questions are distinguished from values; a value is an idea or object an individual regards as worthy, important, or significant. It may also refer to a system of personal attitudes and beliefs. One individual, for example, might value a work of art, and another may not; the one, however, is no less ethical than the other. Or an individual may value the family unit of two parents and children; whereas another might value his or her independence from a family unit. Again, the individual may choose what he or she values. Ethics, on the other hand, are obligations that are often separate from what we might want or choose. In the situations just described we must decide the right or fair course of action.

Strike believes that ethical decision making involves two stages. The first stage requires applying ethical principles to cases, and the second requires judging the adequacy or applicability of the principles (p. 156). We will deal with both these stages in the discussion of particular codes of ethics that follows.

Codes of Ethics

Most of the major professional associations have codes of ethics that help teachers deal with difficult decisions. The codes give teachers some principles they can apply to problems with ethical questions.

The NEA Code of Ethics

The National Education Association's (NEA) Code of Ethics was adopted by its representative assembly in 1975. The preamble of the NEA states that its membership will recognize the worth and dignity of each individual and the importance of nurturing democratic principles and pursuing truth and excellence.

The first principle of the code is commitment to students. This principle states that no student should be subjected to embarrassment or disparagement, nor be unfairly excluded from participation in any program, denied any benefit, or granted any advantage based on race, color, creed, sex, national origin, marital status, political or religious beliefs, family, social, or cultural background, or sexual orientation. It states that educators will not use professional relationships with students for personal advantage or disclose information about students except for compelling professional purposes or when required by law. As part of this principle, teachers are expected to preserve the confidentiality of students, if possible, and make every effort to preserve the student's safety and health.

All the ethical dilemmas posed in the situations discussed on pp. 462–463 involve a teacher's responsibility to students. According to Strike, teachers must apply this principle to each case as the first step of ethical decision making. Let's take the case of Juan. First, if Juan is telling the truth, we are dealing with the preservation of a student's health and safety. We are also dealing with a situation in which the coach may be using students for his own benefit. But we are not sure how to determine if Juan is telling the truth.

The second principle of the NEA code is commitment to the profession. This principle states that educators will respect other educators' reputations, refuse gifts or favors that appear to influence professional decisions, and prevent unqualified persons from entering the profession.

This principle represents the other side of the Juan dilemma. If Juan is not telling the truth, what are the consequences for the other teacher? Since the overriding ethical concern must be for the student, we cannot let the matter drop, but we must proceed in a way that will protect both the student's right to confidentiality and the teacher's right to protection against false accusation. In addition, if what Juan has said is true, the coach is not qualified to teach. Hence, we may use this principle, commitment to the profession, as well as the first, to deal with this very difficult ethical dilemma.

The Canadian Psychological Association Code of Ethics

The Canadian Psychological Association (CPA) in 1986 developed a code of ethics based on moral principles. This code has been widely accepted in Canada and has helpful principles for all teachers. The code is in hierarchical order. Hence, when principles within the code seem to be in conflict, the higher principle takes precedence. The four basic principles of the code are:

Principle I: Respect for the Dignity of Persons
Principle II: Responsible Caring
Principle III: Integrity in Relationships
Principle IV: Responsibility to Society

Larry Eberlein in "Ethical Decision Making for Teachers" (1989) points to the value of the CPA code for teachers and suggests ways in which each of the principles applies to education. According to Eberlein, the first principle, which is much like the first principle of the NEA code, suggests that teachers must respect the worth of all students and that individual differences should neither enhance nor decrease this dignity, which includes a moral right to privacy, self-determination, and autonomy. Furthermore, teachers have the greatest responsibility to protect the dignity of the most vulnerable students. The younger the student, the more precarious these rights; thus the more carefully they should be protected by the teacher.

Let's examine the field trip question using this principle. Because it is the teacher's responsibility to protect the dignity of the most vulnerable, the students with disabilities must be considered first. Therefore, according to this principle, we should consider alternatives to this particular field trip and explain to the students the reason for the decision.

The principle of responsible caring states that the teacher must be competent and not be involved in activities that are harmful to society. A teacher's first concern must be the welfare of the students; secondarily the teacher must be concerned about responsibility to parents, schools, school boards, and the public. Since students are rarely given the right to consent in selected school activities, Eberlein suggests, teachers must be especially mindful of protecting them. In selecting activities, teachers must weigh the likely risks and benefits and choose activities in which the benefits predominate. If harmful effects occur, the teacher must take responsibility for correcting them. According to Eberlein, this assumes that "incompetent action is, by definition, unethical." Competence requires continuous growth in knowledge and evaluation of teaching. Competent teachers are concerned with "both short-term and long-term physical and psychological factors in their students. These include self-worth, fear, humiliation, an interpersonal trust, as well as physical safety, comfort, and freedom from injury" (p. 113).

Since teachers must be concerned about the dignity and worth of students and must demonstrate a caring responsibility, the decision making in Sam's case involves these two principles. We know that Sam has been drinking. Beyond Sam's involvement in athletics, we must be concerned about drinking's potential harm to Sam himself. Therefore, we must help him deal with his drinking problem. The first step is probably to discuss the problem confidentially with him. Beyond this we might suggest that he needs to get help from outside sources. Whether we should tell the coach is a decision that should be made first based on what is best for Sam, second on our mutual respect for the coach, and third on our professional responsibility to school rules. If we believe that it is best for Sam not to tell the coach, this should govern our actions.

All professional relationships formed by teachers require mutual integrity. Expectations of integrity, according to Eberlein, include fairness, impartiality, straightforwardness, avoidance of deception, avoidance of conflict of interest, and the provision of accurate information (p. 113). This principle can be in conflict with the first two. At times, teachers must decide that straightforwardness, for example, is not appropriate if responsible caring is to occur. Because these principles are hierarchical, responsible caring should take precedence. Professional integrity requires accountability for the quality of the work done by the teacher.

Take Reggie's case, for example. We assumed that the guidance counselor was acting out of prejudice because Reggie is black. But there could be another explanation. Given the importance of honoring the guidance counselor's integrity, could we handle this situation in a way that would protect the guidance counselor and also ensure the dignity of Reggie? The first step might be discussing the incident with the counselor. Perhaps this will help us better

"I'll be taking the day off tomorrow, so I'll probably just fax you my homework."

© 1989 by Mike Shapiro

understand the counselor's actions and will lead to a resolution of the problem. If, however, we believe that the guidance counselor is acting out of prejudice, we must let our next actions be governed by what we believe is best for Reggie.

Teaching, as clearly established in this chapter, exists within the context of society. Therefore, the teacher's final responsibility is to use knowledge to benefit society and, thereby, support the first three principles. Teachers should recognize that because social structures have evolved over time, they must convey respect for these and avoid "unwarranted or unnecessary disruptions." The pursuit of changes in the social structure should be carried out only through the educational process. However, according to Eberlein, if social structures ignore the first three principles of the code, "it would be irresponsible for teachers to work within these social structures and not be critical of them" (p. 113).

An examination of the student council dilemma might make this principle clearer. Although our first responsibility is to the students, we do not always have to agree with their opinions in order to respect their dignity. Sometimes the responsibility of caring requires that we teach students things they would rather not learn. Perhaps a demonstration at the board meeting is a good idea, but first they must have the facts. They must examine the rule: its history, its potential positive effects, and its potential negative effects. They must also determine who made the rule and who has the authority to change it. They should examine the process of changing a rule within the system and should understand the consequences of working outside it. Once the students have accomplished all this, they can determine the best course of action. We have honored the dignity of the students, have shown an attitude of caring, have clearly valued the integrity of a professional relationship with the students, have upheld the integrity of a professional relationship with other professionals, and have acted responsibly toward society.

There is no doubt that the social problems analyzed in chapter 12 and the schools' response to those problems as discussed in this chapter lead to the increased involvement of teachers in students' lives. Teachers can no longer be concerned with teaching only content and skills. This is neither possible nor is it ethical. Contemporary teachers must deal with the social issues that affect their students both in and out of the classroom. To do this, teachers must develop or adopt a strong code of ethics and learn how to use that code in dealing with ethical issues.

13.3 POINTS TO REMEMBER

- There are numerous approaches to discipline. They can roughly be grouped into five broad categories: authoritarian models, analytic approaches, behavioristic approaches, teacher-student interaction approaches, and student-centered aproaches.

- As more and more social problems affect the education of students, the involvement of parents in the schools is increasingly important. Schools must reach out to parents through phone calls, notices, and even home visits.

- Teachers must often make decisions that relate to students, their own professionalism, other professionals, and society based on established ethical principles. Many professional organizations have developed codes of ethics for teachers.

FOR THOUGHT/DISCUSSION

1. What are some of the primary objections to school choice? Do you believe they are valid objections? Why or why not?

2. What is the democratic concept behind multicultural education? Which of the approaches to multicultural education identified by James Banks do you feel is the most effective in a classroom?

3. In what ways can the techniques used to teach gifted and talented students be used to reach the disadvantaged or at-risk students?

4. If the parents of many of your students failed to become involved in their children's schoolwork, what specific activities can you think of that might get them interested and prompt them to participate?

FOR FURTHER READING/REFERENCE

Banks, J. 1991. *Teaching strategies for ethnic studies*, 5th ed. Boston: Allyn and Bacon. A discussion of a rationale for a multicultural curriculum and specific teaching strategies for teaching Native Americans, African Americans, Europeans, Hispanics, and Asian Americans.

Brandt, R. S. (Ed.). 1990–1991. Schools of choice? [special issue]. *Educational Leadership* 48 (4). Twenty articles on school choice, pros and cons of school choice, specific examples from five states, and choice in private schools.

Curwin, R., and Mendler, N. 1989. *Discipline with dignity*. Alexandria, VA: Association of Supervision and Curriculum Development. A discussion of principles of classroom management with an emphasis on respect for the dignity of the individual and positive reinforcement.

Glasser, W. 1989. *Students without failure*. New York: Harper and Row. A discussion of how schools can succeed by positive involvement of teachers in leading counseling groups to develop social responsibility.

Massachusetts Advocacy Center and the Center for Early Adolescence. 1988. *Before it's too late: Drop out prevention in the middle grades*. Boston, MA, and Carrboro, NC: Authors. Descriptions of two centers that work with the schools and community using such structured activities as counseling, homework, working after school, and parental involvement to prevent dropping out.

Olmstead, P. O., and Weikart, D. P. (Eds.). 1989. *How nations serve young children: Profiles of child care and education in 14 countries*. Ypsilanti, MI: High Scope Press. A discussion of perceptions of and effects of early child care and education in countries in Asia, Africa, and Europe.

Strike, K., and Soltis, J. F. 1985. *The ethics of teaching*. New York: Teachers College Press. An analysis of ethical dilemmas and specific cases and situations such as sex education, students' rights, and parents' rights.

14 The Political and Legal Influences on Education

In this chapter we will explore the role of the federal, state, and local governments and courts in public education. We will also discuss the influence of businesses and foundations on the public schools, as well as the roles played by professional organizations, teacher unions, and nonpublic schools.

15 Financial and Legal Aspects of Education

While most citizens of this country believe in the democratic ideal of equal education for all, the reality is that the quality of education is hardly equal for all children in all school districts. Because the system of educational funding is so heavily dependent on state and local tax revenues, which in turn are so dependent on the economy in various areas of the country, schools even within the same state receive unequal allotments of money. In this chapter we will examine how funding contributes to quality of education. We will conclude by examining some of the practical legal issues that teachers will encounter in the practice of their profession.

Newton, Mass.—Lauren Bisceglia has stopped buying the sturdy canvas out of which her home-economics students have always made tote bags. "We can't afford that anymore," the Brown Junior High School teacher says.

These days, the totes are cut from cheaper cloth she buys by the pound at a factory-outlet store.

Despite the rising cost of such materials and an increase in the number of students she teaches, Ms. Bisceglia has only $1,800—the same amount she has received for each of the past four years—to buy sewing goods and food supplies for her 300 students.

From: K. Diegmueller, May 29, 1991, 1, 10.

PART VI

Schools and Governance

14

The Political Influences on Education

Howard L. Hurwitz was a principal of a Long Island, New York, school in 1976 when he was suspended from his post by the New York City Schools chancellor for refusing to readmit a suspended student. This anecdote helps illustrate how social and political forces working together can influence the public schools.

I was being brought up on charges of insubordination because I had refused to readmit to my school a student with a long record of disruptive behavior. I knew instantly that if I left my office as ordered, I would never again be the principal of Long Island City High School, or any school. I could not live with that thought.

I reached for my phone and called Peter Vallone. Over a ten-year period I had established close links with the community that reflected the composition of our neighborhood high school—Italians, 40 percent; Greeks, 15 percent; Hispanics, 15 percent; blacks, 10 percent; others, 20 percent, including about 2 percent Asians.

Vallone, a city councilman, was the prime mover in the Astoria Civic Association, a large and strong community where his father had been a judge.

"Hello, Pete. I'm calling to let you know that I've been fired."

Pete dismissed such nonsense with a quip.

"Let me read you a letter from Irving Anker that was just hand-delivered to me."

I read the whole letter. . . .

"What do you want me to do, Pete?"

"Stay there."

Within a half hour, six men entered my office. I recognized a few of them as parents of students in the school. Gerald Nozilo, who was to be the field commander of the operation, told me that I was being barricaded in my office. "No children are coming to this school, Doc, unless you're the principal." They placed a long bench outside of my secretary's office and piled chairs on top of it. We had begun three days and nights of 'round the clock defense of discipline in the schools that electrified the nation.

The episode which made me a national symbol of discipline in the schools was triggered by the outburst of a 16-year-old girl. She screamed at a secretary in the general office who had objected when she took a magazine from the librarian's letter box without permission. . . .

I phoned Mrs. Doe [the girl's mother] and told her that I was sending Jane home, directly.

I then phoned the superintendent who agreed to the suspension. . . .

In the 10 years previous to the Jane Doe suspension I had asked for 25 suspensions. Other principals had asked for hundreds during the same time span. Usually, a student who is suspended is transferred to another school. . . .

470

About an hour after I sent Jane home I phoned to find out whether she had arrived. Jane answered and asked for a transfer to Bryant, a neighboring school. I told her that the suspension was in the superintendent's hands but I would do what I could to obtain the transfer.

I phoned the superintendent to tell him that Jane would accept a transfer, and he said he would make the arrangements. . . . This procedure is resorted to often in order to avoid the long, adversarial hearings mandated by the state legislature. Jane's mother agreed to the transfer. . . .

Two days later, after the superintendent had agreed to the suspension and said he would arrange for the transfer, he phoned. . . . It was his decision to return the suspended student to LIC. . . .

I told him that he had not been a principal for 10 tough years. Therefore, he could not understand how a single student could undermine even a strong principal. . . .

Nevertheless, the superintendent insisted that I accept the girl. I told him flat out that I would not permit her to enter the school. . . .

The next morning I talked separately with the Assistant Principal (Guidance), two counselors, the Attendance Coordinator, the Cutting (truancy from class) Coordinator, and the Dean of Girls. All opposed the return of Jane Doe and urged me not to agree to her return. . . .

The next morning I found Jane Doe, her mother, and a man and woman from the local federally funded poverty agency seated on a bench outside my office door. They had been placed there by the Dean of Boys who had refused to permit Jane to go to classes. . . .

I explained that I had refused to readmit Jane to the school. . . . I called for the assistance of the police officer assigned to the vicinity of the school. When he arrived, I said: "Officer, I am asking you to persuade these people to leave this school. . . ."

Before noon the superintendent's assistant phoned and read a letter from the superintendent to me. . . . The final paragraph stated: "It is now my judgment that [Jane] be returned to Long Island City High School, effective Friday morning. . . ."

Dr. Hurwitz continued to refuse to admit Jane Doe. This began a series of confrontations and litigation between Dr. Hurwitz and the school system that lasted more than a year and a half. The superintendent, threatened by a suit from a local poverty lawyer, continued to demand that Jane return to school, but Dr. Hurwitz refused three times, believing that readmitting her would undermine his authority. The chancellor of the New York City schools then suspended Hurwitz.

The principal's supporters, particularly the parents, agreed with his decision and refused to send their children to class until Hurwitz was reinstated. The superintendent accused Hurwitz of insubordination and called a board of education hearing.

CHAPTER OBJECTIVES

After studying this chapter, you should be able to:

- Explain how the U.S. Constitution gives the states the power to govern education.
- Explain how U.S. congressional legislation affects the schools.
- Describe the president's role in education.
- Describe the U.S. Supreme Court's role in education.
- Explain why the governance of education differs from state to state.
- Explain the role of the states' governors and legislature in education.
- Describe the relationship among state boards of education, chief state school officers, and state education agencies.
- Understand the hierarchy of the state court system.
- Explain the role of the local education agency, local board, and local superintendent in the governance of schools.
- Describe how businesses and foundations influence public education.
- Explain the role of nonpublic schools in U.S. education.

Dr. Hurwitz and his supporters felt that the superintendent's office was trying to placate the Civil Liberties Union and the federally funded poverty workers who supported Jane's readmission, rather than examine the issues involved in the case.

The hearing concluded with a compromise: Dr. Hurwitz's suspension would be lifted, Jane Doe would return to school accompanied by a full-time security guard, and Hurwitz would appear at a second hearing in civil court.

Anxious that boycotting students return to class, Hurwitz agreed with the decision, but called the civil court hearing a "kangaroo court" because the judge refused to hear any witnesses speaking on behalf of Hurwitz's forty years of service or permit Jane Doe's record to be used as evidence. The civil court ruled that Hurwitz should pay a $3,500 fine to the board of education.

The parents wanted to pay the fine, but Hurwitz refused their support and appealed the decision to the New York Supreme Court. The case was heard almost one year later. The Court handed down a judgment "annulling and vacating" the resolution of the board. Hurwitz did not pay the fine, Jane Doe remained in school with a security guard, and left the school at the end of the term without a diploma.

From: Howard L. Hurwitz 1988, *The Last Angry Principal.*

The opening anecdote points out the difficulty in determining who controls the school. The local, state and federal agencies all tried to exert their influence on this case. Not until it reached the state Supreme Court was the case settled. In this chapter we will explore the role of the federal, state, and local governments and courts in public education. We will also discuss the influence of businesses and foundations on the public schools, as well as the roles played by professional organizations, teacher unions, and nonpublic schools.

WHO CONTROLS THE SCHOOLS?

Despite the fact that the power to run the schools is given to the states by the U.S. Constitution, no single branch or level of government exerts complete control over public education. Instead, there is an interactiveness, involving all branches of government at all levels, the courts, and the offices of chancellors, superintendents, and principals, that is based on legislative statutes. **Formal control** is that power delegated to individuals or groups through statute or law. **Informal influence** is exerted by individuals or groups on those who formally possess power to control the schools. These groups have no legal authority but have a strong interest in, or commitment to, the schools.

Teachers have little formal control but can influence the governance of the public schools through their unions and professional organizations. In addition, a variety of special interest groups, such as the Civil Liberties Union and the poverty workers of the opening anecdote, affects what happens in the schools.

472

(continued on p. 474)

FIGURE 14-1

Interactive Network of School Control

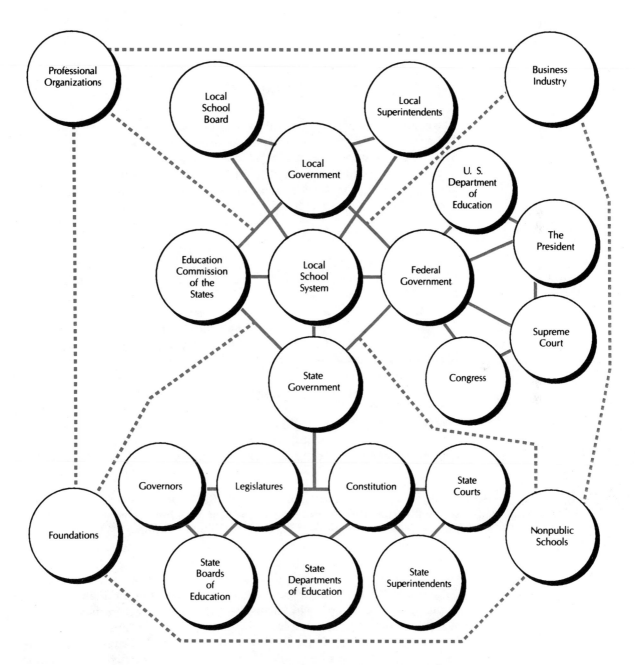

Adapted from: E. Mosher, *Education and American Federalism: Intergovernmental and National Policy Influences* in J. D. Scribner, (Ed.), *The Politics of Education* (National Society for the Study of Education, 1977).

Federal, state, and local agencies all have some jurisdiction over public schools. This chart graphically shows how the various agencies interact with one another to influence policy and procedure in the local public school.

In recent years, the business community and charitable foundations have funded special programs in U.S. public schools and have developed partnerships with the schools to implement some of these programs (see figure 14.1 for a diagram of the interactive network of school control).

ROLE OF THE FEDERAL GOVERNMENT IN PUBLIC EDUCATION

The U.S. Constitution, the federal courts, Congress, the president, and the U.S. Department of Education are the federal forces that influence public education. The Constitution sets the foundation for state control of the public schools. The Supreme Court is the highest authority for interpreting both the federal and state constitutions, legislation, and court decisions. The president recommends legislation to Congress and has the power to endorse or veto legislation enacted by it.

U.S. Constitution and Public Education

Although the U.S. Constitution does *not* mention education specifically, Article I, Section B, states, "The Congress shall have Power to lay and collect Taxes, Duties, Imposts and Excises, to pay the Debts and provide for the common Defense and general Welfare of the United States; but all Duties, Imposts and Excises shall be uniform throughout the United States." The "provide for the general welfare" clause of Article I has been commonly interpreted by the courts to include education.

The Tenth Amendment of the U.S. Constitution defines the states' role in education. "The powers not delegated to the United States by the Constitution, nor prohibited by it to the states, are reserved to the states respectively, or to the people." Since the power to influence education is not delegated to the federal government by the Constitution, the states are given jurisdiction over public education through this constitutional amendment.

The U.S. Congress and Education

The U.S. Congress passes legislation that affects the public schools. Because of the Tenth Amendment, the federal government's involvement in education is indirect rather than direct. However, when congressional legislation involves significant funding attached to specific criteria, federal control over education is increased. The role of Congress prior to the early years of the twentieth century was limited to providing land grants for schools. The Ordinance of 1785 stated: "There shall be reserved the lot No. 16 of every Township for the maintenance of public schools within said Townships." The Northwest Ordinance of 1787 also awarded land grants for schools.

Congressional legislation in the twentieth century has attempted to ensure equal access to public education. The Smith-Hughes Act (1917) allocated millions of dollars for vocational education. The National School Lunch Act (1946) provided funds for free milk and low-cost lunches for children from economically deprived families. Following the Soviet Union's launching of Sputnik, Congress passed the National Defense Education Act (P.L. 85-864) in 1958, giving funds to states, colleges, and universities to improve education in

[Handwritten reproduction of the Preamble and Article I of the U.S. Constitution: "We the People of the United States, in order to form a more perfect Union, establish Justice..." with Sections 1 through 7 in cursive script]

101ST CONGRESS
1ST SESSION

H. R. 3199

To amend title 38, United States Code, to establish a program to provide post-secondary educational assistance to students in health professions who are eligible for educational assistance under the Reserve GI Bill program in return for agreement for subsequent service with the Department of Veterans Affairs.

IN THE HOUSE OF REPRESENTATIVES

AUGUST 4, 1989

Mr. SMITH of New Jersey (for himself, Mr. MONTGOMERY, Mr. STUMP, and Mr. PENNY) introduced the following bill; which was referred to the Committee on Veterans' Affairs

---

A BILL

To amend title 38, United States Code, to establish a program to provide post-secondary educational assistance to students in health professions who are eligible for educational assistance under the Reserve GI Bill program in return for agreement for subsequent service with the Department of Veterans Affairs.

1   *Be it enacted by the Senate and House of Representa-*
2 *tives of the United States of America in Congress assembled,*
3   SECTION 1. SHORT TITLE.
4   This Act may be cited as the "Veterans Health Profes-
5 sionals Educational Amendments of 1989".

The Tenth Amendment to the Constitution gives primary authority over educational issues to the states. The U.S. Congress, however, can initiate legislation, like the bill shown above, that will affect how the states implement policies in their schools, thus giving the federal government an indirect influence on the schools.

mathematics, sciences, and foreign languages. Many scholars of educational law consider this act to be the first attempt of Congress to set educational policy.

The role of Congress in the establishment of educational policy continued to expand into the 1960s and 1970s. Federal legislation increased significantly during this period, primarily to ensure equal educational opportunity for all citizens.

The Economic Opportunity Act (P.L. 88-452) of the Civil Rights Act of 1964 allocated funds for community action programs such as Head Start and provided special assistance to public school districts to implement desegregation. The Elementary and Secondary Education Act (ESEA) (P.L. 89-10) of 1965

CROSS-CULTURAL PERSPECTIVE

'People's Education' in the People's Republic of China

Unlike the United States, there is no question about who controls education in the People's Republic of China. The Chinese system of education is known as "people's education," mass education for all. All legislative power in education is vested in a central authority—the National Ministry of Education. Education is a highly centralized, rational, top-down, linear model. The central government upgraded the ministry in 1985 and reformed it into the State Education Commission. This commission formulates the guiding principles on which *all* education is based, plans the progress of curriculum, coordinates the educational work of different departments, and organizes and guides educational reform for the entire country. This centralized system implements policy throughout the country, guaranteeing standards. However, this centralized system makes "it difficult for local administrators to implement the *mass line*, a form of leadership developed by Mao that involves making decisions based on the will of the people, not the wishes of the party leadership." Nonetheless, governance of all schools in the People's Republic of China remains highly centralized.

From: Su, 1989

established a wide range of compensatory programs, particularly for underprivileged youth from low-income families. These programs included bilingual education, special educational programs for the disabled, Indians, immigrants, and adults; and the establishment of the National Science Foundation (see chapter 6, pp. 170–178, for an extensive discussion of these acts). With federal funding came federal regulations for implementing this legislation in the schools.

Thomas R. Dye believes that the federal government's expanding role in education in the 1960s resulted in "centralized Federalism." Significant federal involvement in education through legislation and funding of special programs had the effect of limiting state control of public education and, thereby, destroying the meaning of the Tenth Amendment of the U.S. Constitution, which gave control of education to the states (Dye 1985, 61).

The President and Education

The U.S. president's effect on public education is more indirect than that of Congress. The president frequently establishes the legislative agenda of Congress and sets the tone for the decisions of the Supreme Court. However, some presidents take more initiative than others in influencing educational policy.

As early as the 1800s, President Thomas Jefferson, highly suspicious of centralized government, claimed that the preservation of democracy required that political power be kept in the hands of the people. He believed that education was the ultimate safeguard of liberty, and that only educated people could maintain and use the institutions designed to protect them from tyranny. Jefferson equated education with democracy: "No other sure foundation can be devised for the preservation of freedom and happiness" (Jefferson 1781–1785).

A century and a half later, John F. Kennedy was responsible for the passage of legislation designed to improve educational opportunities for migrant workers and their families, and to increase funding for classroom construction, teacher salaries, and improvement of instruction in science and mathematics.

Ronald Reagan in the 1980s began to shift congressional concerns away from legislative influence over education. He attempted to return educational control to the states, believing that increased federal spending had not resulted in increased learning as measured by standardized tests. Reagan believed that the schools should return to the basics of discipline, hard work, and homework. He also suggested that federal funds should shift from compensatory programs such as Chapter I of ESEA, designed to provide remedial instruction for students who fall below the poverty line, and Head Start, a preschool program for poverty-level children, to incentive programs such as merit pay for teachers and rewards for schools in which students achieve (State of the Union Address, January 25, 1988). He appointed an articulate secretary of education, William Bennett, to communicate his agenda to the schools, the public, and Congress.

In the late 1980s and early 1990s, President George Bush continued to encourage congressional legislation that would return control of education to the states. He appointed John Chubb, a political scientist from Stanford University and a well-known proponent of President Reagan's positions on education, as full-time presidential adviser on education. In addition, Bush appointed an education advisory committee to meet quarterly and examine educational reform in the context of innovation, accountability, and flexibility. Through a series of education summits involving the state governors, Bush set the tone for increased state funding of public education.

> There are real problems right now in our educational system, but there is no one Federal solution. The Federal government of course has a very important role to play. . . . But I firmly believe that the key will be found at the state and local levels. You are the ones, as governors, who are out there on the firing line. And you see what goes on in the classrooms and in the local school boards and in your state policymaking sessions. Truly, the states are the laboratories of reform in this country and you are the experts. (September 1989, 1455)

In 1979, the **U.S. Department of Education**, headed by the U.S. secretary of education, was elevated to a cabinet-level agency. It was originally established in 1867 as the Federal Department of Education to formalize the government's effort in education. In 1953, it became the U.S. Office of Education and was a part of the cabinet-level Department of Health, Education, and Welfare. In 1979, after extensive lobbying by the National Education Association, whose membership was to make up 10 percent of the delegates to the 1980 Democratic National Convention, President Jimmy Carter established the U.S. Department of Education as a separate cabinet-level department.

The U.S. Department of Education has three separate departments. The Office of Educational Research and Improvement is responsible for conducting research, developing innovative educational techniques, and securing grants. The National Center for Education Statistics prepares the *Digest of Education Statistics* and *The Condition of Education*. These two annual publications are compilations of data about enrollment, finances, outcomes of education, teachers, students, and schools at all levels of education. The Information Services Department provides information to the two other departments, the public, and the media.

U.S. Department of Education

The primary functions of the Department of Education are to support the legislative education agenda of the president and to oversee the implementation of congressional legislation in the public schools. In recent years, the department has assumed the first role through the publication of numerous reports. For example, during the Reagan administration, Education Secretary William Bennett wrote two major reports suggesting that schools should be more concerned with excellence than with equality: *First Lessons*, dealing with elementary education, and *James Madison High School*, dealing with secondary education. Lauro F. Cavazos, education secretary during the first two years of the Bush administration, publicized Bush's contention that parental choice will help make schools excellent, in *Educating Our Children: Parents and Schools Together* and *Choosing a School for Your Child* (see chapter 13 for a discussion of school choice).

U.S. Supreme Court and Education

Article III of the U.S. Constitution provides that "the judicial power of the United States shall be vested in one Supreme Court, and in such inferior courts as the Congress may from time to time ordain and establish." These courts adjudicate all cases arising out of the Constitution, Acts of Congress, and U.S. treaties.

The **U.S. Supreme Court** interprets the Constitution and, therefore, can have significant influence on public education. In fact, during the 1960s, the Supreme Court had such extensive influence that it was called the "black-robed school board." Between 1954 and 1970 two thousand cases involving education were brought before the court, compared to two hundred cases prior to 1954. A classic illustration of its policy-making potential is a decision based on the Fourteenth Amendment. The *Brown v. Board of Education of Topeka et al.* (347 U.S. 483, 1954) case established the role of the public schools in the desegregation of society (see chapter 6, p. 167, for a complete discussion). Although segregation in public schools did not end immediately and many years of unrest followed, the *Brown* decision set educational policy for public schools and contributed to a changing social attitude.

Another important case was *Tinker v. Des Moines Independent Community School District* (393 U.S. 503, 1969), which involved the First Amendment and focused on the school board's refusal to allow students wearing black arm bands to protest casualties in the Vietnam War. The court ruled that students had a constitutional right to protest their government's policies and that the wearing of arm bands simply represented one method of free speech.

This decision and a number of others established students' First Amendment rights, even in public schools. Students now had the right to voice their opinions, even if they were opposed by the majority of school officials.

Changes in the Supreme Court's Interpretation of the Constitution

Despite the fact that decisions of the Supreme Court are based on the Constitution and its amendments, the political composition of the Court changes over time. Supreme Court justices are appointed by the president for life and confirmed by the Senate. These changes in personnel, influenced by politics and policies of the White House, are reflected in the decisions of the Court. An analysis of how the Court has dealt with one educational issue will help illustrate these changes.

Censorship: Supreme Court Decisions

In 1957, the ruling by the Supreme Court in the case of *Roth v. U.S.* (354 U.S. 476, 1957) established a precedent for censorship cases that prevailed until the early 1970s. The majority decision in *Roth* stated, in part, "All ideas having even the slightest redeeming social importance—unorthodox ideas, controversial ideas, even ideas hateful to the prevailing climate of opinion—have full protection of the First Amendment guarantees unless excludable because they encroach upon . . . more important areas."

In 1973, however, the Supreme Court handed down a decision in *Miller v. California* (413 U.S. 15, 24, 1973) that provided a new set of guidelines to determine obscenity:

1. Whether the "average person, applying contemporary community standards" would find that the work, taken as a whole, appeals to prurient interest.
2. Whether the work depicts or describes, in a patently offensive way, sexual conduct specifically defined by the applicable state law.
3. Whether the work, taken as a whole, lacks serious literary, artistic, political, or scientific value.

These guidelines make it very difficult to determine whether a work is obscene. Who is the "average person"? How do we determine "community standards"? What does "contemporary" mean? Who decides?

The *Miller* decision, however, does give increased control to the community and the schools in determining obscenity in censorship cases. Justice William O. Douglas, in a dissenting opinion, expressed concern about this increased control.

> What we do today is rather ominous as respects librarians. The anti-obscenity net now signed by the court is so finely meshed that taken literally it could result in raids on libraries. . . . Libraries, I had always assumed, were sacrosanct, representing every part of the spectrum. If what is offensive to the most influential person or group in the community can be purged from a library, the library system would be destroyed.

The courts, possibly realizing the difficulty in determining a work's obscenity, have moved from an earlier attempt to examine the quality of a work to an examination of an individual's or group's right to select a book. In earlier cases the courts examined the work to determine its appropriateness. In *Keefe v. Geanokos* (418 F.2d 359, 361–362, 1st Cir., 1969), a teacher assigned his students an article from the *Atlantic Monthly* that dealt with student revolts of the 1960s in which the word *mother-fucker* was used several times. The Massachusetts Supreme Court ruled in favor of the teacher. The court said that the article was acceptable since it was written in a scholarly manner and the word was an integral part of the thesis of the article. In a similar case a short autobiographical story, containing the phrase *white-mother fuckin' pig*, was read to a class of tenth graders by teacher Stanley Lindros. In reversing a decision of a lower court, the California Supreme Court said that by reading the article Mr. Lindros was pursuing a "bona fide educational purpose" and no disruption was created by the reading of the story.

In more recent cases, however, especially since *Miller*, the courts' decisions have been based not on the applicability of the work, but rather on the board of education's right to select the material and to remove it from use. Though there have been a few exceptions at the state level to this shift in censorship opinions, in the vast majority of cases the courts have not attempted to judge the material but rather the rights of those selecting it.

The U.S. District Court in Strongsville, Ohio, in *Minarcini v. Strongsville (Ohio) City School District* (541 F.2d 577, 6th Cir., 1976), found that the board of education had not violated the First Amendment freedom of speech rights of its faculty when it rejected the faculty's recommendations for books to be ordered for the school library. The U.S. Court of Appeals upheld the decision, saying that the board's decision was neither "arbitrary" nor "capricious." As in most cases since 1973, the books were not on trial; obscenity was not the issue. Instead, the court based its decision on the legal right of the board of education to decide. In a similar case, *Cary v. Board of Education of Adams-Arapahoe (Colo.) School District* (28-J, 598 F.2d 535, 544, 10th Cir., 1979), the court ruled that the local school board had the right to rule on course content. The case involved a board-approved elective English course in contemporary literature for juniors and seniors. The books for the course were selected by the teacher and the students, but the board objected to several of the selections. In its decision the court agreed that English teachers and students should be permitted to conduct an open discussion of free inquiry. "The student must be given an opportunity to participate openly if he is to become the kind of self-controlled individually motivated and independent thinking person who can function effectively as a contributing citizen." However, according to the court, free inquiry was not the issue at hand; authority to select appropriate materials for the curriculum was. The court decided in favor of the board, claiming that when teachers submit to a collectively bargained contract, they agree to allow the board to decide everything, including the materials to be used in the classroom.

The actual removal of books already in school libraries has been the issue in several court cases. A case that was first heard in 1972, appealed to the U.S. Court of Appeals, and argued before the Supreme Court in 1979 is *President's Council Dist. 25 v. Community School Board No. 25* (457 F.2d 289, 2d Cir., 1972, cert. denied, 409 U.S. 998, 1972). In this case Piri Thomas's *Down these Mean Streets* was removed from all junior high school libraries in a New York school district. The appellate court upheld the lower court's ruling that the power to remove books is in the hands of the board. A similar question was argued in 1979 in Vermont in *Bicknell v. Vergennes Union High School Board of Directors* (475 F.Supp. 615, D.V.T., 1979). The board of education, in ordering two books removed from the school library, called them "obscene, vulgar, immoral, and perverted." The court ruled in favor of the board although it did not agree with the board's opinion of the books (again, the books were not on trial); it affirmed the authority of the elected board to control all curricular matters, including the removal of library books. Librarians, on the other hand, according to the court, do not have the right to control the library collection under the "rubric of academic freedom."

In 1986 the Supreme Court ruled in favor of the school board in a seven-to-two decision in *Bethel School District No. 403 v. Fraser* (106 S.Ct. 3159, 1986). School officials in Spanaway, Washington, had suspended a student for using sexual metaphors in describing candidates for a student government election. Chief Justice Burger wrote in the majority opinion, "Surely it is a highly appropriate function of public school education to prohibit the use of vulgar and offensive terms in public discourse. . . . Schools must teach by example the shared values of a civilized social order."

In January 1988 the Supreme Court, in a five to three ruling, upheld a high school principal's right to censor a student newspaper. In the case *Hazelwood School District v. C. Kulmeir et al.* (U.S. 86-836, 1988), Justice Byron White, writing for the majority, said that while the First Amendment prevented a school from silencing certain kinds of student expression, it did not require a school to promote such expression in plays and publications under the school's auspices. He said that educators may exert editorial control in such instances "so long as their actions are reasonably related to legitimate pedagogical concerns."

It is clear, then, that the opinions of the courts have shifted in censorship cases that relate to education. Earlier cases were decided on the quality of the work, whereas more recent ones have been determined on the right of those in authority to make decisions about the school's curriculum (revised and updated from Reed 1985).

14.1 POINTS TO REMEMBER

- Since the power to influence education is not delegated to the federal government by the Constitution, the Tenth Amendment affirms it is the province of the states.

- Congress influences public education by passing bills to which funding and specific criteria for obtaining the funding are attached.

- The president affects education indirectly through his legislative agenda to Congress.

- The U.S. Supreme Court rules on education cases related to the U.S. Constitution. Court rulings can be extremely influential and affect educational policy.

ROLE OF THE STATES IN PUBLIC EDUCATION

Since the U.S. Constitution does not mention education specifically, it is left to each state to determine how its schools will be governed and maintained. Consequently, there is great variety in the organization and governance of schools from state to state. Utah's constitutional provisions for education, for example, require a "uniform" school system: "The Legislature shall provide for the establishment and maintenance of a uniform system of public schools, which shall be open to all children of the State, and free from sectarian control." In contrast, Virginia's provisions do not require that the state's public schools be uniform but merely that they be free for all children: "The General Assembly shall provide for a system of free public elementary and secondary schools for all children of school age throughout the commonwealth, and shall seek to ensure that an educational program of high quality is established and continually maintained." Differences such as these in the states' constitutional provisions lead to differences in how the schools are governed and maintained within each state.

President George Bush, who wished to be known as the education president, based his proposals for education reform on the recommendations of the Education Commission of the States. At Slanesville Elementary School in West Virginia, the president visits with the 1991 national teacher of the year, Rae Ellen McKee, and her student, Keith Johnson.

Governors The role of the governors in public education is indirect. Like the U.S. president, they primarily set the legislative agenda for their constituency. In all states except North Carolina, the governor also has the right to veto legislation passed by the state legislature.

In the late 1980s, however, the states' governors began to take a more active role in public education. All fifty formed the Education Commission of the States. This commission, together with the National Governors' Association and the Council of Chief State School Officers, developed seven task forces to examine teaching, leadership and management, parental involvement and choice, readiness, technology, school facilities, and college quality. This commission gave the governors a more active voice in educational decision making within the states. In *Time for Results: The Governors' 1991 Report on Education*, the governors state, "Still, state constitutions and laws establish the basic framework for how we operate the schools. So we [the governors of the states] can *change* the way we attract and keep the best possible administrators and teachers. We can change the way our colleges educate our future principals and teachers . . . and we can *change* the way we assess performance" (1986, 5).

In February 1990, the National Governors' Association, under the leader-

A national testing program as proposed by President Bush in his America 2000 plan is intended to provide consistency of educational methods and to ensure that the student and teacher are held accountable for learning. Critics of national testing maintain that it promotes static, narrowly focused learning, and is unfair to those in the lower tracks.

ship of President George Bush and as a result of the work of the task forces of the Education Commission of the States, set six major goals for education that influenced President Bush's proposals known as America 2000 (see chapter 6, p. 190, for a complete discussion). The National Governors' Association also set an agenda for reaching the goals. However, the governors' suggestions will only be enacted if passed into law by each state legislature, defined by each state board of education, and implemented by each state office of education.

State legislatures have broad power to pass laws regarding public education. State and federal courts have affirmed state legislative authority to create and design school districts, raise revenues and distribute funds, control teacher certification, prescribe and evaluate curriculums, mandate attendance laws, and regulate other aspects of school administration. All states require students to attend school between specified ages, typically six to sixteen.

State Legislatures

State legislatures may not delegate law-making powers to subordinate agencies. However, legislatures may establish agencies to carry on the administrative functions of the schools and implement the laws.

(continued on p. 487)

Point/Counterpoint

WE DO NEED A NATIONAL ACHIEVEMENT EXAM

Keith Geiger, head of the National Education Association, is against it. Joe Nathan of the University of Minnesota Center for School Change opposes it. Even Gregory Anrig of the Educational Testing Service doesn't like it. With so many clamoring against a national achievement examination for high-school seniors, why do I support it?

Because we need a reliable way to measure our progress toward the national goals [in America 2000] set by President Bush and the governors. Because employers need a lot more than the high-school diploma to tell them what their applicants have learned. And because even as most indicators tell us that our schools are failing, America continues to spend hundreds of billions of dollars annually on an enterprise that has little or no means of accounting for results.

It's time to develop a national achievement exam, required for all students. Some educators may not agree, but three out of four Americans do. In a 1989 Gallup poll, 77 percent of respondents strongly supported requiring schools to use standardized national testing programs to measure what their students are learning.

Educate America, a group I chair [a special committee of the NEA], recently proposed a national achievement examination for all high-school seniors in public and nonpublic schools. The exam would measure outcomes in six areas: reading, writing, math, science, American and world history, and geography. Individual scores (on a 0–200 scale in each area) would be mailed to students and their parents, as well as colleges and potential employers designated by the students. School-by-school and state-by-state averages would be published, allowing educators and policymakers to focus attention on clear, unambiguous, easy-to-understand results.

At least five reasons compel us to pursue a national exam:

- *Accountability for students.* Students not bound for college have little incentive to work hard in school. They know that prospective employers are likely to ask only for a diploma, and in many schools, that sheepskin is more a proof of attendance than a mark of achievement. But what if students were told that Employer K would be looking at how much math they have learned, or Employer L how well they can construct a paragraph?

A national exam with clear, easily understandable results would have a much more direct impact on job opportunities. It would create an effort-oriented system with a clear message that hard work pays dividends and that tough courses are the path to success. A large part of our efforts nationwide must be to bring that kind of challenging curriculum to all students, particularly those now tracked into dull and watered-down courses.

- *Accountability for schools and states.* With results of the test made public, the $230 billion nationwide education enterprise at long last would be accountable for results. For the first time in history, a reliable, commonly accepted indicator of accountability would be available for every high school in America. Because the results could be compared across schools and states, decisionmakers at all levels could pinpoint where changes were necessary. Depending on the results of these objective indicators, schools could either celebrate success or focus resources where most needed. . . .

- *Raised academic rigor.* A mandatory national exam could help raise academic rigor and expectations for all students. While not a graduation requirement, it would assess what Andrew C. Porter of the Wisconsin Center for Education Research calls "hard content for all students." That's a sharp contrast with most state graduation tests, which assess "easy content for all students." And placing the exam at the end of high school gives a resounding answer to the dreaded classroom question, "Will we have to know this for the test?" Yes, you will have to know it, not just for the test but for your life. All 12 years in school matter.

- *Clear results.* The results would be understood by every American. And they would tell us so much more than Scholastic Aptitude Test scores, which are the most common and the most misused measure of our schools' progress. First, not everyone takes the S.A.T., which is especially true of the non-college-bound. Second, the S.A.T. is a *prospective* test, used to assess the ability to perform college work and specifically designed to be unrelated to the curricula in our high schools. Doesn't it make more sense to use a *retrospective* exam, focusing on achievement and performance, which can clearly assess what schools have taught and students have learned?

- *Quality assessment.* If it's true that testing drives curriculum and teaching, most of today's testing methods are stuck in reverse. They focus on minimums and rely exclusively on simple multiple-choice questions, so it's no wonder they lead to poor teaching practices and irrelevant curricula. It would be a mistake merely to heap one more such test on the pile. But we don't have to settle for that. As the old television show, "The Six Million Dollar Man," proclaimed, "We have the technology . . . we can rebuild."

Educate America's proposal would use state-of-the-art assessment practices and performance measures, including multi-step problems, essays to determine writing performance, open-ended questions that require critical thinking, and passages from literature to measure the ability to read, comprehend, and infer. No doubt, this exam would be more expensive than fill-in-the-dot tests, but economies of scale would keep the cost down to $30 per student, or about $90 million nationwide. That's about 4 cents for every $100 being spent on education in America.

America's school system isn't working. I salute President Bush and the governors for pledging to make it work by setting ambitious goals for the decade. But we will wander toward those goals like the ancient Israelites in the desert unless we have milestones to mark our progress and provide direction. Without that 4-cent commitment, without a mandatory national exam of one sort or another, the promised land of American educational excellence could be another 40 years off.

Thomas H. Kean, former Governor of New Jersey, is president of Drew University in Madison, N.J., and chairperson of Educate America.

From: Kean, 1991

WE DO NOT NEED A NATIONAL ACHIEVEMENT EXAM

U.S. policymakers are besieged with proposals for a national test or examination system. The plans range from a national multiple-choice exam to a complex system of exams which are to be calibrated to one another.

While the examination proposals have significant differences, all are based on the false premise that measurement by itself will produce positive change. Recent history shows this is not true: During the 1980s, U.S. schoolchildren became probably the most over-tested students in the world—but the desired educational improvements did not occur. FairTest research indicates that our schools now give more than 200 million standardized exams each year. The typical student must take several dozen before graduating. Adding more testing will no more improve education than taking the temperature of a patient more often will reduce his or her fever.

The proposals also share the assumption that the United States needs a national exam because our education system is failing to produce workers as skilled as those produced by economic competitors such as Japan and Germany. Education in this country does need major improvements, and not just for economic reasons. But neither Germany nor Japan has a national examination system of the sort being proposed for the United States. In fact, Germany does not even have a national curriculum. If these nations provide a better education to more of their children, it cannot be because they have national tests.

In response to the national-testing proposals, Fair-Test and over two dozen major education, civil-rights, and advocacy groups—including the National Education Association, the National Association for the Advancement of Colored People, the National PTA, the National

Association for the Education of Young Children, the American Association of School Administrators, and the national associations of elementary- and secondary-school principals—released a statement urging "the Bush Administration and the Congress to support education reform by not implementing a national exam at this time." The organizations agree that mandating a national exam is premature at best and could lead to deepening educational disaster.

The scope of the potential damage is most clear in the Educate America proposal. That group seeks to administer a series of six tests to each high-school senior for $30 per student. It also claims its tests would be "state of the art" and include performance-based components. But the Scholastic Aptitude Test, which is entirely multiple-choice, costs $16 for just two tests. At the proposed price, the Educate America plan would have to be a multiple-choice test.

There can be no doubt that schools would be forced to teach to such a test. Yet organizing schooling around multiple-choice tests has been convincingly shown to do great damage to curriculum and instruction. The harm is greatest for students in the lower tracks whose schooling often is reduced to "drill and kill" to raise test scores. This method of instruction virtually guarantees they will not learn higher-order academic thinking skills.

Examination systems like those proposed by the University of Pittsburgh researcher Lauren Resnick and Marc Tucker, president of the National Center on Education and the Economy, do have positive features. Unlike Educate America, their plan calls for performance-based exams and would not be one-test-for-all. Its proponents recognize that we must develop educational standards before we implement an exam and they seem aware that assessment reform cannot be implemented without other educational changes, though the actual proposals fail to address this fact.

Indeed, assessment should be part of school reform—not the controlling force that national-testing proposals make it. By focusing on assessment as the solution to our educational problems, we may well fail to address such critical issues as equity, rigid school governance, low-quality textbooks and curricula, inadequate schools of education, and a lack of useful information about school inputs, processes, and outcomes. To make real use of performance-based assessments requires creating performance-based schools, which in turn requires restructuring, staff development, and new educational materials. . . .

FairTest is also concerned that these examinations could become a national gatekeeper that continues our nation's unfortunate history of unfairly sorting students by race and class. Barring additional changes, it is all too likely that districts will sort students according to their perceptions of how rapidly students will advance toward the "certificate of initial mastery" proposed by Lauren Resnick and Marc Tucker. Such sorting will not spur low-income and minority-group students to improved achievement. . . .

Assessment reform should be incorporated into systemic educational reconstruction at all levels. We must begin by defining the kind of education we want our children to have, including both their daily experiences and the outcomes society desires. On that basis, we can determine how to make the changes in curriculum, instruction, school governance and structure, and assessment required to reach educational goals far more comprehensive than those enunciated by the Bush Administration and the governors.

To do that, the pieces of a reform program must be organized into a coherent whole. Only after we have real experience in implementing the changes will we have the information necessary to make a reasoned decision about a national test. Once these reforms have taken hold in classrooms, schools, districts, and states, there may be no real need for the expense and complexity of a national exam system.

In the interim, we do need changes in assessment, as we need reform in all areas of education. For one, states and districts should stop the incessant, numbing, destructive multiple-choice testing most of them now engage in. They should develop and implement performance-based assessments, but do so while changing curricula, instructional methods and materials, ensuring the staff development of teachers and administrators required to make it work, and involving parents and other members of the community in the process.

The federal government should support improvement efforts that include assessment reform and that build consensus and change from the bottom up, with guidance—not dictates—from national organizations such as the National Council of Teachers of Mathematics or bodies such as the National Education Goals Panel. Support for systemic educational reform would be a far better use of limited federal resources than imposing a national test or examination system would be.

Education can be dramatically improved over the next decade. Assessment reform is part of the way to make the changes, but it is not the magic key. Just testing without ensuring all the other necessary changes is a prescription for failure, a false short-cut that will actually undermine education reform. Public education in the United States can ill afford such an error.

Monty Neill is the associate director of FairTest, the National Center for Fair & Open Testing, located in Cambridge, Mass.

From: Neill, 1991

POSTSCRIPT

One of the major proposals of America 2000 was the design and implementation of a national achievement test in five core subjects, to be given to all U.S. public school students at several grade levels. Kean and Neill have very different responses to this idea.

Governor Kean suggests that the tests, because they will be designed to measure "hard content," will lead to better teaching and more reliable results. Since both authors agree that multiple-choice tests and teaching to these tests diminish student achievement, Kean suggests that the test should include several types of measures. But Neill claims that the tests will have to be multiple choice because of the limited proposed dollar cost per pupil and hence will lead to poorer rather than better teaching.

In addition to the interesting and complex argument about whether a national test will benefit education, there are several elements of this point-counterpoint that make it particularly relevant to the legal processes involved in implementing educational reform. First, President Bush and Secretary of Education Lamar Alexander proposed the national tests based on educational goals for the year 2000 set by the fifty governors. This process clearly shows the role of the president, the secretary of education, and the governors in public education. The President and the governors set the legislative agenda for education, both in the nation and the states. The secretary of education, as a member of the president's cabinet, helps develop this agenda, communicates it to Congress and the public, and should legislation be passed, oversees its implementation in the schools.

This point-counterpoint also reveals the roles of others in the interactive arena of public education. Both authors are players—one a politician turned educator, the other an educator and director of an educational think tank. They publicize their ideas through articles such as the ones above, press releases, and consortiums of like-thinkers such as the one suggested by Neill and the one chaired by Kean. Their influence on education is indirect but can be significant.

Neill mentions another set of players in public education: professional organizations. He specifically refers to the National Council of Teachers of Mathematics, which set standards for mathematics education that are likely to have a significant impact on mathematics instruction.

Kean suggests another important player, the public, which is heard from through opinion polls, special-interest groups such as the Parent-Teacher Association (PTA) (see pp. 498–499 of this chapter for a PTA press release related to this issue), and its collective voice at the ballot box. The public votes for school board members, statewide education officials, and politicians, who often have educational platforms. In the case of the national test, as Kean points out, the majority of the public supports it, and as Neill suggests, a large proportion of the educational community does not. It remains to be seen whether a national test will be implemented and whether it will improve teaching and student achievement.

State Boards of Education

Since it is impossible for legislatures to include in state statutes all the details for administering public schools, most states have boards of education whose role is to set policy and to supply the structure and details necessary for carrying out broad legislative mandates. For example, the legislature might determine that all public school teachers must be tested prior to certification. The state board must determine how and by whom this mandate will be implemented. In some states, members of the board of education are appointed by the governor, and, in others, elected by the citizenry.

Today, Wisconsin is the only state without a state board of education. Hawaii's state board is also its district board of education because it is all one school district. Florida is the only state in which the governor's cabinet is also the state school board. Figure 14.2 illustrates the levels of educational control.

Chief State School Officers

In addition to the state board of education, all states have a designated chief school officer, usually called the superintendent of public instruction or commissioner of education. The duties of the state school officers tend to be regulatory. In some states, they may be required to adjudicate educational

FIGURE 14-2

Hierarchy of Educational Control

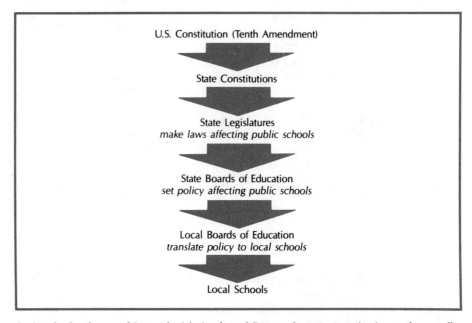

The local schools are subject to legislation based first on the U.S. Constitution and secondly on their own state constitutions. Thereafter, policies and procedures are set by state legislatures and state boards of education, and are processed through the local boards of education to the schools.

controversies. The chief state school officer may also be involved in such activities as long-range planning and educational research.

In half the states, the chief state school officer is selected by the state school board. In other states, he or she may be appointed by the governor or the legislature or elected by the people.

State Education Agencies   State education agencies, often called the state department of education, provide assistance to the public schools and oversee the implementation of legislative enactments and state board policies. They do not set policy and, therefore, do not exert direct control. Most also conduct research and development to improve public education in the state. These agencies consult with the state board, the chief state school officer, the local school board, and, frequently, colleges and universities that offer teacher training. The state education agencies might recommend policy to the state board, which enacts this policy. For example, the state agency that requires teachers to take tests prior to certification might also participate in the following: consultation with the state board and chief state school officer, evaluation of existing tests or development of a new test, field trials of the test, evaluation of the success of the field testing, suggesting to the state board cutoff scores for passing the test, implementation of the statewide testing, recording the results of the test, monitoring each certification candidate's test results, and working with teacher-training institutions to help prepare students to take the test. Twenty-seven states have met legislative mandates for testing of teachers by requiring that applicants take the National Teachers Examination (NTE), a nationally normed, core battery of three tests: general knowledge, communication skills, and professional knowledge. Many states also require that future teachers take a specialty area test which is designed to measure understanding of the content and methods of a specific subject.

Curriculum Decisions

Most states make numerous decisions about their instructional programs. A few write standards regarding instruction into their statutes. However, most state legislatures delegate this authority to the state board of education, which sets broad guidelines and delegates the authority to set specific standards to the state education agency. When these standards are set, they are usually approved by the state board of education and integrated into the curriculum by local school districts.

A few states, however, have more centralized control over curriculum. In North Carolina, for example, a legislative statute requires the state board of education to adopt a course of study for the schools, which is then developed and monitored by the state education agency. The local schools are required to implement this course of study. Such decision making is the exception rather than the rule.

IN THE CLASSROOM

Morris Jefferson was an academic failure in a school where academic failure was commonplace. A sprawling one-story brick building in a barrio on the northwestern outskirts of Houston, the Hollibrook Elementary School sits across the street from a rundown public housing project where the roofs leak and the potholes in the street are large enough to swallow a tricycle. Almost all of the school's one thousand students are poor members of minority groups who live in homes where a language other than English is spoken. The typical Hollibrook student entered kindergarten ill-prepared for academic work and, year by year, slipped farther and farther below grade level. When it came to standardized test scores, Hollibrook was the caboose of the Spring Branch School District.

As a second-grader, Morris was traveling the familiar route. Tall and skinny, with olive skin, big brown eyes, and dark hair cut in bangs over his forehead, he showed a wry sense of humor and a talent for goofy drawings but little enthusiasm for sitting quietly and listening to teachers talk. He neglected his homework assignments and picked fights with classmates. A standardized reading test put him at only the 8th percentile nationally, and by the end of the 1989 school year he had failed to master the full list of "competencies" that the state of Texas requires for promotion to third grade. Morris was, as educators like to put it, "retained."

By September, though, just as Morris was gearing up for his second shot at second grade, major changes were taking place at Hollibrook. The school had a new principal, Suzanne Still, a former special-education teacher whose years of working with struggling young people had convinced her that *all* students, including the Morris Jeffersons of the world, could learn more than most public schools either encourage or expect. One of her first acts was to tack a small sign above the door to her office: "A good principal always remembers what it was like." She then set out to overhaul Hollibrook around principles that were the exact opposite of most of those held dear by the state of Texas, the Spring Branch School District, and a century of American public school tradition.

Instead of putting every student in a class with peers of like ability, as had been the practice for years, she grouped them randomly, even allowing children in various grades to work together in a multiage "pod." Two second-grade teachers got the go-ahead to combine their classes and do team teaching, while three others took on a group of second-graders and agreed to stay with them until they graduate in 1993. Spanish-speaking students worked side by side with Anglos. The school day was no longer divided into regular forty-five- or seventy-two-minute periods, and teachers were encouraged to disregard artificial distinctions between the various academic areas. Students wrote while they were doing math, learned spelling from the social studies teacher, and read for the first half hour of every school day.

Whereas Texas expects its teachers to take their state-approved basal readers and textbooks in hand, start on page one, and work their way through to the last chapter, Still told her faculty to use whatever teaching resources they wanted. Gone, too, was the requirement that teachers file the educational equivalent of flight plans (otherwise known as planning books) so that the principal or a visiting inspector from the State Education Department in Austin could quickly ascertain that on Thursday at 10:15 A.M. "Miss Burpee in 5B" is doing simple division. As a teacher, Still recalls, she "always preferred to work for someone who thought that I had a brain and could think." So at Hollibrook decisions on everything from the hiring of new teachers to the choosing of curriculum materials are now made by committees dominated by teachers. Perhaps most important, Hollibrook adopted the principle of "accelerated learning," which asserts that if students are having difficulty, teachers should give them *more* academic stimulation, not plunk them in "remedial" classes, slow down the learning process, and condemn them to perpetual failure.

Cumulatively the changes at Hollibrook constituted a frontal assault on just about every aspect of traditional school management—how to manage a school, treat teachers, deal with students, organize instruction, and manage time. It was also politically risky. To deal with the threat that some inspector from the state or local school district might show up and call teachers on some technicality, Hollibrook set up an early warning system. Whenever such a visitor showed up at the front office, one of the secretaries unobtrusively meandered over to the nearest classroom, stuck her head in the door and spoke the code word, "Bluebird." The teacher immediately dropped what she was doing and sent a student on the rounds of the other classrooms, like a modern-day Paul Revere, spreading word of the impending danger.

"Bluebird."
"OK."
"Bluebird."
"Thanks."
"Bluebird."
"Got it."

Within minutes, students who were reading on their own in the halls would be recalled to their desks. Officially sanctioned textbooks were pulled from their hiding places in closets and opened prominently on the teachers' desks. To the untrained eye, Hollibrook had become a model of educational orthodoxy. (Fiske, 1991)

State courts are established under the constitutional provisions of each state. Therefore, the structures of judicial systems are remarkably different. They usually include trial, or circuit, courts; courts of special jurisdiction such as juvenile courts; appellate, or appeals, courts; and a supreme court. In the Illinois state court system, for example, the supreme court, with seven judges, hears appeals from the appellate courts. The five appellate courts hear appeals from the circuit (trial) courts. Illinois is divided into twenty-one circuit court districts, which include, among others, chancery-divorce, law, probate, juvenile, criminal, municipal, and county.

State Courts

All state court systems provide some type of administrative appeal for individuals involved in disputes regarding the internal operation of the schools. Although state court systems vary, all require that internal administrative sources of appeal be utilized prior to bringing a case to the courts. Dr. Hurwitz, for example, in the opening anecdote, first used the administrative offices of his school to appeal his case before he brought it before civil court.

Teachers and the State Courts

The following situation is relatively rare in the teaching profession but illustrates the legal procedures available to teachers. Suppose you are a teacher who has been dismissed by the superintendent for "incompetence" based on the principal's evaluation of your teaching. You believe that your firing is unjust and unwarranted and that the principal has been "out to get you" since you disagreed with him on a decision about whether to promote a student. You appeal the decision of the superintendent and your principal to the school board. The school board rules in favor of the superintendent and principal and dismisses you based on causes that have been identified by state law and documented by the principal in his evaluations of your teaching. Because the right of the school board to determine the fitness of teachers has been established by the U.S. Supreme Court, the dismissal is final unless appealed through the state courts.

After obtaining a lawyer through your professional organization, you and your attorney decide to sue the school board, the superintendent, and the principal on the grounds that the evidence is insufficient to prove your incompetence. You take your case to a district circuit court. The circuit court rules that the school board was justified in its dismissal because the state's and the school board's procedures for dismissal were followed and causes for termination were based on statutory grounds. You contend that although the procedures are spelled out, they were not followed in your case, and that the principal's evaluations of you were superficial and vindictive. You and your attorney decide to appeal your case to the appellate court.

The appellate court agrees to hear the case and reverses the decision of the lower court, claiming that the procedures set by the school board were minimally followed. However, your district's procedures explicitly state that a notice of teaching inadequacies must be provided to you and an appropriate opportunity to remedy these must occur prior to dismissal. The appellate court agrees that the list of inadequacies was provided and was based on statutory grounds but that neither time nor support was given to you to help remedy them. Therefore, the school board did not adequately follow its own set policies. The appellate court rules that you must be reinstated and given back pay and damages. The school board decides to appeal the appellate court's decision to the state supreme court. The supreme court refuses to hear the case and the decision of the lower court stands.

State Courts and Constitutional Law

In addition to appeals from cases heard in the lower courts, state supreme courts, like the United States Supreme Court, rule on cases having to do with the constitutionality of legislative actions. In 1989, for example, the Kentucky Supreme Court ruled in *Rose v. The Council for Better Education, Inc.* (Ky., 790 S.W.2d 186, 1989) that the legislature should "re-create and re-establish" the state's precollegiate education system. In the case, brought by sixty-six property-poor school districts, the justices ruled five to two that Kentucky's entire system of school governance and finance violated the state constitution's mandate for an "efficient system of common schools." The court ruled that inequities in state spending for schools violated every student's right to a common education. This court ruling struck down not only the state's financing system but the common-school laws creating school districts, school boards, the state department of education, and laws regarding teacher certification and school construction.

To understand how a state court system works in a case involving constitutional law, it might be helpful to follow *Rose v. The Council for Better Education, Inc.* through the Kentucky courts. The case began in 1984 when it became clear to Arnold Guess, former Kentucky associate state superintendent of public instruction, that neither the governor nor the state legislature would provide needed school finance reform. Guess recruited twenty superintendents from property-poor school districts to discuss an equity suit. The state superintendent, Alice McDonald, said that if the superintendents were able to effect a change in the law through the suit, she would administer it as required by her job.

By March 1985, an equity suit to be filed against the governor, the speaker of the house, the head of the senate, and others able to change the financing of public education in Kentucky was drafted; in November 1985, the suit was filed.

On May 31, 1988, Judge Ray Corns of the Franklin Circuit Court (the trial court) declared school financing in Kentucky unconstitutional. On June 8, 1989, the Kentucky Supreme Court upheld Judge Corns's decision and took it a step further, declaring Kentucky's public schools unconstitutional (interpretation of Rose case based on an article by Barwick 1989).

The court's ruling led to the formation of a task force that provided the governor and the legislature with a blueprint for a total restructuring of Kentucky's precollegiate school system. The plan included the adoption of a performance-based system of rewards and sanctions for schools and teachers, the creation of a professional-standards board for teachers, reorganization of the state education department, the creation of site-based management teams in each school district, at-large election of all local school board members, and a limit to the amount that wealthy districts could spend on schools. The education-reform law was passed by the Kentucky legislature in the spring of 1990.

Appealing Cases to the U.S. Supreme Court

A state supreme court ruling is final unless the case involves an issue related to the U.S. Constitution. If the case is appealed to the U.S. Supreme Court, it may either uphold or overturn the state court's decision. State courts are subservient to decisions of the United States Supreme Court, as illustrated in 1954 in *Brown v. Board of Education* (347 U.S. 483, 1954) when the United States Supreme Court ruled that laws of twenty-one states requiring or permitting racial segregation were in violation of the equal protection clause of the Fourteenth Amendment.

State Attorneys General

The state attorney general may also influence decisions regarding the schools. Usually, he or she will issue an official opinion when consulted by a local authority. For example, if a local school board has a question about the appropriate use of state funds for the purchase of school buses, the board might consult the attorney general, who will research legal questions through statutory law, state and federal law precedents, and state board policy. The opinion will then be forwarded to the official who requested it. How much weight the opinion of the attorney general has in such a case when it is brought to court varies from state to state and case to case. The attorney general's opinion can be important in determining public school policy.

LOCAL EDUCATION AGENCIES

Although the states control public education, the local education agencies (LEA) or school districts administer local public schools. An LEA may be a county, a city, or a district within a large city. Specific decision-making powers are granted to local school boards, which then appoint school administrators to carry out the policies and decisions adopted by the board.

The amount of power given to LEAs varies from state to state. In states with long histories of local control, particularly the New England states, local school boards have a great deal of responsibility for making administrative decisions. In states with centralized control of education, particularly the southern states, local boards function within a strict framework of state legislative mandates. Hawaii makes all decisions regarding the schools on the state level.

Altering LEAs

The state, in giving administrative responsibility to LEAs, does not relinquish control of the state's public schools. In fact, the state may withdraw, through legislative action, any power or authority granted to an LEA. The state may also create LEAs and alter the boundaries of existing school districts.

We can see evidence of how the states redistricted the public schools in the consolidation efforts of the 1950s through the 1970s. The number of LEAs in the United States decreased from 94,426 in 1947 to 31,705 in 1964 in a major reorganization of schools due to consolidation of small districts into larger districts. By 1987–1988 the number of LEAs was only 15,577 (U.S. Department of Education 1990, 90). Consolidation represented the states' attempt to bring better and more equitable services and efficient funding to each LEA.

An interesting example of a state's authority to withdraw administrative power from an LEA occurred in Jersey City, New Jersey, in 1989. The New Jersey state board of education authorized a full state takeover of the Jersey City schools, citing evidence of the district's "total educational failure." This takeover became possible following the passing of a 1988 New Jersey law authorizing state officials to take control of school systems deemed to be what they called "academically bankrupt" and unable to provide a "thorough and efficient" education for the students of the district.

Local School Boards

The local school board is the immediate governing body of an LEA and holds those legal powers granted to it by the state. Its chief responsibilities are to develop and improve the district's educational program, to supply staffing for the schools, to provide and maintain educationally efficient school buildings, to obtain adequate financial resources, to maintain two-way communication with the community, to select a superintendent as the school's chief executive, and to work cooperatively with the superintendent.

School boards usually vary in size from five to nine members with staggered terms, and its members serve without pay or with a nominal salary. School boards must act as a body; individual members cannot make policy on behalf of the board.

Superintendents

The superintendent is the chief executive officer of a school district and is usually appointed by the board of education. The superintendent is responsible for the educational and business administration of all the schools in the LEA, including curriculum, selection and improvement of teachers and key administrators, gathering data on issues of interest to the school board, preparing the school budget, implementation of the budget, implementation of the school board's goals and policies, evaluation of curricular and instructional programs, maintenance of buildings, safety of students and personnel, and transportation of students to and from the schools. In addition, the superintendent is the LEA's primary liaison with the community. Most school districts have a central office with deputy or associate superintendents and a professional staff to assist in these responsibilities.

The delineation of responsibilities can again be seen in the chapter's opening anecdote. Dr. Hurwitz, whose actions brought him into conflict with the local superintendent whose responsibility was to carry out the policies of the board, was eventually relieved of his post as a high school principal. When Hurwitz's appeals to the superintendent did not produce the results Hurwitz desired, he took the next logical step and made a further appeal to the local school board. As is the board's right, it suggested a compromise, including a second hearing before a civil court.

ROLE OF BUSINESSES AND FOUNDATIONS IN EDUCATION

During the 1980s and 1990s, businesses and foundations have had an increased impact on the public schools. Corporate America has historically stood aloof from public schools while complaining about the quality of education, but a new partnership between business and the schools was developed in the late 1970s that led to some recent innovations (Carnegie Foundation for the Advancement of Teaching 1988).

In 1990, the Business Roundtable (BRT), a group representing the chief executive officers (CEOs) of 213 corporations, made a ten-year commitment to the restructuring of education at the state level. Under the leadership of IBM Chairman John Akers, BRT members are volunteering to work with governors, state political leaders, and other interested parties to identify key educational problems, develop strategies for dealing with them, and implement new policy, regulatory, and funding initiatives. BRT is sponsoring a series of CEO-governor dialogues in an effort to support state reform efforts.

One of the more controversial elements of President George Bush's America 2000 plan was the involvement of business in education. He suggested that first, business must establish a list of job-related skill standards to be taught to students. Second, a group of business leaders headed by Paul O'Neill, CEO of Alcoa, pledged to raise at least $150 million to fund research and development teams to work with schools to develop innovative approaches to education. On one hand, these proposals encourage business to determine the practical goals of public education and develop strategies for reaching these goals. Some critics of Bush's proposal, on the other hand, suggest that this gives business too great a role in public education.

Business and the Schools

Most of the involvement of business is currently through funding special programs; however, some businesses are actually becoming involved in the operation of schools. Here are a few examples:

1. Pittsburgh's Allegheny Conference on Community Development awards minigrants to 100 teachers each year to encourage creative teaching. The grants range from $50 to $1,000.
2. General Electric donated a $5 million plant to the Cleveland Board of Education for students to work on assembly lines and be paid for their work.
3. The Oak Forest Bank of Houston gives awards to students who demonstrate outstanding leadership ability.
4. AT&T Bell Laboratories provides scholarships for college-bound students.
5. McDonnell-Douglas Corporation conducts management seminars for administrators and courses in computer science and mathematics for teachers.
6. People's Energy, a natural gas firm in Chicago, sends employees to the public schools to tutor students in reading and mathematics.

7. Nike donated $1 million to the National Foundation for the Improvement of Education to create dropout prevention programs for teachers. The "Just Do It" grants gave $5,000 to $25,000 to teachers for creative programs to motivate students to stay in school.

8. Dewitt Wallace–Reader's Digest Fund has contributed $3 million to the National Board for Professional Standards to hold thirty-six state and regional forums to inform teachers about national certification.

9. The Tandy Technology Scholars Corporation awards a $2,500 stipend to 100 outstanding mathematics, science, or computer science students annually. They also grant $1,000 scholarships to a second group of 100 students.

10. Apple Computers has donated computers to educators and the schools through the Apple Education Grants Program. The program has granted more than $2 million annually in equipment to needy schools nationwide.

11. The Adopt-A-School program is a joint project of the Boston business community and the Boston public schools. Through this program, businesses sponsor schools to help refurbish them, provide computers, and help solve specific school-related problems.

12. The Cleveland business community has formed a partnership with the Cleveland public schools to provide a scholarship to every student who earns it. All students in grades seven through twelve earn deposits toward scholarships for grades in core subjects: $40 for an A, $20 for a B, and $10 for a C. Each grading period students receive a statement of earnings.

13. The Computer Science Corporation, Hazelton Laboratories, Martin-Marietta, and other local businesses in Alexandria, Virginia, contributed $4 million in high-tech equipment to Thomas Jefferson Magnet High School for Science and Technology.

Foundations and the Schools

Foundations, legally chartered funds administered by independent boards of control, are increasingly involved in financing educational projects. Some major recent foundation projects are listed below.

1. The Annie E. Casey Foundation selected five cities to receive a total of $10 million each for programs designed to reduce the number of school dropouts. The five selected cities were required to match the funds of the foundation with equal funds from other sources.

2. The Matsushita Foundation is spending $850,000 a year in no more than ten school districts on five- to ten-year school improvement plans which are designed to restructure schools. Teachers and principals must be involved in the process.

3. The W. K. Kellogg Foundation has set up a twenty-year program with three Michigan communities to address the developmental needs of children.

4. The Ford Foundation is assisting twenty-one cities with a total of $2.3 million to reduce the number of school dropouts.

5. The Lily Endowment has appropriated funds to ten cities to improve middle schools and involve teachers in the planning.

Bo knows Shakespeare

Bo knows philosophy

Bo knows calculus

Bo knows all this stuff because
he learned it in school

Nike is probably the most visible example of corporate involvement in education. Its advertisement with Bo Jackson urges kids to stay in school. While some view this development as a positive step in the relationship between the education a student receives and his or her ultimate role in the working world, critics worry that business may have undue influence on the educational system.

6. The Lily Endowment has given up to $5 million to a coalition of business, political, and educational leaders for educational reform in Indianapolis.

7. The John D. and Catherine T. MacArthur Foundation has contributed $40 million in grants over ten years to support educational improvement and community involvement in the schools.

Although in most instances business has no direct control over the public schools (exceptions being in rare cases when businesses and communities work together to form boards to administer the schools), business exerts a significant influence over public education through funding of special projects, lobbying state legislatures, scholarships to students, providing supplies and materials for schools, and producing educational audiovisuals to be used in the schools.

V I E W P O I N T S

How One Influential Organization Attempts to Influence Education: An Editorial by the President of the National PTA

Several weeks ago, U.S. Secretary of Education Lamar Alexander introduced a "long-range plan" called America 2000, a strategy for moving the nation closer to the realization of the six education goals. This was a bold step personifying the more aggressive leadership for which Alexander is known.

For the 7 million member National PTA, the success of America 2000 will be based on the premise that *every* child has access to an excellent preschool, elementary and secondary education. The plan of America 2000 to research better schools, develop skills clinics, focus on at-risk children, create America 2000 communities, and design more accountable schools deserves attention precisely because the ideas, if pursued with fervor and commitment, hold the hope of an improved public education for *all* students.

The National PTA believes that the Secretary has laid a philosophical and strategic foundation, and as president of the National PTA, I will urge our membership to heed his challenge: that if America 2000 is to work, it will "most of all, take America's parents," who have now become the "demanding shareholders of our schools." As shareholders we want this partnership between the parents and the schools to succeed. Therefore, we offer some suggestions as Mr. Alexander prepares a more detailed plan for Congress.

1. *Parental involvement* must be the cornerstone of America 2000. The report minimizes the parental role, and should recognize that parents play an important part in advocacy, home-school coordination, volunteerism and curriculum decision making. It is not acceptable that parents are referred to only twice in the report at a time when the country attributes academic success to parental participation.

2. *America 2000 should reflect an additional national goal:* "That every elementary and secondary school have a comprehensive parental involvement program by the year 2000."

3. *Child readiness* as articulated by the first national goal should be given greater attention. While the focus of America 2000 is more on the later student years and college, a more comprehensive national policy is required to assure that the schools are ready for our children and that the children are ready for the academic challenges of the 21st century schools. Basic nutrition, pre- and neo-natal care, vaccinations, and quality early care and preschool must be essential components—starting now to reach those children who will be five years of age in 1996.

4. There should be *greater coordination between educational and health services.* For many of our children, basic needs to survive are unmet: nutritional

meals, shelter, physical and mental health care, security and protection must be coordinated with the educational functions. America 2000 should reflect a policy of the *whole* child.

5. The schools of the 21st century will not come on the cheap. If our country can make a $100 billion investment developing a new stealth bomber, America 2000 should be making that same 10 year investment in its children by fully funding Head Start for every preschooler that is eligible.

6. *The issue of testing should not overshadow the issue of education.* While genuine accountability is an essential component of the learning process, the development of testing instruments must come *after* the development of subject matter standards and curriculum. We want President Bush to

be known as the education president rather than the testing president.

Mr. Alexander possesses the leadership to build a national consensus around public education. However, support of private and religious school vouchers will produce divisiveness, an intellectual intrusion that will divert national debate away from school improvement and toward another quick fix scheme. Let us not waste precious time by getting mired in diatribes that will diminish the ability to pursue America 2000 precepts.

As the "concept" of America 2000 takes shape, we urge the Secretary of Education to consider our additions. The parents of America look forward to working with the Administration as we launch "the new beginning."

From: Lynch, May 20, 1991

NONPUBLIC SCHOOLS

The first schools in the United States were private. Even after the establishment of a U.S. public school system, private schools continued to exist, and have grown in numbers from colonial times to the present. The reasons for this growth relate to the nature of nonpublic schools, to the country's democratic creed ("freedom of choice"), societal needs, and governmental forces.

What Are Nonpublic Schools?

Nonpublic schools are of several types: parochial or church-related schools, secular private schools, and independent schools. Parochial schools are funded by churches or other religious communities. Independent schools are "a collection of accredited private schools not supported generally by public funds, religious communities or great bureaucracies" (Esty 1984, 1). Like independent schools, private schools are not supported by public funds or religious communities, but they may be funded by special interest groups and, unlike independent schools, are frequently not accredited by the regional agencies that accredit nonpublic schools.

Enrollment

In 1988, 11.5 percent of all students enrolled in school from kindergarten through grade twelve attended a nonpublic school. The student population in

Nonpublic or private schools have always been one educational choice available to some parents and their children in this country. They may be supported by a special interest group, a church, or a particular segment of society. Because private schools are not supported by either the federal or state government, they are free to pursue their own curriculums and use their own methods of instruction.

nonpublic schools totaled 7.3 percent in 1920, climbing to a high of 13.6 percent in the 1960s, dropping to 12 percent by 1980 (Bennett 1985, 5).

Researchers have attempted to explain why enrollment has fluctuated in nonpublic schools. The increased number of Irish and Italian immigrants caused the number of Roman Catholic schools "to grow from about one hundred in 1840 to about three thousand in the 1880's." Nonpublic school enrollments increased substantially in some parts of the country in the late 1950s and 1960s due to implementation of forced busing for public schools (Kliebard 1969).

In another study to determine why enrollments in fundamentalist Christian schools increased from 160,000 to 347,000 in the late 1970s and 1980s, parents explained why they withdrew children from public school: "Poor academic quality, lack of discipline, and the fact that public schools were promoting a philosophy of secular humanism inimical to their religious beliefs" (Butts 1978). Other parents cite the academic success rate of students attending nonpublic schools to explain why they are willing to invest in their children's education.

A 1989 study conducted by the National Catholic Educational Association and the National Assessment of Educational Progress found that Catholic school children score higher on standardized tests than public school children. Sociologist James Coleman determined that 3.4 percent of children in Catholic schools drop out of school compared to 14.3 percent of public school children. In addition, 83 percent of Catholic school children attend college compared to 50 percent of public school students. Some contend that these statistics are due to the selective nature of Catholic schools. However, the National Catholic

Educational Association insists that Catholic schools enroll 90 percent of all students who apply for admission, and once admitted few are expelled. Albert Shanker, president of the American Federation of Teachers (AFT), claims that it is that 10 percent who make the difference. "Any teacher will tell you that the problem is one or two kids, not everybody" (Rachlin and Glastris 1989, 62).

William Bennett, secretary of education in the Reagan administration, explained that much of the rise in enrollment in nonpublic schools from 12 percent of all students in 1980 to 13 percent in 1983 was due to larger numbers of preschool children counted in the 1983 nonpublic school survey. He noted that the number of children in this age group is growing, and most nursery school children attend nonpublic schools (1985, 5).

Relationship Between States and Nonpublic Schools

Through a U.S. Supreme Court ruling in 1925 (*Pierce v. Society of Sisters*, 268 U.S. 510, 1925), states have been given general authority over nonpublic schools with respect to compulsory attendance, health, safety, and quality of instruction. The "quality of instruction" component of this ruling caused problems in the late 1970s, when some states attempted to enforce legislative mandates requiring the successful completion of minimum competency tests as a requirement for high school graduation. Most nonpublic schools refused to become involved in minimum competency testing on the grounds of separation of church and state. Nonpublic schools were unwilling to fund the administration of the tests in their schools. According to the "High School and Beyond" survey, approximately 68 percent of the public sector schools require successful completion of a competency exam, whereas only 3 percent of the private sector schools have a similar requirement (Kilgore 1985, 119). Since nonpublic schools are not directly funded through tax money, they contend that they are not required to meet legislative mandates, particularly when complying with these mandates requires additional funding that will not be provided to the nonpublic schools through legislative apportionment. Hence, although most nonpublic schools administer standardized tests that are normed through extensive testing done in nonpublic schools, few give state-required competency tests or participate in state testing programs.

Funding Nonpublic Schools

Governance and funding of nonpublic schools are filled with complexities. Finances come from tuition fees, gifts, contributions, grants from churches and sponsors, or endowments rather than from public funds or tax support. Most states are constrained by legislative or constitutional provisions from granting any aid to nonpublic schools, especially to church-related schools, since state funds cannot be used to encourage or support the teaching of religion. But these funding constraints were tested in the late 1960s, when millions of dollars given to the states through the Elementary and Secondary School Act of 1965 were funneled into all types of nonpublic schools for textbooks, libraries, transportation, free milk, low-cost lunches, and health services, causing confusion and conflict in some states and districts since it appeared that public funds were being granted to institutions that paid no taxes because they are nonprofit. State and federal courts ruled that aid went directly to the students in nonpublic institutions instead of the institution itself, thus the funding was not found to be unconstitutional and was allowed to continue.

Many individuals, groups, agencies, and branches of government affect U.S. education. Although the U.S. Constitution gives control and operation of the public schools to the states through the Tenth Amendment, federal and local governments and all levels of the courts are involved in and have some degree of control over education. In addition, nongovernmental agencies, organizations, and businesses influence education through funding, lobbying, and creating task forces to study controversial issues in education. Education in the United States is thus public in its broadest sense—involving government, the courts, and agencies and businesses.

14.2 POINTS TO REMEMBER

- State control of public schools is established in each state's constitution. Therefore, how schools are governed differs from state to state.

- The governor's role in education is indirect, whereas the state legislature's role is direct. The governor sets a legislative agenda. The legislature passes laws that directly affect the governance and administration of schools within the state.

- Legislatures delegate authority to state school boards to translate state statutes into policy. State boards give the policy to state education agencies or departments to develop curriculums. Chief state school officers serve a regulatory function to ensure that local education agencies are implementing state policy.

- Each state has a supreme court, which is the final authority of constitutional law within the state judiciary. The appellate courts hear appeals from the circuit or trial courts. A case related to education is usually heard first by the circuit courts and later appealed to appellate and supreme courts.

- Local school boards are usually elected and oversee the implementation of state policy within the local education agency or school district. The board appoints the superintendent, who is the chief administrative officer of the local school district.

- In recent years, businesses and foundations have been increasingly involved in the public schools, primarily through funding projects of special interest.

- Over 10 percent of all students enrolled in school attend nonpublic schools, providing diversity to U.S. education.

H. L. Schwadron in *Phi Delta Kappan.*

"After 20 years of schooling, your aptitude test shows that you're skilled at just one thing— taking tests."

FOR THOUGHT/DISCUSSION

1. Do you believe a national exam will result in standard academic excellence throughout the United States or a stagnant approach to learning? Explain.

2. In matters of censorship in the schools, on what basis has the Supreme Court made most of its recent decisions? Do you agree with this rule? Why or why not?

3. Do you believe it is appropriate for a state legislature to assume control of a school district? Why or why not?

4. Do you see the role of business in education as a positive or negative factor? Explain.

FOR FURTHER READING/REFERENCE

Blair, L. H., Brounstein, S. L., Hatry, H. P., and Morley, E. 1990. *Guidelines for school-business partnerships in science and mathematics.* Lanham, MO: Urban Institute Press. A discussion of obstacles to and successes of twenty-four school-business relationships across the United States; recommendations for beginning a school-business partnership are presented.

Chubb, J. E., and Moe, T. M. 1990. *Politics, markets, and American schools.* Washington, DC: Brookings Institution. Views of why and how governmental controls present problems for schools; discussions of the author's proposal of parent-school choice as a remedy for school reform.

Hurwitz, H. L. 1989. *The last angry principal.* Portland, OR: Halcyon House. An elaboration of the chapter's opening anecdote that details the author's battle against a school system; a discussion of what the author believes must be done in disciplined schools of excellence.

National Center on Education and the Economy. 1989. *To secure our future: The federal role in education.* Rochester, NY: Author. A report sent to the president and Congress in 1989 to illustrate this group's vision of what the federal role in education in the 1990s should be as well as the role of business and technology.

15

Financial and Legal Aspects of Education

FUNDING EDUCATION
Educational Funding and Politics
Local Funding of Education
State Funding of Education
Federal Funding of Education
Courts, Legislatures, and Equalization of
    Funding

TEACHERS AND THE LAW
Contract Law
Due Process
Freedom of Expression
Academic Freedom
Tort Liability
Copyright Law

STUDENTS AND THE LAW
Equal Educational Opportunity
School Attendance and Student Health
Curriculum
Student Achievement
Freedom of Expression and Assembly
Freedom of Religion
Access to Student Records
Student Discipline
Corporal Punishment
Search and Seizure

NEWTON, MASS.—Lauren Bisceglia has stopped buying the sturdy canvas out of which her home-economics students have always made tote bags. "We can't afford that anymore," the Brown Junior High School teacher says.

These days, the totes are cut from cheaper cloth she buys by the pound at a factory-outlet store.

Despite the rising cost of such materials and an increase in the number of students she teaches, Ms. Bisceglia has only $1,800—the same amount she has received for each of the past four years—to buy sewing goods and food supplies for her 300 students.

As long as the students carry a light load in the elegantly stitched bags, Ms. Bisceglia explains, they will hold up fine. But if they use the totes as book bags, the cloth will tear.

While Ms. Bisceglia's forced economies on tote bags are of relatively minor importance in the scheme of things, they epitomize the plight of the school district that employs her. By scaling back on expenditures, both the home-economics teacher and the Newton public schools are getting the job done, but the financial stress is causing the fabric to fray.

In each of the past three years, district officials have been forced to make cutbacks in staffing, services, and programs in order to erase a budget deficit.

"I see a membrane being stretched very tight," said David Michaud, the district's associate superintendent for elementary education. With each new budget cut, "I fear we're fraying a little closer to the center."

Like most school districts in Massachusetts—and throughout New England for that matter—Newton's financial vitality has been sapped by the region's distressed economy.

Irwin Blumer, superintendent of the Newton schools, contends that the nation's public schools can no longer rely on the vagaries of local property taxes and undependable state revenue for their funding.

"It goes beyond Newton and Massachusetts at this point," he said. "There's something wrong with the whole process.". . . .

Linda Puretz and her husband moved to Newton in 1977—primarily because of the educational system.

"Imagine our feeling 13, 14 years later . . . of being in a situation where the school system is not what we had hoped for," Ms. Puretz said.

A memorandum from the principal of Bowen Elementary School, where Ms. Puretz's children attend school, outlines what they have to look forward to next year: no room for a computer lab, resulting in limited student access; no room for a nurse's office, meaning reduced nursing support; and 5th-grade classes with 28 students and 6th grades with 29 students.

"The large class sizes have shocked people in a way that other cuts haven't, primarily because this is very visible to people," Ms. Puretz said. . . .

Two years ago, the district started charging $25 user fees for high-school students who wanted to play sports. This year, the school committee voted to raise the fee to $50 and to introduce a $25 fee at the junior-high level. Junior-high students will also pay a fee for some music and drama programs. Later this month, the school committee will vote on a $100 user fee for high-school students.

Faculty and staff members will be asked to identify any student who may not be able to afford the fee.

"I will never have—never have—any student who wants to play a sport be prevented from playing a sport because of money," Mr. Blumer said.

But the whole concept does not sit well with the community.

"We're saying, 'Parents, you pay for what the public used to think was for the public good,' " said Jerold Katz, principal of Bowen Elementary.

From: K. Diegmueller, May 29, 1991, 1, 10.

The only thing that can try a father's patience as much as a teenager is a lawsuit. For 22 years Demetrio Rodriguez and the determined parents of the Edgewood School District in San Antonio battled through the courts, trying to change the way in which Texas funds its public schools. In 1973, they reached the U.S. Supreme Court and came within one vote of fundamentally changing all of America's schools. They lost, but in a slightly different guise simply started over again in the courts of Texas.

Last October [1990] they won a famous victory. The state Supreme Court ruled that the school funding for Edgewood was so inadequate and so unfair that it amounted to an unconstitutional denial of a child's right to an equal education. Then, nothing changed. Not until eight months later did the governor and state legislature finally agree on a new plan to help the state's sorriest schools. The change came too late for the Rodriguez household. The deal was cut on June 1, the same day that the last Rodriguez child, Patricia, was graduating from high school. It was a bittersweet moment for her father: "Maybe by the time my grandchildren go to school, they can take advantage of all we have fought for, for so long."

From: G. Carroll, Fall/Winter, 1990–1991, 81.

CHAPTER OBJECTIVES

After studying this chapter, you should be able to:

- Discuss the politics of funding for education.
- Describe how local governments fund education.
- Describe how state governments fund education.
- Explain why school districts are not equally funded.
- Discuss how courts and legislatures are attempting to equalize funding.
- Discuss the federal role in funding education.
- Define block grants.
- Compare and contrast constitutional and statutory law.
- Discuss why contract law is important to teachers.
- Identify the due process rights of teachers.
- Discuss what is meant by academic freedom.
- Define tort liability and negligence.
- Discuss how the copyright laws apply to education.
- Discuss the legal aspects of school attendance and student health.
- Discuss the legal aspects of student achievement and access to student records.
- Explain how court decisions related to students' freedom of expression are evolving.
- Identify court rulings in search and seizure cases.

While most citizens of this country believe in the democratic ideal of equal education for all, the reality is that the quality of education is hardly equal for all children in all school districts. Because the system of educational funding is so heavily dependent on state and local tax revenues, which in turn are so dependent on the economy in various areas of the country, schools even within the same state receive unequal allotments of money. In this chapter we will examine how funding contributes to quality of education. We will conclude by examining some of the practical legal issues that teachers will encounter in the practice of their profession.

FUNDING EDUCATION

How public schools are funded varies from state to state. Some schools receive most of their funding from the local government rather than state or federal sources. For example, over 90 percent of New Hampshire's public school revenues comes from local sources. In other states, however, schools receive most of their funding from the state. Schools in New Mexico and Washington, for example, receive more than 70 percent of their revenue from the state (U.S. Department of Education 1990b, 149). Although the percentage of federal funding for schools also varies, most states receive less than 10 percent of their education revenues from the federal government.

Educational Funding and Politics

We might want to think that educational funding is not affected by politics. Unfortunately, this is not so. In 1978–1979, during the Carter administration, for example, 9.8 percent of all the money spent on U.S. public education came from the federal government, 45.6 percent from the states, and 44.6 percent from local sources. By 1988 there had been a significant shift in the percentage of funding received from each of the three sources: 6.3 percent came from the federal government, 49.5 percent from state funds, and 44.1 percent from local sources (U.S. Department of Education 1990b, 80).

Why these shifts occur is an interesting political phenomenon. The more politically liberal the federal government, the greater the likelihood of more centralized funding for education because state and federal aid programs equalize educational opportunity for students in all schools. The alternative method of funding, local property taxes, is necessarily unequal since the tax base of richer communities is much larger than that of poorer communities. Hence, when politically liberal administrations gain power, the funds for education are equalized by augmenting the tax base of local communities with federal and state grants.

On the other hand, the more politically conservative the federal government, the greater will be decentralized funding for education. Decentralization occurs because of a conservative belief in home rule, keeping the center of government as close to the population as possible. We can see these shifts in funding when we compare federal educational funding during the presidential administrations of Jimmy Carter, a liberal, and Ronald Reagan, a conservative.

Local Funding of Education

Today, local taxation provides the majority of the school funds in half the states. On an average, 43.9 percent of school revenues come from local sources. Ninety-eight percent of that local school revenue is generated from property taxes, which are based on the assessed value of real estate (residential and commercial land and buildings) and personal property (automobiles, jewelry, stocks, and bonds).

Property taxation originated on the United States frontier, where wealth was measured in land. It remains a widely used form of taxation because it produces a fairly stable rate of collection and is difficult to evade. Property taxes are also used to fund other municipal services, such as police, fire, parks, libraries, and municipal roads. Most states have laws that place limits on the property tax rates local school districts can levy—a greater rate requires approval by the voters of the district.

When funding for schools is primarily based on local property taxes, significant inequities develop. The richer the district, the higher the assessed property values; the larger the tax base, the greater the funding for local schools. For example, assume that local school district A has an assessed valuation of $100 million and a 1,000-student school population and that local school district B has an assessed valuation of $50 million for 1,000 students. A

(continued on p. 508)

Point/Counterpoint

STATES SHOULD PROVIDE THEIR OWN FUNDS FOR EDUCATION

Federal control is potentially far more dangerous than state control. Federal funds should flow to the state and be dispersed within the state by state authorities according to state law. The ideal pattern of state aid places the maximum responsibility on the local community; this responsibility means local control and likewise a high local tax rate. The ideal pattern for Federal aid should involve the flow of funds only to those states that have already demonstrated that they have done their utmost from their own resources, and where in spite of the state's effort the funds available per pupil are below a minimum figure.

From: Conant, 1948

THE FEDERAL GOVERNMENT SHOULD PROVIDE PRIMARY FUNDING FOR EDUCATION

The federal government could easily do more to reduce expenditure differences between states.

Many conservatives have opposed such changes, on the grounds that equalizing resources would mean more central financing, and that more central financing would mean more central control. Central control is, in turn, often said to make schools less responsive to local needs. Experience suggests, however, that while central control may make the schools less responsive to the local establishment, whatever that may be, it often makes schools more responsive to other groups. (Blacks in the South are an obvious case in point.) We therefore tend to favor central financing, both as a means of equalizing expenditures and as a way of making local schools somewhat more responsive to groups they have traditionally ignored.

From: Jencks, 1972

POSTSCRIPT

Although these two arguments date from an earlier time, they are both relevant today. Conant's argues the conservative view that in order for local districts to control education, it is essential that they be, whenever possible, the primary source of funding. Jencks's position reflects the liberal view that if educational opportunities are to be equalized, centralized funding of schools is essential. Somewhere between the two is the solution to the problem of equalizing funding and providing equal education for all.

tax rate of $2 per $100 of assessed valuation produces $2 million in school district A and $1 million in school district B. Hence, the schoolchildren in district B receive only half the funding from local property taxes that the children in district A receive.

Other local funding sources for schools include local sales taxes and special room taxes in hotels and motels, if the voters decide to implement them. However, poorer districts are likely to have less flexibility assessing these forms of taxation because few nonresidents spend money there. Therefore, district A is likely to be able to raise more revenue from these types of taxation than district B, making funding of education even more unequal.

States raise revenues for schools primarily through taxes of various kinds. Inequities of funding for education around the country are thus caused by the inability of some states to raise sufficient funds. These people in the state of Connecticut are protesting Governor Lowell P. Weiker's insistence that the legislature pass a budget that includes an income tax.

State Funding of Education

Depending on the formula used, state aid, may help equalize funding among local school districts, which receive, on average, 49.8 percent of their funds from the state. Usually funding is allocated by the state legislature and administered through state departments of education. Often, however, state allocations still do not make up for inequities in local property taxes.

State funds for education come from a variety of tax sources, including one or a combination of the following: sales, income, inheritance, gift, use, and occupation taxes; franchise and license fees; and state lotteries. It is not only the amount of revenue collected that affects the funding of schools but also how that revenue is allocated to local districts.

State Aid Formulas

The allocation of state revenue to local districts occurs through state aid formulas, the two most common of which are a flat grant and an equalization grant. **Flat grants** are usually based on the district's average daily attendance during the previous school year; each district receives the same amount for each student in attendance. Flat grants do not take into consideration variations among school districts in local taxing ability. Adjustments are made, however,

(continued on bottom of p. 510)

TABLE 15-1

Direct General Expenditures Per Capita of State and Local Governments for all Functions and for Education, by Level and State: 1985–1986

State	Total, all direct general expenditures per capita[1]	Education expenditures per capita							
		Total		Elementary and secondary education		Higher education		Other education[2]	
		Amount	As a percent of all functions	Amount	As a percent of all functions	Amount	As a percent of all functions	Amount	As a percent of all functions
1	2	3	4	5	6	7	8	9	10
United States	$2,507.31	$ 874.49	34.9	$ 601.93	24.0	$234.51	9.4	$ 38.05	1.5
Alabama	2,125.47	792.76	37.3	433.43	20.4	257.00	12.1	102.32	4.8
Alaska	9,437.11	2,272.75	24.1	1,660.36	17.6	523.22	5.5	89.17	0.9
Arizona	2,541.10	987.15	38.8	634.02	25.0	323.45	12.7	29.68	1.2
Arkansas	1,842.74	791.31	42.9	586.07	29.1	200.87	10.9	54.37	3.0
California	2,819.84	906.69	32.2	586.62	20.8	288.23	10.2	31.84	1.1
Colorado	2,567.44	949.28	37.0	666.66	26.0	263.92	10.3	18.70	0.7
Connecticut	2,582.47	745.46	28.9	553.52	21.4	149.56	5.8	42.37	1.6
Delaware	2,817.37	1,108.09	39.3	642.31	22.8	382.04	13.6	83.73	3.0
District of Columbia	4,693.58	801.78	17.1	671.15	14.3	130.63	2.8	—	—
Florida	2,123.35	703.51	33.1	523.95	24.7	132.90	6.3	46.66	2.2
Georgia	2,199.36	761.68	34.6	526.46	23.9	210.40	9.6	24.83	1.1
Hawaii	2,698.60	758.74	28.1	441.02	16.3	303.80	11.3	13.92	0.5
Idaho	1,978.24	762.64	38.6	482.40	24.4	245.72	12.4	34.53	1.7
Illinois	2,350.47	796.15	33.9	545.59	23.2	206.59	8.8	43.96	1.9
Indiana	1,995.67	817.67	41.0	529.11	26.5	245.25	12.3	43.31	2.2
Iowa	2,438.22	937.29	38.4	569.69	23.4	331.59	13.6	36.00	1.5
Kansas	2,382.11	935.09	39.3	620.40	26.0	296.92	12.5	17.77	0.7
Kentucky	1,921.15	689.29	35.9	429.72	22.4	209.68	10.9	49.89	2.6
Louisiana	2,423.38	784.48	32.4	521.30	21.5	212.55	8.8	50.63	2.1
Maine	2,302.83	813.36	35.3	556.52	24.2	202.26	8.8	54.58	2.4
Maryland	2,579.95	871.63	33.8	584.78	22.7	249.28	9.7	37.57	1.5
Massachusetts	2,711.17	791.59	29.2	593.95	21.9	157.16	5.8	40.49	1.5
Michigan	2,773.10	1,032.82	37.2	707.09	25.5	295.69	10.7	30.03	1.1
Minnesota	3,048.51	1,005.00	33.0	703.29	23.1	259.95	8.5	41.77	1.4
Mississippi	1,956.54	707.40	36.2	448.70	22.9	221.53	11.3	37.17	1.9

Each state has its own formula for equalizing spending on education in its districts. There is not, however, any formula for equalizing spending among the states. Thus, the states vary greatly on the amount they spend on education.

for special students, such as the disabled, and, in some cases, for school districts with large fluctuations in student population during the school year. **Equalization grants** provide less state money to districts with higher property values than ones with lower property values.

Some states set qualifying or minimum local tax rates, which districts must levy in order to qualify for state funds. This is to avoid wealthy districts using

State	Total, all direct general expenditures per capita[1]	Education expenditures per capita							
		Total		Elementary and secondary education		Higher education		Other education[2]	
		Amount	As a percent of all functions	Amount	As a percent of all functions	Amount	As a percent of all functions	Amount	As a percent of all functions
1	2	3	4	5	6	7	8	9	10
Missouri	1,914.40	704.57	36.8	505.77	26.4	176.52	9.2	22.28	1.2
Montana	2,783.94	1,026.30	36.9	763.53	27.4	213.65	7.7	49.12	1.8
Nebraska	2,394.23	922.91	38.5	615.70	25.7	279.65	11.7	27.57	1.0
Nevada	2,662.87	773.29	29.0	549.73	20.6	197.89	7.4	25.67	1.0
New Hampshire	2,024.25	705.83	34.9	517.90	25.6	167.25	8.3	20.68	1.0
New Jersey	2,797.08	916.63	32.8	710.01	25.4	178.23	6.4	28.39	1.0
New Mexico	2,695.77	1,068.08	39.6	672.92	25.0	365.68	13.6	29.48	1.1
New York	3,615.61	1,037.96	28.7	787.08	21.8	195.38	5.4	55.50	1.5
North Carolina	1,911.11	840.64	44.0	530.13	27.7	279.67	14.6	30.85	1.6
North Dakota	2,706.94	1,040.22	38.4	619.93	22.9	380.07	14.0	40.23	1.5
Ohio	2,289.45	855.85	37.4	612.86	26.8	226.64	9.9	16.36	0.7
Oklahoma	2,228.26	874.22	39.2	585.86	26.3	253.74	11.4	34.61	1.6
Oregon	2,672.48	982.84	36.8	668.51	25.0	290.29	10.9	24.05	0.9
Pennsylvania	2,183.32	771.33	35.3	584.24	26.8	125.38	5.7	61.70	2.8
Rhode Island	2,671.35	840.32	31.5	549.55	20.6	210.76	7.9	80.01	3.0
South Carolina	1,972.05	803.22	40.7	510.62	25.9	244.46	12.4	48.14	2.4
South Dakota	2,253.67	791.62	35.1	568.81	25.2	193.26	8.6	29.56	1.3
Tennessee	1,918.31	651.90	34.0	392.52	20.5	205.06	10.7	54.32	2.8
Texas	2,203.57	926.30	42.0	650.23	29.5	259.82	11.8	16.25	0.7
Utah	2,482.22	1,050.39	42.3	658.98	26.5	352.76	14.2	38.65	1.6
Vermont	2,561.78	987.91	38.6	590.30	23.0	335.19	13.1	62.42	2.4
Virginia	2,212.40	881.59	39.8	601.50	27.2	248.14	11.2	31.94	1.4
Washington	2,564.88	936.35	36.5	612.49	23.9	290.61	11.3	33.25	1.3
West Virginia	2,157.80	832.13	38.6	595.95	27.6	192.74	8.9	43.44	2.0
Wisconsin	2,719.23	1,024.17	37.7	648.19	23.8	337.98	12.4	38.0	1.4
Wyoming	4,472.28	1,666.83	37.3	1,206.73	27.0	429.80	9.6	30.30	0.7

[1] Includes state and local government expenditures for education services, social services and income maintenance, transportation, public safety, environment and housing, governmental administration, interest and general debt, and other general expenditures.
[2] Includes state education administration and services, tuition grants, fellowships, aid to private schools, and special programs.
From: U.S. Department of Education, National Center for Education Statistics, *Digest of Education Statistics* (1989b). Washington, DC: U.S. Government Printing Office, 36.

state equalization funds rather than local funds for public education. Conversely, some state constitutions or laws set ceilings for the amount of local tax dollars that can be spent on public schools. Thus, if districts are below the upper limits, they may authorize new taxes on property; districts whose spending has reached the maximum may not levy new tax monies for schools. Both minimums and maximums are designed primarily to help equalize educational spending across districts within a state. There is, however, no formula for equalizing funding among the states where great diversity still exists. For example, in 1985–1986, Alaska spent over $1,600 per capita on public education, whereas Alabama spent $433 per capita (see table 15.1 on p. 510). Some of this differential can be attributed to the relative cost of living in each state, but large differentials exist even between states with similar costs of living.

Fluctuating State Funding

The level of state support for public education fluctuates depending on the level of federal and local funding available. Until 1930, more than 80 percent of public school revenue came from local districts. However, the percentage of local dollars as compared to state and federal dollars spent on education decreased steadily after 1930. From 1930 through 1960, the states' share of educational funding increased from 16.9 to 39.1 percent of all dollars spent on public education. The percentage of state dollars compared to local and federal dollars spent on education remained relatively constant from the mid-1940s through the mid-1970s. The states' share of educational spending then in-

FIGURE 15-1

Sources of Revenue for Public Elementary and Secondary Schools: 1969–70 to 1987–89

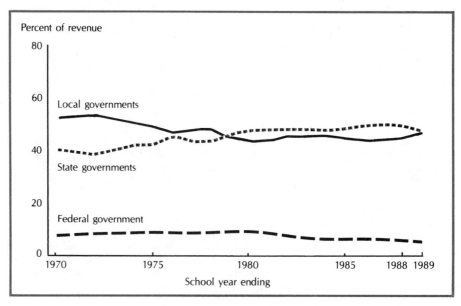

Source: U.S. Department of Education, National Center for Education Statistics, *Statistics of State School Systems; Revenues and Expenditures for Public Elementary and Secondary Education;* and Common Core of Data surveys.

From: U.S. Department of Education, National Center for Education Statistics, *The Condition of Education,* Vol. I (1991). Washington, DC: U.S. Government Printing Office, 88.

Most school systems receive funding from local or state sources. While the states differ in the amount of funding derived from local, state, and federal sources, most states receive less than 10 percent of their funds from the federal government.

creased from 42.2 percent in 1974–1975 to 49.8 in 1986–1987. We can better understand how substantial this increased share is by looking at figure 15.1 on p. 512. While a similar 7.5 percent increase in states' share of educational funding occurred in both time frames, the first occurred over a nearly thirty-year period and the second over only a twelve-year period. When the states' share of educational funding increases, the federal and local shares decrease.

The U.S. Congress has no obligation to provide funding for public education but does so voluntarily. Federal aid to education comes through grants from several federal agencies: the U.S. Department of Education, the Office of Economic Opportunity, the National Science Foundation, the National Endowment for the Humanities, and the National Endowment for the Arts, among others. Funds flow directly from federal agencies and indirectly through state agencies. For example, funding for an educational project for an interdisciplinary program in the humanities might come directly from the National Endowment for the Humanities. This constitutes **direct federal aid**. However, the National Endowment also provides significant funding to each state's endowment, and funding for this same program might come, then, from the state humanities council. This is **indirect federal funding**.

> **Federal Funding of Education**

Federal funds are not meant to support the schools but rather to improve and equalize educational opportunities for all students, and to encourage innovative programs within the public schools.

Federal funds frequently take the form of matching or seed-money grants. These require that state and local districts either match the amount supplied by the federal grant or extend the project funded by the federal government beyond the granted period. In this way, the federal government ensures state and local involvement in the project and its funding.

Many federal grants are **categorical**, meaning they must be spent for specific purposes. Hence, if money is received by a local school district to fund a Chapter I reading program through the Elementary and Secondary Education Act, the district must use the money to support this program and no other.

In 1981 Congress enacted the Educational Consolidation and Improvement Act (ECIA), which consolidated over forty categorical educational funding programs. Two-thirds of these funds had been distributed competitively. However, under ECIA, these funds are now awarded based on each state's share of the nation's school-aged population. Because of adjustments made for small states and territories, no state receives less than 0.5 percent of the total. Eighty percent of the funds flow through the state to local education agencies, rather than directly to local districts, and these must be distributed according to enrollment. The remaining 20 percent can be distributed by the states for discretionary use. These federal grants are called **block grants**. Many groups, particularly the Children's Defense Fund and the Lawyers' Committee for Civil Rights, have been critical of this consolidation. They contend that in the two years following the consolidation program, services for underprivileged children under Chapter I of the Elementary and Secondary Education Act (ESEA) declined because of decreased funding, decreased staff to monitor how funds were used, and increased flexibility in how states and school districts can use the funds. Proponents of ECIA contend that the block grant program cuts down on waste by reducing staff needed to monitor programs and gives states and districts more local control over federal funds.

(continued on p. 516)

CROSS-CULTURAL PERSPECTIVE

A Comparison of Educational Funding

There are numerous ways in which to compare educational spending. Figure 15.2 shows how the United States compares to other industrialized countries who belong to the Organization for Economic Development and Cooperation (OECD) in instructional expenditures per student. Using purchasing power parities (a method of equating currencies and comparing spending levels) as the basis to compare educational spending, the United States spends more per student than any country other than Switzerland, according to a report prepared by the Hudson Institute based on information provided by the U.S. Department of Education.

However, when comparisons are based on public expenditures for education as a percentage of the gross domestic product (GDP = current expenditures), the United States ranks eleventh among the same group of OECD nations, allocating 4.7 percent of GDP to elementary, secondary, and higher education, compared to an average of 5.4 percent in other OECD countries. Figure 15.3 illustrates the percentage of GDP spent by various countries on public education.

From: Perelman, May 1990

FIGURE 15-2

Instructional Expenditures per Student[1] (Pre-K through grade 12)

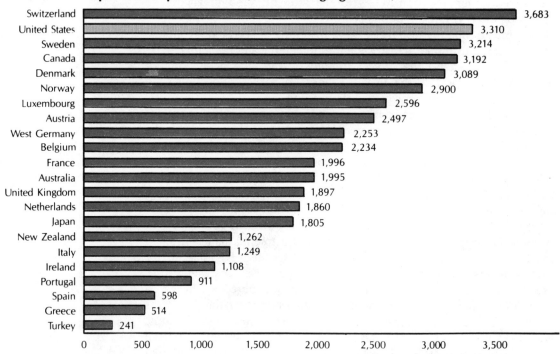

[1]Based on OECD 1985 purchasing power parities (PPP) index.

From: L. J. Perelman, *The "Acanemia" Deception*, Hudson Institute Briefing Paper (No. 120), (May 1990), 4.

When using a formula to equalize monetary exchange rates so that there is the same amount of purchasing power (purchasing power parities) among all the countries, the United States ranks second only to Switzerland in expenditures per student.

FIGURE 15-3

**Public Spending on Education as a Percent of Gross Domestic Product
(Current Expenditures)**

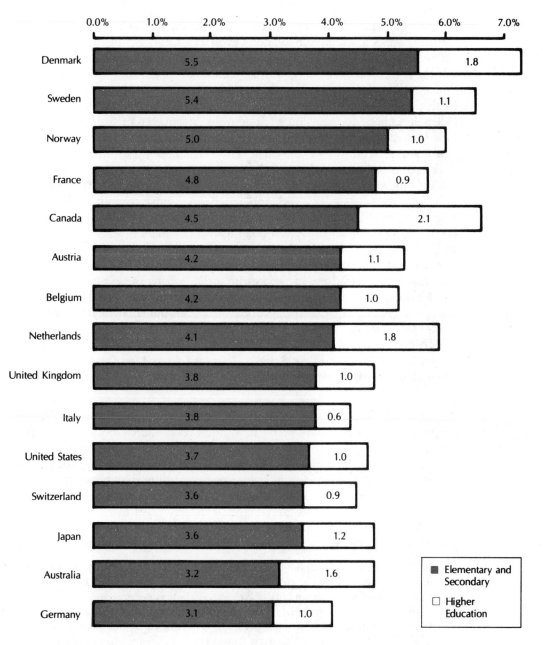

From: Research Department of AFT, *International Comparisons of Public Spending on Education,* February 1991, p. 13.

**When comparing expenditures for education as a percentage of the gross domestic product
(GDP), the United States ranks eleventh among the same group of OECD countries.**

To receive federal funds, even block grants, school districts must comply with federal regulations and guidelines. For example, if the federal government believes there are civil rights violations in a district receiving federal funds, the government may withhold these funds until the alleged violations have been investigated and remedied. Therefore, it can be said that federal funding is the carrot used to encourage school districts to comply with federal standards and guidelines.

In some cases, however, the federal government does more than extend a carrot. It seeks to enforce regulations even in educational institutions that do not receive federal categorical aid for specific programs. For example, Hillsdale College is a private institution in Michigan that has, since its founding in 1844, refused to accept any federal funds. Nonetheless, the U.S. Department of Health, Education, and Welfare (HEW) instituted legal proceedings against Hillsdale College for refusing to submit an "Assurance of Compliance" with Title IX, which is designed to prevent sex discrimination in federally assisted education programs and activities. HEW claimed that although Hillsdale College did not receive direct federal aid, its students received financial aid through four federally funded programs. Hence, according to HEW, Hillsdale indirectly received federal aid and, therefore, must comply with Title IX requirements. In August 1978, an Administrative Law Judge (ALJ) denied HEW's request for an order terminating federal financial assistance to Hillsdale's students, ruling that the regulations relating to the prohibition of sex discrimination in employment were invalid. However, the ALJ found that Hillsdale was a recipient of federal financial assistance because the money provided to Hillsdale's students by the federal government would have otherwise been provided by the college. Both the college and HEW filed exceptions to the ALJ's initial decision. In October 1979, the Reviewing Authority denied Hillsdale's exceptions and granted HEW's exceptions (*Hillsdale College v. Department of Health, Etc.*, 696 F.2d 418, 1982). This case exemplifies the control exerted by the federal government in education.

Courts, Legislatures, and Equalization of Funding	State and federal courts have examined inequities in school funding based on property taxation and have come to various conclusions about the constitutionality of the inequalities of educational opportunities that result. In the California Supreme Court case of *Serrano v. Priest* (5 C.3d 584, 487 P.2d 1241, 96 Cal. Rptr. 601, 1971), the plaintiffs contended that California's heavy reliance on property taxes to fund public education violated the students' Fourteenth Amendment, or equal protection, rights. Property taxes in Baldwin Park, for example, provided $577 per pupil, whereas the property taxes in Beverly Hills provided $1,232 per pupil. The court ruled in favor of the plaintiffs, stating:

> The California public school financing system . . . conditions the full entitlement to [education] on wealth, classifies its recipients on the basis of their collective affluence and makes the quality of a child's education depend upon the resources of his school district and ultimately upon the pocketbook of his parents. We find that such financing system as presently constituted is not necessary to the attainment of any compelling state interest. . . . [I]t denies to the plaintiffs and others similarly situated the equal protection of the laws.

However, in a similar case, *San Antonio Independent School District v. Rodriguez* (411 U.S. 1, 1973), the U.S. Supreme Court disagreed. The Court ruled that a funding system based on the local property tax, even though it provides only minimal educational opportunities to all students, is still constitutional. Justice White, supporting the majority opinion of the Court, stated:

> The method of financing public schools in Texas, as in almost every other state, has resulted in a system of public education that can fairly be described as chaotic and unjust. It does not follow, however, and I cannot find, that this system violates the Constitution of the United States.

In spite of the U.S. Supreme Court's ruling in the *Rodriguez* case, the Texas Supreme Court later found that the state's method of funding public schools violated the state's constitution in *Edgewood Independent School District v. Kirby* (777 S.W.2d, 391 Tex. 1989). The state constitution requires the legislature to "establish, support, and maintain an efficient system of public free schools." The judges ruled that the Texas aid system was unconstitutional: "Property-poor districts are trapped in a cycle of poverty from which there is no opportunity to free themselves. School districts must have substantially equal access to similar levels of tax effort." This ruling effectively overturned the 1973 *Rodriguez* decision in Texas. However, *Kirby* also confirms that each state will have to decide if its own system of funding public education is inequitable based on its own constitution, since the U.S. Supreme Court's ruling in the *Rodriguez* case moved jurisdiction in these matters to the state courts.

Numerous state legislatures have had to deal with the problem of providing equal educational opportunity in all districts. Because some costs such as administrators, facilities, instructional staff, and support services are fixed, small rural school districts tend to spend more per pupil than larger, more urban districts. To minimize the resulting inequities, some thirty states have modified their funding formulas to provide additional revenue to rural school districts. One of these states is Idaho. In 1990, however, this provision was challenged in the Idaho legislature. A proposed change in the district funding formula to give less to rural districts and more to large towns and city schools lost by a vote of 43 to 40, according to Idaho associate superintendent of finance and administration (phone conversation, June 27, 1991). However, in 1991, a suit by rural and larger school districts to determine whether there is "uniformity" and "thoroughness" in the funding formula, as provided by the Idaho State Constitution, was pending.

IN THE CLASSROOM

Camden, New Jersey, is the fourth-poorest city of more than 50,000 people in America. In 1985, nearly a quarter of its families had less than $5,000 annual income. Nearly 60 percent of its residents receive public assistance. Its children have the highest rate of poverty in the United States.

Once a commercial and industrial center for the southern portion of New Jersey—a single corporation, New York Shipyards, gave employment to 35,000 people during World War II—Camden now has little industry. There are 35,000 jobs in the entire city now, and most of them don't go to Camden residents. The largest employer, RCA, which once gave work to 18,000 people, has about 3,000 jobs today, but only 65 are held by Camden residents. Camden's entire property wealth of $250 million is less than the value of just one casino in Atlantic City.

The city has 200 liquor stores and bars and 180 gambling establishments, no movie theater, one chain supermarket, no new-car dealership, few restaurants other than some fast-food places. City blocks are filled with burnt-out buildings. Of the city's 2,200 public housing units, 500 are boarded up, although there is a three-year waiting list of homeless families. As the city's aged sewers crumble and collapse, streets cave in, but there are no funds to make repairs.

What is life like for children in this city?

To find some answers, I spent several days in Camden in the early spring of 1990. Because the city has no hotel, teachers in Camden arranged for me to stay nearby in Cherry Hill, a beautiful suburban area of handsome stores and costly homes. The drive from Cherry Hill to Camden takes about five minutes. It is like a journey between different worlds.

On a stretch of land beside the Delaware River in the northern part of Camden, in a neighborhood of factories and many abandoned homes, roughly equidistant from a paper plant, a gelatine factory and an illegal dumpsite, stands a school called Pyne Point Junior High.

In the evening, when I drive into the neighborhood to find the school, the air at Pyne Point bears the smell of burning trash. When I return the next day I am hit with a strong smell of ether, or some kind of glue, that seems to be emitted by the paper factory.

The school is a two-story building, yellow brick, its windows covered with metal grates, the flag on its flagpole motionless above a lawn that has no grass. Some 650 children, 98 percent of whom are black or Latino, are enrolled here.

The school nurse, who walks me through the building while the principal is on the phone, speaks of the emergencies and illnesses that she contends with. "Children come into school with rotting teeth," she says. "They sit in class, leaning on their elbows, in discomfort. Many kids have chronic and untreated illnesses. I had a child in here yesterday with diabetes. Her blood-sugar level was over 700. Close to coma level. . . ."

A number of teachers, says the nurse, who tells me that her children go to school in Cherry Hill, do not have books for half the students in their classes. "Black teachers in the building ask me whether I'd put up with this in Cherry Hill. I tell them I would not. But some of the parents here make no demands. They don't know how much we have in Cherry Hill, so they do not know what they're missing." . . .

Camden High School, which I visit the next morning, can't afford facilities for lunch, so 2,000 children leave school daily to obtain lunch elsewhere. Many do not bother to return. Nonattendance and dropout rates, according to the principal, are very high.

In a twelfth grade English class the teacher is presenting a good overview of nineteenth-century history in England. On the blackboard are these words: "Idealism . . . Industrialization . . . Exploitation . . . Laissez-faire. . . ." The teacher seems competent, but, in this room as almost everywhere in Camden, lack of funds creates a shortage of materials. Half the children in the classroom have no texts.

"What impresses me," the teacher says after the class is over, "is that kids get up at all and come to school. They're old enough to know what they are coming into." . . .

"President Bush," says Ruthie Green-Brown, principal of Camden High, when we meet later in her office, "speaks of his 'goals' and these sound very fine. He mentions preschool education—early childhood. Where is the money? We have children coming to kindergarten or to first grade who are starting out three years delayed in their development. They have had no preschool. Only a minute number of our kids have had a chance at Head Start. This is the *most* significant thing that you can do to help an urban child if your goal is to include that urban child in America. Do we *want* that child to be included?" (Kozol 1991, 137–142)

15.1 POINTS TO REMEMBER

- The share of local, state, and federal funding shifts depending on politics. The more liberal the federal government, the more likely it will assume a larger share of educational funding; the more conservative, the more likely it will assume less.
- Local governments assume a large share of the funding for public education, which is raised by property and personal property taxes.
- States use aid formulas to fund education. Flat grants are based on average daily attendance; equalization grants are based on the ability of the district to raise funds.
- School districts are not equally funded because poorer districts are unable to provide the same level of funding for education as wealthier districts. Often state formulas do not equalize the funding.
- Courts and legislatures are struggling to equalize educational funding. In some cases, the courts have ruled that property taxes are constitutional for funding schools; in others they have ruled them unconstitutional.
- The federal government has no responsibility to fund education but does so voluntarily through grants for special programs.
- Block grants are provided to the states by the federal government based on the average student population of the state.

TEACHERS AND THE LAW

In any society, the rights of the individual need to be protected. Thus, in the very special microcosm of society that is the classroom, both the rights of the teacher and the rights of the student are determined and legislated by court rulings and legal statutes.

Teachers are both protected by the law and responsible for upholding it. When we talk about the law, we are discussing several things. First, the law of the land is set forth in the U.S. Constitution. Second, the law of each state is established in that state's constitution. These comprise **constitutional law**. **Statutory law** refers to statutes passed by federal and state legislatures. And, finally, **law** refers to our system of jurisprudence, which defends our rights and secures justice in the courts.

Contract Law

State statutes grant to the local school board the decision to employ, assign, or transfer a certified teacher within the school district. A **contract** is an agreement between two or more competent parties to legally create, alter, or dissolve a relationship. A teacher's employment is based on a contract between the teacher and the school board, usually in writing. In order to be valid, contracts must meet certain requirements specified by state law and must have five basic elements: (1) an offer and acceptance, (2) competent parties, (3) consideration,

(4) legal subject matter, and (5) proper form. These requirements constitute *contract law.*

In order to be considered competent, parties must have the legal capacity to enter into a contract. These include a legal school board and a teacher who meets state certification requirements.

Consideration is what one party pays in return for services rendered by the other party. Teaching contracts include a designated salary, a period of time, and identified duties and responsibilities as part of this consideration.

Due Process All U.S. citizens have the constitutionally guaranteed right to **due process**, which protects us from arbitrary governmental action and unreasonable or discriminatory practices. These rights are protected by the Fifth and Fourteenth amendments. The Fifth Amendment states that "no person shall be compelled in any criminal case to be a witness against himself, nor be deprived of life, liberty, or property without due process of the law." The Fourteenth Amendment guarantees that no state shall "deny to any person within its jurisdiction the equal protection of the laws."

Frequently, due process decisions deal with the nonrenewal of teaching contracts. Disputes about contract violations are common in public education. Between 1985 and 1988, in three hundred of the nation's school districts, representing 2 percent of the districts and 6 percent of the pupils, 94 cases were filed by employees against the schools in the area of professional negotiations (Imber and Thompson 1991). In a famous precedent setting case, *Board of Regents v. Roth* (408 U.S. 564, 1972), the U.S. Supreme Court ruled that nontenured teachers who were dismissed at the end of a specified contract had no right to a statement of reasons or a hearing as long as regulations set by the institution and the state were followed.

Tenure is a contractual relationship between a teacher and a school board that can be terminated only for adequate cause and with due process. It is usually awarded after a specified probationary period, usually three to seven years, during which teachers are evaluated by administrators and/or peers. Tenure laws are set by the states and give discretionary power to grant tenure to local school boards. Tenure is a statutory (by law) right rather than a constitutional right, and, therefore, protections and procedures vary among states. Tenure does not give absolute job security to teachers; they may be dismissed for adequate cause, gross misconduct, neglect of duty, mental or physical incapacity, moral turpitude, or financial emergency. These causes are clearly identified by state law. In tenure cases, the courts have attempted to protect the rights of the teachers and at the same time maintain some flexibility for school districts in personnel matters.

Court cases based on an individual's due process rights attempt to establish fair procedures related to life, liberty, or property. For example, in *Board of Regents v. Roth,* the Court ruled that a state university which did not provide a pretermination hearing for a nontenured teacher hired on a fixed contract for one academic year did not violate his due process rights. According to the Court, the life, liberty, or property interests of this individual were not impaired, since he did not have property rights based on tenure or length of service. Therefore, the lack of a pretermination hearing, in this case, did not violate his due process rights.

However, in *Perry v. Sindermann* (408 U.S. 593, 1972), the Court ruled in favor of the plaintiff, who had taught in the Texas state college system for ten years without tenure. Sindermann, who was denied a due process hearing, claimed that he was dismissed because he publicly criticized the college administration. He further claimed that due to his length of service he had de facto tenure. The Court upheld Sindermann's right to a hearing with a statement that, if a case involved freedom of speech, a hearing must be provided. Furthermore, the Court agreed with Sindermann that he had valid property rights based on de facto tenure deriving from length of service.

Hence, the courts have ruled that teachers are entitled to due process of the law prior to dismissal if property rights or an infringement of liberty can be established. Roth established neither; Sindermann established both. Property rights, according to court rulings, are based on tenure, implied tenure, or contract. A liberty issue involves potential damage to the teacher's reputation.

Freedom of Expression

The First Amendment of the U.S. Constitution guarantees every citizen the right to freedom of speech, including the right to criticize government agencies, policies, and actions. In *Pickering v. Board of Education*, (391 U.S. 563, 1968), the U.S. Supreme Court clearly defined a teacher's First Amendment free speech rights.

Marvin Pickering, a high school teacher, published a letter criticizing the school board and superintendent about the way school funds were raised and spent. The school board claimed that his letter damaged its professional reputation and was detrimental to the administration and the operation of the school. Pickering was dismissed. An Illinois court ruled in favor of the school board. Pickering contended that he was protected by the First Amendment and took his case to the Supreme Court. The Court ruled that, although not all Pickering's contentions were correct, his expression of his opinions did not impede his teaching or the operation of the school, and Pickering was reinstated.

This case firmly established the right of teachers to express their opinions about schools and administrators publicly or privately. However, the case did not give teachers the unrestricted right to interfere with the operation of a school system. In cases of freedom of speech, the courts consider whether the action impedes the teacher's performance, undermines his or her effectiveness, or can be considered libelous or slanderous. According to the Pickering decision, "certain forms of public criticism of the superior by the subordinate would seriously undermine the effectiveness of the working relationship between them." Hence, the Court concluded, that discipline might be appropriate in such cases.

Academic Freedom

Academic freedom, protected by the First Amendment, is the right of teachers to speak freely about what they teach, to experiment with new teaching ideas or techniques, and to select appropriate material even though it may be controversial.

The Alabama case *Parducci v. Rutland* (316 F.Supp. 352, Mo., Ala., 1970), established guidelines for academic freedom. Marilyn Parducci assigned Kurt Vonnegut's "Welcome to the Monkey House" to her eleventh-grade class. After the assignment had been made, she was asked by the school administration not to teach the story. Parducci contended that it was of high literary quality, and she had the responsibility to teach it. Parducci was dismissed for assigning "disruptive" material and refusing the advice of her administrators. She claimed that her right to academic freedom was violated.

A federal court found that the school board "failed to show either that the assignment was inappropriate reading for high school juniors or that it created a significant disruption to the educational process." Because Parducci's First Amendment rights were violated, the court ruled that she be reinstated.

However, neither this case nor subsequent cases have guaranteed complete academic freedom. Teachers and librarians must be able to prove that the material or the methods do not interfere with school discipline and that they are appropriate to the age of the students. In fact, in many recent cases, the courts have ruled in favor of the administration (see chapter 14, pp. 479–481) to determine what can be taught and what material can be used.

Tort Liability

Tort liability is defined as a civil wrong perpetrated on the private rights of citizens and consists of three types: negligence, intentional torts, and strict liability. Most school-based court cases deal with negligence. In fact, according to the study "Developing a Typology of Litigation in Education and Determining the Frequency of Each Category," conducted by Michael Imber and Gary Thompson, more negligence suits were filed by students than any other kind. Between 1985 and 1988 in three hundred school districts, 821 negligence suits were filed by students and 131 by teachers (1991). **Negligence** is unacceptable conduct or care that results in personal injury. **Intentional torts** involve assault, battery, desire to inflict harm, and defamation. **Strict liability** occurs when injury results from unusual hazards. For example, strict liability might occur in a science laboratory in which chemicals are improperly stored and one or more students are injured as a result.

Negligence

Negligence may occur when a teacher fails to use proper standards and reasonable care to protect students or doesn't foresee potential harm in a situation and correct it. Negligence is contingent upon the age of the students, the environment, and the type of instructional activity.

Teachers can be found negligent if four things are proved. (1) The teacher had a responsibility to protect the student from injury. (2) The teacher failed to use due care. (3) The teacher's carelessness caused the injury. (4) The student sustained provable damages. Most states have laws that permit school boards to buy insurance to cover negligence assessed against the school district. Likewise, teachers are able to purchase their own liability insurance.

There are many examples of tort cases dealing with negligence. In 1967, a New Jersey child was seriously injured by a paper clip shot by another child on the school grounds prior to school. According to the case, *Clark v. Furch* (567 S.W.2d 451, Mo. App., 1978), children regularly gathered on the school grounds before classes. The court concluded that the principal was aware of the need for supervision during the time between the arrival of school buses and the beginning of school; however, he had not established rules for the students or

A teacher may be found negligent if she or he fails to take reasonable precautions when instructing students or supervising their activities. Not only must this physical education teacher explain how to play this game, but she must be alert to the movements of the students so they don't injure themselves or others.

secured adult supervisors to assist him. The court held that the principal was liable for damages.

In another case, a California student left school without permission and was struck by a motorcycle several blocks from the school. In *Hoyem v. Manhattan Beach School Dist.* (150 Cal. Rptr. 1, 585 P.2d 851, Cal., 1978), the trial court ruled that the school's responsibility ended when the child became truant. However, the California Supreme Court reversed the decision in saying that proper supervision might have prevented the student's truancy and serious injury.

Many negligence cases deal with teachers failing to use due care. In *Landers v. School Dist. No. 203, O'Fallon, Illinois* (383 N.E.2d 645, Ill. App., 1978), an Illinois appeals court ruled that a physical education teacher did not use a reasonable standard of care in requiring an overweight student to perform a backward somersault that resulted in injury. In *Brod v. School Dist. No. 1* (386 N.Y.S.2d 125, App. Div., 1976), a teacher was found negligent when a student was injured trying to complete a high jump at a level considerably higher than he had been able to complete before. Another teacher was found negligent for allowing two male students, one of whom was fatally injured, to participate in a boxing match without prior training while the teacher sat in the bleachers (*LaValley v. Stanford*, 70 N.Y.S.2d 460, App. Div., 1947).

Teachers have successfully defended themselves against negligence suits when they have been able to prove that the child was aware of or should have been aware of the consequences of the actions, but nonetheless participated in the activity. This is known as *contributory negligence*. In these cases the courts attempt to determine whether the teacher has provided due care in anticipating dangers and in warning students against them. In North Carolina, for example, an industrial arts teacher was found not liable when a deaf student injured his eyes while trying to add oil to a hydraulic lift. The court ruled that the teacher did not owe this student greater due care because of his deafness, and since the teacher had instructed the student in the rules of safety, he had provided an appropriate standard of care. The student should have known, based on the teacher's instruction, that the hydraulic lift was to be left alone (*Payne v. Department of Human Resources*, 382 S.E.2d 449, N.C. Ct. App., 1989).

Intentional Torts

Although negligence is the most common tort case filed against schools and educators, cases of assault and battery are not uncommon. In most instances, they involve corporal punishment, but no actual physical contact need take place. *Assault* is an overt attempt to cause fear of physical harm; when assault leads to physical injury, **battery** is committed.

If, however, a teacher uses reasonable force with students, the courts will often rule in favor of the teacher. For example, in *Simms v. School Dist. No. 1* (508 P.2d 236, Ore. App., 1973), a teacher held the arms of a student, leading him toward the door after he refused to leave the room. The student swung at the teacher, thereby breaking a window and injuring his arm. The court ruled that the teacher had used reasonable force with the student and, therefore, had not

---

VIEWPOINTS

Some Types of Negligence Lawsuits Brought Against Teachers and Schools

1. The teacher's lesson plans, left for a substitute, failed to warn of the mischievous nature of a particular student.
2. A physical education teacher failed to warn high school students enrolled in his gym class that there were dangers in the sport of boxing.
3. An elementary school teacher failed to inspect and warn students of potentially dangerous or faulty playground equipment.
4. A school district did not publish rules of bicycle safety.
5. A teacher made a derogatory statement about the conduct of a pupil's parent.
6. Students in an auto repair shop did not check the gas tank before welding on a car.
7. A student died as a result of injuries of unknown causes suffered behind the school building at an after-school dance.
8. The guard [safety device] on a saw in the machine shop was defective.
9. A student attacked a fellow student in the hall during passing time.
10. A delinquent student stabbed a classmate in a classroom before school.
11. A teacher assigned a task that a student was too immature or inexperienced to carry out successfully.
12. A teacher sent a pupil on errands and used the pupil as a student helper to open windows.

From: Cobb 1981, 83–84

committed assault or battery. In other cases a court has ruled in favor of the student. In *Frank v. Orleans Parish School Bd.* (195 So.2d 451, La. App., 1967), for example, a teacher was convicted of assault and battery and the court assessed damages against him when he shook a student against bleachers in a gymnasium and the student sustained a broken arm. The court ruled that the teacher's actions were unnecessary to discipline the student or to protect himself.

Copyright Law

In 1978 P.L. 94-553 (Title 17 USC-copyrights), General Revision of the Copyright Law, completely amended Title 17 of the United States Code, which was adopted in 1909. This recent federal statute has important implications for teachers and schools.

The intent of the copyright law is to promote the creation and dissemination of knowledge and ideas. This intent was established in the U.S. Constitution article I, section 8, clause 8. Today, the phrase "to promote the progress of science and useful arts, by securing for limited times to authors and inventors the exclusive right to their respective writings and discoveries" is broadly interpreted to mean that those individuals who produce artistic and intellectual work should have their financial interests protected by prohibiting others from copying or misusing the work.

The law attempts to balance the interests of the copyright owner and those of the public. The difficulty is in balancing the rights of authors, artists, and scholars who desire to protect their works with the rights of teachers and librarians to disseminate the works. If the law balances these interests, then it encourages both creation and dissemination. Conflicts often arise.

To ensure the fair dissemination of knowledge and ideas, the 1978 copyright law established the concept of **fair use**, which is the right to use copyrighted material in a reasonable manner without the permission of the author. The statute established four criteria for determining whether fair use applies to a particular instance of copying:

1. the purpose and character of the use, including whether such use is of a commercial nature or is for nonprofit educational purposes
2. the nature of the copyrighted work
3. the amount and substantiality of the portion used in relation to the copyrighted work as a whole
4. the effect of the use upon the potential market for or value of the copyrighted work. (Section 107 of P.L. 94-553)

Because of the general nature of these particular criteria, the House Judiciary Committee report (House Report 94-1476) established guidelines for interpreting fair use (see table 15.2).

The fair use concept was tested in the case of *Marcus v. Rowley* (695 F.2d 1171, 1983). In this case a home economics teacher, Eloise Marcus, wrote a thirty-five-page booklet on cake decorating. She copyrighted the booklet and sold most of the 123 copies she had made for $2 each to students in her adult education cake-decorating class. Shirley Rowley took Marcus's class and later developed a Learning Activities Package (LAP) for her high school food-service career classes. Fifteen of the pages in Rowley's twenty-four page unit were copied from Marcus's booklet without permission for use with her students. Rowley had fifteen copies made to use with her students on a nonprofit basis.

TABLE 15-2

Guidelines for Photocopying Material

I. Single Copying for Teachers

A single copy may be made of any of the following by or for a teacher at his or her individual request for his or her scholarly research or use in teaching or preparation to teach a class:

A. A chapter from a book;
B. An article from a periodical or newspaper;
C. A short story, short essay or short poem, whether or not from a collective work;
D. A chart, graph, diagram, drawing, cartoon or picture from a book, periodical, or newspaper.

II. Multiple Copies for Classroom Use

Multiple Copies (not to exceed in any event more than one copy per pupil in a course) may be made by or for the teacher giving the course for classroom use or discussion, provided that:

A. The copying meets the tests of brevity and spontaneity as defined below; and,
B. Meets the cumulative effect test as defined below; and,
C. Each copy includes a notice of copyright.

Definitions
  Brevity
  (i) Poetry: (a) A complete poem if less than 250 words and if printed on not more than two pages, or (b) from a longer poem, an excerpt of not more than 250 words.
  (ii) Prose: (a) Either a complete article, story or essay of less than 2,500 words, or (b) an excerpt from any prose work of not more than 1,000 words or 10 percent of the work, whichever is less, but in any event a minimum of 500 words.

[Each of the numerical limits stated in *i* and *ii* above may be expanded to permit the completion of an unfinished line of a poem or of an unfinished prose paragraph.]

  (iii) Illustration: One chart, graph, diagram, drawing, cartoon or picture per book or per periodical issue.
  (iv) "Special" works: Certain works in poetry, prose or in "poetic prose" which often combine language with illustrations and which are intended sometimes for children and at other times for a more general audience fall short of 2,500 words in their entirety. Paragraph *ii* above notwithstanding, such "special works" may not be reproduced in their entirety; however, an excerpt comprising not more than two of the published pages of such special work and containing not more than 10 percent of the words found in the text thereof, may be reproduced.

Spontaneity
  (i) The copying is at the instance and inspiration of the individual teacher, and
  (ii) The inspiration and decision to use the work and the moment of its use for maximum teaching effectiveness are so close in time that it would be unreasonable to expect a timely reply to a request for permission.

Cumulative Effect
  (i) The copying of the material is for only one course in the school in which the copies are made.
  (ii) Not more than one short poem, article, story, essay or two excerpts may be copied from the same author, nor more than three from the same collective work or periodical volume during one class term.
  (iii) There shall not be more than nine instances of such multiple copying for one course during one class term.

[The limitations stated in *ii* and *iii* above shall not apply to current news periodicals and newspapers and current news sections of other periodicals.]

III. Prohibitions as to I and II Above

Notwithstanding any of the above, the following shall be prohibited:

A. Copying shall not be used to create or to replace or substitute for anthologies, compilations or collective works. Such replacement or substitution may occur whether copies of various works or excerpts therefrom are accumulated or reproduced and used separately.

B. There shall be no copying of or from works intended to be "consumable" in the course of study or of teaching. These include workbooks, exercises, standardized tests and test booklets and answer sheets and like consumable material.

C. Copying shall not:
   (a) substitute for the purchase of books, publishers' reprints or periodicals;
   (b) be directed by higher authority;
   (c) be repeated with respect to the same item by the same teacher from term to term.

D. No charge shall be made to the student beyond the actual cost of the photocopying.

From: House Judiciary Committee, House Report 94-1476, *Congressional Record*, (Washington, DC: U.S. Government Printing Office, September 22, 1976), 68–70.

The intent of the copyright law is to protect both the rights of students to learn and the rights of artists and writers who produced the work. The concept of fair use allows reasonable dissemination of the work. Guidelines for interpreting fair use have been established by the House Judiciary Committee.

Marcus sued for copyright infringement. The appellate court concluded, "The fair use doctrine does not apply to these facts. . . . Rowley's LAP work, which was used for the same purpose as plaintiff's booklet, was quantitatively and qualitatively a substantial copy of plaintiff's booklet with no credit given to plaintiff. Under these circumstances, neither the fact that the defendant used the plaintiff's booklet for nonprofit educational purposes nor the fact that plaintiff suffered no pecuniary damage as a result of Rowley's copying supports a finding of fair use."

Applying the 1978 copyright law to computers, audiovisual materials, and off-the-air taping is another complex issue. In 1980, amendments dealing with the copyright of computer software were added to the law. Making even a single copy of a computer program that is designed for a single user, without a license to do so, violates the law. Even booting up a series of microcomputers with one disk, enabling numerous students to access a program intended for a single user, is illegal. Likewise, it is illegal to make a copy of a software program acquired for preview purposes. However, computer software owners are permitted to make a single copy of a disk for archival purposes.

To understand which uses of audiovisual materials are permitted under the copyright law, teachers must know the meaning of the terms *display* and *perform*. **Display** means to show individual frames of a film or videotape, while **perform** means to run the entire work through a projector or recorder. Teachers may display individual images or perform a work for nonprofit educational purposes as long as the copy was not unlawfully made. To be displayed or performed legally, a work must be part of the instruction by teachers or guest lecturers in an educational, face-to-face setting with students, and it must be a legitimate copy. If, however, a videotape displays the label, "Warning: For Home Use Only," it may be used only in the home.

In 1981 the House Subcommittee on the Courts, Civil Liberties, and the Administration of Justice developed guidelines for off-the-air recording of broadcast programs. The major limitations for use of videotapes in educational settings are that they can be kept for not more than forty-five calendar days after the recording date, at which time the tapes must be erased. They may be shown to students only within the first ten school days of the forty-five day period.

STUDENTS AND THE LAW

Statutes and court rulings also apply to students' rights and responsibilities. First and foremost, students have the right to attend a school that provides each of them an equal educational opportunity. Some educators contend that students also have the right to achieve at a predetermined minimal level as established by the state. Students' rights to freedom of expression, of assembly, and of religion are also protected by the First Amendment, and they have the right to due process in decisions of suspension or expulsion. The parents of students under the age of eighteen have the right of access to their children's school records. Along with these rights, however, students have the responsibility to ensure that their health and behavior do not endanger others. To this end, the state and the school establish laws and rules of discipline and behavior that must be enforced in order to ensure that all students are protected.

Equal Educational Opportunity

The Fourteenth Amendment of the U.S. Constitution guarantees in part that "no State shall . . . deny to any person within its jurisdiction, the equal protection of the laws." Since the 1954 *Brown v. Board of Education of Topeka* (347 U.S. 483, 1954) case, the Supreme Court has ruled that this equal protection clause applies to education. Chapter 6 (pp. 170–178) discusses at length the courts' and legislatures' interpretation of equal educational opportunity.

School Attendance and Student Health

All fifty states have compulsory attendance laws that include penalties for noncompliance. Compulsory attendance requires that all students up to a specified age be educated whether they attend a private or public school or whether they are simply tutored or taught in informal settings, provided the instructors are qualified by the state.

In most states, schools have the right to require that all students be in good health so as not to endanger others. For this reason states have the right to require that all students have specific immunizations.

Even though decisions about whether students can attend school are made by boards of education and the states, parents often object to them. In recent AIDS cases, for example, some parents have questioned whether children with the disease should be allowed to attend school. The federal Centers for Disease Control stresses that AIDS is transmitted only through contact with infected blood or semen and not through ordinary contact with an infected person; therefore, they have recommended, and the courts have agreed, that most AIDS victims be allowed to attend school.

In order to protect the health of its students, schools can require that all students receive certain immunizations. Students with AIDS have presented special problems in many school systems because there is as yet no immunization to protect people against acquiring this disease. And while it can be transmitted only in very limited, specific ways, people have deep-seated, if irrational, fears about it. Ryan White, for example, when he lived in Komomo, Indiana, was forced to stay home and take his classes over a telephone hookup to his school. His mother, Jeanne, assists him.

The law, however, has little control over people's emotions, especially when they involve children and a fatal disease, as demonstrated by the highly publicized cases of Ryan White and the Ray brothers. In Kokomo, Indiana, thirteen-year-old Ryan White, a hemophiliac infected with the AIDS virus, was banned from school. He moved to Cicero, Indiana, where the school and his new classmates welcomed him. In Arcadia, Florida, on August 28, 1987, the home of the Rays was burned to the ground by local people angered that the Rays were sending their three HIV-infected (human immunodeficiency virus), hemophiliac sons to the public schools. Other children infected with AIDS, however, are welcomed into the schools. In Swansea, Massachusetts, an HIV-infected hemophiliac was not only accepted into the school but supported by his friends and neighbors. In Wilmette, Illinois, the parents of a boy with AIDS won over other parents by inviting them into their home and asking for their help. In Chicago, the Mexican-American parents of children in Pilsen Academy initially demonstrated against the school system's decision to allow an anonymous HIV-infected child to attend. Later, however, after receiving information about AIDS from principal William Levin, the parents approved the decision of the board.

Because the issue of AIDS is such an emotional one, many communities have been unable to solve the problems it causes without the involvement of the courts. In some cases, nervous school officials have been unwilling to admit

HIV-infected students into the school without a court order. In other cases, such as the White case in Kokomo, the courts have ruled that the child must be readmitted. Almost unanimously, judges have ruled in favor of the right of the child with AIDS to attend school (Kirp and Epstein 1989, 587).

Curriculum   The courts have ruled that the states not only have the right to develop curriculum as long as federal constitutional guarantees are respected, but also have the right to monitor whether that curriculum is being implemented in the public and private schools of the state. Although few states have constitutional curriculum mandates, most require the state legislatures to make specific curricular determinations. These include:

- Specific topics such as the federal Constitution
- Certain subjects such as U.S. history
- Specific subjects appropriate for the grade level
- Vocational and bilingual education
- Special education for students with disabilities
- Specific subjects required for high school graduation
- Minimal acceptable performance levels for high school graduation

Most legislatures assign the actual development of the curriculum to the state education agency. State statutes usually requires that local boards of education offer the state-mandated minimum curriculum and allows them to supplement it based on local needs unless there is a statutory prohibition. The state education agency usually monitors the board's delivery of the curriculum in local schools.

Challenges to the Curriculum

Parents have frequently challenged the curriculum and materials used by the schools, especially when they deal with sex education. However, the courts have ruled in favor of the board's right to establish such courses based on the state's interest in the health and welfare of its children (*Aubrey v. School District of Philadelphia*, 63 Pa. Cmwlth. 330, 437 A.2d 1306, 1981). Likewise, the right to teach mandatory sex education courses has been upheld even when parents have maintained that they violated their religious beliefs (*Cornwell v. State Board of Education*, 314 F.Supp. 340, D., Md., 1969).

Although most states do not select a single text, most develop a list of acceptable books from which local districts may adopt books. Many cases have challenged the right of local boards to prescribe textbooks. One of the best-known cases, in part because of the violence that surrounded it, took place in Kanawha County, West Virginia, in 1974. Parents protested the board's adoption of an English series that they considered to be godless, communist, and profane. The federal court upheld the school board's right to select books to be used in the schools (*Williams v. Board of Educ. of County of Kanawha*, 388 F.Supp. 93, S.D., W.Va., 1975). See chapter 14, pp. 479–481, for other cases related to censorship of school-related material and For Further Reading/Reference at the end of this chapter for a description of J. Moffett's book that describes this case.

The courts have ruled against curricular requirements that they believe limit an individual's constitutional rights. For example, courts have ruled against legislatures that have attempted to ban specific courses from the curriculum. The first such case occurred in 1923, when the U.S. Supreme Court ruled that the state of Nebraska could not prohibit the teaching of a foreign language in any private or public schools to children who had not yet completed eighth grade. According to the Court, the teacher's right to teach private elementary school students reading in German, the parents' right to employ the teacher to instruct their children, and the children's right to learn were protected under the due process clause of the Fourteenth Amendment (*Meyer v. Nebraska*, 262 U.S. 390, 1923). In 1968 the Court ruled against an Arkansas law that prohibited teaching Darwin's theory of evolution in the public schools, as a violation of the teachers' and students' First Amendment rights (*Epperson v. Arkansas*, 393 U.S. 97, 106, 1968).

Student Achievement

Since the states have been given the right to require attendance and to establish and monitor the curriculum, the public has demanded that schools assume greater responsibility for student achievement. This **accountability** has led to an increased number of educational malpractice suits in which the schools are considered liable for nonachievement of students. Often nonachievement is determined by minimum competency testing programs.

For example, in *Peter W. v. San Francisco Unified School District* (60 Cal. App.3d 814, 131 Cal. Rptr. 854, 1976), a student maintained that the school was negligent in teaching, promoting, and graduating him since he read at only a fifth-grade level. He claimed that his lack of achievement was misrepresented to his parents, who didn't know of his deficiency until he was tested by a private agency after graduation. However, both the trial court and appellate court dismissed charges against the school based on the complexities of the teaching and learning process. This, so far, has been the tenor of all educational malpractice decisions.

Although the schools are unlikely to be held accountable by the courts for specified levels of student achievement, these decisions have clearly indicated that schools can be expected to be accountable for accurately diagnosing student needs and keeping parents informed of student progress. Furthermore, in cases dealing with students with disabilities, the courts have ruled that the school must be able to prove that it is providing appropriate remedial services for them.

Another result of public outcries for academic accountability has been the implementation of competency testing. These proficiency exams, which are now administered in most states, are designed to show that students have achieved basic verbal and computational skills at the time of high school graduation.

Because competency tests were developed to ensure that all students were getting at least a basic education, it is ironic that in the court cases involving competency tests, people have claimed that the tests are discriminatory. For example, in Florida, ten black students who failed the test challenged the law authorizing the test, claiming that the test discriminated against minority students. According to evidence presented in the case, 77 percent of black students failed the math portion of the test compared to 24 percent of white students. Likewise, 26 percent of black students, compared to 3 percent of white students, failed the communication section of the test. The students further claimed that they were not given enough warning to prepare for the test. The court ruled that the test could be used for remedial purposes but not as a prerequisite for graduation until a phase-in period was implemented to prepare students for the test. Although the court disallowed the competency test for graduation purposes, it upheld the state's right to establish academic standards.

Freedom of Expression and Assembly

First Amendment constitutional guarantees of free speech extend to students, as well as to teachers. The U.S. Supreme Court ruled in a landmark free speech decision, *Tinker v. Des Moines Independent School District* (393 U.S. 503, 1969), that the plaintiffs, three public school students, could not be suspended from school for wearing black armbands to class to protest the government's policy in Vietnam. The decision stated that school officials could infringe on students' free speech rights only when the students' opinion and expression thereof materially and substantially interfered with the operation of the school. This includes such behavior as excessive noise, agitation, sit-ins, deliberate disruption of school functions, blocking halls, boycotts, and speech intended to incite disruptive action. The courts have further established that any regulation prohibiting student expression must be specific, publicized, and uniformly applied without discrimination. The ruling in this case became a precedent for other freedom of expression cases that dealt with issues such as distribution of controversial literature and publication of controversial topics in school newspapers (see also chapter 14, p. 481).

In recent years the courts have ruled in favor of the school's right to edit or limit student free expression when students are participating in school-sponsored events. These decisions have focused on an educator's right to control the "style and content of student speech in school-sponsored expressive activities so long as their actions are reasonably related to legitimate pedagogical concerns" (*Hazelwood School District v. Kuhlmeier*, 484 U.S. 260, 1988). In the Hazelwood case, the school principal had forbidden students to print two pages of a school paper, produced as a part of a journalism class, that dealt with student pregnancy and drug use. The Supreme Court ruled that this action did not offend the First Amendment free speech rights since the principal had the right to exercise "editorial control over class material." A Tennessee high school student made fun of a school administrator while delivering a speech as a candidate for student council president. The principal removed his name from the school's ballot. The courts ruled that the principal was exercising appropriate control over student expression in a school-sponsored event (*Poling v. Murphy*, 872 F.2d 757, 6th Cir., 1989).

The courts have also upheld students' right to assembly, based on First Amendment freedoms. This has generally been interpreted to mean that, as long as the operation of the school is not disrupted, students have the right to meet in groups and distribute petitions. School officials can control the time and place of student meetings and circulation of materials, and these rules must be specific, publicized, and uniformly applied.

For example, in *Healy v. James* (408 U.S. 169, 1972), a group of college students, following guidelines, petitioned to have a local chapter of the controversial national organization SDS recognized by the college. (Students for a Democratic Society was an organization actively involved in the student demonstrations of the 1960s and 1970s.) The Student Affairs Committee approved their application, but it was rejected by the college president. The group

The U.S. Supreme Court in *Tinker v. Des Moines Independent School District* (393 U.S. 503, 1969) ruled that the school's right to restrict a student's freedom of expression extends only to behavior that substantially interferes with the normal operation of the school. Mary Beth Tinker and her brother John were instrumental in causing this decision when they and three other students wore black armbands to school to protest the government's policy in Vietnam and to mourn the war dead.

took its case to court based on the denial of First Amendment rights of expression and association arising from denial of campus recognition. Two lower courts ruled that the college had a right to refuse recognition to any group "likely to cause violent acts of disruption" (319 F. Supp. 113, 116). However, the Supreme Court reversed the decision, ruling that not recognizing the group was a violation of the students' rights of free expression and association.

Freedom of Religion

The First Amendment provides two protections of religious freedom. First, the government may not enact legislation establishing a religion and, second, may not interfere with an individual's right to practice her or his religion. The courts have interpreted these freedoms in the schools by ruling that reciting prayers and reading the Bible in school constitute an attempt on the part of the state to establish a religion and violate the religious freedom of those students who oppose the practice.

In 1963, two separate families challenged a Pennsylvania law requiring the reading of ten biblical verses and the recitation of the Lord's Prayer in school, even though their children could be excused from the exercise. In *Abington School District v. Schempp* (374 U.S. 203, 1963) and *Murray v. Curlett* (374 U.S. 203, L.Ed. 2d 844, 83 S.Ct. 1560, 1963), the Supreme Court ruled that it is unconstitutional for a state law to promote religion on school grounds, even when participation is not compulsory.

Access to Student Records

The U.S. Supreme Court has maintained that a right to "liberty" includes a right to "privacy." What this means in terms of students' school records has been the source of controversy.

In many cases, the courts have ruled that potentially damaging information must be expunged from the student's record. In 1974, the U.S. Congress passed the Buckley amendment to the Family Educational Rights and Privacy Act (FERPA), also called the "sunshine law," which stipulates that federal funds may be withdrawn from schools that (1) fail to provide parents with access to their child's records or (2) disseminate information to third parties without parental permission. Parents must also be given the right to a hearing to challenge what is in their child's records. However, a teacher's daily records pertaining to student progress are exempted from the law, as long as the records are in sole possession of the teacher.

Student Discipline

The law is clear in authorizing the state and the schools to establish and enforce rules that protect the property rights of students, to ensure that all students can learn, and to protect students' rights and freedoms. But, historically, the courts have rarely reviewed school disciplinary action. They have instead upheld the right and duty of educators to maintain reasonable discipline. But they have provided guidelines defining appropriate standards for student discipline. In *Public School Law: Teachers' and Students' Rights* (1981), Martha M. McCarthy and Nelda H. Cambron summarize these guidelines:

1. Any conduct regulation adopted should be necessary in order to carry out the school's educational mission; rules should not be designed merely to satisfy preferences of school board members, administrators, or teachers.
2. The rules should be publicized to students and their parents.
3. The rules should be specific and clearly stated so that students know which behaviors are prohibited.
4. The regulations should not infringe on constitutionally protected rights unless there is an overriding public interest to justify the infringement, such as a threat to the safety of other students.
5. A rule should not be *ex post facto* [formulated after the fact]; it should not be promulgated to prevent a specific activity that school officials know is being planned or has already occurred.
6. The regulations should be consistently enforced and uniformly applied to all students without discrimination.
7. Punishments should be appropriate to the offense, taking into consideration the child's age, sex, mental condition, and past behavior.
8. Some procedural safeguards should accompany the administration of all punishments; the formality of the procedures should be in accord with the severity of the punishment. (p. 286)

Corporal Punishment

The U.S. Supreme Court has held **corporal punishment** (physical contact such as striking, paddling, or spanking of a student by an educator) to be constitutional where state law and local board policy permit it. Corporal punishment is statutorily disallowed in Hawaii, Massachusetts, and New Jersey. In California, Illinois, and Montana, educators must get parental permission prior to administering corporal punishment. In other states, such as New York, local districts are permitted to make their own decisions about whether to use corporal punishment and establish how it should be administered. Thus, although corporal punishment is permitted in New York State, New York City prohibits it.

Challenges to the school's right to use corporal punishment on the basis of violation of a student's Fifth or Fourteenth Amendment due process rights are rarely successful. For example, a sixth-grade student was paddled twice by a coach after he was found playing dodgeball when he had been told not to. The coach had warned the student twice and administered the punishment with two witnesses present. A doctor found no physical injury to the student. However, the father filed suit. The lower court and the appeals court found no substantive due process violation (*Wise v. Pea Ridge School Dist.*, 855 F.2d 560, 8th Cir., 1988). Even in a case in which doctors found that the children involved had suffered bruises, the courts ruled in favor of the school. In *Cunningham v. Beavers* (858 F.2d, 5th Cir., 1988), kindergarten students were paddled twice, once by the teacher and once by the principal, for refusing to stop "snickering." After the second paddling they missed six days of school. However, the courts found that their due process rights were not violated.

Search and seizure is an area in which the courts have generally ruled in favor of the school rather than the student. Many of the cases in this area have resulted from the confiscation of drugs from student lockers and have been based on the Fourth Amendment, which protects "individuals against arbitrary searches by requiring state agents to obtain a warrant based on probable cause prior to conducting a search." However, the courts have generally ruled that school officials have the right to search student lockers and personal effects both for educational purposes and for contraband (particularly alcohol, drugs, and weapons) that will disrupt the operation of the school. The search must be based on reasonable suspicion.

Search and Seizure

For example, *New Jersey v. T.L.O.* (469 U.S. 325, 1985) concerned a student whose purse had been searched for cigarettes. When marijuana and evidence that the student was selling drugs were found, the school imposed sanctions on her. Even though her attorney sought to have them removed on the grounds that they violated the student's Fourth Amendment rights, the Supreme Court affirmed the right of the school to search a student based on "reasonable suspicion." The Court further maintained that searches must be "reasonably related to the objectives of the search and not excessively intrusive in light of the age and sex of the student and the nature of the infraction."

Reasonableness is determined by the search methods employed by the school and the extent to which the search is personally intrusive. Bodily searches and searches of locked cars on school grounds require stricter standards. In *Jennings v. Joshua Indep. School Dist.* (869 F.2d 870, superseded, 877 F.2d 313, 5th Cir., 1989), dogs were used to search for drugs in the school parking lot. When one of the search dogs sniffed out a car, the well-publicized policy stated that the student would be asked to open it. If the student refused, a parent would be summoned. If the parent refused, the police would be called. When, after these steps were followed, one student's father refused to open the car, the police took over. After a search warrant was issued and the car searched, nothing was found. The father subsequently sued the school and the police officer. A district court dismissed the complaint against the school, and a jury returned a verdict in favor of the police officer.

Since drug tests involving the use of urine or blood specimens constitute a search under terms of the Fourth Amendment, the courts have been called to rule in cases involving drug tests of interscholastic athletes. In *Schaill v. Tippecanoe County School Corp.* (679 F.Supp. 833, N.D., Ind., 1988), the court upheld the right of the school to administer drug tests to students wishing to compete in interscholastic athletics. In this case, the courts did not require that reasonable suspicion exist, as in other search cases.

Although the courts have ruled in favor of the administration in many of these cases, they have done so for different reasons. In some instances, the courts have ruled that school officials are not state agents but private individuals, and, therefore, the Fourth Amendment is not applicable. In other cases, school officials have been considered state agents, but the courts have applied the rule of *in loco parentis*, meaning that the school has rights in place of parents.

Despite court rulings supporting administrators in searching lockers and personal effects, McCarthy and Cambron maintain that schools should adhere to the following guidelines before conducting searches:

1. If police officials are conducting a search in the school, either with or without the school's involvement, school authorities should ensure that a search warrant is obtained.
2. Students and parents should be informed at the beginning of the school term of the procedures for conducting locker searches and personal searches.
3. Before school personnel conduct a search, the student should be asked to turn over the contraband, as such voluntary submission of material can eliminate the necessity for a search.
4. The authorized person conducting a search should have another staff member present who can verify the procedures used in the search.
5. School personnel should refrain from using strip searches or mass searches of groups of students.
6. Any search should be based on at least "reasonable belief" or "suspicion" that the student is in possession of contraband that may be disruptive to the educational process. (pp. 307–308)

15.2 POINTS TO REMEMBER

- Constitutional law is based on the U.S. and state constitutions; statutory law is based on legislation.
- Contract law relates to agreements between two or more competent parties. Teachers enter into contracts with boards of education when they are employed.
- The due process rights of teachers relate to the contractual relationship between the teacher and the board. Tenured teachers have the right to a statement of reasons and a hearing should their contract be terminated.
- Academic freedom, related to the First Amendment right of free speech, is the right to speak freely about what to teach and to experiment with new teaching techniques.

- Tort liability is a civil wrong. Negligence is one type of tort liability that relates to unacceptable conduct or care resulting in personal injury. Negligence is the most common case brought against teachers.
- Copyright law is designed to both protect and disseminate knowledge and ideas. Teachers must balance their right to disseminate knowledge with the obligation to protect copyrighted material.
- All states have compulsory attendance laws. In addition, states and local boards have the right to decide who can attend school based on health and immunization. The AIDS epidemic has required that school boards carefully examine their policies.

- Students, based on recent court rulings, have the right to expect at least a basic level of achievement. In addition, parents have the right to obtain access to their children's school records.
- In earlier court decisions, the courts tended to rule in favor of the students' right to freedom of speech. Recently, however, courts have ruled in favor of educators' rights to limit free speech if it is judged to be potentially disruptive.
- In search and seizure cases, particularly those related to drugs, the courts have ruled in favor of the right of administrators to conduct searches if there is reasonable suspicion.

FOR THOUGHT/DISCUSSION

1. Do you believe educational opportunities would be better equalized in all school districts if the federal government controlled all revenue allocated to the schools, or if each state controlled its own revenue?

2. If you feel uncomfortable in the presence of someone with AIDS, and if a child with AIDS was assigned to your class, how would you deal with the child to make him or her feel comfortable and welcome? How would you deal with the rest of the class?

3. If *Pickering v. Board of Education* guarantees a teacher's First Amendment rights, how far could you go in publicly criticizing the administration in your school?

4. If you were on duty in the school yard during recess carefully watching the students and one child tripped another resulting in a chipped front tooth, would you be considered negligent? Why or why not?

5. If you suspect one of your students is selling illegal drugs during lunchtime, what steps would you take to see that it stopped?

FOR FURTHER READING/REFERENCE

Alexander, K., and Alexander, M. D. 1984. *The law of the schools, students and teachers in a nutshell.* St. Paul, MN: West Publishing Company. A categorization and synthesis of the legal aspects of schools, students, and teachers. Attendance, the instructional program, due process, freedom of speech and expression, search and seizure, student discipline, people with disabilities, sex discrimination, terms of teacher employment, and teachers' constitutional rights are discussed.

Hartman, W. T. 1988. *School district budgeting.* Englewood Cliffs, NJ: Prentice-Hall. Identification of varying aspects of budgeting at the local level from conception to adoption, from practical to political, together with choices that must be weighed, made, and implemented. The author also discusses how budgeting affects the classroom teacher.

Honeyman, D., Wood, C., and Thompson, D. (Special Eds.). 1988. *Journal of Education Finance* 13 (4), 349–511. This special edition has thirteen articles on school funding in selected states and in the province of Manitoba. Disparities in district spending are discussed in two articles.

Moffett, J. 1988. *Storm in the mountains: A case study of censorship, conflict, and consciousness.* Carbondale: Southern Illinois University Press. A case study of the 1974 Kanawha County, West Virginia, censorship case, in which Moffett was a major player as one of the coauthors of the attacked language arts series. He describes the case from the viewpoints of the administrators, the parents, the community, and the other coauthors of the series.

Thomas, S. B. (Ed.). 1990. *The yearbook of education law, 1990.* Topeka, KS: National Organization on Legal Problems of Education (NOLPE). An annual yearbook that describes relevant legal cases related to the schools, teachers, and students from the preceding year. The yearbook has been published since 1971 and allows teachers to keep up with the legal aspects of education.

Appendixes

APPENDIX 1

HISTORY OF EDUCATION

People	Dates	Events
(*Greek Roots*) Sophists	5th Century B.C.	
Socrates (469–399 B.C.)		
Plato (427–346 B.C.)		
Aristotle (384–322 B.C.)	4th Century B.C.	
(*Roman Roots*) Quintilian (35–95 A.D.)	1st Century A.D.	
St. Augustine (359–430 A.D.)	4th Century A.D.	
(*Medieval Period*) Pierre Abelard (1079–1142)	1100–1400	
St. Thomas Aquinas (1225–1274)		
(*Renaissance Period*) Desiderius Erasmus (1444–1536)	1400–1700	
Martin Luther (1483–1546)		
John Calvin (1509–1564)		
Johann Comenius (1592–1670)		
	1630s–1640s	Hornbook, 1st Elem. Textbook
		First Latin Grammar School established in Boston (1634)
		Harvard University founded, first college in the New World (1636)
	1640–1650	First compulsory education law enacted in Massachusetts (1642)

People	Dates	Events
		"Old Deluder Satan Law" in Mass.
	1680–1700	Private Venture Training Sch.
		New England Primer (1687)
		Quaker School for blacks established in Philadelphia (1700)
(*Early Europeans*) Jean Rousseau (1712–1778)		
Johann Pestalozzi (1746–1827)		Dame Schools (1710)
(*Early Americans*)	1700–1800	
Benjamin Franklin (1706–1790)		Established his English Language Academy
		The Anglican Society for the Propagation of the Gospel in Foreign Parts established charity schools for Southern blacks (1750–1760)
Thomas Jefferson (1743–1826)		"A Bill for the More General Diffusion of Knowledge"—professing equality of educational opportunity (1779)
Noah Webster (1758–1843)		American Spelling Book, "Blue Back Speller" (1783)
		Northwest Ordinance—first federal enactment supporting education (1787)
	1800–1890	Infant schools for children 2–6 emerged (1800)
		First monitorial school in New York City established (1805)
		Town Schools (1820s–1830s)
		Rise of district schools (1830s–1840s)
Andrew Jackson (1767–1845)		Presidency—Rise of common man (1829–1837)

Horace Mann
(1796–1859)

Henry
Barnard
(1811–1900)

William T.
Harris
(1835–1909)

Booker T.
Washington
(1856–1915)

Frederick
Douglass
(1817–1895)

W. E. B. Du-
Bois
(1868–1963)

Jane Addams
(1860–1935)

1895–1900

John Dewey
(1859–1952)

Sunday schools
emerged (1830)

Ray's Arithmetic text
(1834)

McGuffey's Reader
(1836)

Became Secretary of
Massachusetts State
Board of Education
(1837)

Common schools
promoted in Twelve
Annual Reports

Introduced teachers
to views of European
educational re-
formers. First U.S.
Commissioner of Ed-
ucation (1867)

Compulsory school
attendance law
passed in Massa-
chusetts (1852)

Child Labor Law
passed in Massa-
chusetts (1866)

Superintendent of
St. Louis public
schools (1868–1880)
Immigrants assimi-
lated into culture

Kalamazoo Case es-
tablished support for
public high schools
(1874)

Tuskegee Normal
and Industrial Insti-
tute founded (1875)

Leader in abolitionist
movement and edu-
cation of blacks

Promoted education
and advancement for
blacks

Founded Hull House
(1890)

Began laboratory
school at University
of Chicago, begin-
ning of Progressive
Education Movement
(1896)

Plessy v. Ferguson
(separate but equal
schools) (1896)

Mary Bethune
(1875–1955)

George
Counts (1932)

Robert
Hutchins
(1936)

Arthur Bestor
(1956)

Robert
Havighurst
(1957)

Richard
Hofstadter
(1963)

1900–1930

Coeducation in sec-
ondary schools
promoted (1902)

Founded Daytona
Normal School (1904)

Gary Plan (1906)

Progressive Educa-
tion Movement

Smith-Hughes Voca-
tional Education Act
(1917)

Seven Cardinal Prin-
ciples (1918)

1930–1940

Great Depression
with economic cut-
backs and increased
school enrollments

Challenged schools
to meet societal
needs

Education based in
the classic disciplines

1940–1960

Emphasis on science
and technology

*Brown v. Board of Ed-
ucation of Topeka*
(began integration of
schools) (1954)

National Defense Ed-
ucation Act (1958)

Proposed return to
basic skills, aca-
demics

Developmental tasks
of children by ages

Development of the
mind should be the
purpose of second-
ary education

Increased school en-
rollments

1960–1970

Economic Oppor-
tunity Act (1964)

Head Start (1965)

Elementary and Sec-
ondary Education
Act (ESEA) (1965)

James Coleman (1966)	Report on equality of educational opportunity	National Commission on Excellence in Education (1983)	*A Nation at Risk* (1983)
	Hobson v. Hansen (found students in low tracks received inferior education (1967)	Education Commission of the States (1983)	*Action for Excellence* (1983)
	Expansion of the secondary curriculum	John Goodlad	*A Place Called School* (A study reporting similarities and differences among schools) (1984)
	Open classrooms		
	Bilingual Education Act (1968)		
	Smuck v. Hansen (tracking detrimental for those in low track) (1969)	National Governors' Association (1986)	*Time for Results* (established six task forces for the improvement of education to be completed by 1991) (1986)
1970–1980			
Christopher Jencks (1971)	A study on reassessment of the effect of family and schooling	William Bennett (1986–1988)	Wrote three reports for improvements in elementary and secondary education
	Expansion of compensatory education		*First Lessons* (Elementary) (1986) *James Madison High School* (Secondary) (1988) *James Madison Elementary School* (1988)
	Lau v. Nichols (ruled that schools should meet needs of non-English speaking students) (1973)		
	Keyes v. School District No. 1 of Denver (ruled that schools should develop a bilingual-bicultural program) (1973)	The Association for Early Childhood Education (ACEI)	*Right from the Start* (focus on 4–8 year-olds) (1988)
	Title VII of ESEA (Racial balance in schools should be maintained) (1974)		*Hawkins-Stafford Elementary and Secondary School Improvement Amendments* (1988)
	Bilingual Education Act (provided funding for bilingual programs)		Even Start (Improve adult literacy and early education) (1988)
	Education for all Handicapped Children Act (PL 94-142)	Carnegie Council on Adolescent Development (1989)	*Turning Point* (a report for restructuring of middle schools) (1989)
	(IEP's and mainstreaming for handicapped) (1975)		
	Title IX Women's Education Equity Act (sex discrimination must be eliminated) (1978)	National Governors' Association (1990)	*Task Force on Education* (state strategies for achieving the National Education Goals) (1990)
1980–1990			
	Excellence movement		

APPENDIX 2

CURRENT MINIMUM REQUIREMENTS FOR EARNING AN INITIAL CERTIFICATE FOR TEACHING PUBLIC ELEMENTARY AND SECONDARY SCHOOLS

	College B.A. Degree	General Ed. as Specified by SEA	Pedagogical Studies as Specified by SEA	Studies of Subject Matter as Specified by SEA	Pedagogical Studies as Specified by SEA	Basic Skills in Reading	Basic Skills in Mathematics	Basic Skills in Writing	Examination of Teaching Proficiency	Examination of Subject Matter Knowledge	Other
State	1	2	3	4	5	6	7	8	9	10	11
Alabama	x	x	x	x	x	x	x	x		x	(1)
Alaska	x										
Arizona	x	x	x	x	x	x	x^1	x^1	x		
Arkansas	x	x	x	x	x					x	(1)
California	x			x	x	x	x	x		x^1	
Colorado	x	x	x	x	x		x	(2)			(1)
Connecticut	x	x			x	x^1	x^1				
Delaware	x					x	x	x			(1)
Dist. of Columbia	x	x	x	x	x						
Florida	x	x		x	x	x	x	x	x		
Georgia	x	x	x	x	x	x^1	x^1			x^2	
Hawaii	x					x	x	x			
Idaho	x	x	x	x	x	x^1					
Illinois	x	x	x	x	x						
Indiana	x	x	x	x	x						
Iowa	x	x	x	x	x						
Kansas	x	x	x	x	x				x^1		
Kentucky	x	x		x	x	x	x	x	x^1	x^1	
Louisiana	x	x		x						x	
Maine	x	x		x^1	x	x^2					
Maryland	x	x^1		x	x						
Massachusetts	x			x	x						

APPENDIX 2

CURRENT MINIMUM REQUIREMENTS FOR EARNING AN INITIAL CERTIFICATE FOR TEACHING PUBLIC ELEMENTARY AND SECONDARY SCHOOLS

State	College B.A. Degree	General Ed. as Specified by SEA	Pedagogical Studies as Specified by SEA	Studies of Subject Matter as Specified by SEA	Pedagogical Studies as Specified by SEA	Basic Skills in Reading	Basic Skills in Mathematics	Basic Skills in Writing	Examination of Teaching Proficiency	Examination of Subject Matter Knowledge	Other
	1	2	3	4	5	6	7	8	9	10	11
Michigan	x	x	x	x	x						
Minnesota	x	x	x	x^1	x	x^2	x^2	x^2			
Mississippi	x	x	x^1	x	x	x	x	x	x	x	(2)
Missouri	x	x	x	x	x						
Montana	x	x	x	x	x	x	x^1	x			
Nebraska	x	x	x	x	x	x	x	x		x	
Nevada	x	x	x	x	x	x	x^1	x		x^2	
New Hampshire	x	x	x	x	x	x	x	x			
New Jersey	x	x	x	x	x	x	x	x	x	x^1	
New Mexico	x					x	x	x			
New York	x			x^1	x	x^2					
N. Carolina	x	x	x	x	x	x	x	x	x	x	
N. Dakota	x	x	x	x	x						(1)
Ohio	x	x		x	x	x	x	x		x^1	(2)
Oklahoma	x	x	x	x	x	x^1	x^1	x^1		x	
Oregon	x			x	x	x	x^1	x			
Pennsylvania	x										(1)
Rhode Island	x			x^1							
S. Carolina	x	x	x	x	x	x	x	x		x	
S. Dakota	x	x	x	x	x						
Tennessee	x	x	x	x	x	x	x	x			(1)
Texas	x	x		x	x	x^1	x^1	x^1		(2)	

APPENDIX 2

CURRENT MINIMUM REQUIREMENTS FOR EARNING AN INITIAL CERTIFICATE FOR TEACHING PUBLIC ELEMENTARY AND SECONDARY SCHOOLS

State	College B.A. Degree	General Ed. as Specified by SEA	Pedagogical Studies as Specified by SEA	Studies of Subject Matter as Specified by SEA	Pedagogical Studies as Specified by SEA	Basic Skills in Reading	Basic Skills in Mathematics	Basic Skills in Writing	Examination of Teaching Proficiency	Examination of Subject Matter Knowledge	Other
	1	2	3	4	5	6	7	8	9	10	11
Utah	x	x		x	x						(1)
Vermont	x	x	x	x	x	x	x	x			
Virginia	x	x	x	x	x	x	x	x	x	x	
Washington	x	x	x	x	x	x	x	x	x[1]	x[1]	
W. Virginia	x	x		x	x	x	x[1]				
Wisconsin	x	x	x	x	x						
Wyoming	x	x	x	x	x						

APPENDIX 2 FOOTNOTES

ALABAMA
1. Exam of knowledge of concepts common to all teaching areas (including mainstreaming).

ARIZONA
1. Elementary level only.

ARKANSAS
1. NTE Professional Knowledge for both Elementary and Secondary.

CALIFORNIA
1. Exempted from exam if completed a Commission- approved subject matter program.

COLORADO
1. 6 semester hours of recent course work (within the past five years).
2. Basic skills in oral English and written English but no writing sample required.

CONNECTICUT
1. Elementary level only.

DELAWARE
1. Vocational Ed Skills Test for Secondary Vocational Ed Program.

GEORGIA
1. Elementary level only.
2. On-the-job assignment for both levels.

IDAHO
1. Elementary level only.

KANSAS
1. Examination required beginning May 1986.

KENTUCKY
1. Effective 1985–86 school year and thereafter.

MAINE
1. Secondary level only.
2. Elementary level only.

MINNESOTA
1. Secondary level only.
2. Elementary level only.

MISSISSIPPI
1. Elementary level only.
2. National Teachers' Exam.

MONTANA
1. Elementary level only.

NEVADA
1. Elementary level only.
2. Exams are given at the I.H.E. (Institute of Higher Education)

NEW JERSEY
1. As of September 1, 1985.

NEW YORK
1. Secondary level only.
2. Elementary level only.

NORTH DAKOTA
1. North Dakota Native American Studies.

OHIO
1. Secondary level only.
2. Applicants for both Elementary and Secondary Certificates must complete an approved program.

OKLAHOMA
1. Student must show proficiency in reading, writing, and mathematics prior to admission to an approved program. The college assesses for those skills.

OREGON
1. Elementary level only.

PENNSYLVANIA
1. Completion of an approved program and a recommendation by a college are required. Currently Pennsylvania's teacher certification standards are being revised. More specific requirements may be established in the future.

RHODE ISLAND
1. Secondary level only.

TENNESSEE
1. All three sections of the NTE Commons Exam.

TEXAS
1. As of 5-1-84, Pass/Fail level on these tests is required for admission to the institution's program.
2. Certification examinations are required at all levels as of 5-1-86.

UTAH
1. Metric competencies and reading/reading in content fields.

WASHINGTON
1. These exams are not formal, uniform state examinations. Rather, an assessment in the programs.

WEST VIRGINIA
1. Elementary level only.

APPENDIX 3

STATE STANDARDS FOR SECOND-STAGE TEACHER CERTIFICATION

	Is a Second-Stage Certificate Required?		Does Your State Offer a 2nd-Stage Certificate		Standards for the Second-Stage Certificate								Are Changes Contemplated?	
	YES	NO	YES	NO	Intern-ship	Specific Years of Ex-perience	Re-em-ploy-ment	Fifth Year	Master's Degree	Specific Number of Semes-ter Units	State Test	Local District Assess-ment	YES	NO
	1	2	3	4	5	6	7	8	9	10	11	12	13	14
Alabama		x	x						x					x
Alaska		x	x							6 s.u.				x
Arizona	x		x						x or	40 s.u.				x
Arkansas		x		x										x
California	x		x					(1)					x	
Colorado	x		x			3 years						x	x	
Connecticut	x		x			3 years			(1)		(2)	(2)	x	
Delaware	x		x			3 years	x							x
D.C.	x		x			2 years	(1)			(1)				x
Florida	x		x		x						(1)	(1)	x	
Georgia	x		x								(1)	(1)		x
Hawaii	x		x			2 years								x
Idaho		x	x					x or	x					x
Illinois		x		x										x
Indiana	x		x		x or	2 years						x	x	
Iowa		x	x			4 years			x				x	
Kansas	x		x			2 years							x	
Kentucky	x		x		(1)		(1)						x	
Louisiana	x		x			3 years								x
Maine	x		x			4 years	x			30 s.u.			x	
Maryland	x		x			3 years			x or	30 s.u.				x
Massachusetts		x		x										x
Michigan	x		x			3 years				18 s.u.			x	

APPENDIX 3

STATE STANDARDS FOR SECOND-STAGE TEACHER CERTIFICATION

	Is a Second-Stage Certificate Required?		Does Your State Offer a 2nd-Stage Certificate		Standards for the Second-Stage Certificate								Are Changes Contemplated?	
	YES	NO	YES	NO	Internship	Specific Years of Experience	Re-employment	Fifth Year	Master's Degree	Specific Number of Semester Units	State Test	Local District Assessment	YES	NO
	1	2	3	4	5	6	7	8	9	10	11	12	13	14
Minnesota	x		x			1 year								x
Mississippi	x		x		x							x		x
Missouri		x	x							(1)		(1)	x	
Montana		x	x			3 years	x or	x or		30. s.u.	x		x	
Nebraska		x	x			2 years								x
Nevada		x	x			3 years			x					x
New Hampshire	x		x			3 years				(1)		x		x
New Jersey		x		x										x
New Mexico	x		x							8 s.u.			x	
New York	x		x			2 years			x				x	
N. Carolina	x		x			2 years								x
N. Dakota	x		x			18 months	(1)							x
Ohio	x		x			3 years	x			30 s.u.		x	x	
Oklahoma	x		x		x						x	x		x
Oregon	x		x			2 years	x or			30 s.u.		x		x
Pennsylvania	x		x		(1)	3 years				24 s.u.		x		x
Rhode Island	x		x			3 years				6 s.u.				x
S. Carolina		x		x										x
S. Dakota	x		x			1 year						(1)		x
Tennessee	x		x			1 year						x		x
Texas		x	x			3 years				30 s.u.				x
Utah	x		x			2 years						x		x

APPENDIX 3

STATE STANDARDS FOR SECOND-STAGE TEACHER CERTIFICATION

	Is a Second-Stage Certificate Required?		Does Your State Offer a 2nd-Stage Certificate		Standards for the Second-Stage Certificate								Are Changes Contemplated?	
	YES	NO	YES	NO	Intern-ship	Specific Years of Ex-perience	Re-em-ploy-ment	Fifth Year	Master's Degree	Specific Number of Semes-ter Units	State Test	Local District Assess-ment	YES	NO
	1	2	3	4	5	6	7	8	9	10	11	12	13	14
Vermont	x		x				(1)					x	x	
Virginia		x	x			3 years			x				x	
Washington	x		x			3 years			x or	30 su.(1)		x	x	
W. Virginia		x	x			3 years				(1)				x
Wisconsin		x		x										x
Wyoming	x		x			5 years			x					x

APPENDIX 3 FOOTNOTES

CALIFORNIA
1. Fifth year, a course in special education, and a unit in heatlh education.

CONNECTICUT
1. A master's degree or a planned fifth year program.
2. After 7-1-88, the provisional educator certificate is issued for 8 years upon successful completion of beginning educator support and assessment program, which encompasses the professional skills assessment.

DISTRICT OF COLUMBIA
1. Course in computer literacy and tenure.

FLORIDA
1. Pass Florida teacher certification exam and complete the Florida Beginning Teacher Program.

GEORGIA
1. The second stage certificate is issued when the individual passes both the test of knowledge of the teaching field and on-the-job assessment of performance.

KENTUCKY
1. The second stage certificate is issued for one year upon confirmation of employment; upon successful completion of the internship, it is extended to four years.

MISSOURI
1. Completion of the employing district's professional development plan.

NEW HAMPSHIRE
1. Fifty clock hours of staff development.

NORTH DAKOTA
1. Requires 3 positive recommendations by supervisors.

PENNSYLVANIA
1. Induction Program for beginning teachers. School districts may require experienced teachers new to the district to complete the induction program.

SOUTH DAKOTA
1. Successful evaluation by a three-member committee.

VERMONT
1. Issued for 7 years upon recommendation of the Superintendent or the local teacher's certification agency.

WASHINGTON
1. Fourteen of the 30 semester units must be earned after the first year of teaching. The 30 semester units are waived for those with a master's degree.

WEST VIRGINIA
1. Six semester units or salary classification of master's degree plus 30 semester units.

MAJOR NATIONAL EDUCATION ORGANIZATIONS

American Alliance for Health, Physical Education,
Recreation and Dance (AALR)
1900 Association Drive
Reston, VA 22091
(703) 476-3400
Student Membership $28

American Alliance for Theatre and Education (AATE)
Theatre Arts Dept.
Virginia Tech.
Blacksburg, VA 24061
(703) 231-7624
Student Membership $30

American Council on the Teaching of Foreign
Languages (ACTFL)
(Classical and Modern)
Six Executive Blvd., Upper-Level
Yonkers, NY 10701
(914) 963-8830

American Federation of Teachers AFL-CIO (AFT)
555 New Jersey Avenue, NW
Washington, DC 20001
(202) 879-4400
Student Membership—Nat'l $5
State dues vary

American Home Economics Association (AHEA)
2010 Massachusetts Ave., NW
Washington, DC 20036
(202) 862-8300
Student Membership $30

American Speech-Language-Hearing Association
(ASLHA)
10801 Rockville Pike
Rockville, MD 20852
(301) 897-5700
Student Membership $35

Association for Childhood Education International
(ACEI)
11141 Georgia Ave., Suite 200
Wheaton, MD 20902
(301) 942-2433
Student Membership $20

Council for Exceptional Children (CEC)
1920 Association Drive
Reston, VA 22091
(703) 620-3660
Student Membership $24

International Reading Association (IRA)
800 Barksdale Rd.
P.O. Box 8139
Newark, DE 19714
(302) 731-1600
Student Membership $23

International Technology Education Association (ITEA)
1914 Association Drive
Reston, VA 22091
(703) 860-2100
Student Membership $25

Music Teachers National Association (MTNA)
2113 Carew Tower
Cincinnati, OH 45202
(513) 421-1420
Student Membership—Nat'l $4
State dues vary

National Art Education Association (NAEA)
1916 Association Drive
Reston, VA 22091
(703) 860-8000
Student Membership $20

National Association of Biology Teachers (NABT)
11250 Roger Bacon Drive
Reston, VA 22090
(703) 471-1134
Student Membership $18

National Association for Gifted Children (NAGC)
1155 15th St., N.W.,
Suite 1002
Washington, DC 20005
(202) 785-4268
Student Membership $45

National Association for the Education of Young
Children (NAEYC)
1834 Connecticut Ave., NW
Washington, DC 20009
(202) 232-8777 (800) 424-2460
Student Membership $25

National Business Education Association (NBEA)
1914 Association Drive
Reston, VA 22091
(703) 860-8300
Student Membership $15

National Council for the Social Studies (NCSS)
3501 Newark St., NW
Washington, DC 20016
Student Membership $25

National Council of Teachers of English (NCTE)
1111 Kenyon Rd.
Urbana, IL 61801
(217) 328-3870
Student Membership $14

National Council of Teachers of Mathematics (NCTM)
1906 Association Drive
Reston, VA 22091
(703) 620-9840
Student Membership $20

National Education Association (NEA)
1201 16th Street, NW
Washington, DC 20036
(202) 833-4000
Student membership $10

National Middle Schools Association (NMSA)
4807 Evanswood Dr.
Columbus, OH 43229
(614)848-8211
Student Membership $25

National Science Teachers Association (NSTA)
1742 Connecticut Ave., NW
Washington, DC 20009
(202)328-5800
Student Membership $10

Sources: Burek, O. M., Koek, K. E., and Navello, A. (Eds.). (1990).
            Encyclopedia of Associations (24th Ed.). (Volume 1, Part I, Part 2, Part 3).
            Detroit, MI: Gale Research, Inc.

            Buttlar, L. J. (1989). *Education: A guide to reference and information sources.*
            Englewood, CO: Libraries Unlimited, Inc.

            Freed, M. N. (Ed.). (1989). *The Education Desk Reference: A sourcebook of
            educational information and research.* New York: Macmillan.

SUMMARY OF MAJOR REPORTS ON EDUCATION, 1982–1990

The Report	Source	Recommendations	Implementers
A Nation at Risk (1983)	National Commission on Excellence in Education, a group of educators and legislators assembled by Terrell Bell, U.S. Secretary of Education.	1. Schools, colleges, and universities should adopt more rigorous measurable standards and higher expectations for academic performance and student conduct. (This includes higher admissions standards for colleges.) 2. The high school curriculum for all students should include 4 years of English and math, 3 years of science and social studies, 5 years of computer science, 2 years of foreign language for college-bound students. 3. Teaching should be improved by attracting better teachers and paying them more. Higher entrance requirements for preparation programs, scholarships for better students, recognition of "master teachers," and use of outside school resources to alleviate shortages in math and science are suggested. 4. More time should be spent on teaching and learning. The present school day should be used more effectively, the day and year lengthened, and more homework required.	1. Federal government. 2. State and local officials. 3. School boards, principals, superintendents. 4. Citizens, educators, parents, students.
Report of the Task Force on Federal Elementary and Secondary Education Policy (1983)	The Twentieth Century Fund Task Force on Education, a report to the U.S. House of Representatives Budget Committee	1. The federal government should stress better schooling for *all* students. 2. A national master teacher program should be instituted to improve the quality of teachers. 3. Federal "impact" aid should be sent to school systems with large enrollments of immigrant students. 4. The primary language taught in schools should be English; all students should be offered a second language. 5. Schools should offer advanced courses in math and science. 6. School districts should be awarded federal moneys to create small, individual programs for students who are failing.	1. Elementary and secondary schools. 2. Federal government.

The Report	Source	Recommendations	Implementers
Action for Excellence (1983)	Education Commission of the States Task Force on Education, a Denver-based group of governors. The Commission was headed by Governor Hunt of North Carolina.	1. Goals for improving educational performance should be clear, compelling, and widely agreed on. 2. Basic skills should include these competencies: reading, writing, mathematics, science, listening and speaking, computer science, "basic employment," and economic competency. 3. States should have plans for improving the curriculum in grades K-12. 4. The academic experiences of children should be more intense and productive. 5. Instructional management should allow more effective and efficient use of classroom resources. 6. Student progress should be closely monitored. 7. States should change their methods of recruiting, training, and compensating teachers. 8. Certification for teachers and administrators should be changed to reflect new training and recruitment policies. 9. Principals should become curriculum leaders rather than professional bureaucrats. 10. States should foster partnerships between public schools and the private sector. 11. States and corporations should ensure that unserved or underserved students (members of minority groups, women, handicapped, gifted) receive the same quality of education as all other students.	1. State and corporate leaders. 2. Elementary and secondary schools.
Academic Preparation for College (1983)	The College Board, publishers of the College Entrance Examinations.	1. To read critically and analytically and to respond imaginatively. 2. To compute (add, subtract, multiply, and divide) and do statistics, algebra, and geometry. 3. To write English clearly and precisely. 4. To understand the principles, structure, and use of the English language. 5. To speak, listen, and separate fact from fiction. 6. To master fundamental concepts in at least one scientific field through laboratory and field work. 7. To know general political, social, and cultural history, particularly of the U.S. 8. To be proficient in another language. 9. To understand and appreciate different art forms. 10. To program computers for personal use.	Secondary schools.

The Report	Source	Recommendations	Implementers
The Paideia Proposal (1982)	Consortium of nationally recognized liberal arts educators (among them Mortimer Adler).	1. Basic education should be general liberal arts, not vocational, for all students with no electives except a second foreign language. 2. Instruction should have three phases: —Didactic instruction and use of textbooks in language, literature and arts, math and natural science, and history, geography, and social studies. —Coaching to develop intellectual skills in reading, writing, speaking, listening, calculating, problem-solving, observing, measuring, estimating, and criticizing. —Socratic discussion of books and works of art to expand students' understanding of ideas and values. 3. Teachers should be trained in general liberal arts before specializing to teach a particular field. Teachers should be better paid. 4. The principal should provide educational leadership, not manage a business, and should be able to hire and fire teachers and enforce standards of conduct. 5. Preschool tutoring should be established for children from disadvantaged homes. 6. Children with deficiencies should receive special help.	1. Local communities through local school boards. 2. Elementary and secondary schools through school administrators, who are crucial to the process.
America's Competitive Challenge: The Need for a National Response (1983)	The Business-Higher Education Forum, a group of businessmen and high school and college administrators.	1. In order for America to compete in world markets, the current and future work force should be nurtured along with long-term capital investments and technological innovations. 2. The federal government should upgrade and replace obsolete equipment and facilities in universities. 3. The federal government should use tax incentives to get industries to invest in the training and retraining of workers, including apprenticeships. 4. Industries should use academicians as consultants. 5. Universities and industries should collaborate on problem-solving research.	1. Industry and university leaders. 2. Federal government through public policies relating to these problems.
Horace's Compromise (1984)	The National Association of Independent Schools and the National Association of Secondary School Principals	1. Basic competencies in reading, writing, and mathematics should be acquired in elementary schools. 2. High school should be voluntary for all children. It should have a common curriculum for all students, and no tracking should occur.	

The Report	Source	Recommendations	Implementers
Horace's Compromise (1984) (cont'd)		3. The curriculum should include (a) inquiry and expression, (b) math and science, (c) literature and the arts, and (d) philosophy and history. 4. Teachers should assume the role of academic coaches, helping students to pass examinations in specific subjects. Teachers would work with small groups of students in small schools. 5. Students should be able to move through the curriculum at their own speed, without being locked into a grade by their age.	
A Place Called School (1984)	Institute for the Development of Educational Activities and Laboratory in School and Community Education, Grad. Sch., Univ. of Calif., L.A.	1. Use recommended goals for schooling in U.S. to build programs of teaching and learning. 2. Secondary schooling ends and completion certificate at age 16. 3. School begins at age 4. 4. Three phases of non-graded schooling: 4–7 yrs., 8–11 yrs., 12–15 yrs. 5. Mastery learning, cooperative learning, small-group peer tutoring, and individualizing. 6. Good general education in elementary/secondary school. 7. Greater participation of parents/teachers in decision making. 8. Increase salaries/decrease teaching time. 9. Greater articulation/collaboration with colleges/universities.	1. State and local policymakers. 2. State and local school boards. 3. Parents. 4. Colleges and universities.
Teacher Preparation: The Anatomy of a College Degree (1985)	Southern Regional Educational Board	1. All teachers should have a general education. 2. Four years are sufficient if students enter prepared for college work. 3. Elementary teachers should have more academic subjects and majors. 4. Education courses should be 30% of total.	1. Colleges and universities.
A Call for Change in Teacher Education (1985)	National Commission for Excellence in Teacher Education: American Association of Colleges for Teacher Education	1. Rigorous performance standards for admission and graduation from teacher education programs. 2. States and federal governments should recruit qualified candidates for teaching. 3. Special programs should be developed to attract minorities to teaching. 4. Teacher education programs should integrate liberal studies, subject specialization, and content and skills of professional education. 5. The first year of teaching should be an internship.	1. Federal and state governments. 2. Colleges and universities. 3. National Council for Accreditation of Teacher Education. 4. State and local policymakers.

The Report	Source	Recommendations	Implementers
		6. States should encourage and assist in the evaluation of teacher education programs. 7. Rigorous standards for program review should be enforced by states.	
A Nation Prepared (1986)	Carnegie Forum on Education & the Economy	1. State and local policymakers should work with teachers to create schools that provide a professional environment for teaching. 2. A national board for professional teaching standards should be formed. 3. Licensing authority should remain with the states. 4. States should abolish undergraduate degrees in education. 5. Undergraduate programs in the arts & sciences should be evaluated to ensure adequate preparation of teachers. 6. Ensure an increasing number of minority teachers. 7. Salaries should be linked to performance. 8. Salaries should be increased.	1. State and local policymakers. 2. Education Commission of the States. 3. Colleges and universities. 4. Federal and state governments. 5. Corporate leaders and local communities.
Tomorrow's Teachers (1986)	The Holmes Group	1. Establish a 3-tier system of teacher education: the professional and career with tenure and the instructor with a temporary certificate. 2. Develop a graduate professional teacher education program. 3. Connect schools and colleges. 4. Make schools better places for teachers to work. 5. Create standards for entry to the profession.	1. Colleges and universities. 2. Elementary and secondary schools. 3. State and local policymakers.
First Lessons: A Report on Elementary Education in America (1986)	U.S. Department of Education	1. There should be more instructional time in the schedule. 2. Use homework to extend instructional time. 3. Employ creative curriculum strategies. 4. Free teachers to teach. 5. Set school priorities and give parents choices among them. 6. Consider lengthening the school year.	1. State and local policymakers. 2. Elementary schools. 3. Local communities.
Time for Results: The Governors' 1991 Report on Education (1986)	The National Governors' Association: Center for Policy Research and Analysis	1. Teaching, Leadership and Management, Parent Involvement and Choice Readiness, Technology, School Facilities, and College Quality.	1. State governments. 2. State and local policymakers. 3. Corporate leaders. 4. Parents, local communities. 5. Colleges and universities. 6. Elementary/secondary schools. 7. Preschools.

The Report	Source	Recommendations	Implementers
Bringing Down the Barriers: Making America Work (1987)	The National Governors' Association: Center for Policy Research and Analysis	1. Task forces on: Welfare Prevention, School Dropouts, Teen Pregnancy, Adult Literacy, and Alcohol and Drug Abuse.	1. Federal, state, and local governments. 2. State and local policymakers. 3. Elementary and secondary schools. 4. Corporate leaders. 5. Communities.
James Madison High School: A Curriculum for American Students (1987)	U.S. Department of Education	1. Curriculum to include: 4 years of English, 3 years of science, 3 years of math, 3 years of social studies, 2 years of foreign language, 2 years of physical education, 1 year of fine arts, 1 elective in second year, 2 electives in third year, 6 electives in fourth year.	1. State and local policymakers. 2. Secondary schools.
An Imperiled Generation: Saving Urban Schools (1988)	The Carnegie Foundation for the Advancement of Teaching	1. School-based leadership. 2. Accountability: A School Report Card. 3. Small schools in bigger schools. 4. A good beginning in early years. 5. A core curriculum. 6. Flexible arrangements, more time, more options. 7. Good facilities. 8. College-school connections. 9. Corporate connections. 10. Parents as teachers.	1. Elementary and secondary schools. 2. State and local policymakers. 3. Colleges and universities. 5. Parents and local community.
New Voices: Immigrant Students in U.S. Public Schools (1988)	National Coalition of Advocates for Students	1. Better assessment and placement. 2. More bilingual, multicultural, and special education. 3. Better staffing and support services. 4. A better school climate.	1. Federal and state governments. 2. State and local policymakers. 3. Colleges and universities. 4. Local communities.
Right from the Start: A Report on the NASBE Task Force on Early Childhood Education (1988)	The National Association of State Boards of Education	1. Establish early childhood units for 4–8 year-old children in elementary schools. 2. Have a developmentally appropriate curriculum. 3. Improve assessment. 4. Be responsive to cultural and linguistic diversity. 5. Have partnerships with parents. 6. Appropriate training and support for staff and administrators.	1. Preschools and elementary schools. 2. State and local policymakers. 3. Colleges and universities. 4. Federal and state governments. 5. Parents and local community.

The Report	Source	Recommendations	Implementers
James Madison Elementary School: A Curriculum for American Students (1988)	U.S. Department of Education	1. Grades K–3, introduction to: reading, writing, history, geography, civics, math, science, music, visual arts, physical education, and health. 2. Grades 4–6, introduction to: critical reading, U.S. history, world history to Middle Ages, intermediate math and geometry, earth science, life science, physical science, foreign language, music, visual arts, physical education, and health. 3. Grades 7–8, survey of: elementary grammar/composition, literary analysis, world history to 1900, world geography, U.S. Constitution, general math, pre-algebra, algebra, biology, chemistry, physics, foreign language, music and art appreciation, physical education, and health.	1. State and local policymakers. 2. Elementary, middle, and junior high schools.
Turning Points: Preparing American Youth for the 21st Century: The Report of the Task Force on Young Adolescents (1989)	Carnegie Council on Adolescent Development	1. Create small communities for learning, schools within schools. 2. Teach a core academic program. 3. Ensure success for all students. 4. Empower teachers and administrators to make decisions about the experiences of middle grade students. 5. Staff middle grade schools with teachers who are expert at teaching young adolescents. 6. Improve academic performance through fostering the health and fitness of young adolescents. 7. Reengage families in the education of young adolescents. 8. Connect schools with communities.	1. Middle and junior high schools. 2. Colleges and universities. 3. State and local policymakers. 4. Local communities.
Educating Our Children: Parents and Schools Together (1989)	U.S. Department of Education	1. Increase parent choice in selecting schools. 2. Join with parents to improve the schools. 3. Allow parents to participate in decision making. 4. Promote teacher training in parent involvement.	1. State and local policymakers. 2. Parents. 3. Colleges and universities.
Report of the Task Force on Education: State Strategies for Achieving the National Education Goals (America 2000) (1990)	National Governors' Association: Center for Policy Research and Analysis	1. By the year 2000, all children in America will start school ready to learn. 2. By the year 2000, the high school graduation rate will increase to at least 90 percent. 3. By the year 2000, American students will leave grades four, eight, and twelve having demonstrated competency over challenging subject matter including English, mathematics, science, history, and geography, and every school in America will ensure	

The Report	Source	Recommendations	Implementers
Report of the Task Force on Education: State Strategies for Achieving the National Education Goals (America 2000) (1990) (cont'd)		that all students learn to use their minds well, so that they may be prepared for responsible citizenship, further learning, and productive employment in our modern society.	
		4. By the year 2000, American students will be first in the world in mathematics and science achievement.	
		5. By the year 2000, every adult American will be literate and will possess the knowledge and skills necessary to compete in a global economy and exercise the rights and responsibilities of citizenship.	
		6. By the year 2000, every school in America will be free of drugs and violence and will offer a disciplined environment conducive to learning.	

Adapted and updated by the authors from B. Loman, "Improving Public Education: Recommendations From Recent Study Commissions," *Popular Government* (Winter 1985), 14–16.

Glossary

Ability grouping Assigning students to groups based on their ability to learn. 145

Academy A secondary school established in the early nineteenth century for middle class students offering a wide range of subjects. 145

Accommodation A cognitive process by which children change or develop new schemes when a new concept cannot be assimilated into existing schemes (Piaget). 334

Accountability The schools' responsibility for ensuring student achievement. 531

Accreditation Certifying that consistent standards, procedures, and policies are met for operating quality teacher-education programs. 61

Advanced organizers Providing external motivation for learning by beginning a lesson with overall aims, giving examples, and relating the learning to past learning and experiences (Ausubel). 356

Aesthetic need The human need for beauty (Maslow). 335

Aesthetics The study of values in the realm of beauty and art. 198

Affective development The development of values. 40, 172

Age of the common man The years between 1812 and 1865 when tracts of land were free and open to all, resulting in equality of economic and political opportunity. 142

Alternative approaches Varied nontraditional, teacher-training approaches that strive to reduce some of the barriers to entry into teaching. 66

Analytic approach to discipline Discipline approaches that attempt to identify the cause of student misbehavior and then treat the cause(s). 457

Anecdotal observations Informal observations that focus on a specific classroom event, a student, or teaching for a specified period of time. 54

Animism A young child's infusing of the inanimate world with conscious attributes (Piaget). 334

Assertive discipline A classroom management approach in which teachers determine structure and routine, expect appropriate student behavior, develop appropriate consequences for misbehavior, and receive support from administrators and parents. 33

Assimilation A cognitive process by which children integrate new stimuli into an existing scheme (Piaget). 333

Authoritarian model of discipline A teacher-dominated discipline approach in which the teacher sets the rules and requires the students to submit to the teacher's authority. 456

Autonomy Teacher discretion in making decisions related to teaching, curriculum course material, discipline, and evaluation of student work. 90

Axiology A category of philosophic thought dealing with the nature of values. 198

Battery An assault that leads to physical injury. 522

Behaviorism An educational theory based in the philosophical schools of realism and philosophical analysis, that stresses the scientific method, objectivity, immediate results, efficiency, and positiveness. 224

Behaviorist A scientist who bases conclusions exclusively on the observation of behavior. 352

Behavioristic approach to discipline A classroom management approach in which students are reinforced for good behavior. 457

Bell curve A bell-shaped symmetrical distribution in which most performance scores or human attributes fall near the mean (average). 283

Belonging or love need The human need to feel wanted and loved (Maslow). 335

Blended families Families joined together by the marriage of divorced adults in which one or both have children from previous marriages. 389

Block grants The 20 percent of federal public education funds distributed by the states to the schools for their discretionary use (Education Consolidation and Improvement Act, 1981). 513

Career ladder   A hierarchy of levels in a teaching career, each with additional responsibilities and salary; promotion to the next level is based on evaluation of teaching performance and increased responsibilities and levels of education. 98

Categorical grants   Federal grants that must be applied for. 573

Certification   A specified set of state requirements (such as coursework, fieldwork, examinations) that prospective and inservice teachers must complete in order to teach. 58

Child abuse   The physical and/or sexual abuse and the physical neglect and/or emotional maltreatment of children by adults. 400

Child-centered psychology   The study of the stages of children's physical, intellectual, and behavioral development. 273

Child-centered teaching   A teaching style in which the curriculum emerges from the children's interests. 42

Classical conditioning   The development of a conditioned stimulus by pairing a neutral stimulus (no effect) with an unconditioned stimulus (effect) (Pavlov). 352

Cognitive development   The development of concepts. 40, 172

Common school   The ideal of publicly supported education for all students espoused by nineteenth-century educators and businessmen. 143

Compensatory education   The schools' effort to individually compensate for the unequal learning and experiences that students bring to the classroom. 182

Competency   An element of knowledge that is essential if the student is to master the content of the discipline. 279

Competency-based model   A teacher-training approach that requires the development of specific, measurable competencies over a specified period of time. 64

Computer-assisted instruction (AI)   Computer programs that allow students to progress at their own rate by completing a series of complex tasks, each of which receives immediate feedback. 354

Concrete operational period   A period of cognitive development that occurs between the ages of seven and eleven during which children develop the ability to solve problems through reasoning and to think symbolically with words and numbers (Piaget). 334

Conditioned stimulus   The pairing of a neutral stimulus (no effect) with an unconditioned stimulus (effect) to produce the desired effect even after the unconditioned stimulus is removed (Pavlov). 352

Conservation   The cognitive ability to recognize equivalent volume, regardless of the size of the container (Piaget). 335

Constitutional law   The law of the land set forth in the U.S. Constitution and each state's constitution. 519

Content-centered teaching   A teaching style which employs lecturing and formal discussion as a means to cover content coherently and systematically and measure student learning objectively. 40

Content-student-centered learning style   A learning style that balances the objectives of the material to be learned with the needs of the students. 42

Contract   An agreement between two or more competent parties to create, alter, or dissolve a relationship legally. 519

Conventional moral reasoning   Moral judgments that are based on the approval of others, on family expectations, traditional values, laws of society, and loyalty to country (Kohlberg). 336

Cooperative planning   A teaching style in which teachers and students plan together. 42

Corporal punishment   Physical contact such as striking, paddling, or spanking of a student by an educator. 534

Dame schools   Seventeenth-century schools held in private New England homes in which several children gathered to be taught by the woman of the household. 135

Decenter   A cognitive process in which a child learns that his or her perspective is only one perspective (Piaget). 335

Deduction   Logical reasoning that moves from the general to the specific. 199

Deductive teaching   Presenting a lesson in an organized sequence from the general to the specific (Ausubel). 356

Demographic patterns   Population trends due to births, deaths, marriages, etc. 394

Differentiated staffing   Differing levels of responsibility, education, and professional achievements leading to increased professional status and pay. 98

Direct federal aid   Funding that flows directly from federal agencies to the schools. 513

Discipline   The training that leads to the development of self-control, an internal conscience that acknowledges appropriate behavior. 456

Discovery learning   Learning by oneself through discovery rather than through prepared and teacher-presented information (Bruner). 355

Display   To show individual frames of a film or videotape. 525

Due process   A constitutionally guaranteed right protecting citizens from arbitrary governmental action and unreasonable or discriminatory practices. 520

Effective teaching research   The study and examination of classroom teaching behaviors, mainly those that positively influence student performance. 33

Egocentric   Seeing the world as revolving around oneself. 334

Elementary and Secondary Education Act (ESEA)   A federal act to improve educational opportunities for socially and economically disadvantaged students. 173

Emotional disturbance: A condition that adversely affects educational performance over a long period of time. May include one or more of the following characteristics: inability to learn that cannot be explained by intellectual, sensory, or health factors; inability to build or maintain personal relationships; and/or inappropriate types of behavior or feelings. 308

Emotionally exciting teaching style A teaching style in which teachers demonstrate intense excitement and emotion during the teaching/learning process. 40

Enculturation Everything the child does under the guidance of an adult, including formal schooling. 131

English language academy An eighteenth-century prototype for contemporary secondary schools offering practical and vocational courses such as commerce, English, oratory, politics, and mathematics. 141

Epistemology A category of philosophic thought that deals with the nature and universality of knowledge. 197

Equalization grants A state funding formula for public schools that provides those districts with higher property values less state money than those districts with lower property values. 510

Equilibrium A sense of balance that is achieved through the assimilation of new experiences into an existing scheme (Piaget). 333

Essentialism An educational theory based in the philosophical school of realism, asserting that the primary function of the school is the transmission of essential facts. 218

Esteem need The human need for self-respect, achievement, and status. 335

Ethics The study of moral values and conduct. 198

Existentialism A philosophical school that contends reality is lived existence and final reality resides within the individual self. 211

Expository learning Learning that occurs from general to specific, from rule to example (Ausubel). 356

Expository style A teaching style focusing on content and sequence of subject matter, usually from a text; lecturing, direct questioning for student recitation, and structured assignments predominate. 41

Extinguish The disappearance of a response if reinforcement does not occur (Pavlov). 352

Fair use The right to use copyrighted material in a reasonable manner without the permission of the author. 524

Fieldwork Observing, participating, and teaching in classrooms during a teacher-training program. 59

Five-year degree model An undergraduate-graduate five-year approach to teacher training. 65

Flat grants A state funding formula for public schools based on the district's average daily attendance during the previous school year; each district receives the same amount for each student in attendance. 509

Formal control That power delegated to individuals or groups through statute or law. 472

Formal operational period A period of cognitive development that occurs between ages eleven and adulthood during which abstract, logical, and hypothetical reasoning are developed (Piaget). 335

Freedmen's Bureau Established by Congress to work with voluntary organizations to provide basic education for blacks who had been slaves. 153

General education Education for all, but not necessarily equal education. 132

Head Start A federally funded, comprehensive child development program for three- to five-year-olds from low-income families. 170

Hornbook The first elementary notebook made of transparent paper from flattened cattle horns, used for teaching the alphabet, syllables, and the Lord's Prayer. 134

Idealism A traditional philosophical school that contends that reality consists of an idea, a nonphysical essence, and that the development of the mind and self are primary. 202

Incentive pay Increased compensation for success in teaching, and additional responsibilities and levels of education; also called performance-based. 94

Indirect federal funding Federal funding that flows first through state education agencies and then to the schools. 513

Individual education program (IEP) An individually designed educational program for physically, mentally, and emotionally handicapped students, and for those with special learning disabilities. 176

Induction Logical reasoning that moves from the specific to a general conclusion. 200

Infant schools Seventeenth-century schools for young children, ages two to six, whose mothers worked in factories. 144

Inferential style A teaching style that stimulates and encourages student participation, self-direction, and independence through the use of a variety of techniques such as inquiry, discovery, simulations, and experimentation. 42

Informal influence Attempted control exerted by individuals or groups who have no legal authority, but who have a strong interest or commitment to schools, and who try to sway opinions of those who have the formal power to control. 472

Instructor-centered teaching A teaching style in which the teacher is the ego ideal and socializing agent, modeling ways learners should approach a particular field or subject. 40

Instrumental learning An organism is able to repeat a response if reinforcement (food, money, praise) occurs; also called operant conditioning (Skinner). 353

Integrated An approach which unifies a number of subjects or fields of study into one topic. 287

Intentional torts A type of tort liability that involves assault, battery, desire to inflict harm, and defamation. 524

Interview A planned fact-finding technique in which an attempt is made to obtain information through direct questioning. 54

Knowledge or understanding need The human need to understand one's environment (Maslow). 335

Latchkey children Children who come home from a school to a house without adult supervision. 450

Latin grammar school A seventeenth-century Boston classical secondary school established for young men. 135

Law The U.S. system of jurisprudence and the courts, which are utilized in defending one's rights and securing justice. 519

Law of effect If an act leads to a satisfying change in the environment, the likelihood that the act will be repeated in similar situations increases; but if the act does not lead to a satisfying change, the likelihood that the act will be repeated decreases (Thorndike). 353

Learning disability: A disorder in one or more of the basic psychological processes involved in understanding or in using spoken or written language, which may manifest itself in an imperfect inability to listen, think, speak, read, write, spell, or do mathematical calculations. 308

Learning outcomes Learning skills that can be categorized into four types of results: attributes, motor skills, verbal data, and cognitive strategies (Gagne). 357

Learning style The manner in which various elements in one's environment affect learning. 362

Learning-centered teaching style A teaching style that strives to balance concern for students, curriculum, and materials to be covered. 42

Liberal arts model A teacher-training approach that requires an arts and sciences major, general education course work, and a professional education component; emphasis is on the development of thinking skills. 63

Linguistic analysis A branch of philosophical analysis that deals with language, particularly grammar and structural linguistics, and logic. 214

Logic A category of philosophic thought dealing with the nature of reasoning. 199

Logical empiricism A branch of philosophical analysis based on experimentation and observation. 214

Magnet schools Schools with focused themes, such as the arts, math, and science, and multiculturism; com-monly designed for purposes of integration and par-ental choice. 184

Mainstreaming Participation of handicapped students in regular educational programs. 176

Major premise A general statement or fact from which logically inferred conclusions are deduced. 199

Master teachers A group of teachers who are given increased leadership responsibility, including leader-ship of a team working on curriculum and instruction and guiding new teachers; also called mentor, lead, or head teachers. 99

Maxim A commonly held belief. 197

Mental disability A below-average intellectual func-tioning that exists concurrently with deficits in adap-tive behavior; it manifests itself during a child's developmental period, adversely affecting his or her educational performance. 311

Merit pay An annual bonus or reward given to selected teachers and other school personnel for recognized professional achievement. 97

Metaphysics A category of philosophic thought that speculates on the nature of ultimate reality, searching for the principles of human existence. 196

Minor premise A particular fact. 200

Modeling A theory of observational learning in which a child learns through imitation and observation of adults (Bandura). 354

Monitorial schools A system whereby master teachers train advanced students to teach beginning students, thus making it possible to educate large numbers of children efficiently and inexpensively. 145

Multicultural education The idea or concept that all students, regardless of race, gender, or social class, have the same opportunity to learn in school; an educational reform movement; an ongoing process that gives all students equal access to educational achievement. 444

Multitudinousness The historical concept of breadth of educational opportunity. 130

National Assessment of Educational Progress (NAEP) A congressionally mandated periodic testing program of the level of student learning. 364

Naturalism An educational philosophy that claims that environment plays a crucial role in individual develop-ment and that it could be shaped through reason and science. 128

Negligence A type of tort liability that involves unac-ceptable conduct or care that results in personal injury. 522

Neutral stimulus A stimulus that has no effect on the responder (Pavlov). 352

Noncustodial parent Following a divorce, the parent who does not have custody of the children. 388

Nonemotional teaching style A teaching style in which teachers conduct class in a subdued, unemo-tional tone; learning is dispassionate but significant. 40

Normal schools Teacher training schools established in the early to mid-nineteenth century. 142

Object permanence A cognitive skill that allows young children to recognize that an object may exist even though it cannot be seen (Piaget). 334

Operant conditioning The operation of an organism on its environment during learning; also called instrumental learning (Skinner). 353

Paidocentric A child-centered psychological theory developed by G. Stanley Hall. 273

Pais, paidas A Greek word for the upbringing of the child. 274

Parochial schools Schools supported by religious organizations; they originated in the Middle Atlantic colonies during the seventeenth century. 138

Parsons schools Endowed free schools for women in parishes or districts of the Southern colonies in the seventeenth century. 136

Perennialism An educational theory based in the philosophical schools of idealism and realism that stresses the great works of the intellectual past and the ability to reason. 218

Perform To run the entire work through a projector or recorder. 525

Performance-based Increased compensation for success in teaching and additional responsibilities and levels of education; also called incentive pay. 96

Philos A Greek word meaning love. 196

Philosophical analysis Analysis which classifies and verifies phenomena in order to define reality. 214

Physiological need The human need for food, health, warmth, and shelter (Maslow). 335

Politicization The historical concept that schools are a force for political change. 130

Popularization The historical concept of schooling for all. 130

Positive ethos The development of both intellectual and moral character by a school. 237

Postconventional moral reasoning Socially agreed-upon standards of individual rights and democratically determined laws that are the basis of moral behavior (Kohlberg). 336

Pragmatism A philosophical school that contends that humans and their environment interact, both being responsible for that which is real. 209

Preconventional moral reasoning Moral judgments that are based on the expectation of rewards and punishment (Kohlberg). 336

Preoperational period A period of cognitive development that occurs between the ages two and seven during which children acquire language and learn to represent the environment with objects and symbols (Piaget). 334

Principle of inclusion A cognitive process of the concrete operational stage in which the child can reason about the relationship between classes and subclasses (Piaget). 335

Private schools Schools supported by private rather than by public funds; they originated in the Middle Atlantic colonies during the seventeenth century. 138

Private venture training schools Schools developed in the late seventeenth century by businesses and trades in the Middle Atlantic colonies to train skilled workers such as navigators, surveyors, accountants and printers. 139

Progressive movement A late nineteenth-century educational movement based on the educational theory of progressivism, which attempted to bring the disenfranchised into the schools. 150

Progressivism An educational theory, based on the philosophical school of pragmatism, believing that curriculum and teaching methodologies should relate to students' interests and needs. 219

Realism A philosophical school that seeks knowledge and understanding about the nature of reality and of humankind and attempts to interpret people's destiny based on that nature. 206

Reconstructionism An educational theory, based on the philosophical school of pragmatism, contending that the purpose of education is to reconstruct society. 222

Reinforce The occasional presentation of the unconditioned stimulus with the neutral stimulus to encourage the continuation of the desired effect (Pavlov). 352

Reinforcement A reward (such as food, money, praise) used to encourage a direct response. 353

Republicanism A political theory founded on the principle that government arises from the consent of the governed. 140

Reversal A cognitive process that allows children to work a problem backwards (Piaget). 335

Safety need The human need to feel safe (Maslow). 335

Scheme An organized pattern of behavior or thought that children formulate as they interact with parents, agemates, teachers, and the environment (Piaget). 333

Schoolmen Medieval philosophers who advocated educational methods of open-ended questioning, independent learning, and sensory learning. 127

Self-actualization Reaching one's highest potential (Maslow). 335

Sensorimotor period A period of cognitive development which occurs between birth and two years and is marked by the development of reflexes and responses (Piaget). 334

Seven cardinal principles A 1918 National Education Association report that recommended a nonclassical secondary curriculum for noncollege-bound students. 149

Shared identity Teachers and students share similar characteristics, making teaching easier. 32

Short-cycle family A family that produces children approximately every 14 years. 392

Single-parent family A family group headed by one parent. 385

Social disintegration A belief of social reconstructionists that society is in a severe crisis, caused by the unwillingness of humans to reconstruct institutions and values to meet existing needs. 223

Socratic method A teaching method that uses systematic doubt and questioning to get at underlying, universal meanings. 126

Sophists The earliest of Greek educators who taught grammar, logic, and rhetoric to educate the citizenry so they could become legislators. 126

Sophos A Greek word meaning wisdom. 196

Statutory law Statutes passed by federal and state legislatures. 519

Strict liability A type of tort liability that occurs when injury results from unusual hazards. 522

Structured observations Objective, formal observations of a predetermined classroom event, student, or teacher; data recorded using a prepared format such as a checklist. 54

Student-centered approaches of discipline Classroom management approaches of discipline that give students maximum freedom within limits; the teacher provides the appropriate environment and resources commensurate to the children's stage of development. 457

Student-centered teaching A teaching style in which instruction is tailored to the needs of the student. 41

Subject-centered teaching A teaching style similar to content-centered in that it focuses on covering the subject matter; differs in that student learning is not central. 41

Sunday school A church-sponsored, nineteenth-century school held on Sundays for children who worked at low-paying jobs during the week, designed to teach them basics of reading, writing, and religion. 144

Synectics Making the strange appear familiar, and the familiar appear strange; usually carried out in a small group setting in which students attempt to solve complex problems. 455

Systematic observation Planned, objective, goal-oriented observation of different classroom situations over an extended time period. 53

Task-oriented A teaching style in which materials, competencies, and appropriate levels of students' progress are prescribed. 40

Tax credit An amount equal to a percentage of school tuition that can be subtracted from federal and/or state income taxes. 441

Teacher accountability Personal responsibility for instructional quality as measured by such things as observations and student progress on standardized tests. 95

Teacher empowerment Teacher autonomy in making decisions that affect students, teachers, and schools; including selection of texts, promotion and retention of students, selection of teachers and administrators, etc. 91

Teachers' college model A teacher-training approach that emphasizes teaching methodology and fieldwork in an education specialty such as middle school mathematics; emphasis is on the development of teaching skills. 62

Teacher-student interaction approach to discipline A discipline approach in which the teacher and student work together employing structured discussion to find causes of student misbehavior. 457

Teacher-student-centered learning style A learning style in which both the teacher and student share equally in the planning of instruction. 42

Teaching style The unique way teachers organize instruction based on their philosophy of teaching and learning. 39

Tenure A contractual relationship between a teacher and a school board that can only be terminated for adequate cause and with due process procedures. 520

Theory of verification A branch of philosophical analysis that states that empirical propositions may be verified either directly or indirectly. 214

Time-on-task A strong focus on attention to the completion of tasks related to clearly stated instructional objectives. 240

Tort liability A civil wrong that pertains to the private rights of citizens and consists of three types: negligence, intentional tort, and strict liability. 522

Town schools Seventeenth-century schools established to provide elementary education for all New England children. 135

Tracking Ability grouping that places students based on academic performance, which includes school-based performance and scores on standardized achievement tests. 179

Unconditioned response An untaught response to a stimulus (Pavlov). 352

Unconditioned stimulus A stimulus that automatically provokes a response (Pavlov). 352

U.S. Department of Education A cabinet-level governmental agency representing a formalized federal effort in education with three major divisions: the Offices of Educational Research and Improvement, the National Center for Education Statistics, and the Information Services Department. 477

U.S. Supreme Court A body of judges, nominated by the president and confirmed by Congress, who interpret the Constitution and thereby can have significant influence on public education. 478

Valid inference Logical reasoning that allows one to determine if stated inferences about an experience or issue are valid.

Vernacular schools Schools established by the New Amsterdam Dutch settlers during the seventeenth century for teaching, reading, and writing in their native language. 138

Vouchers A receipt equal to the average per-pupil cost for educating a child in a specific area's public schools that can be redeemed from the government by the school in which the child is enrolled. 441

References

Abington School District v. Schempp, 374 U.S. 203 (1963).

Adler, M. J. 1982. *The Paideia proposal: An educational manifesto.* New York: Macmillan.

_____. 1983. *Paideia problems and possibilities.* New York: Macmillan.

Alan Guttmacher Institute. 1981. *Teenage pregnancy: The problem that hasn't gone away.* New York: Author.

_____. 1987. *Pregnancy, birth, and abortion rates in U.S., other countries.* Washington, DC: Author.

Alexander, A. April 4, 1991. Head Start: Initiation, federal funding, participation [telephone interview]. Atlanta, GA: Regional Head Start Office.

Alexander, K., and Alexander, M.D. 1984. *The law of schools, students and teachers.* St. Paul, MN: West Publishing.

Allen, J. 1991. League endorses status quo. *Business/Education Insider* 8 (March), 1.

Allen, P. 1989. Let your students lead you. *Learning* (September), *18* (2), 4.

Allen, R. W. 1990. Legislative limits on certification requirements: Lessons from the Texas experience. *Journal of Teacher Education* 41 (4), 26–32.

American Association of Colleges for Teacher Education. June 1989. *Alternative preparation for licensure: A policy statement.* Washington, DC: Author.

_____. 1989. *Rate III teaching teachers: Facts and figures.* (Research about Teacher Education Project). Washington, DC: Author.

American Association of School Administrators. 1988. *Women and minorities in school administration.* Arlington, VA: Author.

American Broadcasting Company (ABC). June 10, 1991. "Morning News," "Deaths resulting from crime in New York City," and "Deaths in the Persian Gulf War."

American Federation of Teachers, AFL-CIO. 1989. *Survey and analysis of salary trends, 1989.* Washington, DC: Author.

_____. 1990a. *Constitution of the American Federation of Teachers, AFL-CIO.* Washington, DC: Author.

_____. 1990b. *Convention report 1990.* Washington, DC: Author.

_____. 1991. *Survey and analysis of salary trends, 1991.* Washington, DC: Author.

American Student Council Association. 1990. *NAEP Survey of Student's Beliefs.* Alexandria, VA: Author.

Anderson, L. W. (Ed.). 1989. The effective teacher: Study guide and readings. New York: Random House.

Andrew, M. D. 1990. Differences between graduates of 4-year and 5-year teacher preparation programs. *Journal of Teacher Education* 41 (2), 45–51.

Ansberry, C. 1989. Learning by doing: After 23 years, foxfire still teaches practical skills with homespun methods. *Wall Street Journal* (March 31), R-24.

Apple, M. 1985. Making knowledge legitimate: Power, profit, and the textbook. In *Current thought on curriculum,* Ed. A. Molnar, 75. Alexandria, VA: Association for Supervision and Curriculum Development.

Apple, M., and King, N. R. 1977. What do schools teach? In *Humanistic education,* Ed. R. H. Weller, 29–63. Berkeley, CA: McCutchan.

Aristotle. 1899. *The politics,* Trans. B. Jowett. New York: Colonial Press.

_____. 1984. Politics, book VIII. In *The complete works of Aristotle.* Vol. 2, Ed. J. Barnes, 2121. Trans. B. Jowett. Princeton, NJ: Princeton University Press. Original work published 310 B.C.

Armstrong, L. S. 1991. Census confirms remarkable shifts in ethnic makeup. *Education Week* (March 20), 1, 16.

Association for Childhood Education International. 1991. Two pillars of education reform. *ACEI Exchange* 59 (4), 2.

Aubrey v. School District of Philadelphia, 63 Pa. Cmwlth. 330, 437A.2d 1306 (1981).

Austin-Martin, G., Bull, D., and Molrine, C. 1981. A study of the effectiveness of a pre-student teaching experience in promoting positive attitudes toward teaching. *Peabody Journal of Education* 58 (3), 148–153.

Ausubel, D. F. 1986. *Educational psychology: A cognitive view.* New York: Holt, Rinehart and Winston.

Ayer, A. J. 1982. *Philosophy in the twentieth century.* New York: Random House.

Ayers, William. 1990. Rethinking the profession of teaching: A progressive option. *Action in Teacher Education* 12 (1), 1–6.

Bailyn, B. 1960. *Education in the forming of American society: Needs and opportunities for study.* New York: Vintage.

Bane, M. J. 1976. *Here to stay: American families in the twentieth century.* New York: Basic Books.

Banks, J. A. 1989. Integrating the curriculum with ethnic content: Approaches and guidelines. In *Multicultural education: Issues and perspectives,* Ed. J. A. Banks and C. A. M. Banks, 189–207. Boston, MA: Allyn and Bacon.

_____. 1991. *Teaching strategies for ethnic studies,* 5th ed. Boston: Allyn and Bacon.

_____. March 1, 1991. Multicultural imperative. Paper presented at Conference on Cultural Diversity, University of North Carolina at Asheville.

Barnow, B. 1973. *Evaluating project Head Start.* Madison, WI, Madison Institute for Research on Poverty (ERIC Document Reproduction Service No. ED 106404).

Barwick, W. 1989. A chronology of the Kentucky case. *Journal of Education Finance* 15 (2), 136–141.

Bastian, A., Fruchter, N., Gittrell, M., Greer, C., and Haskins, K. 1986. *Choosing inequality.* Philadelphia: Temple University Press.

Beale, H. K. 1936. *Are American teachers free?* New York: Scribner.

Beaudry, M. L. 1991. Post-Carnegie developments affecting teacher education: The struggle for professionalism. *Journal of Teacher Education* 41 (1), 63–70.

Becker, H. J. 1985. The computer and the elementary school. *Principal* 64 (5), 32–34.

Becker, S. 1962. The nature of a profession. In *Education for the professions: The sixty-first yearbook of the National Society for the Study of Education,* pt. 2, Ed. N. B. Henry, 4–42. Chicago: University of Chicago Press.

Beilan v. Board of Public Education, School District of Philadelphia, 357 U.S. 399 (1958).

Bennett, W. J. 1985. *The condition of education.* Washington, DC: U.S. Government Printing Office.

_____. 1986. *First lessons: A report on elementary education in America.* Washington, DC: U.S. Government Printing Office.

_____. 1987a. *James Madison High School: A curriculum for American students.* Washington, DC: U.S. Government Printing Office.

_____. 1987b. *What works: Research about teaching and learning,* 2nd ed. Washington, DC: U.S. Government Printing Office.

_____. 1988a. *American education: Making it work.* Washington, DC: U.S. Government Printing Office.

_____. 1988b. *James Madison Elementary School: A curriculum for American students.* Washington, DC: U.S. Government Printing Office.

Bentrup, K., Rienzo, B. A., Dorman, S. M., and Lee, D. D. 1990. Cooperative learning: An alternative for adolescent AIDS education. *Clearing House* 64 (2), 107–111.

Bergquist, W., and Phillips. S. R. 1975. *A handbook for faculty development.* Washington, DC: Council for the Advancement of Small Colleges.

Berkeley, G. 1950. *A treatise concerning the principles of human knowledge.* LaSalle, IL: Open Court Publishing.

Berliner, D. C. 1989. The executive functions of teaching. In *The effective teacher,* Ed. L. W. Anderson. New York: Random, 105–112.

Bestor, A. 1955. *The restoration of learning.* New York: Alfred A. Knopf.

Bestor, A. 1985. *Educational wastelands: The retreat from learning in our public schools,* 2nd ed. Chicago: University of Illinois Press.

Bethel School District No. 403, Fraser 106 S.Ct. 3159 (1986).

Betts, F. 1991. U.S.–Japan comparisons called misleading. *Educational Leadership* 48 (6), 5.

Bicknell v. Vergennes Union High School Board of Directors, 475 F.Supp. 615 (D.V.T., 1979).

Biehler, R. F. 1978. *Psychology applied to teaching.* 3rd ed. Boston: Houghton Mifflin.

Biehler, F., and Snowman, J. 1982. *Psychology applied to teaching,* 4th ed. Boston: Houghton Mifflin.

_____. 1986. *Psychology applied to teaching,* 5th ed. Boston: Houghton Mifflin.

Bigge, M. L. 1982. *Educational philsophies for teachers.* Columbus, OH: Merrill.

Biklen, S. K. 1983. *Teaching as an occupation of women: A case study of an elementary school.* Syracuse, NY: Education Designs Group.

Bilingual Education Act of 1968 (P.L. 94-127).

Binder, F. M. 1974. *The age of the common school, 1830–1865.* New York: Wiley.

Bitter, G. 1989. *Microcomputers in education today.* Watsonville, CA: Mitchell.

Blair, G. 1990. Men vs. women: Imagine two men in a board-room. *Business Month* (October), 43, 44, 49.

Bloom, B. S. 1968. *Learning for mastery.* Los Angeles: Center for the Study of Evaluation.

_____. 1976. *Human characteristics and school learning.* New York: McGraw-Hill.

_____. 1981. *All our children learning: A primer for parents, teachers, and other educators.* New York: McGraw-Hill.

_____. 1984. The search for methods of group instruction as effective as one-to-one tutoring. *Educational Leadership* 42 (9), 5.

Bloom, B. S., et al. 1956. *Taxonomy of educational objectives, handbook I: Cognitive domain.* New York: David McKay.

Blue, T. 1986. *The teaching and learning process.* Washington, DC: National Education Association.

Blunt v. Marion Country School Board, 515 F.2d 951 (5th Cir., 1975).

Board of Education v. Rockaway Township Education Assoc. 120 N.J. Super. 564, 295A. 29 380 (1972).

Board of Regents v. Roth, 408 U.S. 564 (1972).

Bobbitt, F. 1924. *How to make a curriculum.* Boston: Houghton Mifflin.

Boe, E. C. April 9, 1990. *Teacher incentive research with SASS.* Paper presented at the meeting of the American Education Research Association. Boston, MA.

Bohannan, L. 1966. Shakespeare in the bush. *Natural History* 75 (7), 28–33.

Bolin, F. S., and Falk, J. M. 1987. *Teacher renewal: Professional issues, personal choices.* New York: Teachers College Press.

Bond, H. M. 1966. *The education of the Negro in the American social order.* New York: Octagon Books.

Boocock, S. S. 1980. *Sociology of education: An introduction.* New York: Macmillan.

Borrowman, M. L. 1961. Traditional values and the shaping of American education. In *The sixtieth yearbook of the National Society for the Study of Education,* Ed. N. B. Henry, 144–159. Chicago: University of Chicago Press.

Bossert, S. T. 1985. Effective elementary schools. *Reaching for excellence: An effective school's sourcebook,* Ed. R. M. Kyle, 39–53. National Institute of Education (No. 400-81-0004). Washington, DC: U.S. Government Printing Office.

Bourne, R. S. 1916. *The Gary schools.* Boston: Houghton Mifflin.

Bourne v. Northwest Allen County School Corp., 532 N.E.2d 1196 (Ind. Ct. App., 1989).

Bouvier, L. F., and Agresta, A. J. 1987. The future Asian population of the United States. In *Pacific bridges: The new immigration from Asia and the Pacific Islands,* Ed. J. T. Fawcett and B. V. Carino. New York: Center for Migration Studies.

Boyer, E. L. 1983. *High School.* New York: Harper and Row.

Braddock, J. H. 1990. Tracking the middle grades: National patterns of grouping for instruction. *Phi Delta Kappan* 71 (6), 445–449.

Bradley, A. 1990. Chicago reforms to get $40 million from MacArthur. *Education Week* (October 17), 1, 22.

Brameld, T. 1950. *Ends and means in education: A midcentury appraisal.* New York: Harper Brothers.

———. 1971. *Patterns of educational philosophy: Divergence and convergence in culturological perspective.* New York: Holt, Rinehart and Winston.

Brandt, R. M. 1990. *Incentive pay and career ladders for today's teachers.* Albany, NY: State University of New York Press.

Brett, P. 1990. France makes universities the center of its new approach to teacher education. *Chronicle of Higher Education* (October 31), A39, A42.

Brod v. School Dist. No. 1, 386 N.Y.S.2d 125 (App. Div., 1976).

Brookover, W., et al. 1977. *Schools can make a difference.* East Lansing, MI: College of Urban Development, Michigan State University.

Brooks, D. M., and Kopp, T. W. 1989. Technology in teacher education. *Journal of Teacher Education* 40 (4), 2–7.

Brophy, J., and Evertson, C. 1974a. Process-product correlations. In *Texas effectiveness study: Final report* (Research Report No. 74-4). Austin: University of Texas,

R&D Center for Teacher Education (ERIC Document Reproduction Service No. ED 091 0943).

———. 1974b. *The Texas Teacher Effectiveness Project: Presentation of non-linear relationships and summary discussion* (Research Report No. 74-6). Austin: University of Texas, R&D Center for Teacher Education. (ERIC Document Reproduction Service ED 099 345).

———. 1976. *Learning from teaching: A developmental perspective.* Boston: Allyn and Bacon.

Brophy, J., and Good, T. 1984. *Looking into classrooms.* 3rd ed. New York: Harper and Row.

———. 1986. *Teacher behavior and student achievement.* In *Handbook of research on teaching,* 3rd ed., Ed. M. C. Wittrock, 328–375. New York: Macmillan.

Brown, B. F. 1984. *Crisis in secondary education: Rebuilding America's high schools.* Englewood Cliffs, NJ: Prentice-Hall.

Brown v. Board of Education of Topeka, 347 U.S. 483 (1954).

Brubacher, J. 1966. *A history of problems in education,* 2nd ed. New York: McGraw-Hill.

Bruder, I. 1989. Future teachers: Are they prepared? *Electronic learning* (January–February), 32–39.

Brumbaugh, R. S. 1964. *The philosophers of Greece.* New York: Thomas Y. Crowell.

Bruner, J. S. 1960. *The process of education.* New York: Vintage.

Buechler, M. March 1990. Alternative certification for teachers. *Policy Bulletin No. 7.* Bloomington, IN: Consortium on Education Policy Studies.

Bull, B. L. 1990. The limits of teacher professionalism. In *The moral dimensions of teaching,* Ed. J. I. Goodlad, R. Soder, and K. A. Sirotnik, 87–129. San Francisco: Jossey-Bass.

Bullock, H. A. 1967. *A history of Negro education in the South: From 1619 to the present.* Cambridge, MA: Harvard University Press.

Bullough, R. 1988. Evaluation and the beginning teacher: A case study. *Education and Society* 6 (1, 2), 71–78.

Bureau of Labor Statistics. 1988. *Current population survey, 1988.* Washington, DC: Author.

Burt, M. R., and Cohen, B. E. 1989. *American homeless: Numbers, characteristics and programs that serve them.* Washington, DC: Urban Institute Press.

Bush, G. 1989. Remarks at the education summit, welcoming ceremony in Charlottesville, Virginia. In *Weekly Compilation of Presidential Documents* 25 (39), 1454–1463. Washington, DC: U.S. Government Printing Office.

Bush, R. N. 1967. The science and art of educating teachers. In *Improving teacher education in the United States,* Ed. S. Elam, 35–62. Bloomington, IN: Phi Delta Kappan.

Butler, J. D. 1966. *Idealism in education.* New York: Harper and Row.

Buttery, T. J., Haberman, M., and Houston, W. R. 1990. First annual ATE survey of critical issues in teacher education. *Action in Teacher Education* 12 (2), 1–7.

Button, H. W., and Provenzo, E. F., Jr. 1983. *History of education and culture in America*. Englewood Cliffs, NJ: Prentice-Hall.

Butts, R. F. 1978. *Public education in the United States: From revolution to reform*. New York: Holt, Rinehart and Winston.

Butts, R. F., and Cremin, L. A. 1953. *A history of education in American culture*. New York: Holt, Rinehart and Winston.

Campbell, R. F., Cunningham, L. L., and McPhee, R. F. 1965. *The organization and control of American schools*. Columbus, OH: Charles E. Merrill.

Campbell, R. F., Cunningham, L. L., Nystrand, R. O., and Usdan, M. D. 1985. *The organization and control of American schools*, 5th ed. Columbus OH: Charles E. Merrill.

Cannell, J. J. 1989. *How public educators cheat on standardized tests: The "Lake Wobegon" report*. Albuquerque, NM: Friends of Education. ERIC Document Reproduction Service No. ED 314 454.

Canter, L., and Canter, M. 1977. *Assertive discipline*. Santa Monica, CA: Canter and Associates.

Carnegie Council on Adolescent Development, Carnegie Corporation of New York. 1989. *Turning points: Preparing American youth for the 21st century*. Washington, DC: Author.

Carnegie Forum on Education and the Economy. 1986. *A nation prepared: Teachers for the 21st century* (Report of the Task Force on Teaching as a Profession). New York: Author.

Carnegie Foundation for the Advancement of Teaching. 1988a. *The condition of teaching: A state-by-state analysis*, 3rd ed. Princeton, NJ: Author.

_____. 1988b. *An imperiled generation: Saving urban schools*. Lawrenceville, NJ: Princeton University Press.

_____. 1990. *The condition of teaching: A state-by-state analysis*. Princeton, NJ: Author.

Carnoy, M., and Levin, H. M. 1985. *Schooling and work in the democratic state*. Stanford, CA: Stanford University Press.

Carroll, G. Fall, Winter 1990. Who foots the bill? *Newsweek* (special issue), 81–85.

Cary v. Board of Education of the Adams-Arapahoe School District, 28-J, 598 F.2d 535, 544. (10th. Cir., 1979).

Cavazos, L. V. 1989a. *Choosing a school for your child*. Washington, DC: U.S. Department of Education.

_____. 1989b. *Educating our children: Parents and schools together*. Washington, DC: U.S. Department of Education.

Center for Population Options. 1986. *Teenage sexuality, pregnancy and parenthood*. Washington, DC: Author.

_____. 1987. *Estimates of public costs for teenage childbearing, 1986 Report*. Washington, DC: Author.

Center for the Study of Social Policy. 1991. *Kids count data book: State profiles of child well-being*. Washington, DC: Author.

Centers for Disease Control. 1988. Guidelines for effective school health education to prevent the spread of AIDS. In *Morbidity and Weekly Report Supplement 37* (S-2), 1–14.

Chabator, K. J., and Montgomery, S. H. 1972. *Second year evaluation of an American management association pilot program: Adapting and testing business management development programs for educational administrators*. Syracuse University. Maxwell Graduate School of Education, ERIC Document Reproduction Service No. ED 072543.

Chance, W. 1986. " . . . *The best of educations": Reforming America's public schools in the 1980's*. Chicago: John D. and Catherine T. MacArthur Foundation.

Chenfield, M. B. 1987. *Teaching language arts creatively*. 2nd ed. San Diego: Harcourt Brace Jovanovich.

Children's Defense Fund. 1990. *Children 1990: A report card, briefing book, and action primer*. Washington, DC: Author.

_____. 1991. *Child poverty in America*. Washington, DC: Author.

Children in Philadelphia factories. August 20, 1830. Mechanics Free Press. Columns 3, 4, p. 2.

Childs, J. 1972. *Education and the philosophy of experimentalism*. New York: Ayer.

Chira, S. 1990. Princeton student's brainstorm: A peace corps to train teachers. *New York Times* (June 20), A1, B7.

_____. 1991a. Bush presses bill allowing parents to choose schools. *New York Times* (April 19), A1, B7.

_____. 1991b. Bush's education vision. *New York Times* (April 20), 1, 8.

_____. 1991c. The rules of the marketplace are applied to the classroom. *New York Times* (June 12), A1, B5.

_____. 1991d. Teaching history so that cultures are more than footnotes. *New York Times* (July 10), A17.

Chubb, J. E., and Moe, T. M. 1990. *Politics, markets, and America's schools*. Washington, DC: Brookings Institution.

Clark, C. M. 1989. Research into practice: Cautions and qualifications. In *The effective teacher: Study guide and readings*, Ed. L. W. Anderson, 113–121. New York: Random House.

Clark v. Furch, 567 S.W.2d 457 (Mo. App., 1978).

Clewett, A. S. 1988. Guidance and discipline: Teaching young children appropriate behavior. *Young Children* 43 (4), 26–31.

Cobb, J. J. 1981. *An introduction to educational law*. Springfield, IL: Charles C. Thomas.

Cohen, D. L. 1989. Middle schools gain "focus" on child. *Education Week* (June 21), 1, 20.

Cohen, S. A., Ed. 1978. *Education in the United States: A documentary history*. Vols. 1–3. New York: Random House.

Coleman, J. 1966. *Equality of educational opportunity*. Vol. 1. Washington DC: U.S. Government Printing Office.

Collins, M., and Tamarkin, C. 1982. *Marva Collins' way*. Los Angeles, CA: Jeremy P. Tharcher.

Collins, R. 1984. Head Start: A review of research with implications for practice in early childhood education. Paper presented at the Annual meeting of the American Educational Research Association, New Orleans, LA, April 23–27, 1984. (ERIC Document Reproduction Service No. ED 24.5833).

Combs, A. W. 1982. Affective education or none at all. *Educational Leadership* 34 (7), 495–497.

Comenius, J. A. 1897. The great didactic. In *The great didactic of John Amos Comenius*, Ed. and trans. M. W. Keatinge. London, England: Adam Black. Original work published 1657.

_____. 1956. *The school of infancy*, Ed. E. M. Eller. Chapel Hill: The University of North Carolina Press. Original work published 1633.

_____. 1968. Orbis Pictus. In *The Orbis pictus of John Amos Comenius*, Ed. C. W. Bardeen. Detroit, MI: Singing Tree Press. Original work published 1659.

Committee for Economic Development. 1991. *The unfinished agenda: A new vision for child development and education.* New York: Author.

Compton, N., Duncan, M., and Hruska, J. 1987. *How schools can help combat student pregnancy.* Washington, DC: National Education Association.

Conant, J. B. 1948. *Education in a divided world.* Cambridge, MA: Harvard University Press.

_____. 1959. *The American high school today.* New York: McGraw-Hill.

_____. 1962. *Thomas Jefferson and the development of American public education.* Berkeley: University of California Press.

Conroy, P. 1972. *The water is wide.* Boston: Houghton Mifflin.

Corcoran, T. B. 1985. Effective secondary schools. In *Reaching for excellence: An effective school's sourcebook*, Ed. R. M. Kyle, 71–97. National Institute of Education (No. 400-81-0004). Washington, DC: U.S. Government Printing Office.

Corey, S. J. 1944. The poor scholar's soliloquy. *Childhood Education* 64 (3), 150–151.

Cornwell v. State Board of Education, 314 F.Supp. 340 (D. Md., 1969).

Council of Chief State School Officers. 1988. Teacher preparation: Coursework requirements. *Policies and practices questionnaire: State education indicators.* (MOO-C.C.S.S.O.) Washington, DC: Author.

Council of State Directors of Programs for the Gifted. 1987. *The 1987 state of the states gifted and talented education report.* Washington, DC: Author.

Counts, G. 1969. *Dare the schools build a new social order?* New York: John Day (orig. ed. 1932).

Cremin, L. 1990. *Popular education and its discontents.* New York. Harper and Row.

Cremin, L. A. 1951. *The American common school: A historical conception.* New York: Teachers College Press.

_____. Ed. 1957. *The republic and the school: Horace Mann on the education of free men.* New York: Bureau of Publications, Teachers College, Columbia University.

_____. 1964. *The transformation of the school: Progressivism in American education, 1876–1957.* New York: Alfred A. Knopf.

_____. 1970. *American education: The colonial period, 1607–1783.* New York: Harper.

_____. 1980. *American education: The national experience, 1783–1876.* New York: Harper.

_____. 1988. *American education: The metropolitan experience, 1876–1980.* New York: Harper and Row.

_____. 1990. *Popular education and its discontents.* New York: Harper and Row.

Crowley, J. C. 1970. Letter from a teacher. *Massachusetts Teacher* (September–October), 34–38.

Cruickshank, D. R. 1988. Profile of an effective teacher. In *Education: Annual editions, 87/88*, Ed. F. Shultz, 216–221. Guilford, CT: Dushkin Publishing Group.

Cubberly, E. P. 1919. *Public education in the United States.* Boston: Houghton Mifflin.

_____. 1920. *Readings in the history of education.* Boston: Houghton Mifflin.

_____. 1925. *An introduction to the study of education and to teaching.* Boston: Houghton Mifflin.

Cullum, M. 1990. Cartoon: Spell school funding. *Birmingham News* (May 7), 2C.

Cunningham v. Beavers 858 F.2d (5th Cir., 1988).

Cyran, J. 1987. The banning of corporal punishment. *Childhood Education* 63 (3), 146–63.

Darling-Hammond, L. 1984a. *Beyond the commission reports: The coming crisis in teaching.* Santa Monica, CA: Rand.

_____. 1984b. The Toledo (Ohio) public school intern and intervention programs. In A. E. Wise, L. Darling-Hammond, M. W. McLaughlin, and H. T. Bernstein (authors), *Case studies for teacher evaluation: A study of effective practices*, 119–166. Santa Monica, CA: Rand.

_____. 1988. Accountability and teacher professionalism. *American Educator*, 1 (1), 8–13, 38–43.

Darling-Hammond, L., and Berry, B. 1988. *The evolution of teacher policy.* Santa Monica, CA: Rand.

Darling-Hammond, L., Hudson, L., and Kirby, S. N. 1989. *Redesigning teacher education: Opening the door for new recruits to science and mathematics teaching.* Center for the Study of the Teacher Profession (R-3661-FF/CSTP). Santa Monica, CA: Rand.

Davis, J. D. 1974. *Coping with disruptive behavior.* Washington, DC: National Education Association.

deLone, R. H. 1979. *Small futures: Children, inequality, and the limits of liberal reform.* New York: Harcourt, Brace Jovanovich.

DeLong, T. J. 1987. Teachers and their careers: Why do they choose teaching? *Journal of Career Development*, 14 (2), 118–125.

deMauro, D. 1989–1990. *Sexuality education 1990: A review of state sexuality and AIDS education curricula.* New York: Sex Information and Education Council of the United States (SIECUS).

Denham, C., and Lieberman, A., Eds. 1980. *Time to learn. A review of the beginning teacher evaluation study.* (Report No. EA 12 947). Washington, DC: National Institute of Education (DHEW). (ERIC Document Reproduction Service No. ED 192 454).

Devor, J. W. 1964. *The experience of student teaching.* New York: MacMillan.

Dewey, J. 1902. *The child and the curriculum.* Chicago: University of Chicago Press.

_____. 1915. *The school and society.* Chicago: University of Chicago Press.

_____. 1928. *Democracy and education.* New York: Macmillan.

Dewey, E., and Dewey, J. 1915. *Schools of tomorrow.* New York: Dutton.

Dickens, C. 1960 [1859]. *A tale of two cities.* New York: New American Library.

Diegmueller, K. 1991. A case in point: District fears quality is suffering as it cuts closer to the bone. *Education Week* (May 29), 1, 10, 11.

Douglass, F. 1962. *The life and times of Frederick Douglass.* New York: Macmillan. Original work published 1850.

_____. 1970. *My bondage and my freedom.* Chicago: Johnson Publishing. Original work published 1855.

Downing, J., and Harrison, T. C., Jr. 1990. Dropout prevention: A practical approach. *School Counselor* 38 (1), 67–73.

Downs, R. B. 1974. *Horace Mann.* New York: Twayne.

Doyle, D. P. 1989a. Business and the schools. *Business Week* (special advertising section), E24–E31, E45–46, E90.

_____. 1989b. Endangered species: Children of promise, student as worker. *Business Week* (special advertising section), E121.

Duffy, B. 1986. Putting teachers to test [an interview with Albert Shanker]. *U.S. News and World Report* (July 21), 58.

Duke, D. L. 1984. *Teaching: The imperiled profession.* Albany: State University of New York Press.

Dunn, K. J., and Dunn, R. S. 1987. Dispelling outmoded beliefs about student learning. *Education Leadership* 44 (6), 56–72.

Dunn, R. S., and Dunn, K. J. 1979. Learning styles/ teaching styles: Should they . . . can they . . . be matched? *Education Leadership* 26 (4), 238–244.

Dunn, R., Gemake, J., Jalali, F., and Zenhauser, R. 1990. Cross-cultural differences in learning styles of elementary-age students from four ethnic backgrounds. *Journal of Multicultural Counseling and Development* 18 (2), 68–93.

Durham, M. 1989. Swapping chalk for cheese: Teachers over the wall. *London Sunday Times* (June 4), F4.

Dye, T. R. 1985. *Politics in states and communities,* 5th ed. Englewood Cliffs, NJ: Prentice-Hall.

Eberlein, L. 1989. Ethical decision making for teachers. *Clearing House* 63 (3), 125–129.

Eby, J. 1931. *Early Protestant educators.* New York: AMS Press.

Eck, A. 1990. [July telephone interview: Number of teachers leaving profession]. Washington, DC: Bureau of Labor Statistics.

Economic Opportunity Act (EOA) of 1964 (P.L. 88-452).

Edgewood Indep. School Dist. v. Kirby, 777 S.W.2d 391 Tex. (1989).

Edmonds, R. 1979. Effective schools for the urban poor. *Educational Leadership* 37 (2), 15–27.

Education Commission of the States. 1983. *Action for excellence.* Denver, CO: Rand.

Education for All Handicapped Children Act of 1975 (P.L. 94-142).

Education Week staff. 1990a. Nike donates $1 million to N.F.I.E. drop-out prevention program. *Education Week* (September 19), 2.

Educational Testing Service. 1988a. *The mathematics report card: Are we measuring up? Trends and achievement based on the 1986 national assessment.* (Project of the National Center for Education Statistics, U.S. Department of Education). Princeton, NJ: Author.

_____. 1988b. *The science report card: Elements of risk and recovery: Trends and achievement based on the 1986 national assessment.* (Project of the National Center for Education Statistics, U.S. Department of Education). Princeton, NJ: Author.

_____. 1990a. *The reading report card, 1971–88: Trends from the nation's report card.* (Project of the National Center for Education Statistics, U.S. Department of Education). Princeton, NJ: Author.

_____. 1990b. *The U.S. history report card: The achievement of fourth-, eighth-, and twelfth-grade students in 1988 and trends from 1986 to 1988 in the factual knowledge of high-school juniors.* (Project of the National Center for Education Statistics, U.S. Department of Education). Princeton, NJ: Author.

_____. 1990c. *The writing report card, 1984–88: Findings from the nation's report card.* (Project of the National Center for Education Statistics, U.S. Department of Education). Princeton, NJ: Author.

Edwards, T. K. 1988. Providing reasons for wanting to live. *Phi Delta Kappan* 70 (4), 296–298.

Egan, K. 1990. Ethical codes: A standard for ethical behavior. *NASSP Bulletin* 74 (2), 59–62.

Einstein, A. 1954. *Ideas and opinions.* New York: Crown.

Eisner, E. W. 1985. *The educational imagination: On the design and evaluation of school programs,* 2nd ed. New York: Macmillan.

Elam, S. M. 1990. The 22nd annual Gallup poll of the public's attitudes toward the schools. *Phi Delta Kappan* 72 (1), 41–55.

Elementary and Secondary Education Act of 1965 (P.L. 89-10).

Ellis, J., Ed. 1867. *The Work of Ann Bradstreet,* 269–270. Charlestown, MA.

Ellison, L. 1990–1991. The many facets of school choice. *Educational Leadership* 48 (4), 37.

Emans, R. L. 1987. Abuse in the name of protecting children. *Phi Delta Kappan* 68 (10), 740–743.

Epperson v. Arkansas, 393 U.S. 97, 106 (1968).

Epstein, J. L. 1988. Parent involvement: State education agencies should lead the way. In *"Drawing in the family": Family involvement in the schools,* 1–4. Denver, CO: Education Commission of the States.

Erasmus, D. 1904. Depueris instituendis. In *Erasmus concerning education.* Cambridge MA: Cambridge University Press. Original work published 1518.

Erikson, E. H. 1963. *Childhood and society,* 2nd ed. New York: W. W. Norton.

Esty, J. C. 1984. *Annual report of the president: Independent schools and public interest.* Washington, DC: National Association of Independent Schools. Unpublished manuscript.

Etzoni, A. 1969. *The semiprofessions: Teachers, nurses and social workers.* New York: Free Press.

Evertson, C., Anderson, C., Anderson, L., and Brophy, J. 1980. The Texas junior high school study: Relationship between classroom behavior and student outcomes in junior high math and English classes. *American Educational Research Journal,* 17 (1), 43–60.

Evertson, C. M., and Green, J. L. 1986. Observation as inquiry and method. In *Handbook of research on teaching,* 3rd ed., Ed. M. C. Wittrock, 162–213. New York: Macmillan.

Fadely, J. L., and Hosler, V. N. 1983. *Case studies in left and right hemispheric functioning.* Springfield, IL: Charles C. Thomas.

Fagan, T. W., and Heid, C. A. 1991. Chapter I program improvement: Opportunity and practice. *Phi Delta Kappan* 72 (8), 582–585.

Fallows, J. 1989. *More like us: Making America great again.* Boston: Houghton Mifflin.

Family Life Matters. Fall 1990. *Newsletter of the New Jersey network for family life education.* (No. 11). (Available from the Center for Community Education, School of Social Work, Rutgers, State University of New Jersey, Building 4087, Kilmer Campus, New Brunswick, NJ 08903.)

Feibleman, J. 1946. *The revival of realism.* Chapel Hill: University of North Carolina Press.

Feiman-Nemser, S., and Fischer, L. I. 1979. Styles in teaching and learning. *Educational leadership* 36 (4), 245–254.

Feiman-Nemser, S., and Floden, R. E. 1986. The cultures of teaching. In *Handbook of research on teaching,* 3rd ed., Ed. M. C. Whittrock, 505–526. New York: Macmillan.

Feinberg, W. 1990. The moral responsibility of public schools. In *The moral dimensions of teaching,* Ed. J. I. Goodlad, R. F. Soder, and K. A. Sirotnik, 155–187, San Francisco: Jossey-Bass.

Fenstermacher, G. D. 1990. Some moral considerations on teaching as a profession. In *The moral dimensions of teaching,* Ed. J. I. Goodlad, R. F. Soder, and K. A. Sirotnik, 130–151. San Francisco: Jossey-Bass.

Fischer, B. B., and Fischer, L. 1979. Styles in teaching and learning. *Educational Leadership* 26 (4), 245–254.

Fischer, L., and Sorenson, G. P. 1985. *School law for counselors, psychologists, and social workers.* New York: Longman.

Fischer, L., Schimmel, D., and Kelly, C. 1981. *Teachers and the law.* New York: Longman.

Fiske, E. B. 1989. Wave of the future: A choice of schools. *New York Times* (June 4), 32.

_____. 1991. *Smart schools, smart kids. Why do some schools work?* New York: Simon and Schuster.

Flanders, N. 1970. *Analyzing teacher behavior.* Reading, MA: Addison-Wesley.

Flanders, N., and Simon, A. 1969. Teacher effectiveness. In *Encyclopedia of educational research,* 4th ed., Ed. R. Ebel, 426–437. New York: Macmillan.

Flavel, J. H. 1982. Structures, stages, and sequences in cognitive development. In *The concept of development: The Minnesota symposia on child psychology,* vol. 15, Ed. W. Collins. Hillsdale, NJ: Erlbaum.

Flexner, A., and Bachman, F. 1918. *The Gary schools.* New York: General Education Board.

Foltz, R. G. 1989a. Speak the language of possibility. *Learning* (September), 16.

_____. Ed. 1989b. Teach the art of success. *Learning 89* [special issue] (September), 10.

Fox, L. H. 1979. Programs for the gifted and talented: An overview. In *The gifted and talented: Their education and development* (Seventh–eighth yearbook of the National Society for the Study of Education), Ed. A. H. Passow, 104–126. Chicago, IL: University of Chicago Press.

Frank v. Orleans Parish School Bd., 195 So.2d 451 (La. App., 1967).

Franklin, B. 1978. Proposals relating to the education of youth in Pennsylvania. In *Education in the United States: A documentary history.* Vol. 1, Ed. S. Cohen, 495–504. New York: Random House. Original work published 1744.

Freidson, E. 1986. *Professional powers: A study of the institutionalization of formal knowledge.* Chicago: University of Chicago Press.

French, W. M. 1964. *America's educational tradition.* Boston: Heath.

Froebel, F. 1889. *The education of man,* Trans. W. Hailman. New York: Appelton.

Frymier, J. 1988. Understanding and preventing teen suicide: An interview with Barry Garfinkle. *Phi Delta Kappan* 70 (4), 290–293.

Fulghum, R. 1986. *All I really need to know I learned in kindergarten: Uncommon thoughts on common things.* New York: Ballantine.

Fuller, M. L. 1989. Delayed parenting: Implications for schools. *Childhood Education* 66 (2), 75–77.

Furth, M., Bredeson, P. V., and Kasten, K. L. 1982. *Commitment to teaching: Teachers' response to organizational incentives.* Madison: Wisconsin Center for Educational Research.

Futrell, M. H. 1989. *An open letter to America on schools, students, and tomorrow.* Washington, DC: National Education Association.

Gage, N. L. 1978. *The scientific basis of the art of teaching.* New York: Teachers College Press.

_____. 1990. Dealing with the dropout problem. *Phi Delta Kappan,* 72 (4), 280–285.

Gage, N. L., Belgard, M., Dell, D., Hiller, J., Rosenshine, B., and Unruh, W. 1968. *Explorations of the teacher's effectiveness in explaining* (Tech. Rep. No. 4). Stanford, CA: Stanford University, Center for Research and Development in Teaching.

Gagne, R. M. 1970. *The conditions of learning*, 2nd ed. New York: Holt, Rinehart and Winston.

Gagne, R. M., and Briggs, L. J. 1965. *Principles of instructional design*, 2nd ed. New York: Holt, Rinehart and Winston.

Galambos, E. C. 1985. *Teacher preparation: The anatomy of a college degree*. Atlanta, GA: Southern Regional Education Board.

_____. February 15, 1991. Results of Southern Regional Education Board's (SREB) proposals for teacher preparation. [Telephone interview with authors].

Gallagher, M. 1990. Women: The glass-ceiling excuse is so much nonsense. *Business Month* (October), 42–43.

Gallup, A. M. 1988. The 22nd annual Gallup Poll of the public's attitudes toward the schools. *Phi Delta Kappan* 70 (4), 34–46.

_____. 1990. The 22nd annual Gallup Poll of the public's attitude toward the schools. *Phi Delta Kappan* 72 (2), 41–55.

Gallup, A. M., and Elam, S. M. 1988. The 20th annual Gallup Poll of the public's attitude toward the schools. *Phi Delta Kappan* 70 (1), 33–46.

Gallup Organization. March 1991. *Teenage suicide study*. Princeton, NJ: Author.

Gandara, P. 1989. "Those" children are ours: Moving toward community. *Today: Issues '89* [special edition] (January), 38–49.

Garcia, R. 1978. The multiethnic dimension of bilingual-bicultural education. *Social Education* 42 (6), 492–493.

Gardner, D. P. 1983. *A nation at risk: The imperative for educational reform*. Washington, DC: U.S. Government Printing Office.

Gardner, J. W. 1961. *Excellence: Can we be equal and excellent too?* New York: Harper and Row.

Gatto, J. T. 1991. The 6-lesson schoolteacher. *Whole earth review* 96–100.

Gauss, J. 1962. Evaluation of Socrates as a teacher. *Phi Delta Kappan* (January), back cover).

Geiger, K. 1991. The six education goals: America's children cannot wait. *Education Week*, 12.

Gelman, D. 1990. A much riskier passage. [special issue] *Newsweek* (Summer/Fall), 10–17.

Gelman, R., and Gallistel, C. R. 1978. *The young child's understanding of numbers: A window on early cognitive development*. Cambridge, MA: Harvard University Press.

Gest, T. 1989. Victims of crime. *U.S. News and World Report* (July 31), 16–19.

Gilchrist, R. 1989. *Effective schools: Three case studies of excellence*. Bloomington, IN: National Education Service.

Gilligan, C. 1988. Adolescent development reconsidered. In *Mapping the moral domain: A contribution of women's thinking to psychological theory and education*, Ed. C. Gilligan, J. V. Ward, J. M. Taylor, and B. Bardige, vii–xxxix. Cambridge, MA: Center for the Study of Gender Education and Human Development.

Girl Scouts of America. 1990. *Beliefs and moral values of American children*. New York: Author.

Giroux, H., and Purpel, D., Eds. 1983. *The hidden curriculum and moral education*. Berkeley, CA: McCutchan.

Glasser, W. 1969. *Schools without failure*. New York: Harper and Row.

Glenn, M. 1982. *Class dismissed: High school poems*. New York: Ticknor and Fields.

Gloeckler, L. C., and Cianca, M. 1986. Expectations for quality and achievement in special education. *Educational Leadership* 44 (1), 31.

Glosoff, H. L., and Koprowicz, C. L. 1990. *Children achieving potential: An introduction to elementary school counseling and state-level policies*. Alexandria, VA: American Association for Counseling and Development.

Golden, C. 1985. Understanding the gender gap. *New Perspectives* 17 (4), 142.

Good, C. 1959. *Dictionary of education*. New York: McGraw-Hill.

_____. Ed. 1973. *Dictionary of education*, 3rd ed. New York: McGraw-Hill.

Good, T. L., and Brophy, J. E. 1986. School effects. In *Handbook of research on teaching*, 3rd. ed., Ed. M. C. Wittrock, 570–602. New York: Macmillan.

Good, T. L., and Grouws, D. 1975. *Process-product relationships in fourth-grade mathematics classrooms* (Final Report: National Institute of Education Grant NIE-G-00-3-0133). Columbia, MO: University of Missouri, College of Education.

Goodlad, J. I. 1983. The problems of getting markedly better schools. In *Bad times, good schools*, Ed. J. Frymier, 59–77. West Lafayette, IN: Kappa Delta Pi.

_____. 1984. *A place called school: Prospects for the future*. New York: McGraw-Hill.

_____. 1990a. The occupation of teaching in schools. In *The moral dimensions of teaching*, Ed. J. I. Goodlad, R. Soder, and K. A. Sirotnik, 3–34. San Francisco: Jossey-Bass.

_____. 1990b. *Teachers for our nation's schools*. San Francisco: Jossey-Bass.

Gordon, E. W. 1974. The political economics of effective schooling. In *Equality of educational opportunity*, Ed. L. P. Miller and E. W. Gordon, 445–459. New York: AMS Press.

_____. 1989. An interview with Nancy Rabianski-Carriuolo on learning styles in different cultures. *Journal of Developmental Psychology* 62 (6), 18–19.

Gordon, W. J. J. 1971. *Synetics*. New York: Collier Books.

Gorney, C. 1985. The bilingual education battle. *Washington Post National Weekly Edition* (July 29), 6–10.

Goslin, D. A. 1965. *The school in contemporary society*. Chicago: Scott, Foresman.

Graham, E. 1990. Bottom-line education: A business-run school in Chicago seeks to improve learning without a big rise in costs. *Wall Street Journal* (February 9), R24, R26–R27.

Graham, P. 1989. The other certification: More benefits than risks? [special edition] *N.E.A. Today* 76 (6), 75–78.

Grant, G. 1985. Schools that make an imprint: Creating a strong positive ethos. In *Challenge to American schools*, Ed. J. D. Bunzell, 127–143. New York: Oxford.

Grant, V. 1990. [July 19 telephone interview: Number of teachers leaving the profession]. National Center for Education Statistics. Washington, DC: U.S. Department of Education.

Grasha, A. F. 1972. Observations on relating goals to student response styles and classroom methods. *American Psychologist* 27 (8), 144–147.

Graubard, S. R. 1984. Preface to the issue, "values, resources, and politics in America's schools." *Daedalus* 113 (4), v–xi.

Green, J. (Ed.). 1985. *Conversations: 20 years in American education*. Denver, CO: Education Commission of the States.

Greene, M., Ed. 1967. *Existential encounters for teachers.* New York: Random House.

Greenwood, G. E., and Parkway, F. M. 1989. *Case studies for teacher decision making.* New York: Random.

Griese, A. A. 1980. *Your philosophy of education: What is it?* Santa Monica, CA: Goodyear.

Grube, G. M. A. 1935. *Plato's thought.* Boston, MA: Beacon Press.

Guralnik, D. B., and Friend, J. S., Eds. 1968. *Webster's new world dictionary of the American language.* New York: World Publishing.

Gutek, G. L. 1968. *Pestalozzi and education.* New York: Random House.

_____. 1988. *Philosophical and ideological perspectives on education.* Englewood Cliffs, NJ: Prentice-Hall.

Gutman, A. 1987. *Democratic education.* Princeton, NJ: Princeton University Press.

Haberman, M. 1988. *Preparing teachers for urban schools* (Fastback 267). Bloomington, IA: Phi Delta Kappan Educational Foundation.

Hall, A. G. 1981. Points picked up: One hundred hints on how to manage a school. In *Teaching school: Points picked up,* Ed. E. W. Johnson, 209–216. New York: Walker.

Hall, E. W. 1956. Metaphysics. In *Living schools of philosophy,* Ed. D. R. Runes, 130. Ames, IA: Littlefield, Adams.

Hamilton, J. G. D., Ed. 1926. *The best letters of Thomas Jefferson.* Boston: Houghton Mifflin.

Hamilton, V. L., Blumenfeld, P. C., Akoh, H., and Miura, K. 1989. Citizenship and scholarship in Japanese and American fifth grades. *American Educational Research Journal* 26 (1), 44–72.

Hanby-Sikora, C. February 19, 1991. *Technology in teacher education at the Center for Excellence in Education at Indiana University.* [Telephone interview with authors].

Haney, W. 1987. An estimation of immigrant and immigrant student population in the United States as of October 1986. (Unpublished paper for immigrant student project). Boston, MA: Boston College.

Harbaugh, M. 1985. Who will teach the class of 2000? *Instructor* 94 (1), 31–36.

_____. 1990. Celebrating diversity. *Instructor* 100 (2), 44–48.

Harlan, L. R. 1972. *The Booker T. Washington papers* address to the Cotton States Exposition in Atlanta, 1895, Vol. 3, 621. Urbana: University of Illinois Press.

Harris, L., and Associates. 1988. *The Metropolitan Life survey of the American teacher: Strengthening the relationship between teachers and students.* New York: Metropolitan Life Insurance Company.

_____. 1990. *The Metropolitan Life Survey of the American teacher: Preparing schools for the 1990's.* New York: Author.

Harris, W. T. 1898. *The theory of education.* Syracuse, NY: Bardeen.

Hauser, M., Fawson, C., and Lathan, G. 1990. Chinese education: A system in transition. *Principal* 69 (3), 44–45.

Havighurst, R. J. 1957. *Society and education.* Boston: Allyn and Bacon.

Hawkins, J. D., Jones, C. L., and Battjes, R. J. 1985. Childhood predictors and the prevention of adolescent substance abuse. In *Etiology of drug abuse: Implications for prevention,* Ed. C. L. Jones and R. J. Battjes, 85. Washington DC: U.S. Government Printing Office.

Hawkins and Stafford Elementary and School Improvement Amendments of 1988 (P.L. 100-297-20, USC 2701, 2741, 2744).

Hawley, W. D., Austin, A. E., and Goldman, E. S. 1988. *Changing the education of teachers.* Atlanta, GA: Southern Regional Education Board.

Hazard, W. R. 1978. *Education and the law: Cases and materials on public schools,* 2nd ed. New York: Free Press.

Hazelwood School v. C. Kulmier et al., U.S. 86-836 (1988).

Hazelwood v. Kuhlmeir, 484 U.S. 260 (1988).

Head Start Bureau. 1988. *Head Start reaches out.* Washington, DC: U.S. Department of Health and Human Services.

Heafford, M. 1967. *Pestolozzi: His thoughts and its relevance today.* London: Methuen.

Healy v. James, 408 U.S. 169 (1972).

Heitz, T. 1989. How do I help Jacob? *Young children* 45 (1), 11–15.

Helge, D. 1990. *A national study regarding at-risk students.* Bellingham, WA: National Rural Development Institute.

Heller, K., Holtman, W., and Messick, S. (Eds). 1982. *Placing children in special education: A strategy for equity.* Washington, DC: National Academy of Sciences Press.

Helm, V. M. (1986). *What educators should know about copyright. Fastback 33.* Bloomington IN: Phi Delta Kappan Educational Foundation.

Hennig, M., and Gardin, A. 1977. *The managerial woman.* Garden City, NY: Anchor Press.

Henry, M. 1988. The effect of increased exploratory field experiences upon the perceptions and performance of student teachers. In *Action in teacher education: Tenth-year anniversary issue, commemorative edition,* Ed. J. Sikula, 93–97. Reston, VA: Association of Teacher Educators.

Herbart, J. F. 1970. Outlines of educational doctrine. In *Foundations of education in America: An anthology of major thoughts and significant actions*, Ed. J. W. Noll and S. P. Kelly, 205–208. New York: Harper. Original work published 1901.

Herndon, J. 1969. *The way it spozed to be.* New York: Simon and Schuster.

Herndon, J. 1971. *How to survive in your native land.* New York: Simon and Schuster.

Herndon, N. 1988. Parents who are boys: Some American boys accept responsibility for their babies. *Christian Science Monitor* (May 23), 25–26.

Hersch, P. 1991. Teen epidemic: Sexually transmitted diseases are ravaging our children. *American Health* (May), 42–46.

Hetherington, E. M., and Parke, R. D. 1986. *Child psychology: A contemporary viewpoint.* New York: McGraw-Hill.

Hill, G. M., Leslie, D., and Snider, W. C. 1991. Shifting priorities in the high school physical education curriculum. *High School Journal* 74 (3), 168–172.

Hill, P. T. 1990. The federal role in education: A strategy for the 1990's. *Phi Delta Kappan* 71 (5), 398–404.

Hilliard, A. 1982. *Strengths: African-American children and families.* City College of New York: City College Workshop Center.

———. 1989. Teachers and cultural styles in a pluralistic society. *Today: Issues '89* [special edition] (January), 65–69.

Hillsdale College v. Department of Health, Education, and Welfare et al., 696 F.2d 418 (1982).

Hirsch, E., Jr. 1987. *Cultural literacy: What every American needs to know.* Boston, MA: Houghton Mifflin.

Hobson v. Hansen, 269 F.Supp. 401 (DDC, 1967).

Hobson v. Hansen, 327 F.Supp. 844 (DDC, 1971).

Hodgkinson, H. L. 1989. *The same client: The demographics of education and service delivery systems.* Washington, DC: Institute for Educational Leadership, Center for Demographic Policy.

Hofstadter, R. 1963. *Anti-intellectualism in American life.* New York: Alfred A. Knopf.

Holmes, O. W., Jr. 1923. Law and social reform. In *The rational basis of legal institutions*, Vol. 11, Modern Legal Philosophy Series, 198, Littleton, CO: Rothman.

Holmes Group. 1986. *Tomorrow's Teachers.* East Lansing, MI: Author.

Holt, J. 1964. *How children fail.* New York: Pitman.

———. 1967. *How children learn.* New York: Dell.

———. 1970. *What do I do Monday?* New York: Dutton.

———. 1972. *Freedom and beyond.* New York: Delta.

Hooker, C. P. (Chr.) 1983 *West's education law reporter.* St. Paul, MN: West Publishing.

House Judiciary Committee, 1976. House report 94–1476. *Congressional Record.* Washington, DC: U.S. Government Printing Office.

Howe, L. P. 1972. *The future and the family.* New York: Simon and Schuster.

Howey, K. R., and Gardner, W. E. 1983. *The education of teachers.* New York: Longman.

Howey, K. R., and Zimpher, N. L. 1989. *Profiles of preservice teacher education: Inquiry into the nature of programs.* Albany: State University of New York Press.

Howick, W. H. 1971. *Philosophies of Western civilization.* Danville, IL: Interstate Printers.

Hoyem v. Manhattan Beach School Dist., 150 Cal. Rptr. 1, 585 P.2d 851 Cal. (1978).

Hudgins, H. C., Jr., and Vacca, R. E. 1985. *Law and education: Contemporary issues and court decisions*, 2nd ed. Charlottesville, VA: Mitchie.

Hunter, E. 1985. Under constant attack: Personal reflections of a teacher educator. *Phi Delta Kappan* 67 (3), 222–224.

Hurwitz, H. L. 1988. *The last angry principal.* Portland, OR: Halcyon House.

Hutchins, R. M. 1936a. *Higher learning in America.* New Haven, CT: Yale University Press.

———. 1936b. *No friendly voice.* Chicago: University of Chicago Press.

———. 1968. *The learning society.* New York: Praeger.

Imber, M., and Thompson, G. 1991. Developing a typology of litigation in education and determining the frequency of each category. *Educational Administration Quarterly* 27 (2), 225–244.

Instructor Magazine. 1986. *Instructor Curriculum Attitude Study Report.* New York: Scholastic Inc.

Isaacs, F. 1990. Is teaching for you? *Parade* (November 18), 11–13.

Jackson, P. W. 1968. *Life in classrooms.* New York: Holt, Rinehart and Winston.

———. 1986. *The practice of teaching.* New York: Teachers College Press.

Jacobson, S. L. 1989. Merit pay incentives in teaching. In *Crisis in teaching: Perspectives on current reforms*, Ed. L. Weiss, P. G. Altbach, G. P. Kelly, H. G. Petrie, and S. Slaughter, 111–128. Albany: State University of New York Press.

Jalengo, M. R. 1985. When young children move: Manolo's new country. *Young children* 40 (60), 51–56.

James, W. 1912. *Talks to teacher on psychology: And to students on some of life's ideals.* New York: Henry Holt.

———. 1958. *Talks to teachers: On psychology; and to students on some of life's ideals*, Ed. P. Woodring. New York: Norton.

Jefferson, T. 1781–1785. *Notes on the state of Virginia, Query XV*, 94.

———. 1936. Letter to Nathaniel Burwell. From Missouri Historical Society, 1936. Correspondence of Thomas Jefferson, 1788–1826, Vol. 3. In S. K. Padover, *The complete Jefferson*, 1985. New York: Duell, Sloan & Pierce. Original work published March 14, 1818.

———. 1943. Notes on Virginia and other writings. In *Alexander Hamilton and Thomas Jefferson*, Ed. F. C. Prescott, 134. New York: American Book Company. Original work published 1781–1785.

———. 1954. Bill 79 of 1779 for the more general diffusion of knowledge. In *The papers of Thomas Jefferson*, Ed. J. P. Boyd, 526–543. Princeton, NJ: Princeton University Press. Original work published in 1779.

Jencks, C. 1972. *Inequality: A reassessment of family and schooling in America*. New York: Basic Books.

Jennings, L. 1989. Inadequate teacher training is cited as a cause of unreported child abuse. *Education Week* (September 6), 16.

Jennings v. Joshua Indep. School Dist., 869 F.2d 870 (1989).

Joel, B. 1977. Just the way. In *The Stranger*, 27. New York: Bradley.

Johansen, J. H., Collins, H. W., and Johnson, J. A. 1982. *American education: An introduction to education*, 4th ed. Dubuque, IA: Wm. C. Brown.

Johns, R. L., Morphet, E. L., and Alexander, K. 1983. *The economics and financing of education*, 4th ed. Englewood Cliffs, NJ: Prentice-Hall.

Johnson, C. 1963. *Old-time schools and school-books*. New York: Dover.

Johnson, L. B. 1965. President Lyndon Johnson's call upon Congress to pass elementary and secondary education act. *89th Congress, 1st Session* (House Document No. 45). Washington, DC: U.S. Government Printing Office.

Johnson, S. M., and Nelson, N. C. W. 1989. Conflict and compatibility in visions of reform. In *Crisis in Teaching: Perspectives on current reforms*, Ed. L. Weis, D. G. Altbach, G. P. Kelly, H. G. Petrie, and S. Slaughter, 141–155, Albany: State University of New York Press.

Johnston, J. D., and Knapp, C. L. 1971. Sex discrimination by law: A study in judicial perspective. In *Educational policy and the law*, Ed. D. L. Kirp and M. G. Yudof, 526. Berkeley, CA: McCutchan.

Johnston, J. S., Jr., Spalding, J. R., Paden, R., and Ziffren, A. 1989. *Those who can: Undergraduate programs to prepare arts and sciences majors for teaching*. Washington, DC: Association of American Colleges.

Johnston, L. 1986. *Monitoring the future study: Questionnaire responses from the nation's high school seniors*. Ann Arbor: University of Michigan.

Johnston, L., Bachan, J. G., and O'Malley, P. M. 1990. *Monitoring the future study: Drug abuse among high-school seniors*. (Conducted for the National Institute on Drug Abuse). Ann Arbor: University of Michigan's Institute for Social Research.

Joyce, B., and Weil, M. 1972. *Models of teaching*. Englewood Cliffs, NJ: Prentice-Hall.

Joyce, B. R., Hersh, R. H., and McKibbin, M. 1983. *The structure of school improvement*. New York: Longman.

Kant, I. 1956 [1788]. *Critique of practical reason*, Trans. L. W. Beck. New York: Bobbs Merrill.

———. 1959 [1785]. Foundations of the metaphysic of morals. In *Fundamental principles of the metaphysics of ethics*, Trans. L. W. Beck. New York: Bobbs Merrill.

Katz, J. 1974. *Education in Canada*. London, England: David and Charles.

Katz, M. B. 1968. *The irony of early school reform*. Cambridge, MA: Harvard University Press.

Kauchak, D., and Eggen, P. D. 1989. *Learning and teaching: Research based methods*. Boston, MA: Allyn and Bacon.

Kean, T. H. 1991. Do we need a national achievement exam? Yes! To measure progress toward national goals. *Education Week* 10 (31), 28, 36.

Keefe v. Geanokos, 418 F.2d 359, 361–362 (1st Cir., 1969).

Kennedy, J. 1962. President's message on education to the Congress of the United States. In *Public papers of the presidents of the United States*, 101–117. Washington, DC: U.S. Government Printing Office.

Kennedy, M., Birman, B., and Demaline, R., Eds. 1986. *The effectiveness of Chapter I services*. Office of Educational Research and Improvement. Washington, DC: U.S. Government Printing Office (ERIC Document Reproduction Service No. ED 281919).

Keogh, B. K. 1983. Classification, compliance and confusion. *Journal of learning disabilities* 16 (1), 25.

Keppel, F. 1966. *The necessary revolution in American education*. New York: Harper and Row.

Keyes v. School District No. 1, Denver, 414 U.S. 883 (1973).

Kidder, T. 1989. *Among school children*. Boston: Houghton Mifflin.

Kilgore, S. G. 1985. Educational standards in private and public schools. In *Education on Trial*, Ed. W. J. Johnston, 103–121. San Francisco: ICS Press.

Kilpatrick, W. 1933. *The educational frontier*. New York: Arno Press.

Kirp, D. 1989. *Learning by heart: AIDS and schoolchildren in America's communities*. New Brunswick, NJ: Rutgers University Press.

Kirp, D., and Epstein, S. 1989. AIDS in America's schoolhouses: Learning the hard lessons. *Phi Delta Kappan* 70 (8), 584–593.

Kirp, D., Epstein, S., Franks, M. S., Simon, J., Conway, D., and Lewis, J. 1989. *Learning by heart: AIDS and schoolchildren in America's communities*. New Brunswick, NJ: Rutgers University Press.

Kirp, D., and Yudof, M. G., Eds. 1974. *Educational policy and the law: Cases and materials*. Berkeley, CA: McCutchan.

Kleinfeld, J., and Noordhoff, K. 1988. *Teachers for Rural Alaska (TRA) program assessment report* (Report No. RC 017 045). Fairbanks: Alaska University, Center for Cross-Cultural Studies. (ERIC Document Reproduction Service No. ED 306055).

Kliebard, H. (Ed.). 1969. *Religion and education in America: A documentary history*. Scranton, PA: International Books.

Kluener, M. M. 1984. Teacher education programs in the 1980s: Some selected characteristics. *Journal of Teacher Education* 34 (4), 33–35.

Knapp, J. L., Nergney, R. F., Herbert, J. M., and York, H. L. 1990. Should a master's degree be required of all teachers? *Journal of Teacher Education* 41 (2), 27–37.

Knapp, M. S., and Shields, D. M. 1990. Reconceiving academic instruction for the children of poverty. *Phi Delta Kappan* 71 (10), 752–758.

Kneller, G. F. 1964. *Introduction to the philosophy of education.* New York: John Wiley and Sons.

Knight, E. February 20, 1991. *Status of a masters degree for initial teacher certification.* [Telephone interview with authors].

Knight, G. R. 1982. *Issues and alternatives in educational philosophy,* 2nd ed. Berrien Springs, MI: Andrews University Press.

Koerner, J. D. 1968. *Who controls American education?: A guide for laymen.* Boston, MA: Beacon Press.

Kohl, H. R. 1967. *On teaching.* New York: Shocken.

———. 1969. *The open classroom.* New York: Random House.

Kohlberg, L. 1981. *Essays on moral development: The philosophy of moral development: Moral stages and the idea of justice,* vol. 1. New York: Harper and Row.

Kozol, J. 1991. *Savage inequalities: Children in America's schools.* New York: Crown.

Krathwohl, D. R., Bloom, B. S., and Masin, B. R. 1964. *Taxonomy of educational objectives, handbook II: Affective domain.* New York: David McKay.

Kulik, C. L., and Kulik, J. 1982. Effects of ability grouping on secondary school students: A meta-analysis of evaluation findings. *American Education Research Journal* 19 (3), 415–428.

Kyle, R. M. J., Ed. 1985. *Researching for excellence: An effective schools sourcebook.* Washington, DC: U.S. Government Printing Office.

Lamm, R. D. 1986. Task force on parent involvement and choice. In L. Alexander (Chr.), *Time for results: The governors' 1991 report on education,* 65–91.

LaMorte, M. W. 1987. *School law: Cases and concepts.* Englewood Cliffs, NJ: Prentice-Hall.

Landers v. School Dist. No. 203, O'Fallon, Illinois, 383 N.E.2d 645 (Ill. App., 1978).

Lau v. Nichols, U.S. 938, 483 F.2d (9th Cir., 1973).

LaValley v. Stanford, 70 N.Y.S.2d 460 (App. Div., 1947).

Lee, S., Luppino, J., and Plionis, E. 1990. Keeping youth in school: A follow-up report. *Children Today* 19 (2), 4–7.

Leo, J. 1990. The heartbreak that is New York. *U.S. News and World Report* (September 24), 37.

Lerner, B. 1985. Our black-robed school board: A report card. In *Challenge to American schools,* Ed. J. H. Bunzell, 169–187. New York: Oxford University Press.

LeTendre, M. J. 1991. Improving Chapter I programs. *Phi Delta Kappan* 72 (8), 577–580.

Levine, D. U., and Havighurst, R. J. 1989. *Society and education,* 7th ed. Boston: Allyn and Bacon.

Levy, J. 1985. Right brain, left brain: Fact and fiction. *Psychology Today* 19 (4), 38–44.

Lieberman, M. 1986. *Beyond public education.* New York: Praeger.

Lindner, B. 1987. *Family diversity and school policy.* Denver, CO: Education Commission of the States.

———. 1988. *Drawing in the family: Family involvement in the schools.* Denver, CO: Education Commission of the States.

Lochhead, C. 1988. Homeless in America; All alone, with no home. *Insight* (May 16), 8–18.

Locke, J. 1964. *John Locke on education,* Ed. P. Gay. New York: Teachers College Press.

Lodge, R. C. 1970. *Plato's theory of education.* New York: Russell and Russell.

Lortie, D. C. 1975. *Schoolteacher: A sociological study.* Chicago: University of Chicago Press.

Loughrey, M. E., and Harris, M. B. 1990. A descriptive study of at-risk high school students. *High School Journal* 73 (4), 187–193.

Louis, K. S., and Van Velzen, B. A. M. 1990–1991. A look at choice in the Netherlands. *Educational Leadership* 48 (4), 66–72.

Louv, R. 1990. *Childhood's future: Listening to the American family, new hope for the next generation.* Boston: Houghton Mifflin.

Lundgren, U. F. 1985. Curriculum from a global perspective. In *Current thought on curriculum,* Ed. A. Molnar, 119–135. Alexandria, VA: Association for Supervision and Curriculum Development.

Lynch, A. T. May 20, 1991. *News release from the National PTA.* Chicago, IL: National PTA.

Mabbett, B. 1990. The New Zealand story. *Educational Leadership* 47 (6), 59–61.

MacCracken, M. 1976. *Lovey: A very special child.* New York: J. B. Lippincott.

Macmillan, D. L., Keogh, B. K., and Jones, R. L. 1986. Special education research on mildly handicapped learners. In *Handbook of research on teaching,* 3rd ed., Ed. M. C. Wittrock, 686–721. New York: Holt, Rinehart and Winston.

Macrorie, K. 1984. *Twenty teachers.* New York: Oxford University Press.

Manatt, R. P. 1981, November. *Manatt's exercise in selecting teacher performance evaluation criteria based on effective teaching research.* Albuquerque, NM: National Symposium for Professionals in Evaluation and Research.

Mann, H. 1867. *Lectures and annual reports on education (1837–1848).* Cambridge, MA: Cornhill Press.

Marcus v. Rowley, 695 F.2d 1171 (1983).

Marland, S. P., Jr., 1972. *Education of the gifted and talented,* vol. 1. Report of the Congress of the United States by the U.S. Commissioner of Education, 2. Washington, DC: U.S. Government Printing Office.

Marriott, M. 1990. A new road to learning: Teaching the whole child. *New York Times* (June 13), A1, B7, B8.

Marsiglio, W. 1988. Commitment to social fatherhood: Predicting adolescent males' intentions to live with their child and partner. *Journal of Marriage and the Family* 50 (2), 427–441.

Maslow, A. 1970. *Motivation and personality.* New York: Harper and Row. (orig. published 1954).

Massachusetts Advocacy Center and the Center for Early Adolescence. 1988. *Before it's too late: Dropout prevention in the middle grades.* Boston, MA, and Carrboro, NC: Authors.

Mathews, J. 1988. *Escalante: The best teacher in America.* New York: Henry Holt.

Matyas, M., and Kahle, J. 1986. "Equitable precollege science and mathematics: A discrepancy model." 1. Paper presented at the Workshop on Underrepresentation and Career Differentials of Women in Science and Engineering. Washington, DC: National Academy of Sciences.

McAshan, H. A. 1979. *Competency-based education and behavioral objectives.* Englewood Cliffs, NJ: Educational Technology Publications.

McCarthy, B. 1980. *The 4 Mat system: Teaching to learning styles with the right/left mode techniques.* Oak Brook, IL: EXCEL.

McCarthy, M. M., and Cambron-McCabe, N. H. 1987. *Public school law: Teachers' and students' rights,* 2nd ed. Boston, MA: Allyn and Bacon.

McEnany, J. 1986. Teachers who don't burn out. *Clearing House* 60 (2), 84–88.

McGrath, J. J. 1988. Goycochea: Tough, caring principal. *San Diego Tribune* (December 6), D-1, D-2.

McLaughlin, M. W., and Shields, P. M. 1988. Involving low-income parents in the schools: A role for policy? In *"Drawing in the family": Family involvement in the schools,* 5–12. Denver, CO: Education Commission of the States.

McMillen, M. M. April 19, 1990. *Characteristics of public and private school teachers.* Paper presented at the meeting of the American Educational Research Association, Boston, MA.

McNeil, J. D. 1977. *Curriculum: A comprehensive introduction.* Boston: Little, Brown.

McSordad, J. O. 1883. An indignant taxpayer. January 27, 1833. *School Journal* 25 (4), 53. In Foy, R. 1968. *The world of education.* New York: Macmillan.

Mearns, H. 1958. Johnny. In *Creative power: The education of youth in the creative arts,* Ed. H. Mearns, 46. New York: Dover.

Medley, D. M. 1982. Teacher effectiveness. In *Encyclopedia of Educational Research,* 5th ed., Ed. H. E. Mitzel, 1894–1903. New York: Free Press.

Medley, D., and Mitzell, H. 1963. Measuring classroom behavior by systematic observation. In *Handbook of research on teaching,* Ed. N. L. Gage, 247–328, Chicago: Rand McNally.

Menacker, J., Weldon, W., and Huritz, E. 1989. School order and safety as community issues. *Phi Delta Kappan* 71 (1), 39–56.

Mernit, S. 1990. Kids today. *Instructor* 100 (2), 44–48.

Merrow, J. 1989. *Learning in America series. Part III: A transcription.* Overland Park, AR: Strictly Business.

Messerli, J. 1972. *Horace Mann: A biography.* New York: Knopf.

Metropolitan Life Insurance Company. 1985. *The Metropolitan Life survey of former teachers in America* (conducted by Louis Harris and Associates) (fieldwork: April–June 1985). New York, NY: Author.

_____. 1988. *The Metropolitan Life survey of the American teacher: Strengthening the relationship between teachers and students.* New York: Author.

_____. 1989. *The Metropolitan Life survey of the American teacher 1989.* New York: Author.

_____. 1990. *The Metropolitan Life survey of the American teacher 1990.* New York: Author.

Metzger, M.T., and Fox, C. 1986. Two teachers of letters. *Harvard Educational Review* 56 (4), 351–354.

Meyer v. Nebraska, 262 U.S. 390 (1923).

Miller, A. 1990. Work and what it's worth. *Newsweek* [special issue] (Summer/Fall), 29–33.

Miller, J. 1983. *The educational spectrum.* New York: Longman.

Miller, J. A. 1991. Bush strategy launches "crusade" for education: National exam system, new schools included. *Education Week,* (April 24), 1, 26.

Miller, J. P., and Seller, W. 1985. *Curriculum: Perspectives and practices.* New York: Longman.

Miller v. California, 413 U.S. 15, 24 (1973).

Minarcini v. Strongsville, 541 F.2d 577 (6th Cir., 1976).

Ministry of Education and Science (MOW). 1988. *Newsletter on freedom of education in the Netherlands.* Dociform 22 E. Zoetermeer: Ministrie van Onderwizs au Wetenschappen (MOW).

Mitchell, A. 1989. Old baggage, new visions: Shaping policy for early childhood programs. *Phi Delta Kappan* 70 (9), 664–672.

Mitchell, D. E., and Peters, J. J. 1988. A stronger profession through appropriate teacher incentives. *Educational Leadership* 46 (3), 74–78.

Mohr, M. H. 1989. The joy of learning. *Wall Street Journal Reports* (March 31), R36.

Molnar, A., Ed. 1985. *Current thought on curriculum.* Alexandria, VA: Association of Supervision and Curriculum Development.

Moore, G. E. 1953. The defence of common sense. In G. E. Moore, *Some main problems of philosophy.* London: Allen and Unwin.

Moore, M. T., Walker L. J., and Holland, R. P. 1982. *Finetuning special education finance: A guide for state policymakers.* Princeton, NJ: Educational Testing Service.

Morris, V. C. 1961. *Existentialism in education: What it means.* New York: Harper and Row.

Morrow, L. 1988a. Through the eyes of children: Bianca. *Time* (August 8), 49–51.

_____. 1988b. Through the eyes of children: Josh. *Time* (August 8), 55–57.

Morsink, C. 1986. Research on teaching: Opening the door to special education classrooms. *Exceptional Children* 53 (1), 32–40.

Mosher, E. K. 1977. Education and American Federalism: Intergovernmental and national policy influences. In *The politics of education,* Ed. J. D. Scribner, 94–124. Chicago, IL: National Society for the Study of Education.

Mozert v. Hawkins County Public Schools, 765 F.2d, (6th Cir., 1985) on remand CIV-Z-83-401 (E.D. Tenn., 1986).

Murray v. Curlett, 374 U.S. 203, L.Ed.2d 844, 83 S.Ct. 1560 (1963).

National Association of State Boards of Education. 1988. *Right from the start: A report on the NASBE task force on early childhood education.* Washington, DC: Author.

National Board for Professional Teaching Standards. 1989. *Toward high and rigorous standards for the teaching profession: Initial policies and perspectives of the National Board for Professional Teaching Standards.* Washington, DC: Author.

National Center for Education Statistics, U.S. Department of Education. 1987. *Digest of education statistics.* Washington, DC: U.S. Government Printing Office.

———. 1988a. *The condition of education.* (Report No. CS 88–623). Washington, DC: U.S Government Printing Office.

———. 1988b. *Digest of education statistics.* Washington, DC: U.S. Government Printing Office.

———. 1989a. *The condition of education: Vol. 1: Elementary and secondary education.* (CS 89-650) Washington, DC: U.S. Government Printing Office.

———. 1989b. *Digest of education statistics,* 25th ed. (NCES 89-643). Washington, DC: U.S. Government Printing Office.

———. 1990a. *The condition of education. Vol. 1: Elementary and secondary education* (NCES 90–681). Washington, DC: U.S. Government Printing Office.

———. 1990b. *Digest of education statistics.* (NCES 91-660). Washington, DC: U.S. Government Printing Office.

———. 1990c. *Projections of education statistics to 2001: An update.* (NCES 91–683). Washington, DC: U.S. Department of Education.

National Coalition of Advocates for Children. 1988. *New voices: Immigrant students in U.S. public schools.* Boston, MA: Author.

National Coalition of Advocates for Students. 1988. *New voices: Immigrant students in U.S. public schools.* Boston, MA: Author.

National Commission for Excellence in Education. 1983. *A nation at risk: The imperative for educational reform.* Washington, DC: U.S. Government Printing Office.

National Commission for Excellence in Teacher Education. 1985. *A call for change in teacher education.* Washington, DC: American Association of Colleges for Teacher Education.

National Committee for the Prevention of Child Abuse. April 1991. *Current trends in child abuse reporting and fatalities: The results of the 1990 annual 50 state survey.* Chicago, IL: Author.

National Council for Accreditation of Teacher Education. 1990. *NCATE Standards, procedures, and policies for the accreditation of professional education units.* Washington, DC: Author.

National Education Association, Commission on the Reorganization of Secondary Schools, 1918. *Cardinal principles of secondary education.* Washington, DC: U.S. Bureau of Education.

National Education Association. 1977. *The new copyright law: Questions teachers and librarians ask.* Washington, DC: author.

———. 1989a. *NEA handbook, 89–90.* Washington, DC: Author.

———. 1989b. *NEA today* (September), 19–26. Washington, DC: Author.

———. 1990a. *Estimates of school statistics, 1989–90.* Washington, DC: Author.

———. 1990b. NEA supports nontraditional routes to teacher licensure. *Proceedings of the 128th Annual Meeting of the National Education Association.* Press release July 3–8, 1–2. Kansas City, MO: Author.

National Governors' Association. 1986. *Time for results: The governors' 1991 report on education.* Washington, DC: Author.

———. 1987a. *Making America work: Bringing down the barriers.* Washington, DC: Author.

———. 1987b. *Making America work: Productive people, productive policies.* Washington, DC: Author.

———. 1990a. *Educating America: State strategies for achieving the national education goals.* (Report of the Task Force on Education). Washington, DC: Author.

———. 1990b. *Report of the task force on education.* Washington, DC: Author.

———. 1990c. *The state of the states' children.* Washington, DC: Author.

———. 1990d. *An overview of state policies affecting adolescent pregnancy and parenting.* Washington, DC: Author.

National Institute on Alcohol Abuse and Alcoholism. 1979. *Here's looking at you, two.* Rockville, MD: Author.

National School Boards Association. 1990. *A survey of public education in the nation's urban school districts, 1989.* Alexandria, VA: Author.

Natriello, G., McDill, E. L., and Pallas, A. M. 1990. *Schooling disadvantaged children.* New York: Teacher's College Press.

Neil, A. S. 1960. *Summerhill.* New York: Hart.

Neill, M. 1991. Do we need a national achievement exam? No. It would damage, not improve, education. *Education Week* 10 (31), 28, 36.

Nelson, F. H. 1991. *International comparison of public spending on education.* Washington, DC: American Federation of Teachers, AFL-CIO.

Nevi, C. 1987. In defense of tracking. *Educational Leadership* 44 (60), 24–26.

New Jersey v. T.L.P., 469 U.S. 325 (1985).

New York Times staff. 1990. An international agenda for children. *New York Times* (October 1), A10.

Newsweek staff. 1990. The new teens: What makes them different? [special issue]. *Newsweek* 115 (Summer/Fall), 27.

Nicholas, A. 1988. Hidden minorities. *Instructor* 98 (2), 51.

Nicklin, J. 1991. Alternative teacher education project draws mixed reviews in first year of placing recent college graduates in schools. *The Chronicle of Higher Education,* A21.

North Carolina Department of Public Instruction. 1989. "Task force on excellence in secondary education." Raleigh, NC: Author. (Unpublished report).

Oakes, J. 1985. *Keeping track: How school structures inequality.* New Haven, CT: Yale University Press.

Oakley, A. 1981. *Subject women.* New York: Pantheon.

Office of the Federal Register, National Archives and Records. 1990. *Code of federal regulations: Education 34,* parts 300–399. Washington, DC: Author.

Olson, L. 1989. Study of nontraditional routes to teaching finds ranks boosted, questions on quality. *Education Week* 8 (31), 1, 26.

Orlich, D. C., Harder, R. J., Callahan, R. C., Kracas, C. H., Pendergrass, R. A., and Keogh, A. J. 1985. *Teaching strategies.* Lexington, MA: D. C. Heath.

Ornstein, A. C. 1985. Teachers as professionals: News vistas. *Curriculum Review* 24 (4), 9–12.

———. 1990. *Strategies for effective teaching.* New York: Harper and Row.

Ornstein, A. C., and Levine, D. U. 1989a. Class, race, and achievement. *Journal of Teacher Education* 40 (5), 17–23.

———. 1989b. Social class, race, and school achievement: Problems and prospects. *Journal of Teacher Education* 37 (1), 17–22.

Ovando, C. J. 1989. Language diversity in education. In *Multicultural education: Issues and perspectives,* Ed. J. A. Banks and C. A. M. Banks, 208–227. Boston, MA: Allyn and Bacon.

Ozmon, H., and Craver, S. 1976. *Philosophical foundations of education.* Columbus, OH: Merrill.

Pang, V. O. 1990. Asian American children: A diverse population. *Educational Forum* 55 (1), 50–64.

Parducci v. Rutland, 316 F.Supp. 352 (MD Ala., 1970).

Parnell, D. 1978. *The case for competency-based education.* Bloomington, IL: Phi Delta Kappan.

Parris, J. 1989. Sequoyah writes. *Asheville Citizen Times* (October 26), 1, 8.

Partridge, P. H. 1968. *Society, schools and progress in Australia.* London: Pergamon.

Passow, A. H. 1979. Educational policies, programs and practices for the gifted and talented. In *The gifted and talented: The seventy-eighth yearbook of the National Society for the Study of Education,* Ed. A. Harry Passow, 97–104. Chicago: University of Chicago Press.

Payne v. Department of Human Resources, 382 S.E.2d 449 (N.C. Ct. App., 1989).

Pearson, J. 1989. Myths of choice: The governor's new clothes? *Phi Delta Kappan* 70 (10), 821–823.

Peddiwell, J. A. 1939. *The saber-tooth curriculum.* New York: McGraw-Hill.

Perelman, L. J. May 1990. The "acanemia" deception. *Hudson Institute Briefing Paper* (No. 120), 4–27.

Perkins, H. 1969. *Human development and education.* Belmont, CA: Wadsworth.

Perrin, J. 1990. The learning styles project for potential dropouts. *Educational Leadership* 48 (2), 23–24.

Perrone, V. 1991. On standardized testing. *Childhood Education* 67 (3), 131–142.

Perry v. Sinderman, 408 U.S. 593 (1972).

Persell, C. 1977. *Education and inequality: The roots and results of stratification in America's schools.* New York: Free Press.

Persell, C., and Cookson, P., Jr. 1982. The effective principal in action. In *The effective principal: A research summary,* 42–53. Reston, VA: National Association of Secondary School Principals.

Pestel, B. C. 1990, June. Teaching is not an art, it is a science. *Journal of Chemical Education,* 67 (6), 490.

Peter W. v. San Francisco Unified School District, 60 Cal. App.3d 814, 131 Cal. Rptr. 854 (1976).

Peterkin, R. S. 1990–1991. What's happening in Milwaukee? *Educational Leadership* 48 (4), 50–51.

Peterson, D. 1990. Pinning down empowerment: Eight teachers speak out on education's hottest topic. Ed. D. Dillon. *Instructor* 99 (5), 26–36.

Pettijohn, T. E. 1989. *Psychology: A concise introduction,* 2nd ed. Guilford, CT: Dushkin.

Phenix, P. H. 1958. *Philosophy of education.* New York: Holt, Rinehart and Winston.

Piaget, J. 1952. *Child's conception of number.* London: Humanities Press.

Pickering v. Board of Education, 319 U.S. 563 (1968).

Pico v. Board of Education of Island Trees Free School District, 474 F.Supp. 387 (E.D. NY., 1979).

Pierce, J. 1837. Report on the superintendent of public instruction of the State of Michigan. *Senate Journal.* Doc. No. 7, 229–232. In Cohen, S. A. 1974. *A history of colonial education: 1607–1776.* New York: Wiley.

Pierce v. Society of Sisters, 268 U.S. 510 (1925).

Pigford, A. B. 1990. Instructional grouping: Purposes and consequences. *Clearing House* 63 (6), 261–263.

Pitman, K. 1985. *Preventing children having children.* Washington, DC: Children's Defense Fund.

P.L. 64-347. 1917. Smith-Hughes Vocational Education Act.

P.L. 85-864. 1958. (National Defense Education Act).

P.L. 88-452. 1964. (Economic Opportunity Act of the Civil Rights Act).

P.L. 89-10. 1965. (Elementary and Secondary Education Act).

P.L. 91-230, Section 206. 1970. (Gifted and Talented).

P.L. 100-297, Title IV, Part B. 1988. (Gifted and Talented Students Act).

Planchon, P. 1990. *Highlights of minority data from the schools and staffing survey, 1987–88.* Washington, DC: U.S. Department of Education, National Center for Education Statistics.

Planned Parenthood Federation. 1986. *Teenage pregnancy.* New York: Author.

Plessy v. Ferguson, 163 U.S. 537 (1896).

Plevin, A. 1988. *Education as a career.* Washington, DC: National Education Association.

Poling v. Murphy, 872 F.2d 757 (6th Cir., 1989).

Popenoe, D. 1991. Breakup of the family: Can we reverse the trend? *USA Today* 119 (2552), 50–53.

Postman, N., and Weingarter, C. 1969. *Teaching as a subversive activity.* New York: Delacorte.

Power, E. J. 1982. *Philosophy of education: Studies in philosophies, schooling, and educational policies.* Englewood Cliffs, NJ: Prentice-Hall.

President's Council, Dist. 25 v. Community School Bd. No. 25, 82 (1982).

Price, K. 1967. *Education and philosophical thought,* 2nd ed. Boston: Allyn & Bacon.

Puglisi, D. J., and Hoffman, A. J. 1978. Cultural identity and academic success in a multicultural society: A culturally different approach. *Social Education* 42 (6), 495–498.

Pulaski, M. A. S. 1971. *Understanding Piaget: An introduction to children's cognitive development.* New York: Harper and Row.

Pulliam, J. D. 1976. *History of education in America,* 2nd ed. Columbus, OH: Merrill.

_____. 1986. *History of education in America,* 3rd ed. Columbus, OH: Merrill.

_____. 1991. *History of education in America,* 5th ed. New York: Macmillan.

Purkey, S. C., and Smith, M. S. 1983. Effective schools: A review. *Elementary School Journal* 83 (2), 427–453.

Purpel, D. E. 1989. *The moral and spiritual crisis in education: A curriculum for justice and compassion in education.* Granby, MA: Bergin and Garvey Publications.

Quintilian. 1970. De Institutione Oratoria. In *Foundations of education in America: An anthology of major thoughts and significant actions,* Ed. J. W. Noll and S. Kelly, 41–45. New York: Harper and Row. Original work discovered A.D. 96 and first published 1416.

Rabianski-Carriuolo, N. 1989. Learning styles: An interview with Edmund W. Gordon. *Journal of Developmental Education* 13 (1), 18–20, 22.

Rachlin, J. 1989. Opening the school doors. *U.S. News and World Report* 106 (18), 62.

Rachlin, J., and Glastris, P. 1989. Of more than parochial interest. *U.S. News and World Report* (May 22), 61–62.

Rafferty, M. 1962. *Suffer little children.* New York: Signet.

_____. 1963. *What they are doing to your children?* New York: New American Library.

Ranbom, S. 1985. Schooling in Japan: Harnessing education for growth. *Education Week* (February 20), 12–24.

Rasinski, T. Y.; and Padak, N. D. 1990. Multicultural learning through children's literature. *Language Arts* 67 (6), 576–580.

Ravitch, D. 1983. *The troubled crusade.* New York: Basic Books.

_____. 1984. A good school. *American Scholar* 53 (4), 480–493.

_____. 1985. *The schools we deserve.* New York: Basic Books.

Reagan, R. January 25, 1988. State of the union address. In *Public papers of the presidents of the United States: Ronald Reagan,* 79–80. Washington, DC: U.S. Government Printing Office.

Ream, M. H. 1977. *Status of the American public school teacher.* Washington, DC: National Education Association.

Reed, A. J. S. 1985. *Reaching adolescents: The young adult book and the school.* New York: Holt, Rinehart & Winston.

Reed, S., and Sautter, R. C. 1990. Children of poverty: The status of 12 million Americans. *Phi Delta Kappan* 71 (10), K2–K11.

Reiff, G. 1985. *The 1985 fitness study: Conducted for the president's council on physical fitness.* Washington, DC: U.S. Government Printing Office.

Reinhardt, E. 1960. *American education.* New York: Harper and Row.

Reinhartz, J., and VanCleaf, D. 1986. *Teach-practice-apply: The TPA instructional model, K-8.* Washington, DC: National Education Association.

Renzulli, J. S. 1977. *The enrichment triad model: A guide for developing defensible programs for the gifted and talented.* Mansfield Center, CT: Creative Learning Press.

Resnick, L. B. 1977. Assuming that everyone can learn everything, will some learn less? *School Review* 85 (3), 445–452.

Richmond, G. 1988. The future school: Is Lowell pointing us toward a revolution in education? *Phi Delta Kappan* 71 (3), 232–236.

Rickover, H. G. *Education and freedom.* New York: Dutton.

Rimer, S. 1990. Slow readers sparkling with a handful of words. *New York Times* (June 19), B1, B34–36.

Rittenmeyer, D. C. 1986. *School reform: Can it succeed?* Paper presented at the annual meeting of the Association of Teacher Educators, Atlanta, GA.

Rock, D., Ekstrom, R., and Goetz, M. 1984. *Excellence in high school education: Cross-sectional study, 1972–1980, final report.* Princeton, NJ: Educational Testing Service.

Rogers, C. 1983. *Freedom to learn for the 80's.* Columbus, OH: Merrill.

Rohlen, T. P. 1983. *Japan's high schools.* Berkeley: University of California Press.

Rollins v. Blair, 767 P.2d 328 (Mont., 1989).

Rose v. The Council for Better Education, Inc. KY, 790 S.W.2d 186 (1989).

Rosenholtz, S. J. 1986. Career ladders and merit pay: Capricious fads or fundamental reforms? *Elementary School Journal* 86 (4), 513–527.

Rosenshine, B., and Furst, N. 1971. Research in teacher performance criteria. In *Research in Teacher Education,* Ed. B. O. Smith, 37–72. Englewood Cliffs, NJ: Prentice-Hall.

Rosenthal, R., and Jacobsen, L. 1968. *Pygmalion in the classroom: Teacher expectation and pupils' intellectual development.* New York: Holt.

Roth v. U.S., 354 U.S. 476 (1957).

Rothman, R. 1988a. "Computer competence" still rare among students, assessment finds. *Education Week* (April 13), 1, 20.

_____. 1988b. Teachers vs. curriculum in Philadelphia. *Education Week* (March 27), 1, 20, 26.

_____. 1990. Ford study urges new test system to "open the gates of opportunity." *Education Week* (May 30), 1, 12.

Rousseau, J.-J. 1979 [1762]. *Emile, or on education*, Trans. A. Bloom. New York: Basic Books.

Rubin, L. J. 1985. *Artistry in teaching*. New York: Random House.

Runes, D. D., Ed. 1983. *Dictionary of philosophy*. New York: Philosophical Library.

Russell, A. M. 1991. The twelfth annual working woman salary survey: Women vs. men. *Working Woman* (January), 66–71.

Russell, B. 1903. *The principles of mathematics*. Cambridge, MA: Cambridge University Press.

_____. 1926. *Education and the good life*. New York: Boni and Liveright.

Ryan, M. 1990. "I needed to show them who I was." *Parade Magazine* (August 19), 12, 13.

San Antonio Independent School District v. Rodriguez, 411 U.S. 1 (1973).

Sanders, J. W. 1977. *The education of an urban community*. New York: Oxford University Press.

Sartre, J.-P. 1956. *Being and nothingness*, Trans. H. E. Barnes. New York: Philosophical Library.

_____. 1957. *Existentialism and humanism*. New York: Philosophical Library.

Schaill v. Tippecanoe County School Corp., 679 F.Supp. 833 (N.D. Ind., 1988).

Schetter, W. 1987. *The Netherlands in perspective: The organization of society and environment*. Leiden: Martinus Nijhof.

Schumacher, E. F. 1980. *Good work*. New York: Harper and Row.

Sedlak, M., and Schlossman, S. 1986. *Who will teach? Historical perspectives on the changing appeal of teaching as a profession*. Santa Monica, CA: Rand.

Select Committee on Children, Youth, and Families, U.S. House of Representatives, 101st Congress, 1st session. September 1989. *U.S. children and their families: Current conditions and recent trends, 1989*. Washington, DC: U.S. Government Printing Office.

Serrano v. Priest, 5 C.3d 584, 487 P.2d 1241, 96 Cal. Rptr. 601 (1971).

Sexuality Today Newsletter. March 9, 1987. *Newsletter of Sexuality Today*. (Available from 2315 Broadway, New York, NY 10024.)

Shafritz, J. M., Koeppe, R. P., and Soper, E. 1988. *Dictionary of education: Facts on file*. New York: Oxford.

Shanker, A. 1987. The making of a profession. In *Education 87/88: Annual editions*, Ed. F. Schultz, 196–204. Guilford, CT: Dushkin.

_____. 1990. Restructuring the teaching profession and our schools. In *What teachers need to know*, Ed. D. A. Dill, 203–224. San Francisco: Jossey-Bass.

_____. 1991. A new national strategy: Education 2000. *New York Times* (April 21), E7.

Sharpes, D. K. 1987. Incentive pay and the promotion of teaching proficiencies. *Clearing House* 60 (486), 406–408.

Shaw, G. B. 1903. Maxims for revolutionists. In *Man and superman: A comedy and a philosophy*, 203. New York: Brentano's.

_____. 1916. *Pygmalion*. London: Constable and Company.

Shevin, M. S. 1989. Mild disabilities: In and out of special education. In *Schooling and disability: Eighty-eighth yearbook of the National Society for the Study of Education, Part III*, Ed. D. Biklen, D. Fergusen, and A. Ford, 77–105. Chicago: University of Chicago Press.

Shulman, J. and Colbert, J. Eds. *The Intern Teacher Casebook* 1988.

Shurtleff, N. B., Ed. 1853. Massachusetts school law of 1647. *Records of the governor and company of Massachusetts Bay in New England*. Vol. 2, pp. 6–7. Boston: Order of the Legislature.

Simms v. School Dist. No. 1, 508 P.2d 236 (Ore. App., 1973).

Sirotnik, K. A., and Goodlad, J. I. 1985. The quest for reason amidst the rhetoric of reform: Improving instead of testing our schools. In *Education on trial*, Ed. W. Johnson, 277–296. San Francisco: ICS Press.

Sizer, T. R. 1984. *Horace's compromise: The dilemma of the American high school*. Boston: Houghton Mifflin.

Skinner, B. F. 1968. *The technology of teaching*. New York: Appleton-Century-Crofts.

Slavin, R. E. 1987. *Mastery learning reconsidered*. Report No. 7. Baltimore, MD: Johns Hopkins University. Center for Social Organization of Schools. ERIC Document Reproduction Service No. ED 294 891.

_____. 1988. *Education psychology*, 2nd ed. Englewood Cliffs, NJ: Prentice Hall.

Slavin, R. E., Karweit, N. L., and Madden, N. A. 1990. *Effective programs for students at risk*. (Center for Research on elementary and middle schools, the Johns Hopkins University). Boston: Allyn and Bacon.

Sleeter, C. E., and Grant, C. A. 1988. A rationale for integrating race, gender, and social class. In *Class, race, and gender in American education*, Ed. L. Weiss, 144–160. Albany: State University of New York Press.

Smith, B. O., Stanley, W. O., and Shores, J. H. 1957. *Fundamentals of curriculum development*, rev. ed. Yonkers-on-Hudson, NY: World Book.

Smith, M. H. 1847. "The ark of God on a cart" [a sermon]. In *The Bible, the rod, and religion in the common school*. Boston: Redding.

Smuck v. Hobson, 408 F.2d 175 (DC Cir., 1969).

Snider, W. 1988. School choice: New, more efficient "sorting machine"? *Education Week* (May 18) 1, 8.

Soars, R., and Soars, R. 1973. *Classroom behavior, pupil characteristics and pupil growth for the school year and summer*. Gainesville: University of Florida, Institute for Development of Human Resources.

_____. 1978. *Setting variables, classroom interaction and multiple pupil outcomes* (Final Report Project No. 6-04332). Washington, DC: National Institute of Education.

Sockett, H. 1990. Accountability, trust, and ethical codes of practice. In *The moral dimensions of teaching*, Ed. J. I. Goodlad, R. F. Soder, and K. A. Sirotnik, 224–250. San Francisco: Jossey-Bass.

Solman, P. 1989. *Learning in America series. Part III: A transcription*. Overland, AR: Strictly Business.

Soltis, J. F. 1968. *An introduction to the analysis of educational concepts*. Reading, MA: Addison Wesley.

Southern Regional Education Board. 1986. *Major reports on teacher education: What do they mean for the states?* Atlanta, GA: Author.

_____. 1991. *Linking performance to rewards for teachers, principals and schools: The 1990 SREB career ladder clearinghouse report*. Atlanta, GA: Author.

Spencer, H. 1927. *Education: Intellectual, moral and spiritual*. New York: D. Appleton.

Sperry, R. 1968. Hemisphere deconnection and unity in conscious awareness. *American Psychologist* 23 (4), 723–733.

Spring, J. 1972. *Education and the rise of the corporate state*. Boston: Beacon.

_____. 1986. *The American school: 1642–1985*. New York: Longman.

Spruill, Julia C. 1972. *Women's life and work in the Southern colonies*. New York: Norton.

Stallings, J., Cory, R., Fairweather, J., and Needles, M. 1977. *Early childhood classroom evaluation*. Menlo Park, CA: SRI International.

_____. 1978. *How to change the process of teaching basic reading skills in secondary schools*. Menlo Park, CA: SRI International.

Stallings, J., and Kaskowitz, D. 1974. *Follow-through classroom observation evaluation, 1972–1973* (SRI Project URU-7370). Stanford, CA: Stanford Research Institute.

Stedman, L. 1988. The effective schools' formula still needs changing. *Phi Delta Kappan* 69 (6), 439–442.

Steller, A. W. 1988. *Effective schools research: Practice and premise*. Bloomington, IN: Phi Delta Kappan Educational Foundation.

Stephan, W. G., and Feagin, J. R., Eds. 1980. *School desegregation: Past, present and future*. New York: Plenum.

Stern, Ed. 1987. *The condition of education*. Washington, DC: U.S. Government Printing Office.

Stiles, L. J. 1960. Instruction. In *Encyclopedia of educational research*, Ed. C. W. Harris, 710. New York: Macmillan.

Stinnett, T. M., and Huggett, A. J. 1963. *Professional problems of teachers*, 2nd ed. New York: Macmillan.

Strather, D. B. 1985. Adopting instruction to individual needs: An eclectic approach. *Phi Delta Kappan* 68 (4), 307–310.

Strike, K. 1988. The ethics of teaching. *Phi Delta Kappan* 70 (2), 156–158.

Su, Z. 1989. People's education in the People's Republic of China. *Phi Delta Kappan* 70 (8), 614–618.

Sunal, D. W. 1976. *A comparison of two pre-professional programs in the department of early childhood elementary education*. University of Maryland. (ERIC Document Reproduction Service No. ED 139 624).

Taba, H. 1962. *Curriculum development*. New York: Harcourt.

Tannebaum, A. 1980. *Reaching out: Advocacy for the gifted and talented*. New York: Teachers College Press.

_____. 1983. *Gifted children: Psychological and educational perspectives*. New York: Macmillan.

Tanner, D., and Tanner, L. 1975. *Curriculum development*. New York: Macmillan.

_____. 1980. *Curriculum development: Theory into practice*, 2nd ed. New York: Macmillan.

Thomas, S. B., Ed. 1989. *The yearbook of education law, 1989*. Topeka, KS: National Organization on Legal Problems of Education.

_____. 1990. *The yearbook of education law, 1990*. Topeka, KS: National Organization on Legal Problems of Education.

Thompson, L. H. 1991. *Within school discrimination: Inadequate Title VI enforcement by Education's Office for Civil Rights*. Washington, DC: U.S. General Accounting Office.

Thorndike, E. L. 1931. *Human learning*. Cambridge, MA: MIT Press.

_____. 1932. *The fundamentals of learning*. New York: Teachers College Press.

Tifft, S. 1989a. The fight over school choice. *Time* (March 13), 54.

_____. 1989b. The lure of the classroom, *Time* (April 19), 69.

Tinker v. Des Moines Independent Community School District, 393 U.S. 593 (1969).

Title VI of the Civil Rights Act of 1974 (Bilingual Education) (P.L. 93-380).

Title VII of the Civil Rights Act of 1979 (Racial Discrimination) (P.L. 93-517).

Title IX of the Civil Rights Act of 1975 (Women's Equity Act) (P.L. 95-561).

Toch, T., and Levine, A. 1991. Schooling's big test. *U.S. News and World Report* (May 6), 63, 64.

Tower, C. C. 1987. *How schools can help combat child abuse and neglect*, 2nd ed. Washington, DC: National Education Association.

Towers, R. 1987. *How schools can help combat student drug and alcohol abuse*. Washington, DC: National Education Association.

Troike, R. C. 1975. *Improving conditions for success in bilingual education programs*. In *A report of the compendium*, 2. Arlington, VA: Center for Applied Linguistics.

Tryneski, J. 1990/1991. *Requirements for certification of teachers, counselors, librarians, administrators*. 55th ed. Chicago: University of Chicago Press.

Turner, R. 1979. The value of variety in teaching styles. *Educational Leadership*, 36 (4), 257–258.

Turner, R. L. 1990. An issue for the 1990's: The efficacy of the required master's degree. *Journal of Teacher Education* 41 (2), 38–44.

Urschel, J. 1991. Why not let teachers really teach? *USA Today* (October 4), 11A.

U.S. Department of Commerce, Bureau of the Census. 1986. *Statistical abstract of the United States*, 106th ed. Washington, DC: U.S. Government Printing Office.

_____. 1988. *Current population reports*, Series P-60. Washington, DC: U.S. Government Printing Office.

_____. 1990a. *Marital status and living arrangements: March 1989*. Population statistics. series P-20. No. 445. Washington, DC: U.S. Government Printing Office.

_____. 1990b. *Money income and poverty status in the United States, 1989*. Current population reports series P-60N0168. Washington, DC: U.S. Government Printing Office.

_____. 1990c. *Per capita income in 1987, ranked by state*. Washington, DC: Author.

_____. 1990d. *School enrollment—social and economic characteristics of students: October 1988 and 1987*, Series P-20, No. 443. Washington, DC: Author.

_____. 1990e. *Statistical abstract of the United States*, 110th ed. Washington, DC: U.S. Government Printing Office.

_____. 1990f. *United States population estimates, by age, sex, race, and Hispanic origin: 1980–1988*. Washington, DC: U.S. Government Printing Office.

_____. 1991. *Statistical Abstract of the United States*, 111th ed. Washington, DC: U.S. Government Printing Office.

U.S. Department of Education. 1987. *The condition of education*. Washington, DC: U.S. Government Printing Office.

_____. 1991. Thirteenth Annual Report to Congress on the Implementation of the Individuals With Learning Disabilities Education Act. *To assure the free appropriate public education of all children with disabilities*. Washington, DC: author.

U.S. Department of Education, National Center for Education Statistics. 1980. *Digest of education statistics*. Washington, DC: U.S. Government Printing Office.

_____. 1986. *Digest of education statistics*. Washington, DC: U.S. Government Printing Office.

_____. 1987. *What works: Research about teaching and learning*, 2nd ed. Washington, DC: U.S. Government Printing Office.

_____. 1988a. *The condition of education*. (CS89-625) Washington, DC: U.S. Government Printing Office.

_____. 1988b. *Digest of education statistics*. (CS88-600). Washington, DC: U.S. Government Printing Office.

_____. 1989. *Digest of education statistics*. (NCES-89-643). Washington, DC: U.S. Government Printing Office.

_____. 1990. *Characteristics of private schools: 1978–88*. (NCES 90-080). Washington, DC: Author.

U.S. Department of Health and Human Services, Division of HIV/AIDS. 1986. *Objectives for the nation*. Washington, DC: Author.

U.S. Department of Labor, Bureau of Labor Statistics. 1988. *Employment and earnings, 1987*. Washington, DC: U.S. Government Printing Office.

U.S. Equal Opportunity Commission. 1988. *State and local government information report*. Washington, DC: U.S. Government Printing Office.

Valente, W. D. 1980. *Law in the schools*. Columbus, OH: Charles E. Merrill.

Vanderbilt University, Office of Teacher Education. 1990. *Associated Master of Arts in Teaching*. Nashville, TN: Author.

Vazquez, C. 1989. Teach the art of success. *Learning* (September), 10.

Verstegen, D. A. 1990. Efficiency and economies-of-scale revisited: Implications for financing rural school districts. *Journal of Education Finance* 16 (2), 159–179.

Wadsworth, B. J. 1984. *Piaget's theory of cognitive and affective development*, 3rd ed. New York: Longman.

Walberg, H. J., Schiller, D., and Haertel, G. D. 1979. The quiet revolution in educational research. *Phi Delta Kappan*, 61 (4), 179–183.

Wall Street Journal staff. 1986. Governors opt for choice of schools. *Wall Street Journal* (August 26), 14.

Walters, E. 1988. A test that never fails. *The Progressive* (August), 52 (18), 12, 13.

Wang, M. C., Reynolds, M. C., and Walberg, H. J. 1986. Rethinking special education. *Educational Leadership* 43 (1), 26–31.

Warner, W. L., Havighurst, R. J., and Loeb, M. B. 1944. *Who shall be educated?* New York: Harper and Row.

Webb, L. D., McCarthy, M. M., and Thomas, S. B. 1988. *Financing elementary and secondary education*. Columbus, OH: Merrill.

Westinghouse Learning Corporation. 1969. *The impact of Head Start: An evaluation of the effects of Head Start on children's cognitive and affective development*. Athens: Ohio University (ERIC Document Reproduction Service No. ED 036321).

White, E. E. 1902. *Report of the U.S. commissioner of education*, 1247–1250. Washington, DC: U.S. Government Printing Office.

White, M. 1987a. Japanese education: How do they do it? *Principals*, (March), 19–20.

_____. 1987b. *The Japanese educational challenge: A commitment to children*. New York: Free Press.

Whitehead, A. N. 1959. *The aims of education and other essays*. New York: Macmillan.

Wigginton, E., Ed. 1972. *The foxfire book*. Garden City, NY: Doubleday.

William T. Grant Foundation Commission on Work, Family, and Citizenship. 1988a. *The forgotten half: Non-college youth in America*. Washington, DC: Author.

_____. 1988b. *The forgotten half: Pathways to success for America's youth and young families*. Washington, DC: Author.

Williams, D. L., and Chaukin, N. F. 1989. Essential elements of strong parent involvement programs. *Educational Leadership* 47 (2), 18–20.

Williams, K. 1991. Multicultural music: The need, the action, and the future. *Delta Kappa Gamma Bulletin 57* (2), 15–18.

Williams, R. 1987. Schooling in an addicted society. *Educational Leadership,* 45 (6), 36–37.

Williams v. Board of Educ. of County of Kanawha, 388 F.Supp. 93 (S.D. W. Va., 1975).

Wise, A. E., Darling-Hammond, L., McLaughlin, M. W., and Bernstein, H. T. 1984. *Case studies for teacher evaluation: A study of effective practices.* Santa Monica, CA: Rand.

Wise v. Pea Ridge School Dist., 855 F.2d 560 (8th Cir., 1988).

Witkin, G., with Hedges, S. J., Johnson, C., Guttman, M., Thomas L., and Moncreiff, A. 1991. Kids who kill. *U.S. News and World Report 110* (13), 26–31.

Wolf, J. S., and Stephens, T. M. 1989. Parent/teacher conferences: Finding common ground. *Educational Leadership 47* (2), 28–31.

Woodward, W. H., Ed. 1904. *Erasmus concerning education.* Cambridge: Cambridge University Press. Original work published 1522.

Woolfolk, A. E. 1987. *Educational psychology,* 3rd ed. Englewood Cliffs, NJ: Prentice Hall.

Worsnop, R. 1991a. How choice plans operate in the states. *CQ Researcher 1* (1), 269.

———. 1991b. School choice: Would it strengthen or weaken public education in America? *CQ Researcher 1* (1), 253–276.

Wright, C., and Nuthall, G. 1970. Relationships between teacher behaviors and pupil achievement in three experimental elementary science lessons. *American Educational Research Journal,* 83 (6), 67–75.

Wynne, E. 1981. Looking at good schools. *Phi Delta Kappan 62* (5), 377–381.

Yinger, R. J., and Hendricks, M. S. 1990. An overview of reform in Holmes Group institutions. *Journal of Teacher Education 41* (2), 21–26.

Young, M. F. D. 1971. Knowledge and control. In *Knowledge and control,* Ed. M. F. D. Young, 30. London: Collier-Macmillan.

Zais, R. S. 1976. *Curriculum: Principles and foundations.* New York: Harper and Row.

Zettel, J. J. 1979. Gifted and talented education over a half-decade of change. *Journal for the Education of the Gifted 13* (6), 14–37.

Zinn, M. B., and Eitzen, D. S. 1987. *Diversity in American families.* New York: Harper and Row.

Zirkel, P. A., and Richardson, S. N. 1988. *A digest of Supreme Court decisions affecting education,* 2nd ed. Bloomington, IN: Phi Delta Kappa Educational Foundation.

Zirkel, P. A. 1990. Know your copy rights: Teachers have special freedom and responsibilities. *Teacher Magazine, I* (8) 68, 69.

Name Index

Subject Index

Page references in **bold** indicate glossed terms.

Credits & Acknowledgments

Staff

Developmental Editor M. Marcuss Oslander
Copy Editor Al Metro
Production Manager Brenda S. Filley
Art Editor Pamela Carley Petersen
Designers Harry Rinehart and Charles Vitelli
Typesetting Supervisor Libra Ann Cusack
Typesetter Juliana Arbo
Editoral Assistant Diane Barker
Graphic Assistant Meredith Scheld
Photo Research Wendy Connal
Systems Manager Richard Tietjen